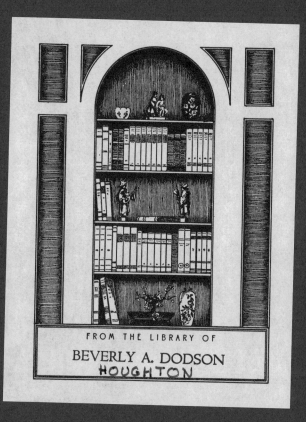

A Modern Introduction to the Family

Edited by

NORMAN W. BELL and EZRA F. VOGEL

A Modern Introduction to

THE FAMILY

THE FREE PRESS OF GLENCOE

Preface

There is no dearth of literature both academic and applied, on the family. Numerous professions are actively working and writing on this subject. Despite the great amount of work done, the field has been slow in developing a systematic body of theory and data. In some academic circles, perhaps because of the prominence of applied interests, the family is not regarded as a suitable, or fashionable, area for specialization. Practitioners, on the other hand, often feel that those with "pure" interests have little to contribute to their "applied" endeavors. We believe that these conclusions are false and detrimental to all concerned. This volume has a dual aim: to introduce a tentative theoretical conception which will systematically organize a wide variety of family phenomena, and to present selected readings within this conceptual context. These readings do not prove that the conceptual scheme is the best possible, but only illustrate its utility.

The readings can be used independently of the conceptual scheme advanced; they will, we trust, provide a representative selection of many streams of thought and interest in the field. Within the confines of a single volume, it is impossible to give representation to all specialized interests. Thus, we have omitted several special areas that are relevant and will be of central concern to some students. We have, for instance, not given adequate space to the too-often neglected early writers in this field. We have omitted completely demographic studies of either a descriptive or analytical nature. Finally, we have not attempted to include material pertaining to the application of knowledge in the clinical professions, in policy development, or in marriage and family-life education. On the other hand, we have attempted to select material without regard to the boundaries of academic disciplines, to present economic, anthropological, and psychiatric, as well as sociological studies.

We hope that the conceptual scheme advanced will be applicable, with appropriate modification of specific terms, to any society. We have not tested whether this is so. Although this volume includes some cross-cultural studies, we have drawn chiefly from the more accessible and familiar literature on American society.

This book would not have been possible without the help of many people. Florence Kluckhohn, Talcott Parsons, and John Spiegel have been our principal intellectual mentors. Many helpful suggestions have been made by David and Kathleen Aberle, Robert Blood, Jack Buerkle, Kent Geiger, Reuben Hill, Frank Jones, Marion Levy, Jesse Pitts, Albert

Reiss, and Neil Smelser. The authors of the various selections and their publishers have been very co-operative in making the selections available for reprinting.

We should also like to thank Gerda Andrews, Kathryn Matsis, Janet Pinkerton, and Carol Fitzgerald for assistance in the production of the manuscript; and Jeremiah Kaplan for his encouragement, co-operation, and patience.

Norman W. Bell,
Cambridge, Massachusetts

Ezra F. Vogel,
Tokyo, Japan

Contents

Part III—Internal Processes of the Family

Part IV—Family and Personality

A Modern Introduction to the Family

Toward a Framework for Functional Analysis of Family Behavior

NORMAN W. BELL and EZRA F. VOGEL

In this essay, the editors present a framework within which a wide variety of materials on the family, drawn from a variety of disciplines, may be systematically organized. The framework is a structural-functional model cast in a transacting systems mold. This framework, still in a programmatic stage, is the basis for the organization of the rest of this book.

Terms and Terms of Reference

The family is a popular but not well-organized field of special interest. Many reasons, rational and nonrational, could be adduced to account for this state of affairs: the difficulties in investigating the intimate details of what is regarded as a private, sometimes almost sacred, part of life; the push felt (especially by the adolescent) in an individualistic society to leave the parental family behind; the great variety of interests in the family, with the resulting inability of one profession to lay claim to it as its own area, and so on. Another significant reason is the lack of a clear and consistent referent for the word "family." This common word, with its many emotional overlays, means many things to different people. If the word is to be used as a concept in scientific discourse, it must be given a stable and precise meaning.

In this chapter, we shall regard the family as a structural unit composed, as an ideal type, of a man and woman joined in a socially recognized union and their children. Normally, the children are the biological offspring of the spouses, but, as in the case of adopted children in our society, they need not necessarily be biologically related. This social unit we shall call the *nuclear family* or simply the *family*. This unit is familiar and easily identifiable in American society, and it is the expected household unit.[1] In accordance with current usage, we shall use *family of orientation* to designate the nuclear family in which a person has, or has had, the status of a child, and *family of procreation* in which a person has, or has had, the status of parent. *Extended family* is used to refer to any grouping, related by descent, marriage, or adoption, that is broader than the nuclear family.

If the nuclear family is a unit found in all societies, it is a stable point of reference for systematic analysis. Despite arguments to the contrary, we maintain that it is such a universal unit. The nuclear family may not be the normal household unit; it may be imbedded in an extended-family unit, but we contend that it is always identifiable as a unit, both to outside observers and the actors themselves. Again, the nuclear family may not exist in all individual instances, or even in whole segments of a society, but we know of no society in which the family does not exist as an institutionalized pattern.

Starting with the nuclear family as a stable point of reference, we attempt to spell out the patterned relationships and processes in those "structures" existing within the family, between the family and broader social units, and between the family and personality. Our approach will be a structural-functional one, producing a conceptual framework that may allow a theory to be built. The nature and problems of the "functional" approach cannot be explicated here, but understanding what follows in this chapter presumes some acquaintance with this approach.[2]

Another concept basic to our approach is that of the *social system*. A system, as *Webster's Unabridged Dictionary* defines it, is ". . . an organization or assemblage of objects united in some form of regular interaction or interdependence. . . ." A social system is such an aggregation— of persons, or for some purposes, of roles.[3] The family as a social system is not a closed system, existing in isolation. Rather, it is an open system which sustains relationships with other systems in the total transactional field.[4] What is treated as a system is a heuristic matter. For some purposes, the nuclear family may be treated as an undifferentiated system; for other purposes, one might want to view it as a system composed of several subsystems—such as the husband-wife subsystem, the parent-child subsystem, the sibling subsystem, etc. For still other purposes, each of these subsystems might be treated as a system in its own right. The nuclear family may also be treated as a subsystem of some larger system, e.g., an extended-kinship system. If analysis is to be careful, it is essential to be explicit about what system is being referred to.

Analysis cannot rest with identifying systems and describing the structure of their relationships. This would result in a static picture which had form without content, anatomy without flesh. We will attempt to add the dynamics by identifying the *interchanges* that take place between and within systems.[5] Interchanges, like imports and exports, are always two-way processes, although they may not be exactly balanced in the short run.

A Brief History of Family Studies

Before presenting a comprehensive structural-functional model of family behavior, it will help to review the problems of constructing a model, by examining the history of previous studies. No comprehensive history of the forerunners in this field exists.[6] The present account can only sketch the broadest outlines. In the history of family sociology, there have been several different "models," fashioned as much by political, religious, and philosophical ideologies as by accepted canons of science. In the late nineteenth century, when family sociology was just beginning, social Darwinism dominated the field of interest. The basic issues of research were such problems as whether human societies were originally promiscuous or monogamous, and whether families were originally matriarchal or patriarchal. These questions about the origin and development of the human family required the use of historical documents, folklore, and myths. To the extent that families were studied directly, they were studied in broad compass only in the "most primitive" societies. The assumption was that the family systems of these contemporary "primitive" societies were most similar to the earlier forms of the family, and that a study of these families would shed light on the origin and development of the human family. The contemporary family, like the rest of society, was assumed to be the culmination of the long evolutionary process, and not in need of direct study. The results of these investigations were inconsistent and inconclusive. Morgan and Engels uncovered examples of "promiscuity" and "group marriage" in primitive societies, while Westermark produced evidence to show that primitive and even ape families were monogamous and faithful. While Sir Henry Maine amassed evidence to show that patriarchy was found in early forms of the family, Bachofen and Briffault produced evidence that matriarchy preceded patriarchy. Because the evidence was never clear cut and both sides could find data to support their ideology, the issues were never settled. In the process of these disputes, a vast historical-ethnological literature was uncovered, and some interest in the family, as an object of serious scientific inquiry, was developed. In addition, there was an increase in the interest in ethnographic techniques for direct study of families in primitive societies.

The rapid social changes of the time called attention to the problems of the contemporary family, particularly the problems of poverty and suffering which were readily visible. For the liberal humanitarians such as Rowntree and the Webbs, one important aspect of the reform process was to document the actual conditions of "life and labour" in the cities of Europe and America.

These studies of poverty and spending blossomed in European industrial centers and followed somewhat later in the United States, when economic adversity struck large numbers of immigrants. Such studies and the many studies of "consumption" that followed tended to be narrowly focused on the economic conditions of the family. The structure and processes in the broader society were either ignored or discussed in such non-specific and static terms as place, racial character, and subventions or rights against the community, employer, or government. Despite the narrow focus, valuable findings did result. In the hands of persons with wide-ranging interests, such as LePlay and his followers Zimmerman and Black in America, comparative studies did lead to well-based generalizations. However, such studies tended to concentrate on the disadvantaged lower classes or backward groups. The approach was less easily adapted to the growing middle classes, among whom family forms were changing and problems emerging.

Early in the twentieth century, other problems, just as disturbing as poverty, became apparent. Divorce and separation were increasing, the birth rate was declining, women were spending more time outside the home, and the "individuation" of family members was proceeding to a point where the continued existence of the family as a group was seriously in doubt. These problems were usually investigated "from a distance," through the statistics on divorce, crime, illegitimacy, family size, and birth rates. The final answers, however, could not be given by such research, but by thoughtful essays. Such essays, arguing that the family was disintegrating or was blossoming into a new era, were often perceptive reflections on the family and contemporary society. Although their perspective was much broader than later studies of the family, they were not always supported by, and did not lead to, systematic investigations. Furthermore, they still were in large part an expression of a particular ideological stance.

In the same period, a new problem, more appropriate for research, came into prominence. As "individuation" proceeded, it was recognized that more than satisfactory economic conditions was necessary for families to be stable and family members "adjusted." Comfortably situated families had problems of personal and sexual adjustment, and they were turning to "expert" sources outside the family for consultation and help.

The pressing desire for help which became apparent in the 1920's led to the first large-scale investigation of the contemporary middle-class family. However, there was still much resistance to investigation of the more intimate details of family life, and direct observation was rarely attempted. More usually, the wife, or a child in college, was asked to record certain objective facts about his family and some attitudes of his own on a questionnaire, or a physician accumulated observations on his patients. This research was heavily focused on individual adjustment, a subject which has dominated family sociology ever since. The central concept of this research was Burgess' definition of the family as a "unity of inter-acting personalities." This approach minimized the importance of social structure, by its concentration on the attitudes of individual members, and obscured the organic unity of the family as a group, by focusing on dis-crete attitudes, background factors, or particular subsystems. Unity was recognized only at the psychological level. Psychoanalytic notions were selected, simplified, and combined with the social psychological theories of G. H. Mead and others to give impetus to this movement. In short order, a very extensive literature[7] was produced by psychiatry, social work, and kindred professions; a literature in which correlations were established between ". . . a piece of the child and a piece of the parent."[8] However, as a whole, the research problems were not related to problems of general theory, but to more immediate practical problems raised by the fields of family counseling, child guidance, and "education for marriage." Great attention was given, in the choice of problems and in presentation of results, to the enormous public desire for advice on family matters. The attempt to meet these demands often led to the neglect of more theo-retically significant research and a relatively uncritical acceptance of the research that had been done.

The impact of the depression and World War II once more forced a broader view of the family, by calling attention to the intimate relationship between the family and contemporary external social systems. However, these studies were usually approached from the older standpoint of the adjustment and happiness of individual family members, or of individual families. Typically, a study focused on the way in which a particular group of families responded to a particular crisis, such as depression, unemploy-ment, war separation and reunion, illness, and death. There was no attempt to treat systematically the relationship between the family and external social systems. Even the comparison of families of different ethnic and social classes has usually been social analysis of different patterns of family re-lationship and childrearing, not of how the characteristics of the family system fit into the context of the society, or of how personality is related to the structure of the family. If there was any resort to a model, it was most frequently to "stages in the life cycle," a common-sense but arbitrary set of divisions never related to any theoretical system.

Recently, there has been an increasing interest in the details of family life, even those which are private and commonplace, and in trying to de-velop new and more general conceptualizations of the family, as well as appropriate methods of investigation. There have been a number of studies that have attempted to treat the family as a social system, and that are concerned with the relationships between the family's structure and functioning and external systems, on the one hand, and between the family and the individual, on the other hand. It is principally such studies that the present volume brings together.

Functions of the Nuclear Family

There has been much confusion as to whether "the functions of the family" refer to functions the family performs for other social institutions, the wider society, the individual personality, or simply to activities* performed within the family. The family has functions which relate to each of these other systems, and it is important to be clear about which functions pertain to which system. With regard to the total society, the family may serve such general functions as replacing members, primary socialization, and maintaining motivation for participation within the society. There are, also, specific functions which the family performs for each of t'he other social systems. For instance, the family discharges basic personality-formation, status-conferral, and tension-management functions for an individual member. Moreover, since functional interchanges seldom operate in one direction only, it is necessary to ask what functions are performed for the family by each other system in return.

Any general analysis of family functions is complicated by the many variations in concrete family functions within different societies, and by further variations among families in a given society. Frequently, however, the variation, or the change over time in a given society, is grossly exaggerated because the reference point is not clear and constant. For instance, it is often said that the "functions" of the family are being lost in modern society, but it is not clear whether the nuclear family or the extended family is the unit under consideration. In some primitive and agrarian societies, the family is said to have (or have had) major economic, political, religious, and educational duties, but in many cases these are (or were) functions of the extended family, not the nuclear family. In more complex societies, these functions are performed not by the extended family, but by specialized institutions organized on other bases than kinship; the nuclear family's relationship with these institutions has become more important, while the relationship with the extended family has become less important. Although the nuclear family seldom operates as a unit of direct economic production in contemporary industrial societies, the same is true for the nuclear family in many other societies. Moreover, certain activities and functions performed by the nuclear family in industrial societies have increased in recent decades. For example, the care of infants, household maintenance, and individual tension management, formerly performed in large part by the extended family or the community, are now almost exclusively the province of the nuclear family.

Failure to distinguish the extended family from the nuclear family has confused other issues—for example, that of authority. The "patriarchal

---

* We shall use the term "activities" to refer to specific behavioral acts or sequences and patterns of acts, and "function" to refer to the more general consequences of activities.

family" vested strong authority in one person, but the authority often was over the extended family and was restricted to certain specialized activities. The persons in any one nuclear family were subject to the authority of the patriarch for some purposes, but in other respects they might have had considerable freedom. Often, the father who did have this patriarchal authority in the extended group did not have much authority over his own nuclear family. Even the patriarch's authority frequently had little relationship to many specific household activities. Just as the extended family's functions may be taken over by specialized institutions, so the authority formerly in the hands of the patriarch is now in the hands of specialized institutions. This may mean considerable change in the locus of authority outside the nuclear family, but does not necessarily mean drastic change within the nuclear family.

Although misunderstandings result from confusing the nuclear family and the extended family, there are obviously many variations in nuclear-family functions in different societies. Perhaps the main differences between family functions in various societies are associated with the extent to which the society is structurally differentiated. In primitive societies, there are relatively few concrete social systems, and these social systems are not fulfilling specialized functions for the society. Rather, a wide variety of functions is performed by a small number of groups, such as the extended family, the clan, or the community. Since membership in these groups often overlaps, members interact with each other in a wide variety of ways. Because of the extremely frequent contacts and the importance of the kin group or community, very close and complex relationships develop. In such a situation, the boundaries between the nuclear family and other groups are not sharp and clear, in contrast to the boundaries of the contemporary urban nuclear family. Where the boundaries of the nuclear family are relatively blurred, many persons may be involved in the activities of the nuclear family—even in sexual activities—so there is little independence or privacy. But even in these relatively undifferentiated societies, the nuclear family is never completely fused with other groups; in some circumstances and for some purposes, the nuclear family is quite distinct and "walls of privacy" separate it from others. There are always some privacies and privileges, such as full, regular sexual privileges or rights of inheritance, that are reserved for the members of the nuclear family.

By comparison, in modern industrial societies, the nuclear family has become specialized as have other social institutions. In the educational sphere, for example, the nuclear family is becoming almost exclusively responsible for primary socialization and socialization for family participation, but it does not provide the formal education to equip a person for more specialized activities outside the family. Indeed, in the United States, parents have been prevented by law from assuming the responsibilities of educating their children, even when the parents' capability is unquestioned. Despite these variations, the nuclear family always performs certain functions for external social systems and, in turn, is rewarded by these other social systems. It is beyond the scope of the present paper to examine all the variations of family activities and the various functions these activities serve. Some of the major lines of variation in functions will be noted briefly, and the following analysis will focus on certain common characteristics of the functional relations between the nuclear family and external social systems.

1. THE NUCLEAR FAMILY AND OTHER SOCIAL SYSTEMS

The nuclear family's internal activities and the functions they serve are always intimately related to the position of the family in society. Hence, before taking up the activities internal to the nuclear family, it is necessary to examine the relationship between the nuclear family and other social systems.

This relationship can be conceived of as a series of functional interchanges. Some sort of balance is achieved in this interchange, between those contributions made by the family and those received by the family, even though the balance is not necessarily stable or perfect, particularly in the short run. The interchanges need not consist of concrete goods, but may consist of behavior and behavior response. For example, a nuclear family may live up to the standards of family life regarded as proper by the surrounding community. Because the family is respectable, the community rewards it with a certain status and prestige. This can be considered an interchange, just as the exchange of money income for labor services by family members is an interchange. It is not even necessary to have direct interaction for an interchange to take place. For example, if a family knows they are given community status by performing a certain activity, they may perform it and gain in status even if members of the community do not directly communicate this fact to the family. In some instances, the significant interchanges may be negative as well as positive—for example, a withholding of goods and services, hostile attitudes, or a poor reputation. The family, or some external system, may refuse to reciprocate, or may reciprocate in a partial way. Though the concrete interchanges may vary greatly, there is a certain mode of relationship and certain general expectations surrounding the relationship between the family and these external systems.

In these interchanges, the external systems regard the nuclear family to some extent as a corporate, separate unit, and all other persons or units are regarded, at least from a certain point of view, as outsiders. The individual family member then is viewed as a representative of his nuclear family, and the actual interchanges between the family and the external systems may take place either as a family acting as a unit or as an individual acting as a representative of his family.

There are certain functional problems which any social system must solve concerned with the adaptation, goal gratification, integration, and pattern maintenance of the system; functional subsystems to meet these problems[9] can be identified for any society. These subsystems may be termed respectively the economy, the polity, the community, and the value system. The same kind of functional problems arise within the family, but again it is important to be clear about the reference points, since there is no one-to-one relationship between fulfilling a function for society and fulfilling the analogous function for the nuclear family. For example, what the nuclear family receives as a contribution from the polity may help solve not only goal gratification problems within the nuclear family, but adaptive, integrative, and pattern-maintenance functions as well. This section is concerned with the functional subsystems of a society in relation to the nuclear family. The functional subsystems should not be thought of as having concrete structural referents. A given functional subsystem may consist of different types of structural units. For example, in some societies the economy may consist of such concrete groups as business firms and governmental agencies. In other societies, the economy may consist of such concrete groups as the extended family or the community. Following is a chart briefly stating the basic interchanges between the nuclear family and the major functional subsystems of a society.

a. The Nuclear Family and the Economy.—The economy may be defined as that part of a society which is concerned with the creation and distribution of valued goods and services. One interchange between the nuclear family and the economy is the contribution of labor by the nuclear family in exchange for rewards for services. The family of orientation must have provided the individual with a certain minimum of basic skills before he can enter into the labor market, a minimum which has been rising, at least insofar as opportunities for education are concerned. The individual must have a certain degree of emotional integration and control sufficient to allow him to operate adequately, and he must have certain basic information about, and attitudes toward, work that are essential to the performance of his tasks in the economy. In addition to providing the individual with this basic motivation and the basic skills, the family must then allocate certain of the performance capacities of its members to the economy.

In the case of the highly industrialized society, it is usually money wages that are received for the labor contributed by the nuclear-family member. In more primitive societies, the reward for labor may be goods and services or an informal (and perhaps even non-verbal) understanding that the group will give the laborer and his family assistance under certain circumstances. In some instances, the nuclear family does not directly

The Interchanges Between the Nuclear Family
and the Functional Subsystems of Society

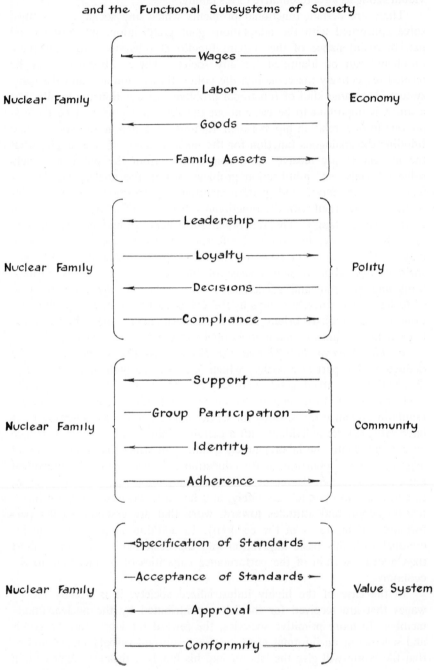

contribute labor services to the economy, but only contributes finished or semifinished products. This is the case in many farm families and in home industry. The finished product is in part a representation of labor services, and in exchange for these products, the nuclear family receives wages or the functional equivalent of wages.

In this interchange of labor for wages, various adjustments are made by the nuclear family, by the firms involved, and by the economy in general. In this way, the terms of the interchange, not only concerning the amount of wages and services but also the "conditions of employment," are established. Even in relatively impersonal industrial societies, the wages are determined not only by the laws of supply and demand, but in part by the needs and demands of the family. Some of these considerations are institutionalized in laws or union contracts regulating minimum wages, working hours and conditions, the dismissal rights of employers, etc. In some societies, family needs are explicitly recognized in policies of differential remuneration for workers depending on family responsibilities. In the United States, differential exemptions from income taxes serve the same ends. In addition, the business firm ordinarily has certain other responsibilities to the worker and his family. For example, a firm ordinarily provides special considerations of time and money when family problems or important family activities occur, such as marriage, birth, funerals, and the like, and it may offer help in arranging housing, meal, and even recreational facilities. Because large formal organizations have much greater power than the individual worker, special organizations such as labor unions develop to insure that these various demands of the worker and his family are being met by large firms. While such formally organized adjustments are primarily applicable to modern industrial society, the same types of adjustments are also found, and may even be more comprehensive, in less developed societies.

Similarly, there are certain adjustments which the nuclear family must make to the demands of the firm, in regard to when and where labor services shall be rendered. Principally, this means that the family must give encouragement and the necessary facilities to the wage earner, so that he can continue his participation in the economy. In many modern industrial societies where there is a heavy emphasis on productivity, a relatively large adjustment has to be made by the family to the economy, compared to societies where economic productivity is not regarded as so important. It may also mean than even internal family activities will tend to be modeled on and adapted to the economic roles in the society. The professionalization of the "housewife" and the extent, clearest in the upper-status levels, to which she, the family, and the home become adjuncts to the husband's career, is a case in point. This is in contrast to other societies where the family has much more importance relative to the economy, and economic roles tend to be modeled on family roles. In some societies, meeting the demands of the economy may require the nuclear family to move from one place to another in accord with the shifts in the labor market. In such cases as "the wives of management" or the minister's wife in our own society, the wife may be required to give fairly direct help in the husband's work. In less developed societies, the assistance given by the family to the wage earner may be even greater. Furthermore, the family member must be fairly regular in attendance at work, and at times of "rush season" the worker may be absent from home for particularly long times to fulfill his commitments to the employer. The family must adjust to these things and assist the worker in meeting such demands as the occupational sphere may place on him. It may even require some modification of the nature and extent of the worker's commitment to his nuclear family. The economy necessarily requires, for effective participation within it, that the family permit the wage earner some independence. A worker who always takes his family troubles to work with him or who is so attached to his family that he can't meet the demands of his work will usually find the returns from his labor limited. Conversely, as the selection from Bakke (9) shows, when unemployment cuts off wages, a train of events affecting virtually all areas of family life is set in motion.

In the consumption interchange, the family exchanges its assets for consumer goods. Compared to employment, purchasing ordinarily involves less commitment between the family and any single business firm. A family usually purchases its goods from a variety of sources, at least in the urban setting, while labor services are performed in connection with one or two firms. The conditions of employment are often decided directly between the firm and the family member, and the family member may have considerable commitment to the firm; conditions of purchasing are often governed by purely ecological considerations, particularly in modern society. Hence, consumer co-operatives, for example, have not assumed the importance of labor unions.

The family's purchases are governed in large part by the supplies available in the economy; ordinarily the family's purchases, and even its desires for purchases, are within the frame of reference of the goods available. Any individual family has relatively little power in deciding the terms of this interchange, except as their wishes are judged by the firm to be important for accomplishing its purposes, usually profit-making. While any individual family's wishes may not be important, and no organization represents their wishes, still the mass behavior of families may require adjustments on the part of the economy, as Reisman and Roseborough (selection 12) show in their analysis of changes in family composition. In contemporary society, through such mechanisms as advertising and opinion-polling, business firms are able to control and preplan these activities even when there are changes in the family's desires.

In primitive societies, in any concrete instance, these two functional interchanges may be combined into one, i.e., goods are received for performances rendered, and all the considerations mentioned above will come into play in this single interchange. In such societies, the economy may have relatively little independence from the community, and this interchange may be governed by community considerations rather than considerations of the economy and the family alone. For example, a person who has an important position in the community may be given rewards much higher than his economic contribution merits. Of course, the reverse may also occur. Certainly in industrial societies, and probably in primitive societies, some positions are remunerated far lower than their occupants could earn in alternative positions. The sacrifice involved for a successful lawyer to become a Supreme Court Justice is a case in point.

b. The Nuclear Family and the Polity.—Every social system has some type of administration of its activities to attain the system goals. The subsystem which fulfills these functions for the society may be termed the polity; in contemporary societies, this approximates roughly what is referred to as government. It is not coterminous with government since a government may perform other functions (as, for example, economic), and other institutions such as a clan or lineage may serve polity functions for the society. Ordinarily, the family acts as a unit in relation to the polity, as is suggested, for example, by the fact that husbands and wives and even, as Maccoby (selection 15) shows, youth tend to vote for the same party, and by the solidarity of the family in relation to the totalitarian societies, which Geiger finds (selection 14). The nature of societal leadership requires that policies be made at a very general level, not permitting the refinements of variable adjustment that may be possible between the individual family and the economy. While a family may decide to have the wage earner change jobs if his employment situation is not satisfactory, and is able to shop around for consumer goods and services, it does not have the same option in relation to the polity. Since governing bodies typically are given a mandate to remain in power for one or more years, and since they (if elected) are elected by a large number of constituents with many different interests, the burden of adjustment may be on the family. In the first interchange with the polity, the family contributes loyalty in exchange for leadership. At a very minimum, the members of the nuclear family recognize the legitimacy of the political order and signify a loyalty to the regime sufficient for its policies to be carried out. In return for this, the society provides a variety of advantages to the family through its leadership—legal protection and regulation, legitimacy, and the like.

In the typical case, the family's loyalty goes far beyond recognizing the legitimacy of the regime and includes active commitment to the polity.

Because the polity often represents most directly the goals of society, it often becomes a particularly appropriate symbol of the society, and the family may attach a great deal of cathexis to the polity. At normal times, this cathexis may be relatively latent, but in times of threat, this loyalty becomes extreme, and the family may be willing to forego many routine gratifications. The austerity programs or military service in war times are indications of the extent of the family's loyalty to the polity in times of emergency. Even though this exchange is usually a relatively inactive one, compared to the interchange between family and economy most of the time, it is expected that the leadership will work to provide optimum conditions for the society, which in turn will provide direct and indirect benefits for the nuclear family.

To some extent, there is always a gap between the interests of the family and the interests of the state. In general, the time perspective of a single nuclear family is much shorter than the time span of the state. For example, state expansion, austerity programs for basic state development, military programs, and the like, frequently require sacrifices from the nuclear family for which there is little immediate motivation. Perhaps the ideal is that the family will be sufficiently motivated to provide the loyalty without fear of coercion by the state. And because the nuclear family cannot expect the refinements of adjustment from the polity as from the economy, there must be some mechanism for dealing with the process of alienation of the family from the government.[10] At the very deepest level, there is normally a commitment to the society which is relatively unquestioned, and alienation is channeled in ways which do not threaten the regime, for example, through attachment to alternate political parties in a country with political parties, or through identification with purges, "self-criticisms," etc. in totalitarian countries. Again, in the typical state of affairs, this interchange is relatively latent, but it assumes great significance if a sufficient number of members are seriously disloyal to the regime, which must then endeavor to regain loyalty. The situation is analogous to hunger not being an important drive except when there is a shortage of food.

On the second level of interchanges between the polity and the family, the family supplies compliance in exchange for decisions made by the polity. Since the typical family has little power to influence decisions at the societal level, the polity is often interested less in family opinions than in the extent to which the family will comply with the decisions of the polity. This depends, in part, on the polity's ability to deal successfully with the problems of society. In some relatively undeveloped countries, and even some developed ones, part of a regime's difficulty is not so much the problems of opposition, but the ability of the polity to deal with the problems facing the society well enough to inspire the specific forms of compliance needed. If the polity is able to cope successfully with these problems, and the family is willing to comply with a wide range of governmental decisions, the polity decisions must provide considerable benefits to the family. Thus, in the modern state which has taken over the management of many of the affairs of the society, the state must also provide very broad welfare benefits to the family in order to obtain the compliance of the individuals.

In individualistically oriented western societies, we are accustomed to thinking of the person as relating to the polity as a separate individual. It is clear that in many ways the individual is the significant unit in the eyes of the polity. Appearances may be deceptive, however. In fact, there is probably a good deal more homogeneity and solidarity among the members of a family than we commonly assume. There are too, other solidary units which relate to the polity—peer groups, ethnic groups, political clubs, and so on. Such groups may mediate the relations of the family and the polity, but the family is always operative in some way. Because the family is stable, compared to many other concrete units, and because family sentiments tend to become associated with attitudes toward the polity, the family is always a unit of importance. This is most evident at the symbolic level, with leaders striving to present themselves as "solid family men (or women)," and to gather support by favoring the "family farm" or the values of strong family life. But the polity's orientation to the family is also evident in its decisions and policies, which protect the privacy of the home, refuse to compel spouses to testify against each other, distribute welfare benefits in relation to the family's condition, and, as Litwak illustrates (selection 17), act in various ways to inhibit the dissolution of marriages.

c. The Nuclear Family and the Community.—All social systems face the problem of integrating various parts and activities of the system; this problem is solved by institutionalizing patterns of behavior and by using mechanisms of social control to motivate members to conform to these patterns. The subsystem of society concerned with this problem may be termed the community, defined not as a single concrete group, such as a village or neighborhood, but as diffuse affective relationships of varying extensiveness, including the various social networks discussed in the selection by Bott (35). In primitive societies, the community usually consists of a very small number of concrete groups such as a village or kin group; in modern industrial societies, instead of such close-knit groups, there are many different "communities" based on such criteria as common participation in an industrial firm or religious group, common interests, physical proximity, or previous membership in other social systems.

Even in simpler societies where a single group or a few overlapping groups constitute the community and the polity, there is often a functional differentiation between the community and the polity. For example, a patrilineal lineage may serve as a political unit, and the kin group as the community.[11] Whether one single group serves as both the polity and the community, or whether there is a variety of different "communities," the diffuse affective bond to the community serves to integrate the family into the society.

As one of the functional interchanges, the nuclear family participates in community activities in exchange for the support of the community. Daily interaction, gifts, special kindnesses, and the like, come to symbolize the solidarity of the bonds among families. These favors imply an obligation of the receiver to the giver, and to the community in general. Often these reciprocal obligations between the family and the community are relatively latent and come to have real significance only in times of difficulties or crises.

Ordinarily, the community reinforces the bonds of solidarity within the nuclear family, but it may also prohibit the family from such intensive involvement in its own internal processes that it withdraws from participation in community affairs. Thus, from the viewpoint of the community, both strains and involvements within the family must be kept below a certain level, so as not to interfere with community activities. However, ordinarily there is a wide range of permissiveness for the nuclear family which does not participate in community activities; because of the nature of the close affective bonds, there is usually room for subtle adjustments and permissions on the part of the community not possible on the part of the economy or polity. For example, not only is the family exempt from participation in community activities at times of birth, marriage, death, and serious internal family problems, but the community offers social support to the family, just as society gives special exemptions and therapy to the "sick" person.

In the other functional interchange, the community gives the nuclear family an identity in exchange for adherence to community patterns. At a minimum, the family is recognized as a legitimate part of the society, and usually the community provides the family with a specific status position, along with appropriate standards of behavior and rewards for behavior which accord with these norms. The identity provided by this membership and a specific position within the group gives the family a feeling of belonging and prevents anomie. When the society is relatively stable and the "community" is a relatively closed network, identity may not be a serious problem. However, in a very mobile, highly industrialized society, with a variety of concrete "communities" wherein there is no clear, stable identity, there may be a considerable problem in maintaining an identity consistent with multiple and changing group memberships.

In exchange for identity, the nuclear family adheres to and makes concrete the community patterns. While various members of the nuclear family have differential commitment to various segments of a "community" or to different "communities," at a minimum the nuclear family gives tacit permission to its members to behave in accord with these various standards. In many cases, the family may actively encourage or even require adherence to such standards. If the family's ties to the community are very strong, this adherence to group standards is not regarded by the family as a duty or obligation, but simply as a natural expression of the family's solidarity and of its solidarity with the community. As Durkheim argued, this attachment to the group strengthens adherence to the norms. Through its participation in community activities and through the support it receives from the community, a family is motivated to adhere to the norms of the community, including norms regarding its own stability. Just as a family's identity consists not only of membership in a given community but of a certain status within this community, so the nuclear family adheres to standards appropriate to this particular position.

The relationship between the nuclear family and the community also has many implications for the family's relationships with the rest of the society, i.e., the community becomes a reference group for the family and its relationship with other social institutions. For example, the style of life supported by the community becomes an important basis for the pattern of relationships between a family and the economy. The political attitudes of the community similarly become an important basis for the relationship between the family and the polity. The community also is the reference group for relationships with the basic value standards of the society.

d. The Nuclear Family and the Value System.—No society, however simple, can persist in an orderly fashion without general orienting principles. These principles are at a higher level than the concrete patterns for governing specific behavior, and they constitute a reference point and *raison d'etre* for the more concrete patterns of behavior. From basic alternatives facing any society, such as what is the nature of man, and how should man relate to fellow man, each society must select certain solutions which serve as guides for behavior.[12] Value patterns do not simply influence family behavior, but there is an active interchange between the family and the value system, and problems arising from attempting to live up to values may lead to modifications and changes in the basic value patterns.

While it is true that some societies have more flexible values permitting adaptability to contemporary situations, as a whole, the ultimate values have considerable stability over time. Even the phenomena of shame or "other-directedness" signify the variety, not the absence, of internalized values. A society may have value conflict, but there is usually some fundamental agreement about the hierarchy of values underlying even the conflict, what Durkheim called the "noncontractual elements of contract." Despite the existence of value conflicts, the value system works toward achieving a certain amount of order between the various value elements in a society.

The significance of the nuclear family, with regard to the society's value system, stems from the fact that the nuclear family is the smallest social unit responsible for the preservation of the value system. It is the nuclear family's duty to see that new members are socialized into the basic value system. The family is peculiarly suited for this task, by virtue of the prolonged dependency of the human infant and the intensity and priority of relationships within the family. The greatest part of this socialization goes on implicitly, as Schneider and Homan's study of kinship terminology (selection 37) brings out. The family also has a significant part in insuring that all members continue to abide according to the societal values.

An exchange between the nuclear family and the value system takes place in that the value system specifies standards and the nuclear family accepts them—at a more general level than the community's specification of norms and the family's adherence to them. The value system defines what behavior is legitimate and desirable. Religion, in the broad sense, fulfills a part of this function, which is distinct from many other activities that may be associated with a single religious group. The ultimate values in a society may also be embodied in certain aspects of the educational system, particularly if there is no specific religious education in the society. The nuclear family accepts the standards presented by these representatives of the ultimate values of society. Ordinarily, children internalize these values through relationships in the family, and the nuclear family thus aids in the preservation of these values.

A second interchange between the nuclear family and the value system occurs when the value system gives approval and the nuclear family supplies conformity. Not only do the representatives of the value system specify what the values are, but they offer approval for conformity to these values. Ordinarily, this approval or disapproval is internalized within the personality at an early age, and the internal sanction operates to select and reject, to approve or disapprove of alternative behaviors. The values apply to the acceptability of the family as a whole in accordance with the value system, as well as to the acceptability of any given member. To the extent that a family behaves in accord with the value system, it can regard itself with corresponding esteem. This internalization is reinforced by the community, which operates to see that the nuclear family conforms, at least to some measure, with the more specific norms derived from basic values.

Because the nuclear family is concerned with approval, both internal and external, it strives to maintain a satisfactory relationship with the societal value system. Typically, this means conformity to the basic values. If there is not strict conformity, then there is, ordinarily, an attempt to establish a relationship with the value system through modification of the basic values. Because the basic value system changes very slowly, the attempts at modification have relatively little success in the short run, and various rationalizations develop to define the behavior so that it seems really to be conforming with the basic values. Often, there is some cleavage between the ideal value system of the society and the specific concrete norms enforced by the community. In this case, the nuclear family may conform to the basic value system of the society, but be considered a nonconformist or a superconformist by the community; or the family may violate basic values in exchange for community acceptance. The nuclear family is also considered responsible, to some extent, for the conformity of the family members. In the case of young children this responsibility may be stated and enforced very explicitly. Aside from the responsibility of socializing new members, the nuclear family is ordinarily considered at least partially responsible, by other groups in society, for maintaining the conformity of its members.

2. INTERNAL FAMILY ACTIVITIES

In order to participate in these interchanges with external social systems, certain activities must be performed within the nuclear family. The nuclear family must carry on internal activities related to these external exchanges, and it must perform other internal activities directly for its own benefit. Most activities carried on in the family have functional significance for the family itself *and* external systems, and the various functions fulfilled can be separated only analytically. Similarly, activities of external systems have implications for the family, but external-system activities are not sufficient in themselves to guarantee stability and smooth operation. The two approaches are, therefore, complementary, neither standing by itself.

The general functional problems facing the family are analogous to those facing the society as a whole, and those facing any other social system. In the case of the nuclear family, the functional problems may be termed task performance, family leadership, integration and solidarity, and pattern-maintenance. In examining these internal activities, it should be kept in mind that meeting a function within a family does not necessarily lead to the fulfillment of the analogous function for the society. Moreover, any given interchange between the economy and the family, such as the granting of wages in return for the performance of services by family members, may involve internal activities such as family leadership, integration and solidarity, and pattern-maintenance, as well as task performance. Similarly, the goods received from the external systems may have implications for all the subsystems in the family.

a. Task Performance.—Task performance within the nuclear family always occurs in the context of the family's relationships with external systems. The internal activity is governed in part by the requirements of the external interchanges and in part by the amount of goods obtained in the external interchanges. In addition, internal task performance is related to internal family characteristics, such as the standard of living and the solidarity and integration of relationships within the family. These tasks cannot be performed except as they are made consistent with the existing patterns of interpersonal relationships within the family. This is partly a problem of obtaining the motivational commitment of the family members for the performance of the tasks, and this can only be done as they are related to other family goals.

The goods obtained from the external systems are never completely ready for consumption when they come into the nuclear family, and some must be cared for if they are to continue to be used by the family. At a minimum, nuclear family members participate in the care and maintenance of family possessions, although in the extreme case this may merely mean seeing that no damage comes to these possessions. Typically, however, maintaining equipment requires a variety of other services such as cleaning, repairing, or improving the family's possessions. In addition to maintaining equipment, the nuclear family performs a variety of tasks which may be referred to as "finishing." Additional preparation making goods ready to use adds to their value. Additional preparation may include such things as cleaning and cooking food, installing equipment, sewing, "do-it-yourself" operations, and the like. It may involve selection, transportation, and placing of facilities in a particular location so that they may be justly distributed and conveniently used within the family.[13]

If there are dependent members of the family, then other members are expected to perform various tasks in connection with their welfare. The family is, at least to some extent, responsible for the technical problems of childcare as well as socialization. In many cases, it is responsible for the care of other dependents such as the sick or aged, although as the paper of Parsons and Fox (28) demonstrates, various changes have taken place in the urban family which make it more difficult for the family to carry out these tasks itself.

To some extent, the relationships within the family develop as a result of the nature of task activity. For example, if productive activities performed within the family require close interaction between family members, then one would expect family bonds to be very strong,[14] particularly if there is considerable interdependence between members in the performance of these tasks. If there is a high degree of interdependence and a member would have difficulty obtaining a livelihood elsewhere, his bond to the family is likely to be extremely difficult to sever. However, if the bonds are strictly of this instrumental nature and affective ties are weak, then the family bonds are not likely to survive instrumental changes.[15]

If there are major task activities performed within a family, the nature of the task may also require that appropriate standards exist between family members to regulate their activities. For example, if technical standards of efficiency apply, this will have various implications for family relationships. Typically, the nuclear family performs a wide variety of task and non-task activities; at times the requirements of affective relationships take precedence over the relationships required by task performance. There are various possible ways of reconciling the differences between the affective relationships and the relationships required for effective task performance. Relationships between family members may be based part of the time on these efficiency standards, and on more diffuse affective standards at other times. If these tasks require a considerable amount of time within the family and rather rigidly controlled relationships, considerable affect may be expressed outside the nuclear family (to mistresses or peers, for example), and the members may restrict their relationships with each other to relatively formal and technical tasks. However, if the norms about task performance become very strong, they may govern the performance of tasks regardless of their efficacy, or members may feel compelled to work even if it is not necessary to work to maintain their standard of living. The selection by Aberle and Naegele (10) suggests how the standards of the work world may pervade family activities, particularly through the father.

In addition to the problem of the influence of tasks on the norms governing family relationships, there is the problem of distributing tasks within the family. To some extent, this distribution appears to be based on certain biological factors. The biological nature of the mother-child bond ordinarily leads the mother to perform tasks connected with the child, particularly when it is small, and the father to perform (frequently away from the home) activities that, directly or indirectly, will produce the needed goods and services. This division of labor is, as Zelditch argues (selection 26), evidently universal, and a fundamental principle of family life the world over. It usually means that the mother is more economically dependent upon the father than vice versa. The availability of the mother in the home ordinarily leads to her performing other incidental tasks in the home. To be sure, these biological factors are handled differently in different cultures, and there are a number of other situational and social factors which govern the performance of various tasks. For example, if the family activities require a great amount of relatively unskilled labor, it is likely that children may be required to participate in them. Also, the relative skill of individual members influences the way in which tasks are assigned. However, the various social values governing the relative status of man and woman, parent and child, also greatly influence the division of labor, and the strength of these values may also govern the flexibility or rigidity in role allocation.

Just as the performance of these tasks depends in part on the solution to other functional problems facing the family, so does task performance have implications for solving other functional problems of the family. For example, performing tasks together may strengthen family solidarity and reinforce family values. The nature of the task may require one person to assume greater leadership, and if one family member makes an unusually valuable contribution to family tasks, he may be given higher status. Conversely, if he fails in some important way, his status may be lowered.

b. Family Leadership.—Because the family is a stable group with the same membership over a relatively long period of time, its division of leadership is ordinarily rather clearly structured. For example, parents have clear-cut leadership over children. However, because of the complex nature of the family and the wide variety of activities within it, many subtle considerations are involved in its leadership, depending on such things as the particular activity pursued, the present family situation, the needs of family members, and the willing (though not necessarily conscious) turning over of leadership in certain affairs to other members.

If a minor problem develops, disturbing the usual pattern of relationships, the individual concerned may simply assume the leadership required for solving the problem. Other problems involve more than one person, and certain major issues, such as family size, life-plans for children, and inheritance, clearly involve several or all family members. These problems require leadership of the entire family, either by some member of the family or by someone acting for the family.

It is usual to think of the solution to these problems as a result of conscious decision-making processes. While family members may be conscious of their problems and various possible solutions, often, as noted in the selection by Spiegel (29), solutions are reached without a conscious decision-making process and may be in conflict with consciously desired goals. An equilibrium may be restored as a result of manipulations analogous to those in power-politics. One party may attempt to induce another to behave in the desired way by a variety of techniques, such as exploiting the coalition patterns within the family. The familiar case of the child who forms an alliance with the favored parent, when the other refuses his wishes, is one example; many other manipulations and coalition patterns are used to reinforce one's position in the family or to achieve the desired pattern of relationships.

Even if decision-making is conscious, it is not a simple matter of obtaining the desired number of votes before action can be taken. Because of the long period of intimate relationships between the family members, various subtle considerations enter into the process. For example, the person in the group most flexible on a given topic may yield to another less flexible, regardless of the power position. Maintaining the motivational level of group members is so important that efforts are often made to maintain motivation regardless of the power position of the members. Families which have "no disagreements," or which solve their problems "democratically," are often those families with sufficient solidarity and sufficiently accepted patterns that subordinating certain wishes or desires is not felt as a sacrifice, or even as problematic. Thus, the solution is successful, not because of the decision-making process but because of the commitment and motivation of family members.

While it is true that certain family members are often granted more power than other members of the family, this authority has often been overestimated and oversimplified, particularly in the discussions of "matriarchy" and "patriarchy."[16] One of the reasons for this is the assumption that the person who receives deference necessarily has the power to lead. Although one family member may receive formal deference from others, this does not necessarily mean that he has the power to ensure that his opinions are carried out by others. Often the person who exercises the greatest actual leadership is one who "works behind the scenes." Even if the one receiving the most deference formally makes the decisions, the critical issues in the decision may, in fact, have been settled by other members of the family. The person receiving greater deference may have the right of leadership when he desires it, but may not take a prominent part in the ordinary decisions, and often his decisions are concerned only with certain aspects of family behavior. In this area of activities, as in task activities, a differentiation of authority spheres usually develops.

In addition, the power of an individual has often been overestimated because of lack of awareness of the fact that the solution to problems may be predetermined by the social structure, even though the reaffirmation of this structure may be regarded as a conscious decision by the participants. While the person who receives great deference may formally enunciate this agreement, this does not necessarily mean that he has played an important leadership role.

Nor is the authority figure usually absolute and responsible to no one. It may be true that the "authority figure" in the family is invariably obeyed at the conscious level, but if he were to attempt to exert his authority in ways not considered legitimate by other members of the family, he might not be obeyed. The appearance of absoluteness is derived from the fact that the "authority" does not go beyond bounds of what is considered legitimate and proper by the others. Other family members usually have many subtle ways of influencing or of subverting the decisions of the authority.

It is true, however, that in some cases considerable power may be vested in one person. In the large family, co-ordination may require greater centralization of power in the hands of one or two persons. This is particularly true if the nuclear family performs a wide range of adaptive tasks or if the relationships with the community place heavy demands on the family. To be effective in meeting these external demands or internal tasks may require rapid co-ordination and the willingness of members to abide by the decisions made by the appropriate person, if only for the time being.

Concern with the formal process of decision-making also tends to overlook the decision of nondecision, postponement of decision, or of contended decision, as is also noted in the selection by Spiegel (29). Just as there are noncontractual elements of contract, so there are elements of decisions which are accepted but not formally agreed to. If one family member behaves in a certain way relevant to other family members, and if other family members continue to remain in the system without protesting effectively, this means that they have to some extent recognized the behavior of the other as legitimate. In effect, silence is assent, but protest may also be a way of giving assent. If the structure of family relations is relatively stable, and if one member continually expresses protest without attempting to exercise further sanctions, he may in effect be accepting the situation the way it is. Protest can be a way of giving implicit approval at the same time that explicit disapproval may permit an expression of feelings of alienation or a reinforcement of official values or "face-saving." Similarly, threats to use sanction power, without actually using sanction power, may be a modified way of expressing protest without actually initiating change. Situations of indecision may themselves be routinized into a relatively stable equilibrium. Such situations may be perpetuated, and the new "decision" may only result in a continuation of the previous equilibrium. Some of the complexities and subtleties of these leadership patterns are examined in the paper by Vogel and Bell (30).

c. Integration and Solidarity.—For a group to maintain close relationships between members over a long period of time requires some commitment and feelings of solidarity. For example, one of the functions of romance, especially early in marriage, can be to provide a feeling of solidarity even when economic interdependence of the spouses and external social systems do not exert strong sanctions for the continuance of the family. In turn, as Durkheim has shown, solidarity gives members the motivation to abide by the norms. If there is little solidarity within the family, the obligations imposed by the group may seem oppressive, but if there is a great deal of solidarity, the obligations may be accepted as natural and not even felt as obligations. In addition, feelings of solidarity are very important in dealing with individual tensions and personality problems.

To some extent, the mere process of interaction, even when frustrating to the individuals involved, is related to solidarity; over a long period of time, the meeting of expectations leads to a feeling of faithfulness which adds to solidarity. Furthermore, there are certain activities particularly significant for family solidarity. One obvious case, discussed in the Bossard and Boll selection (34), is the family ritual or the family celebration. The performance of certain specific routines at mealtime, in which the family unites as a whole, gives the family a feeling of solidarity; special family holidays, such as birthdays and special occasions, also serve to give the family a feeling of solidarity. It is true that some of these larger celebrations, such as weddings, christenings, funerals, and the like, serve to unite the entire extended family as well as the nuclear family. But there are many occasions, for example, a Sunday dinner, family prayers, or family television-viewing, which can reinforce the solidarity of the nuclear family. Just as political campaigns serve to strengthen the bonds between members of the same political parties, at the expense of bonds between members of nonpolitical groups and perhaps of the whole nation, so these family occasions serve to strengthen the loyalty to the family group over ties to peer groups, occupational groups and the like.

While the importance of ritual activities for family solidarity has long been recognized, there are many other family symbols of family solidarity. For example, family photographs or photograph albums, family vacation experiences, favorite jokes and stories, family secrets, family history, endurance of hard economic times, and the like are remembered and treasured, in large part because of their significance for family unity and solidarity. It has long been recognized that family furnishings are symbols of social-class membership; it has been less common to note the extent to which certain family possessions, hope chests, heirlooms, and even the family house or car can serve as concrete symbols of family solidarity. These possessions unite the family by presenting a common pattern of taste and symbolizing the unity of the particular family. Experience of affect and sexual relationships also operate to give greater solidarity to relationships within the family. Aside from the purely physical aspects of sex, the sexual relationship serves to express and reinforce certain ties within the family. Other expressions of affection, such as physical contact, politeness, and "consideration," also help to express and maintain ties of family solidarity.

Both as a result of, and to promote these feelings of solidarity, the family attempts to preserve the motivational commitment of its members. If a family member is losing interest in family activities in ways considered inappropriate, the family will apply various sanctions, either positive or negative, to renew the individual's participation. Any lack of motivation is always a potential threat to the entire group, and the family cannot let deviance from family norms occur, without attempting to supply motivation to correct this deviance or at least making clear that such behavior is unacceptable. The selection from Cousins (32) explores some of these patterns.

The requirements of, and problems in, maintaining integration differ for different family members. Families place restrictions on the expression of solidarity, since unlimited expression of affect would interfere with the solution of other functional problems. For example, it may interfere with the effective performance of family tasks requiring behavior inconsistent with considerations of solidarity. In the case of family leadership, too-strong ties between parents and certain children may interfere with effective leadership in the family. As Kingsley Davis notes (selection 31), this is one of the important reasons for the existence of the incest taboo. But it is important to note that this restriction on closeness of ties between mother and son goes far beyond simply an incest taboo, as reflected, for example, in the negative sanctions toward a "mama's boy" or "playing favorites" beyond legitimate expectations.

Because of the strength of family ties, there are very strong pressures operating to prevent group disintegration, as noted in studies of family responses to stress.[17] The family appears to have a certain level of tension tolerance. When tensions become so severe as to threaten the group with disintegration, there is often a sudden rallying of forces to unite the family by dealing with the threat to the family's solidarity. These family "coping mechanisms" operate in ways very similar to individual personality mechanisms.

The same phenomenon occurs not only in response to crises such as illness or disaster or separation by war, but to all action by people outside the family that threatens to disrupt the family system. For example, it has been noted (selection 14) that in a police state, the family strongly pulls together in response to threats from the outside regime and fights to preserve its ties of solidarity. Ordinarily, there are certain intimacies shared only among members of the family, and the exclusiveness of these intimacies requires that outsiders be prevented from intruding and disrupting the ties of family solidarity. If an outsider becomes very close to one of the family members and this threatens to disrupt the ties of family members to each other, there may be a sudden rallying of family forces and a complete break between the family and the person or group that has threatened the solidarity of the family. Such a sharp break is usually required, however, only when the solidarity of the family is very tenuous and subject to disintegration.

If separation occurs as a result of voluntary decisions on the part of family members, usually it is only after serious attempts to "make it work," and it is only after these efforts at rallying or rescuing group solidarity fail that the system is finally disbanded. Even in times of family conflict, solidarity is taken very seriously by the members, and the severity of the conflict that can be endured reflects the strength of these solidarity ties.

Not only are these pressures for solidarity expressed directly within the family, they are reflected in attitudes about families in general. Part of the negative reaction toward prostitution and divorce springs from the threat to family solidarity which they constitute. If divorce and separation were to be freely and easily permitted for others, this would involve a potential threat to one's own family solidarity. The continued negative attitude toward divorce and separation serves to reinforce the stability of one's own family and to insure that the threat does not come "too close to home." When divorce does occur, there are institutionalized pressures, especially strong for women, as Goode (selection 25) points out, to reconstitute a family group.

External societal institutions are also concerned with maintaining family solidarity, and the family may be aided directly and indirectly in preserving itself by these institutions. However, if family members accept the legitimacy of external institutions and have differential commitment to them, this may itself interfere with family solidarity. The conflicting reference groups for husband and wife or parents and children, for example, may lead to mutual alienation from the family. This can be an important problem in societies undergoing fundamental change or in groups undergoing rapid change within a society, as were the Poles described by Green (selection 48).

d. The Family Value System.—Through their relationships with each other, family members come to have certain expectations about how other members should behave; these expectations are associated with feelings of rightness or wrongness. Specific expectations are related to more general standards, and together they constitute a system of values for organizing and giving direction to various family activities. This value system provides a hierarchy of goals and a body of rules for their attainment. These are valued far beyond their mere utility in solving specific problems. The family attempts to maintain this value system, because it gives meaning and purpose to specific family activities.

While the societal value orientations are more general and govern all of society's basic values, the family value system is more specific and governs only behavior among family members and how they, as family representatives, should relate to outsiders. For example, while a society may have certain dominant and variant values, the family's values may be related only to the variant values of the society. It is also possible for children and their parents to have different general values,[18] but if the family is to continue to exist, there must be some agreement about the values which serve as a basis for and regulate family activities. The values of a family are not entirely, or even necessarily, conscious, except when there is conflict or when they are made explicit in the socialization process. Even in the socialization process, values are often taught through relationships and examples rather than by explicit precept. In spite of unconsciousness and the fact that many logical inconsistencies may exist, values must be sufficiently consistent to provide orderly family relationships. Because a family in most societies does make many adjustments to its individual members, these expectations are often individualized and based on a combination of personal idiosyncrasies and family experiences; even so, they nevertheless involve shared feelings of rightness and wrongness.

All behavior within the family is subject to the same type of legitimation. The leadership, task performance, solidarity, and division of labor, in any of these spheres, all take place within the context of the family's over-all value system. This value system is governed in part by the family's place in the society and its relationship to other social systems. But, as noted in the selection by Naegele (33), the right to express various emotions between members in the family, permission to escape routine responsibilities, special privileges, and division of labor, are also subject to definitions of what is considered legitimate. Within the framework of shared values, which Bott's selection (35) discusses, there may occur quite disparate values. The selection from Seeley, Sim, and Loosley (36) emphasizes how disparate the values of men and women can become, not without causing problems and difficulties in understanding, but without destroying the family.

Often there is a disparity between what is explicitly legitimate and what is implicitly accepted as legitimate. For example, if a husband suddenly gets angry at his wife, the wife may feel that the anger is not justified in terms of the family value system and may state this explicitly, but she may legitimize his anger because of special considerations and not apply sanctions against the expression of anger. A person may be expected to do something and even be explicitly criticized if he does not, but there may be implicit recognition of the difficulty of the task, and the person may, in fact, be excused. It is sensitivity to the implicit definitions of legitimacy that children often so cleverly recognize, to the dismay of their parents.

The effect of values is, ordinarily, to conserve existing patterns or at least to slow down the process of change. This is partly because family leaders were socialized in earlier values, partly because family members are committed to a given value system, and partly because the value system requires some consistency. However, values are not completely impervious to change. Indeed, while they change slowly, values are constantly being re-evaluated in the light of appropriateness, in solving the problems which arise in the family. While a solution which is wholly out of tune with family values may not be permitted, there may be a gradual process of weakening of some family values, and other values may develop which are more appropriate to contemporary conditions and which do not interfere greatly with other family values.

Any change, however, may potentially upset the system of values so that there is usually careful explanation and rationalization of the changes in the light of other values. Since the family is a small group with informal ties, the demand for rationality is usually not so acute as in larger organizations. If anything, the family value system can permit more flexibility, because the demands of logic and consistency are not so severe. However, in the event of family conflict or strains, the family values become more conscious, and in such a case there is a greater attempt to achieve consistency in the definitions of the value system.

It is in accord with group values that certain members of the family, and certain activities, are rewarded with varying amounts of prestige. Typically, the one who best represents the family values is the one who receives the most prestige within the family. In stable societies, this assignment may be made routinely on the basis of age and/or sex, but in other societies it may vary, depending on how well the various family members live up to their value system.

3. FAMILY AND PERSONALITY

So far we have considered the processes internal to the family, and the processes of the family's relations with wider units as systems of social action. Frequent reference has been made throughout to the importance, for these systems, of the articulation between the system and personality. If a social system is to operate successfully, the members must have, to a considerable extent, similar orientations to the group and activities within it, to themselves, and to each other member, and they must have motivational commitments sufficient to maintain the system and to meet its functional requirements. On the other side of the coin, it has been suggested that personality develops not entirely, but to a considerable extent, within the matrix of the family system and is maintained by the family. Now, personality can be conceived of as a system of activities, orientations, motivations, etc., which has some internal cohesion, as well as a tendency to have and maintain boundaries. In this section, a very tentative formulation of some relationships between personality, as a system, and the family, as a system, will be offered.

At this level of analysis, the problem of keeping clear one's point of reference is especially acute. On the one hand, in many interchanges the family is but a mediator between the personality and broader systems outside of the family; on the other hand, some interchanges are not primarily with the whole family but with subsystems, for example the mother-child subsystem, within it. Another problem, also alluded to earlier, is that many interchanges of the family and personality tend to remain unconscious as long as the process operates smoothly; when problems arise the relationships reveal themselves much more readily. This is reflected in the readings, most of which concern aberrations in the process of development and maintenance of some stability of personality. Still another difficulty is that personality has been investigated in most detail by another discipline, which has developed a conceptual system different from that employed here and lacking extensive articulation with the latter. In psychoanalytic and psychiatric literature, attention has been focused mainly upon the relationships of one personality to another, in particular mother and child,[19] with relatively little attention to the relationship of the family as a system and personality. Even so, it has been possible to locate readings which give some attention to family patterns and to how an individual personality is related to them.

It is not within the scope of this essay to undertake a revision of personality theory consistent with the structural-functional approach adopted here. Rather, personality will be treated as an undifferentiated system having interchanges with the various functional subsystems of the family, just as, in the first section, the family was treated as a unitary system having interchanges with the functional subsystems superordinate to it.

a. Task Performance.—Task activities in the family have to do with adapting to the instrumental requirements of living—providing and utilizing food, shelter, other possessions, etc., organizing the activities of various members to carry out such tasks, and organizing motivation and trained performance capacities to insure that they are carried out. As we have seen, the division of labor in this sphere by sex and generation is a basic structural characteristic of the family in all societies. The family, if it is to develop its members' personalities adequate for them to advance into the "outside world," must then give individuals the opportunity for graded involvement in, or identification with, task activities, and insure that learning takes place. This assignment of tasks must be appropriate to, and not above or below, the intellectual, physical, and attitudinal capacities of the individual. The paper by Freedman and associates (44) outlines the vicious circle which may be set up if the family is not properly oriented to the capacities of the individual. By these means, the personality achieves an organization which ranges far beyond the immediate skills and attitudes acquired. It acquires a structuring of trained capacities and attitudes which has much broader significance. As Plant develops (selection 40), the family's adaptation to space can affect the individual's whole personality, particularly his perception of, and attitudes toward sex. Similarly, some conception of and identification with the father's occupation must take place. Since the father's occupation is frequently far removed from the family, and from the child's experience, under certain circumstances aberrations in the child's adaptation to this may occur, as Bettelheim and Sylvester discuss (selection 39).

The personality does not acquire the structures appropriate to task performance solely through actual experience. A wide range of activities, from being read fairly tales, to playing with father on his day off, or observing him bid goodbye to mother on workdays, contribute to the formation of the appropriate attitudes, etc. Still, the assignment of tasks within the family, and the sanctions experienced by carrying them out (or failing to do so) do play an important part in the personality development. How important they are will vary with the emphasis and value given, in the family and in the society generally, to task performance functions.

The significance of the family's adaptive functional subsystem is not by any means restricted to the developing personality. Even the most mature adult personalities require some support and recognition, if they are to preserve the proper orientations to work and maintain the appropriate flow of motivational energy. Of course, this support comes not solely from the family, but consistent lack of support and validation can affect the personality, as Bakke (selection 9) also shows in relation to the unemployed man. Nor is this a one-way process. Personality structure, along with family values and varying conditions, affects the organization of tasks in the family. Severe personality problems in one spouse may require the wife to become the wage-earner, or may lead the husband to perform most maternal activities. Even in less dramatic situations, personality affects the structure of task activities; family activities may have to be restructured to accommodate to the personality of a member, averting internal strain and maintaining motivational commitment.

b. Family Leadership.—The modes of meeting the leadership problems of co-ordination and authority which the family develops similarly have wide-ranging effects upon the developing and the developed personality. Psychoanalytic theory holds that attitudes and orientations to authority figures are laid down early in life and are basic elements of the whole personality. Henry's findings (selection 42) on the relation of the authority structure of the family and the individual's proclivities for self-blame support this proposition. More generally, it would be expected that the person or persons with greatest authority would have greater ability to establish patterns of family activities suited to their personality needs. There are, of course, limits to this freedom, set by the support requirements of, and alienative potentials in, the personalities of other members.

Since personality is acquired through the process of accepting roles assigned by parents, the child is particularly susceptible to deviant development when parents express their conflicts by assigning inappropriate roles in implicit ways. The process of assigning roles is an important part of the leadership functions in a family; when there is a coincidence of impulses of the parents at a covert level, so that there is both implicit stimulation for certain behavior and implicit permission of it, the results can be very traumatic for the child's personality. The paper by Kaufman, Peck, and Tagiuri (43) illustrates the possible results when such role assignments are made. It is worth noting that in their cases the fathers as well as the daughters were involved in the sexual acting-out, suggesting that it is not only the personality of the young child which is distorted by the family process described.[20]

    c. Family Integration and Solidarity.—The need of the family to maintain some integration of the activities and sentiments of its members also plays upon the individual personality and, in turn, is affected by it. It can be asserted with justification that minimum integration is essential if socialization is to take place. Without quite intense bonds among members, the motivational leverage necessary to encourage children to give up dependency strivings, for instance, would not exist; in any event, all persons forever bear the mark of how their families handled problems of integration and solidarity. The Oedipal conflict is a good illustration of how deeply into personality structure the nature of each person's integration into the family runs.

    There is probably a fairly wide range of degrees of integration which can be produced and tolerated by stable personalities. Still, analogous to the psychoanalytic principle of overdetermination, both too much and too little integration can have deleterious effects. The family is always faced with particular problems of this nature since personalities change over time. The intense solidarity that may be effective when the child is a dependent infant may be incapacitating when the child is old enough to be breaking away from the family and forming emotional ties to outsiders. In a society in which social and geographic mobility are valued characteristics, the family needs to be flexible and capable of finding alternate modes of preserving its solidarity.

    Integration can be problematic for personality, not only by being too scarce or too abundant but by being created and maintained artificially. The paper of Lidz, *et al.* (47) relates schizophrenia to an underlying lack of integration between parents, which is denied on the surface at the price of distortions of reality.

    d. Family Value System.—From the family value system, the individual derives direction and the standards which become internalized as part of his personality. When there is consistency of values and consistent affirmation of them, the individual develops a consistent superego, through modes described at a general level by Parsons (selection 51). However, if the child receives inconsistent rewards, or is rewarded in terms of inconsistent values, then he is likely to develop superego "lacunae," as noted in the selection by Giffin, Johnson, and Litin (50).

    Much of the process of acquiring values goes on unconsciously, and thus there tends to be a good deal of continuity from one generation to the next. This continuity includes conflicts as well as conflict-free areas of values, as the Giffin, Johnson, and Litin paper also suggests. There is not, however, inevitable replication; modification can and does occur. Influences, from peer groups, other reference groups, and situational factors, have some impact on personality structure, independently of the family value system, though usually such influences can be expected to be mediated by the family. Variation, and even innovation, may also occur through the selective transmission of values to different children. The earlier selection by Vogel and Bell (30) presents some considerations of this process in pathological cases.

Concluding Remarks

This essay has attempted to provide the broad outlines of a conceptual model which can be applied to various levels of family phenomena. This schema is not yet a systematic "theory," from which emerges testable hypotheses. Rather, it is a way of systematically relating phenomena often left disconnected, and of giving a more acute awareness of the many layers and levels of the context within which specific problems are embedded. As such, the test of its utility will be in application to empirical problems.

PART I

Introduction

1   *The Universality of the Nuclear Family*

GEORGE PETER MURDOCK

Professor Murdock is an outstanding proponent and practitioner of the comparative method. On the basis of an analysis of 250 societies, he concludes that the nuclear family is universal. To explain this generalization, Murdock looks to the conditions without which societies and their cultures could not persist. Though the family may serve various other functions, four are universal—sexual, economic, reproductive, and educational—and no society has developed an institutionalized pattern within which these functions are fulfilled by units other than the family.

The family is a social group characterized by common residence, economic co-operation, and reproduction. It includes adults of both sexes, at least two of whom maintain a socially approved sexual relationship, and one or more children, own or adopted, of the sexually cohabiting adults. The family is to be distinguished from marriage, which is a complex of customs centering upon the relationship between a sexually associating pair of adults within the family. Marriage defines the manner of establishing and terminating such a relationship, the normative behavior and reciprocal obligations within it, and the locally accepted restrictions upon its personnel.

Used alone, the term "family" is ambiguous. The layman and even the social scientist often apply it undiscriminatingly to several social groups which, despite functional similarities, exhibit important points of difference. These must be laid bare by analysis before the term can be used in rigorous scientific discourse.

Three distinct types of family organization emerge from our survey of 250 representative human societies. The first and most basic, called herewith the *nuclear family*, consists typically of a married man and woman with their offspring, although in individual cases one or more additional persons may reside with them. The nuclear family will be familiar to the reader as the type of family recognized to the exclusion of all others by our own society. Among the majority of the peoples of the earth, however, nuclear families are combined, like atoms in a molecule, into larger aggregates. These composite forms of the family fall into two types, which differ in the principles by which the constituent nuclear families are affiliated. A *polygamous*[1] *family* consists of two or more nuclear families affiliated by plural marriages, i.e., by having one married parent in com-

From George Murdock, *Social Structure* (New York: The Macmillan Co., 1949), pp. 1-11. Copyright 1949 by The Macmillan Co., and used with their kind permission.

mon.[2] Under polygyny, for instance, one man plays the role of husband and father in several nuclear families and thereby unites them into a larger familial group. An *extended family* consists of two or more nuclear families affiliated through an extension of the parent-child relationship rather than of the husband-wife relationship, i.e., by joining the nuclear family of a married adult to that of his parents. The patrilocal extended family, often called the patriarchal family, furnishes an excellent example. It embraces, typically, an older man, his wife or wives, his unmarried children, his married sons, and the wives and children of the latter. Three generations, including the nuclear families of father and sons, live under a single roof or in a cluster of adjacent dwellings.

Of the 192 societies of our sample for which sufficient information is available, 47 have normally only the nuclear family, 53 have polygamous but not extended families, and 92 possess some form of the extended family. The present chapter will concern itself exclusively with the nuclear family.

The nuclear family is a universal human social grouping. Either as the sole prevailing form of the family or as the basic unit from which more complex familial forms are compounded, it exists as a distinct and strongly functional group in every known society. No exception, at least, has come to light in the 250 representative cultures surveyed for the present study, which thus corroborates the conclusion of Lowie:[3] "It does not matter whether marital relations are permanent or temporary; whether there is polygyny or polyandry or sexual license; whether conditions are complicated by the addition of members not included in *our* family circle: the one fact stands out beyond all others that everywhere the husband, wife, and immature children constitute a unit apart from the remainder of the community."

The view of Linton,[4] that the nuclear family plays "an insignificant role in the lives of many societies," receives no support from our data. In no case have we found a reliable ethnographer denying either the existence or the importance of this elemental social group. Linton mentions the Nayar of India as a society which excludes the husband and father from the family, but he cites no authorities, and the sources consulted by ourselves for this tribe do not substantiate his statement. Whatever larger familial forms may exist, and to whatever extent the greater unit may assume some of the burdens of the lesser, the nuclear family is always recognizable and always has its distinctive and vital functions—sexual, economic, reproductive, and educational—which will shortly be considered in detail. It is usually spatially as well as socially distinct. Even under polygyny a separate apartment or dwelling is commonly reserved for each wife and her children.

The reasons for its universality do not become fully apparent when the nuclear family is viewed merely as a social group. Only when it is analyzed into its constituent relationships, and these are examined individually as well as collectively, does one gain an adequate conception of the family's many-sided utility and thus of its inevitability. A social group arises when a series of interpersonal relationships, which may be defined as sets of reciprocally adjusted habitual responses, binds a number of participant individuals collectively to one another. In the nuclear family, for example, the clustered relationships are eight in number: husband-wife, father-son, father-daughter, mother-son, mother-daughter, brother-brother, sister-sister, and brother-sister. The members of each interacting pair are linked to one another, both directly through reciprocally reinforcing behavior and indirectly through the relationships of each to every other member of the family. Any factor which strengthens the tie between one member and a second also operates indirectly to bind the former to a third member, with whom the second maintains a close relationship. An explanation of the social utility of the nuclear family, and thus of its universality, must consequently be sought not alone in its function as a collectivity but also in the services and satisfactions of the relationships between its constituent members.

The relationship between father and mother in the nuclear family is solidified by the sexual privilege which all societies accord to married spouses. As a powerful impulse, often pressing individuals to behavior disruptive of the co-operative relationships upon which human social life rests, sex cannot safely be left without restraints. All known societies, consequently, have sought to bring its expression under control by surrounding it with restrictions of various kinds. On the other hand, regulation must not be carried to excess or the society will suffer through resultant personality maladjustments or through insufficient reproduction to maintain its population. All peoples have faced the problem of reconciling the need of control with the opposing need of expression, and all have solved it by culturally defining a series of sexual taboos and permissions. These checks and balances differ widely from culture to culture, but without exception a large measure of sexual liberty is everywhere granted to the married parents in the nuclear family. Husband and wife must adhere to sexual etiquette and must, as a rule, observe certain periodic restrictions such as taboos upon intercourse during menstruation, pregnancy, and lactation, but normal sex gratification is never permanently denied to them.

This sexual privilege should not be taken for granted. On the contrary, in view of the almost limitless diversity of human cultures in so many respects, it should be considered genuinely astonishing that some society somewhere has not forbidden sexual access to married partners, confining them, for example, to economic co-operation and allowing each a sexual outlet in some other relationship. As a matter of fact, one of the societies of our sample, the Banaro of New Guinea, shows a remote approach to such an arrangement. In this tribe, a groom is not permitted to approach his young wife until she has borne him a child by a special sib-friend of his father. Certain peasant communities in eastern Europe are reported to follow a somewhat analogous custom. A father arranges a marriage for his immature son with an adult woman, with whom he lives and raises children until the son is old enough to assume his marital rights.[5] These exceptional cases are especially interesting since they associate sexual rights, not with the husband-wife relationship established by marriage, but with the father-mother relationship established by the foundation of a family.

As a means of expressing and reducing a powerful basic drive, as well as of gratifying various acquired or cultural appetites, sexual intercourse strongly reinforces the responses which precede it. These, by their very nature, are largely social, and include co-operative acts which must, like courtship, be regarded as instrumental responses. Sex thus tends to strengthen all the reciprocal habits which characterize the interaction of married parents, and indirectly to bind each into the mesh of family relationship in which the other is involved.

To regard sex as the sole factor, or even as the most important one, that brings a man and a woman together in marriage and binds them into the family structure would, however, be a serious error. If all cultures, like our own, prohibited and penalized sexual intercourse except in the marital relationship, such an assumption might seem reasonable. But this is emphatically not the case. Among those of our 250 societies for which information is available, 65 allow unmarried and unrelated persons complete freedom in sexual matters, and 20 others give qualified consent, while only 54 forbid or disapprove premarital liaisons between nonrelatives, and many of these allow sex relations between specified relatives such as cross-cousins.[6] Where premarital license prevails, sex certainly cannot be alleged as the primary force driving people into matrimony.

Nor can it be maintained that, even after marriage, sex operates exclusively to reinforce the matrimonial relationship. To be sure, sexual intercourse between a married man and an unrelated woman married to another is forbidden in 126 of our sample societies, and is freely or conditionally allowed in only 24. These figures, however, give an exaggerated impression of the prevalence of cultural restraints against extramarital sexuality, for affairs are often permitted between particular relatives though forbidden with nonrelatives. Thus in a majority of the societies in our sample, for which information is available, a married man may legitimately carry on an affair with one or more of his female relatives, including a sister-in-law in 41 instances. Such evidence demonstrates conclusively that sexual gratification is by no means always confined to the marital relationship, even in theory. If it can reinforce other relationships as well, as it commonly does, it cannot be regarded as peculiarly conducive to marriage or as alone accountable for the stability of the most crucial relationship in the omnipresent family institution.

In the light of facts like the above, the attribution of marriage primarily to the factor of sex must be recognized as reflecting a bias derived from our own very aberrant sexual customs. The authors who have taken this position have frequently fallen into the further error of deriving human marriage from mating phenomena among the lower animals.[7] These fallacies were first exposed by Lippert[8] and have been recognized by a number of subsequent authorities.[9]

In view of the frequency with which sexual relations are permitted outside of marriage, it would seem the part of scientific caution to assume merely that sex is an important, but not the exclusive, factor in maintaining the marital relationship within the nuclear family, and to look elsewhere for auxilliary support. One such source is found in economic co-operation, based upon a division of labor by sex.[10] Since co-operation, like sexual association, is most readily and satisfactorily achieved by persons who habitually reside together, the two activities, each deriving from a basic biological need, are quite compatible. Indeed, the gratifications from each serve admirably to reinforce the other.

By virtue of their primary sex differences, a man and a woman make an exceptionally efficient co-operating unit.[11] Man, with his superior physical strength, can better undertake the more strenuous tasks, such as lumbering, mining, quarrying, land clearance, and housebuilding. Not handicapped, as is woman, by the physiological burdens of pregnancy and nursing, he can range farther afield to hunt, to fish, to herd, and to trade. Woman is at no disadvantage, however, in lighter tasks which can be performed in or near the home, e.g., the gathering of vegetable products, the fetching of water, the preparation of food, and the manufacture of clothing and utensils. All known human societies have developed specialization and co-operation between the sexes roughly along this biologically determined line of cleavage.[12] It is unnecessary to invoke innate psychological differences to account for the division of labor by sex; the indisputable differences in reproductive functions suffice to lay out the broad lines of cleavage. New tasks, as they arise, are assigned to one sphere of activities or to the other, in accordance with convenience and precedent. Habituation to different occupations in adulthood and early sex typing in childhood may well-explain the observable differences in sex temperament, instead of vice versa.[13]

The advantages inherent in a division of labor by sex presumably account for its universality. Through concentration and practice each partner acquires special skill at his particular tasks. Complementary parts can be learned for an activity requiring joint effort. If two tasks must be performed at the same time but in different places, both may be undertaken and the products shared. The labors of each partner provide insurance to the other. The man, perhaps, returns from a day of hunting, chilled, unsuccessful, and with his clothing soiled and torn, to find warmth before a fire which he could not have maintained, to eat food gathered and cooked by the woman instead of going hungry, and to receive fresh garments for the morrow, prepared, mended, or laundered by her hands. Or perhaps the woman has found no vegetable food, or lacks clay for pottery or skins for making clothes, obtainable only at a distance from the dwelling, which she cannot leave because her children require care; the man in his ramblings after game can readily supply her wants. Moreover, if either is injured or ill, the other can nurse him back to health. These and similar rewarding experiences, repeated daily, would suffice of themselves to cement the union. When the powerful reinforcement of sex is added, the partnership of man and woman becomes inevitable.

Sexual unions without economic co-operation are common, and there are relationships between men and women involving a division of labor without sexual gratification, e.g., between brother and sister, master and maidservant, or employer and secretary, but marriage exists only when the economic and the sexual are united into one relationship, and this combination occurs only in marriage. Marriage, thus defined, is found in every known human society. In all of them, moreover, it involves residential cohabitation, and in all of them it forms the basis of the nuclear family. Genuine cultural universals are exceedingly rare. It is all the more striking, therefore, that we here find several of them not only omnipresent but everywhere linked to one another in the same fashion.

Economic co-operation not only binds husband to wife; it also strengthens the various relationships between parents and children within the nuclear family. Here, of course, a division of labor according to age, rather than sex, comes into play. What the child receives in these relationships is obvious; nearly his every gratification depends upon his parents. But the gains are by no means one-sided. In most societies, children by the age of six or seven are able to perform chores which afford their parents considerable relief and help, and long before they attain adulthood and marriageability they become economic assets of definite importance. One need only think here of the utility of boys to their fathers and of girls to their mothers on the typical European or American farm. Moreover, children represent, as it were, a sort of investment or insurance policy; dividends, though deferred for a few years, are eventually paid generously in the form of economic aid, of support in old age, and even, sometimes, of cash returns, as where a bride-price is received for a daughter when she marries.

Siblings[14] are similarly bound to one another through the care and help given by an elder to a younger, through co-operation in childhood games which imitate the activities of adults, and through mutual economic assistance as they grow older. Thus, through reciprocal material services, sons and daughters are bound to fathers and mothers and to one another, and the entire family group is given firm economic support.

Sexual cohabitation leads inevitably to the birth of offspring. These must be nursed, tended, and reared to physical and social maturity if the parents are to reap the afore-mentioned advantages. Even if the burdens of reproduction and childcare outweigh the selfish gains to the parents, the society as a whole has so heavy a stake in the maintenance of its numbers, as a source of strength and security, that it will insist that parents fulfill these obligations. Abortion, infanticide, and neglect, unless confined within safe limits, threaten the entire community and arouse its members to apply severe social sanctions to the recalcitrant parents. Fear is thus added to self-interest as a motive for the rearing of children. Parental love, based on various derivative satisfactions, cannot be ignored as a further motive; it is certainly no more mysterious than the affection lavished by many people on burdensome animal pets, which are able to give far less in return. Individual and social advantages thus operate in a variety of ways to strengthen the reproductive aspects of the parent-child relationships within the nuclear family.

The most basic of these relationships, of course, is that between mother and child, since this is grounded in the physiological facts of pregnancy and lactation and is apparently supported by a special innate reinforcing mechanism, the mother's pleasure or tension release in suckling her infant. The father becomes involved in the care of the child less directly, through the sharing of tasks with the mother. Older children, too, frequently assume partial charge of their younger siblings, as a chore suited to their age. The entire family thus comes to participate in child care, and is further unified through this cooperation.

No less important than the physical care of offspring, and probably more difficult, is their social rearing. The young human animal must acquire an immense amount of traditional knowledge and skill, and must learn to subject his inborn impulses to the many disciplines prescribed by his culture, before he can assume his place as an adult member of his society. The burden of education and socialization everywhere falls primarily upon the nuclear family, and the task is, in general, more equally distributed than is that of physical care. The father must participate as fully as the mother because, owing to the division of labor by sex, he alone is capable of training the sons in the activities and disciplines of adult males.[15] Older siblings, too, play an important role, imparting knowledge and discipline through daily interaction in work and play. Perhaps more than any other single factor, collective responsibility for education and socialization welds the various relationships of the family firmly together.

In the nuclear family or its constituent relationships, we thus see assembled four functions fundamental to human social life—the sexual, the economic, the reproductive, and the educational. Without provision for the first and third, society would become extinct; for the second, life itself would cease; for the fourth, culture would come to an end. The immense social utility of the nuclear family and the basic reason for its universality thus begin to emerge in strong relief.

Agencies or relationships outside of the family may, to be sure, share in the fulfillment of any of these functions, but they never supplant the family. There are, as we have seen, societies which permit sexual gratification in other relationships, but none which deny it to married spouses. There may be extraordinary expansion in economic specialization, as in modern industrial civilization, but the division of labor between man and wife still persists. There may, in exceptional cases, be little social disapproval of childbirth out of wedlock, and relatives, servants, nurses, or pediatricians may assist in childcare, but the primary responsibility for bearing and rearing children ever remains with the family. Finally, grandparents, schools, or secret initiatory societies may assist in the educational process, but parents universally retain the principal role in teaching and discipline. No society, in short, has succeeded in finding an adequate substitute for the nuclear family, to which it might transfer these functions. It is highly doubtful whether any society ever will succeed in such an attempt, utopian proposals for the abolition of the family to the contrary notwithstanding.

The above-mentioned functions are by no means the only ones performed by the nuclear family. As a firm social constellation, it frequently, but not universally, draws to itself various other functions. Thus it is often the center of religious worship, with the father as family priest. It may be the primary unit in land-holding, vengeance, or recreation. Social status may depend more upon family position than upon individual achievement. And so on. These additional functions, where they occur, bring increased strength to the family, though they do not explain it.

2   *Variations in the Human Family*

CLYDE KLUCKHOHN

Empirically, there is a wide range of variation in the specific characteristics of families. This is not to say that the variation is unlimited and random; as Murdock argues, there are universal aspects. In an address to applied workers, Professor Kluckhohn, a distinguished anthropologist, emphasizes the variation that occurs along several dimensions.

Variations in the human family are interesting and are important both from scientific and from practical standpoints. However, anthropology has tended to overemphasize the differences at the expense of the similarities. Fascinated with the exotic and obsessed with the new principle of cultural relativity, anthropologists have tried to show that the gamut of variability was limitless. Earlier systematic studies seemed to indicate that this was indeed the case. There was the discovery of the extended family system, of the fact that, even in Europe, ultimogeniture existed along with primogeniture; of "visit marriage" in which the man retains residence in his own group. There were those few societies in which two or more men might be married to one woman. But claims for a socially accepted complete promiscuity or for "group marriage" have not stood up under closer scrutiny. And matriarchy, in the strict sense of the term, has turned out to be a myth. What is true is that the formal and informal power of the mother—both within the family and in political and economic affairs affecting the group as a whole—is greater in some societies than in others. Similarly, the claim that there were groups in which the father had no social relationship to his children is now seen as an extravagant overstatement of a considerable range of variation in the extent of that relationship.

The first generalization to be made, then, is that all variations in the form and functioning of the human family could, until recently, be seen as variations on a basic theme. No aspect of the universal culture pattern has been more clearly delimited than that of the family. The family was always and everywhere an agency for the protection and training of the child and for the care of the aged and the infirm. The manner and extent of this training and care varied considerably, but the basic function was constant. In every society the family was the fundamental institution for the

Clyde Kluckhohn, "Variations in the Human Family," reprinted from *The Family in a Democratic Society* (New York: Columbia University Press, 1949), pp. 3–11.

transmission of those patterned ways of living which anthropologists call culture.

The past tense has been used advisedly in the preceding sentences; for the traditional philosophy of the family has been threatened in recent decades. Both in Europe and in the United States, the function of protection for the aged, the infirm, and the distressed is being taken over more and more by the state. Greatly increased geographical mobility, changed patterns in regard to employment of married women, and other economic developments make it impossible to regard this long-established functional continuity as still a constant. Under modern urban conditions, both men and women can enjoy opportunities (which previously were easily accessible only in family life) without surrendering their independence or assuming family responsibilities.

Every culture legalizes an enduring union between two or more persons of the two sexes explicitly for purposes of parenthood. This nuclear or biological family is never completely submerged in any extended family system. The social approval of sexual union does not in any society constitute in and of itself a marriage or a family. The legitimization of sexuality between husbands and wives, like that prohibition of sexual relations between all other members of the biological family which is an almost constant feature of the human family, is everywhere conceived, not as an end in itself, but as a means to the physical nature and cultural training of children.

There is nothing mysterious or supernatural about these pan-human regularities in cultural patterns for the family. They bear an understandable relationship to certain inescapable facts in the human situation. Children inevitably go through a period of helplessness. Sickness and old age render adults dependent again. These are biological "givens," which all cultures must face. In the same way, it is a biological fact that men are ordinarily stronger physically than women and that women are for longer or shorter periods incapacitated by events of their reproductive cycle. Sexual competition within the immediate family could hardly fail to lead to suffering and to disruption of the family. Hence, the restriction of sexuality to husbands and wives may be regarded as one of those aspects of the universal culture pattern that is based upon countless millennia of trial-and-error learning. Exceptions are limited to a few ruling groups and, possibly, to the society of old Iran.

With some qualifications, then, for the contemporary situation in Europe and America, it can be said that there are certain constancies in the functions of the human family. There are also certain regularities in form. The ideal in all human groups has been long-term marriage—though not necessarily between only two partners. The elementary family has ever been conceived as based upon the primary relations of children and parents, with parents related to each other, in the last analysis, through their children.

Finally, there are psychological universals. The Freudian description of the Oedipus situation and of sibling rivalry is basically right, even though there are formal variations of this psychological theme; that is, the older person of opposite sex to whom a male child is drawn may be the sister or an aunt, and the older person of the same sex toward whom there exist ambivalent feelings may be an uncle rather than the father. But psychoanalysis has correctly pointed to some inevitable features of the psychodynamics. These words from an Indonesian informant of Cora DuBois suggest one kind of basis for the universality:

> Wives are like our mothers. When we were small our mothers fed us. When we are grown, our wives cook for us. If there is something good, they keep it in the pot until we come home. When we were small, we slept with our mothers. When we are grown, we sleep with our wives. Sometimes when we are grown, we wake in the night and call our wives "mother."

It is no accident that in many cultures the term for "sweetheart" is identical with, or similar to, the word for "mother" or "sister."

Within this basic psychological-formal-functional pattern, variations are of three general types. The first may be termed cross-cultural and refers to those differences in blueprints for family living that are standardized as part of the historic tradition of a people. These cross-cultural variations relate in part to the form of the family, in part to its functions.

There are the well-known marriage forms of monogamy, polygyny, and polyandry. These themselves have many variants. While every culture tends to define marriage as ideally permanent, there are many societies, such as our own, in which the behavioral pattern must be realistically described as "serial monogamy." Polygyny ranges from a standard of two or, at most, three wives to the Mohammedan limit of four or the hundreds held by certain African and Asiatic potentates. It is interesting, however, that in these cases only a few women are ordinarily considered wives in the full sense. In some African tribes, for instance, there are only three legal wives —"the head," "the arm," and "the leg"—and the children of concubines are formally ascribed to one of these three. The plural marriage may be to sisters or to non-related women or to a woman and her daughter by a previous marriage. In polyandry, also, the marriage of the woman may be to brothers or to nonbrothers. Monogamy, on the whole, appears mainly in the simpler societies and in those where the normal sex ratio is not disturbed. Hobhouse, Wheeler, and Ginsberg found monogamy in only 66 societies as against polygyny in 378 and polyandry in 31.

In addition to the marriage pattern, the form of the family is structured by the size of the group included in various social and economic arrangements. The biological family may customarily live alone with the occasional addition of a widowed grandmother or grandfather or collateral relative. Or, the family may be extended to include various relatives on the father's or mother's side of the family or both. Typically, a matrilineal extended family is made up of a grandmother, her husband, her married daughters, their husbands, and their children. In many societies considered matrilineal, however, this typical picture is seldom actualized in all its details. One married daughter lives with her husband's people, or she and her husband and children live as an isolated family unit. One or more sons bring their wives and children to reside with the matrilineal group. In almost every case, membership in what W. Lloyd Warner has called the "family of orientation" continues to some extent when the adult joins in founding a new "family of procreation." Matrilineal, patrilineal, and bilateral families represent ideal types rather than clear-cut forms that apply without qualification to every family in a community.

The forms of family organization prescribed by cultural patterns have consequences that are in the strict sense social rather than cultural. A cultural pattern that provides for sisters and their husbands and children living together in one place determines the nature of interpersonal relations in ways other than dictating economic co-operation, stating that children of sisters shall call each other by sibling terms, behave toward each other as do biological brothers and sisters, etc. The sheer size of the face-to-face group of relatives makes for variation in family life. If the child grows up with a maximum of, say, ten other individuals whom he addresses as "brother" and "sister," the number of personal adjustments he must make is very different from the number that would be necessary in an extended family, where he might have fifty or sixty "brothers" and "sisters." Similarly, any family system involving plural marriages is distinctive, not only because the culture accepts multiple spouses, but also because the interaction rate in a dyadic relationship is different from that in a triadic, tetradic, or still higher set. The addition of each person increases the number of persons in simple arithmetical progression, but the number of personal relations increases in the order of triangular numbers. Of course, this quantitative dimension is enormously complicated by the emotional quality of each given relationship.

It is convenient and in accord with usual practice to restrict the term "family" to that group of relatives who have habitual face-to-face dealings. Thus, only the biological families of orientation and procreation and the extended family are included, and such wider units as the clan, phratry, and moiety are excluded. But it should be noted that this conception is an artifact of the Western cultural tradition. The vocabularies of certain nonliterate languages do not include a term that corresponds to our biological family, and some fail even to distinguish the extended family from the whole group of individuals, whether personally known or not, whom one addresses by kinship terms. The distinction between actual mother and mother's sister or classificatory mother can always be and is expressed —when context makes it necessary—by such circumlocutions as "mother from whose body I came" and the like. Yet the concept of a particular group of individuals to whom one's actual biological relations are closest is often not explicit. The secondary parenthood and siblingship implied by a classificatory kinship terminology merges at every point with the relationships we call the "immediate family."

Two family systems can, of course, have approximately the same form but allot the functions within the family organization very differently. The families of the Navaho, Zuñi, and Hopi Indians are all extended, matrilineal, matrilocal. However, the cultural image of the ideal family is not identical in these three cases. The official head of the Navaho family is the father, though emotional and informal authority may actually rest largely with the mother. With the Hopi, authority is, in theory, divided between the mother and her brothers. In practice, the father has a good deal. The Zuñi system falls somewhere between the Navaho and the Hopi. In respects other than that of authority there is also a great and subtle range of variation, both formalized and unformalized. The obligations and expectations of each family member, the tolerated deviations, the stereotypes of ideal role fulfillment—all of these bear a relationship to the formal structure but cannot be predicted solely on the basis of knowledge of the forms.

The second major type of variation may be called the intracultural. In spite of the existence of ideal patterns defining family life for a total society there tend to grow up behavioral patterns that differentiate local or regional groups, economic groups, religious groups, and class groups. In our own society, for example, the existence of a generalized pattern for family organization and behavior is attested to by uniformities in the picture portrayed in national advertisements, radio programs, and moving pictures. Yet the development of well-established, class-typed family patterns has been shown by Warner, John Dollard, Allison Davis, and others. Among the Navaho, polygyny is an accepted pattern of the aboriginal culture. But the actual incidence of polygyny varies widely as between regions where the primary economic base is agricultural, pastoral, or a mixture of these two.

The third principal type of variation may be called idiosyncratic. In no society, however homogeneous, nor in any given segment of that society, is any one family precisely identical with any other. No two individuals play the culturally defined role of mother in precisely the same way. In one family the mother happens, for reasons not culturally controlled, to be much older than the father. To another family the father brings the experience of a previous unhappy marriage. In societies where children are ordinarily born every two or three years, one parent is sterile for a period. Or, if some of the children in a sequence die at an early age, the constellation of that family is unmistakably altered. It is because of a combination of determinants of this order that no particular family ever passes on "*the* culture." Each family transmits its private variant of the culture. And herein lies a fertile source of culture change.

The cause of all these variations in human family life cannot be subsumed in any simple formula. There is some degree of correlation between economic patterns and family organization. Where population density is one to the square mile or less and where livelihood depends on intimate knowledge of the country, the normal form of the family is the simple patrilineal family, with families joined together in bands or hordes. But the correlation is by no means one to one. All kinds of cultural patterns have a way of persisting long after the institutions or circumstances which gave them adaptive value have disappeared. Family patterns may be radically altered as the consequence of widespread acceptance of a new religious cult. This acceptance, in turn, may be determined by a temporary set of economic conditions or other situational factors. Many cultural forms are the product of historical accidents. A variation in family life may, for instance, arise originally as an idiosyncratic variation. A father of a special constitutional type marries a woman who is psychopathic. They manage to work out a form of mutual adjustment for themselves and their children. Most often this particular form would disappear with the end of this particular biological family. But, if the father in question happens to succeed to the chieftainship through the accidental death of his older brother, or if a son of the family founds a new religion, an accidental variant might become the "sacred institution" of a whole people, to be blindly defended and carefully perpetuated.

The practical lessons to be drawn from the foregoing by the applied social scientist (the social worker, for example) would seem to be the fol'owing: First, the stuff of human nature is, after all, basically the same because of similarities in human biology and in the conditions of human life. The tailoring is different, and this is significant in making judgments as to how human needs can most effectively be satisfied, as to what incentives will work with one group and not another, as to the meaning of a specific human act. However, the applied social scientist must not be taken in by cultural stereotypes any more than by the simplest, common-sense view of human nature, which is ordinarily a projection of values and beliefs that are local in time and in space. There are patterned variations, whether regional or class or economic, within most cultures. Moreover, there are idiosyncratic variations that sometimes bear only the most general resemblance to the cultural blueprint. In other words, knowledge of a culture or of some segment of that culture can be very useful for general orientation, but one can never expect to drop a perpendicular from the abstracted culture patterns to the behavioral forms existing in a particular family. Finally, the applied social scientist will do well to remember the multifarious causes of variations in human family life. Knowing this, the social worker can steer a difficult but necessary middle course between proper respect for traditional ways of living, as related to the total life design of a group, and absolute acceptance of specific tailorings which usually turn out, after all, to be by-products of adventitious historical events.

Anthropologists have, on the whole, been preoccupied with the more bizarre variations in human family life, such as polyandry. It is now necessary to analyze the subtler differences, to compare, for example, the romantic individualism of American marriage with French marriage which is conceived as a treaty of alliance between two families. What are the formal and functional and psychological differences between family councils of the Chinese and the Japanese type? How do the family patterns of rural Europeans alter after a generation of adaptation to urban life in New York? The case records of social workers are rich in materials for analysis of the answers to such questions as these. Probably social workers are in the best position to make the next advances in our knowledge of variations in the human family.

3   *The Transformation of the Family*

FREDERICK ENGELS

For Frederick Engels, Karl Marx's collaborator, the family was another vestige of the iniquitous capitalist system. In the writings of Lewis Morgan on family forms among American Indians, and of other early anthropologists, Engels found evidence to support his view that the family as known in Western civilization was not the original, "natural," form. In accordance with the logic of dialectic materialism, once the proletariat had seized the means of production and the communistic state was established, the family, as we know it, would disappear. The treatise from which this selection is taken was one of the influences leading Soviet Russia to attempt, in the 1920's, to abolish the family.

We have three main forms of the family, corresponding in general to the three main stages of human development: for savagery, group marriage; for barbarism, the pairing family; for civilization, monogamy supplemented by adultery and prostitution. Monogamy was the first form of the family not founded on natural, but on economic conditions, viz., the victory of private property over primitive and natural collectivism. Supremacy of the man in the family and generation of children that could be his offspring alone and were destined to be the heirs of his wealth—these were openly avowed by the Greeks to be the sole objects of monogamy. For the rest, it was a burden to them, a duty to the gods, the state, and their own ancestors, a duty to be fulfilled and no more.

Monogamy, then, does by no means enter history as a reconciliation of man and wife, and still less as the highest form of marriage. On the contrary, it enters as the subjugation of one sex by the other, as the proclamation of an antagonism between the sexes unknown in all preceding history. In an old unpublished manuscript written by Marx and me in 1846, I find the following passage: "The first division of labor is that of man and wife in breeding children." And today I may add: The first class antagonism appearing in history coincides with the development of the antagonism of man and wife in monogamy, and the first class oppression with that of the female by the male sex. Monogamy was a great historical progress. But by the side of slavery and private property it marks, at the same time, that epoch which, reaching down to our days, takes with all progress also a step backwards, relatively speaking, and develops the welfare and advancement of one by the woe and submission of the other.

Reprinted from Frederick Engels, *The Origin of the Family, Private Property, and the State*, trans. Ernest Untermann (Chicago: Chas. H. Kerr & Co., 1902), pp. 79–100 *passim*.

We are now approaching a social revolution in which the old economic foundations of monogamy will disappear just as surely as those of its complement, prostitution. Monogamy arose through the concentration of considerable wealth in one hand—a man's hand—and from the endeavor to bequeath this wealth to the children of this man to the exclusion of all others. This necessitated monogamy on the woman's, but not on the man's, part. Hence, this monogamy of women in no way hindered open or secret polygamy of men. Now, the impending social revolution will reduce this whole care of inheritance to a minimum by changing at least the over-whelming part of permanent and inheritable wealth—the means of production—into social property. Since monogamy was caused by economic conditions, will it disappear when these causes are abolished?

One might reply, not without reason: Not only will it not disappear, but it will rather be perfectly realized. For with the transformation of the means of production into collective property, wage labor will also disappear, and with it the proletariat and the necessity for a certain statistically ascertainable number of women to surrender for money. Prostitution disappears and monogamy, instead of going out of existence, at last becomes a reality—for men also. Furthermore, if one removes the economic considerations that now force women to submit to the customary disloyalty of men, women will be placed on an equal footing with men. All present experiences prove that this will tend much more strongly to make men truly monogamous than to make women polyandrous.

At all events, the situation will be considerably altered. With the transformation of the means of production into collective property, the monogamous family ceases to be the economic unit of society. The private household changes to a social industry. The care and education of children becomes a public matter. Society cares equally well for all children, legal or illegal. This removes the care about the "consequences" which now forms the essential social factor—moral and economic—hindering a girl to surrender unconditionally to the beloved man. Will not this be sufficient cause for a gradual rise of a more unconventional intercourse of the sexes and a more lenient public opinion regarding virgin honor and female shame? And finally, did we not see that in the modern world monogamy and prostitution, though antitheses, are inseparable and poles of the same social condition? Can prostitution disappear without engulfing at the same time monogamy?

The indissolubility of marriage is partly the consequence of economic conditions under which monogamy arose, and partly the consequence of tradition from the time when the connection between this economic situation and monogamy, not yet clearly understood, was carried to extremes by religion. Today, it has been perforated a thousand times. If marriage founded on love is alone moral, then it follows that marriage is moral only as long as love lasts. The duration of an attack of individual sex-love varies considerably according to the individual disposition, especially in men. A positive cessation of fondness or its replacement by a new passionate love makes a separation a blessing for both parties and for society. But humanity will be spared the useless wading through the mire of a divorce case.

What we may anticipate about the adjustment of sexual relations after the impending downfall of capitalist production is mainly of a negative nature and mostly confined to elements that will disappear. But what will be added? That will be decided after a new generation has come to maturity: a race of men who never in their lives have had any occasion for buying with money, or other economic means of power, the surrender of a woman; a race of women who have never had any occasion for surrendering to any man for any reason but love, or for refusing to surrender to their lover from fear of economic consequences. Once such people are in the world, they will not give a moment's thought to what we today believe should be their course. They will follow their own practice and fashion their own public opinion about the individual practice of every person—only this and nothing more.

4   *The Attempt to Abolish the Family in Russia*

NICHOLAS S. TIMASHEFF

In the 1920's the newly established communistic state instituted a program aimed at abolishing the family as it existed in Western civilization. Had the experiment worked, the universality of the family could no longer have been maintained. Professor Timasheff traces how the program, like many other programs of economic and political change, failed and finally had to be abandoned.

In their attempts to create a new culture, the revolutionists always meet resistance. This resistance is displayed by individuals, but they resist because they have been molded by mighty institutions through which social structure and culture are perpetuated. In modern society, these pillars of society are the family, the school, and the church. From the standpoint of the revolutionists, two of them, the family and the church, are hopeless, for it is their very nature to preserve tradition. But the school might perhaps be transformed into an instrument of cultural revolution.

Hence, for those who are eager to endow a nation with a new culture, a definite program of action follows: they must loosen the family ties; they must destroy or at least weaken the church; and they must transform the school into an accelerator of cultural revolution. This was the natural program of the Communists while they performed their Great Experiment.

With respect to the family, the destructive attitude is sometimes denied by pro-Communist writers outside of Russia.[1] The reason is obvious; the value of the family is beyond question, say, in this country, and a regime which is hostile to it cannot count on many sympathizers. But in 1919, an authoritative representative of the regime said: "The family has ceased to be a necessity, both for its members and for the State." A few years later, another high dignitary declared that the Communists had to undermine the family, "this formidable stronghold of all the turpitudes of the old regime."[2] And acts were still more conclusive than words.

The family, which was to be destroyed, was of the patriarchal type. In old Russia, marriage was a religious institution. Only religious marriage and divorce were recognized, so that the rules of the corresponding religious communities were exclusively applied. The superiority of the husband over the wife was legally recognized, but there was no joint property of the consorts.[3] The wife received the husband's last name, but the Russians emphasized that, in contradistinction to the West, their women never were addressed as "Mrs. John Doe"; their first names had to be used. Parental authority was strong; up to the age of twenty-one, children needed parental consent for marriage and quite a few other significant acts. Naturally, the institution of inheritance existed. Thus, the strong family structure prevailed; this was especially the case among the peasants and the lower-middle class, whereas among the upper classes, the intellectuals, and the workers there was a well-expressed tendency to weaken the family ties.

This stronghold of the old order, this instrument of culture tradition, was attacked by the Communists from the very start of their rule.[4] The general tendency was to destroy the stable character of marital relations and make marriage as easily soluble as possible. Naturally, marriage was liberated from all bonds with religion: after a certain date, church weddings ceased to be accorded any legal effect. Instead of going to church, the prospective consorts had to apply for "registration" of their marriage to local boards established for that purpose. Measures were taken to deprive the registration of the character of an impressive ceremony. The boards were usually located in some dark and abject room of an office building, and no words about the significance of marriage were uttered by the officials.

The most drastic change concerned divorce: in contradistinction to the old law which made it so difficult, the decrees of December 17 and 18, 1917, permitted every consort to declare that he wanted his marriage to be canceled. No reasons were to be given to the board. Receiving the application, it had to grant the cancellation immediately if there was mutual consent; if this was not the case, divorce was to be granted by the court, but this was a meaningless formality, since the court had to do it at the request of each consort, even if the other one opposed it. If one of the consorts was absent, he or she was notified by a postcard.

In addition to this, incest, bigamy, and adultery were dropped from the list of criminal offenses. Abortion was explicitly permitted by the decree of November 20, 1920, provided that it was performed by an approved physician in a state hospital. Under these conditions, the physician had to accede to requests for abortion even if no valid reasons could be established. Under war communism, inheritance ceased to exist.

When marriage can be canceled by means of a postcard, when there is no distinction between legitimacy and illegitimacy, when inheritance is unknown, parental authority is naturally weakened, and this effect was one of the purposes of the measures described. In official propaganda, the idea was persistently emphasized that children had to obey their parents only insofar as the parents complied loyally with the directions of those in power. This signified, among other things, that unless they wanted to risk placing themselves in a dangerous position, parents could not oppose the propaganda of the Marxist doctrine, including atheism, to which the children were exposed at school. There they were taught to do their best to re-educate their parents in the Communist spirit and denounce them to the authorities if they displayed a marked counterrevolutionary attitude. Numerous family tragedies evolved on that basis, the state backing the children against the parents. Time and again the idea was publicly discussed as to whether family education ought not to be abolished and replaced by education in state institutions. Reluctantly, the idea was rejected as impractical, at least for the period of transition.

During the NEP,[5] a partial restoration of the family could be expected, if the Marxist doctrine were correct and monogamy and the strong family were the counterpart of the individualistic manner of production. There was actually one almost unavoidable concession; this was the restoration of inheritance. But in contrast with the Marxist scheme, the attack on the family was rather strengthened. A new Family Code was prepared in 1925, and the draft was submitted to an informal discussion. Voices from the countryside were unfavorable, but this did not stop the government, and the new code was enacted as of January 1, 1927. The main innovation was the introduction of the institution of "the non-registered marriage," legally equal to the registered one. This meant that courts and boards were obliged to consider every union of a man and woman as marriage provided that at least one of the following conditions were present: (1) durable cohabitation; (2) common menage; (3) declaration of the relationship before third persons, or (4) mutual support and common education of the children. The unforeseen effect was the legalization of bigamy: applying the new law, the Supreme Court prescribed the division of the estate of a deceased man between his registered and nonregistered wife.[6]

The period of the Second Socialist Offensive was characterized by additional efforts to uproot the traditional structure of the family. The labor law of the period made it obligatory to accept any job imposed on the individual, and often husband and wife were assigned work in different towns. To the complaint of a teacher that she was artificially separated from her husband, the Labor Board replied that divorce was easy and that she probably could find another husband in the place of her occupation. In Stalingrad, it was decided to create "socialist suburbs" consisting of houses without apartments for family life, replaced by single rooms, refectories, and nurseries. The plan fell through because nobody but bachelors agreed to live in such suburbs.

The antifamily policy was crowned by partial success: around 1930, on the average, family ties were substantially weaker than they had been before the revolution. But this partial success was more than balanced by a number of detrimental effects unforeseen by the promoters of the Communist experiment. About 1934, these detrimental effects were found to endanger the very stability of the new society and its capacity to stand the test of war. Let us review these effects.

1. The abuse of the freedom of divorce and abortion resulted in an ominous decrease of the birth rate. No natality figures have ever been published for the crucial years, but in 1937, the population proved to be 13 million behind expectation, so that around 1934, the deficit must already have been large. To what extent this was due to the freedoms just mentioned cannot be established. But the following figures speak for themselves: in 1934, in the medical institutions of the city of Moscow, 57 thousand children were born, but 154 thousand abortions were performed; in 1935, already under changing conditions, the figures were 70 thousand, and 155 thousand. As to divorce, the frequency of which also pushes down the birth rate, the following figures were reported from Moscow: in 1934, in 100 marriages there were 37 divorces, and in the first half of 1935, there were 38.3 divorces.[7]

2. The dissolution of family ties especially of the parent-child relations threatened to produce a wholesale dissolution of community ties, with rapidly increasing juvenile delinquency as the main symptom. In 1935, the Soviet papers were full of information and indignation about the rise of hooliganism, i.e., of crimes in which the sadistic joy of inflicting pain on somebody or destroying something of value was paramount. Everywhere, wrote the papers, gangs invaded workingmen's dwellings, ransacked them, and destroyed or spoiled what they did not take away; if somebody dared to resist, he was mercilessly killed. In trains, the hooligans sang obscene songs; to prolong the fun, they did not permit travelers to alight at their destinations if they had not finished singing. Sometimes the schools were besieged by neglected children; other times gangs beat the teachers and attacked women, or regularly fought against one another.

3. Finally, the magnificent slogans of the liberation of sex and the emancipation of women proved to have worked in favor of the strong and reckless, and against the weak and shy. Millions of girls saw their lives ruined by Don Juans in Communist garb, and millions of children had never known parental homes.

The disintegration of the family did not disturb the Communists, since this was precisely what they wanted to achieve, but they were disturbed by quite a few collateral effects of the disorganization. The unfavorable trend of the population figures threatened to undermine both the labor supply and the strength of the nation at arms—for wars to be waged by the next generation. In the specific circumstances of 1934, the waste of human energy in juvenile delinquency, the combat against it, and love affairs, and the accumulation of unfavorable attitudes among the victims of the new family order—or perhaps disorder is the correct word?—could no longer be tolerated: they undermined the strength of the nation for the war which was straight ahead. The unfavorable development had to be stopped, and to achieve this the government had no other choice but to re-enforce that pillar of society which is the family. These were the main lines of development:

1. Contrary to the teachings of the previous years, young people were instructed to consider marriage "as the most serious affair in life," since in principle it should be a union for life. Statements such as follow, which never could have appeared in the course of the Communist experiment, now daily adorned the Soviet papers and magazines: "There are people who dare to assert that the Revolution destroys the family; this is entirely wrong: the family is an especially important phase of social relations in socialist society. . . . One of the basic rules of Communist morals is that of strengthening the family. . . . The right to divorce is not a right to sexual laxity. A poor husband and father cannot be a good citizen. People who abuse the freedom of divorce should be punished." And actually, in 1935, the Soviet government started to prosecute men for rape who "changed their wives as gloves," registering a marriage one day and divorce the next. *Pravda* told the following story:

Engineer P. seduced a girl by promising to marry her. When symptoms of pregnancy appeared, the girl reminded him of his promise. His reply was: "Look, dear, you are the seventh girl in my life to whom the same unpleasant thing has occurred. Here is a letter from another woman who is also bearing a child of mine. Could I marry her, too?" The girl insisted, but the engineer terminated the discussion by saying: "Forget about marriage. Do as you like. Here is money to pay for an abortion." Having told the story, the paper added: "This man should be tried, and his trial ought to be a 'demonstrative trial.' " [8]

In the official journal of the Commissariat of Justice these amazing statements may be found:

> The State cannot exist without the family. Marriage is a positive value for the Socialist Soviet State only if the partners see in it a lifelong union. So-called free love is a bourgeois invention and has nothing in common with the principles of conduct of a Soviet citizen. Moreover, marriage receives its full value for the State only if there is progeny, and the consorts experience the highest happiness of parenthood. [9]

To inculcate the rediscovered value of marriage into the minds of the younger generation, not only the negative method of deterrence by trials and producing indignation by well-chosen stories was used, but also the positive method of glorifying marriage by well-staged ceremonies; perhaps one could speak of "demonstrative marriage." Here is a story from *Izvestia*. The people involved are a *kolhoz* brigadier, V., and the first parachutist among *kolhoz* girls, B. The scene is Northern Caucasus, one of Russia's granaries.

The romance lasted about two years. In the beginning, V. hated B.

He did his best to organize a shock brigade,[10] but she preferred dancing and diverted the energy of youth towards that futility. When V. saw that he was unable to discourage that attraction he joined the movement, even started helping young people organize dances and athletic performances, and in return was helped by them in work. Then suddenly, when B. made her first jump, V. decided that life without her would be valueless, and proposed to her. She accepted. The secretaries of the regional and local party organizations decided to sponsor the marriage. Stimulated by them, the collective farm took over all preparations and decorated the village beautifully for the great day. The people's commissar for agriculture was invited to come. He could not accept, but congratulated the young people by wire and offered them a magnificent gift, a phonograph and a set of records.

The story is continued in *Pravda*. Early in the morning guests started arriving. Among them were leaders of the party, the Soviets, and the economic organizations, as well as the champion of the girl parachutists of the Union. About noon, a score of airplanes appeared in the sky. The betrothed were offered a ride, after which they were enthusiastically acclaimed by the crowd. About five o'clock, 800 guests were invited to dinner. Tables were overloaded with mutton, hams, ducks, chickens, pies, and other dishes. After a while the regional party secretary rose and made a speech congratulating the V.'s on their marriage, the most serious step in their lives. He expressed the hope that they would live in perfect unity and procreate an abundant Bolshevik progeny. The 800 present rose and drank to the health of the newlyweds. The people danced and rejoiced far into the night.[11]

Was not this an invitation to millions of young people to reconsider those ideas about marriage which, until quite recently, they were taught as belonging to the very essence of the doctrine? To re-enforce the new ideas, very simple, but probably very effective symbolic means were used. The registration offices ceased to be filthy places. Now, young people found them clean, comfortable, well furnished; the officers became polite, friendly, underlining the seriousness of the act. Marriage certificates started being issued on decent paper, no longer on wrapping paper, as was the case previously. For a small additional sum, the newlyweds could receive a marriage certificate designed by artists.[12] Then, in the fall of 1936, wedding rings started being sold in Soviet shops.[13] Since these rings are used in church weddings, this novelty could be interpreted as an invitation, on the part of the government, to have the civil marriage, or registration, re-enforced and made almost indissoluble by the church.

2. The freedom of divorce was first curtailed and then almost abolished. The first phase appears in the law of June 27, 1936, which introduced a number of inhibitions. It calls for the summoning of both parties when a divorce is to be registered.

Moreover, according to the law of September 28, 1935, the fact of divorce must be marked in the passports and birth certificates of the consorts. Commenting on this regulation, *Izvestia* expressed the hope that before marrying a "fluttering scoundrel," a girl would ask him to produce his papers and then perhaps renounce the honor of becoming his thirtieth bride.[14]

Finally, the fee for divorce which previously had been rather nominal was substantially raised; instead of three rubles, one had to pay 50 rubles for the first divorce, 150 for the second, and 300 for the third and each subsequent divorce.

The effect of the antidivorce drive may be measured by the following figures: in the course of the second half of the year 1936, the number of divorces in the Ukraine was 10,992, against 35,458 in the second half of 1935;[15] in other words, it decreased more than three times.

The second phase appears in the decree of July 8, 1944.

> Prospective applicants for divorce will henceforth be obliged to state their reasons and satisfy the courts that these reasons are serious and valid. Both parties must appear personally before a lower court which hears all the evidence and then seeks to determine if it cannot effect a reconciliation. If this is believed impossible, the petition can be carried to a higher court. Witnesses must be heard in both courts. The divorce fees have been raised to 2,000 rubles.

It is probable that the courts, obeying the government's directions, will demand very good reasons and irrefutable evidence to grant a divorce. In consequence, obtaining a divorce in Russia will probably become more difficult than in many states of this country.

Moreover, the decree of July 8, 1944, abolished the institution of "unregistered marriage" introduced in 1926. Now, only "registered marriage" is legally recognized; as a corollary, the "bourgeois" distinction between legitimate and illegitimate children has reappeared in Soviet law. In addition to this, "the research of paternity" has been explicitly forbidden, so that illegitimate children and their mothers will receive no alimony. Very definitely, this will prove a mighty deterrent to extra-marital relations, insofar as girls are concerned.

3. The freedom to dispose of unborn children through abortions no longer exists. Early in 1935 a campaign against abortion was started. Articles began to appear in Soviet papers written by high medical authorities explaining the harm which abortion, especially repeated abortion, inflicts on women.[16] Praising maternity, these authorities declared that the longing for children had suddenly reappeared among the women of the Soviet Union—a manner of saying that now Stalin wanted them to bear as many children as possible. Trials resulting in severe sentences finished the careers of persons operating clandestine "abortaria": their very emergence disclosed that, without change in the law, Soviet hospitals no longer

performed abortion at the simple request of the pregnant woman. Finally, a draft law prohibiting abortion was published and offered for public discussion. Numerous objections were raised, mainly based on intolerable dwelling conditions. Nevertheless, the law of June 27, 1936, abolished the freedom of abortion which had been considered one of the highest achievements of Communism by many pro-Communists.

Repealing the notorious law of November 20, 1920, the new law prohibited abortion in all cases except where there was danger to life or health of the pregnant woman or danger of hereditary transmission of serious sickness. As in the former law, only medical men were permitted to perform the operation. Pressure exerted on a woman to induce her into abortion was declared a crime punishable by two years in prison. To make more childbearing possible, the law promised a large extension of the network of maternity hospitals, day nurseries, and kindergartens. Maternity grants were increased, and special allowances were promised to mothers of six or more children.[17]

4. The peculiar parent-child relationship which had obtained under the Communist experiment, and which granted superiority to the children, was reversed to one which is considered normal in the world; once more, children have to recognize the authority of their parents. Obviously, the change could not be effected through legal enactment, and the method of persuasion through propaganda was used exactly in the same manner as it was used to stabilize marriage. Statements like these could be found almost daily on the pages of Soviet papers, beginning with the spring of 1935:

> Young people should respect their elders, especially their parents. . . . The respect and care of parents is an essential part of the Comsomol[18] morals. . . . One must respect and love his parents, even if they are old-fashioned and do not like the Comsomol.[19]

In 1939, the official journal of the Union Prosecutor declared:

> Sound moral ideas must be inculcated into the minds of young persons. They must know that lack of care for their parents is found only among savages and that in every civilized society such conduct is considered dishonest and base.[20]

To corroborate these ideas, the journal cited the laws of Solon and Xenophon's works.

The method of positive demonstration was also used, and Stalin himself found it necessary to set the example. In October, 1935, he paid a visit to his old mother living in Tiflis,[22] and in the detailed accounts of this visit signs of love and respect to the old lady by the leader of the world proletariat were emphasized. A high degree of intimacy in family relations was displayed through the reproduction of such questions as: how did Stalin's children like the jam made for them by their grandmother. Another day Stalin appeared in one of Moscow's gardens with his children, something he had never done previously. Up to that time, the majority of Soviet citizens did not even know that Stalin had any children.

Gradually, the unlimited freedom granted to young people under the Communist experiment was curbed. One of the most conspicuous items in the process has been the decree of July 15, 1943, excluding children below the age of sixteen from evening perfomances in theaters and movies.

To strengthen parental authority, an indirect method has been used in the new inheritance law of March 20, 1945. While previous laws limited possible heirs to direct or adopted descendants, consorts, and needy dependents, the new law broadens this list to include parents, brothers, sisters, and public organizations. Although according to the new law the testator may not deprive his minor children or jobless heirs of their rightful portion, its impact on the family is clear: the greater the freedom to dispose of one's estate, the greater is the authority of the head of the family relating to presumptive heirs.

5 Is the Family Universal?
—The Israeli Case

MELFORD E. SPIRO

Professor Spiro has intensively studied life in an Israeli kibbutz. These communal settlements, while not characteristic of the whole society, provide a test of the proposition of the universality of the nuclear family. If Murdock's definitions are strictly applied, the kibbutz has no family, except as it is one big, extended family. However, socially regulated patterns of mating exist, and children are recognized as the offspring of particular couples. This suggests to Spiro that the family fulfills functions for the individuals which may be stronger, even more universal, than those fulfilled for the society. In his addendum, Spiro considers whether Murdock's definition of the family is adequate, and whether a redefinition of what constitutes the family would not remove this seeming exception.

The universality of the family has always been accepted as a sound hypothesis in anthropology; recently, Murdock has been able to confirm this hypothesis on the basis of his important cross-cultural study of kinship. Moreover, Murdock reports that the "nuclear" family is also universal, and that typically it has four functions: sexual, economic, reproductive, and educational. What is more important is his finding that no society "has succeeded in finding an adequate substitute for the nuclear family, to which it might transfer these functions."[1] In the light of this evidence, there would be little reason to question his prediction that "it is highly doubtful whether any society ever will succeed in such an attempt, utopian proposals for the abolition of the family to the contrary notwithstanding."[2]

The functions served by the nuclear family are, of course, universal prerequisites for the survival of any society, and it is on this basis that Murdock accounts for its universality.

Without provision for the first and third (sexual and reproductive), society would become extinct; for the second (economic), life itself would cease; for the fourth (educational), culture would come to an end. The immense social utility of the nuclear family and the basic reason for its universality thus begins to emerge in strong relief.[3]

Although sexual, economic, reproductive, and educational activities are the functional prerequisites of any society, it comes as somewhat of a surprise, nevertheless, that all four functions are served by the same social

Reprinted from Melford E. Spiro, "Is the Family Universal?" *American Anthropologist*, LVI, No. 5, Part 1, 839–846, with the kind permission of the publishers. This selection has been brought up to date for its insertion in the present volume.

group. One would normally assume, on purely a priori grounds, that within the tremendous variability to be found among human cultures, there would be some cultures in which these four functions were distributed among more than one group. Logically, at least, it is entirely possible for these functions to be divided among various social groups within a society; and it is, indeed, difficult to believe that somewhere man's inventive ingenuity should not have actualized this logical possibility. As a matter of fact this possibility has been actualized in certain utopian communities—and it has succeeded within the narrow confines of these communities. The latter, however, have always constituted subgroups within a larger society, and the basic question remains as to whether such attempts could succeed when applied to the larger society.

Rather than speculate about the answer to this question, however, this paper presents a case study of a community which, like the utopian communities, constitutes a subgroup within a larger society and which, like some utopian communities, has also evolved a social structure which does not include the family. It is hoped that an examination of this community —the Israeli *kibbutz*—can shed some light on this question.

A *kibbutz* (plural, *kibbutzim*) is an agricultural collective in Israel whose main features include communal living, collective ownership of all property (and hence, the absence of "free enterprise" and the "profit motive"), and the communal rearing of children. *Kibbutz* culture is informed by its explicit, guiding principle, "from each according to his ability, to each according to his needs." The family, as that term is defined in *Social Structure,* does not exist in the *kibbutz,* in either its nuclear, polygamous, or extended forms. It should be emphasized, however, that the *kibbutzim* are organized into three separate national federations, and though the basic structure of *kibbutz* society is similar in all three, there are important differences among them. Hence, the term *kibbutz,* as used in this paper, refers exclusively to those *kibbutzim* that are members of the federation studied by the author.[4]

As Murdock defines it, the family is a social group characterized by common residence, economic cooperation, and reproduction. It includes adults of both sexes, at least two of whom maintain a socially approved sexual relationship, and one or more children, own or adopted, of the sexually cohabiting adults.[5] The social group in the *kibbutz* that includes adults of both sexes and their children, although characterized by reproduction, is not characterized by common residence or by economic cooperation. Before examining this entire social group, however, we shall first analyze the relationship between the two adults in the group who maintain a "socially approved sexual relationship," in order to determine whether their relationship constitutes a "marriage."

Murdock's findings reveal that marriage entails an interaction of persons of opposite sex such that a relatively permanent sexual relationship is maintained and an economic division of labor is practiced. Where either of these behavior patterns is absent, there is no marriage. As Murdock puts it:

> Sexual unions without economic co-operation are common, and there are relationships between men and women involving a division of labor without sexual gratification . . . but marriage exists only when the economic and the sexual are united in one relationship, and the combination occurs only in marriage.[6]

In examining the relationship of the couple in the *kibbutz* who share a common marriage, and whose sexual union is socially sanctioned, it is discovered that only one of these two criteria—the sexual—applies. Their relationship does not entail economic co-operation. If this be so—and the facts will be examined in a moment—there is no marriage in the *kibbutz,* if by marriage is meant a relationship between adults of opposite sex, characterized by sexual and economic activities. Hence, the generalization that, "marriage, thus defined, exists in every known society,"[7] has found an exception.

A *kibbutz* couple lives in a single room, which serves as a combined bedroom-living room. Their meals are eaten in a communal dining room, and their children are reared in a communal children's dormitory. Both the man and the woman work in the *kibbutz,* and either one may work in one of its agricultural branches or in one of the "service" branches. The latter include clerical work, education, work in the kitchen, laundry, etc. In actual fact, however, men preponderate in the agricultural branches, and women, in the service branches of the economy. There are no men, for example, in that part of the educational system which extends from infancy to the junior-high level. Nor do women work in those agricultural branches that require the use of heavy machinery, such as trucks, tractors, or combines. It should be noted, however, that some women play major roles in agricultural branches, such as the vegetable garden and the fruit orchards; and some men are indispensable in service branches such as the high school. Nevertheless, it is accurate to state that a division of labor based on sex is characteristic of the *kibbutz* society as a whole. This division of labor, however, does not characterize the relationship that exists between couples. Each mate works in some branch of the *kibbutz* economy, and each, as a member (*chaver*) of the *kibbutz,* receives his equal share of the goods and services that the *kibbutz* distributes. Neither, however, engages in economic activities that are exclusively directed to the satisfaction of the needs of his mate. Women cook, sew, launder, etc., for the entire *kibbutz,* and not for their mates exclusively. Men produce goods, but the economic returns from their labor go to the *kibbutz,* not to their mates and themselves, although they, like all members of the *kibbutz,* share in these economic returns. Hence, though there is economic co-operation between the sexes within the community as a whole, this co-operation does not take place between mates because the social structure of this society precludes the necessity for such co-operation.

What then is the nature of the relationship of the *kibbutz* couple? What are the motives for their union? What functions, other than sex, does it serve? What distinguishes such a union from an ordinary love affair?

In attempting to answer these questions, it should first be noted that premarital sexual relations are not taboo. It is expected, however, that youth of high-school age refrain from sexual activity; sexual intercourse between high-school students is strongly discouraged. After graduation from high school, however, and their election to membership in the *kibbutz,* there are no sanctions against sexual relations among these young people. While still single, *kibbutz* members live in small private rooms, and their sexual activities may take place in the room of either the male or the female, or in any other convenient location. Lovers do not ask the *kibbutz* for permission to move into a (larger) common room, nor, if they did, would this permission be granted if it were assumed that their relationship was merely that of lovers. When a couple asks for permission to share a room, they do so—and the *kibbutz* assumes that they do so—not because they are lovers, but because they are in love. The request for a room, then, is the sign that they wish to become a "couple" (*zug*), the term the *kibbutz* has substituted for the traditional "marriage." This union does not require the sanction of a marriage ceremony, or of any other event. When a couple requests a room, and the *kibbutz* grants the request, their union is *ipso facto* sanctioned by society. It should be noted, however, that all *kibbutz* couples eventually "get married" in accordance with the marriage laws of the state—usually just before, or soon after, their first child is born—because children born out of wedlock have no legal rights according to state law.

But becoming a couple affects neither the status nor the responsibilities of either the male or the female in the *kibbutz*. Both continue to work in whichever branch of the economy they had worked in before their union. The legal and social status of both the male and the female remain the same. The female retains her maiden name. She not only is viewed as a member of the *kibbutz* in her own right, but her official registration card in the *kibbutz* files remains separate from that of her "friend" (*chaver*)— the term used to designate spouses.[8]

But if sexual satisfaction may be obtained outside of this union, and if the union does not entail economic co-operation, what motivates people to become couples? It seems that the motivation is the desire to satisfy certain needs for intimacy, using that term in both its physical and psychological meanings. In the first place, from the sexual point of view, the average *chaver* is not content to engage in a constant series of casual affairs. After a certain period of sexual experimentation, he desires to establish a relatively permanent relationship with one person. But in addition to the physical intimacy of sex, the union also provides a psychological intimacy that may be expressed by notions such as comradeship, security, dependency, succorance, etc. And it is this psychological intimacy, primarily, that distinguishes couples from lovers. The criterion of the couple relationship, then, that which distinguishes it from a relationship between adults of the same sex who enjoy psychological intimacy, or from that of adults of opposite sex who enjoy physical intimacy, is love. A couple comes into being when these two kinds of intimacy are united in one relationship.

Since the *kibbutz* couple does not constitute a marriage because it does not satisfy the economic criterion of marriage, it follows that the couple and their children do not constitute a family, economic co-operation being part of the definition of the family. Furthermore, as has already been indicated, this group of adults and children does not satisfy the criterion of common residence. For though the children visit their parents in the latter's room every day, their residence is in one of the children's houses (*bet yeladim*), where they sleep, eat, and spend most of their time.

More important, however, in determining whether or not the family exists in the *kibbutz* is the fact that the physical care and the social rearing of the children are not the responsibilities of their own parents. But these responsibilities, according to Murdock's findings, are the most important functions that the adults in the family have with respect to the children.

Before entering into a discussion of the *kibbutz* system of collective education (*chinuch meshutaf*), it should be emphasized that the *kibbutz* is a child-centered society, par excellence. The importance of children, characteristic of traditional Jewish culture, has been retained as one of the primary values in this avowedly antitraditional society. "The parents' crown" is the title given to the chapter on children in an ethnography of the Eastern European Jewish village. The authors of this ethnography write:

> Aside from the scriptural and social reasons, children are welcomed for the joy they bring beyond the gratification due to the parents—the pleasure of having a child in the house. A baby is a toy, the treasure, and the pride of the house.[9]

This description, except for the scriptural reference, applies without qualification to the *kibbutz*.

But the *kibbutz* has still another reason for cherishing its children. The *kibbutz* views itself as an attempt to revolutionize the structure of human society and its basic social relations. Its faith in its ability to achieve this end can be vindicated only if it can raise a generation that will choose to live in this communal society, and will, thus, carry on the work that was initiated by the founders of this society—their parents.

For both these reasons the child is king. Children are lavished with attention and with care to the point where many adults admit that the children are "spoiled." Adult housing may be poor, but the children live in good houses; adult food may be meager and monotonous, but the children enjoy a variety of excellent food; there may be a shortage of clothes for adults, but the children's clothing is both good and plentiful.

Despite this emphasis on children, however, it is not their own parents who provide directly for their physical care. Indeed, the latter have no responsibility in this regard. The *kibbutz* as a whole assumes this responsibility for all its children. The latter sleep and eat in special children's houses, they obtain their clothes from a communal store; when ill, they are taken care of by their "nurses." This does not mean that parents are not concerned about the physical welfare of their own children. On the contrary, this is one of their primary concerns. But it does mean that the active responsibility for their care has been delegated to a community institution. Nor does it mean that parents do not work for the physical care of their children, for this is one of their strongest drives. But the fruits of their labor are not given directly to their children; they are given instead to the community which, in turn, provides for all the children. A bachelor or a couple without children contribute as much to the children's physical care as a couple with children of their own.

The family's responsibility for the socialization of children, Murdock reports, is "no less important than the physical care of the children."

> The burden of education and socialization everywhere falls primarily upon the nuclear family. . . . Perhaps more than any other single factor collective responsibility for education and socialization welds the various relationships of the family firmly together.[10]

But the education and socialization of *kibbutz* children are the function of their nurses and teachers, and not of their parents. The infant is placed in the infants' house upon the mother's return from the hospital, where it remains in the care of nurses. Both parents see the infant there; the mother when she feeds it, the father upon return from work. The infant is not taken to its parents' room until its sixth month, after which it stays with them for an hour. As the child grows older, the amount of time he spends with his parents increases, and he may go to their room whenever he chooses during the day, though he must return to his children's house before lights-out. Since the children are in school most of the day, however, and since both parents work during the day, the children—even during their school vacations—are with their parents for (approximately) a two-hour period in the evening—from the time that the parents return from work until they go to eat their evening meal. The children may also be with their parents all day Saturday—the day of rest—if they desire.

As the child grows older, he advances through a succession of children's houses with children of his own age, where he is supervised by a nurse. The nurse institutes most of the disciplines, teaches the child his basic social skills, and is responsible for the "socialization of the instincts." The child also learns from his parents, to be sure, and they too are agents in the socialization process. But the bulk of his socialization is both entrusted, and deliberately delegated, to the nurses and teachers. There is little doubt but that a *kibbutz* child, bereft of the contributions of his parents to his socialization, would know his culture; deprived of the contributions of his nurses and teachers, however, he would remain an unsocialized individual.

As they enter the juvenile period, pre-adolescence, and adolescence, the children are gradually inducted into the economic life of the *kibbutz*. They work from an hour (grade-school students) to three hours (high-school seniors) a day in one of the economic branches under the supervision of adults. Thus, their economic skills, like most of their early social skills, are taught them by adults other than their parents. This generalization applies to the learning of values, as well. In the early ages, the *kibbutz* values are inculcated by nurses, and later by teachers. When the children enter junior high, this function, which the *kibbutz* views as paramount in importance, is delegated to the "homeroom teacher," known as the "educator" (*mechanech*), and to a "leader" (*madrich*) of the inter-*kibbutz* youth movement. The parents, of course, are also influential in the teaching of values, but the formal division of labor in the *kibbutz* has delegated this responsibility to other authorities.

Although the parents do not play an outstanding role in the socialization of their children, or in providing for their physical needs, it would be erroneous to conclude that they are unimportant figures in their children's lives. Parents are of crucial importance in the *psychological* development of the child. They serve as the objects of his most important identifications, and they provide him with a certain security and love that he obtains from no one else. If anything, the attachment of the young children to their parents is greater than it is in our own society. But this is irrelevant to the main consideration of this paper. Its purpose is to call attention to the fact that those functions of parents that constitute the *conditio sine qua non* for the existence of the "family"—the physical care and socialization of children—are not the functions of the *kibbutz* parents. It can only be concluded that in the absence of the economic and educational functions of the typical family, as well as of its characteristic of common residence, that the family does not exist in the *kibbutz*.

It is apparent from this brief description of the *kibbutz* that most of the functions characteristic of the typical nuclear family have become the functions of the entire *kibbutz* society. This is so much the case that the *kibbutz* as a whole can almost satisfy the criteria by which Murdock defines the family. This observation is not meant to imply that the *kibbutz* is a nuclear family. Its structure and that of the nuclear family are dissimilar. This observation does suggest, however, that the *kibbutz* can function without the family, because it functions as if it, itself, were a family; and it can so function because its members perceive each other as kin, in the psychological implications of that term. The latter statement requires some explanation.

The members of the *kibbutz* do not view each other merely as fellow citizens, or as coresidents in a village, or as co-operators of an agricultural economy. Rather they do view each other as *chaverim,* or comrades, who comprise a group in which each is intimately related to the other, and in which the welfare of the one is bound up with the welfare of the other. This is a society in which the principle, "from each according to his ability, to each according to his needs," can be practiced, not because its members are more altruistic than the members of other societies, but because each member views his fellow as a kinsman, psychologically speaking. And just as a father in the family does not complain because he works much harder than his children, and yet he may receive no more, or even less, of the family income than they, so the *kibbutz* member whose economic productivity is high does not complain because he receives no more, and sometimes less, than a member whose productivity is low. This principle is taken for granted as the normal way of doing things. Since they are all *chaverim,* "it's all in the family," psychologically speaking.

In short, the *kibbutz* constitutes a *gemeinschaft*. Its patterns of interaction are interpersonal patterns; its ties are kin ties, without the biological tie of kinship. In this one respect it is the "folk society," in almost its pure form. The following quotation from Redfield could have been written with the *kibbutz* in mind, so accurately does it describe the social-psychological basis of *kibbutz* culture.

> The members of the folk society have a strong sense of belonging together. The group . . . see their own resemblances and feel correspondingly united. Communicating intimately with each other, each has a strong claim on the sympathies of the others.
>
> . . . .
>
> The personal and intimate life of the child in the family is extended, in the folk society, into the social world of the adults. . . . It is not merely that relations in such a society are personal; it is also that they are familial. . . . the result is a group of people among whom prevail the personal and categorized relationships that characterize the families as we know them, and in which the patterns of kinship tend to be extended outward from the group of genealogically connected individuals into the whole society. The kin are the type persons for all experience.[11]

Hence it is that the bachelor and the childless couple do not feel that an injustice is being done them when they contribute to the support of the children of others. The children *in* the *kibbutz* are viewed as the children *of* the *kibbutz*. Parents (who are much more attached to their own children than they are to the children of others) and bachelors, alike, refer to all the *kibbutz* children as "our children."

The social perception of one's fellows as kin, psychologically speaking, is reflected in another important aspect of the *kibbutz* behavior. It is a striking and significant fact that those individuals who were born and raised in the *kibbutz* tend to practice group exogamy, although there are no rules that either compel or encourage them to do so. Indeed, in the *kibbutz* in which our field work was carried out, all such individuals married outside their own *kibbutz*. When they are asked for an explanation of this behavior, these individuals reply that they cannot marry those persons with whom they have been raised and whom they, consequently, view as siblings. This suggests, as Murdock has pointed out, that "the *kibbutz* to its members *is* viewed psychologically as a family to the extent that it generates the same sort of unconscious incest-avoidance tendencies" (private communication).

What is suggested by this discussion is the following proposition: although the *kibbutz* constitutes an exception to the generalization concerning the universality of the family, structurally viewed, it serves to confirm this generalization, functionally and psychologically viewed. In the absence of a specific social group—the family—to whom society delegates the functions of socialization, reproduction, etc., it has become necessary for the entire society to become a large extended family. But only in a society whose members perceive each other psychologically as kin can it function as a family. And there would seem to be a population limit beyond which point individuals are no longer perceived as kin. That point is probably reached when the interaction of its members is no longer face-to-face; in short, when it ceases to be primary group. It would seem probable, therefore, that only in a "familial" society, such as the *kibbutz,* is it possible to dispense with the family.

Addendum, 1958

This is, quite obviously, an essay in the interpretation, rather than in the reporting of data.[12] After rereading the paper in 1958, I realized that the suggested interpretation follows from only one conception of the role which definitions play in science. Starting with Murdock's inductive—based on a sample of 250 societies—definitions of marriage and family, I concluded that marriage and the family do not exist in the *kibbutz,* since no single group or relationship satisfies the conditions stipulated in the definitions. If I were writing this essay today, I would wish to explore alternative interpretations as well—interpretations which, despite Murdock's definitions, would affirm the existence of marriage and the family in the *kibbutz*. Hence, I shall here very briefly outline the direction which one alternative interpretation would take.

The *kibbutz,* it should be noted first, does not practice—nor does it sanction—sexual promiscuity. Each adult member is expected to form a more-or-less permanent bisexual union; and this union is socially sanctioned by the granting of a joint room to the couple. The resulting relationship is different from any other adult relationship in the *kibbutz* in a number of significant features. (1) It alone includes common domicile for persons of opposite sex. (2) It entails a higher rate of interaction than is to be found in any other bisexual relationship. (3) It involves a higher degree of emotional intimacy than is to be found in any other relationship. (4) It establishes (ideally) an exclusive sexual relationship. (5) It leads to the deliberate decision to have children. These characteristics which, separately and severally, apply uniquely to this relationship, not only describe its salient features but also comprise the motives for those who enter into it. The couple, in short, viewed either objectively or phenomenologically, constitutes a unique social group in the *kibbutz*.

What, then, are we to make of this group? Since economic co-operation is not one of its features, we can, using Murdock's cross-cultural indices, deny that the relationship constitutes marriage. This is the conclusion of the foregoing paper. In retrospect, however, this conclusion does not leave me entirely satisfied. First, although we deny that the relationship constitutes a marriage, it nevertheless remains, both structurally and psychologically, a unique relationship within the *kibbutz*. Moreover, it is, with the exception of the economic variable, similar to those distinctive relationships in other societies to which the term marriage is applied. Hence, if I were writing this paper today, I should want to ask, before concluding that marriage is not universal, whether Murdock's inductive definition of marriage is, in the light of the *kibbutz* data, the most fruitful, even for his large sample; and if it were agreed that it is, whether it ought not to be changed or qualified so as to accommodate the relationship between *kibbutz* "spouses." Here I can only briefly explore the implications of these questions.

If the stated characteristics of the *kibbutz* relationship are found in the analogous relationship (marriage) in other societies—and I do not know that they are—it is surely apposite to ask whether Murdock's definition could not or should not stipulate them, as well as those already stipulated. For if they are found in other societies, on what theoretical grounds do we assign a higher priority to sex or economics over emotional intimacy, for example? Hence, if this procedure were adopted (and assuming that the characteristics of the *kibbutz* relationship were to be found in the marriage relationship in other societies) we would, since the *kibbutz* relationship satisfies all but one of the cross-cultural criteria, term the *kibbutz* relationship "marriage."

Alternatively, we might suggest that Murdock's definition of marriage, as well as the one suggested here, are unduly specific; that cross-cultural research is most fruitfully advanced by means of analytic, rather than substantive or enumerative, definitions. Thus, for example, we might wish to define marriage as "any socially sanctioned relationship between non-sanguineally-related cohabiting adults of opposite sex which satisfied felt needs—mutual, symmetrical, or complementary." A non-enumerative definition of this type would certainly embrace all known cases now termed "marriage" and would, at the same time, include the *kibbutz* case as well.

In the same vein, and employing similar definitional procedures, alternative conclusions can be suggested with respect to the family in the *kibbutz.* Although parents and children do not comprise a family, as Murdock defines family, they nevertheless constitute a unique group within the *kibbutz,* regardless of the term with which we may choose to designate it. (1) Children are not only desired by *kibbutz* parents, but, for the most part, they are planned. (2) These children—and no others—are called by their parents "sons" and "daughters"; conversely, they call their parents—and no other adults—"father" and "mother." (3) Parents and children comprise a social group in both an interactional and an emotional, if not in a spatial, sense. That is, though parents and children do not share a common domicile, they are identified by themselves and by others as a uniquely cohesive unit within the larger *kibbutz* society; this unit is termed a *mishpacha* (literally, "family"). (4) The nature of their interaction is different from that which obtains between the children and any other set of adults. (5) The rate of interaction between parents and children is greater than that between the children and any other set of adults of both sexes. (6) The psychological ties that bind them are more intense than those between the children and any other set of adults of both sexes.

Here, then, we are confronted with the same problem we encountered with respect to the question of *kibbutz* marriage. Because the parent-child relationship in the *kibbutz* does not entail a common domicile, physical care, and social rearing—three of the stipulated conditions in Murdock's definition of family—we concluded that the family does not exist in the *kibbutz.* But, since parents and children comprise a distinct and differentiated social group within the *kibbutz,* I am now not entirely satisfied with a conclusion which seems, at least by implication, to ignore its presence. For, surely, regardless of what else we might do with this group, we cannot simply ignore it. We can either perceive it, in cross-cultural perspective, as a unique group, and invent a new term to refer to it, or we can revise Murdock's definition of family in order to accommodate it.

Should the latter alternative be preferred, it could be effected in the following way. The stipulation of "common residence" could be qualified to refer to a reference, rather than to a membership, residence; and this is what the parental room is, for children as well as for parents. When, for example, they speak of "my room" or "our room," the children almost invariably refer to the parental room, not to their room in the communal children's house. If, moreover, the educational and economic functions of the family were interpreted as responsibilities for which parents were either immediately or ultimately responsible, the *kibbutz* parent-child unit would satisfy these criteria as well. For, though parents do not provide immediately for the physical care of their children, neither do they renounce their responsibility for them. Rather, they seek to achieve this end by working jointly rather than separately for the physical welfare of all the children—including, of course, their own.

Similarly, though the parents have only a minor share in the formal socialization process, they do not simply give their children to others to be raised as the latter see fit. Rather, socialization is entrusted to specially designated representatives, nurses and teachers, who rear the children, not according to their own fancy, but according to rules and procedures established by the parents. In short, though parents do not themselves socialize their children, they assume the ultimate responsibility for their socialization. Interpreted in this way, the relationship between *kibbutz* parents and children satisfies Murdock's definition of family.

To conclude, this addendum represents an alternative method of interpreting the *kibbutz* data concerning the relationship between spouses, and among parents and children. I am not suggesting that this interpretation is necessarily more fruitful than the one adopted in the paper. Certainly, however, I should want to examine it carefully before concluding, as I previously did, that marriage and the family are not universal.

6   *Is the Family Universal?*
—The Nayar Case[1]

E. KATHLEEN GOUGH

The Nayar, in a period prior to the British control of India, were supposed not to have a true family system. Though the Nayar, like the kibbutzim, did not constitute a total, self-contained society, they are another test of the universality of the nuclear family. On the basis of extensive field and historical research. Dr. Gough concludes that there is some differentiation between the ritual and the de facto husband. Hence, there is at least a minimal recognition of the role of husband-father as having a special relationship to the wife and children defined in terms of marriage and paternity.

The problem of a satisfactory definition of marriage has vexed anthropologists for decades and has been raised, but not solved, several times in recent years. Over time, it became clear that cohabitation, ritual recognition, definition of sexual rights or stipulation of domestic services each had too limited a distribution to serve as a criterion for all the unions anthropologists intuitively felt compelled to call "marriage." For good reason, therefore, The *Notes and Queries*[2] definition of 1951 makes no reference to any of these: "Marriage is a union between a man and a woman such that children born to the woman are recognized legitimate offspring of both parents."

Admirably concise though it is, this definition too raises problems in a number of societies. The Nuer institution of woman-marriage-to-a-woman would be a case in point. Here, both parties to the union are women, yet as Evans-Pritchard[3] has shown, the legal provisions of the union are strictly comparable to those of simple legal marriage between a man and a woman. Few, therefore, would question Evans-Pritchard's logic in calling this union a marriage.

The *Notes and Queries* definition contains two criteria: that marriage is a union between one man and one woman, and that it establishes the legitimacy of children. Nuer woman-marriage does not conform to the first criterion, but it does to the second. At this point the problem therefore becomes: is a definition feasible which would insist only on the second criterion, that of legitimizing children?

In Europe,[4] Dr. Edmund Leach initiated the most recent chapter in this discussion,[5] and rather than review its whole history it is pertinent

Reprinted by permission of the Council of the Royal Anthropological Institute, from the *Journal of the Royal Anthropological Institute*, Vol. LXXXIX (1959), Part 1.

for me to take up the argument where he and others have left it. In effect, Dr. Leach answered "No" to the question posed above. He argued not only against the vagueness of the phrase "legitimate offspring" but also against any use of potential legal paternity as a universal criterion of marriage. He concluded in fact that no definition could be found which would apply to all the institutions ethnographers commonly refer to as marriage. Instead, he named ten classes of rights[6] which frequently occur in connection with what we loosely term marriage, added that "one might perhaps considerably extend this list," and seemed to conclude that since no single one of these rights is invariably established by marriage in every known society, we ought to feel free to call marriage any institution which fulfills any one or more of the selected criteria.

There is, surely, a quite simple logical flaw in this argument. For it would mean in effect that every ethnographer might extend at will Dr. Leach's list of marital rights, and in short define marriage in any way he pleased. This may be legitimate in describing a single society. But I would argue that for purposes of cross-cultural comparison, we do need a single, parsimonious definition, simply in order to isolate the phenomenon we wish to study.

In support of his argument against using the legitimizing of children as a universal criterion of marriage, Dr. Leach cited the Nayar case. On the basis of two of my papers on the Nayars,[7] he stated that the Nayars traditionally had "no marriage in the strict (i.e., *Notes and Queries*) sense of the term but only a 'relationship of perpetual affinity' between linked lineages.[8] The woman's children, however they might be begotten, were simply recruits to the woman's own matrilineage." He stated further, "The notion of fatherhood is lacking. The child uses a term of address meaning 'lord' or 'leader' towards *all* its mother's lovers, but the use of this term does not carry with it any connotation of paternity, either legal or biological. On the other hand the notion of affinity is present, as evidenced by the fact that a woman must observe pollution at her ritual husband's death."[9] Later Dr. Leach concluded that "among the matrilineal matrilocal Nayar, as we have seen, right J (to establish a socially significant 'relationship of affinity' between the husband and his wife's brothers) is the only marriage characteristic that is present at all."[10]

This paper has two objectives. It will begin by analyzing traditional Nayar marital institutions and thereby showing that in fact the notion of fatherhood is not lacking and that marriage does serve to establish the legitimacy of children. My analysis will, I hope, not only dispose of a misinterpretation on Dr. Leach's part, but will in general clarify what has always proved a crucial but difficult borderline case for theorists of kinship. The paper will conclude with a new definition of marriage which will again make the status of children born to various types of union critical for decisions as to which of these unions constitute marriage. The ulti ·

mate aim is not of course simply to re-define marriage in a dogmatic way to suit a particular case, for definitions are tools of classification and not aims of research. The aim is to show that there *is* a common element not only in the institutions anthropologists have confidently labelled "marriage" by the *Notes and Queries* definition, but also in some unusual cases to which that definition does not apply. Whether we call the element "marriage" does not much matter provided it is made explicit, but it would probably be convenient to do so.

Nayar Marriage in Central Kerala

This account will refer to Nayars in the former kingdoms of Calicut, Walluvanad, and Cochin, in the center of the Malabar Coast or Kerala. In the northernmost kingdoms (Kolattunad, Kottayam) and probably also in the southernmost kingdom of Travancore, Nayar residence appears to have been avunculocal even before the period of British rule, marriage was optionally polygynous but not polyandrous, and individual men appear to have had definite rights in and obligations to their children. Full information is not available for these northernmost and southernmost kingdoms in the pre-British period. But it seems probable that in the northern kingdoms at least, even the *Notes and Queries* definition of marriage was applicable to the Nayars. It was certainly applicable in the latter half of the nineteenth century for which I have accounts from informants.

My account of marriage in the central kingdoms is a reconstruction of a state of affairs which appears to have been general before 1792 when the British assumed government of the Coast. As I have shown elsewhere[11] Nayar kinship was slowly modified in the nineteenth century and more rapidly in the twentieth. But in remote villages the traditional institutions persisted until toward the end of the nineteenth century, and were remembered by a few of my older informants. Their reports are not contradicted and are substantially corroborated by writings of Arab and European travellers of the fifteenth to eighteenth centuries.

In this account I shall use the terms "marriage," "husband," and "wife" without definition. My reasons for doing so will appear later.

In each of the three central kingdoms, the Nayar caste was divided into a number of ranked subdivisions characterized by different political functions. Chief of these were (a) the royal lineage, (b) the lineages of chiefs of districts, (c) the lineages of Nayar village headmen, and (d) several subcastes of commoner Nayars. Each of these last either served one of the categories (a) to (c) or else served patrilineal landlord families of Nambudiri Brahmans. I shall deal first with the commoner Nayars of category (d).

There were present in each village four to seven exogamous matrilineages of a single subcaste of commoner Nayars. They owed allegiance to the family of the head of the village, which might be a patrilineal Nambudiri family, a Nayar village headman's matrilineage, a branch of the lineage of the chief of the district, or a branch of the royal lineage. The commoners held land on a hereditary feudal-type tenure from the headman's lineage, and in turn had authority over the village's lower castes of cultivators, artisans, and agricultural serfs. Each retainer lineage tended to comprise some four to eight property-owning units which I call property-groups. The property-group formed a segment of the total lineage and was usually composed of a group of brothers and sisters together with the children and daughters' children of the sisters. The members owned or leased property in common, lived in one house, and were under the legal guardianship of the oldest male (*kāranavan*) of the group. Both the property-group and the lineage were called *taravād*.

Nayar men trained as professional soldiers in village gymnasia, and for part of each year they tended to be absent from the villages in wars against neighboring kingdoms or for military exercises at the capitals. Only the *kāranavan,* the women and the children of the property-group remained permanently in their ancestral homes.

The Nayars of one village or of two adjacent villages formed a neighborhood group (*kara* or *tara*) of some six to ten lineages. Each lineage was linked by hereditary ties of ceremonial co-operation with two or three other lineages of the neighborhood. These linkages were reciprocal but not exclusive, so that a chain of relationships linked all the lineages of the neighborhood. The lineages linked to one's own were called *enangar;* the total neighborhood group, the *enangu.* At least one man and one woman of each linked lineage must be invited to the house of a property-group for the life-crisis rites of its members. Its linked lineages were also concerned if some member of a lineage committed a breach of the religious law of the caste. It was their duty at once to break off relations with the offending lineage and to call a neighborhood assembly to judge and punish the offense. Its linked lineages thus represented the neighborhood group as a whole to the offending lineage and were special guardians of its morality. Sometimes, in small neighborhoods, the commoner Nayar lineages were all *enangar* to each other, but in larger neighborhoods this was not feasible, for the heads of property-groups would have had too many ceremonial obligations to fulfill.

The linked lineages played their most important role at the prepuberty marriage rites (*tālikettukalyānam*) of girls.[12] At a convenient time every few years, a lineage held a grand ceremony at which all of its girls who had not attained puberty, aged about seven to twelve, were on one day ritually married by men drawn from their linked lineages. The ritual bridegrooms were selected in advance on the advice of the village astrologer at a meeting of the neighborhood assembly. On the day fixed they came in procession to the oldest ancestral house of the host lineage. There, after various ceremonies, each tied a gold ornament (*tāli*) round the neck of his ritual bride. The girls had for three days previously been secluded in an inner room of the house and caused to observe taboos as if they had menstruated. After the *tāli*-tying each couple was secluded in privacy for three days. I was told that traditionally, if the girl was nearing puberty, sexual relations might take place. This custom began to be omitted in the late nineteenth century, but from some of the literature it appears to have been essential in the sixteenth and seventeenth centuries. At the end of the period of seclusion, each couple was purified from the pollution of cohabitation by a ritual bath. In Calicut and Walluvanad each couple in public then tore in two the loin-cloth previously worn by the girl during the "cohabitation" period, as a token of separation. This rite appears to have been omitted in Cochin. In all three kingdoms however the ritual husbands left the house after the four days of ceremonies and had no further obligations to their brides. A bride in turn had only one further obligation to her ritual husband: at his death, she and all her children, by whatever physiological father, must observe death-pollution for him. Death-pollution was otherwise observed only for matrilineal kin. In Cochin, even if their mother's ritual husband never visited his wife again, her children must refer to him by the kinship term *appan*. Children in the lower, patrilineal castes of this area used this word to refer to the legal father, who was presumed also to be the biological father. In Walluvanad and Calicut I did not hear of this verbal usage and do not know by what term, if any, Nayar children referred to their mother's legal husband.

The prepuberty *tāli*-rite was essential for a girl. If she menstruated before it had been performed, she should in theory be expelled from her lineage and caste. In fact, however, my informants told me that in such a case the girl's family would conceal the fact of her maturity until after the rite had been performed. But it was a grave sin to do so and one which would never be publicly admitted.

The *tāli*-rite marked various changes in the social position of a girl. First, it brought her to a social maturity. She was now thought to be at least ritually endowed with sexual and procreative functions and was henceforward accorded the status of a woman. After the rite, people addressed her in public by the respectful title *amma*, meaning "mother," and she might take part in the rites of adult women. Second, after the *tāli*-rite a girl must observe all the rules of etiquette associated with incest prohibitions in relation to men of her lineage. She might not touch them, might not sit in their presence, might not speak first to them and might not be alone in a room with one of them. Third, after the *tāli*-rite and as soon as she became old enough (i.e., shortly before or after puberty), a girl received as visiting husbands a number of men of her subcaste from outside her lineage, usually but not necessarily from her neighbor-

hood. In addition she might be visited by any Nayar of the higher subcastes of village headmen, chiefs or royalty, or by a Nambudiri Brahman.
All of these relationships were called *sambandham*. Among commoner
Nayar women, however, the great majority of unions were with men of
commoner subcaste.

Relations between any Nayar woman and a man of *lower* Nayar subcaste, or between any Nayar woman and a man of the lower, non-Nayar
castes, were strictly prohibited. If a woman was found guilty of such a
relationship her lineage's *enangar* carried the matter to the neighborhood
assembly. This temporarily excommunicated the woman's property-group
until justice had been done. In the nineteenth century and early this
century the property-group was re-accepted into the caste only after its
kāranavan had dismissed the woman from her household and caste, never
to return. In pre-British times a woman so dismissed became the property
of the king or chief and might be sold into slavery with foreign traders.
Alternatively, however, the men of her property-group had the right,
sometimes exercised, to kill both the woman and her lover and thus
preserve the good name of their lineage.

After the ritual marriage, the bridegroom need have no further contact
with his ritual wife. If both parties were willing, however, he might enter
into a sexual relationship with his ritual bride about the time of her puberty. But he had no priority over other men of the neighborhood group.
There is some uncertainty as to the number of visiting husbands a woman
might have at one time. Writers of the sixteenth and seventeenth centuries
report that a woman usually had some three to eight regular husbands
but might receive other men of her own or a higher caste at will. Hamilton,
in 1723, stated that a woman might have as husbands "twelve but no
more at one time."[13] As late as 1807, Buchanan reported that Nayar
women vied with each other as to the number of lovers they could obtain.[14]
A few of my older informants could remember women who had had
three or four current husbands, although plural unions were being frowned
upon and had almost died out by the end of the last century. There appears to have been no limit to the number of wives of appropriate subcaste whom a Nayar might visit concurrently. It seems, therefore, that a
woman customarily had a small but not a fixed number of husbands from
within her neighborhood, that relationships with these men might be of
long standing, but that the woman was also free to receive casual visitors
of appropriate subcaste who passed through her neighborhood in the course
of military operations.

A husband visited his wife after supper at night and left before breakfast next morning. He placed his weapons at the door of his wife's room,
and if others came later they were free to sleep on the verandah of the
woman's house. Either party to a union might terminate it at any time
without formality. A passing guest recompensed a woman with a small

cash gift at each visit. But a more regular husband from within the neigh-borhood had certain customary obligations. At the start of the union, it was common although not essential for him to present the woman with a cloth of the kind worn as a skirt. Later he was expected to make small personal gifts to her at the three main festivals of the year. These gifts included a loin-cloth, betel-leaves and arecanuts for chewing, hair-oil and bathing-oil, and certain vegetables. Failure on the part of a husband to make such a gift was a tacit sign that he had ended the relationship. Most important, when a woman became pregnant, it was essential for one or more men of appropriate subcaste to acknowledge probable paternity. This they did by providing a fee of a cloth and some vegetables to the low-caste midwife who attended the woman in childbirth. If no man of suitable caste would consent to make this gift, it was assumed that the woman had had relations with a man of lower caste or with a Christian or a Muslim. She must then be either expelled from her lineage and caste or killed by her matrilineal kinsmen. I am uncertain of the precise fate of the child in such a case, but there is no doubt at all that he could not be accepted as a member of his lineage and caste. I do not know whether he was killed or became a slave; almost certainly, he must have shared the fate of his mother. Even as late as 1949, over a hundred and fifty years after the establishment of British rule, a Nayar girl who became pregnant before the modern marriage ceremony was regarded as acting within the canons of traditional religious law if she could simply find a Nayar of suitable subcaste to pay her delivery expenses. But if no Nayar would consent to this she ran the danger of total ostracism, with her child, by the village community. I heard of several cases in which such a girl was driven from her home by her *kāranavan* at the command of the subcaste assembly. Her natal kinsmen then performed funeral rites for her as if she had died. In each case the girl took refuge in a town before or shortly after her child was born.

Although he made regular gifts to her at festivals, in no sense of the term did a man maintain his wife. Her food and regular clothing she ob-tained from her matrilineal group. The gifts of a woman's husbands were personal luxuries which pertained to her role as a sexual partner—extra clothing, articles of toilet, betel and arecanut—the giving of which is associated with courtship, and the expense of the actual delivery—not, be it noted, of the maintenance of either mother or child. The gifts continued to be made at festivals only while the relationship lasted. No man had obligations to a wife of the past.

In these circumstances, the exact physiological fatherhood of a child was often uncertain, although, of course, paternity was presumed to lie with the man or men who had paid the delivery expenses. But even when physiological paternity was known with reasonable certainty, the genitor had no economic, social, legal or ritual rights in, nor obligations to, his children after he had once paid the fees of their births. Their guardianship, care and discipline were entirely the concern of their matrilineal kinsfolk headed by their *kāranavan*. All the children of a woman called all her current husbands by the Sanskrit word *acchan* meaning "lord." They did not extend kinship terms at all to the matrilineal kin of these men. Neither the wife nor her children observed pollution at the death of a visiting husband who was not also the ritual husband of the wife.

In most matrilineal systems with settled agriculture and localized matrilineal groups, durable links are provided between groups by the interpersonal relationships of marriage, affinity and fatherhood. The husbands, affines, fathers, and patrilateral kin of the members of the matrilineal group have customary obligations and rights that, over time, serve to mitigate conflicts between the separate matrilineal groups. The Nayars had no such durable institutionalized interpersonal links. This does not mean that men did not sometimes form strong emotional attachments to particular wives and their children. My information indicates that they did. I know, for example, that if a man showed particular fondness for a wife, his wife's matrilineal kin were likely to suspect the husband's matrilineal kin of hiring sorcerers against them. For the husband's matrilineal kin would be likely to fear that the husband might secretly convey to his wife gifts and cash which belonged rightfully to his matrilineal kin. This suspicion was especially rife if the husband was a *kāranavan* who controlled extensive property. Informal emotional attachments did therefore exist between individuals of different lineages. But what I wish to indicate is that among the Nayars, these interpersonal affinal and patrilateral links were not invested with customary legal, economic or ceremonial functions of a kind which would periodically bring members of different lineages together in mandatory forms of co-operation. Four special kinship terms did apparently exist for use in relation to affines acquired through the *sambandham* relationship—although, as I have said, there were no patrilateral terms for kin other than for the mother's husbands. All men and women currently engaged in *sambandham* unions with members of ego's property-group, and all members of the property-group of these individuals, were collectively referred to as *bandhukkar* ("joined ones"). A current wife of ego's mother's brother was addressed and referred to as *ammāyi*, and a wife of the elder brother as *jyeshtati amma* (literally, "elder-sister-mother"). Finally, the own brother and the *sambandham* husband of a woman employed the reciprocal term *aliyan* to refer to each other but used no term of address. All the current *bandhukkar* of a property-group were invited to household feasts, but as individual affines they had no ceremonial or economic obligations and were not obliged to attend. As representatives of *enangar* lineages, however, some of these same individuals might be obliged to attend feasts and to fulfill ceremonial obligations as *enangar*. But as particular affines they had no obligations. In place, therefore, of institutionalized, interpersonal patri-lateral and affinal links, the Nayars had the hereditary institution of linked lineages. Whether or not, at a particular time, sexual relationships existed between individuals of linked lineages, the linked lineages must fulfill their obligations at household ceremonies and give neighborly help in such emergencies as birth and death. In the patrilineal and double unilineal castes of Kerala, precisely the same obligations are fulfilled by the matri-lateral kin and affines of individual members of the patrilineal group. The linked lineages of the Nayars must therefore, I think, be regarded as having a relationship of "perpetual affinity," which carried the more formal functions of affinity and persisted through the making and break-ing of individual sexual ties.

The Nayars of this area were thus highly unusual. For they had a kin-ship system in which the elementary family of father, mother, and children was not institutionalized as a legal, productive, distributive, residential, socializing or consumption unit. Until recent years, some writers have thought that at least as a unit for some degree of co-operation in economic production and distribution, the elementary family was universal. This view has been put forward most forcibly by Murdock.[15] Radcliffe-Brown, however, was one of the earliest anthropologists to observe that if the written accounts of the Nayars were accurate, the elementary family was not institutionalized among them.[16]

I turn briefly to marital institutions among the higher Nayar subcastes of village headmen, district chiefs and royalty. At various times during the pre-British period these lineages were accorded political office and set themselves up as of higher ritual rank than the commoner Nayars. The ritual ranking between these major aristocratic subdivisions was fairly stable, but the mutual ranking of lineages within each subdivision was in dispute. Most village headmen acknowledged the ritual superiority of district chiefs, and most chiefs, of the royal lineage. But some village headmen disputed among themselves for ritual precedence and so did many chiefs. As a result, each of these aristocratic lineages tended to set itself up as a separate subcaste, acknowledging ritual superiors and inferiors but acknowledging no peers. Over time moreover, following vicissitudes of political fortune, such lineages could rise or fall in the ritual hierarchy. It was in these lineages therefore that hypergamous unions became most highly insti-tutionalized, for most of these lineages refused to exchange spouses on equal terms. Instead, most of them married all their women upwards and all their men downwards. Women of the village headmen's lineages entered *sambandham* unions with chiefly, royal or Nambudiri Brahman men. Men of these lineages had unions with commoner Nayar women. Chiefly women had unions with royals or Nambudiris; chiefly men, with the women of village headmen's or commoner lineages. Royal women for the most part had unions with Nambudiri Brahmans of the highest rank. A few, especially in Calicut, however, had unions with men of older and ritually higher-ranking royal lineage which had through conquest become politically subordinate to their own. Among Nambudiri Brahmans, only eldest sons were permitted to marry Nambudiri women and beget children for their own families. Younger sons of Nambudiri households might have *sambandham* unions with Nayar women of any subcaste.

In all of these hypergamous unions the visiting husband owed the same periodic gifts to his wife as in the case of equal unions between persons of the same commoner subcaste. The husband in a hypergamous union was also held responsible for payment of delivery expenses at the birth of a child to his wife. Hypergamous unions differed from "equal" unions in that in the former, the husband, being of higher ritual rank, might not eat in the house of his wife. The husband was also prohibited from touching his wife, her children or her other kinsfolk during the daytime while he was in a state of ritual purity. Finally, although children called their mother's higher caste husband by the term *acchan* plus the caste title, Nayars as a whole were not permitted to use affinal terms toward the Nambudiri husbands of their womenfolk, nor did Nambudiris address or refer to their Nayar wives' brothers as affines. Nayars insisted however that a *sambandham* union with a Nambudiri Brahman was of the same character as a *sambandham* union with a Nayar of equal subcaste. It seems that from the legal point of view we must also judge it to be so, since the Brahman husband, like the Nayar, was responsible for payments at the birth of a child to his Nayar wife. During my fieldwork, the three Nambudiri Brahmans whom I was able to question closely on this subject told me that from *their* point of view only marriage to a Nambudiri woman with Vedic rites could be regarded as true marriage and that *sambandham* unions with Nayar women were a kind of concubinage. There seems to me no reason why we should not regard these latter unions as concubinage from the point of view of the Brahmans and (since they fulfilled the conditions of Nayar marriage) marriage from the point of view of the Nayars. This seems to me, in fact, the only possible interpretation, since the Brahmans are patrilineal and the child of a Brahman-Nayar union is not legitimized into the Brahman caste. The contrast from the Brahman point of view appears most sharply in the case of an eldest son, who may marry one or more Nambudiri women with Vedic rites and may also have liaisons with one or more Nayar women. The Brahman wife's children are of course fully legitimized into the Brahman caste from birth. But the Nayar wife and her children traditionally had no rights of patrilineal descent or inheritance whatsoever, might not enter the kitchen of the Brahman house and might not touch its inhabitants.

Consistent with the difference in direction of *sambandham* unions,

the *enangar* institution in these aristocratic Nayar lineages differed somewhat from that in the commoner subcastes. In general, an aristocratic
Nayar lineage had as *enangar* two or more lineages of a subcaste higher
than itself from which its women were wont to draw husbands in the
sambandham relationship. The linked lineage relationship was in these
cases not reciprocal. A chiefly lineage might act as *enangar* for the lineages
of one or two village headmen, but had as its own *enangar* one or two
chiefly or royal lineages of higher rank than itself. Nambudiri Brahman
lineages acted as *enangar* for the highest ranks of chiefs and royalty. In
this case, too, the aristocratic Nayar lineage had of course no reciprocal
ritual obligations towards the Brahman families with which it was linked.
The functions of these aristocratic *enangar* were, as far as I can detect,
the same as in the case of commoner Nayars. In particular, men of the
higher-ranking *enangar* lineages tied the *tāli* at the prepuberty marriage
of aristocratic girls—appropriately, for it was from these and other higher-
ranking lineages that the girls would later draw visiting husbands. Plural
unions were customary in these aristocratic lineages as among commoner
Nayars. Obviously, however, the choice of husbands became more and
more restricted as one ascended the scale of ranked subcastes, and at
the top of the Nayar hierarchy it was restricted to Nambudiri Brahmans.

I turn now to my interpretation of Nayar marital institutions. To accomplish this it is necessary to classify the rights and obligations obtaining
between "spouses" and between "fathers" and their "children." These fall
into two categories: those of the *tāli*-rite and those of the *sambandham*
union. In relations between spouses of the *tāli*-rite, the important rights are
those of the woman. The ritual husband had, it is true, apparently at one
time the right to deflower his bride. But the accounts of many writers indicate that this right was not eagerly sought—that in fact it was viewed with
repugnance and performed with reluctance. The ritual husband also had the
right that his ritual wife should mourn his death. But we may assume that
this right had more significance for the wife than for the husband, for it
was not attended by offerings to the departed spirit. These could be
performed only by matrilineal kin. The ritual bride's rights were complementary to her husband's, but for her they were of supreme importance.
She had, first, the right to *have* a ritual husband of her own or a superior
subcaste before she attained maturity. Her life depended on this, for if
she was not ritually married before puberty she was liable to excom-
munication and might possibly be put to death. She held this claim
against her subcaste as a whole exclusive of her lineage, or (in the case
of aristocratic lineages) against a higher subcaste. This group must,
through the institution of linked lineages, provide her with a ritual husband
of correct rank and thus bring her to maturity in honor instead of in
shame. It was the duty of her lineage kinsmen to see to it that some

representative from their linked lineage fulfilled this right. The ritual wife's second right was that of observing pollution at the death of her ritual husband. I interpret this as a mark of proof that she had once been married in the correct manner and that this ritual relationship had retained significance for *her* throughout her ritual husband's life.

The *tāli*-tier had no rights in his ritual wife's children except that they observe pollution at his death. From the child's point of view, however, his mother's ritual husband must have been a figure of great symbolic significance. For a child whose mother had no ritual husband could not acquire membership in his caste and lineage at all. The birth of a child before his mother's *tāli*-rite was absolutely forbidden and, in the nature of the case, can scarcely have happened. If it did occur, mother and child must certainly have been expelled and were probably killed. The child's observance of pollution for his mother's ritual husband—like the use of the kinship term *appan* in Cochin—was a formal recognition that, for ritual purposes, he had been "fathered" by a man of appropriate caste.

Turning to the *sambandham* union, it seems clear that the husband had no exclusive rights in his wife. He had only, in common with other men, sexual privileges that the wife might withdraw at any time. Again it is the wife's rights which are important. The wife had the right to gifts from her husband at festivals—gifts of little economic value but of high prestige value, for they established her as a woman well favored by men. But most significant was the woman's right to have her delivery expenses paid by one or more of her husbands of appropriate caste—that is, to have it openly acknowledged that her child had, as biological father, a man of required ritual rank. Her matrilineal kinsmen could if necessary press for the fulfillment of this right in a public assembly of the neighborhood; in cases of doubtful paternity any man who had been currently visiting the woman could be forced by the assembly to pay her delivery expenses. But if no man of appropriate rank could be cited as potential father, woman and child were expelled from their lineage and caste.

The *sambandham* father had no rights in his wife's children. Here again, however, the child had one right in his possible biological fathers—that one or more of them pay the expenses associated with his birth, and thus entitle him to enter the world as a member of his lineage and caste.

It is clear therefore that although the elementary family of one father, one mother and their children was not institutionalized as a legal, residential, or economic unit, and although individual men had no significant rights in their particular wives and children, the Nayars did institutionalize the concepts of marriage and paternity and give ritual and legal recognition to both. It is here that I must contradict Dr. Leach's interpretation of the situation, for it is not true that "the notion of fatherhood is lacking" nor is it true that "a woman's children, however they might be begotten, were simply recruits to the woman's matrilineage."[17] For unless his mother was ritually married by a man of appropriate caste, and unless his biological paternity was vouched for by one or more men of appropriate caste, a child could never enter his caste or lineage at all.

It is interesting also to notice that the Nayars were aware of the physiological function of the male in procreation and attached significance to it, for they expected a child to look like his genitor. Like all the higher Hindu castes of India, they based their belief in the moral rightness of the caste system in part upon a racist ideology which involved the inheritance of physical, intellectual, and moral qualities by a child from both its natural parents, and which held that the higher castes were, by virtue of their heredity, superior to the lower castes. It was ostensibly for this reason that the Nayars forbade with horror sexual contacts between a Nayar woman and a man of lower caste, and that they expelled or put to death women guilty of such contacts. This racist ideology also provided a motive for hypergamous unions, for Nayars of aristocratic lineages boasted of the superior qualities they derived from royal and Brahmanical fatherhood.

Moreover, although individual men had no significant customary rights in their wives and children, marriage and paternity were probably significant factors in political integration. For hypergamous unions bound together the higher subcastes of the political and religious hierarchies. Multiple sexual ties, as well as the *enangar* relationship, linked office-bearing lineages to each other and to their retainers in a complicated manner. And Nayar men phrased their loyalty to higher-ranking military leaders, rulers and Brahmans in terms of a debt owed to benevolent paternal figures whose forebears had collectively fathered them and whose blood they were proud to share. The generalized concept of fatherhood thus commanded the Nayar soldier's allegiance to his wider caste unit, to the rulers of his village, chiefdom and kingdom and to his religious authorities. It was associated with tender loyalty and with fortitude in war.

I regard Nayar unions as a form of marriage for two reasons. One is that, although plural unions were customary, mating was not promiscuous. Sexual relations were forbidden between members of the same lineage on pain of death. It was also forbidden for two men of the same property-group wittingly to have relations with one woman, or for two women of the same property-group to have relations with one man. (This rule of course automatically excluded relations between a man and his biological daughter.) Further, relations were absolutely prohibited between a Nayar woman and a man of lower subcaste or caste. These prohibitions are directly connected with my second and more important reason for regarding these unions as marriage, namely that the concept of legally established paternity *was* of fundamental significance in establishing a child as a member of his lineage and caste.

Granted that Nayar unions constituted a form of marriage, we must,

I think, classify them as a clear case of group-marriage. This was the interpretation to which I inclined in 1952[18] and it is, I now think, the only interpretation which makes sense of the descriptive material I have presented. The *tāli*-rite, as I see it, initiated for each individual Nayar girl a state of marriage to a collectivity of men of appropriate caste. First, the rite ceremonially endowed the girl with sexual and procreative functions. (The mock menstrual seclusion before the rite is relevant to this, i.e., it is the actual defloration.) Second, the woman's natal kinsmen surrendered the newly acquired rights in her sexuality, though not in her procreative functions, to a male representative from outside her lineage. This is apparent in that rules of etiquette associated with incest prohibitions came into force from this date. Third, rights in the woman's sexuality were received by her *enangar* as representative of the men of his subcaste as a whole. This appears in that the individual *enangar,* as a special sexual partner, was dismissed at the end of the ceremonies and might approach the woman again only as one among a series of equal husbands. In the commoner subcastes, the *enangar* was of the same subcaste as the woman, and through him as representative, sexual rights in the woman were conferred on all men of her subcaste as a collectivity. Fourth, the *tāli*-rite, by providing the woman with a ritual husband who (in my view) symbolized all the men of his subcaste with whom the woman might later have relationships, also provided her children with a ritual father who symbolized the correctness of their paternity. The children acknowledged their debt to him by mourning at his death.

The later *sambandham* unions, by this interpretation, involved the claiming of sexual privileges by men all of whom were potential husbands by virtue of their membership in a subcaste. The husbands had, however, no individually exclusive rights and could be dismissed at the woman's wish. Their duties as members of their caste were to provide the woman and her lineage with children and to acknowledge their potential biological paternity through birth-payments which legitimized the woman's child.

The Definition of Marriage

I have called the Nayar unions marriage because they involved the concept of legal paternity. It is clear however that such a form of group-marriage will not fit the *Notes and Queries* definition of "a union between *a* man and *a* woman such that children born to the woman are recognized legitimate offspring of both parents" (my italics). For legitimacy, in the case of the Nayar child, required both a ritual father and a "legalized genitor" of appropriate rank, and indeed a child might have more than one "legal genitor"[19] if two or more men had jointly paid the expenses of his birth.

As a tentative move toward a new definition that will have cross-cultural validity and that will fit the Nayar and several other unusual cases, I suggest the following: "Marriage is a relationship established between a woman and one or more other persons, which provides that a child born to the woman under circumstances not prohibited by the rules of the relationship, is accorded full birth-status rights common to normal members of his society or social stratum."

A few footnotes to this definition may help to vindicate its inevitably clumsy phraseology. "One or more persons" (in place of "a man") will bring into the definition both group-marriage of the Nayar type and also true fraternal polyandry.[20] It also brings within the definition such unusual types as woman-marriage-to-a-woman. "Under circumstances not prohibited by the rules of the relationship" would bring into the definition various problematic cases. It is possible, for example, that there are patrilineal societies in which a husband may legally repudiate a child illicitly begotten upon his wife by another man, without divorcing the wife herself. In this case the previous establishment of the marriage would *not* ensure full birth-status rights to the child, for the rules of the marriage relationship would have been broken through the circumstances which led to his birth. "Full birth-status rights common to all normal members" is a compressed reference to all the social relationships, property-rights, etc. that a child acquires at birth by virtue of his legitimacy, whether through the father or through the mother. For patrilineal societies the phrase "full birth-status rights" will include the rights that a child acquires in his *pater* as a person and in his *pater's* group. It will include, that is to say, the legitimization of fatherhood—or more precisely, of "father-sonhood." The phrase is, however, broader than any concept of specific rights in a particular father. It will therefore take care of a case like the Nayar, in which all rights are acquired *through* the mother but in which a relationship must be established between the mother and one or more other persons in order for these matrilineal rights to be ratified. Such a process may be called the legitimization of motherhood, or more precisely of "mother-sonhood." Moreover "full birth-status rights" is, I think, not only broader but more precise than "recognized legitimate offspring," to the vagueness of which Dr. Leach took exception. The inclusion of "society or social stratum" makes allowances for class or caste systems in which birth-status rights vary between strata. The case of the Nayars, who are a matrilineal caste in a predominantly patrilineal society, is an obvious example of this.

It should also perhaps be pointed out that this definition does not state that full birth-status rights *cannot* be acquired by a child expect through the marriage of its mother, but only that marriage provides for the acquisition of these rights. The definition does not therefore exclude societies like the Nuer in which a man may legitimize the child of an unmarried woman upon payment of a legitimization fee, without becoming married to the mother.[21]

Prince Peter has objected to the *Notes and Queries* definition and, by implication, to any definition which would make the legitimization of children through the mother's relationship to another party the distinctive characteristic of marriage.[22] His reason for objecting is that in some societies like the Toda, "marriage and legitimacy of the children can be looked upon as two different and separate concepts, and it may be necessary to go through a ceremony of legitimization of the offspring (the Toda *pursütpimi* ceremony) in order to establish who is the legal father, because marriage rites are insufficient in themselves to do this." However, it seems from Rivers' account that precisely what distinguishes the institution that Prince Peter translates as "marriage" (*mokh-vatt*) from that which he translates as "concubinage" (*mokhthoditi*)[23] is that a "husband" holds the right to legitimize some or all of his "wife's" children by the *pursütpimi* ceremony, whereas a lover in the *mokhthoditi* union, being of a different endogamous group from the woman, does not hold this right.[24] A husband acquires the right to perform the *pursütpimi* ceremony, it seems, by virtue of arranged marriage to an infant or through payment of cattle to a former husband or to a group of former husbands of the wife. The Toda marriage union, at its inception, does therefore provide that a child born to the woman (under circumstances not prohibited by the rules of the relationship) *must be* legitimized before his birth; the *pursütpimi* ceremony confirms his legitimacy by attaching him to a particular father and giving him rights in the father's patrilineal group. In the Toda case again, therefore, the concept of legal paternity is *the* distinguishing characteristic of marriage, even though the individual husband, because of polyandry, may be permitted to legitimize only some and not all of the children born to his wife. The Toda case, therefore, fits my definition, whether we regard the *pursütpimi* ceremony as the final one of a sequence of marriage rites, or as a legitimizing act which, under circumstances not prohibited by the rules of the relationship, one or another of the woman's husbands in legally obliged to fulfill.[25]

I do not argue that all societies must necessarily be found to have marriage by my definition. There may yet turn out to be whole societies —or more probably whole social strata—in which children acquire no birth-status rights except through their mother, by the simple fact of birth. There seems no doubt, for example, that some slave populations do not have marriage in this sense of the term. What I do wish to suggest, however, is that for most of the societies for which we now have information, including the Nayar, marriage as I have defined it is a significant relationship, distinguished by the people themselves from all other kinds of relationships. My definition should therefore enable us to isolate marriage as a cross-cultural phenomenon, and from there to proceed to the more exciting task: that of investigating the differential circumstances under which marriage becomes invested with various other kinds of rights and obligations. Some of the most important of these Dr. Leach has already listed for us.

7 The Stability of the American Family System

TALCOTT PARSONS

By the 1930's, many critics held that the American family was experiencing a one-way loss of many of its traditional functions and viewed this social trend with alarm. Professor Parsons, a noted sociological theorist, examines the issue from a system point of view. Parsons is, thus, oriented to interchanges rather than one-way flows, and to the relationships among systems rather than the state of a single one. He produces evidence that the family, far from declining, is a very vital pattern, even though it is undergoing changes; and, rather than losing its functions, the family is becoming more specialized in an increasingly differentiated society.

The American family has, in the past generation or more, been undergoing a profound process of change. There has been much difference of opinion among social scientists, as well as among others concerned, as to the interpretation of these changes. Some have cited facts such as the very high rates of divorce, the changes in the older sex morality, and until fairly recently, the decline in birth rates, as evidence of a trend to disorganization in an absolute sense. Such considerations as these have in turn often been linked with what has sometimes been called the "loss of function" of the family.[1] This refers to the fact that so many needs, for example that of clothing, which formerly were met by family members working in the home, are now met by outside agencies. Thus, clothing is now usually bought ready-made; there is much less food-processing in the household, there is a great deal of commercial recreation outside the home, etc.

That changes of a major character have been going on seems to be beyond doubt. That some of them have involved disorganization of a serious character is clear. But we know that major structural changes in social systems always involve strain and disorganization, so the question of evaluating symptoms of disorganization is one of how much is a general trend to disorganization as such, and how much is what may be called the "disorganization of transition."

Certain facts about the most recent phases of development seems to us to throw doubt on the thesis of general disorganization. First, after the postwar peak, the upward trend of divorce rates has been checked, though

Reprinted from Talcott Parsons and Robert F. Bales, *Family, Socialization and Interaction Process* (Glencoe, Ill.: The Free Press, 1955), pp. 3–9. Copyright 1955 by The Free Press of Glencoe, Illinois.

it is too early to judge what the longer-run trend is likely to be. To judge the impact of the instability of marriages, the distribution of divorces by duration of marriage and by relations to children is just as important as the absolute numbers. As the figures show, by and large divorces are, and continue to be, concentrated in the early periods of marriage and in childless couples. Even though married before and divorced, once people settle down to having children, there is a relatively high probability that they will stay together.[2]

Second, divorce certainly has not led to a general disillusionment with marriage, so that people prefer to stay single or not to try again. In spite of a situation where it has become economically easier for single women to support themselves independently than ever before, the proportion of the population married and living with their spouses is the highest that it has ever been in the history of the census and has risen perceptibly within the recent period.

Third, although up to the mid-thirties there had been a progressive decline in birth rates (until, on a long-run basis, the population was for a time no longer fully reproducing itself), by now it has become clear that the revival of the birth rate which began in the early forties has not been only a matter of catching up the deficit of war-time, but has reached a new plateau on what appears to be a relatively stable basis.[3] This is certainly suggestive of a process of readjustment rather than of a continuous trend of disorganization.

In this connection, it should be remembered that the immense increase in the expectancy of life since about the turn of the century has meant that continuance of the birth rates of that time would have led to a rate of population increase which few could contemplate with equanimity. The transition, from a high birth rate–high death rate population economy to one where low death rates have to be balanced by substantially lower birth rates than before, is one of the profoundest adjustments human societies have ever had to make, going as it does to the deepest roots of motivation. In processes of such magnitude, it is not unusual for there to be swings of great amplitude to levels which are incompatible with longer-run stability. There is at least a good case for the view that the low birth rates of the nineteen-thirties—not of course confined to the United States—constituted the extreme point of such a swing, and that extrapolating the trend up to that point simply failed to take account of adjustive processes already at work. At any rate, the recent facts have shifted the burden of proof to him who argues that the disorganization of the family is bringing imminent race suicide in its wake.

There is a further bit of evidence which may be of significance. The family, after all, is a residential unit in our society. If the family were breaking up, one would think that this would be associated with a decline of the importance of the "family home" as the preferred place to live of the population. Recent trends of development seem to indicate that far from family homes being "on their way out," there has, in recent years, been an impressive confirmation that even more than before this is the preferred residential pattern. The end of World War II left us with a large deficit of housing facilities. Since then, once the shortages of materials were overcome, there has been an enormous amount of residential building. In this building, as is indicated by the figures, the single family house occupies an extraordinarily prominent place.[4] It seems that the added mobility given our population by modern means of transportation, especially in making possible a considerable geographical distance between place of residence and place of work, has led to a strengthening of the predilection to have a "home of our own." In the face of a level of geographical and occupational mobility which makes permanence of residential location highly problematical, this is a most impressive phenomenon.

The situation with which we are concerned may be summed up by noting again that, in spite of divorces and related phenomena, Americans recently have been marrying on a unprecedented scale. They have been having children, not on an unprecedented scale, but on one which, by contrast with somewhat earlier trends, is unlikely to be without significance. Third, they have been establishing homes for themselves as family units on a very large scale. Since the bulk of home-provision has been on the financial responsibility of the couples concerned, it seems unlikely that the having of children is a simple index of irresponsibility, that we have, as Professor Carver used to put it, produced a generation of "spawners" as contrasted with "family-builders."[5]

There are certain very important elements of constancy in the structure and in the functional significance of the family on a human cultural level. These elements of constancy are by no means wholly or even mainly a reflection of its biological composition. But this view is, in our opinion, by no means incompatible with an emphasis, in other respects, on certain important elements of variation in the family. The set of these latter elements, on which we wish now to focus attention, is that concerned with the level of structural differentiation in the society.

It is a striking fact of sociological discussion that there has been no settled agreement on either of two fundamental problems. One is the problem of the structural and functional relations between the nuclear family on the one hand, and the other elements of the kinship complex in the same society. Structural analysis of kinship is, we feel, just reaching a point where the importance of clear discriminations in this field is coming to be appreciated. Second, there has been no clear conception of what are the important "functions of the family." Procreation and childcare are always included, as is some reference to sexual relations, but in addition there are frequent references to "economic" functions, religious functions, and various others.

There has been little attempt to work out the implications of the suggestion that there are certain "root functions" which must be found wherever there is a family or kinship system at all, while other functions may be present or not according to the *kind* of family or kinship system under consideration, and its place in the structure of the rest of the society.

The aspect of this problem in which we are particularly interested concerns its relations to the problem of structural differentiation in societies. It is well known that in many "primitive" societies there is a sense in which kinship "dominates" the social structure; there are few concrete structures in which participation is independent of kinship status. In comparative perspective, it is clear that in the more "advanced" societies a far greater part is played by non-kinship structures. States, churches, the larger business firms, universities, and professional associations cannot be treated as mere "extensions" of the kinship system.

The process by which non-kinship units become of prime importance in a social structure, inevitably entails "loss of function" on the part of some or even all the kinship units. In the processes of social evolution, there have been many stages by which this process has gone on, and many different directions in which it has worked out.

Our suggestion is, in this perspective, that what has recently been happening to the American family constitutes part of one of these stages of a process of differentiation. This process has involved a further step in the reduction of the importance in our society of kinship units other than the nuclear family. It has also resulted in the transfer of a variety of functions from the nuclear family to other structures of the society, notably the occupationally organized sectors of it. This means that the family has become *a more specialized agency than before,* probably more specialized than it has been in any previously known society. This represents a decline of *certain* features which traditionally have been associated with families; but whether it represents a "decline of the family" in a more general sense is another matter; we think not. We think the trend of the evidence points to the beginning of the relative stabilization of a *new* type of family structure, in a new relation to a general social structure, one in which the family is more specialized than before, but not in any general sense less important, because the society is dependent *more* exclusively on it for the performance of *certain* of its vital functions.

We further think that this new situation presents a particularly favorable opportunity to the social scientist. Because we are dealing with a more highly differentiated and specialized agency, it is easier to identify clearly the features of it which are essential on the most general level of cross-cultural significance. The situation is methodologically comparable to the relation between the emergence of modern industrial economy and the problems of economic theory. The high level of differentiation, of economic from non-economic processes under modern conditions, has made possible a kind of natural experimental situation which has been crucial to the development of modern economic theory.

PART II

The Family and External Systems

8   *The Impact of Urban Civilization upon Negro Family Life*

E. FRANKLIN FRAZIER

In America, the adaptive sector of society is accorded great importance and tends to be emphasized more strongly than other subsystems of the society. It should follow, then, that this aspect of society exerts a strong influence on the family. Professor Frazier gives an account of how the Negro family has adapted to its marginal position in the economic and social setting of urban centers. Frazier believes that many of the characteristics of the Negro family which have been ascribed to the primitiveness, or even lack of morality, of Negroes, are in fact adaptations to the particular circumstance in which they are forced to live.

The urbanization of the Negro population during the present century has effected the most momentous change in the life of the Negro since his emancipation. During the first three decades of the century, nearly two and a half million Negroes moved from the rural South into the urban areas of the North and the South.[1] Public attention has been directed to the northward movements because they were dramatized by the mass migrations to northern industrial centers during World War I; whereas, the million or more Negroes who drifted into southern cities attracted little or no attention.[2] However, the shift from country to city in both the North and the South has been accompanied by profound changes in the Negro's behavior and general outlook on life. Because of the fundamental role of the family in social organization, the study of the Negro family offers the most fruitful approach to an understanding of these important changes in the social and cultural life of the Negro.

Reprinted from *American Sociological Review*, II (1937), 609–18, with the kind permission of the author and the publishers.

Although the great majority of Negroes who have migrated to urban areas have been simple peasant folk, the economic and cultural differences among the migrants as a whole have determined largely the kinds of accommodation which they have made to their new environment. Therefore, on the basis of a large body of documentary material we shall undertake first to describe four fairly distinct types of traditional patterns of family life found among the Negroes who make up communities in American cities.[3] There is first the maternal family pattern which is found in its purest and most primitive form in the rural South. By a maternal pattern of family organization we mean a family that is based primarily upon the affectional ties and common interests existing between the offspring and the mother who is the head of the family. As one would expect, many of these families owe their origin to illegitimacy, often involving several men. In such cases the man's or father's function generally ceases after impregnation; and if he continues to show interest in the woman and the offspring, his contacts are casual and his contributions to the household are of the nature of gifts. But he has no authority in the family and the children may not even be aware of his relationship to them. This type of family pattern has existed since the days of slavery when the mother was the dominant and most stable element in the Negro family. Even after emancipation, which resulted in a general loosening of social bonds, the Negro mother continued in her accustomed role unless perchance the father acquired some interest in his family. The high rate of illegitimacy among southern Negroes represents family mores and folkways that have their roots in a natural maternal family organization that flourished dur-·ing slavery.

The second type of family pattern shows many of the characteristics of the traditional family pattern of the American whites. In fact, the histories of the families of this type provide the source materials for studying the genesis of the traditional family type. It is possible to trace, in the histories of some Negro families, the actual process whereby the father's interest in the family became consolidated with the common interests of the various members of the family group of which he was the recognized head. In some cases traditions in these families go back to the time when the family was still in slavery. Where conditions were favorable to stable family life, the father's interest in his family was often bound up with his status among the slaves, as well as his trusted position in relation to the whites. The moralization of his behavior was further facilitated by incorporation into the household and church of his master or the Negro's own church. Under such circumstances, the transition from serfdom to freedom did not result in a breakdown of family relations. In fact, when the father began working as a free man, his authority was undisputed in his family. It has been upon such families that the development of the race as a whole in respect to character and culture has depended.

The third type of family pattern is sharply differentiated in regard to social heritage from the great mass of the Negro population. These families originated in the communities of free Negroes, usually of white and Negro and sometimes Indian ancestry, that existed in various parts of the country during pre-Civil War times. Many of these families not only achieved stability but also assumed an institutional character. The founders of these families inherited in some cases wealth from their white ancestors and generally showed the advantages of educational opportunities and white contacts. The families were as a rule patriarchal in organization with the female members playing roles similar to those of the slave-holding class in the ante-bellum South. Pride in white ancestry exercised considerable influence on their conception of themselves and their role in relation to the Negroes of unmixed blood and of slave origin. Many of the old established families in the North sprang from this group, families which were often forced to migrate before as well as after the Civil War in order to maintain their self-respect and secure advantages for their children.

We come finally to the fourth class of families who have been relatively isolated from the main currents of Negro life. These families originated in isolated communities of persons of Negro, white and Indian ancestry, and branches and remnants of these families may still be found in these communities, which are located in Alabama, North Carolina, Ohio, New Jersey, and New York. They are not a homogeneous group but are classified together because they show certain common characteristics. Usually they regard themselves as a distinct race from the Negroes and show in their behavior the clannishness of an isolated group. Their family organization is sternly patriarchal and is usually closely tied up with the religious organization of the community. Negro families that have their roots in such communities generally show in their behavior the influence of their peculiar cultural heritage.

Before considering the significance of these various patterns of family life in the accommodations which the Negro family has made to the urban environment, let us turn our attention to the sex behavior and familial life of the thousands of solitary men and women who have found their way into the towns and cities of the North and South. It is necessary to distinguish this group from the great body of black migrants, because their attitudes towards sex and family life have resulted from their mobility and emancipation from the most elementary forms of social control. Such a group of men and women have formed a part of the Negro population since the confusion and disorder following the Civil War. Although, after emancipation, the great mass of the Negro population settled down under a modified form of the plantation system, a fairly large number of Negro men and, to a less extent, Negro women continued to wander about in search of work and new experience. The size and character of this migratory element has been continually affected by the condition of southern agriculture and industry. On the other hand, when mass migrations were set in motion by demands of northern industries during and following World War I, many unattached men and women were among the migrants.

When the present economic crisis disrupted the economic life of the rural South, as well as that of industrial areas, the number of these un-attached migrants was greatly augmented. A study by the Works Progress Administration showed that for the country as a whole, unattached Negro transients constituted 7 to 12 per cent of the total during the nine-month period, August, 1934 through April, 1935.[4] In Chicago, during the first six months of 1934, 1,712 of the 10,962 unattached persons registered with the Cook Country Bureau for Transients were Negro men and women. In the Harlem area of New York City, during the period from December, 1931 to January, 1936, there were 7,560 unattached Negro men registered with the Emergency Relief Bureau.[5] However, these figures include only those unattached Negro men and women who have sought relief; they leave out of account the thousands of roving men and homeless women who support themselves by both lawful and unlawful means.

Although we cannot describe in detail the various types of sexual unions which these migratory men and women form in the course of their wander-ings from city to city, we may safely draw some conclusions concerning the general character of their sex behavior and mating. In a sense, one may say that the "Blues," those distinctive creations of the black trouba-dours in our industrial civilization, epitomize the sex and family behavior of this class. In these songs, the homeless, wandering, intermittent black workers sing of their disappointments and disillusionment in the city. An oft-repeated cause of this disillusionment is the uncertainty and instability of romantic love, if one might apply the term to the emotions of these migratory men and women. Yet, in a very real sense, one might say that in these songs one can discover the origin of romantic sentiments among the great masses of the Negro population. These songs record the spontaneous responses of strange men and women to each other in an unfamiliar environment. More important still, they reveal an awakening imagination that furnishes a sharp contrast to the unromantic matings of Negroes in the isolated peasant communities of the rural South.

It is not our purpose to give the impression that the "Blues" furnish historical data on the sex and familial behavior of this migratory group. Through life-history documents, we have been able to distill from these songs their true significance. We find that in many cases these men begin their migratory careers by going first to nearby sawmills or turpentine camps, in order to supplement the landlord's allowances to their families. In fact, if one goes to one of the "quarters" near a sawmill in the South, one may find these foot-loose men and women living out the stories of their loves and disappointments which have become fixed in the "Blues." On the whole, their sexual unions and matings are characterized by impulsive behavior. However, just as their natural impulses urge them to all forms of anti-social behavior, spontaneous sympathy and tender emotions create the temporary unions which these men and women often form. In this connection one should not overlook the fact that a recurring theme of these songs is the longing for the intimate association of kinfolk, or wife and children, who have been left behind. Although the temporary unions which these men and women form are often characterized by fighting and quarreling, they supply a need which these wanderers feel for warm and intimate human association.

If the sawmill closes or the man feels the "itch" to travel, or some "Black Ulysses" from the outside world lures him by stories of a more exciting existence or a tale of fabulous wages in a nearby city, he takes to the road. In some cases, the girl may follow to the next city; but in the end she loses her temporary lover. During the course of their wanderings, these men may pick up lonely Negro women in domestic service who gratify their sexual longings and provide them with temporary lodging and food. While these men are acquiring sophistication in the ways of the city, they are becoming thoroughly individuated men. By the time they reach Chicago, Detroit, or New York, they have learned how to survive without labor. Some of them have acquired the art of exploiting women for their support. Girls who have run away from their homes in the South and sought adventure in these large cities often become, in spite of their callousness and boasted toughness, the tools of these men. However, these same women sometimes, during their sentimental reflections, disclose a hidden longing for the security and affection of their families, or betray an abiding attachment to an illegitimate child that they have left with a parent or relative during their wanderings.

From this migratory group of men and women, we turn now to the great mass of the Negro migrants who have come to the city in family groups or in remnants of family groups. This movement was at its peak during World War I when not only whole families but entire communities picked up their meager possessions and joined the flight from the semifeudal conditions of the South to the modern industrial centers of the North. One can get some notion of the volume of the tide of black humanity that overwhelmed the comparatively small Negro communities in northern cities by considering the increases in the Negro population of the four principal cities to which these migrants were attracted. Between 1910 and 1920, the Negro population of Detroit increased 611.3 per cent; that of Chicago, 148.2 per cent; that of the Borough of Manhattan in New York City, 80.3 per cent; and that of Philadelphia, 58.9 per cent. The immediate effect of the inundation of Negro communities in northern cities was conflict with the white population in contiguous areas. However, the subsequent expansion of the Negro communities proceeded in accordance with the natural growth of these cities.

What especially interests us in regard to the expansion of these Negro communities is that, through selection, various elements of the population have become segregated, thus causing the spatial organization of these communities to reflect their economic and cultural organization. In the case of Chicago, it was possible to divide the Negro community into seven zones of about a mile in length indicating its southward expansion along and parallel to one of the arterial highways radiating from the center of the city.[6] The selection which had taken place during the expansion of the Negro population was indicated by the decline in the percentage of southern-born Negroes and of illiteracy, the decrease in the proportion of persons engaged in unskilled labor and domestic service and the percentage of women employed, and a corresponding increase in the percentage of mulattoes in the population and of persons in professional and public service in the successive zones. A similar selection was found in the Harlem Negro community in New York City. However, whereas the Chicago Negro community in its expansion has cut across the concentric zones of the larger community and shows the impress of the larger community, the Harlem Negro community has expanded radially from the area where Negroes first settled and has assumed the same pattern of zones as a self-contained city.[7]

When the Negro family is studied in relation to the economic and cultural organization of these communities, we are able to obtain a rough measure, at least, of the Negro's success in the struggle to support himself or family and attain a normal family life. Therefore, let us consider first the question of family dependency. From the records of the United Charities it appears that under normal conditions between 8 and 9 per cent of the families in the poorer areas of Chicago are dependent upon charity. However, the rate of family dependency showed a progressive decline in the successive zones marking the expansion of the community. In the seventh zone only 1 per cent of the families were dependent.[8] Although we do not possess comparable data for Harlem, we know that prior to the crash in 1929 between 25 and 30 per cent of the "under care" families handled by the Charity Organization Society in an area in New York City including a part of Harlem were Negro cases. The present economic crisis has tended to emphasize the precarious economic situation of a large percentage of Negro families in our cities. According to the 1933 report of the Federal Emergency Relief Administration, as high as 85 per cent of the Negro families in some cities were receiving relief. The percentage of Negro families receiving relief was highest in such highly industrialized areas as Toledo, Akron, and Pittsburgh, where large numbers of Negroes are employed in unskilled labor; the percentage in Chicago and New York was around 46 per cent and 30 per cent respectively.

In the case of the Harlem community, we are able to study the incidence of relief in relation to the spatial organization of the Negro area.

During the first week of September, 1935, there were 24,292 Negro families on Home Relief, this being 43.2 per cent of the 56,137 Negro families in this area. However, the incidence of relief varied considerably in the zones marking the outward expansion of the community from its center. The percentage of families receiving relief declined rapidly from 70.9 per cent in the central zone to 28.4 per cent in the outermost zone. This is of special interest because, although in some areas of the peripheral zone were found some of the poorest Negro families in the entire community, the incidence in these areas did not vary greatly from the average for the zone as a whole. The only explanation that occurs to us is that the family groups that tended to be segregated in the peripheral zones were better able to meet collectively the economic crisis than the single, unattached, separated, and widowed men and women who tended to congregate in the center of the community. This selection was shown in the marital status of the population in the various zones. The percentage of single men declined in the successive zones outward from 42.6 to 31.1 per cent and that of single women from 30.9 to 23.5 per cent. On the other hand, the proportion of men and women married increased from about 50 per cent each to 64 per cent for the men and to 60 per cent for the women.[9] A similar tendency was discovered in the case of the Negro community in Chicago.[10]

The selection and segregation of the population with reference to marital status coincides with other processes of organization and disorganization of Negro family life in the city. In Chicago, home ownership was closely correlated with family stability, whereas, in Harlem, with its apartments and multiple dwellings, it was not significant. Similarly, the relationship between family organization and disorganization and the spatial organization of the Negro community was more evident in Chicago with its relatively simple pattern than in Harlem with its more complex pattern. For example, the desertion and non-support rates declined regularly from two and a half per cent of the total families in the poorer zone near the Chicago loop to less than one half of one per cent in the outermost zone. Although a similar tendency in regard to desertions was discernible in the Harlem Negro community, the various zones did not show the same degree of cultural homogeneity as the Chicago zones. Thus, in Chicago the delinquency rate declined from 42.8 per cent in the zone of considerable family and community disorganization near the center of the city to 1.4 per cent in the outermost zone of stable family life and home ownership. However, in Harlem, no such decline in the successive zones of population expansion was discernible in regard to juvenile delinquency. It would require a more intimate study of the character and culture of the various zones in order to determine the relationship between community factors and juvenile delinquency. Nevertheless, it is apparent that as a result of competition, various elements of the Negro population in both cities are selected and segregated in a way which enables the student to get some measure of the processes of organization and disorganization.

This is seen most clearly in regard to the question of the survival of the Negro in the city. The low fertility of Negro women in cities has been shown in a number of studies. According to Thompson and Whelpton, Negroes in large cities, including Chicago and New York, "were not maintaining their numbers on a permanent basis in either 1920 or 1928."[11] Lately, Clyde Kiser has found that the fertility of Negro women in a health area in New York was lower than that of white women of similar and higher occupational status in several urban communities.[12] However, if we study the fertility of Negro women in relation to the organization of the Negro community, some important facts are revealed. For example, in Chicago in 1920, the highest ratio of children under five to women of child-bearing age, i.e., 15 to 44, was found in the two peripheral zones, or the areas of stable family life and home ownership. The ratio was higher in these zones than in the zones where the poorer migrant families settled and almost twice as high as the ratio in the bright-light area with its cabarets, saloons, and houses of prostitution.[13]

Harlem offers even more striking evidence of the influence of selective factors on the survival of the Negro in the city. In 1920, the ratio of children under 5 to 1,000 women from 20 to 44 years of age increased in the successive zones outward from the center of the community from 109 in the first to 274 in the fifth, with a slight variation in the fourth. However, in 1930, the ratio of children increased regularly from 115 in the first to 462 in the outermost zone. This latter figure is about the same as the ratio in towns with from 2,500 to 10,000 population. Differential survival rates were revealed also in the ratio of deaths to births in 1930 in the various zones. In the central zone, the population was dying out, there being 112 deaths to each 100 births. However, the ratio of deaths to births declined in the successive zones until it reached less than 50 to 100 in the areas near the periphery of the community. Looking at the situation from the standpoint of births alone, we find that in 1930 there was one child born to each 25 women, 20 to 44 years of age, in the central zone. From this zone outward, the number of women of child-bearing age per child born declined regularly until it reached eight in the outermost zone. Thus the survival of the Negro in the city seems to be influenced by the same selective factors which determine the spatial organization and social structure of the Negro community.

Let us return now to the four traditional patterns of family life described above and consider them in relation to the selective process at work in these communities. The first or maternal type of family offers little resistance to the disintegrating forces in the urban environment. Because of their poverty, these families are forced to seek homes in the poorer sections of the Negro community. Moreover, since these families are supported solely by the mother who is generally employed in domestic service or at unskilled labor, they easily slip into the ranks of those dependent upon charity. The children suffer not only from the lack of parental control but are subjected to the vicious environment of disorganized areas. Consequently, many of the boys become members of delinquent gangs, while the girls are guilty of sex delinquency, which often leads to unmarried motherhood.

In these same areas may be found the poorer families of the paternal type. In these families, as well as those of the maternal type, a large percentage of the mothers are forced to be wage earners. Whether they maintain their paternal organization depends upon a number of factors, including the vitality of family traditions, the security and regularity of employment of the father, the development of common interests, and the degree to which these families are integrated into the institutions of the Negro community. But it often happens that the father's interest in his family rests upon some immediate interest or is based upon mere sympathy and habit. Under such circumstances, if the father loses his job or if he develops new interests in the urban environment that are antagonistic to the common interests of his family, he may easily join the ranks of the large number of Negro deserters. In this connection, it should be pointed out that the families inhabiting these blighted areas are free from the censure of public opinion, as well as other types of communal control. On the other hand, those families that succeed in maintaining a community of interest or develop new ambitions for their children generally move, if their economic resources permit, towards the periphery of the Negro community. Their movement at first may be just beyond the area of extreme deterioration and poverty.

It may take another generation for these families to reach the periphery of the Negro community where one finds the families of the third type —those having a background of several generations of stable family life and firmly rooted traditions. It was old mulatto families of the third type who sometimes fled before the onrush of the uncouth Negroes from the South to areas beyond the borders of the Negro community. But as a rule they sought the periphery of the Negro community as is shown in the case of the seventh zone in Chicago, where half of the inhabitants were mulattoes.[14] Then, too, sometimes these old established families have isolated themselves and have regarded with mixed feelings of contempt and envy the rise of the ambitious elements in the lower and, on the whole, darker elements in the Negro population. But, just as in the rigorous competitive life of the northern city, the poor and illiterate Negroes with no other resources but their folk culture are ground down by disease, vice, and poverty, those possessing intelligence and skill and a fund of family traditions find a chance to rise beyond the caste restrictions of the South.

Thus, there has come into existence in these cities a fairly large middle-class element comprised of the more ambitious elements of the second type of families and representatives of the third type with a few descendants of the fourth type of families. Their pattern of family life approaches that of the white middle class. It is the emergence of this class which accounts largely for those orderly and stable areas on the periphery of the Negro communities in our cities. In between such areas and the areas of extreme deterioration where family disorganization is highest, there are areas of a mixed character in which the more stable and better paid industrial workers find homes.

In view of the process described here, it is not surprising that in the area occupied by the middle-class families, there may be on the average more children, as for example in Chicago, than in the areas of extreme poverty and family disorganization. In the case of the Harlem community which resembles in its spatial organization a self-contained city, relatively large family groups of working-class as well as middle-class status tend to become segregated on the periphery, though they occupy different areas. In the center of the Harlem community, which is essentially a non-family area, one may find the emancipated from all classes and elements.

Our discussion points to a number of conclusions which may be stated briefly as follows. First, it seems inevitable that, as long as the bankrupt and semifeudal agricultural system in the South continues to throw off men and women who lose the restraints imposed by a simple folk culture, there will be a class of roving Negroes who will live a lawless sex and quasi-family life. Secondly, the great mass of migrants who, as a rule, manage to preserve remnants of their family organization must face in the competitive life of the city a severe struggle for survival and, at the same time, be subjected to the disintegrating forces in the urban environment. The fate and fortunes of these families will depend upon both their economic and their cultural resources. Many of the poorer families that are held together solely by the affectional ties between mother and children, will be ground down by poverty and the children will be scattered and are likely to become delinquent. Those families in which the father's interest rests upon no firmer basis than some passing attachment, or mere sympathy and habit, may suffer a similar fate. But, if such families succeed in becoming integrated into the institutional life of the community and have sufficient income to avoid dependence upon charity, they may achieve a fair degree of stabilization. On the other hand, the economically better-situated families, in which the father's interest is supported by tradition and tied up with the common interests of the family, may resist the disintegrating effects of the city, and some of the children will enter the middle class. The traditions of these families will become merged with the traditions of mulatto families, many of free origin, who once formed an upper social class. The economic and cultural organization of the Negro community which emerges as the result of competition indicates the selective influence of the urban environment on these various family heritages.

9   *The Cycle of Adjustment to Unemployment*

E. WIGHT BAKKE

During the 1930's, Professor Bakke carried on intensive studies* of the impact of the economic depression and unemployment on workers and their families. Failure of the economy to make available a job for the father and a regular income for the family, Bakke suggests, upsets a wide variety of established habit patterns of the family and its members. The established patterns become inappropriate for the new conditions and altered patterns must be developed. Once initiated, the processes of change ramify through the whole system, as old patterns break down and are surrendered, and as new patterns are experimented with, found successful and solidified. Thus, a straight-forward event in the family's relations with the outside, economic world requires readjustments in all functional subsystems of the family.

The adjustments made to unemployment by any particular family are not the adjustments of a typical family to a typical unemployment situation. Nevertheless, all of the families studied had at least two problems. One was the necessity for readjustment of the employment pattern within the family group, and the other was the necessity for making adjustments in expenditure when income was curtailed.

Facing these problems effectively involved adjustments in many of the practices and attitudes upon which family relations are built. It involved adjustments in:

1. Means of support
2. Employment and job outlook
3. Expenditures
4. Community associations and activities
5. Foresight and planning
6. Rationalization of position and maintenance of moral standards.

It would not be surprising, therefore, if the practices and readjustments within families were to have certain tendencies in common. These common tendencies did appear, although the length of time which passed before they were distinguishable in any particular case varied from family to

---

* These studies are reported at length in the volume from which this selection was taken and a companion volume, *The Unemployed Worker* (New Haven: Yale University Press, 1940). Editors.

family. Several stages were discernible: (1) momentum stability, (2) unstable equilibrium, (3) disorganization, (4) experimental readjustment, and (5) permanent readjustment.

All of the twenty-four families observed went through these five stages in their attempts to solve the problem of self-maintenance. They varied in the length of time they spent in each period and in the amount of community assistance they received in the process. None of the families, however, applied for such help until they had reached the third stage, that of disorganization. Half never applied at all, and for all but one the receipt of relief was only temporary. This one family appears to have accepted the inevitability of maintenance from the public treasury in the face of a disabling illness in the case of the head and the lack of any family sources of support.

The significant fact is that loss of income through unemployment is followed by the exploration and use of numerous available devices to restore that income by individual and collective effort and to revise the pattern of economic and social life in accordance with the degree of success or failure in this attempt. The early stages of this readjustment are attended by real frustration as present possibilities are compared with the former pattern of life, as the customary techniques of getting a livelihood are proved ineffective, and the pattern of family and community relationships is altered by the removal of the normal amount of cash necessary for its maintenance. The frustration involved in readjustment becomes less acute as the passage of time dulls the sharpness of the comparison of former and present possibilities, and as the need for an active attack on present problems centers the interest and attention on today's opportunities rather than on yesterday's achievements.

The readjustment takes place, however. None of the families stayed for long in the disorganization stage. The end of that period was marked in the economic sphere by the striking of a balance between available income and the accepted standard of living. Adjustment from both angles was important. New earning opportunities or relief allowances on the one hand and revised expenditure wants on the other approached more closely to each other. The amount of relief available set a minimum below which adjustment in expenditure wants need not fall. It is difficult to escape the conclusion that the primary factors involved in the striking of the new balance were the willingness and ability of the workers and their families to readapt their standards, devise new practices, and adjust their relationships and activities to the necessities imposed upon them. The energy and thought of the family itself are the chief resources upon which the com-

Abridged from E. Wight Bakke, *Citizens Without Work*, pp. 154–225 *passim*. Copyright 1940 by the Yale University Press, and used with the kind permission of the author and publishers.

munity must count for the maintenance of the family as an independent economic unit.

In a monetary economy in an urban industrial setting, however, this process must be undergirded with financial resources sufficient to maintain life. The best efforts some of the families could make did not result in that much financial reward. They turned to the public treasury for help. But it is worth noting that such a move was merely one among the many moves the families were making in their attempts to meet the obligations our culture places upon the family, and that it followed a vigorous attempt to escape recourse to charity.

It is relevant to recall also that the move was taken only after a considerable period of failure to secure sufficient financial resources through individual and collective efforts. Only one-fourth of those found unemployed in 1933* had applied for relief two years later. Forty per cent of those who finally applied for the first time waited over two years after the layoff before taking that step. Only 30 per cent had applied within twelve months of the beginning of their unemployment. The efforts to find ways of keeping the family a self-supporting unit did not cease; but support itself is a more imperative need than the idea that the form of support should involve no community help.

Another observation was that the economic changes are accompanied by social changes in family and community relationships. Economic resources provide not only food and shelter but also the means of establishing and maintaining the satisfying relationships and status of a social nature within the family and in the community. These in turn support the incentives which stimulate men in their economic practices. A reduction in economic resources tends to undermine the power of family and community relationships to support economic ambition. At the same time, however, satisfactory "living" is largely defined in terms of these relationships. The desire to retain or restore them can be counted on to stimulate economic effort directed toward maintaining as nearly as possible the pattern of living termed proper and desirable by our culture.

The pattern of relations and practices within the family itself must undergo change in order to deal with the readjustments recorded above.

Stage I. Momentum Stability

The description given to this period suggests that the pattern of family relationships remains relatively undisturbed and on very much the same basis as before unemployment. The family proceeds under the momentum of the customary ways. The division of labor within the home is

---

* In the sample of 2,007 New Haven families selected for investigation by the Institute of Human Relations in that year.

scarcely altered. If the chances of re-employment at his regular firm are slight, the head of the family may be out looking for a job; nevertheless, this activity is a substitution for the time he formerly spent at work. Since the mornings are the best time to look for work, he is likely to have a considerable amount of time to spend around the home in the afternoon, and in some cases this results in his availability for odd jobs around the place; but he does about the same amount of domestic work as he would ordinarily do on Sundays or holidays. Occasionally, he gives more assistance in the matter of shopping. Otherwise, however, the tasks of the several members of the family remain very much the same as before.

Some change occurs in the type of relationships and activities in which the family shares. The husband's daily experiences and interest in job possibilities provide the whole family with fresh subjects for conversation. The husband remains at home a greater proportion of the time, and, since his presence there is normally purposeless, it is not particularly satisfactory to anybody concerned except to the younger children. Families are likely to think twice before spending money on recreation, and consequently there is a minor curtailment here of activities normally carried on outside the home.

At this point, new discipline problems or training problems with respect to the children seldom arise. The children and the father see more of each other, and frequently share in more home recreational relationships than before. We find that in almost every case in this initial period the bonds between the father and children are somewhat strengthened.

In general, it is probably true that during this period the necessity of considering the children first and of facing new problems increases the stability of the relationships between the husband and wife. All integrating factors and symbols of family solidarity, such as ritual and established relationships, common goals of effort, family pride, ideals and codes of behavior, the furnishing of the house, remain very much the same. Frequently, a common resentment shared by both the husband and the wife, sometimes by the children, that the husband has been discriminated against in the layoff adds to the factors drawing the members closer to each other.

The wife censures her husband very little; she tends to accept whatever explanation he gives for the loss of his job—favoritism, slack work, discrimination, or whatnot—and supports her husband loyally both in his presence and to her friends. We feel certain that, unless this loss of a job is the last of a series of events which has tended to disturb the equilibrium of family life, during this period the integration of family life is actually strengthened.

Eventually, however, worry resulting from lack of success in finding a job and from the increasingly severe adjustments which have to be made to a reduced income increases and tends to destroy the customary degree of consideration and regard for each other. With such a development this period draws to a close. The most important factor in determining its length is the amount of resources which the family has to call upon. As resources diminish, the severity of the adjustment increases.

Stage II. Unstable Equilibrium

The chief change in the division of labor during this period is likely to result from the fact that the wife tries her hand at gainful work. Usually she is doing something in the home, such as ironing curtains or taking in washings. Less frequently, she may be seeking gainful employment outside the home. In any case, her activities take her time away from the domestic duties and make it necessary for her to place those duties upon other members of the family. Usually this means upon the children, because during this period the husband is engaged in a more intensive search for work, and lacks the time to spend around the home even if he had the inclination or the enthusiasm for such work. There is some difference of opinion as to whether or not unemployment resulted in a greater amount of domestic work on the part of the husband. One wife put the impression of several in these words: "You know, there is something in the fact that a busy man can always find time to do more. But a man who isn't doing anything doesn't find time even to do that." Probably just as important, however, is the fact that in many cases the hold of custom is strong. Both husband and wife feel that any thoroughgoing redistribution of domestic duties somehow is not a proper procedure; the customary division of labor is well rooted. Unemployed men assumed very few tasks commonly accepted by them as women's work beyond those with which they normally helped. Household repairs, gardening, and the like received somewhat more attention. But these involved no change in the cultural pattern.

Whatever earnings are coming into the family purse now are channeled through the wife's hands even if before that time she had not managed the purse completely. The wife assumes a greater degree of responsibility for management and for distributing the available income. The husband, considerably discouraged and tired out by his search for work, usually takes this excuse to withdraw from his parental responsibilities in other respects, so that decisions as to the activities of the several members of the family customarily descend upon the mother also.

These changes in the division of labor involve a challenge to the status and the roles of the several members, and these are progressively altered. The husband's status in the eyes of both wife and children tends to decline. The status of the mother increases; her decisions become more important, and her enlarged functions give a basis in reality for her heightened prestige. Earning children, and in particular the older children who may have been supplementary earners prior to unemployment but who are now contributing a larger share of their earnings to the family purse, also find that their function in the family is more important. This increased importance is very frequently out of harmony with the normal submission of their own desires to decisions of the parents. The mother is usually more willing to admit the need for giving them greater prestige and recognition than is the father, who resents this change in status.

No new tactics for the solution of family affairs are highly developed during this period, but there are increasing opportunities for the wife to come into conflict with her husband and for children to come into conflict with their parents over such new tactics as must be used. What methods of earning the wife uses, whether or not the husband is diligent in work-seeking activities, how the available cash shall be distributed, and in particular whether "social-front" and "social-contact" expenditures shall be kept up in preference to expenditures not involving the prestige of the family before the outside world are all troublesome matters. What shall be done about the increasing load of debt and credit? What shall be done about the outside activities of the family, particularly recreational affairs? Decisions on such questions which might have been more or less automatic when regular income was provided by the head of the family now become matters for continued debate. As long as there are still some resources in savings or in credit available to the family these decisions do not become pressing, but the opportunities they offer for conflict are obvious.

The necessity for undertaking a special campaign for funds every time a necessary expenditure must be made places a tremendous strain upon the organizational and planning abilities of the family. It is little wonder that the usefulness of planning appears to be challenged. Said a former steam fitter: "It just isn't safe to plan. You're tempting Providence in making any sort of plans. It seems that once you do, fate only goes against you."

The rearrangement of domestic affairs necessitated by unemployment must be carried on in the midst of such an emergency-dominated, energy-consuming, and failure-charged atmosphere. One of the most serious blows to stability is found in the way in which the routine of family life is disorganized, even at an early stage in the experience with unemployment. The lack of regularity in the family program is resented, even though silently, by all. It tends to destroy the normal comfort and satisfaction of life within the family group.

At the same time that satisfaction in the home is being decreased and the normal routine disrupted, mutual activities outside the home and with friends have to be curtailed. Mutual activities offered opportunity for interaction valuable in making the family a unit and for relieving any tensions and difficulties that might arise. These relationships outside the home now tend to become individual rather than mutual.

The roots of training and discipline problems in the family are grounded in factors which it is not our present task to explore. Yet it is worth noting that at this period in unemployment the customary solutions of those problems operate with increasing difficulty. In the first place, parental authority is geared to the status of parents relative to their children. As we have seen, that status undergoes definite change. The father is no longer performing his basic function of provider on which his authority is primarily based. At the same time, supplementary earners, in view of their increased importance as providers, frequently expect and demand somewhat less control of their affairs. Elder daughters in particular are resentful of the continued authority of the father when they are actually, in many cases, taking his place as breadwinner. The father, in order to meet this challenge to his authority, is likely to become increasingly arbitrary, and, if his authority had been well established prior to his unemployment, he is likely to be successful for a time, the older children yielding rather than making an open revolt.

The respect for parents was frequently increased, however, by the obvious evidence that they were willing to go without in order to save their children from a too violent adjustment in their manner of life. Indeed, in a number of cases, children indicated that their regard for their parents had been greatly stimulated by this fact.

In the second place, the subjects over which it is necessary to exercise authority are increased by unemployment. In this matter, also, the older children of earning age are most implicated. It is they who have to stop school, curtail their normal social activities most of which involve expenditures, go without adequate clothes for their activities, and, in addition, devote a larger share of any earnings to supplying the family exchequer. In all these matters, they must be persuaded to do the thing necessary for the best interests of the whole family. Frequently dissatisfaction arose between the older and the younger children on the question of what was likely to appear to the former as favoritism. Parents tried to protect the younger children "who couldn't be expected to understand" while expecting co-operation to a larger extent from the others.

In the third place, the normal function of expenditures as rewards and punishment is severely handicapped. The case of clothing economies is to the point. Obviously the desires of the children must more frequently meet denial than satisfaction. The use of the granting or withholding of new clothes as a reward or punishment is curtailed. The visible evidence of appreciation or disapproval of the children's conduct is vitiated by the difficulty of making any expenditure at all. Any existing rivalries between children are difficult to reduce by well-timed and justly distributed expenditures on clothes.

Finally, the atmosphere in the home, charged as it is with discouragement of the parents in the face of unaccustomed problems, is not conducive to a happy solution of parent-child relationships. For instance, the ordinary relationships of parents and children with respect to co-operation on their schoolwork or parents' attempts to straighten out social or educational problems of the children are made more difficult when the parents are under the stress of having to make all these other decisions. What is ordinarily a somewhat pleasant, if at times an exhausting, undertaking now is done under a strain which causes the parents to resent it. Several parents who had what might be called problem children in school commented on the fact that now they didn't have any energy or patience left for trying to solve their difficulties. "It was all right when your whole day wasn't a problem, but when that's the case, then you don't have the same patience and interest as you did before. You resent it."

In spite of her other worries, however, normally the mother acts as peacemaker between the father and the children and bolsters by her increased authority his declining prestige. Whatever she may say to him—and her criticism of him during this period is likely to increase—she defends the father before the children. Conflicts between parents and children are considerably reduced, also, by the fact that the parents are trying to absorb the stress of readjustment and save the children from unfortunate and depressing facts which might stimulate their restlessness and revolt.

In every family, there exist observable symbols of family unity which play an effective part in stabilizing family relationships. These symbols are not destroyed at this period of unemployment, but they are under severe attack. Ritual events are still carried out, although on a basis of somewhat reduced expenditure. The holiday seasons, customary times for much of this ritual, brought a particular awareness of changed circumstances. Christmas tree, exchange of gifts, and family feasts cannot be continued on the old scale. Equally important is the effect of the curtailing of expenditures for such items as Easter baskets and presents for different members of the family.

Several parents indicated that, from the point of view of maintaining family pride, the children's clothes were almost more important than those of the parents. Said one mother: "We can go to early Mass where no one will see us, but the children are out with other children, and they would bring shame on us if they were not properly dressed."

It is not possible now to relieve the tensions arising within the family through outside contact, recreation, small surprises, and like tactics. The forces which are destructive of family integration are constantly in operation. It can hardly be expected, for example, that the satisfaction of husband and wife in mutual association would escape unscathed from such circumstances, or that their mutual affection and regard would be undiminished. It seems clear that the amount of association that husband and wife want with each other is conditioned by the customary routine of the husband's work schedule. That means that he is usually at home in the late afternoon and evening only. Even if he is on a night schedule, he normally sleeps during the day, so that he is not in constant contact with his wife. If their association in the home during unemployment were to be pleasant, a whole new division of labor would have to be drawn up, accepted, and practiced until it became customary and satisfactory. Apparently this shift of the husband to domestic duties is desired neither by the husband nor by the wife. She is conditioned as much as he is to the fact that the husband's business is to earn money and not to do the household tasks. Several of the wives expressed the wish that their husbands would help them more, but very frequently they would add, "but I suppose I'd lose my respect for him if he did." Even when some experimentation is carried on in this matter of getting the husband accustomed to domestic work, his ineptness and the mistakes he makes as frequently lead to conflict as to satisfaction. After a while, the wife is glad to have him out from under foot and do the work herself.

All of the women with whom we talked tried for considerable periods to excuse and to rationalize their husbands' inability to get jobs, but most of them were obviously making an effort to do so. Said one woman: "I don't blame him. I know no one else around here is working, but it's awfully hard not to." Whatever might be said in criticism of the husband at home, however, the wife usually defended him before outsiders.

As the customary habits enforcing a normal status and the co-operation methods of dealing with problems are unable to survive in the midst of increasing difficulties, they are abandoned and are not yet supplanted by substitute habits and methods. Probably the best indication of the terminus of this particular period is the evidence that the children are going to have to face the necessity of marked readjustment.

Stage III. Disorganization

This period is merely an exaggerated manifestation of the tendencies noted in the previous period, that of unstable equilibrium. The family usually does not stay long in this period. Very quickly the forces of readjustment are felt, and those forces, present even from the beginning of unemployment, take hold. A period of temporary readjustment rapidly comes out of the period of disorganization. If the period does not end quickly, the likelihood is that the family will be destroyed as a unit.

The division of labor of the previous period is maintained. Unless the husband has found a considerable amount of part-time work, the wife definitely takes over the responsibility for managing and planning. All earnings that are coming into the family are now channeled through her, and she has complete charge of them. Since the husband has not yet found a job, he is so involved in his awareness of his own failure and so depressed by his loss of confidence in his own ability and his own future that he cannot focus his attention on family problems. The result is that most of the decisions fall to the wife.

Within the family the status of the husband and father as the head of the family has suffered tremendously. Decisions which are taken for granted and which require very little discussion when the husband is earning normally are raised to huge proportions and take an inordinate amount of time when the husband is out of work. They furnish, often for long periods of time, the subject for dispute and for interrupting the normal satisfactory character of family life.

By the time the family has reached this period, practically all mutual activities outside the home and with non-members of the family have ceased. Even satisfying relations within the home have been reduced to a minimum. For one thing, "No one has any heart for it"; they cannot keep their minds off their troubles. In several cases, the sale of items used in such family activities naturally canceled the activity.

The children are disciplined chiefly now by power authority. Both the father and mother have become dogmatic in their orders and seek by arbitrary control to obtain obedience which would not ordinarily be given to them on the basis of the natural respect the children have for them. The supplementary earners are definitely resentful of the amount that they are having to contribute to the family, and are in revolt against any restraint as well as against the obligations that are placed upon them. There is practically no common sharing of activity between the children and parents, and indeed among all the children except very young ones any activity is almost completely individualistic. The children feel an increasing amount of shame for their parents, comparing them, chiefly the father, with those of other children. Shame rather than pity seems to characterize their attitude at this point.

Very few symbols of family unity remain to give even a superficial indication of family integration. Ritual has been given up with the exception of a few deeply ingrained traditional observances on holidays, and the observance of these is so limited by lack of funds as to give little satisfaction. Many intrafamily activities for mutual aid are now burdens instead of the privileges of a larger family. The family pride in its social position now becomes silly and is discarded along with the practices and expenditures which were intended to give some validity to the objective evidence of that status.

Relations between husband and wife are under extraordinary strain during this period. Wives are no longer publicly vocal about their loyalty to their husbands. They more frequently criticize him openly to the family or to "girl friends." Husbands in retaliation blame their wives for poor management, both in the past and in the present. Each blames the other for past mistakes. Old conflicts that have long been suppressed are revived, and much attention is paid to the contemplation of what might have happened if husband or wife had been more wise and foresighted in the past. The wife frequently questions the sincerity of her husband's search for work and expresses suspicion that he is loafing. In return, the husband challenges her understanding of his real problem and asks her if she thinks she could do any better. Few criticisms are withheld, even in the presence of children and friends. The mother does not defend the father, as she did prior to this period, from criticism by the children. She herself is now the target for their resentment in view of the fact that her decisions with respect to expenditures and the kind of activities the minor members of the family can engage in must now severely curtail satisfactory life for those involved.

The difficulties of home life themselves, however, are not sufficient to cause the man and wife to separate under any ordinary circumstances. It is only the presence of an alternative possibility of going home to mother, or being supported by a rich uncle, or something of the kind, which causes the matter to be even seriously considered. The usual reaction is to make some kind of adjustment to the home situation and make the best of it. Besides, divorces cost money.

In the developing of methods to live as satisfactorily as possible on relief, the family finds a common goal of effort through which functional integration is secured. But at the moment the questions merely furnish new perplexities to already overburdened minds. And as long as there is some possibility that the family may break up, no real organization is possible. When the decision has been made either to break up or to "stick it out," the family can start on its process of reorganization with some hope for success.

Stage IV. Experimental Readjustment

The period we have just described cannot continue for long. If the family continues to live together under the same roof, some working relationships have to be established. An important prerequisite to these is the common, but usually unspoken, acceptance of the fact that the achievements of the past can no longer be made the standards for satisfaction of achievements in the present.

The wife's part in management and planning is still most important, but the husband begins to share more in these efforts, particularly if he has succeeded in finding some opportunity to earn. Much depends upon the degree to which the work activities in which he is participating relieve him from the contemplation of failure. The division of labor made necessary by the readjustment in contributions to the family welfare has now become somewhat more normal and sufficiently recognized so that the mother can see the gaps in the domestic management provisions and make assignments to them.

The precise mutual activities and interests of the several members, which we saw were so nearly destroyed as unemployment progressed, are seldom restored. But one can witness at this period the process by which such materials are woven into the fabric of family life. The routine has become somewhat more satisfactory. Once again the family becomes a help to its members in facing their individual problems. Every point at which such help occurs adds a stone to the foundation of family solidarity. Whatever pattern of discipline and practice has been established tends to become habitual, and therefore there is less need for the assertion of dogmatic authority. Moreover, since the family is making a somewhat better adjustment to its economic problems, some degree of respect of children for parents is restored. The older earning children, now becoming accustomed to their large contribution to the family exchequer, become less resentful and assist in discipline problems. The school children have somewhat recovered from the shock of having their parents ridiculed and now begin to defend them.

One of the first signs that the family is recovering from the period of disorganization is the re-establishment of ritual events although on a somewhat less expensive basis. Also the importance of common goals reasserts itself as a force binding the family together. Very frequently, the family becomes more conscious of itself as a unit, defending its members against the impacts of the judgment and criticism of outsiders. A common enemy, as well as a common goal for action, can act as an integrating factor.

The mutual respect for and appreciation of one's mate so thoroughly challenged in preceding periods cannot be immediately and fully restored. But criticisms once so outspoken are withheld, and each begins to make allowances for the points of view and states of mind and comfort of the other. Even if criticisms are aired, one or the other is very likely to let them go so that they do not cause a continued quarrel.

Husbands in particular played an important role in this situation. In not every case were they willing to grant the wife credit for the way in which she handled her increased responsibilities and functions. Frequently they were quite outspoken on this matter, however, and their appreciation added salve to whatever wounds had been made in the relationship. Disagreements between husband and wife, and even fights between husband and wife, do not necessarily indicate that the family is not a strong institution.

Of course, by this time any censure has begun to appear as practically useless and as making matters worse. Consequently, if any degree of mental control still exists, criticisms may be reduced for this reason. However, there are very real reasons why blame is not so frequently offered. We are inclined to think that the fact that the wife looks for work is a very important factor in decreasing her criticisms of her husband. Once she has been out looking for work and finds out how hard it is, she is less inclined to blame him for not finding work. In every case where the wife looked for work, this result was observed. Blame is normally stimulated by comparison of present achievements with past achievements, and as the distance from the past increases there is less reason and less opportunity for blame. It seems less appropriate than the devotion of attention to the present or future adjustment and the assessment of one's success or failure in terms of his present activities.

Moreover, rationalization of the position of the head of the family has proceeded far enough to take the edge off censure. The decisions of the mother as to expenditures, which were so frequently productive of criticism by the children, have become accepted as necessary, and, in any case, as customary, and criticism of her and of the father is reduced.

Work relief in many cases provided the self-maintenance foundation on which this period of experimental readjustment rested. This fact deserves particular comment. Many of the attacks on the stability of the family unit were weakened when the head of the family was certified for a WPA job. Once more his wages are the chief source of support. He is the breadwinner, the provider. Earnings of supplementary earners can once more be allocated to the personal needs of that individual by family decision. The necessary choices in expenditures can be made in family council from which outsiders are excluded. If those expenditures include items considered important to the satisfactory relations between family members—surprises, symbolic family events, common recreation—the only restraint is one which is self-imposed. Less rationalization is needed to explain the fact that "father can't get a job." To those outside the family circle, he goes daily to work. Even within the family circle the restoration of a more normal division of labor and routine is possible. Lacking a private job for the head, work relief furnishes the family with the best possible substitute under the circumstances. Having observed our families under conditions of unemployment with no public help, or with that help coming from direct and from work relief, we are convinced that after the exhaustion of self-produced resources, work relief is the only type of assistance which can restore the strained bonds of family relationship in a way which promises the continued functioning of that family in meeting the responsibilities imposed upon it by our culture. We have observed a few families finding a new level of integration and stability on the assumption of continued expectancy of direct relief. Stability is not restored in such a case, however, unless family objectives have been severely modified, unless the family has established itself among a group of associates similarly situated and has come to think of the relief check as the probably permanent substitute for the pay envelope. Even so, family stability is scarcely furthered unless agreement on such matters is found among all members. Nor is the institution thus re-created the sort which provides the kind of common life conducive to the satisfactory functioning of its members in a democratic community.

Stage V. Permanent Readjustment

The aspects of this particular period are not essentially different from those of the last. They are simply continued and strengthened. However, the period is characterized by several features which are worth noting. Conflict situations rooted in the transition in the standard of living have practically disappeared. Instead of concentrating upon a comparison of the past with the present, the attention is focused upon the present and future problems. Rationalizations of the changed position of the family have been accepted without serious question and give a satisfactory explanation of the present status of the family. Goals of common effort once more appear and become the source of common interest and the objective to which individuals will subordinate their own personal wishes. Family activities of a recreational sort are renewed, and such recreation becomes less individualized and more frequently a common enterprise of the whole group. The discipline pattern which is consistent with the new authority relationships within the family is accepted by all and, with the exception of the ordinary conflicts arising from the exercise of any discipline, little trouble is found in this quarter.

10   *Middle-Class Fathers' Occupational Role and Attitudes toward Children*

DAVID F. ABERLE and KASPAR D. NAEGELE

Enduring relationships such as those that develop between the family and the economic system have far-reaching effects, effects which may not be germane to the relationship itself. In the previous selection Bakke discussed how the fact of unemployment impinged upon diverse areas of family life. In the present selection, Professors Aberle and Naegele discuss how employment affects a father's relationships with his children. An occupational role, they argue, develops in the role occupant a particular set of values and attitudes, which in turn shape the expectations the father will hold for his children and how he will evaluate the behavior the children do show.

This paper will consider the relationship between the occupational role of the middle-class male and his aims and concerns in the socialization of his children. The approach is deliberately one-sided. We will deal almost entirely with fathers and scarcely at all with mothers, and we will highlight other aspects of the socialization process at the expense of such matters as feeding practices, toilet training, and sexual training.[1] There is no intention of denying the worth of approaches other than that exemplified here. We wish only to stress what seem to be neglected, though obvious and common-sense, aspects of the question of socialization.

We will define socialization for the purpose at hand as the process of inculcating in individuals the skills, traits, and value attitudes associated with the performance of present or anticipated roles.[2] There are a number of ways of stating problems concerning socialization. One approach is to ask what are the *effects* of certain types of socialization experience. Considerable strides have been made along these lines, in analyzing, for example, the effects of "basic disciplines" such as weaning, toilet training, and sexual training. The effects of aggression and dependency training are also receiving attention. Some work has been undertaken regarding the effects of particular kinds of parent-child relationships on the socialization process. When attention is turned to the *causes* of certain types of treatment of the child, there is a tendency in psychiatric and mental health work to investigate the causes of pathological parental behavior and to find its sources in the childhood experiences of the parents: to see that in various complex and unconscious ways parents are repeating, or undoing, or working out

Reprinted from *The American Journal of Orthopsychiatry*, XXII (April, 1952), 366–78, with the kind permission of the authors and publishers.

problems derived from their own childhood. There is no desire to eliminate either of these approaches. But the focus here will be on an aspect of socialization so obvious that it is sometimes forgotten: the relationship between the adult role of the individual and his orientation to his children.

In every society, parents aim to raise their children to become adults capable of assuming the typical adult roles and of being integrated into the social system. Consequently, we can expect that within any given social group there will be similarities in the goals and practices of socialization. Similarity of goals depends partly upon the relative uniformity of the parents' long-range expectations as to what sorts of positions the children will ultimately occupy and what consequent skills, attitudes, and qualities they must ultimately possess, and partly on the relative uniformity of the definition of the succession of roles intermediate between infancy and adulthood.[3] Similarities in means depend partly on the fact that they "make sense" to the parents in terms of the goals hoped for and partly on the effects of having one's efforts inspected by one's neighbors. (In addition to these conscious and semiconscious expectations, parents are influenced by a variety of unconscious factors, derived from both idiosyncratic and general experience. Furthermore, any particular socialization regime has consequences for personality unanticipated by the socializing agents. These unanticipated consequences sometimes take the form of particular types of deviations common in the society, sometimes of "quirks" commonly found in "normal" members of the group.) All in all, child rearing is future-oriented to an important extent. The picture of the desired end product is importantly influenced by the parents' experiences in the adult world, as well as by their childhood experiences. When adult experience changes under the impact of major social change, there is reason to believe that there will ultimately, though not necessarily immediately, be shifts in the socialization pattern as well. The adult's experiences tell him what attitudes, skills, and qualities his child must have to fit into the adult role system. And the parent is likely to consider his child's present behavior as a prognostication of his probable adult behavior. The parent's evaluation of the child's behavior, however, proceeds not only by direct extrapolation, but also by vaguer and less conscious processes, in which the connection between present and future behavior is more indirectly and symbolically reckoned.

These rather obvious matters are sometimes forgotten by the psychiatrically oriented—or rather, fall far into the background—in the interests of analyzing more complex and interesting problems of psychopathological behavior. But it is with these things in mind that we shall approach the question of the middle-class father. And perhaps it should be said that one reason we are stressing the father is that he, too, is forgotten or recedes into the background in the face of the overwhelming focus on the mother in recent work.

This presentation is based on data collected in the course of research carried out for the Human Relations Service, a group interested in preventive psychiatry, located in a suburb of Boston, with both clinical and research functions. The authors of this paper, respectively a social anthropologist and a sociologist, have recently completed interviews with both parents in a series of more than twenty families. Each family had at least one child in a particular nursery school in the community. The parents were selected for our research because, after meetings of their group where members of the Human Relations Service spoke, they expressed willingness to serve as subjects. The group is middle class by our subjective impressions and by rating according to Warner's Index of Status Characteristics.[4] The members range from upper-middle class to lower-middle class. Incomes run from about $20,000 per annum to about $3,700. One family lives in a two-family house, and the remainder in single-family dwellings, all in "good" neighborhoods. For the most part, the fathers are professional men, major and minor executives of medium to large business concerns, owners of businesses, and salesmen (not including house-to-house sales). Only one man is on an hourly wage rate, and the group includes no skilled, semiskilled, or unskilled laborers. Most of the men are college-educated, and the remainder have technical training beyond the high-school level. Most of the wives are college educated. The school itself is "progressive." All of the men have risen in status in the course of their careers, and almost all feel that they have not yet reached their ceilings.

Since the families are middle class, what is said here is restricted in its implications to the middle class, with no necessary assumption that the remarks that follow have wider application and with some reason to believe that they do not. Most of the families are "normal," in the sense that few parents have sought or appear to need psychiatric advice, few children have appeared in psychiatric facilities, and there are no startling deviations from the norm in the patterning of adult roles.

One of us interviewed the fathers in these families, seeing them ordinarily for two evening-long interviews in their homes. The other interviewed the mothers. Information regarding the mothers will be presented separately and is used only for background data here.

That part of the project which was concerned with the fathers had as its aim the investigation of the relationship between the father's occupational role and his behavior in the home. More specifically, it was hoped that a connection could be established between the particular satisfactions and strains of each father's occupational setting and his behavior toward his wife and children. While minor relationships of this kind seem to exist, the data appear to illuminate somewhat more general questions. Before discussing them, we must stress the tentative character of subsequent remarks. The investigation was exploratory in nature, and the number of cases small. Matters which turned out to be quite important later on were not included in the initial interview schedule. And that schedule was long enough so that some questions were overlooked in interviewing some fathers.

It became clear in the course of research that the relationship which some fathers could see between their job situation and their behavior in the home was trivial, that some fathers could find no connection, and that still others flatly rejected the idea that there could be any connection. There is good reason for this. In the first place, many features of our social system stress the separation of the occupational and the domestic role. In urban middle-class America, there is a deliberate boundary between home and job.[5] This only seems obvious because we all participate in this sort of setup. In the majority of the world's societies, production and consumption units overlap greatly, and the extended or nuclear family is likely to be a basic organized unit of production and consumption. In our middle-class society, universalistic standards[6] ideally govern the selection of individuals for occupational positions: competence—what you can do—rather than who you are, is, or ideally should be, crucial for occupational recruitment, advancement, or firing. Family connections are theoretically irrelevant to the allocation of occupational role in the majority of middle-class occupations. There are institutional barriers against nepotism in many organizations, personal fortune and company funds are kept distinct, and of course place of employment and home are ordinarily separate. One's home life may actually affect job performance, positively or negatively. But the effects of home life are treated as irrelevant in many organizations, or as intrusive: something to be recognized only in order to dispel it—such is the role of the psychological consultant in many firms. For many reasons, modern complex industrial bureaucratic society requires this separation, institutionalizes it, makes of it a virtue—and the fathers in our group respond in terms of this norm.

Second, a man is bewildered when he is asked to consider the relationship of his behavior and attitudes on the job to those in the home. For him the two worlds are incommensurable. The occupational world is one of clearly delimited responsibility and authority, of judgment of individuals on the basis of what they can do, rather than who they are, of initiative and persistence, usually of competition, and a world where aggressiveness—in the layman's sense—pays off. In the domestic world, however, there are no such clear-cut limits on authority and responsibility; children are to be loved and cared for because they are one's children, and not because of their accomplishments or deserts; competition and aggressiveness are considered inappropriate techniques for gaining one's ends; and ideally emotional warmth, relaxation, and the like are to be maximized. Thus the techniques required for dealing with other individuals and making a success in the occupational world differ point by point from the techniques for dealing with wife and children and making a success of family life and the raising of sons and daughters. It is true that the standards of the occupational world "infect" behavior in the family in many ways, not all of which can be mentioned here. But in terms of ideal patterns, the two spheres are far apart. Hence the unwillingness or inability of fathers to see a relationship need not surprise us. But neither need it deter us from seeking a connection. When we consider the investment of time and effort in the occupational sphere, we are entitled to assume that the eight or more hours a day spent on the job may affect behavior during the other hours of the day. We shall see that while the father attempts to leave the office behind him, at home he represents the occupational world to his family (this is particularly clear in the interviews with mothers) and evaluates his children in terms of his occupational role.

We would assume that fathers in this group would be oriented toward their sons in terms of an expectation that they will ultimately occupy positions in the middle-class occupational structure, and toward their daughters with the expectation that they will not. The data confirm this assumption. Without exception, fathers desire college training for their boys. One father says that one of his sons may not be college material and that in this case he should not take up space in college—but he considers this a shocking statement. For girls, the majority of fathers plan a college education, but there is considerably more willingness to admit that the child may not go, either because she does not want to, or because she may get married first.

As for the sons' future occupation, fathers always say initially that they have "no plans" for their children. Further questioning always shows that "no plans" means that any occupation is all right, *if* it is a middle-class occupation. It means that either a professional or a business career is all right. (In the same way, "no plans" with regard to college means, any *good* college, usually with certain limitations as to what constitutes a good college.) Skilled wagework is never mentioned. This drastic limitation is completely unconscious for the fathers. From their point of view, this restriction is identical with "no plans." It might be mentioned that if fathers were asked whether academic work represented a possible career for the boy, they tended to reject it. One accepted it as a possibility; one said that it would be fine for his oldest son, since he was shy, irresponsible, bookish, and needed a woman to look after him. Three rejected it contemptuously. It is evident from the rejections, as well as from one of the acceptances, that it is not just a matter of meager financial reward; many a middle-class father does not consider the academic role to exemplify appropriate masculine behavior.[7]

As for the daughters, over half of the fathers who discussed the point would accept the possibility of a career for their daughters, but only as a possibility. Most of these men would prefer that their daughters marry, or expect them to, and the remainder of the group reject a career out of hand. Only two fathers wanted their daughters to know how to earn a livelihood, and both of them have wives who are working or did work during married life.

These findings are "normal" and "obvious" only because we are so deeply imbedded in the life which these fathers represent. Note that no father envisages downward mobility for his son. Also, though many of our fathers come from social and occupational backgrounds quite different from those they now occupy, it is their own present status, derived from adult experience, which they project into the future for their children. So far, then, our assumptions are supported by the data.[8]

One complication is introduced. Fathers do expect their sons to move in the same general occupational world that they do. But in our society occupational choice is theoretically free, and particular occupational positions are achieved, not inherited. Fathers should not, and in most cases cannot if they would, plan their children's precise future—since almost no one can guarantee a particular niche to his son. That means that fathers cannot foresee exactly what skills, values and personality traits are going to be useful for their sons—something that is possible in many other societies. Nor can they plan precisely what steps their sons should take to reach this unknown future. Consequently, in evaluating their sons' present behavior they can only focus on general character traits conducive to success, on symbolic manifestations of those traits, and on a modicum of success in school as an almost essential step toward middle-class occupational status. A different future, marriage, is envisaged for girls, and we can expect a different evaluation of present behavior.

In the light of fathers' expectations for the future, let us examine some typical concerns that fathers express about the present behavior of their children. It must be stated at once that when we say that a child's behavior is a matter of concern to the father, this does not mean that the child is, or will become, a problem by psychiatric standards. It means only that the child's behavior is disvalued, is a matter of worry and mild anxiety, is something that the parent would like to change, for the sake of the child (though his own convenience may also be involved). It should also be mentioned that it is possible for a father to become seriously concerned over behavior which a clinician might consider normal, to overlook behavior which might be considered portentous by a clinician, and to pass off some troubling behavior on the assumption that it is "just a stage."

Fifty-six children are involved: 29 boys and 27 girls. The age range is from 13 years to a few months for boys and from 10 years to a few months for girls. Fathers may not subject very young infants to evaluative comment of the sort we are about to discuss, but this begins early in the child's life. There are many more statements of concern involving boys, and the emotional strength of these concerns is considerably greater with respect to boys than with respect to girls.

The question of securing obedience, and of annoyance at disobedience runs through virtually all the interviews and will not be discussed. The recurrent concerns expressed involve lack of responsibility and initiative, inadequate performance in school, insufficiently aggressive or excessively passive behavior, athletic inadequacies, overconformity, excitability, excessive tearfulness, and the like, possible involvement in homosexual play, and "childish" behavior.[9] In all of these categories more boys were objects of concern than girls; in some, many more boys and in some, no girls at all were mentioned. Of course no parent expressed concern about all these things in any one child or even in any one family. But the total tendency clearly indicates that such behaviors as have been mentioned are negatively evaluated when they appear in male children. Similarly, satisfactory performance in these areas of behavior was more often mentioned for boys than for girls. Fathers are pleased if their boys display responsibility and initiative, perform well in school, stand up for themselves, show athletic ability, emotional stability, and so on. Only one father does not want his boys to be particularly athletic. Far less concerns, we have said, are expressed regarding girls. Satisfactions with girls, though they do include school performance, moral sexual behavior, and the like, seem to focus strongly on the girls' being "nice," "sweet," pretty, affectionate, and well liked. For both boys and girls, of course, fathers hope for normal personalities, good adjustment, likeability, and popularity.

But all of the traits we have mentioned as matters of concern are—from the father's point of view—prognosticators, direct or indirect, of adult traits which will interfere with success in middle-class occupational life. The ideal-typical successful adult male in the middle-class occupational role should be responsible, show initiative, be competent, be aggressive, be capable of meeting competition. He should be emotionally stable and capable of self-restraint. These qualities are part of the value structure of the occupational world, they are involved in the role definitions of that world, and fathers' discussions of their own jobs show that these qualities have great significance for them. This does a great deal to explain the difference between the father's concern with his son's behavior and with his daughter's. He worries about failures in these areas and is happy over successes, because of his future expectations for his sons. He does not worry so much about his daughters because they will occupy different roles, toward which he has a somewhat vaguer orientation. Occupational career is not taken seriously, marriage is the primary hope and expectation, the same sorts of demands are not made, and the father does not seem to fuss too much as to whether his young daughter will ultimately be a good mate. If she is a sweet little girl, this is enough. We do find that there is some concern with these matters in girls and that one father is disturbed by his daughter's lack of aggressiveness. But by and large, though the girls are undoubtedly less athletic, less aggressive, and more tearful and emotional than the boys, this does not bother the father. These qualities do not predict failure in the adult feminine role

—quite the reverse. In fact some fathers are troubled if their daughters are bossy—a term not used for any of the boys. Though we know that some of the boys are holy terrors in their play groups, no father shows any concern lest his son be a bully, and some proudly mention that they guess the boy is a bit of a devil. (It might be noted that though the "bad boy" is a stereotype of American life, ambivalently but never wholly negatively regarded, there is no corresponding stereotype for a girl, the phrase "bad girl" having quite different connotations.) We will not deal here with mothers' concerns, but it can be said that mothers do react to what they consider excessive aggression in boys and that mothers show more concern with girls than do fathers.

Fathers' concern with athletic ability requires a little further discussion. This is a case of indirect and symbolic meaning of present behavior. Fathers are not concerned with athletics because they want their boys to grow up to be professional athletes, but because failure along these lines seems to symbolize for the father inability to be properly aggressive and competitive, now and in the future. The threat of homosexual play is, of course, very complex in its meaning, but in part it hints at something passive, inadequate and unmasculine, and in part seems to mean "sneaky"—evasive, dishonest, shady—behavior.

Projection into the future is not intended as a total explanation of the father's concerns. A son's present failures reflect on the father as a father, and this is important. In addition, we see conscious and half-conscious identification with sons in several fathers, and it is undoubtedly present in many more. Some of our most critical or most concerned fathers remark that the boy is "like me," or "reminds me of myself when I was his age." In a sense, we might say that whereas the father's present situation represents to him his son's probable future situation (broadly speaking), the son's present behavior may represent to the father his own past. This identification may produce nurturant behavior. But the identification may result in a highly ambivalent reaction: perhaps difficulties now observed in the son were once successfully overcome by the father, sometimes after a struggle, and these may now be unconsciously reactivated. The identification may thus intensify the degree to which the father attempts to counteract the disturbing behaviors in his son, attempting at the same time to stifle the same tendencies in himself.

It might be mentioned that our sample indicates that fathers become more concerned with male first-born children than with female first-born children, and that subsequent male children, whether they follow boys or girls, are less likely to be foci of concern for fathers. This might be partly connected with the identification phenomenon noted above, since conscious identification is mentioned more often in connection with male first-born children than with other sons.[10] But there are many—too many—other ways to interpret this particular finding, and on the basis of our small sample we are reluctant to choose among them.

We see a good deal of evidence, then, for the belief that fathers' attitudes toward their sons' behavior are different from those toward their daughters'. It is relatively easy to account for a good deal of this difference on the basis of the fact that the father is oriented toward his son as the future occupant of a middle-class occupational role, for which certain behaviors are of great importance—something about which he has direct experience—and toward his daughter as the future occupant of a different middle-class role, that of mother and wife, for which his own standards are less exacting and less well formed in terms of the girl's present behavior.

This does not mean that because the father uses present behavior as a prognosticator for the future it is a good prognosticator. It has been pointed out that he may well stress the unimportant, disregard fairly severe symptoms, and at times simply reckon present behavior as a "stage." Nor do our findings mean that boys are subject to more strains than girls, or are more likely to be problems in adult life, or the reverse. They only point to a particular relationship: that between father's occupational role, his future expectations for his children, and his evaluation of their conduct. The nature of that relationship has been discussed. What are its broader implications?

On the theoretical level, it is hoped that this paper points to the desirability of much more minute inquiries aimed at relating socialization practices (about which we have said little), aims of socialization, parents' evaluation of children's behavior at various age levels, and parents' long-range expectations, to parents' adult roles, occupational and other, and to the values connected with those roles. Let us turn our attention not only to the effects of socialization practices in a group, but to the causes of those patterns. For, far from being fortuitous with respect to the remainder of the social system, many or most of those patterns are somehow integrated with it. The broad outlines of some of these relationships are recognized and have been explored empirically, as in the work of Davis and Havighurst, who have compared certain socialization practices as between class and caste groups and related those practices to the social position of the parents.[11] The present paper works within a class, rather than by comparing two classes, and gives explicit attention to differences of expectations as between boys and girls. A tremendous amount of work, however, remains to be done on these and on more subtle and intricate issues.

Many questions in this general area pressed for our attention in the course of research. Some have been omitted here for lack of space, and some because the data were insufficient for extended discussion. But a few might be mentioned as suggestive of the sorts of problems remaining for analysis. Parents often express a certain ambivalence regarding the use of physical techniques in discipline—an ambivalence probably related to middle-class rejection of force as a means of settling interpersonal tensions or organizational difficulties. This rejection, in turn, has ramifications in the characteristics of role systems in the middle class. The question of means of socialization, largely neglected here, brings to mind the disagreements we sometimes saw between husband and wife as to what means shall be used, and the problem of analyzing to what extent these differences reflect a real difference of opinion regarding goals and to what extent only a disagreement as to the path to be followed to reach a jointly agreed-upon goal. If the latter is the case, what are the factors which make one technique more congenial to the father, and a different one to the mother? We find a close relationship between these disagreements and another striking phenomenon: faddism in child-rearing techniques. Much of the faddism seems to center about two apparently opposed techniques of child-rearing. One (the older) stresses scheduled feeding, early sphincter training, and, in general, responsibility and self-control. The other (and more recent) emphasizes demand feeding, late sphincter training, and concern for spontaneity and lack of severe inhibitions. Do these two approaches in fact reflect utterly diverse values, or are they simply two aspects of the same general value: individualism, with its responsibility aspect and its freedom aspect, here, as in other areas of life, in tension with each other?

Regardless of the issues about which faddism centers, we must ask how it is possible to have fads in child-training procedures. One factor seems to be the high valuation in our society placed on antitraditionalism, which is associated with the stress on science, rationalism, and progress. This anti-traditionalistic attitude opens up the possibility of experimentation, change and faddism in child training, as in other aspects of social life—though there are other social reasons for the existence of faddism as a general phenomenon. A thorough analysis of faddism in child-rearing would also involve analysis of the adult feminine role in our society. These examples and partial interpretations only suggest the wealth of problems lying ready at hand. So, finally, this paper represents a very small contribution to a very large potential field: the relating of socialization practices to general American values, to class values, to role orientations, and the like, with due regard for the effects of adult, as well as childhood experiences, in determining parents' attitudes and behavior toward children and with due attention to unconscious and symbolic connections as well as conscious ones.

The approach used in this paper has implications for preventive psychiatric work, as well as for research. We see that fathers consider their sons' present behavior directly or symbolically indicative of probable future behavior, but we know that they may overstress minor defections and overlook serious symptoms. This stresses the need for pushing forward current work in educating the public. To ensure rapid referral of disturbed children, and perhaps even more important, to allay parental anxieties, guidance must be provided not only to mothers, but also to fathers, which will give them a more precise understanding of the prognostic significance of present behavior for the future.

The matter of faddism, briefly touched on here, highlights another practical issue. In a sense the specialist views child training as a technological problem and believes that, like other technological problems, it can at least be improved by scientific analysis, which, he expects, can provide more effective techniques than those of common sense. Many middle-class parents have absorbed this attitude. Technological change always creates some discomfort in those who have to learn new ways, and parents are no exception. Lacking the security derived from the belief that customary behavior is adequate, they seek security by following to the hilt—or attempting to follow—the current recommendations of specialists, who now assume for the parents the authority once vested in tradition. These recommendations change, and parents attempt to change with them. In this way faddism grows out of insecurity and the use of the specialist's recommendations in the effort to attain fixity. But along with the effort to follow the specialist goes an ambivalence toward him; for, it seems, each psychiatrist is held responsible for the shifts of opinion of the last twenty years. Thus faddism poses three problems for preventive psychiatry: the careful evaluation of their recommendations, to test their validity; the assuaging of the anxiety created in parents by "styles" in child-rearing; and fence-mending with respect to public relations.

One last point stands out with great clarity. In the course of research we found what many other workers must have observed: fathers with an ultimate faith in psychiatry and preventive psychiatry but with marked resistance to some of the advice they had received in public meetings conducted by psychiatrically oriented—and well-qualified—individuals. Their complaints, in addition to faddism, seemed to center about excessive self-consciousness induced in parents and too much emphasis on spontaneity and de-inhibition rather than on discipline and responsibility. In the light of what has been said about the occupational sphere and about fathers' concerns, these complaints become intelligible. It would be too limited a view to consider such complaints only as manifestations of hostility toward the children. Rather, the "spontaneity" regime threatens the fathers because to them it means the possibility of raising children who cannot adapt to the world as the fathers know it. From a practical point of view, then, efforts to educate parents regarding socialization practices must be accompanied by at least equally intensive efforts to understand the meaning to the parents of the socialization practices they now use, to understand the threats which a change would mean to them, and to show them (when such is the case) that their goals are not subverted, but supported by suggested changes. Otherwise we can anticipate reactions to attempted change in the form of ambivalence, over-complicated performance, resistance, or rejection of the changes proposed.

11   *The Effects of the Wife's Employment on the Family Power Structure*

ROBERT O. BLOOD, JR.,

and ROBERT L. HAMBLIN

Engels viewed the status of women in the home as similar to that of the proletariat exploited by the capitalist owner of the "means of production," and predicted that one day they would be freed from this "serfdom." Many others, including both the proponents of women's rights and the decriers of women's freedom to neglect their homes and families, have had similar ideas: that participation in the occupational world would alter the nature of leadership or authority in the home. Professors Blood and Hamblin have tested this notion in their study comparing families in which the wife is employed and others in which she is not. They fail to find that employment of the wife significantly alters the power structure of the family. In the same connection, a paper in Part IV by Eleanor Maccoby may be mentioned. Her careful review of the literature fails to confirm that the employment of the mother outside the home in itself has harmful influences on the personality development of her children.

The purpose of this paper is to test some hypotheses regarding the effects of the wife's employment on the power relationships between the husband and wife as shown in marital attitudes and behavior.

In a study of married and divorced couples, Jacobson found substantial variation in the respondents' views about the power which should be wielded by the husband and the wife.[1] Jacobson described these role conceptions as varying along a continuum from "traditional" to equalitarian. Sociologists generally agree that American marriages have shifted toward greater husband-wife equality. Presumably this change from a husband-dominated toward an equalitarian power structure has not occurred haphazardly. Such a change should be traceable to other changes in the family's relationship to its environment.

The basic hypothesis we wish to test is that the "husband-dominated" family becomes more equalitarian as a result of the wife's employment outside the home. Since an increasingly large proportion of wives work during the first years of marriage this hypothesis has widespread implications for our understanding of contemporary family life.

Power is often defined as the share group members have in originating group policy.[2] Theoretically, power varies with control (the relative ability of group members to sanction one another).[3] When the wife works, she

Reprinted from *Social Forces*, XXVI (May, 1958), 347–52, with the kind permission of the authors and Williams and Wilkins Co., the publishers.

presumably increases her ability to sanction or control because of the financial contribution she makes to the family. Hence, her status should be improved both with respect to her expected power (i.e., her authority) and her actual power.[4]

The above hypothesis was tested in an *ex post facto* experiment. A questionnaire containing scale items and questions designed to measure the several independent and dependent variables as well as fifteen control variables was pretested on sixty couples.

A larger quota sample was then selected according to the following criteria: (1) The wives in half of the marriages were employed full time outside of the home. The other half were full-time housewives. (2) Each couple had been married at least one year but not more than six years. (3) The wives had been in their present role (that is, a full-time housewife or working wife) at least a year at the time of being interviewed.

Upper division students at the University of Michigan who were enrolled in the Sociology Department's course on marriage were given a two-hour training period, after which they administered the questionnaires to each couple individually. The respondents were drawn from the home towns of the students, primarily in the state of Michigan.

Coding and computational operations were performed by experienced personnel. Preliminary cross tabulations were made using the experimental variable, each control variable, and the dependent variables. Those control variables which showed a consistent association with the dependent variables in these preliminary tabulations were controlled in the *ex post facto* experiment. These control variables were: (1) socio-economic class, (2) relative education of husband and wife, (3) absolute education of wife, (4) independent unearned income of wife, (5) number of children, (6) religious affiliation (Catholic vs. other), (7) number of years married, and (8) the number of years the wife had been in her present role. The frequency distributions of each of these eight variables were matched in the two experimental groups (i.e., working wives and non-working wives). When the controls were applied, 160 of the original 350 couples remained. The greatest shrinkage occurred when the two variables of number of children and years in present status were controlled.[5]

The power structure of a family should be related to husband-wife expectations about authority, i.e., to legitimized power. When a group member is expected by other members to originate group policy, he is said to have authority. These authority expectations ought to change with the actual power relationship. Sociologists from Marx to Weber agree that expectations (which are one aspect of ideologies) tend toward consistency with actual behavior patterns, although there is some disagreement as to which changes first.

If relative power does vary with control over the flow of resources into the group, then these empirical hypotheses ought to obtain: (a) On the average, working wives change toward equalitarian authority expectations more than do housewives. (b) On the average, husbands of working wives change toward equalitarian authority expectations more than do husbands of housewives.

To measure changes in authority expectations, 18 of the 28 items of Jacobson's original scale were included in the questionnaire.[6] The instructions to the respondents were as follows:

1. What are your present attitudes toward the statements below? Choose the response for each statement which indicates what you believe is right as a matter of principle.
2. What were your attitudes toward the above statements before you started going with your spouse?

Of the 18 items, 10 were judged to be authority-relevant and 7 of the 10 authority items proved to be scalable.

In constructing this Guttman-type scale, the "now" responses of a random sample of 50 wives were used. The scale was then checked for reproducibility on the "before" responses of another 50 wives, the "now" responses of 50 husbands, and the "before" responses of another 50 husbands. The coefficients of reproducibility averaged .91.

The changes revealed were in the predicted directions. The working wives more often change toward equalitarian authority expectations, whereas the housewives more often change toward traditional authority expectations. The husbands of the working wives also change more often toward equalitarian authority expectations whereas more husbands of housewives change toward traditional authority expectations. However, the latter difference is not statistically significant.

Let us turn now to the actual power structure of these families. Families usually make a number of important decisions each year. Either the husband or wife may make the initial suggestion which eventually becomes family policy. Suggestions as to what ought to be done are the usual way of originating group policy. Hence, the number of initial suggestions of the husband or wife which become family decisions indicates the share each partner has in originating group policy.[7] If control does determine power in the family, another empirical hypothesis ought to obtain. On the average, working wives have a larger percentage of adopted suggestions than do housewives.

The percentage of adopted suggestions was obtained by formulating 30 questions of the following general form: "The last time you decided ———— ————, who first suggested what you finally decided to do?" Included were questions about selecting a home, having a baby, buying an automobile, planning a family vacation, and buying insurance. This original list of questions was presented to two Marriage classes who served as judges for picking out those questions which involved "important" family decisions. The students achieved considerable consensus on 18 items.

These items were included in the questionnaires as a power scale. Both the husband and wife were asked to respond independently according to these instructions:

> The following questions ask whether it was the husband's or wife's initial idea which was accepted when certain decisions were made. Please place an "H" in the blank preceding the question if the husband made the initial suggestion, a "W" if the wife made the initial suggestion or an "0" if you have never made this kind of decision since getting married.

A reliability check on a random sample of 100 couples revealed that, on the average, each husband-wife pair gave identical responses on 86 per cent of the items.

Although the working wives did average a greater percentage of adopted suggestions as predicted in the above empirical hypothesis, the difference is unreliable.

During some preliminary studies, it became apparent that most wives would like their husbands to do more around the house than the husbands are currently doing. There is a continuous (although, in most cases, a mild) power struggle between husbands and wives over the share of the housework which the husband will do. The resolution of this power struggle over housework may give another measure of the relative power of husbands and wives.

Because she shares in the responsibility for economic support of the family, the working wife can appeal to her husband to share in the house-keeping tasks on grounds of fairness. By contrast, the housewife has less of a basis for appealing to her husband to help with the housework. There-fore, the following empirical hypothesis may be formulated: Husbands of working wives, on the average, do a greater proportion of housework than husbands of housewives.

The husband's proportion of housework was obtained by listing twelve household tasks—for example, doing the dishes, cooking meals, and shopping for groceries. The husband was asked to estimate how many hours a week he spent doing each of these twelve tasks. The wife was asked to make a similar estimate for herself. These two estimates gave a total from which the husband's proportion was calculated.

As predicted in the empirical hypothesis, the husbands of working wives did, on the average, a greater *proportion* of the housework than husbands of housewives. It is appropriate to ask, however, whether the husbands of working wives actually do a greater *amount* of housework than the husbands of housewives. Perhaps their larger proportion results from a decrease in the total amount of housework done in these families. Examination of our data shows, however, that there is no significant difference in the total number of hours of housework reported in working-wife families and housewife families. Thus, not only do the husbands of working wives do a greater proportion of the housework, but they are actually doing more housework than the husbands of the housewives.

In view of the fact that working wives do not have appreciably more influence in decision-making, the greater help with housework provided by their husbands needs re-examination. Perhaps this housework should not be interpreted as evidence of the working wife's ability to force her husband to help against his will so much as his voluntary and necessary response to the situational pressures arising from the wife's inability to get the housework done without his help.[8]

On the whole, the power structure of both groups of families seems to be remarkably equalitarian. Further research might reveal that two-income families operate more syncratically whereas the more differentiated division of labor in one-income families leads to more autonomous (but still equalitarian) decision-making in different spheres of influence.[9]

The equalitarian decision-making pattern corresponds to the general tendency of both groups of husbands to shift their role conceptions in an equalitarian direction. Perhaps masculine attitudes are more influential than feminine ones in determining the balance of power in the family.

On the other hand, the significantly differentiated shifts in role conceptions in the two groups of wives may foreshadow a later shift in the balance of power. Four years (the average duration of the wives in their roles to date) may be too short a time for the wife's employment to affect her power, especially since young couples often view her employment as a temporary expedient. Further research needs to be done with couples who have been married a longer period of time. Even so, the working wives in this study have so nearly equal power already that it is difficult to visualize much increase in the future.

Despite the ideological shifts related to the wife's employment or nonemployment, our over-all evaluation of these two groups of marriages points to a smooth-working pattern of getting the necessary tasks done by whoever is available—without either partner feeling superior or inferior in power no matter who does what.

Such a conclusion throws doubt on the extent to which theories of economic determinism of power apply to the contemporary American family. Moreover, the substantial dispersion of the actual balance of power within our two groups suggests that other factors are far more predictive of family power than the factor of economic control.[10]

This inapplicability of theories of economic determinism of family power structure may reflect the fact that the family is a primary group governed by different principles from those present in secondary organizations. Cooley suggests that power wielded on any basis other than skills tends to destroy moral unity—in this case the conjugal love of husband and wife.[11] Our data suggest that the working wife tends to feel that she is entitled to more authority as a result of her work. However, in actual decision-making practice, she fails to use this economic lever, perhaps intuitively recognizing that to do so would impair the couple's solidarity. If Cooley's analysis is correct, this means that the marriage partner with the greater skill or competence in a particular area is most apt to have his suggestions adopted, thus introducing a wide variability in power structure into marriages of particular authority expectations and/or role structures.

This study suggests, then, the importance of viewing the family as a primary group governed by moral imperatives which may make inappropriate the applicability of some theories derived from the analysis of large-scale social organizations.

12   *Careers and Consumer Behavior*

DAVID RIESMAN
and HOWARD ROSEBOROUGH

The family and the adaptive subsystem of the society, we have maintained, sustain two-way relationships. The previous papers in this section have given more attention to the impact of the economy on the family than vice versa. This article by Professors Riesman and Roseborough, sociologists with legal and economic training respectively, addresses itself more to the other side of the picture. They develop the view that the family, by having conceptions of what is an appropriate life-style for it, a life-style which has a "career" of its own, and by conveying these life-styles to the young, exerts a significant shaping force upon what is demanded of production facilities. The family's influence goes further than influencing demand through shaping consumer behavior; the family also shapes how much of the family's available labor services the economy can "consume" and under what conditions.

We have in this paper availed ourselves, perhaps too freely, of Professor Lincoln Clark's encouragement to present the conference with a congeries of questions, impressions, and more or less educated guesses concerning the life cycle of consumption in America—a large order. Following anthropological practice in monographs, where the life cycle is described from birth to death, we shall proceed chronologically, from the child as consumer-trainee to the young and not-so-young adult, the old, and the decedent. The members of preliterate tribes, however, cannot usually be said to have careers; and careers, in the sense of a life plan wrapped around an occupation, complicate consumption and lead us into the bewildering variety of social class consumption patterns. Moreover, tribes are not supposed to change (at any rate, the ethnographer is there for only a moment of history), while we have had in mind throughout our work the historical issues of what is changing in career styles and consumption styles. Since we cannot write a symphonic score and introduce these many themes concurrently, this paper demands of its audience that they keep more than one idea in mind at a time.

I

In the summer of 1954, the Kroger Food Foundation made an experiment. They turned several dozen pre-teen boys and girls loose in a supermarket, telling them they could take twenty items for free, without any

---

Reprinted with permission from Lincoln H. Clark (ed.), *Consumer Behavior* (New York: New York University Press, 1955), II 1–18.

limits on what they chose. (According to the sponsors, the idea was based on the rather fantastic suggestion of a "world's fair for children" in *The Lonely Crowd,* a suggestion of how consumer free choice might be developed.) Recorders, human and mechanical, observed the proceedings and a group of social scientists are now examining the results. What was immediately evident, however, was that the children, in addition to picking up watermelon and pop for immediate consumption, filled their carts with the very sorts of things their mothers might have taken, such as sacks of flour and meats and vegetables. They did not select—perhaps in that setting they did not feel quite entitled to—the cameras and other toys which the supermarket, as a one-floor department store, carries in addition to groceries, nor did they pick as much candy and ice cream as had been predicted.[1] It would seem as if anticipatory socialization[2] had occurred, in which these children had been trained, at home and by the media (perhaps at school, too, in the "junior home economics" of a book like *Let's Go Shopping*), to view themselves as prospective householders and to take an adult role. (We don't mean to imply that this socialization was the result of deliberate parental or societal decision—many of the parents would no doubt have been surprised to see how "well" the children behaved when on their away-from-home good behavior.)

At the same time, it may be likely that the parents of these children were involved in what we might term "retroactive socialization," in that meals reflected children's tastes as influenced by the media and each other, with breakfast cereals or Coca-Cola serving both age groups (much as many comic books do). For today, it is our belief, a general lowering of barriers in going on: between the age grades, between the sexes, between regions of the country, and between social classes, with the prospect in view of a fairly uniform middle-majority life style becoming a major American theme with variations.

The *theme,* a set of goods and services including such household items as furniture, radios, television, refrigerator, and standard brands in food and clothing, shows a considerable uniformity throughout American society: it encompasses the (steadily rising) national standard of living. Some seek to level up to it, and some level down, with the result that quality differences are minor, and expense-concealing rather than class-revealing. The *variations* include both embroideries and elaborations on this standard package and, more importantly, the setting given this package by the home and neighborhood; the neighborhood in turn involves such class-bound services as schools, churches, clubs, and civic amenities. While possession of the standard package, the theme items, carries membership in the broad band of the American middle class, the variations identify one as the possessor of a specific life style, localized by region, subclass, ethnic group, and occupation. Social mobility in America is made easier by the ability of the family, through minor variations (in terms of expense and complexity), to adapt the standard package to a new peer group—much as one can buy parts that will make one's Ford look much like a Mercury.

In childhood and adolescence, one builds the standard package into one's anticipations, and the young married couple will expedite its acquisition—at first, or ordinarily, in an apartment. But by young adulthood anticipation begins to assume, at least in the white-collar strata, a more specific form, for the husband's occupational peers and superiors, and to a lesser extent the wife's neighbors and friends, provide models for what the family's style will be at the peak of the husband's career; it is here, of course, that variations enter. Meanwhile, as the husband advances in his career and as children arrive, the package will be moved, probably geographically, possibly socially, nearer to the community that symbolizes his final occupational status. As we shall see, this destiny is compressed for the skilled worker; it may be protracted until late-middle age for the corporate vice-president. Even so, parts of the "dwelling complex"—the schools, clubs, cars, plus inconspicuous elaborations of the standard package —will be acquired in anticipation of the career peak.

This is not the only cycle for consumer behavior: we propose the hypothesis that it is increasingly typical. There are, of course, many Americans even today who have made money faster than they could possibly anticipate; their resocialization does not begin until after they are rich, and often it is painful.[3] Others have their anticipations so structured by their subculture as virtually to eliminate discontinuities and discretionary areas; for an example, we can refer to a study, which is in some ways the antithesis to the Kroger experiment, by the social psychologist Manford Kuhn.

Kuhn asked a group of Amish and of matched non-Amish children in Iowa what gifts they would most want to have. The "American" children wanted toys: dolls, electric trains, and so on (these being things, of course, their parents expect them to want). The Amish children, rigorously brought up on first-class farms and, save for baseball, not allowed to share in the general youth culture, wanted such things as a team and wagon, an oven, a tractor. Though 11 or 12 years old, they already saw themselves as grownups; indeed, only by anticipatory socialization that deprived them of what many Americans would consider a normal childhood, could the Amish youngsters be kept "to home," safe from the seductions of the urban and secular world. Moreover, for them as for their parents, useful producers' goods such as handsome tractors and barns moderated the consumption asceticism of the sect, and permitted reward of the faithful in fine equipment useful if not essential in agricultural success. Indeed, only in a rural area can children enjoy and use adult equipment in quite this way, in which increasing access to the world of work becomes, like Tom Sawyer's fence, a kind of eventful fair whose pleasures only pall with time; but by then the Amish are mostly hooked, unprepared in tertiary skill or in energizing consumer passions to enter the middle-majority market. They are ready in turn to become unyielding Amish parents, relatively unaffected by retroactive socialization and hence compelling their children to imitate them unequivocally; the age-grade barriers remain firm, and the children, short of occasional instances of revolt, must accept the adult world on adult terms.

The Amish are, we suggest, an exception to many of the generalizations one might develop about the consumption career of Americans. But before we leave them aside, we should underline the point about their expensive farm equipment, in order to foreshadow our discussion of "conspicuous production," a kind of corporate consumption in which the energies displaced from individual consumption by sumptuary rules are channeled into impressive or luxurious or stagey ways of doing business. Early observers noticed that American farmers tended to overmechanize, as contemporary observers might notice that American manufacturers may tend to oversplurge on new plants and machine tools, and perhaps the Amish have been ever so slightly of this world in this so-easily rationalized area of producers' vanity.[4]

II

Anticipatory socialization (or what some social psychologists prefer to call role-taking in the sense of playing at a role in fantasy) occurs at all ages and in all areas. It occurs, of course, in all cultures, but what is striking about American life is that people are prepared for roles their parents have not played, indeed, that no one yet has played: they are prepared, in terms of motivation and social skill (a large component of "know-how"), for jobs not yet invented and for consumption of goods not yet on the market. (If children are to surpass their parents, both the job market and the goods market *must* expand.) It would appear that the children in the Kroger food store experiment had learned at home about the basic food necessities, and also to distinguish secular shopping days from ceremonial gift occasions, and it would seem in general that what they learn from their parents is a kind of basic set of domestic arrangements: foods as "necessities," furniture as a quantitative rather than stylistic concept, and the "need" for such durable home furnishings as stoves, refrigerators, and television sets. In contrast, what they learn from their peers is a set of styles and moods of consumption, "affective" consumption beyond and around the basic domestic items.[5]

We can, quite speculatively, connect this progression with Eliot Freidson's observation that children from kindergarten years through the second grade prefer contact with the media in company with their families; in practice this means that in early years they prefer television to going to the movies or reading comic books. The nature of much television advertising—foods, soaps, cars, refrigerators, furniture, brand-name clothes, even beer and cigarettes—educates the child, as well as his parents, in what goes with what in the "domestic economy" of the average American; he also learns what his parents think about all this. By the sixth grade, the children prefer the movies, and their own company while viewing them. The movies introduce them to a larger and more complex world of affects and relations, of styles and skills—a new or modified context for the possessions advertised in the other media.[6] Likewise, the jobs these children will begin to hold in adolescence will ordinarily be in the tertiary areas—soda-jerking, baby-sitting, delivering goods and telegrams, camp counseling, waiting on table, and so on—rather than in the primary or secondary areas. This is consonant with our general picture of adolescence as a time of gregarious, consumption-oriented activity, as a time of sports, music, dancing, dating. The school system itself increasingly comes to terms with this youth culture by seeking to turn out teenagers "adjusted to life" in terms of citizenship and consumption rather than mathematics and welding; in part, of course, this represents a triumph of liberal-arts abundance over traditional and technological demands, while in part it represents a breaking down of the barriers between school and not-school.[7] Indeed, the school itself, like other "tertiary" buildings (bars, resorts, and plants and offices of companies engaged in "conspicuous production"), is frequently more modern than the home: it prepares one for the ranch house, for the relaxed style.

We may restate this in Parsonian terms.[8] The child learns at home, with assistance from the media (principally television), the goal-directed elements of consumption; of course he also acts as an opinion leader, influencing his parents, for instance, away from any notion that water, as compared with pop or a cola drink or Koolade, is a potable substance for children. He learns from his peers (with assistance from the movies) the expressive elements in consumption, the affective embroidery about the basic package that he takes as given in the home. He learns in school something of the adaptive functions of consumption; he becomes prepared to take his place in neighborhood affairs by courses in civics or in home economics, and by the general group-oriented atmosphere of the newer schools. However, he probably learns much less than formerly about what (continuing to paraphrase Parsons) we might define as integrative purchasing, including the allocation of savings to insurance and other investments. Katona's evidence that, in all strata, life insurance amounts to 3–4 per cent of income[9] would seem to indicate that people are not taught to save the way they are taught to spend; if Janet A. Fisher could repeat in a decade her study of age-graded patterns of spending and saving,[10] we might expect to find saving and investment less prevalent than today in the younger age groups, and static "zero saving" (as against dissaving) less prevalent than today even among those over 65. As something amounting to tenure (seniority in the lower ranks, tacit mutual protection against discharge in the upper) spreads to the non-academic population, people will look increasingly to their employers rather than to their own efforts for financial security in old age, and consumption will increasingly move toward making life now, comfortable and "well rounded." (Even the serious-minded young, for whom well-roundedness in the conventional sense is not an ideal, are not concerned with the distant future in terms of goal-directed investment in their own careers and nest eggs, but rather in terms of the state of the world in general or of its underprivileged portions, near and far.)

Something of this sort, we suggest, forms the social-psychological background of instalment buying, not among the traditionally "improvident" hand-to-mouth, or television-set-to-bedroom, lower strata, but among the middle classes who would in earlier days have saved up for durable goods. Marriage itself, so to speak, is now bought on the instalment plan, following the "anticipatory socialization" of going steady from the seventh grade on: people are marrying younger than ever, without waiting until the man is settled in his career, much less until the woman has a dowry. And, once married, even though wage equalization brings high starting incomes, the young adults are trained to spend up to and beyond them in rapidly accumulating the full package they have learned in general to consider basic. As Marvin Sussman shows, the parents on both sides will help out if they can (they do not want to lose their young so young), by tactful gifts in money, in kind, and in services such as baby-sitting.[11] New items and revisions of older models can be gleaned from *House Beautiful, Better Homes and Gardens, American Home,* and other service magazines that, as Lloyd Warner found, are widely read in the middle and even the lower strata.[12]

These and other media, it goes without saying, have enormously accelerated the transmission of fashions between the classes, the regions, and the age grades. Dr. Harriet Moore of Social Research, Inc., informs us that the average anticipated life of living- and dining-room furniture has shrunk from twelve to seven years within the last two decades. As Americans live longer, their possessions (from "grandfather watches" to refrigerators) would seem to succumb to obsolescence faster. In more general terms, the immediate indulgence that was once a lower-class characteristic, in comparison with the delayed and calculated future-oriented saving of the middle class, has now infiltrated the middle class so that increased income increments are spent rather than saved—and, indeed, dissaved through instalment buying. We might speculate that the child who has been somewhat permissively brought up, who has had a hand in family consumer choice, who has earned and spent substantial sums in the teen-age period of ersatz grownup culture will as a young married person assume as a right many of the items that for his parents were delayed and planned-for luxuries. The capital equipment for domesticity with which such a person starts out must now be, for millions of people, very substantial; it is paid for during the early years of marriage, as well as maintained and expanded by "do-it-yourself" activities in leisure from the paid job; there is little saved up with which to educate the new generation or to protect the old from inclement weather; indeed, an air conditioner may soon be added to the standard package.

The teenager's electric shaver, his jalopy or classy convertible, the young couple's washing machine and dryer—there is in some of these purchase an element of *rites de passage,* a sort of self-declared initiation in a culture that has notoriously not systematized the age grades. Parents can no longer, with the drop in barriers, raise their children on a lower standard of living than their own, or see them start out in marriage at a markedly lower status—any more than those rare women who still have servants can keep them on a cheaper diet than their own. By the same token, children rebelling against their parents seldom abandon the standard package, but rather reject some of the parental variations on it; even a few such modifications are enough to alter the style or *Gestalt.*

Evidence for the breakdown of generational differences is less easy to come by than evidence for the breakdown of regional ones. Russell Lynes recently discovered, in talking with Sears Roebuck officials, that they no longer put out regional catalogues and that, in furniture, there are almost identical tastes in all sections of the country, so that if a certain sofa covering is chosen by 50 per cent of the purchasers in New England it will hit 49 per cent in the Southwest and 52 per cent in Oregon. Likewise, Eric Larrabee has recently observed that pizza dishes have spread to Midwest towns that have never seen an Italian; an ethnic homogenization of taste must of course accompany the regional one.

III

A number of studies, including those of Kuznets on the shares of the upper-income groups and those published in *Fortune's* series on the Great American Market,[13] indicate the increasing pace of homogenization of possessions between the top ranks of factory workers (notably where there is more than one employed person per spending unit) and the lower ranks of the professional, managerial, and entrepreneurial people. A study done by S. Stansfeld Sargent in Ventura, California, indicates that the "dwelling complex" of a skilled worker will not differ in any obvious way from that of an air-plant physicist—even life style differences seemed minimal.[14] To be sure, those parts of California where everyone is new may be a special case, but we do believe that the differences between the social and occupational strata are coming more and more to lie primarily in consumer attitudes, not in consumer behavior or the objects bought at any given moment; more precisely, the attitudes influence behavior only when the whole life cycle is taken into account. To a degree, for the office and factory workers, the "poverty cycle" that B. Seebohm Rowntree found in York, England, a half century ago[15] still holds, though at a far higher level: an early peak is reached, followed by a plateau and a slow decline—modified, to be sure, by the secular rise in real income, especially among factory workers.[16] However, Warner Bloomberg, Jr., a thoughtful participant-observer of factory life, has commented on differential meanings of the cycle for men and for their wives. He points out that the young man, before marriage, has been well supplied with funds, often living at home: "he may well indulge in tailor-made suits, expensive whiskies, and high-priced restaurants if they also are not high falutin' . . . always more object- than experience-oriented, with fun correlated with expenditure of money, even in sex—the more high-priced the woman, the better she must be."

"This period," he continues, "is usually brief, ending as soon as he marries, though the emphasis on recreation as a highly valued activity remains: that is, he will continue to want to have his sports, his nights with the boys for cards and drinks, his dancing, etc. However, he must now acquire the capital goods of a home or apartment to be furnished (he already has a car). Over a period of time he becomes more and more engrossed and expert in the 'consumption' of these hard commodities and the recreation-orientation slowly subsides under the pressure of family obligations and the nagging of his wife. But once the most difficult period, financially, of the marriage is over, the emphasis on recreation returns, especially travel, sports, and the like, although those who acquire homes (and the number has been increasing at a fantastic rate) are forever involved in the purchase, repair, and replacement of the hard goods of the domicile and of the car—involved as buyers and users (and stealers, we might add) of tools, since 'do it yourself' has been part of their occupational culture for a long time."[17]

While, for the men, graduation from (or early leaving of) high school brings liberation, even if followed by the gradual constrictions of domesticity, for the girls the end of high school is viewed with real distress, for it means the end of the pleasant round of dates and opening of the unromantic prospect of early marriage (in this stratum, the seamy side of marriage cannot be hidden from the young). While in an earlier day all they expected of marriage was a pay check, a home in repair, and a spouse who behaved himself, they now have learned—anticipatory socialization again—to look forward to wider alternatives; for one thing, they can protect themselves by their own jobs from having to marry the first man who asks them (nor are they, with contraception, so likely to have to marry because pregnant). "More often than not," Bloomberg observes, "the girls who cry at night as graduation approaches have been introduced to a vague but compelling notion of a richer life, mainly through the mass media and the high schools. More than any others in the working class, they are experience-oriented rather than object-oriented. The men, still in the main occupied vocationally by thing-centered jobs and avocationally by the traditional skills of the hunter or the ball player or the homebuilder, are a big drag on the largely unformulated desire of these girls to build into their lives some *expertise* in consumership which, by an emphasis on experience, could provide the variety and alternation in routines which they believe to be enriching.[18] Travel comes the closest to doing this for both of them, and the working people are getting to be great travelers as time and money permit."[19] No wonder that travel agents have begun to be aware of the guidance function they control; a group of them, recently organized for adult education at the downtown branch of the University of Chicago, met with Reuel Denney to discuss the emotional aura in which people increasingly were buying their way, often on the instalment plan, "from here to eternity." Travel becomes a recurrent second honeymoon, a compensation for the disillusion built into the first by the contrasting expectations of the worker and his bride; and no doubt the home itself, as the man works his evenings and week ends around it, also reflects these tensions and some "built-in" compensations for them.

To return to the life cycle of the educated strata: here it is not contrasting expectations drawn from the youth culture, but the role of the corporation or other large employer in dictating a specific style of life, that creates adult tensions between the spouses. At one level, brilliantly portrayed by William H. Whyte, Jr., of *Fortune,*[20] are the wives of management who cannot drive Cadillacs because the fuddy-duddy president drives a Buick; a little lower down are the wives who must hear their husbands groan on returning from a business trip because the latter must conceal the fact that they live much better "abroad," on the expense account, than their wives can afford to at home, on a mere salary. Still more unhappy are the wives of the Negro school principals described by a student in a recent seminar: These principals are required by their position to live in a large house and to drive a good car (though not too large and too good) but their salaries have not kept pace and they have had to take outside jobs; since these (dairy farmer, trucker, redcap, bellhop, bartender, gas station attendant, and so on) are too lowly for school principals to hold, they must do so under an assumed name and in a neighboring community. The strain on both spouses, caught in a status conflict and in a series of concealments, can well be imagined.

In general, we believe that, despite the foreshortening of time perspectives in all social classes, the middle-managerial groups still take a good deal longer than the working classes to acquire the full domestic package; and they also, again unlike the working classes, cut down on the size and housekeeping demands of this package as they age. Thus, a study done under Everett Hughes in Chicago indicated that the middle-class person usually begins his adult life in an apartment, where he may live for the first several years of marriage; then in his late twenties or early thirties he buys a house (and the neighborhood to go with it) in which to raise his children; after the children have grown and flown, the house becomes a heavy burden, and the bereft couple move back to an apartment, though of a different cast, so that the cycle does not quite end where it began. (In Chicago, he is perhaps also more likely than the working-class person to move because Negroes have "invaded" his neighborhood, for he clings less tenaciously to real estate, including "his" church, and more tenaciously to the values of non-violence.) Though people when they buy their homes are not fully conscious of the likelihood they will stay in them at most for two decades, the general pattern in their milieu certainly casts its shadow before.

While a house cycle of some sort may be characteristic of the middle class as a whole, at least in large cities, ambivalence about putting down "roots" is especially characteristic of the younger executive groups that Whyte has studied for *Fortune*. He notices that they would engender criticism by premature purchase of an overimpressive menage (even if a private income, rather than a bet on future advance, could sustain the cost), and that their careers would also be jeopardized by overcommitment to a particular peer group and neighborhood, which might tie them too closely to people whose careers may not prove commensurate with their own. On the other hand, Charlie Grey is invited by his boss to migrate to a fashionable suburb and to join an expensive country club before he feels quite ready to swing it (though the boss has decided, in a self-fulfilling prophecy, that he *is* ready for the move); accepting, he passes the point of no return.

In terms of family life, this means that, while the husband is to some extent stabilized by his career line within or among firms in a given field or set of fields, his wife and children must be prepared for moves and for the domesticity of transciency, though with only limited knowledge of, let alone satisfactions from, the occupational culture that imposes these requirements. As W. H. Whyte has observed, a man's move up is almost always also a geographic move, and if the wife is not to redo her hair and replan her life while she packs, she must subtly anticipate the promotions her husband may or may not get, while not antagonizing the current peers or baiting the current superiors who see in the consumption field no less than in the office the margins that distance them from their prospective successors. In the new locale, the children (whose own life cycle may not jibe comfortably with this) will attend a slightly different school, the parents join a slightly different club, meanwhile rearranging the standard package in the home so that old objects carried by the moving van will combine into a new *Gestalt*.

Those among us who pull up stakes with difficulty should not, of course, read our own malaise into the transients for whom schools and the army have already provided anticipatory experience. Moreover, in the middle strata of which we are talking, the growing interregional uniformity of the country, doubtless in part the product of mobility and migration, and of the effective system for distributing goods and services, makes moving easier financially and psychologically.

To be sure, there remain millions of people, not only Amish, who do not buy the standard package, much less transport it, either because they fall far below the $4,000–$7,500 per year range that *Fortune* speaks of as the Great American Market, or because they have not been trained to want it. Thus, there certainly remain in less free-floating parts of the country many working-class folk who will use increments of income to buy real estate, not for living only, but for social security, and who will reject many of the amenities in and around the standard package as irrelevant. That is, people in the working class do not see the home as an expendable consumer good but as an investment for old age—something like the West Room into which the Irish peasant retires when his heir takes over the farm. Likewise, workers may buy happenstance items that, in a different combination, form part of the middle-class standard package, but these items will reflect special earning-power bonanzas and may even be compensations, as the Negro Buick or Cadillac sometimes is, for inability to buy the standard package as an entity and an identity.

At the other end of the social scale, the upper end, the standard middle-majority package operates as a different sort of pressure: not as an aspiration, not as something one prepares for in imagination or in childhood paradigms, but as a limitation, as a kind of sumptuary guide. Contrary to the situation described by Veblen, it does not seem to us to be the members of the upper class who dictate life styles, which then filter down; these residuary legatees of the past are influenced as much as they influence, and the location of style leadership, like other leadership, is ramified and, to our mind, obscure. The upper Bohemians have a hand in it, as avocational counselors, just as the upper middlebrows have a hand in diffusing high style to the general population through the mass media. The upper-class youngster in school wears blue jeans and drives an old car; on graduation he wears Uncle Sam's jeans; save in a few enclaves, he avoids high fashion. If he enters the corporate hierarchy, it is, as already pointed out, his official rather than his genealogical ranks that will determine the make of car he drives. (As far as the academic hierarchy goes, we recall the profuse apologies of an instructor at a Kansas college for driving a Lincoln—he explained he had got it cheap; and in Cambridge were heard many wry comments on a colleague who drove a red Jaguar.) On the whole, in a tug-of-war between the occupational culture and the social-class-and-kinfolk culture, the former is likely to win out. The father of one of the authors, a consulting internist, felt compelled to appear for consultations in patients' homes in a car at least the equal of the doctor's who called him in, much as he disliked display; he ironically referred to the car as his "delivery wagon." (In his own office, where other colleagues would be less embarrassed, he could afford shabbiness.) In one of our Kansas City interviews, a housewife bitterly and repeatedly complained about her husband's air-conditioned Cadillac, which he insisted was necessary for selling trips. One investigator recounted the violent objection of a group of clerks in a large city bank when management insisted on their wearing white collars; though many of them had originally come into the bank because of its genteel white-collar aspects, they felt envious both of the salaries and the shirts worn by the working class and if they could not have the one, at least wanted the comfort and economy of the other!

As we have just said, the upper-class person entering on an occupation will have to be careful not to carry with him his class consumption patterns. This is not easy for him since some of these patterns are bred in the bone, so to speak, in his accent and the way he looks and carries his body. But he must make the effort because of the still far-from-evaporated cultural defensiveness of the middle-class businessman, for whom a Harvard accent is not only a doubtful idiosyncrasy but an aggressive one. Provided he conforms in the office, the upper-class businessman may find a hobby on which his excess income may be spent without rivalry-creating inflation of his life style; that is, he will early buy the standard package in one of its more elaborate and expense-concealing variations and then look around for something to collect—a cause or charity, possibly—or have more children and educate them better than the average for the class, or even save something. But, in general, the standard package operates here as a restriction on gaudiness, in part because the older sorts of conspicuously flamboyant objects (footmen, for instance) are no longer made, and in part because equalitarian ideologies influence people to level down as well as to level up. The main, and not insignificant, difference is that the upper-class person will carry the standard package lightly, expand it more quickly, and renew or discard it more ruthlessly, whereas the person of lesser income and less assured position will strain under the load and be toppled by unemployment, serious illness, or miscalculation.

IV

Everett Hughes has described (in conversation) a company that brought in its Harvard Business School graduates too soon for its own industry position. Individuals have even less leeway for miscalculation in seeking status through consumption, and they have far less chance of recourse to government to bail them out, unless they have gone the way of whole strata that possess political leverage. Despite the extent of childhood training for consumption, there are some omissions—how to buy a house, for instance, is seldom discussed. Professor Bossard in his studies of family life has stated the children reflect the influence of their parents when they are in turn parents, and act as they think their parents would have.[21] This often works, but by no means always; we may recall Crevel, in Balzac's *La Cousine Bette,* who, having admired when young the mansion of his employer and dreamed of a house just like that, when he did become rich "with eyes closed and purse open he went straight to Grindot [the same architect]," an architect then completely forgotten. "So," Balzac writes, "dead glory lives on, supported by retrospective admiration." More usual, in America, will be the case where the parents' home pattern is not opulent enough for the children, or relevant to altered moral climates; this largest of durables is in some ways least attended to (in terms of such problems as are admirably spelled out by Robert Woods Kennedy in *The House and the Art of Its Design*).[22] Like the hobby-boat builder recently described in *Time* whose boat could not be got out the door of the shack in which he built it, some home buyers may not allow enough room for all the developments of their married life. Some failures in anticipation they can repair by their own carpentry, but some may involve the neighborhood, the school, the transport possibilities, and they may find themselves overinvested and overcapitalized when they should be able to pull up stakes.

It is true, as we have already noted,[23] that the young married proto-executives in the Park Forests of America become very adept at pulling up stakes, and at being at home everywhere and nowhere. They learn to adapt to the neighborhood and to adapt the neighborhood to themselves, and this is made possible by the very existence of the standard package, items of which can be bought or serviced or transported anywhere. It is rather like a theater in the round, or omnipurpose stage, or like those two-piece outfits advertised in *Seventeen* or *Charm* or *Mademoiselle* that can be modified to fit almost any occasion. But it is also true that these young people who have invested so much capital in a style of life (including, as a major element in style, their marriage to each other) have withdrawn a certain modicum of their energies from their careers as such. They have done this, in the first place, along with the rest of the population, by not working such long hours; the whole suburban package depends, in large measure, on the two-day week end. In the second place, they have rearranged somewhat the career commitments both of the husband and the wife. The latter agrees to earn money only to support the family in the manner to which it has, in anticipation, become accustomed; she enters the labor market to bring home a new car, a new room, a vacation canoeing in Minnesota, but not to "have a career" in the sense of seeking status and satisfaction in job advancement and enlarged work horizons. The former, the husband, agrees to earn enough money to keep the standard package away from the repossessors, and, since the standard package grows in size as new products come on the market or old ones develop new angles (as cars have done), to keep up with its elaborations. For this, he needs merely to get on a seniority ladder—and the recent survey of young people made by the Social Research Service of Michigan State College, indicated that they think seniority the fairest way of distributing promotions. That is, seniority plus fringe benefits from the wife's working will keep the family up with the rising standard of living.

But beyond that the husband need not go, and in fact may be discouraged from going by his wife. Russell Lynes, in "What Has Succeeded Success,"[24] discusses the results of a survey of women college students and recent graduates. Typical is the comment of a University of Texas girl: "I think definitely that a job should not consume your life. It should be one in which you are interested and which enables you to live a well-rounded life." Says another: "I want my husband to be ambitious but not dangerously so"; and still another: "I don't want him to have such a high executive position that it would ruin his health or personal relationships with his friends or family." Presumably, too, she would not want him to have so high a personal standard of living as to put strains on friends or family.

We may conclude that the American economy is poised between the ease with which people move from one income gradient to a higher one along well-worn and hence anticipated steps, and the frictions that family and friendship create for the markedly mobile individual. In a recent article on the strains on kinship which mobility creates—the old problem of the "poor relation"—LeMasters describes a family that got rich quick during the war as the result of the boom in building; they moved to a nice suburb and traded in an old Plymouth on a new Buick, and their children, entering a new and wealthier high school, helped educate them to their new fortunes, while the parents' siblings were left far behind.[25] The author does not observe that the shift from Plymouth to Buick is not only one of price but perhaps even more one of style: the Chrysler line, as recent market researches tend to show, appeals to the sedate and stable, while the General Motors line appeals to the more ambitious and flashy; thus, the move to Buick is not quite the same, on the average, as the move to, say, De Soto. (The Ford line is again something else: a "hot" engine for the young people of all ages, a vehicle perhaps for maleness rather than mobility.) General Motors and Chrysler devotees are, in other words, like Republicans and Democrats, partly accidental aggregates and partly prisoners of different self-images. (We suggest that the devotees of Consumers Union are perhaps like the political "independents" in such a constellation, who make it a point to look at the machine and not at the Briggs or Fisher personality!) But at the same time, as this instance implies, there may be shifts of identity in the course of the life cycle; we can imagine this builder ending up with a Mercury convertible after having dowered his children with Oldsmobiles and Buicks, to show himself that he is still quick on the uptake.

V

There is a lack of any thoroughgoing histories of individual consumption careers in which one might align in parallel columns the job history, the family history, and the consumer history, and relate these in turn to general cultural developments that link the life cycle with the cycle of the husband's industry or with the social fate of his ethnic and other identities. Talking recently with a group of young German industrialists, one of the authors was told of a frequent practice among middle-aged executives who feared they might be slipping: they would sink their savings into a baronial mansion, buy a Mercedes-Benz, and otherwise move into a new stratosphere of luxury, in a desperate hope either to salvage their careers or to compensate for feared occupational downgrading; they could do this in part because among contemporary Germans thrift has become even less conceivable than for Americans, and they might as well go out in a blaze of glory. On the other hand, the University of Chicago's research among older people in Kansas City has turned up a few elderly individuals who cannot bring themselves to live out their lives on an annuity basis: intellectually they know "you can't take it with you," but emotionally they cannot adjust to the altered value of the dollar and are too old either to learn carpentry or to appreciate paying carpenters for an hour's work what they once learned to regard as a good day's wage. We do not know whether such people loom large in George Katona's surveys; what is striking to us is how rare is this provincial reaction, as against the many people whose lifelong anticipatory socialization prepares them to spend now what they have now, and more besides. One of our Kansas City respondents, whose existence had been wrapped up in her daughters' social life, when asked what she did when the daughters married and moved away said that she slept more—and redecorated the living room. Still another became more active in church work—and redecorated the vestry.[26] As such women get still older, it will be interesting to see what, if any, arrangements they make for caskets and grave lots; Robert Habenstein, making a study of a career of the funeral director, has observed a growing vogue for caskets which cradle the dead on cushions, as well as for hearses which do not jolt the body—though on the whole there is evidence that, despite the revival of church-going, the standard of dying has hardly kept pace with the standard of living.[27]

VI

Having now followed the individual from childhood to the grave, we would like in these concluding remarks to touch on the specter of uniformity, both in careers and in consumer behavior, that specter which haunts so much of our, and European, thinking about America. At the outset, it should be clear that whatever uniformities do exist are at least in part defenses against the no less prevalent instabilities of the life cycle. Thus, the rising standard of living inevitably alters the character of the neighborhoods in which people live; neither restrictive covenants nor landscaping can bring permanence. Usually, the only way to stay figuratively in the same place is to keep moving. This is true on the career side too: the more people seek security in large, pension-bestowing organizations, the more likely they are to be shunted around the country, or at least to have to be emotionally prepared for such moves; this is because the large organization, providing for its own future, does so by diversification, decentralization, and a large research and development program, including executive development.

The new suburbs to which people in such organizations move are heavily age-graded. Levittown outside Philadelphia, for instance, has few children over 15 and few adults over 45.[28] A householder in this situation is not likely to plant trees to shade his prospective great-grandchildren. (Such uniformities of instability are only in small degree the product of atomic threats and insecurities.) The shifts in the labor force implicit in what we have said mean that parents cannot plan their children's specific careers any more than they can plan their living rooms. At most, they can head them toward a range of careers within a broad middle-class spectrum of permissibility, and they do this by sending them to school and college and seeking to instill the motivations currently in demand.

What is left of the old-family upper class is an exception to all this. A number of these families possess summer estates—private arboreta— with homes for all the children, homes that upper-middle-class children, brought up on the contemporary standard package in vacations, might consider shabby. Likewise, Charles C. McArthur, studying the career plans of Harvard students, discovered that those, and only those, from upper-class homes and the "St. Grottlesex" preparatory schools knew what they were going to be—and became it: they followed in their father's or uncle's footsteps as lawyers, doctors, trustees; they carried these occupations almost as inherited occupations, and often against their personal preferences.[29]

In general then, the upper-class person is prepared for what lies ahead because of a certain constriction of choice and aspiration. By contrast, McArthur's research shows that the mobile upper-middle-class boy's career aims are apt to be vague: his aptitudes predict what will become of him occupationally better than any statements he makes. He hasn't been there, in terms of a parental model; what he wants is to achieve and maintain a certain style of life, within the range of his limitations and capacities. In much the same way, he is prepared to become a consumer of the standard package as this may have developed up to the time when he is ready to enter the market: there will be a kind of ecumenical freedom about his consumption, not bound to sectarian or parental dogma.

Indeed, one of the few restrictions on the consumption of the mobile person is the resistance of the upper class to the *arrivistes* by exercise of the strategy of conspicuous underconsumption; in this way the already arrived attempt to impose their own limits on those who would become their peers. So it occasionally happens that a man of working-class or lower-middle-class origins who has risen fast to the possibility of splendor, and hopes by splendor retroactively to compensate for his origins and the frustrations of his rise, discovers soon after he has begun flamboyant spending that this devoutly-longed-for goal is now looked down upon. Anticipatory socialization has played a trick upon him: he rose from the working class by learning to postpone gratifications, but the working class taught him what gratifications to seek; now these, when he at last "deserves" them by striking oil or the F.H.A., are once more denied him. He may as a result spend part of his fortune supporting politicians who attack snobs, the elite, Easterners, and Harvard men generally; and this is especially likely when so many people have made money so fast that he is not a lone Great Gatsby seeking admission to an established Society, but finds many of his new peers in the same boat as he, capable of extrapolating the tycoon pattern decades after the demise of Newport, Bar Harbor, and Tuxedo Park.

For such people—whatever uniformities there may be in the beholder's eye—there are real choices to be made both in career and consumption; inheritance, far from foreshadowing the way, merely indicates what is not to be done, not to be bought.

In any event, we must disabuse ourselves of the common notion that mass production, in the contemporary sense, is responsible for consumer uniformity. A dozen decades ago, Alexis de Tocqueville observed the American preoccupation with comfort, as well as occasional revivals of "fanatical spiritualism" in protest against it. He wrote:

> In democratic society the sensuality of the public has taken a moderate and tranquil course, to which all are bound to conform: it is as difficult to depart from the common rule by one's vices as by one's virtues. Rich men who live amid democratic nations are therefore more intent on providing for their smallest wants than for their extraordinary enjoyments; they gratify a number of petty desires without indulging in any great irregularities of passion; thus they are more apt to become enervated than debauched.[30]

This was long before people had cars with automatic steering!

Thus it seems that it was only in the Gilded Age that enormous disparities—between a Hearstian castle and a hovel—existed in American consumption; indeed, as we have become relatively emancipated both from grinding poverty and grinding inhibition, and as, in the same development, we mix work and play, youth and age, and the sexes, we lack the resources as well as the limits that would make "great irregularities of passion" seem appealing; only in our entertainers, including our political figures, do we look for these—many of them seem living substitutes for a historical novel. Tocqueville was writing, we are inclined to think, less about an extant America pictured in reportorial detail and more about an ideal-typical "America," an abstraction based on his imagination of what society would look like where egalitarian tendencies predominated. This involved him in the danger that we, his successors, also face: of standardizing our image of standardization to fit our constructed type; and Americans, trained in adaptability, may also co-operate with their interpreters. While we agree with Tocqueville that great irregularities, whether for good or evil, tend to be weeded out, does it follow that the great middle belt is thereby made more uniform?

We must notice, first of all, that the flexible and adaptive uniformity of this belt, to the degree it exists, is a departure from the traditionalism of the two social extremes. For instance, the lower-class diet, in its regional and ethnic enclaves, is highly standardized. In most countries, peasant customs quaint to the observer are uniforms to the observed. When this "standard package" crumbles in the revolutions of taste brought about by the media and mobility (and the anticipatory socializations these bring in their wake), the first consequences are distressing; W. J. Cash speaks of "the thin jazziness which seems to be the necessary concomitant of industrialization everywhere";[31] and the Delta-born Negro, making $100 a week at Inland Steel in Chicago, may seek to imitate at once the Negro rich as pictured in *Ebony* and his memory of Snopes-like planters of a generation ago. In seeking to be "quality," he will hardly study *Consumers Union Reports,* but will leave one standardization to pursue another; his children, however, may be free to make somewhat more discriminating choices.

The traditionalism of the residual upper class has, of course, never imposed peasant monotony on its members, and even the occupational monotony of careers already referred to exists as a pattern to rebel against. On the consumption side, Richard Coleman's ongoing study of Kansas City society indicates that there are a considerable number of sets—the horsey set, the music-and-culture set, the civic-minded set, and so on—all of which overlap in terms of families, neighborhoods, and occupations but subdivide in terms of age-equivalent friendship cliques pursuing a wide gamut of leisure interests, vacationing in different spots and in different ways, and welcoming by virtue of similarity of interest newcomers, properly introduced, brought to Kansas City by expanding and decentralizing commerce and industry. Very possibly, this is a way of saying that Kansas City has no true upper class, in the sense of a stratum with a markedly nonmiddle-class life style; in the much larger city of Baltimore, it is our impression that society is far more inaccessible and tightly knit, with proper consumption grooves more deeply cut: thus, stables seem to be staples. But this only would tend to confirm our judgment that the rising middle class engulfs the old upper class, modifying its idiosyncrasies while giving its young people the much wider range of middle-class life styles to choose among.

With this preface, let us take one more look at our "standard package" of middle-class consumer items. For each family, the items have a somewhat different history, once we go beyond the increasing group that comes with the house or apartment as part of a complex: this coffee table is ancestral, that mat on the wall collegiate, and the new cover on the Sears borax sofa was glimpsed in a *Harper's Bazaar* read at the hairdresser's. More important, each of these items, and each area in and around the house, is differentially tinged with affect: for some the kitchen may be the center of consumer drama, for others the garden, for still others the rumpus room. The standard package allows for both expansiveness and expressiveness, even while (to return to our Parsonian metaphors) it represents one's integration into the society and allows, once it is bought and paid for, further goal-directed moves in preparation for an open-ended future.

Even so, it can be argued that these differences within the frame of the standard package are fairly marginal; it is in the leisure area beyond the package, for which the package is only a home base, that greater differences exist. No single leisure pursuit (if we except television-viewing) enlists as much as half the population, including vacation auto travel, which, according to A.A.A. estimates, brought 66,000,000 Americans onto the highways last year. Spectator sports such as baseball appealed to about 10 per cent of the population in 1952, movies and drive-ins to about 35 per cent, fishing and hunting to many millions, but no majority, even of males. (These percentages must be compared with the much higher ones reported by Katona for non-consumer behavior, such as the 80 per cent who own some life insurance.) Lyman Bryson, in *The Next America,*[32] has described the new millions of enthusiasts for the arts, and Reuel Denney in a penetrating essay has suggested how the hi-fi passion of American scientists allows them to identify at once with the gadgeteering do-it-yourself impulse and with partially imported high culture, thus modifying both.[33] Denney writes:

> The scientist modifies class conformist consumption of gadgets by setting forth in his consumption pattern a gadget quite his own. The scientist, oriented more toward things than persons, finds a "thing" to become passionate about which has the delicate qualities of a human organism and the function of conveying one of the greatest of the human arts. The scientist puts pressure into his social life because of his "social distance" at work from his clients among workers and consumers, and from the preoccupations of his co-elite among the industrial managers [for whom the scientist and his technical adjuncts are often counters in a game of conspicuous corporate consumption]. The scientist seeks clear and simple symbols of consumption because, being highly mobile.

> he shares with the executive class rapid geographical and class moves
> through regions of disparate styles of consumption. The scientist . . . seeks
> to display consumption in items that are less invidious than distinctive.
> In this sense, he has an ascetic moral of consumption.[34]

Nevertheless, Denney concludes, the scientist's "occupational progress
seems to have been faster than his ability to define himself outside his
work."[35] The advertising man who is so often the scientist's enemy within
a company has probably had more influence even on the latter's leisure
and consumption than his own corps has had.

Studies of consumer purchases of durables indicate that each new
addition to the standard package has taken less prelude time to reach
peak sales, and the same is probably true of industrial capital goods. The
"organizational revolution" in communications and advertising is in large
measure responsible for this: Americans can hardly escape "consumer
literacy" even if of a more rhetorical sort than *Consumers Union Reports*
teaches. As the early enthusiasm of the newly literate vanishes, and as
the standard package becomes S.O.P. for the middle millions, can we
continue to look mainly to our large organizations for inventive spending
of the surplus, whether on big, glamorous bombers or bomb plants, on
big, glamorous superhighways, or on the increasingly standardized
elements of conspicuous corporate production? We doubt it. The scientist
who has given us our model of the hi-fi fan—so much so that this equipment can now also be bought as part of the standard package—may be
looked to for other consumption and leisure pioneering.

13   *Family Structure and Economic Change in Nineteenth-Century Europe*

H. J. HABAKKUK

The family influences the economy in ways other than the relatively direct and immediate ones described by Riesman and Roseborough. Professor Habakkuk discusses the influence that family patterns had on economic development in one period of European history. Habakkuk argues that several aspects of family structure, of which the inheritance system is discussed extensively, affect the supply of capital and labor, and also the mobility and growth of the population, thereby influencing economic development. In this day of concern with "underdeveloped" countries, such considerations are still relevant.

The scholars of continental Europe have devoted much attention to the social consequences of rules and customs of inheritance, and there exists a large body of work of this subject by lawyers and agricultural historians.[1] The purpose of this paper is to consider, in the light of this European evidence, the possible significance of such rules and customs for economic development in the nineteenth century.

The peasant families of western Europe had two conflicting aims: to keep the family property intact and to provide for the younger children. Families differed very widely, from region to region, both in the relative importance they attached to these two aims and in the methods they customarily adopted to achieve them. At one extreme, the ownership property descended intact to a succession of elder sons, who had complete discretion in what provision they made for the younger members of the family. At the other extreme, the ownership was divided between all the children in equal shares. The best example of the former limiting case is provided by England, where the owner had complete freedom to will his property as he pleased, and where, in the absence of a will (or a settlement), the entire property was inherited by the eldest son. Something like the latter limiting case is to be found in France under the Napoleonic Code, which severely restricted the share of property which an owner could leave by will to a single heir and in the absence of a will provided for equal division between the children.

The English case was exceptional; nowhere else in western Europe did the owner enjoy such freedom of testamentary disposition, and nowhere

Reprinted from *The Journal of Economic History*, XV, No. 1 (1955), 1–12, with the kind permission of the author and publishers.

else were the younger children, in cases of intestacy, void of any claim on the family property; in other countries, the portion that a landowner could freely dispose of—the *quotité disponible*—was limited by law, and the children all had a claim to some share in the property. Among the continental countries, however, there were considerable differences in the size of the *quotité disponible,* that is, in the extent to which an owner could favor a single heir. The law was complicated; the *quotité* varied according to the number of surviving children, sometimes also according to the nature of the property involved, whether it had been inherited or acquired. Any precise generalization about the geography of these differences is therefore impossible. But, as a rough approximation, we can say that proprietors in most states of Germany and Italy could will a greater part of their property to a single heir than was the case in France, Russia, Spain and Portugal, Holland, Belgium, and the Rhine provinces.[2]

The law on this point did not invariably afford an adequate index of actual practice. Owners varied in the extent to which they availed themselves of their testamentary powers. The French sociologist Le Play argued that where an owner could not freely dispose by will of at least half of his property, the practice of making wills disappeared, and the property descended according to the rules on intestacy. If this was the case—and it is difficult to be sure, because very little systematic study has been made of habits of will-making—areas in which the *quotité disponible* was small would have had an even stronger bias towards equality. For the exercise of testamentary power was generally in favor of a single heir, while the rules on intestacy tended to have an equalitarian effect. The position was further complicated by the fact that in many areas the succession to the property was commonly settled during the life of the parents and that the substance as well as the timing of such settlements was subject to considerable variation. In some parts of Germany, for example, the parents customarily transferred ownership to a single heir, during their lifetime, on a valuation of the property, and left to his discretion the size of the provision for the younger children. In other areas, the succession and the provision for the children was specified in detail in a settlement made on the marriage of the parents.

Besides differences in the *extent* of provision for younger children, there were differences in the *form* in which the provision was made. Sometimes they took their share in land, sometimes in money; sometimes they had a choice between the two, and sometimes the choice was made for them by law or convention. When the younger children took their provision in the form of land, they might physically divide their share of the property—that was the presumption in the countries to which the Napoleonic Code applied—or they might work their shares in common. If they took money, as was commonly the case in many parts of Germany, their shares might be calculated on the sale value of the property (*Verkehrswert*) or on lower valuation, its *Ertragswert,* the brother and sister valuation.[3]

Broadly speaking, actual physical division of the property was most general in the countries of the Napoleonic Code. Over most parts of Germany, outside the Rhineland and Thuringia, the property descended intact to a single heir, who was charged with the payment of compensation (*Abfindung*) to his younger brothers and sisters. But there might be considerable variations within a single region: islands of inheritance by a single heir in areas where the predominant rule was division, and vice versa.[4] There were also changes over time in inheritance systems; in the properous years before 1914 there was, in middle Germany, some increase in the area over which the single-heir rule of inheritance prevailed.[5]

We are therefore not dealing with two sharply distinguished systems of inheritance, coinciding exactly with well-defined geographical areas, though within the limits of this paper I shall have often to assume that this was the case. We have, instead, a wide range of compromise between two principal aims of family policy. Nor did different inheritance systems, even when they differed widely, invariably produce widely different results. A farm left to an eldest son, but burdened with heavy payments to his younger brothers and sisters who remained living on the farm with him, might in appearance not differ greatly from the farm, the ownership of which was divided among heirs, but which was by agreement worked by them as a single unit. A farm divided among heirs, one of whom bought out the interests of the rest, might for many intents and purposes look like a farm left to a single heir, but burdened with compensation for his younger brothers and sisters.

Nevertheless, there were important differences in inheritance systems from one region to another, and these left permanent marks on the social and economic structure. The influence of an inheritance system was very widely diffused. It affected the distribution of property, and thus the nature of the market. It influenced the type of agriculture and the level of agricultural efficiency. It was not without importance for the supply of capital: I have sometimes suspected, for example, that the development in England of forms of marriage settlement that provided for daughters by assuring them capital sums contributed greatly to the development of the English mortgage market in the seventeenth century. In particular, inheritance systems exerted an influence on the structure of the family, that is, on the size of the family, on the relations of parents to children and between the children; and it is with the economic significance of this fact that I am now concerned.

There are a number of interesting problems in this field. One might consider, for example, the effect of family structure on entrepreneurial decision. In the early stages of industrialization, the family was the commonest form of economic enterprise throughout western Europe, both where industrial development was rapid and where it was slow. How far was the success of its performance influenced by differences in internal structure? Were German entrepreneurial families more successful than the French simply because they worked in a more favorable external environment, or did it have something to do with differences in the legal rights of the father, and of the sisters and younger brothers, who were also the uncles and aunts and nephews and nieces? Is the wicked uncle the villain of the economic plot? How far do the legal relations of the family repeat themselves in the family concern? I meant originally to consider these questions, but, conscious of how much a novice I am in entrepreneurial history, decided to escape, under cover of the exigencies of space, to a ground more familiar to me. I propose, therefore, to consider the effect of the property relations between members of a family first on its demographic behavior and second on its geographic mobility.

Almost all the writers on this subject agree that rules of inheritance have a profound influence on population growth. But they differ as to the nature of this influence. French demographers have generally been inclined to argue that, in their country, the provision for equal division, in the Napoleonic Code, tended to retard population growth.[6] The peasant who worked to keep his property intact had a powerful incentive to limit the number of children between whom his property would be divided. Friedrich List, on the other hand, in his analysis of the migration from Württemburg in the early nineteenth century, suggested that the application of the Napoleonic Code in the Rhineland had stimulated marriages and hence births.[7] In eighteenth-century Bavaria, division of properties was advocated specifically as a means of encouraging population growth, and most German writers lean towards the view that the single-heir system tended to restrain the birth rate.[8] In a peasant society, so the argument runs, children did not marry until they could establish a home; equal division of the family property enabled all the children to acquire an establishment and therefore to marry, whereas inheritance by a single heir made it difficult in a rural society for younger children to set up on their own and therefore condemned many of them to celibacy.

Clearly, it is difficult to bring these views to the bar of empirical verification. Inheritance by a single heir meant one thing in an area where land was still sufficiently plentiful for younger sons to acquire new farms of their own and marry and something quite different where it persisted in a crowded area where the younger children were compelled to remain at home unmarried. A recent study of marriage in France shows that in the remoter regions where the traditional obligation to maintain the social standing of the family was generally recognized, the younger children were often voluntarily celibate, despite their legal ownership of the family property; whereas, in other areas where more "liberal" and modern ideas prevailed, equal division enabled the younger children to acquire their own establishments and marry. And the influence of equal division was not only modified by moral ideas; it had one consequence where properties were still substantial and quite different consequences where fragmentation had already proceeded far. It is therefore difficult in the extreme to disentangle the effects of the rules of succession from the many other circumstances that influence population growth. The general direction of the influence exerted by these rules can, however, be distinguished. In the single-heir areas the owner had relatively slight inducement to limit the number of his children; but his brothers and sisters tended to remain unmarried. In an area of equal division, on the other hand, it was easier for all the heirs to marry, though they may have had some incentive to limit the number of *their* children in order to avoid progressive fragmentation. The typical family in the single-heir region tended, therefore, to consist of the owner and his wife with a large number of children, surrounded by a penumbra of celibate uncles and aunts, younger brothers and sisters. The typical family in the equal-division regions tended to consist of man and wife with a smaller number of children, but with fewer celibates. My own belief—to state summarily what ought to be argued further—is that, other things being equal, the higher proportion of marriages under the latter system was likely to produce in the aggregate more children than the fewer but more productive marriages of the former. I suggest, that is, that the single-heir system tended to retard population growth and division to promote it.

The writers on inheritance systems also differed when they came to discuss the second question—the effect of different inheritance systems on the mobility of population. To this problem much more direct attention was paid, for it was relevant to one of the most controversial developments in the later nineteenth century, the flight from the land; and consequently a large body of evidence was assembled on the point. Little of this evidence is entirely unambiguous, for it is difficult to isolate the effects on mobility of inheritance systems from the effects, for example, of the distribution of property: all the more difficult because the distribution of property was influenced by inheritance systems. To take a specific case, it is not easy to decide whether large numbers migrated from East Prussia because it was an area of *Anerbensitte,* inheritance by a single heir, or because it was, for reasons that had not a great deal to do with rules of inheritance, an area of large estates.

But this much is clear, that a good deal of the discussion was cast in the wrong terms. The question was not one of mobility versus immobility, but of different types of mobility. Long-distance migration, for seasons or short periods, was common throughout Europe, whatever the prevailing rules of inheritance. There is something to be said for the view that equal division promoted such migration, which was the method by which the sons of a peasant household who enjoyed a certain expectation of a share in the patrimonial property could acquire money to enlarge their holdings and supplement their family income. But, in any case, this sort of migration was not of primary importance for economic change, for it was essentially temporary. Seasonal migration was not an escape from the peasant family but a condition of its survival. The peasant went, not to acquire a new occupation in a different society, but to improve his position in the old.

Of much greater importance were the permanent migrations, and where these migrations are concerned there is a reasonably evident distinction between the influence of different systems of inheritance. There are a number of instances of large-scale permanent migration from areas of division. Where division led to a considerable morselization of properties and to a rapid growth of population, a succession of poor harvests might break down the normal resistances and lead to a sudden, explosive, and permanent exodus. South Germany in the early nineteenth century is a case in point. But the inhabitants of division areas were not likely, in the absence of such severe pressure, to respond readily to demands for permanent industrial labor in regions distant from their homes. In the first place, not only was the peasant himself rendered immobile by his property; his sons were deterred from permanent migration by the certainty of succeeding to a share of their family property. Secondly, in these areas, the market in small parcels of land was more active, and the chances of even a landless laborer acquiring some property were brighter than they were in areas where farms descended to a single heir. The retentive effect of property was thus very widely diffused. Finally, though in these areas the peasants often found ways, by agreement, to circumvent the worst excesses of morselization, the division of property did tend to create a class of peasants too poor to find their living outside the village, even had they wished to do so. The poverty of areas of division, as well as the wide diffusion of property rights, might hinder mobility.[9]

By comparison, the inhabitants of single-heir regions responded more easily to a demand for permanent industrial labor. The typical peasant families of these regions tended to contain a higher proportion of celibates, and single men were more likely than families to leave their villages permanently. It was only when there was a breakdown of social morale, such as there was in Ireland in the 1840's, that whole families migrated in large numbers. Moreover, the fact that the share of the younger children was under this system provided in the form of money facilitated their permanent movement away from the family holding. Generally speaking, moreover, the younger children in these areas were not debarred from compounding for their expectations during the lifetime of their parents. This was in Germany a recognized institution—the *Erbverzichtsvertrag*—and it gave the younger members of German families much greater freedom to leave the family home early in their life than was available in France, where the prohibition of the *pacte de renonciation* was one of the main principles of the law relating to succession.

There is, thus, a broad contrast. The one system provided for the younger children usually on a more generous scale but in a form that tethered them to peasant society; the other generally provided less generously but in a form that allowed the younger children to leave that society for good. The division areas may have tended to have the densest populations in relation to their capacity, but they were populations which it was difficult in normal times to induce permanently to leave the area. The population in single-heir areas may have been less dense, but it was more capable of permanent movement.

Czechoslavakia provides an example of the effect of inheritance systems on mobility. The west of Czechoslovakia—Bohemia, Silesia, and northern and western Moravia—belonged to the great East German *Anerbengebiete;* property went to a single heir. The east of Czechoslovakia—southwestern Moravia, Slovakia, and Ruthenia—was an area of division. In Slovakia, where division had created extremely small holdings, it was common for the sons of a peasant household, after marriage, to leave their homes and wives and emigrate. In the 1930's, in one district of 45,000 inhabitants, 3,000 worked as miners outside the district, 3,000 as seasonal agricultural laborers, and 1,500 as building workers. But their intention was not permanent settlement away from the district; it was to earn enough money to set themselves up as farmers or to supplement the family earnings at home. "In many parts of Slovakia this type of emigration was so widespread that the existence of whole villages was based upon it."[10] But *permanent* migration from the family seems to have been commoner in the western parts of Czechoslovakia. Before the development of industry, the younger sons remained unmarried and worked with the lord of the manor or became agricultural wage-earners. With the development of an industrial and urban society they found new employments. Some of them entered the professions, for since the parental holdings in this region remained undivided, the peasant was often wealthy enough to educate his younger sons. "Thus the Historical Provinces, where estates are passed on to a single heir, unlike the Slovak regions, where estates are divided among the heirs, provided a heavy quota of peasants for the liberal professions calling for a secondary university education."[11]

Now for the effects of these differences in mobility on economic change, on the form and speed of industrial development. In early industrial society, labor was probably a higher proportion of total costs than, in general, it is today, and, in societies that were still predominantly peasant and where transport facilities were few, geographical mobility of labor was certainly lower. The terms on which labor was available to industry were therefore a more decisive influence on the location of industry than it is in modern Europe. Where the peasant population was relatively dense but immobile, industry tended to move to the labor; where the peasant population was more mobile, even if less fertile, the industrialist had much greater freedom to choose his site with reference to the other relevant considerations.

But it is a question not only of the location of industry but of its type.

The practice of division of property was favorable to the development of local industry in the home or small workshop, for it tended to create a population with time for by-employments. The relation between division and domestic industry was not indeed a one-way relation. In some areas it was not so much that division facilitated industrial by-employments, as that the independent existence of domestic industry diminished resistance to division; because nonagricultural by-employments were available, properties could be divided and still be capable of maintaining families. Such a case was Schleswig Holstein, predominantly an area of the single heir, in which the practice of division was concentrated in the fishing villages along the western coast. In most cases, however, the practice of division appears to have arisen independently of the customs of local domestic industry, and it is a reasonable conjecture in some cases that it directly promoted the development of such industry. It is, for example, perhaps not entirely a coincidence that the medieval woolen textile industry should have flourished in East Anglia, a region of partible inheritance.[12]

Whether or not inheritance customs had much to do with the early distribution of local domestic industry, division did greatly influence the capacity of that type of industry to resist the competition of the factory in the nineteenth century. To attract labor permanently from peasant families in areas of division the factory had to offer a wage sufficiently high to compensate them for renouncing their prospects of rising in peasant society; this fact limited the range of operations over which the factory could successfully compete with domestic industry, decentralized in the small workshop and the home and drawing its labor from local peasant families of the neighborhood.

The clearest example of the effect of labor immobilities is Russia in the later nineteenth century where, largely because of the existence of the *mir,* the factory failed to make headway against the village industry. The persistence of old forms of industry in France and the wide geographical diffusion of French industry are also, in considerable measure, to be ascribed to immobilities arising from the structure of the French family. It is significant that England, the country of the earliest factories and regions of industrial concentration, was the country where, with a few minor exceptions, younger children had no claim at common law to any share of their father's estate, that is, had only such claims as might be specifically granted them my special agreement—for example, at the time of their parents' marriage. And if space allowed, I think it could be shown that the prevalence of *Anerbensitte* over most of nineteenth-century Germany outside the Rhineland and Thuringia was a significant influence in the rapid development of German industry.

The two features I have been discussing—the mobility of a population and its capacity to increase—are closely related. I have argued that a peasant community in which the single-heir system prevails is likely—with the important proviso of other things being equal—to be mobile but un-prolific in comparison with one in which division prevails. But because of its capacity to send forth its younger sons to become part of a permanent industrial labor force, the single-heir system made a powerful indirect contribution to population increase. It retarded population increase in the country but accelerated it, and to a greater extent, in the towns and areas of industrial concentration. For in all the western European countries, the industrial wage-earners were the most prolific class. They were not restrained by traditional views, which in peasant societies subordinated marriage to the purposes of the maintenance of the family; a higher proportion of them married, and they married younger. And once the initial stages of industrialization had got under way, the natural increase from this source very greatly diminished the extent to which the further expansion of industry needed to depend upon continued migration from the countryside.

In the years before 1914, a large amount of writing was devoted to a discussion of a third consequence of inheritance systems for economic change—their influence on the efficiency of agriculture. It was argued by the opponents of equal division that it starved the land of capital. Regions of division were regions of land hunger; small peasants, anxious to add acre to acre, bid up the price of land to an excessively high level and often mortgaged in order to buy. As a result, the savings of the peasants were not applied to improving their properties but to extending them; in substance, that is, the savings of the fortunate peasants went in absorbing the fragments thrown on the market by the less fortunate members of their own class. Moreover, the flow of outside capital into agriculture was impeded because the high price of land made capitalists reluctant to buy. On the other hand, it was argued by the defenders of division that the single-heir system often had equally bad effects on agricultural efficiency; where the property descended to a single heir who was charged with an obligation to compensate the younger children with sums of money calculated on the market value of the property, it might become heavily burdened with debt and so starved of capital.[13]

Wherever the truth of this argument about the effect of inheritance systems on productivity may lie,[14] it is probable that any given increase in productivity in the regions of equal division tended to exhaust itself in an increase in population, and to accelerate the process of division; whereas an equivalent increase in the single-heir areas was more likely to increase the surplus available for sale to the nonagricultural population. The agriculture of a single-heir region was therefore more capable of responding to the increased demands for food which arose in the course of industrialization.

I have described three ways in which a feature of family structure influenced economic development. I am very conscious not only of having restricted myself to one feature only but also of not having assessed the magnitude, as opposed to the direction, of the influences which flowed from it. I would only say that most of the models produced by the economists who observed the early stages of European industralization assigned an important place to population and food supply, and that, since inheritance systems had an influence on both these, they ought to be considered among the factors that determined the rate at which industrialization got under way in the different parts of Europe and the forms it assumed.

14 Changing Political Attitudes in Totalitarian Society: A Case Study of the Role of the Family

KENT GEIGER

Professor Geiger's paper illustrates how the form and nature of political control that characterizes the larger society impinges upon the family. As he sees it, the emphasis upon the state and the use of coercive techniques that exist in the Soviet Union, produces actual and potential conflict between parents and children. This conflict, in turn, tends to maintain the state's totalitarian power and the ideology which supports it. In the light of this apparently weak position of the Soviet family in the formation of political attitudes, it is interesting to re-examine the articles on Russia in the introductory section. Engels predicted the radical transformation of the family, even its disappearance. Timasheff shows how the attempt to abolish the family failed and had to be reversed. But perhaps the failure and reversal left a residue, seen in the condition Geiger describes.

I

There is general agreement among Western scholars that the modern totalitarian state is distinguished in part by its possession of a unitary and systematically elaborated ideology. While it will be found that expert opinions vary considerably in regard to the importance of the role played by ideology in the origin and continuation of totalitarianism,[1] there is little question but that the ruling power of the totalitarian society is not indifferent to the relationship between national ideology and popular attitudes. Indeed, history shows that the rulers of twentieth-century totalitarian states have devoted considerable effort to the development among their citizenries of attitudes of acceptance toward the social philosophies and goals associated with their regimes.

However, a realistic sense of the limits to which popular psychology

Reprinted from *World Politics*, VIII (January, 1956), 187–205, with the kind permission of the author and publishers.

can, in the short run, be reshaped has seemed to direct the totalitarian leadership sooner or later into feeling that the older generation will not respond to the desired extent and that major emphasis should be placed upon the recruitment of youth. Thus, we find in the writings of the totalitarian ideologues that considerable importance is attached to the increasingly great devotion and loyalty expected of the younger generations. We also find that state-sponsored, closely controlled youth movements have been characteristic of totalitarianism.[2]

But here the aim of the totalitarian state collides with an obstacle. In the crucial early years, children are trained and their personalities shaped predominantly within the family, and the family is not a public, but a private, association of individuals. Within the family, interpersonal relations and behavior tend, in the main, to be governed by the force of tradition, that is, by relatively inflexible norms which frequently are not in accord with those viewed favorably by the totalitarian regime. Therefore, the rapid and radical changes in the orientation of youth fostered by the totalitarian dictatorship are virtually certain to clash with certain of the traditionally sanctioned attitudes of parents.[3] This situation is not infrequently considered prototypical of parent-youth relations in modern totalitarian societies and has become known in popular parlance as the "struggle" between family and state for the minds of the young.

In this struggle (as popularly conceived), it cannot be denied that the totalitarian state disposes of powerful resources for shaping the minds of the young in the desired direction. These include a carefully controlled school system, the suffusion of the output of the mass media with propaganda themes, and, of course, the closely supervised youth organizations. On the other hand, the resources of the family are frequently seen as equally strong; they include the presumed complete control of parents over children in the earliest years and influence achieved through mutual ties of loyalty and affection at later ages.

It is the purpose of this article to explore the dimensions of this contest of forces, with special attention to the way in which the situation is viewed and managed by parents in a totalitarian society. The data to be presented enable us to make some estimate of the degree of success attained by one contemporary totalitarian state, the U.S.S.R., in modifying and controlling for its own purposes this aspect of the process of socialization of young persons within the family.

II

Ideally, of course, investigation of such a problem would be conducted on the spot, but the Soviet Union, unfortunately, has been exceptionally vigorous in denying western investigators access to its population. However, owing to circumstances associated with World War II, it has become possible in the last few years to make extensive use of political refugees as first-hand sources of information about the Soviet Union. The data to be analyzed below were obtained from former Soviet citizens who were interviewed in Germany and in the New York City area, in 1950 and 1951, by members of the Harvard Project on the Soviet Social System. There is no doubt that former Soviet citizens who are now refugees in the West constitute a group which in certain respects must be considered unique and which is far from a random sample of the Soviet population still resident in the U.S.S.R. In particular, by their very presence in the West and by virtue of their prolonged exposure to western influence, we may assume that they are considerably more hostile toward the Soviet regime and its institutions and ideas than the rank and file of the Soviet people. But such a fact does not preclude their effective use as sources of information about the Soviet system if sufficient account is taken of the bias and if care is exercised in the way the results are interpreted.

To investigate the impact of the Soviet system on the transmission of political attitudes within the Soviet parent-child relationship, data were obtained with two different instruments and from two different refugee sub-samples. The first group of materials consists of extended life-history interviews with 141 Soviet young persons who were born in the period 1915–29. Project interviewers were instructed to cover at some time during the course of the two or three days of the interview the role of the respondent's parents in the development of his attitudes toward the Soviet regime and its works. For the bulk of respondents, this proved to be a topic of considerable meaning and interest, and they freely discussed their relationships with their parents vis-à-vis the Soviet regime.

The first part of the analysis which follows will be devoted to the responses secured in interviews from these young people. They were members of families from all social levels, of both rural and urban residence, and include a few representatives of the Soviet minority nationalities, although 93 per cent of the total were members of the dominant Slavic majority—Great Russian, Ukrainian, and White Russian. Although occasional quotations from persons outside the 1915–29 age range will be given for illustrative purposes, the percentage figures and tables from the interview materials represent exclusively the responses of the younger persons in the interview sample.

The second body of data was obtained with the use of a check-list questionnaire from persons who were themselves parents in the U.S.S.R. and whose first child was born in the 1915–30 period. Thus, in terms of age, these respondents correspond roughly to the parental generation of the young persons in the life-history sample. Their responses, which will be discussed after the results of the interviews are presented, serve in part as a check on the validity of the latter.

III

As a starting point for the analysis of the family-state relationship, let us consider the descriptions of parental attitudes toward the Soviet regime given by the sample of young refugee respondents. Most frequently, as might be expected from this group, the respondents reported that their parents were likely to show hostility, skepticism, or a lack of appropriate enthusiasm in regard to the Soviet regime. For example:

> My father always spoke openly. Prior to the war he said that the purges, the closing of the churches, the collective farms, and the 1940 labor laws were all slavery. (23-year-old male, father a shop foreman)[4]

In fact, 94 of the 141 cases available, or 67 per cent, said that their parents had had predominantly anti-Soviet attitudes. At the other extreme, only 9, or 6 per cent, reported that their parents had been in the main pro-regime. The remaining 27 per cent gave no information about the attitudes of their parents, gave inconsistent or contradictory information, or did not live in families as they grew up.

Of the 103 young persons who gave adequate responses to the question, then, 91 per cent came from families in which the parents had been at heart anti-Soviet in feeling while living in the U.S.S.R. This was a situation which posed a sharp problem for the parents: How, if indeed at all, should they teach their children to understand the real nature of the Soviet regime? How far should they go in transmitting openly their own attitudes and values to their children? As a Soviet mother put it:

> . . . in raising our son we immediately faced the question: Should we raise him in the spirit of the Soviet Union or not? At that time we were changing our views toward the Soviet Union; we were both strongly against the Soviet power. (64-year-old female, doctor)

In the meantime, other forces were at work—forces which served to restrict the parents' freedom of choice. Since school, youth organizations, informal peer groups, cinema, radio, and reading materials of all description strive to make the young person a loyal adherent to the works and symbols of the Soviet order, it is not surprising that children were regularly led in the direction of enthusiastic acceptance of bolshevik ideology. In fact, within the anti-Soviet family there frequently appeared a young political activist who did not hesitate to display his sentiments:

> The child comes to the conviction that the Communist propaganda tells the truth, and if he hears from his parents the opposite opinion, he feels insulted and tries to explain these things to his parents, who are not politically conscious. In short, he becomes a convinced Communist, a Pioneer, fired by the Pioneer literature, activism, and so on. (57-year-old male, accountant)

Actually, for very young children, the matter of "parental influence" was pretty much a closed issue, since divulgence of suspect interpretations and sentiments to the partly developed consciousness and incomplete sense of responsibility of the child could have serious repercussions. One of the most widely cited norms of family conduct under Soviet conditions was the requirement that nonconforming attitudes were not to be expressed in front of small children:

> Everyone was afraid of his children. A small child can betray his parents unwittingly, and therefore my parents were always careful in what they said before me and my brother. (20-year-old female, father a secondary-school teacher)

In the close and continuous interaction within the family, this constituted a problem which could not be lightly dismissed. Gross differences in regard to emotionally significant value orientations between persons in intimate relationships are hard to tolerate. In fact, such differences set forces in motion which in the end serve either to make homogeneous the values of the individuals concerned or to disrupt the relationship because of a distressing increase in interpersonal tension.

The distribution of power in the parent-child relationship is generally thought of as markedly asymmetrical; indeed, a good part of the process of socialization can be seen as the exercise of power and influence by the parent in the interest of transmitting his own attitudes to his children. Under Soviet totalitarianism, however, it is clear that parents could not easily control the views of their young children. Moreover, the problem areas in the parent-child relationship applied not only to matters which a westerner would consider "political" and in which, it might be argued, children have little interest or involvement, but to matters which had traditionally been of central importance to the parent-child relationship. Two stand out as of particular relevance —the mode in which parental authority was exercised and the transmission of traditionally hallowed attitudes toward religion and the church. Consider, for example, the following comments:

> . . . they told you you have no right to punish a child. And if a child was punished, he would go and complain to the authorities. (51-year-old male, unskilled worker)

> . . . in the schools they were developing a child of the worst sort. There were denunciations, lack of respect for elders, and denial of God. (51-year-old male, bookkeeper)

The psychological immaturity of children thus constituted a definitely weak link in the family's struggle against the state and provided in effect a point of entry into the family for elements of the totalitarian ideology. Such a situation must be reckoned as a basic source of tension in the prewar Soviet family. In the Project materials, it was a prominent target for parental complaints. However, as the child grew older, the situation changed. From the age of 12 to 15 or 16, when an enlarged sense of awareness and personal responsibility had developed, it was possible, if the parent so desired, to open more fully the channels of communication between himself and his child. From the parental point of view, only then could the child be "trusted" with information which clearly showed a gap between family values and the official sponsored ideology:

> (Was your child a member of the Komsomol?) No. Komsomols are young people in their teens—that is to say, children who are already able to reason. Consequently, at that age they may be influenced by their parents. (47-year-old male, office clerk)

To explore the way in which Soviet parents managed their relationships with older children, the reactions of "anti-Soviet" parents were sorted into categories. These fell into three groups. The most numerous, occurring in 67 out of the 94 cases of anti-Soviet parents, or 71 per cent, was that group in which the parents reportedly took the youngsters into their confidence and freely communicated to them their doubts about and antipathies to the regime.[5] The following are typical of the responses in this category:

> The strongest influences in my life were those of my mother, my father, and my grandmother. All of them were always opposed to the Soviet government, and I, of course, was raised in such opposition. (28-year-old male, father an engineer)

> Since my early childhood our family had been anti-Soviet, and very often I heard my parents say that now the situation was no good, and that before it had been better. (29-year-old male, father a store clerk)

The second group consisted of those families in which the parents were reported to be relatively uncommunicative about their attitudes toward the regime. There were 18 of these—19 per cent of the total. An example is:

> . . . my father never told me, "Here is what it says in the paper, but the fact is this." He never talked about political matters. My father was in no way in accord with the Soviet regime, but he was always silent about it. (26-year-old female, father a director of postal-telegraph office)

A reservation about this category must be entered in terms of the inherent difficulty of "hiding" a deeply felt sentiment from one's family intimates. Some of the respondents did in fact indicate that although nothing was said, they "knew" what the parental view was. For example:

> The parents avoid direct talk on political questions. They only try to strengthen the child in his general moral position. (Were there any discussions between you and your parents?) What kind of discussions could there be? I was just a kid, but they tried to deflect my attention from Communism by making me read classical literature or other instructive

and interesting books rather than the Pioneer literature. (Did you know their political views?) They did not tell me that, but I felt that it did not support the view which was developing in me. (How did you know that?) My feeling was quite definite. I tried to propagandize them and show them they didn't understand. (Did they oppose your ideas?) They did not oppose me directly. They only said, "Wait until you get older and then you will understand more." (And did this influence you?) It did not influence me directly, but it put some doubt in me. These words and remarks became more frequent and they accumulated. (When did they start accumulating?) Between the age of 10 and 15 years. . . . (24-year-old male, father a stage director in theater)

Finally, the least numerous group, 9 or 10 per cent of the total, was composed of the individuals whose parents adapted to this problem by supporting the official doctrines of the regime:

How were we educated? We were educated in the spirit of Communism, the Soviet Union only, we did not know anything else. . . . My parents were afraid to tell about life under the Tsarist regime. . . . My father was very enclosed within himself in the family. He never told about the past. He always said, "You must do what you are told to do." (23-year-old male, father a trust director)

How may one explain the differences revealed by these patterns? For the open and frankly anti-Soviet response, in the majority of cases little rationale was offered. This can be accounted for in part by the anti-Soviet milieu in which the respondents had been living for some time, that is, the Western world, in the context of which the interviews took place. The reporting of an anti-Soviet atmosphere in the family was a response more likely to be approved by DP groups and also by western interviewers, and apparently most respondents felt that an overtly expressed anti-regime attitude did not have to be justified in terms of other values or aspects of the family's situation. However, there does seem to have been a prior motivational element in the picture which, although not mentioned by the respondents, helps to account for the predominance of the openly anti-Soviet pattern. This is the trait of impulsiveness, the spontaneous emission of feelings with little regard for their consequences. For instance:

My mother often cursed the Communists, and said, you should excuse the expression, "It is the Communists who——over everything." And my brother was a Komsomol and a Party member. My mother would often say, "We have gone through so much, and for what? We have nothing and we never will. During Tsarist times we lived better." Sometimes we got fed up with her raving and told her to keep quiet. (Did she say such things even when your brother was around?) Yes. She would say, "Our comrades! What have they done for us? We have gotten nothing good from them." She would say this every day and she would always cry. My mother felt that she had lived better before. Then she often had arguments with my brother over religion, too. (27-year-old male, mother a waitress separated from husband)

Further evidence of such lack of future-oriented calculation is to be found in the fact that in 29 of the 67 cases in the openly anti-Soviet group, the frank expression of parental views did not win over the child, but led instead to conflict or enhanced the seriousness of an already existing conflict. According to these respondents, parental opposition to the ideas they learned at school brought them into a position where they rebelled against their parents and rejected their values. For example:

> Whenever I stayed with my family, I quarreled with my parents, especially my father. He tried to tell me that the Party line was nothing but a lie, that I should open my eyes and see what's behind it all. But I had faith. I was very young and thus very enthusiastic and I thought my parents were old, clinging to old-fashioned ideas, that they couldn't see the truth, that they couldn't understand our new socialist reforms. (33-year-old female, father a physics teacher)

Here is another sample of parent-child tension over political opinions:

> When I started to go to school, the agitation and propaganda began in my life. They used to say we lived better than anybody anywhere. School had a very great influence on me. I did not believe anything my mother said about their having a servant and a cow and everything. Mother often used to tell me about this. She would tell me about her mother and her father and how satisfied they were with their life. But when I joined the Pioneers I was torn away from my family. I doubted that my mother told me the truth, because they [at school] used to tell me about the exploiters before the Revolution and that people were not able to live. (30-year-old male, mother a cook, widowed in 1930)

There is no doubt but that with increasing age the intellectual maturation of the child made him both more fully interested in political ideas and also potentially able to admit and handle the conflict between his parents' views and the outlook broached in extra-familial contexts. On the other hand, another accompaniment of aging is emotional maturation, and in modern industrial societies one of the central problems connected with emotional maturation concerns the "emancipation" of the child from close emotional ties with his parents. Such emotional emancipation is a process which ordinarily accompanies adolescence and thus occurs concurrently with the young person's greater consciousness of his parents' political views. If the latter are dissonant with those which he has learned to idealize in school and youth group organizations, then they will become the focus for conflict with his parents. Consequently, it is quite plausible and probable that in Soviet society emotional problems of the parent-youth relationship become "politicized" to an exceptional degree or, to put it the other way around, that a great proportion of parent-youth conflicts over differing political viewpoints can be explained as a displacement associated with the struggle to overcome dependency feelings which are no longer culturally approved.

Nonetheless, the central point to be noted in the parent-child relationship in those families in which parents frankly expressed their anti-regime sentiments is the high frequency with which political differences were a sore point and the widespread tendency of children to reject their parents' views.

Let us turn now to those parents who did not express their views so openly. Although they themselves were in fact opposed to the regime, they adopted either a "neutral" or a "pro-Soviet" position in regard to the ideological development of their children. The predominant explanation given for such parental behavior was expressed in terms of how best to contribute to the present and future welfare of the child:

> My mother never tried to convince me of the rightness of her ideas. She was extremely cultured and knew I had to live my own life, that I had to live in Soviet society, and she did not wish to make it difficult for me. (32-year-old male, mother a typist, widowed in 1928)

In a number of interviews respondents who were themselves parents in the U.S.S.R. responded in effect in the same way:

> (What kind of character did you try to impart to your child?) I will tell you exactly what my attitude was. Inasmuch as we were living in the Soviet Union, we knew that our children would have to continue to live in the Soviet Union even after we were gone, and so we tried to introduce them to Communist ideas. What can I say about the education of our children? It was of a different sort than I would have preferred, but I didn't object. (59-year-old female, scientific research worker)

In a few cases, a different explanation was offered—namely, that the frank transmission of their own feelings to their children would have jeopardized the physical or economic welfare of the parents themselves:

> In the majority of instances, the influence of parents on their children was insignificant in the Soviet Union. Many questions of ethics are absorbed by the children in school from their classmates and the school's environment, and the parents are forced to accept it. Otherwise there can be very serious consequences. For instance, one can be reported for "political discussions." (54-year-old male, university professor)

> (What was your attitude toward religion?) We did not have any icons in our house. All depended on my father. In the position he was in we could not have done it. My father's sister was a very religious woman and she always laughed at us because we were godless. (What was his internal attitude toward religion?) Since my father occupied a good position, he could not display any religious feelings. Maybe they [the parents of the respondent] talked somewhat differently between themselves. I couldn't know it, but it was not in our presence. We, the young people, were educated in an anti-religious spirit. (23-year-old male, father a trust director)

Finally, there is some indication that still another explanatory condition deserves mention. The modal type of family in the U.S.S.R. is a small, structurally isolated[6] group in which emotional intimacy is highly valued. In such circumstances it becomes especially important to maintain expected levels of mutual acceptance and stability in interpersonal relations. For this reason, it may be supposed that Soviet parents were not infrequently moved to avoid serious conflict with their children simply in order to maintain peace and harmony within the family. Moreover, the burden of adaptation or adjustment could be seen as rightfully belonging more to them than to their children, since by virtue of their age and experience they were better able to "understand" the reasons for the attitudinal patterns of their children than were their children able to appreciate the parental point of view. Moreover, in the adolescent period during which the child is engaging in the struggle to become emotionally independent from his parents, he may be notably unwilling to compromise those principles he calls his own. For these reasons, it is perhaps not too surprising that some Soviet parents were likely to engage in a measure of adaptation to the views of the younger generation and were willing to pay the price of suppressing their dissatisfaction with the Soviet system.[7] The most popular private rationalization for this seems to have been something on the order of: "Someday they'll find out the true state of affairs for themselves."

The result obtained from analysis of reported parental attitudes in the families of these 94 young respondents appears to be an important datum for appraisal of the role of the family in Soviet totalitarian society, for it indicates that in a majority of cases anti-Soviet parents were unwilling or unable by their own efforts to raise anti-Soviet children. Twenty-seven, or 29 per cent of the 94, seem to have made little attempt to do so and either did not contradict what their children learned in school or in fact reiterated and reinforced what they had learned there. As a justification of this attitude, the predominant view in this group was that the children should be raised for their own good, or for the good of the family as a whole, in the spirit of the social system in which they had to live. And of the 67 parents who were reported as attempting to influence their children in an anti-Soviet direction, 29 of the 67 cases, or 43 per cent—a not inconsiderable proportion—were relatively unsuccessful. If these 29 are added to the two groups of families in which the parents, in effect, co-operated with the regime, 27 in all, the resulting 56 families constitute 60 per cent of the total number of 94 respondents with anti-Soviet parents. Now, if the 9 respondents who came from predominantly pro-Soviet families are also added to this number, the proportion of families represented by young respondents in the interview sample which were relatively powerless to oppose effectively the pressures of the Soviet system is even greater—65 out of 103, or 63 per cent. Considering the circumstances under which the interviews were conducted and the disaffected, political-refugee status of the respondents, this is indeed a remarkable finding and testifies in sinister fashion to the ability of the Soviet regime to destroy ideological opposition even within the private family group.

It is not necessary that the above result stand alone, for rough corroboration was obtained from a different group of refugees and with the use of a different instrument. Sixty-six respondents who had themselves been parents in the U.S.S.R. were administered paper-and-pencil questionnaires concerned primarily with their experiences in family life. The first child of these respondents was born in the 1915–30 period; thus they comprise a group which corresponds in age quite closely to that of the parents of the young respondents whose experiences were examined above. These former Soviet parents were confronted with the following check-list question:

> How did you explain to your child(ren) those events in the U.S.S.R. whose negative side was clear to you, such as purges, repressions, the Terror, etc.?
>
> a—I explained to them as best I could in such a fashion that they would see no contradictions between what I told them and what they heard in school.
> b—I told them the complete truth although it contradicted the things they were taught in school.
> c—I tried as best I could to avoid such topics and remained silent.
> d—Something else. (Please explain)

Results were as follows: the most frequently chosen responses were "c," indicated by 36 per cent of the group, and "b," also chosen by 36 per cent. Five per cent chose alternative "a," and nine persons, or 14 per cent, answered in their own terms ("d") or checked more than one response. Five, or 9 per cent, did not answer.

This tabulation merits several comments. In the first place, it indicates that not only when the situation is reported from the point of view of the child, but also from the point of view of the parents themselves, a sizable proportion of Soviet parents were not able or not willing to express their views to their children with complete frankness. Indeed, it suggests that parents are quite a bit less willing than are children to signify the presence of overt opposition to the Soviet regime within the home.

Also indicated is the fact that parental attitudes as characterized by young people tend to be concentrated at the extremes of the three major response patterns, while parental attitudes as characterized by parents themselves are bunched more on the middle, or non-committal, alternative. This difference may be in part a function of the way in which the information was gathered. In the interview situation, because of the use of probes by the interviewer, the respondent may have felt more pressure to characterize the attitudes of his parents as either actively "for" or "against" than was felt by the questionnaire respondents. However, another interpretation is possible: the tabulation may reflect the fact that the same process is being viewed, and interpreted, from two different points of view within the family—points of view which are in themselves different. Parental silence on vital topics may be seen *by the parent* as a compromise solution to the conflict between his own negative attitude and the more positive interpretation of the Soviet scene which he feels is expected of him by his children. But such behavior may be seen *by a young person* as behavior corresponding to the old Russian proverb, "Silence gives consent," or, more likely, as failure to respond in the prescribed way and thus as opposition to the regime.

The first major conclusion suggested by both sources of data is that the regime was quite successful in opposing the anti-Soviet views of parents and thus in molding the attitudes of young people. Clearly, the first step in the process consisted in gaining the loyalty of children at an early age. The predominant reaction to this on the part of parents was a feeling of fear and helplessness. Little could be done to prevent their indoctrination. As their children grew older, however, and developed a sense of responsibility for the welfare of their parents, it was possible to introduce them to nonconformist ideas. But as might be expected, and as these data indicate, by this time it was in many cases too late, and if the parents persisted in contradicting what the children had learned in school, conflict was likely to develop. Parent-youth conflict, actual and potential, then served as a social pressure within the family which often led to greater parental conformity with the attitudes and values of the new Soviet culture. It therefore actually served the purposes of the regime by helping to weaken the family as a source of opposition to bolshevik ideology.[8]

It is perhaps of greater import, however—particularly in view of the anti-Soviet bias of the respondents in this case—to emphasize that such a substantial number of parents made no attempt to pit their strength against the tide of events while they were in the U.S.S.R. and failed to oppose the new Soviet *Weltanschauung* even within the privacy of their homes. They thus collaborated with the regime in spite of themselves in the task of developing their children into loyal young Soviet citizens. It is in fact quite probable that political conformity in this sense has been for some time the modal response among the population still resident in the Soviet Union.

Still and all, the fact remains that in some cases Soviet parents failed to surrender to the course of events and within the home actively resisted the new ideas propagated by the Soviet regime. This raises the question: Which were the families more likely to become "Sovietized," and which were those internally more resistant to the new ideas? To some degree, of course, the answer to this question depends upon the pattern of specific experiences undergone by the members of the family under consideration. For instance, the arrest and sentencing for political reasons of a member of a family made it difficult for the rest of the family to maintain any semblance of a neutral or pro-Soviet orientation.[9] However, consideration of certain more general aspects of Soviet social conditions and social structure leads one to expect significant differences in this regard among the various Soviet socio-economic groups.

In both samples dealt with, the young life-history respondents and the questionnaire respondents of the parental generation, the variation by socio-economic group was in the same direction—quite conclusively favoring the Soviet peasant family as furnishing the most active anti-regime family environment. On the other hand, the least actively anti-regime family is the white-collar-level family of intelligentsia and employees.

How may these differences be explained? In the first place, area of residence is an important factor. The school system, the youth-group organizations, and the mass communications media through which the regime's agitation and propaganda are mediated are much more effectively developed in urban areas than in the Soviet countryside.[10] Therefore, the young people in the cities, and probably to some degree the entire urban population, tend to be much more influenced by current ideology than do their country peers. It is of course not only in totalitarian societies that social change occurs more rapidly in the city than in the country. Insofar as such pressures are effective, we would expect to find a stronger trend toward conformity among urban parents than among rural parents.

Closely connected is the strength of the traditional peasant orientation toward religion and the relative weakness of religious attitudes among the urban population.[11] Essential contradictions between bolshevism and traditional religious views quite effectively precluded the adoption of other than an anti-Soviet frame of reference within a strongly religious household.

The latter consideration also applies in some measure to social group differentiation among the urban population. Owing to the rapid rate of urbanization characterizing recent Soviet history[12] and the fact that newly urbanized peasants generally become workers, a positive attitude toward religion and other attitudinal and behavioral patterns of the peasantry tend to be found more frequently in the urban working class than among the urban non-manual population.

It is also widely recognized that Soviet society since the mid-1930's has become highly stratified[13] and that the material lot of the Soviet peasant and worker has been a hard one. Hence one might expect parents in these categories to manifest genuine hostility toward the Soviet regime purely on the basis of neglected "class interests."[14]

One additional factor deserves mention. It concerns the close connection in Soviet society between access to and retention of responsible, well-paid jobs and attitudes of political orthodoxy. Soviet parents who were highly placed in the Soviet system usually felt they could ill afford to take any chances in jeopardizing their position. Thus part of the price paid by the Soviet upper class for their material advantages was a greater degree of ideological conformity, genuine or simulated, whereas the lower classes seemed to have the compensatory advantage of being allowed more liberty to blow off steam. In their case, politically deviant beliefs and attitudes could be shrugged off by Soviet authorities as a case of the "backwardness of the masses."

The implications of this class difference in family patterns extend in several directions. In the first place, it is apparent that it is in some measure misleading to make general and unqualified statements about the role of "the family" in changing political attitudes. The role of the family evidently varies considerably from class level to class level. Second, since overtly expressed opposition to the regime on the part of parents varies inversely with class level, we would expect parent-youth solidarity in terms of political conflict also to vary inversely with social class level. The best data available indicate that at least for the urban population such is actually the case. Solidarity in Soviet "intelligentsia" families apparently is greater than in families of lower ranking nonmanual categories (bookkeeper, schoolteacher, clerk, etc.) and in these latter greater than in worker-level families.[15] Finally, it is quite likely that considerable variegation as well as a high incidence of underlying ambivalence characterize the political attitudes of the young people in the peasant- and working-class groups. Particularly in the case of the peasant youth, ambivalent feelings about the Soviet regime seem to have given rise to the typical reaction of political apathy, a trend which is related in mutually supporting fashion to the weakness of rural Komsomol and Party organizations.

IV

The broad problem with which this paper has been concerned has been the struggle between totalitarian state and family for the control of the mind of youth. The prewar Soviet Union has served as a test case, and the data have been furnished by Soviet political refugees. If the experiences reported by such persons differ from those of the rank and file of the Soviet population, it may be assumed that they incline in the direction of more parental hostility toward the Soviet government. Thus any conclusion reached which seems to be favorable to the aims of the Soviet regime would probably be even more strongly substantiated if it were possible to investigate the problem within the contemporary U.S.S.R. itself.

A basic conclusion is warranted. The family has on the whole not been a significant force in resisting the ideological indoctrination of Soviet young persons. While there is some evidence that politically tinged parent-youth conflict was a prominent feature in the prewar Soviet family, of equal or greater importance is the fact that Soviet parents so frequently minimized such conflict by their adaptive-conforming responses to the regime's ideology. Although a number of considerations must enter into a full explanation, two deserve special prominence since they underline essential differences between the totalitarian and the democratic way of organizing society. The first is the systematic use of coercion and terrorism as a means of inducing conformity. In substantial measure, Soviet parents went along with the Soviet regime because they feared to act otherwise. Secondly, the family, like an army, travels on its stomach—and the Soviet regime holds the key to the larder. Under Soviet conditions, in which all opportunities are government opportunities, attitudes of political conformity have come to be seen as a basic prerequisite for the obtaining of the good things of life—education, good jobs and, ultimately, decent food, clothing, and shelter.

It is also of some interest to note that the connection between a semblance of political loyalty and personal welfare is most relevant for parents in the upper-class family and that it plays a less prominent role in the worker and peasant family. This reflects a general feature of social structure in contemporary urban industrial society. Adaptation and close conformity to the needs of the existing order are part of the cost involved in the attainment and preservation of high status and its privileges.

A final commentary on the findings reported above takes us back to the general question of evaluating the role of the family in resisting the creation of those homogeneous political attitudes associated with totalitarianism. To what extent can the present results be generalized to other totalitarian societies? It is probable that the Soviet regime in the years preceding World War II enjoyed less mass support than any other totalitarian system of modern times. If the family was of so little importance in blocking the influence of externally induced sources of attitudinal change in this extreme case, one might conclude that it can be reckoned as even less significant a conservative force in other totalitarian societies. But popular support is only one factor. The realities of the Soviet scene differ in a number of additional respects from those obtaining in other systems of the totalitarian type. In the extent to which basic social changes[16] have been carried through, in the isolation of the population from outside influences, and in the very longevity and manifest stability of the system itself, the Soviet experience has as yet not been matched by other regimes. The implications of such contrasts as these suggest that the Soviet pattern cannot easily be generalized to other totalitarian systems. For they emphasize the fact, which has been a consistent interpretive motif in this case study, that parental action within the family is partly determined by factors over and above traditionally grounded personal predispositions.

15 The Family and the Political Behavior of Youth

ELEANOR E. MACCOBY,
RICHARD E. MATTHEWS,
and ANTON S. MORTON

The picture which Maccoby, Matthews, and Morton draw of the influences of the family on the political opinion of youths in America stands in sharp contrast to the Russian situation that Geiger described. The authors of the present article see the family as having a potent influence, more potent than friends or fellow workers, on the political attitudes and behavior of young people. Implicit in this account of the American family's contribution to the formation of political attitudes (and ultimately to the political system) is the less authoritarian and coercive nature of the political leadership of American society.

In each presidential election occurring in the mid-twentieth century, approximately one-ninth of the people eligible to vote are young people who are eligible to cast a presidential ballot for the first time, having had their twenty-first birthdays since the last presidential election. These young people are of great interest to social scientists and political practitioners alike, not only because they constitute a large enough group to carry considerable weight in any particular election outcome, but because it is possible that the political allegiances which they form early in their voting careers will be perpetuated for many years and thus have an impact upon a series of elections. We do not know a great deal about changes in the voting pattern of individual citizens or groups of citizens as they grow older and accumulate voting experience. Nor do we know how many elements of the political ideology formed in late adolescence and early adulthood are retained for a lifetime. It is a resonable hypothesis, however, that young people, being less bound than older people by habit and old political ties, will be more responsive to the political pressures of the moment, so that they might play a greater role in mediating political change than their elders.

What do we already know concerning the political behavior of young people? With varying degrees of certainty, the following facts have been fairly well established:

Reprinted from *Public Opinion Quarterly*, XVIII, No. 1 (1954), 23–39, where it appeared under the title, "Youth and Political Change," with the kind permission of the authors and publishers.

1. A smaller percentage of young people go to the polls than do people in older age groups.[1]
2. In his choice of candidate, a young person tends to be similar to his parents.[2]
3. Despite the agreement with their parents, young people as a group have been more Democratic in party choice than older voters, at least since 1936.[3]

An interesting question is whether the young person's preference for the Democratic party means that he is less conservative in his ideology than older voters. In general, of course, there is a correlation between the liberal-conservative dimension and party choice, but the existing evidence does not point as strongly to a liberal ideology among the young as might be expected. Centers found a slight tendency for young people among the upper occupational groups to be more liberal, but among the laboring groups the young were no more liberal than the old.[4] Lazarsfeld found greater conformity to one's group with increasing age, so that older Catholics were more strongly Democratic, old Protestants more strongly Republican, than younger people in these two religious groups. He suggested that increasing age brings about greater social conservatism, rather than greater political conservatism.[5]

In any case, an anomaly in the existing findings remains to be explained, and this is the fact that youth is consistently more Democratic than the older generations, while at the same time young people tend to follow in the political footsteps of their parents. Lubell has proposed an interesting hypothesis to explain this situation.[6] He points out that over the last two decades, children of immigrants have come of age; their parents were not eligible voters. Furthermore, the working-class urban masses, with their higher birth rate, have contributed disproportionately to each new crop of first-time voters. Possibly, young people vote proportionately just as their parents do, and it is the differential rates of population growth among the different social classes which explain the fact that young people as a whole have been consistently more Democratic than the older age groups. On the other hand, it is possible that young people tend to start their political careers with a more "left" or liberal ideology and become more conservative as they grow older and acquire a larger stake in the existing state of affairs. Possibly, both these factors operate jointly to produce a high proportion of Democrats among the young.

Some important questions to be answered by research, then, are (1) To what extent do young people follow their parents' lead politically? (2) When they do differ from their parents in politics, do they move primarily in the Democratic direction, or are there counter-balancing changes in both directions? and (3) When the young person does take up a political position different from that of his parents, what are some of the psychological and sociological variables associated with the change? The present study has been focused upon these questions, in an effort to advance our understanding of the political behavior of young people.

The study was conducted in Cambridge, Massachusetts, just after the presidential elections of November, 1952. Interviews were conducted with 339 people aged 21–24 inclusive—a group eligible to vote in a presidential election for the first time in 1952. Originally, a probability sample of people within the desired age range was selected from the police lists of Cambridge, which are compiled in January of every year and are intended to record the name, age, and sex of every adult resident of Cambridge at the time of listing. In the course of interviewing, however, the list was found to be badly out of date and consequently the young people finally interviewed cannot be considered to be a representative sample of the young people of Cambridge.[7] However, the main objective of the study was not to produce descriptive statistics about Cambridge but to examine relationships between variables. For such purposes, the range of the sample is more important than its representativeness.

By way of background for the report which follows, it may be useful to present here the voting record for the city of Cambridge in the 1952 elections:

76 per cent of those eligible to vote cast a ballot in the presidential contest

41.8 per cent voted for Eisenhower (among those voting for one of the two major Presidential candidates)

35.5 per cent voted for Lodge, the Republican senatorial candidate

37.1 per cent voted for Herter, the Republican candidate for Governor.

It may be seen that even in a year in which the Republicans swept the country and in which Eisenhower carried the state of Massachusetts (which has been Democratic for many years), Cambridge remained heavily Democratic. The margin for the Democrats was smaller than in previous years, however.

The following report must be interpreted, then, in the light of the fact that the study was conducted in a Democratic stronghold (predominantly working class) in a year which saw a major swing toward the Republican Party.

National-poll data have consistently shown that youth are more Democratic than older age groups. This was true even in 1952, although Eisenhower carried a much larger proportion of the young vote than had earlier Republican candidates. It has not been clear, however, whether individuals change during their lifetime (switching from the Democratic to the Republican Party as they grow older), whether the ranks of the Democrats in the young age bracket are being swelled through the higher birth-rate in the lower socio-economic status (SES) urban groups and by the arrival at voting age of the children of immigrants, or whether both factors are operating.

If it is true that people change party allegiance in the Republican direction as they grow older, then it should follow that young people, as a group, would be more Democratic than their own parents. To check this, young voters were asked for their own party preferences and their choice of presidential candidates; they were also asked these two items of information about each of their parents.[8] Of course, there were some instances in which the young person had lost contact with a parent or for some other reason did not know his parents' political preferences.

In the results, there was a high agreement between the party choice of the young voter and that of his parents, but the agreement was higher when the parents were Democrats. This would suggest a slight shift on the part of the younger generation as a whole toward the Democratic Party, if there were as many Republican as Democratic parents.

In a Democratic stronghold like Cambridge, there are so many more sets of Democratic than Republican parents, that the small proportion of young people switching from Democratic to Republican Party allegiance more than offsets (numerically) the larger proportion of young people switching from the Republican allegiance of their parents into the Democratic party, so that over the sample as a whole, there were slightly fewer (not significantly) Democratic young people than Democratic parents. On the whole, however, the agreement of young people with the party choice of their parents is high: 74 per cent of those who can report their fathers' party preference prefer the same party, and 76 per cent choose the same party as their mothers'. In 86 per cent of the cases where the parents are both of the same party, son or daughter chooses that party.

Parenthetically, it should be noted that there is no evidence of the traditional "father dominance" in political matters. There are only 21 instances in the sample in which the father and mother disagree on their choices of political party, but when they do, the young person is slightly more likely (not significantly) to follow the mother's preference than the father's. When agreement with parents is studied according to the sex of the child, it appears that while the daughters are most responsive to the influence of the mother, sons are as likely to follow the mother as the father when parents disagree.

While we have seen considerable agreement between political preferences of the first-time voter and those of his parents, there exists a group of young people who choose a different party or a different presidential candidate than their parents, or both. What are the forces which might influence a young person to abandon the political orientation of his parents? The first step in studying this problem was to develop a score which would reflect the extent to which the young person had changed from the political position of his parents. This score is called the Index of Political Change. Six items of information were considered for the score: the respondent's party choice and presidential choice, his mother's party choice and presidential choice, and his father's party choice and presidential choice. Numerical values were assigned to each difference between the young person and either of his parents, and these values were added, so that the highest score on political change would go to the young person who differed with both parents on both candidate and party choice. Differences on party choice were given twice as much weight as differences on candidate choice, on the assumption that party choice is a more pervasive indicator of political position than the preference for any particular candidate. Shifts away from the parents' political preferences were also labeled according to whether they were shifts away from a Democratic position and toward a Republican position, or vice versa.

What factors might produce a change on the part of the young person from the political orientation of his parents? The first hypothesis tested was one related to youthful rebellion. It has been popularly assumed that some young people are radical because they are throwing off the shackles of parental authority in their late adolescence. A reasonable assumption would be that the more rigid the control which the parents attempt to exercise over the teen-aged youth, the more he will feel the impulse to rebel and reject parental values when he is in a position to do so. An attempt was made in the current study to measure the strictness and rigidity of control exercised by the parents over the respondents when they were in their teens and something about the reaction of the young person to his parents' effort at control.

It was found to be the children of the parents who attempt to exercise strictest control who most often change away from the political preference of their parents.

The highest conformity to parental political values was found among the group who were subject to moderate parental control. For the young person who is left rather completely on his own, conformity is less—presumably because his decisions are made more independently of family knowledge or influence. And conformity is also less for the rigidly-controlled group. Thus we see that maximum conformity by the young person to the political values of his family occurs when his parents have been neither laissez faire nor authoritarian in their dealings with him—when they have taken an interest in him and attempted to guide him but have used moderate pressure via persuasion rather than strong pressure by command or force.

Although there are too few cases to make a definitive test, it is interesting that the effects of parental training methods on political conformity seem greatest when the parents have a high level of interest in politics. Presumably, when parents do not consider politics important, their children will choose some other area of values in which to signify their loyalty or register their protest.

Among the strictest families, the change is largely toward being more

Republican than the parents. This is unexpected, since "adolescent revolt" has been presumed to lead to leftward, rather than rightward, movement. It must be noted, however, that the strictest parental control was found at the lower SES levels, where the parents are heavily Democratic in political orientation. If the young person is to adopt a different set of political values than that of his parents, he *must* change toward the Republican party, unless he wants to go into the fringe parties, which very few young people do. (Only one member of our sample voted for the Progressive Party candidate.)

The fact that parental control is stricter in the low SES[9] group raises the question whether the relationship between parental control and political change could be an artifact of SES: that is, possibly both political change and strict control are found mostly at the lower SES levels, in which case of course the relationship between control and change would be difficult to interpret. Analysis shows that political change is slightly more common at the *upper* SES levels, so that this relationship is not an artifact of SES.

It is true, however, that the relationship between the degree of parental control and the frequency of the young people's change away from parental politics is found almost exclusively at the lower SES. That is, among the working-class group, young people changed most from their parents' political positions when parental control was strict and when the young people resented this fact. At the higher SES levels, this tends not to be the case.

It appears, then, that when young people at the lower SES level change away from the political preferences of their parents, the change is at least partly motivated by revolt against over-strict control. At the upper SES level, while there is as much or more change on the part of young people, it is not a function of the atmosphere in the home where they grew up, and other factors must be sought.

What about the depth, or generality, of the change away from parental politics which is engendered in the "revolt" group? Possibly, these young people simply give themselves a different party label from their parents, or choose a different presidential candidate, without changing any of the ideology which one would ordinarily expect to underlie political preferences. Possibly, on the other hand, the spirit of revolt goes much deeper and takes the form of a basic shift in ideology (toward the right or left) which is then reflected in vote and party choice. Unfortunately, the study provided no measure of the ideology of the young voter's parents. The young voter himself, however, was asked three questions adapted from Centers' ideology questions,[10] and it is possible to compare the "revolt" group with the "non-revolt" group at a given SES level in their ideology.

There is a shift in the conservative direction among the young people who resent parental control and who were shown earlier to be changing away from the party preference of their parents (changing largely in the direction of becoming more Republican). Two other ideology questions, one on public versus private ownership of power facilities and one on security versus individual initiative, both showed shifts in the same direction on the part of the "revolt" group, although the shifts were somewhat smaller. It appears likely, then, that shifts away from parental political preferences on the part of young people who resent parental control are accompanied by (or perhaps preceded by) some changes in general politico-social attitudes.

We have been examining parental influence on voting. What about the influence of the young person's peers: friends, fellow-workers, and spouse? It was shown that the young voter agrees on choice of party most highly with his spouse, next most highly with his friends, and least often with his fellow-workers.

Seventy-seven per cent of the married young voters had the same party preference as their spouses; 64 per cent had the same party preference as the majority of their friends, and 46 per cent of those who worked agreed in party choice with the majority of their fellow-workers. In a heavily Democratic area like Cambridge, Republican young people cannot or do not surround themselves as easily with like-minded friends and fellow-workers as do the Democrats, or else, possibly the young Republicans tend to assume that the people around them are Democrats unless they have positive knowledge to the contrary.

Of course, the amount of agreement on party choice does not tell anything about the extent and direction of influence. Possibly, the higher agreement with friends than fellow-workers means that people have more freedom of choice as to friends than fellow-workers and that they tend to choose like-minded friends. Another possibility is that friends exert more influence upon each other—change one another's minds about politics more—than do members of work groups.

In an effort to trace lines of influence, the young voter was asked how much he talked about politics with his friends, fellow-workers, and spouse. The amount of political discussion was fairly high with friends and spouse, lower with fellow-workers, where we have seen that there is less agreement on party preference. When we relate the amount of discussion to the amount of agreement on politics, we find that people who prefer the same party as their fellow-workers tend to talk politics with them quite a bit, while those who have a political position different from their fellow-workers' less often engage in political discussion at work. The opposite situation tends to hold true within the home of young married couples: when they disagree on politics, they discuss them extensively, while with agreement, politics become a less central subject of discussion. Among friends discussion is as common when they are of a different party as when they are of the same party.

The findings on political discussion are interesting when viewed from the standpoint of group dynamics. A hypothesis among students of group dynamics[11] is that when a group is highly cohesive and a topic is central to the attainment of group goals, disagreement will produce discussion and mutual influence. If a group is not cohesive, and/or the topic is not central to its goals, disagreement will cut off discussion of the topic or lead people to leave the group. Among the peer groups studied here it is reasonable to assume that the husband-wife team is the most cohesive, the group of friends the next most cohesive, and the work group the least cohesive in terms of the strength of the individual's desire for the approval of the group. The centrality of politics as a topic relevant to the functioning of the group is difficult to assess for these three groups, but we might expect that politics is least relevant to the work group, which has presumably been brought together for other reasons than agreement on politics, while friendships and marriage ties are presumably formed at least partly because of like-mindedness on a number of issues. Of course, if one views political alignment as an expression of membership in an economic interest group, one's political position *could* be viewed as central to the functions of his work group. In any case, our data suggest that the husband-wife team is a cohesive group and that political agreement is important to the smooth functioning of the group, so that disagreement produces discussion and mutual influence. On the other hand, the work group is either not cohesive or political views are irrelevant to the functions of the group, for disagreement on political matters cuts down discussion and thus prevents the work group from being a potent source of political influence. The friendship group occupies a position mid-way between the spouse and the work group in the extent of its probable influence in political matters.

We have seen that the young voter less often agrees with his friends on politics than he does with his parents. It is interesting, however, that the friends appear to exert more influence if the young person is resentful of parental control.

While the number of cases is small, there is evidence of interaction between home atmosphere and the influence of friends: once the psychological ground work for change is laid in over-strict home control, the young person becomes more responsive to the political orientation of his friends in his choice of party and candidate.

A factor which might produce change away from the political orientation of the young voter's parents is social mobility. Presumably, if the young person moves up or down the socio-economic scale, he begins to take on the values of the group into which he has moved. The upwardly-mobile young people (those having higher-level jobs than their fathers) can be compared with the "charter members" of the class into which they move and with the nonmobile people in the classes from which they came.[12] The question to be answered by the data in this: Are mobile young people politically more like the group from which they came or the group into which they have moved?

An important fact discovered is that the mobile young people seldom consider themselves independents: they seem to make a definite party choice more often than nonmobile people. But apart from this, the upwardly-mobile people are more Republican than the class from which they came and are similar to the class into which they have moved. Similarly, when it comes to candidate choice, the upwardly-mobile group has adopted the behavior of its destination group: in fact, they chose Eisenhower more often than their peers and considerably more often than their group of origin.

The downwardly-mobile group, on the other hand, presents quite a different picture. These people do not adapt themselves to the political preferences of their new social milieu; they are more like the class from which they originate than the class into which they move. In fact, if anything, they are more Republican than their class of origin. It appears, then, that those who move up the social scale seek to identify themselves with the political values of the higher group, but those who move down cling to the symbols of their former status. It should be noted that those in the downwardly-mobile group still have a chance of reaching the status from which they came: a young person of 21–24 years of age who has a poorer job than his father may yet achieve as good a job in later years. However, the young person who has already obtained a better job than his father is likely to remain at a higher status.

How deep do the changes of political orientation go among mobile young people? The study included only three questions on ideology, and therefore only an initial exploration of this question is possible; but analysis of the answers to these questions shows that the increasing Republicanism of the upwardly-mobile young people is by no means always accompanied by what might be considered appropriate ideological changes. For example, when asked where their sympathies usually lie in a strike, 73 per cent of the upwardly-mobile young people say they side with the workers, as compared with 71 per cent in the class where they originated and only 49 per cent in the class they have moved into. On the other hand, they are somewhat more likely than their class of origin (not quite significantly) to favor individual initiative instead of government-backed security. Downwardly-mobile young people, on the other hand, even though they do not take on the party labels and voting preferences of the lower group into which they move, do take on some of the ideology of this lower group: 69 per cent of downward mobiles side with the workers in a strike, as compared with 68 per cent of the group into which they have moved and 43 per cent of the group from which they have come. Downwardly-mobile young people are also considerably more in favor of government ownership of large power facilities and slightly more security-minded than the class from which they came.

Lubell has assumed that most of the children of foreign-born parents, as they move up the economic scale, will take their Democratic party orientation with them. We see that while a good many of them become Republicans, they retain some of the ideology which might predispose them to return to the Democratic party. That is, their new party choice could be considered unstable at this age level, since it is not grounded in the system of beliefs most compatible with it, and either the party preference or the ideology should be subject to change on the basis of future events. Similarly, the downwardly-mobile young people, while not currently changing their party and vote, are undergoing ideological changes which might predispose them to later shifts. A longitudinal study would be of the greatest value for following out the threads of change with mobility, as would a study conducted in a year when the general political swing was toward the Democrats instead of toward the Republicans.

We have seen that at the lower SES levels political change is related to resentment of family authority, but that at the upper SES levels this is not the case. Yet there is as much or more change away from parents' political positions among the upper SES young people. What might be some of the sources of change in this group? One possible source is the better education of the high SES group.

Of the college graduates in the sample, 58 per cent changed to some degree from the political position of their parents, while only 28 per cent of those who did not graduate from high school did so. Even when socioeconomic status is held constant, this relationship holds: at each class level, the better-educated young people change more.

The direction of the changes which occur with education are of some interest. At the lower education levels, the direction is clearly toward the Republicans, while among the college group more young people shift in the Democratic than the Republican direction. Of course, college students tend to come from the upper-income brackets, from parents of predominantly Republican preferences, and so if they change, it must be in the Democratic direction. But it must be borne in mind that the college-educated young people include not only those from upper SES families, but also include a sizeable group of upwardly-mobile young people from lower SES families. These upwardly-mobile young people, as we have seen earlier, tend to change in the Republican direction. It is therefore especially striking that there is as much shift in the Democratic direction (especially in a predominantly Republican year) as occurs among the college group. Is there a general tendency for college education to move people to the left politically? Previous findings on this point have not been conclusive. Newcomb's Bennington study showed students becoming more "liberal" during their years at college, but this study was done during the depression years.[13] Havemann and West, on the other hand, found that the people who had been out of college longest were the most heavily Republican.[14] Possibly, college exercises a temporary pro-Democratic influence, with graduates returning to the Republican fold as they grow older. It must be remembered, however, that the group studied by Havemann and West who had been out of college longest had been in college during conservative times. The people more recently out of college had gone through their intellectually formative years during depression and "New Deal" or "Fair Deal" years. The difference between the two groups may be due, therefore, to entirely different factors than age itself.

The data from the present study do not shed much light on the problem of change in college versus after college. It is true that much of the pro-Democratic shifts in our college group occur among young people who are still in college.[15] But those who remain in college are largely people who have chosen professional careers which require graduate work, and those who leave after a B.A. degree are largely those who choose to go into business. The greater Republican leanings of the latter group, then, need not reflect a growing conservatism after leaving college, but may reflect a difference in political viewpoints which exists throughout college between business-oriented and professionally-oriented students.

Regardless of the direction of change, college education is associated with change away from parental politics. How does education function to bring about political change? Presumably, in the course of obtaining an education, the young person is exposed to a wider variety of points of view and more information, so that he is able to make political choices on the basis of "rational" considerations, rather than simply on the basis of family tradition (or revolt against family tradition). If education actually functions this way, political change among the well educated should be accompanied by appropriate changes in ideology, while for the lesser educated, the relationship of ideology to change should not be so close. Examination of the replies to the limited number of ideology questions in this survey shows this is the case: among the college group, those who changed in the Republican direction are considerably more conservative on the items measured than those who remained Democrats, and those who changed in the Democratic direction are more liberal than those who remained Republicans. Among the groups with lesser education, the differences are by no means so clear: political change does not seem to be so consistently a function of ideology. Of course, we must not overlook the possibility that college-educated people rationalize their ideologies *after* changing their party preferences, out of a need for consistency which is more compelling for them than for people of lesser education.

In this survey, therefore, the following findings emerged:

1. Agreement on candidate and party choice is highest between the young person and his family (parents and spouse), next highest with his friends, and least high with his fellow-workers. Findings on the amount of discussion of politics between the young person and each of these groups suggest that fellow-workers are not very influential in the formation of the young person's political opinions, while parents and spouse are of great importance.

2. Among the lower socio-economic groups, rejection of parental political values is associated with strict discipline in the home. The highest conformity to parents' politics occurs in the homes where the parents exercise moderate control over the young people—being neither authoritarian nor completely laissez faire.

3. Young people who are socially upwardly-mobile tend to adopt the political behavior of the group into which they have moved, becoming more Republican. Downwardly-mobile young people, on the other hand, are *not* similar to their new social milieu in their choice of candidate and party; rather, they remain as Republican, or more so, than the class from which they came.

4. The voting and party choice of mobile young people is not generally accompanied by appropriate ideology. The upwardly-mobile young people, while voting like their new social group, retain a good part of the ideology of the group from which they came. Downwardly-mobile young people take on some of the ideology of their new social class, while retaining the voting patterns of the group where they originated.

5. Young people who are well educated change away from the political orientation of their parents more often than poorly-educated young people. Among the better-educated, political change tends to be accompanied by appropriate changes in ideology, while for the poorly-educated, this is less often the case: in this group, political change appears to have a less "rational" basis.

16 Political Issues and Husband-Wife Interaction

JAMES G. MARCH

Dr. March has carried out an experimental investigation of husband-wife interaction over various types of political issues. He finds, as predicted, that husbands and wives tend to specialize in different areas of politics. In the context of this section, we should like to go one step further and suggest that this specialization within the family means that husbands and wives contribute differently to the political realm of the wider society.

The importance of the family-oriented behavior for the study of political attitudes and political action has been conceded by most students of politics at least since the time of Plato. This report describes a technique designed to examine some aspects of the decision-making balance of power within a married couple as it is revealed in the discussion of different questions of public policy.

In thinking about the family as a political institution, one needs to avoid both the over- and the under-estimation of its uniqueness. Since it conforms to a general definition of a group as a relatively stable pattern of interaction among a number of individual actors who exhibit reciprocal feelings of solidarity, the family can be conceived to be one species of the genus group, sharing with a variety of other patterns of interaction the broad characteristics of a social system.[1] At the same time, the cultural importance, intimate nature, and dyadic character of the family clearly differentiate it from other systems with which it is comparable on the generic level of abstraction.

From the point of view of political attitudes, the power system within the family, as within other groups, is definable in terms of a number of dimensions. Most obvious among these is the dimension utilized in the usual description of a power relationship—the disparity of power between the interacting individuals. Such a characterization of a relationship, however, may be inadequate unless it is related to the range of situations involved.[2] In situation S, A has X influence over B with regard to policy P. In order to describe the power relationship between A and B, we need to define not only X but also S and P.

Reprinted from *Public Opinion Quarterly*, XVII, No. 4 (1953), 461–70, where it appeared under the title, "Husband-wife Interaction over Political Issues," with the kind permission of the author and publishers.

The experimental technique described below is designed to facilitate the measurement of influence (X) given the twelve different combinations of four types of situation (S) and three policy areas (P). It was hypothesized that the influence pattern between a husband and wife would vary from situation-to-situation and from policy-to-policy and that the general character of the variability was predictable from our understanding of the family as a relatively stable system of interaction, that system being of considerable importance both to the individuals performing roles within the family and to the culture within which the family functions.

These hypotheses were generated from a consideration of (a) the reasons for specialization in co-operative groups, (b) the continuing importance of the family for individual behavior, (c) the probable low importance of public policy as a focus of family attention and involvement, and (d) the sex-typing of political responsibilities in contemporary American culture.

In the hypothesis of differential influence from one policy area to another, it is suggested that if both husband and wife have mobilized political interests, they will tend to specialize in attitudinal competences in their relations with each other.

The reasons for such specialization in the family are considered to be the same as the reasons for specialization in any group. Specialization in co-operative groups can be conceived to have three major sets of consequences:

1. Those relating to the goals in terms of which the group is organized. In general, the maximization of goal-achievement is attained through the division of labor and specialization.[3]
2. Those relating to the individual personality systems that are linked together by the group. Within limits, it seems probable that specialization may increase both the independence and the sense of indispensibility of the individual. To the extent that it has this consequence, it is ego-constructive.[4]
3. Those relating to the interaction pattern of the group itself. Specialization, by reducing the area of joint activity, would appear to reduce at the same time the possibility of conflict within the group.[5]

If we accept these as some of the major consequences of specialization within groups, it seems reasonable to predict a tendency toward specialization within the family. As an intimate group within which each spouse needs to achieve a position of relative status and in which disagreement must be curtailed, the family represents a realm of interpersonal relations in which the avoidance of conflict has maximum advantages.

Moreover, politics and political attitudes are areas of intrafamily interaction in which a division of labor is particularly appropriate. From the point of view of the family, these are generally marginal areas—scarcely important enough to organize in such a way as to offer a potential threat to internal harmony.

Traditionally, the division of labor utilized within the American family has allocated political matters to the husband. In addition, it seems probable that this continues to be the pattern within substantial elements of American society today. In the last hundred years, however, the ideology of political equality between the sexes has been accepted by significant numbers of both men and women, has gradually been formulated into the legal code of the country,[6] and, there is reason to believe, has altered the form of specialization within the family, particularly among urban, middle-class, college-educated families. With the transference of politics from the exclusive domain of the husband to the joint concern of both husband and wife, sub-specialization may occur.

Sub-specialization following any set of subject divisions would meet the requirements of the family as a functioning system, but since the family exists within a culture in which there have been, and are, certain expectations about female political activity, those areas in which a wife's influence tend to be greatest were expected to correspond to those areas in which female participation has had the longest history of legitimacy.

For the purposes of the present experiment, three policy areas were considered: (1) foreign affairs, (2) labor affairs, and (3) local affairs. In general, an ordering of these three areas of political discussion according to the criterion of "history of legitimacy" would take form:

1. Local affairs
2. Foreign affairs
3. Labor affairs

The prediction, therefore, was that among these three the wife would tend to be most influential in dealing with local affairs and least influential in dealing with labor affairs.

This ranking of influence according to policy areas was understood to represent a cultural norm, forming an equilibrium point for the on-going influence system within the family. At a given point in time, however, the influence relationship between husband and wife might, for a number of reasons, vary from this point of equilibrium. In particular, it was predicted that, in any policy area, if either spouse involved his, or her, ego by making a prior commitment on a particular question, he (or she) would tend to expand his participation in the discussion of that question within the family. This prediction was deduced both from the importance of avoiding conflict within the family and from the marginality of politics for the family.

These general predictions with regard to differential influence were translated into the experimental predictions indicated below. The experimental technique utilized the three areas of public policy listed above as prototypes of the variable P (policy) and four different commitment situations as prototypes of the variable S (situation). It was designed to permit the examination of the differences in X (one spouse's influence over the other) under twelve different combinations of P and S.

In view of the theoretical formulations indicated above, it was necessary to construct a technique which would permit the examination of intrafamily influence under a variety of circumstances. Since it seemed desirable to limit this preliminary investigation to families in which the wife's interest in public affairs was relatively great, the present study was restricted to a markedly atypical universe—couples in which the wife was a member of the League of Women Voters in an eastern suburban town. A random sample was drawn from that universe. Each experimental session took place in the home of the participant involved, requiring a maximum of about two hours and an average of about ninety minutes.

The procedures used represent a variation of the "revealed differences" technique developed by Fred L. Strodtbeck.[7] Twelve problems of public policy were presented to each couple. Of these twelve problems, four were concerned with labor policy, four with foreign policy, and four with local policy. A sample problem is given below:

> Recently there has been speculation about the course of action the United States will pursue toward communist China. Many people appear to have strong ideas on this subject.
> a. Some people say that we are stalemated in our relations with China, that economic measures are ineffective against that country, and that we ought to institute limited military attacks on the China mainland.
> b. Some people say that it is relatively pointless to talk about "China policy" since the problem lies in Moscow rather than in China.
> c. Some people say that we ought to recognize a lost battle when we see one and abandon any hope of stopping communist expansion in Asia.
> d. Some people say that we can seize the initiative against China without risking war if we limit ourselves to economic sanctions. They urge this course of action.
> e. Some people say that since we have stopped communist expansion in Asia without a general war, we ought not to risk war by pressing any sort of economic or military offensive against China.
> Which one of the positions above comes closest to representing your position?

After the procedure of the study had been explained in general terms, the wife and the husband were each given six of the problems. Each was asked to consider the problems given to him without discussing them with his spouse and to indicate a decision on them. The problems thus submitted to the individuals were selected in such a way that *both* husband and wife recorded an individual decision on three of the problems, the *wife only* recorded an individual decision on three of the problems, the *husband only* recorded an individual decision on three of the problems, and *neither* husband nor wife recorded an individual decision on three of the problems.

The questions were so distributed among the four different commitment situations (i.e., both, husband, wife, neither) and the three subject areas (i.e., labor, local, foreign) that each of the twelve problems represented a unique combination of factors.

After both had made their individual decisions, the husband and wife were asked to discuss each of the twelve problems with each other and to arrive at a *joint decision* for each. The couple was alone during this discussion, their remarks being recorded mechanically. The order in which the problems were discussed was determined by standard randomization procedures and was systematically varied from couple-to-couple.

Earlier in this paper a general hypothesis of the probable difference in influence patterns expected in different policy areas and under different commitment situations was indicated. In general, it was predicted that, in a husband-wife discussion, the husband's influence would be greatest on labor-policy questions, least on local-policy questions; greatest where he alone was committed in advance, least where his wife alone was committed in advance.

To test these predictions, it was necessary to establish a feasible connection between the concept of influence and some measurable characteristic of group interaction. It was expected that in the stable, two-person situation represented by a married couple the participation differences between individuals would tend to be minimized. Neither person could, for long, abstain from the conversation. Consequently, even extremes in influence might be reflected by only moderate disproportion in discussion participation. Nevertheless, there was reason to believe that the complexities of interpersonal relations within this group could be tapped by focusing attention on some crucial types of remarks. Studies by Strodtbeck have indicated that leadership within a married couple is usually characterized by high level participation and a distinctive excess of opinion-giving and orientation-giving remarks.[8] These studies provided reasonable basis for believing that the more influential one spouse was, the more likely he would be to provide information or clarification, to define the situation, to evaluate and analyze the question, to give direction, and to express his own opinion. In short, the operational nexus between the influence variable and the discussion situation lay in the hypothesis of a positive relationship between underlying influence and the expression of opinion-giving and orientation-giving remarks.[9] The proportion of instrumental-adaptive answers directed by the husband to the wife, one would expect, would tend to be ranked (a) in decreasing order by policy area as follows: Labor > Foreign > Local; and (b) in decreasing order by commitment situation as follows: Husband > Both-Neither > Wife.

In all, the co-operation of nine couples was secured, but a recording failure in one case reduced the working sample for most purposes to eight couples. The recorded remarks of each couple were analyzed according to Bales's interaction process analysis categories.[10] In general, the basic unit in the Bales recording technique is a simple declarative sentence, although a laugh or an extended pause may be scored.[11] Bales's twelve categories are indicated below:

A. Positive Expressive-Integrative Acts
   (1) *Shows solidarity,* raises other's status, gives help, reward
   (2) *Shows tension release,* jokes, laughs, shows satisfaction
   (3) *Agrees,* shows passive acceptance, understands, concurs, complies
B. Instrumental-Adaptive Answers
   (4) *Gives suggestion,* direction, implying autonomy for other
   (5) *Gives opinion,* evaluation, analysis, expresses feeling, wish
   (6) *Gives orientation,* information, repeats, clarifies, confirms
C. Instrumental-Adaptive Questions
   (7) *Asks for orientation,* information, repetition, confirmation
   (8) *Asks for opinion,* evaluation, analysis, expression of feeling
   (9) *Asks for suggestion,* direction, possible ways of action
D. Negative Expressive-Integrative Acts
   (10) *Disagrees,* shows passive rejection, formality, withholds help
   (11) *Shows tension,* asks for help, withdraws out of field
   (12) *Shows antagonism,* deflates other's status, defends or asserts self

The primary interest here was in the Instrumental-Adaptive Answers (categories 4, 5, and 6). In total, the eight couples were scored as having made 3546 acts in these categories, 55 per cent of those being initiated by the husbands.

There was no discernible tendency for the husband's contribution to vary consistently from one commitment situation to another. Consequently, no support was found for the prediction of differential influence according to commitment situation. Future experiments with this general technique could well be altered, therefore, either to eliminate this type of variable or to undertake to accentuate the ego involvement in a commitment. The latter procedure might properly be considered a precondition to the former.

On the other hand, the consistency with which the husband's proportion of opinion-giving and orientation-giving remarks was highest on labor questions and lowest on local questions was striking. It will be recalled that the prediction made was that the rank order would be: 1- Labor; 2- Foreign; 3- Local. The results offer significant support for the prediction at the .01 level of significance.[12]

In addition, each of the eighteen[13] individuals involved in the study was asked to examine a list of eight different areas of public policy that might be considered by "a group such as the League of Women Voters." Each was asked to list the three "most appropriate for discussion within the League of Women Voters of ————————" and the three "least appropriate." Seven of the nine wives and eight of the nine husbands placed questions of local government on the "most appropriate" list. Eight of the wives and all nine of the husbands listed labor policy as one of the "least appropriate."

The rank correlation coefficient between the rankings made by the husbands and those made by the wives is significant at the .01 level of significance.[14] Assuming that the procedure solicited an articulation of a latent conception of the appropriate sex-typing of political affairs, it offers persuasive confirmation of the conclusions to be drawn from the variation in the husband-wife contribution to the "problem-solving" remarks during their interaction over the experimental questions.

These data would seem to indicate that within the social and cultural groups represented by this sample, the sharing of political power between a husband and wife tends to result in a form of specialization in which each spouse has more or less clearly defined areas of competence.[15] Occasionally, this type of subject-matter specialization was explicitly acknowledged during the experimental session. More frequently, the differential characteristics of the sharing of power either were not formally introduced into the discussion or were explicitly denied. One would suspect that the tendency to ignore or deny the implications of the consistent variation in the expression of opinion-giving and orientation-giving remarks, whether or not the proximate factor was a failure to perceive the actual existence of the variation, stemmed ultimately from a conflict of the influence pattern with some common formulations of feminist and democratic ideology.

If such a pattern is present in other local League of Women Voters organizations, it may offer at least a partial explanation of the apparent contradiction between the picture of the League (common in League councils) as a forum for discussing and acting on important questions of public policy and the picture of the League (common in non-League circles) as an organization through which excess female energy is directed into harmless channels.

In any event, insofar as these data illuminate the political system of the family, they also have implications for political behavior on a wider scale. From the point of view of the individual, the family is one of several reference groups in terms of which the situation is habitually defined for political action. If the present thesis of intrafamily specialization is correct, the extent to which competing reference groups will be able to influence the behavior of either spouse in a family such as those studied here will depend in part on the subject-matter under consideration.

17   *Divorce Law as Social Control*

EUGENE LITWAK

Laws may be thought of as the embodiment of the directions in which a society would like to lead its members and the means adopted for so doing. In his discussion of divorce law, Professor Litwak brings out that law does indeed operate in this "leadership," or direction-giving fashion. Litwak carries the argument further to show that law makes its force felt in various ways.

This paper will address itself to the problem of law as a means of social control. More specifically the question is: to what extent can divorce law be used to prevent de facto family breakup, i.e., the situation where marital partners are separated formally or informally. This paper will not concern itself with an equally relevant problem: is breakup good or bad?

If law is to act on human behavior, it should provide an environment which will enable the deviant or potential deviant to internalize the values embodied in the law or it should provide an environment which will force the deviant to conform by systematically placing blocks in his achievement of his deviant values, whenever he violates the law.

In searching for environments, both social and psychological, which lead to breakup one is confronted by an impressive number of items which have been related to breakup.[1] Though the list is long it is thought that all of these factors actually act upon the family members in one of four ways. These have been called de facto breakup by conflict, de facto breakup by indifference, de facto breakup by opportunity, and continuance by fiat.

Breakup by conflict can be exemplified by the case in which the husband was raised with the value of leisure as paramount and the wife with the value of status. The wife might view the husband as a shiftless time-waster while the husband might view the wife as a vain status-striver. Other things being equal, this will lead to a higher probability of breakup.

Breakup by indifference has been most thoroughly discussed in connection with Ogburn's theory[2] that the family is losing its functions. The less the husband and wife depend on each other the greater are their chances of splitting up.

Breakup by opportunity refers to the number of contacts between

Reprinted from *Social Forces*, XXIV (March, 1956), 217–23, where it appeared under the title, "Three Ways in which Law Acts as a Means of Social Control: Punishment, Therapy, and Education: Divorce Law a Case in Point," with the kind permission of the author and Williams and Wilkins Co., the publishers.

members of the opposite sex. Thus, where the husband's job throws him into contact with women (e.g., traveling salesman), where husband and wife are separated (e.g., during wars, etc.) a high probability exists for one of the spouses to meet other potential spouses. Other things being equal, this is likely to lead to breakup.

The fourth mode is that which is called continuance by fiat. It refers to the fact that a high value is placed on marriage per se. In our society the Catholic considers marriage a sacrament and therefore places a great value on marriage per se, and, other things being equal, the very religious Catholic would be less likely to divorce.

These four modes are thought to encompass all of the factors which relate to family breakup. At the same time they are sufficiently different so that the same law might have entirely different effects depending on

Figure 1. Ways in Which Types of Law Affect Different Kinds of Family Breakup

TYPES OF BREAKUP	TYPES OF LAW		
	Law as punishment	Law as therapy	Law as education
Breakup by Conflict	Penalties are so great that people have an incentive to reconcile their conflict.	Allows fundamental conflicts to breakup; other conflicts are settled through the process of therapy.	Seeks to develop personal abilities so that individuals can deal with conflicts or will be less likely to marry people who conflict with them.
Breakup by Indifference	Forces one spouse to depend on the other as a condition of breakup; forces the guilty spouse to depend on the innocent for seeing the child.	Attempts to point out areas of mutual need.	Attempts to develop the ability to share oneself with others without fear of losing one's identity.
Breakup by Opportunity	Provides penalties if the guilty party remarries; forces the guilty party to wait before remarriage.	Does nothing.	Does nothing.
Breakdown of Fiat	Does nothing except insofar as publicity of punishment increases the strength in which a value is held.	Does nothing except point up value of marriage per se if the client holds it.	In the hands of a social system which holds the value of marriage per se it inculcates this value.

which of these four modes characterizes the family. Laws will be analyzed as mechanisms of social control in terms of their ability to affect these four modes of marriage breakup and stability.

Three types of law will be discussed: that which we have called law as punishment, law as therapy, and law as education.

Law as Punishment

Punishment is defined in this paper as the deliberate and public blocking of the deviant's ability to achieve his goals if he violates those embodied in the law. The law as punishment might act in three ways. It might deter the deviant by threatening the values he holds dear; it might act as a learning device and force the deviant to internalize the values of the law; and it might serve through the publicity of punishment to reinforce the values of the non-deviants. The law as punishment, by definition, stresses the first but it also affects the others.[3]

Historically the idea that divorce is a punishment seems to rest on the general Christian doctrine that marriage is a good per se, which can be broken only by a sinner.[4] Today the idea of divorce as a punishment for guilty parties is maintained in the divorce law of some states. This is exemplified by laws which say that the amount of alimony should be based on the extent of guilt,[5] that the disposition of the children should be decided on the basis of who is innocent,[6] that the guilty party should not be able to remarry for given periods of time (sometimes for life),[7] and by forcing the prosecution of the guilty party in a criminal action rather than in a civil action.[8]

What are the possible limitations of the law as punishment for affecting family breakup? Six possible situations will be discussed. These are as follows:

1. The punishments established by the law cannot reach basic values of the deviant.
2. Where the society has conflicting values the innocent as well as the guilty suffer by punishment.
3. Where there is a deviant group rather than a deviant individual, punishment might lead to a martyr effect and boomerang, causing further deviation.
4. Under certain value systems punishment is by definition not apropos, which leads to the refusal of the innocent party through collusion, perjury, etc., to press the punishment.
5. The simple learning theory implied is not sufficient to bring about changes in values of the deviant.
6. The punishment law will not act as a deterrent where the deviant feels there is little chance of getting caught no matter how efficient the law might actually be.

The law as punishment might fail where it is unable to provide sufficiently serious blocks to the deviant's values. This point is quite easily seen in political deviation and has been virtually sloganized by Patrick Henry's famous "Give me liberty or give me death." Insofar as the maximum block the law could bring was death and insofar as liberty was a greater value than life to Patrick Henry, the law as punishment would have been ineffectual in deterring him from initiating deviant behavior. In the field of divorce, the law fails to act as a means for preventing breakup insofar as people feel that they would prefer the penalties of paying a little more alimony, waiting a longer time to remarry or even having their children taken away from them than live in a marriage which violates their values of love, companionship, and freedom of choice.

A second interrelated point and one reason why the law cannot find blocks to deviant values is that, ideally, punishment should only be directed at the deviant and never at the non-deviant if it is to achieve social control. However, where individuals have conflicting values, punishment of the criminals many times rebounds on the innocent as well. For instance, the criminal who is thrown in jail has to be supported out of funds which the conforming member would like to use for such things as better schools, leisure time activities, health, etc. In this sense, the punishment of the criminal is also felt as a punishment by the conformist.

In our society, the value that marriage is a good per se has gone together with such values as marital chastity, good treatment of children, preservation of health, etc. Where there is a clash in these values, the cost of maintaining the value that marriage is a good per se is (after a certain point) greater than the rewards of maintaining the value. For instance, should the husband be a drunkard who cannot make a living, then any divorce law which seeks through punishment to keep the marriage together will uphold the value of marriage as a good per se but it will also result in violations of other values. It not only punishes the husband but might also punish the innocent wife. It forces her to live in poverty or in danger of her life, etc. Insofar as the law as punishment punishes the innocent (conformist) as well as the guilty (nonconformist), it will not be effective as a means of social control.

Another factor which enters into the consideration of the effectiveness of punishment is the extent to which the deviant is an isolate or a member of a deviant group. In a society such as ours which is made up of groups having some overlapping values and some conflicting values the concept of the deviant group is quite apropos. For instance, the Catholic Church is at odds with most of the populace on the question of divorce, yet in other matters such as foreign policy, interracial freedom, etc., it might be in complete harmony.[9] In some states, Catholics are a deviant group as far as marriage values are concerned, and in others they are non-deviant group.

Where deviant groups rather than individuals are being considered, the mechanism of control which Durkheim and Mead[10] refer to might work in reverse. They point out that publicity of punishment provides an opportunity for the conforming members of the society to reaffirm their values publicly. This public confirmation in turn leads to greater reaffirmation of these same values. However, where there is a deviant group, a member of which is punished publicly, it is recognized, particularly in political deviation, that such public punishment leads to the martyr effect. In short, it provides an opportunity for the deviant group as well as the conformist to affirm their values publicly. The public punishment boomerangs. It promotes greater cohesion within the deviant group and, thus, a breakdown of social control.

It is possible that the public punishment administered in divorce cases might lead to reaffirmation of marriage as a good per se. Lichtenberger points out that, at the turn of the century, concentrated attention on the rising rate of divorce led to changes in the law which made them even more stringent. This would seem to fit the Mead-Durkheim thesis. Yet a more common-sensical assertion, which seems to fit our social situation more completely, is that the more people heard about divorce, the more people got divorced, the more they accepted divorce as legitimate. This is especially true where the divorces come from the power groups of the society.[11]

Still another factor is interrelated to the above. The idea that divorce is punishment for the guilty rests to a great extent on the notion that marriage is a sacrament and therefore a good per se. However, if marriage is considered as based primarily on love, companionship, and freedom of choice, and only secondarily on being a good per se, punishment becomes literally a meaningless concept to the married couple. Thus, a wife who might not want her husband to leave but feels he has a moral right to, might not want to take advantage of the law as punishment to demand the maximum alimony she can get; she might permit the husband to visit the children, even though he has no right to under the law, etc. Where the person who is defined by the law to be the innocent party refuses to recognize punishment as a legitimate mode of orientation in marital separation, then punishment loses all threat to the guilty spouse. Also, under these circumstances, as pointed out by many lawyers, the rules of litigation, condemnation, and collusion actually serve to prevent reconciliation and reduce the effect of law as a means of social control.[12]

Another factor which mitigates against punishment as a means of control is where the violation is due to a personality element which is a consequence of long and constant social interaction. In such a situation the simple conditioning theory of change which law as punishment implies would not be enough to affect the behavior of the deviant. Rather, constant punishment would be required in much the same manner and with as much energy as the Chinese displayed in their treatment of American prisoners to get them to change their basic orientations. Thus the ability of a man to control his temper will not be increased by a threat of paying alimony to his wife.

Somewhat in the same vein is the assertion that it is not always possible for the "guilty" person to correctly assess the possibility of getting punished. He is quite willing to do something which might bring about punishment if he *feels* that the chances of being punished are small or that the punishment is not severe. The fact that he will have to pay alimony without having any of the privileges of marriage will not act as a preventive if the husband cannot visualize prior to his decision the consequence to his standard of living, being without his children, etc.

Despite the various limitations mentioned above about the possible utility of punishment as a means of social control, it is not the intention to say it cannot act as such. There are too many cases, such as the agrarian laws of Russia, our own tax laws, etc., where the law can and does act as a means of social control. If the situation is crucial there is no reason why some of the limitations mentioned above might not be altered by society. Even the data of Lichtenberger indicate the effectiveness of laws which are extremely severe.

The divorce laws strive to achieve control through reduction of the four modes of breakup: breakup by conflict, breakup by indifference, breakup by opportunity, and breakdown of marital fiat.

The law of punishment only indirectly faces the problem of breakup by conflict. If the married couple realizes that it is very difficult to get a divorce and that they must stay together, then they will attempt much harder to reconcile their conflicts. In this sense, the law promotes a harmony of values.[13]

The law of punishment controls breakup by indifference in several ways. It basically tries to link several values to the marriage relationship. For instance, it might make the guilty spouse completely dependent on the innocent one for the privilege of being with his children.

The law as punishment seeks to control breakup by opportunity directly by refusing the guilty party the right to remarry.[14] This reduces his opportunity of finding another spouse. The law as punishment will prevent the breakdown of marital fiat only in the sense that the Meadian theory would hold—that public punishment serves to strengthen the values of society and where society places a value on marriage per se.

Law as Therapy[15]

A basic premise of law as therapy is that people seek divorce because of serious emotional problems. Therefore, any legal procedure seeking to control divorce should provide that the spouses see a therapist. What are the advantages and disadvantages of the law as therapy? In the previous section, we have outlined six conditions which if present might lead to ineffectiveness of the law as punishment. Therapy by definition avoids several of the conditions which make law as punishment ineffective. It does not worry about finding blocks for deviant values, since it focuses on internalization of societal values. It reduces by definition the problem of trying to treat interpersonal relationships in terms of guilt and punishment when it has no such meaning to the participants. By taking the marital dispute out of the public court and putting it into the private chambers of the therapist, it reduces both the boomerang character of the martyr effect as well as the re-enforcing effect on social values suggested by Mead *et al.* It very definitely attempts to meet the objections of trying to bring about change in the deviant's basic pattern by use of a simplicistic psychological theory.

The major contribution of the law as therapy is that it brings to bear upon the deviant a more focused kind of pressure for internalizing the values of society. It provides a highly trained social worker to replace the former personality expert—the judge. And presumably it brings along more effective psychological techniques roughly called therapy. It presumably affects breakup by indifference and by conflict directly. It does this by clarifying the source of conflict and ways of evading further conflict, and by developing the personality of the individuals so that they can share emotionally with each other. This is especially important in view of the fact that affection is, according to some schools of thought, the major bond holding the western industrialized family together.

The second major area of contribution by therapy is that it assumes that marriage is primarily based on the values of love, companionship, and freedom of choice, and only secondarily based on the notion that it is a good per se. Operationally, this means that conciliation—and if that fails, arbitration—are the techniques used rather than litigation. People can meet together and talk out their differences without fear of collusion or need for perjury.

In the hands of a religiously oriented therapist, it might even prevent the breakdown of marital fiat. The law as therapy has little to do with preventing marital breakdown by opportunity.

Law as therapy has several shortcomings. In a report of the Swedish divorce law, which includes many of the ideas of the law as therapy, several major evasions of the law were noted.[16] The basis for these evasions is that the law as therapy usually goes into operation only after the couple have really committed themselves to their hostilities or to new spouses. This means they will not co-operate with the therapist. Since much of modern therapy, to be effective, requires co-operation of the clients, much of the therapy session advocated by law becomes perfunctory. Secondly, when people do not believe in therapy, they view it as a punishment and evade it in the same manner as other forms of punishment. Thirdly, the law as therapy is rather expensive and ineffectual in cases of fundamental personality factors which lead to conflict, or inability to share one's self with another. The policy under the law as therapy is usually to allow breakup where major changes in personality are required.

The difficulties mentioned above are not considered fundamental. It is conceivable that new developments in the methods of therapy might remove them as problems. The fundamental objection to the law as therapy is that it tends to locate deviation within the individual. It fails to recognize that the faults of marriage need not lie within the persons involved but might well be a product of the regular societal system of socialization.[17] For instance, it has been pointed out that, in our middle-class culture, men and women are systematically raised with conflicting concepts of their roles and those of their future spouses.[18] These conflicting concepts of role are a basis for marital conflict. Ogburn[19] has pointed out that in our regular societal development the increasing tendency for families to lose their functions lays the basis for breakup through indifference. These facts have meant that the social system has produced spouses who systematically have a high probability of developing conflicts, being indifferent, meeting new spouses, and who place a low value on marriage per se.

Law as Education

The law as education is one type of law which is designed to meet this objection. It, in a sense, recognizes that the individual's ability to handle himself is a consequence of the regular institutional processes. Unlike the other two types of law, it does not wait until the deviant act has occurred before becoming operative. Illustrations of the law as education exist in many areas of life. Most licensing laws are law as education. For instance, the laws which demand that doctors have a certain amount of education and pass certain examinations before they can practice would illustrate the law as education. The marriage licensing laws insofar as they view minimum age limits as being an index of a person's competence might be thought of in terms of law as education.

In considering the law as education it becomes apparent that certain factors which affect family breakup would be rather difficult to alter by law. Or, put somewhat differently, the environments the law presents cannot compete so easily against such factors as urbanization, industrialization, wars, and depressions. Any law as education would have to take such factors as a given.

If one takes a modern industrial society as a given, then the systematic development of individual capacities is one area in which the law as education might play a major role. Law as education is basically concerned with developing environments which allow individuals to internalize given values.

In the past, the law as education has been thought of as a panacea. For any ills in the society the answer has been education. However, usually a very narrow viewpoint has been taken of the educational processes—they have been thought of primarily in terms of the traditional classroom lecture systems. It has been assumed that exposure to facts is tantamount to their acceptance. Because the notion of education has been so closely tied to the lecture method of information exposure, there is a historic backlog of failures.

It is only when looking at recent investigations into learning processes that one gets a sense that incorporation of facts for use in real life situations is far more than mere exposure to those facts.[20] Much greater use should be made in education of those processes which sociologists have called socializing processes. It is the learning which takes place gradually, imperceptibily, and informally, through participation in common group endeavors.

With this in mind, courses in family living can be thought of as applied courses in social psychology. Each course is in this sense a study in personality development. The technique for evaluation of this change and for bringing it about should be far more sophisticated than straight lectures and factual examinations given at the end of the class, as is now the case in most schools.

One socio-psychological theory which might be incorporated into the processes of education is that of Foote and Cottrell.[21] It rests fundamentally on the proposition that the individual's personality is a function of his interaction with others and is not fixed but capable of infinite development and variation. There is reason to believe that such a systematic development of interpersonal competence might have an effect on family breakup[22] since it takes as a given condition a rapidly changing environment which is one of the chief characteristics of the industrialized urban community in which we now live and which is thought to be the chief institutional source of breakup. Moreover, it suggests types of learning environments which approximate the regular socializing experiences and which are at the same time capable of systematic mass disseminations.[23]

Insofar as the law requires all individuals to attend schools and insofar as school systems have courses in family living and insofar as these courses take cognizance of modern social-psychological developments on learning behavior, these laws might become the most powerful aids in preventing family breakup.

If the law as education is successful, it does everything other types of law will do plus locating responsibility in the institutional structure. Its chief limitation in the past was that the learning environments it presented to the individual have never seriously been able to compete with the other environments to which they were exposed—job, family, peer groups, etc.

Conclusion

Although the law has been discussed as being either that of punishment, therapy, or education, in actual fact laws have elements of all of these. Furthermore, different occasions might at any given time make one more effective than another.

The present discussion has been limited to presenting the law as a means of social control in terms of six conditions. It has not, for instance, discussed the interaction between the enforcement agents and the deviants. It has not considered systematically the effects of various ways into which society can be organized into power structures and the differential effects of these power structures on the enforcement of laws. Yet these would provide crucial limitations on some of the generalizations made in this paper.

The intent of this paper has been to indicate two things. First, that a single set of laws—divorce laws—have different ways of effecting social control—through punishment, therapy, and education. Secondly, that the dependent variable which the law seeks to control, family breakup, is complex. There are different kinds of breakup—breakup by conflict, indifference, opportunity, and marital fiat. The matching of type of law and type of breakup will lead to the maximum form of social control.

18 Introduction to the Analysis of Kinship Systems

A. R. RADCLIFFE-BROWN

The analysis of kinship systems has traditionally been the province of the anthropologist, a province into which other social scientists have seldom ventured. This is unfortunate, since the kinship system establishes much of the context of the nuclear family's ties to the surrounding community, the ties to non-kin as well as kin. The range and degree of control which the kinship system exerts varies widely, but in no society is it insignificant. Even in American society, where the nuclear family is structurally isolated and the kinship system receives little emphasis, its effects are present, as the paper by Schneider and Homans in Part III suggests. Professor Radcliffe-Brown was one of the foremost students of kinship systems. His "Introduction to the Analysis of Kinship Systems," presented here in abridged form, is a summary statement of the basic dimensions of kinship systems. In it, he brings out the many ways in which the kinship system of a society patterns the interchanges between the family and other social systems.

A study of kinship systems all over the world by the method of comparative analysis reveals that, while there is a very wide range of variation in their superficial features, there can be discovered a certain small number of general structural principles which are applied and combined in various ways. It is one of the first tasks of a theoretical study of kinship to discover these principles by a process of abstractive generalization based on analysis and comparison.

We have first of all to try to get a clear idea of what is a kinship system or system of kinship and marriage. Two persons are kin when one is descended from the other, as, for example, a grandchild is descended from a grandparent, or when they are both descended from a common ancestor or ancestress counting descent through males and females.

The term "consanguinity" is sometimes used as an equivalent of

Abridged from "Introduction" to A. R. Radcliffe-Brown and Daryll Forde (eds.), *African Systems of Kinship and Marriage*. Copyright, 1950. Published by the Oxford University Press on behalf of the International African Institute.

"kinship" as above defined, but the word has certain dangerous implications which must be avoided. Consanguinity refers properly to a physical relationship, but in kinship we have to deal with a specifically social relationship. The difference is clear if we consider an illegitimate child in our own society. Such a child has a "genitor" (physical father) but has no "pater" (social father). Our own word "father" is ambiguous because it is assumed that normally the social relationship and the physical relationship will coincide. But it is not essential that they should. Social fatherhood is usually determined by marriage. Kinship therefore results from the recognition of a social relationship between parents and children. Where the term "descent" is used in this essay, it will refer not to biological but to social relations. Thus the son of an adopted person will be said to trace descent from the adopting grandparents.

A part of any kinship system is some system of terms by which relatives of different kinds are spoken of or by which they are addressed as relatives. The first step in the study of a kinship system is to discover what terms are used and how they are used.

There is one type of terminology that is usually referred to as "descriptive." In systems of this type, there are a few specific terms for relatives of the first or second order, and other relatives are indicated by compounds of these specific terms in such a way as to show the intermediate steps in the relation. It is necessary in any scientific discussion of kinship to use a system of this kind. Instead of ambiguous terms such as "uncle" or "cousin," we have to use more exact compound terms such as "mother's brother," "father's sister's son," and so on. Descriptive terminologies in this sense, i.e., those using specific terms and compounding them, are to be found in some African peoples.

In the "classificatory" system of kinship terminology, a single term is used for two or more kinds of relatives, who are thus included in a single terminological category. This may be illustrated by the English system of the present day. The word "uncle" is used for both the father's brother and the mother's brother and also by extention for the husband of an "aunt" (father's sister or mother's sister). Similarly, with such terms as "nephew," "niece," "cousin," "grandfather," etc.

In various systems, the principle of classification may be applied over a wide range of relationship. Thus, a first cousin of the father, being his father's brother's son, whom he therefore calls "brother," is classified with the father, and the same term "father" is applied to him. His son in turn, a second cousin, is called "brother." By this process of extension of the principle of classification, nearer and more distant collateral relatives are arranged into a few categories and a person has many relatives to whom he applies the term "father" or "mother" or "brother" or "sister."

The most important feature of these classificatory terminologies was pointed out long ago by Sir Henry Maine. "The effect of the system," he wrote, "is in general to bring within your mental grasp a much greater number of your kindred than is possible under the system to which we are accustomed."[1] In other words, the classificatory terminology is primarily a mechanism which facilitates the establishment of wide-range systems of kinship.

There is more to it than this, however. Research in many parts of the world has shown that the classificatory terminology is used as a method of dividing relatives into categories which determine or influence social relations as exhibited in conduct. The general rule is that the inclusion of two relatives in the same terminological category implies that there is some significant similarity in the customary behavior due to both of them, or in the social relation in which one stands to each of them, while inversely the placing of two relatives in different categories implies some significant differences in customary behavior or social relations.

A kinship system presents to us a complex set of norms, of usages, of patterns of behavior between kindred. In attempting to define the norms of behavior for a particular kind of relation in a given system, it is necessary to distinguish different elements or aspects. As one element in a relation, we may recognize the existence of a personal sentiment, what may be called the affective element. Thus we may say that in most human societies a strong mutual affection is a normal feature of the relation of mother and child, or there may be in a particular society a typical or normal emotional attitude of a son to his father. It is very important to remember that this affective element in the relation between relatives by kinship or marriage is different in different societies.

We may distinguish also an element that it is convenient to refer to by the term "etiquette," if we may be permitted to give a wide extension of meaning to that word. It refers to conventional rules of outward behavior. What these rules do is to define certain symbolic actions or avoidances which express some important aspect of the relation between two persons. Differences of rank are given recognition in this way. In some tribes of South Africa it would be an extreme, and in fact unheard of, breach of the rules of propriety for a woman to utter the name of her husband's father.

An important element in the relations of kin is what will here be called the jural element, meaning by that the relationships that can be defined in terms of rights and duties. Where there is a duty there is a rule that a person should behave in a certain way. A duty may be positive, prescribing actions to be performed, or negative, imposing the avoidance of certain acts. We may speak of the "performance" of a positive duty and the "observance" of a negative duty. The duties of A to B are frequently spoken of in terms of the "rights" of B. Reference to duties or rights are simply different ways of referring to a social relation and the rules of behavior connected therewith.

In speaking of the jural element in social relations, we are referring to customary rights and duties. Some of these in some societies are subject to legal sanctions, that is, an infraction can be dealt with by a court of law. But for the most part, the sanctions for these customary rules are what may be called moral sanctions sometimes supplemented by religious sanctions.

Two persons who are kin are related in one or another of two ways: either one is descended from the other, or they are both descended from a common ancestor. It is to be remembered that "descent" here refers to the social relationship of parents and children, not to the physical relation. Kinship is thus based on descent, and what first determines the character of a kinship system is the way in which descent is recognized and reckoned.

One principle that may be adopted is the simple cognatic principle. To define the kin of a given person, his descent is traced back a certain number of generations, to his four grandparents, his eight great-grandparents, or still further, and all descendants of his recognized ancestors, through both females and males, are his cognates. At each generation that we go backwards, the number of ancestors is double that of the preceding generation, so that in the eighth generation a person will have sixty-four pairs of ancestors (the great-grandparents of his great-great-grandparents). It is, therefore, obvious that there must be some limit to tracing kinship in this way. The limit may simply be a practical one depending on the inability to trace the genealogical connections, or there may be a theoretically fixed limit beyond which the genealogical connection does not count for social purposes.

Another way of ordering the kindred may be illustrated by the system of ancient Rome. Within the body of a person's recognized cognates certain are distinguished as agnates. Cognates are agnates if they are descendants by male links from the same male ancestor. In the Roman system, there was the strongest possible emphasis on agnatic kinship, i.e., on unilineal descent through males.

In some other societies, there is a similar emphasis on unilineal descent through females. With such a system, a person distinguishes from the rest of his cognates those persons who are descended by female links only from the same female ancestress as himself. We can speak of these as his matrilineal kin.

There are few, if any, societies in which there is not some recognition of unilineal descent, either patrilineal (agnatic) or matrilineal or both. Thus, in the modern English system surnames descend in the male line. In many countries, in a mixed marriage, children acquire by birth the nationality of the father, not that of the mother. But what matters in the study of any society is the degree of emphasis on the unilineal principle and how it is used.

One important way in which the unilineal principle may be used is in the formation of recognized lineage groups as part of the social structure. An agnatic lineage consists of an original male ancestor and all his descendants through males of three, four, five, or *n* generations. The lineage group consists of all the members of a lineage alive at a given time. A woman belongs to the lineage of her father, but her children do not. With matrilineal reckoning, the lineage consists of a progenetrix and all her descendants through females. A man belongs to his mother's lineage, but his children do not. Lineage groups, agnatic or matrilineal, are of great importance in the social organization of many African peoples.

It is desirable to illustrate by examples the differences in the ordering of kindred as the result of relative emphasis on the cognatic principle or on the unilineal principle. As an example of a cognatic system, we may take the kinship system of the Teutonic peoples as it was at the beginning of history. This was based on a widely extended recognition of kinship traced through females as well as males.

The arrangement of kin by degrees of nearness or distance was based on sib-ship (English *sib,* German *Sippe*). A man's sib were all his cognates within a certain degree. No two persons can have the same sib, though for two unmarried full brothers, A and B, every person who was sib to A was sib to B, and A and B were sib-kinsmen of one another. A person cannot be said to "belong" to a sib or be a member of a sib in the sense in which he can be said to belong to a lineage or a clan or a village community.

The sib was thus an arrangement of kindred as it were in a series of concentric circles, with the person whose sib it was at the center. One circle included all those kin with whom marriage was forbidden. It is difficult to discover exactly where this was. In some Teutonic systems and in ancient Wales, it is said that the prohibition against marriage extended to "the fifth degree." This would seem to include all third cousins, but the matter is not quite clear.

"Sib" may be defined as meaning computable cognatic relationship for definite social purposes. We have seen that it was used for fixing the degrees within which marriage was forbidden. After the introduction of Christianity, the relation between godparents and godchildren was included under sib. The godfather and godmother were "god-sib" (modern "gossip") to their godchildren and marriage between them was forbidden. Sib-ship also regulated the inheritance of property. Persons who were not related to a deceased person within a certain degree had no claim to inherit.

We are concerned with the ways in which different societies provide an ordering of the kin of an individual. One way is by tracing kinship equally and similarly through males and through females. There is a close approximation to this in modern European societies and in some primitive societies. In various societies, we find some greater or less emphasis placed on unilineal descent, but there are many different ways in which this principle can be applied. It is, therefore, misleading to talk about matrilineal and patrilineal societies as was formerly the custom of anthropologists. Some more complex and systematic classification is needed to represent the facts as they are.

Within the elementary family, there is a division of generations; the parents form one generation, the children another. The normal relation between parents and children can be described as one of superordination and subordination. This results from the fact that children, at least during the early part of life, are dependent on their parents, who provide and care for them and exercise control and authority over them. Any relationship of subordination, if it is to work, requires that the person in the subordinate position should maintain an attitude of respect towards the other. The rule that children should not only love but should honor and obey their parents is, if not universal, at least very general in human societies.

The relation between the two generations is usually generalized to extend beyond the range of kinship. Some measure of respect for persons of the generation or age of one's parents is required in most if not all societies. In some East-African societies, this relation is part of the organization of the society into age-sets. Thus, among the Masai, sexual intercourse with the wife of a man belonging to one's father's age-set is regarded as a very serious offense amounting to something resembling incest. Inversely, so is sexual connection with the daughter of a man of one's own age-set.

If the exercise of authority on the one side, however, and respect and obedience on the other were simply, or even primarily, a matter of relative age, we should expect to find these features markedly characteristic of the relations between grandparents and grandchildren. Actually, we find most commonly something almost the opposite of this, a relation of friendly familiarity and almost of social equality.

One aspect of the structural principle with which we are here concerned is that one generation is replaced in course of time by the generation of their grandchildren. In the passage of persons through the social structure which they enter by birth and leave by death, and in which they occupy successive positions, it is not, properly speaking, children who replace their parents, but those of the grandparents' generation are replaced by those of the grandchildren's generation. Another aspect of the same principle is that the two generations are regarded as being in a relation, not of superordination and subordination, but of simple friendliness and solidarity and something approaching social equality. This may sometimes result in what may be called the merging of alternate generations, a structural principle of fundamental importance in the native tribes of Australia and in some Melanesian peoples. A man with his "father's fathers," his "son's sons," and his "brothers," in the classificatory sense, form a social division over against his "fathers" and "sons," who constitute another division.

Where the principle makes itself apparent in some African peoples is in a peculiar feature of the kinship terminology, whereby the term that primarily means "wife" is applied by a man to his granddaughters or his grandmothers, and a woman applies to her grandson the term meaning "husband." Or on the other hand, among the Nandi of East Africa, the term *kamet* refers in the first instance to the mother and her sisters (first ascending generation), but the mother's brother's daughter is also called *kamet* and is addressed by the same term of address as the mother. Correspondingly, the term *imamet* refers primarily to the mother's brother, but is also applied to the mother's brother's son. Further, the children of the mother's brother's son, who belong to the first descending generation, are also called "mother's brother" and "mother."

This peculiar type of terminology has been found in a number of societies in different parts of the world, and is called by anthropologists the Omaha type. Its widespread occurrence shows that it cannot be regarded as the product of some accident of history; we should seek some theoretical explanation. It can be regarded as a method of expressing and emphasizing the unity and solidarity of the patrilineal lineage group. A man belongs to a patrilineal lineage. He is closely connected with his mother's lineage, which plays an important part in his life, second only to that of his own. His connection with that lineage, being through his own mother, is with the first ascending generation. By the terminology, he treats all the members of that group, through three (or more) generations, beginning with that of his mother, as belonging to a single category; the females are "mothers" to him and the males are "mother's brothers." For all these persons, and for the group as a whole, he is a "sister's son." Thus, in its relation to this person, the lineage of three generations is a unity; we can therefore speak of the structural principle that is applied in these systems as the principle of the unity of the lineage.

In a previous section the classificatory terminology in general was interpreted as a way of recognizing the principle of the unity of the sibling group. The special Omaha form of the classificatory system is here interpreted as a way of recognizing the unity of the lineage group. Thus a single method of interpretation is applied throughout, and this gives a simplification or economy of theory. If the whole question were merely one of the use of terms of relationship the subject would not be of any importance; but it is here held that the terminology is used as a means of ordering relationships for social purposes, and of this there is already abundant evidence.[2]

Every kinship system provides each person in a society with a set of dyadic (person-to-person) relationships, so that he stands, as it were, at the center of a narrower or wider circle of relatives. During his life, the body of his relatives is constantly changing by deaths and births and by marriages—his own marriage and the marriages of his relatives.

In many societies, the kinship system also includes a different kind of structure by which the whole society is divided into a number of separate groups, each consisting of a body of persons who are or who regard themselves as being a unilineal body of kindred. Such kinship groups are moieties, clans and lineages. Moieties, by which the society is bisected, do not exist in Africa except amongst the Galla, though they are important in some parts of the world. The distinction between clan and lineage is that in a lineage group each member can actually, or at least theoretically, trace his genealogical connection with any other member by descent from a known common ancestor, whereas in a clan, which is usually a larger body, this is not possible. A moiety may be divided into clans and usually is so. Clans may be divided into subclans, and clans or subclans, may be divided into lineages. A lineage of any considerable size is usually divided into branches, which are themselves smaller lineages, and these again may be subdivided. For structures having successive segmentations the term "polysegmentary" has been suggested.

It is usual to apply the term "clan" to both patrilineal and matrilineal groups, but some American ethnographers use the term "clan" only for matrilineal groups and "gens" for patrilineal. There are, of course, many different kinds of clan systems, but the term should be used only for a group having unilineal descent in which all the members regard one another as in some specific sense kinsfolk. One way of giving recognition to the kinship is by the extensive use of the classificatory terminology, so that, in a system of patrilineal clans, a man regards all the men of his clan as being classificatory "fathers," "brothers," "sons," "grandfathers," or "grandsons." Frequently, but not universally, the recognition of the kinship bond uniting the members of the clan takes the form of a rule of exogamy which forbids marriage between two members of the same clan. Where clans are divided into subclans it may be only to the smaller group that the rule of exogamy applies.

If we look at a structure of clans or lineages from the point of view of an individual it appears as a grouping of his relatives. In a patrilineal system the members of his own clan are his agnatic kinsfolk, and the nearest of these to him are the members of his own lineage. The members of his mother's clan or lineage are also his kin, through his mother. He may apply to them the appropriate classificatory terms, and in some systems he may be forbidden to marry any woman of his mother's patrilineal clan. The members of his father's mother's clan and his mother's mother's clan may also be recognized as relatives, and those of his wife's clan or lineage may all have to be treated as relatives by marriage.

A clan system, however, also provides a division of the tribe into a number of distinct separate groups, each having its own identity. The clans may then, as groups, play an important part in the social, political, or religious life of the tribe. The extent to which they do this depends on the degree to which they are corporate groups. A group may be spoken of as "corporate" when it possesses any one of a certain number of characters: if its members, or its adult male members, or a considerable portion of them, come together occasionally to carry out some collective action—for example, the performance of rites; if it has a chief or council who are regarded as acting as the representatives of the group as a whole; if it possesses or controls property which is collective, as when a clan or lineage is a land-owning group. In parts of Africa it is very common to find that land is held or owned by lineage groups, which are thus corporate groups.

Professor Gluckman regards the absence of corporate kin groups (clans or lineages) as an important distinguishing characteristic of a number of tribes of Central Africa. The typical corporate group in that region is a village constituted by the persons who attach themselves to a headman. This group is an open, not a closed group; that is, individuals or families may join or leave it, moving from one village to another. It is usual that a number of the inhabitants of a village at any time should be related, either by cognatic ties or through marriage with the headman or with one another, but they do not form a unilineal kin group, which is by its constitution a "closed" group.

Some of these tribes have clans, patrilineal in some instances, matrilineal in others, but the clans are dispersed and not corporate. Thus, the Ila and Bemba and other tribes have dispersed matrilineal clans. The members of one clan are scattered through the tribe; they do not ever come together to take any kind of collective action, and have no single authority (headman or clan council). They have no positive clan rites; the identity of the clan, and its unity as a separate group of kindred, is maintained by negative ritual observances common to all the members, such as refraining from killing or eating a certain animal (the "totem" of the clan). A member of the clan does not know all the other members, but if two persons meet who know or discover that they belong to the same clan they are expected to behave towards one another as kinsfolk, and since all members are kin they may not intermarry. It does not seem that in these tribes matrilineal lineages are given social recognition except in royal families.

The unilineal principle of reckoning relationship in one line (male or female) is utilized in a great variety of ways in different kinship systems. Where it is used to create a system of clans it facilities that wide-range recognition of relations of kinship to which there is a tendency in many societies. A person will thereby find himself connected by specific social ties, subject to established institutional modes of behavior, with a large number of other persons. In the absence, or weak development, of political structure this gives an effective system of social integration. It is not possible to provide such very wide range in a system based on cognation, since that implies the tracing of genealogical relationships through all lines. But even more important is that unilineal reckoning makes it possible to create corporate kin groups having continuity in time extending beyond the life of an individual or a family. There are innumerable social activities that can only be efficiently carried out by means of corporate groups, so that where, as in so many non-literate societies, the chief source of social cohesion is the recognition of kinship, corporate kin groups tend to become the most important feature of social structure.

Thus, it is the corporate kin group, whether clan, subclan, or lineage, that controls the use of land, whether for hunting, for pastoral life, or for cultivation; that exacts vengeance for the killing of a member, or demands and receives an indemnity. In the sphere of religion the kin group usually has its own cult, whether of its ancestors or connected with some sacred shrine. A continuing social structure requires the aggregation of individuals into distinct separated groups, each with its own solidarity, every person belonging to one group of any set. The obvious instance is the present division of the world into nations. In kinship systems, cognatic kinship cannot provide this; it is only made possible by the use of the principle of unilineal descent.

In order to understand the African customs relating to marriage, we have to bear in mind that a marriage is essentially a rearrangement of social structure. What is meant by social structure is any arrangement of persons in institutionalized relationships. By a marriage, certain existing relationships, particularly, in most societies, those of the bride to her family, are changed. New social relations are created, not only between the husband and the wife, and between the husband and the wife's relatives on the one side and between the wife and the husband's relatives on the other, but also, in a great many societies, between the relatives of the husband and those of the wife, who, on the two sides, are interested in the marriage and in the children that are expected to result from it. Marriages, like births, deaths, or initiations at puberty, are rearrangements of structure that are constantly recurring in any society; they are moments of the continuing social process regulated by custom; they are institutionalized ways of dealing with such events.

We tend, unless we are anthropologists, to judge other people's customs by reference to our own. To understand African marriage, we must remember that the modern English idea of marriage is recent and decidedly unusual, the product of a particular social development. We think of a marriage as an event that concerns primarily the man and woman who are forming a union and the state, which gives that union its legality and alone can dissolve it by divorce. The consent of parents is, strictly, only required for minors. Religion still plays some part, but a religious ceremony is not essential.

We may compare English marriage with the following account of a "wedding" in early England.[3]

> If people want to wed a maid or a wife and this is agreeable to her and to her kinsmen, then it is right that the bridegroom should first swear according to God's right and secular law and should wage [pledge himself] to those who are her forspeakers, that he wishes to have her in such a way as he should hold her by God's right as his wife—and his kinsmen will stand pledge for him.
>
> Then it is to be settled to whom the price for upfostering her belongs, and for this the kinsmen should pledge themselves.
>
> Then let the bridegroom declare what present he will make her for granting his desire, and what he will give if she lives longer than he does.
>
> If it is settled in this way, then it is right that she should enjoy half the property, and all if they have a child, unless she marries another man.
>
> All this the bridegroom must corroborate by giving a gage, and his kinsmen stand to pledge for him.
>
> If they are agreed in all this, then let the kinsmen of the bride accept and wed their kinswoman to wife and to right life to him who desires her, and let him take the pledge who rules over the wedding.
>
> If she is taken out of the land into another lord's land, then it is advisable that her kinsmen get a promise that no violence will be done to her and that if she has to pay a fine they ought to be next to help her to pay, if she has not enough to pay herself.

The marriage here is not any concern of the state or political authorities; it is a compact between two bodies of persons, the kin of the woman who agree to wed their daughter to the man, and his kinsmen who pledge themselves that the terms of the agreement will be carried out. The bridegroom and his kinsmen must promise to make a payment (the "marriage payment") to her father or other legal guardian. He must also state what present he will give to his bride for permitting the physical consummation of the marriage; this was the so-called "morning-gift" to be paid after the bridal night. There was further an agreement as to the amount of the dowry, the portion of the husband's wealth of which the wife should have the use during her lifetime if her husband died before her. The agreement is concluded by the giving of the *wed,* the symbolic payment made by the bridegroom and his kin to the woman's kinsmen.

In modern England, the pledge or gage, in the form of a "wedding" ring, is given, not to the bride's kinsmen when the marriage arrangement is made, but to the bride herself at the wedding ceremony. The change in custom is highly significant. The "giving away" of the bride is a survival of something which at one time was the most important feature of the ceremonial of marriage.

An African marriage is in certain respects similar to the early English marriage described above. The dowry or dower does not exist in Africa, though writers who do not know, or do not care about, the meanings of words use the term "dowry" quite inappropriately to refer to the "marriage payment."[4] There is also in Africa nothing exactly corresponding to the English "morning-gift" regarded as a payment for accepting sexual embraces, though it is usual for the bridegroom to give gifts to his bride. The two other features of the early English marriage are normally found in African marriages. Firstly, the marriage is not the concern of the political authorities but is established by a compact between two bodies of persons, the kin of the man and the kin of the woman. The marriage is an alliance between the two bodies of kin based on their common interest in the marriage itself and its continuance, and in the offspring of the union, who will be, of course, kin of both the two kin groups. The understanding of the nature of this alliance is essential to any understanding of African kinship systems. Secondly, in Africa generally, as in early England, and in a great number of societies in ancient and modern times in all parts of the world, a marriage involves the making of a payment by the bridegroom or his kin to the father or guardian of the bride. Africans distinguish, as we do, between a "legal" marriage and an irregular union. A legal marriage, by which the children who will be born are given definite "legitimate" status in the society, requires a series of transactions and formalities in which the two bodies of kin, those of the husband and those of the wife, are involved. In most African marriages, as in the early English marriage, the making of a payment of goods or services by the bridegroom to the bride's kin is an essential part of the establishment of "legality."

In what follows, the term "marriage payment" will be used for the major payment or payments made by the bridegroom to the wife's kin. Where there is a payment from the wife's kin to the husband this will be called the "counter-payment." The rule in many African societies is that if there is a divorce the marriage payment and the counter-payment must be returned. There are qualifications of this; for example, in some tribes where on divorce there are children and they belong to the father the marriage payment may be not returnable, or returnable only in part. Also, there are tribes in Africa in which, instead of a payment in goods, the bridegroom must serve for his wife by working for her kin, just as Jacob served his mother's brother Laban seven years for each of the two sisters, Leah and Rachel, his cousins, whom he married (Genesis xxix). This service, the equivalent of the marriage payment or of part thereof, is of course not returnable if there is divorce.

In Africa, an unmarried woman is in a position of dependence. She lives under the control and authority of her kin, and it is they who afford her protection. Commonly, if she is killed or injured, her guardian or her kinsfolk can claim an indemnity. At marriage she passes to a greater or less extent, which is often very considerable, under the control of her husband (and his kin), and it is he (and they) who undertake to afford her protection. If she is killed or injured by third parties it is now the husband and his kin who can claim an indemnity. The woman's kin, however, retain the right to protect her against ill treatment by her husband.

To understand African marriage, we must think of it not as an event or a condition but as a developing process. The first step is usually a formal betrothal, though this may have been preceded by a period of courtship or, in some instances in some regions, by an elopement. The betrothal is the contract or agreement between the two families. A most important stage in the development of the marriage is the birth of the first child. It is through the children that the husband and wife are united and the two families are also united by having descendants in common.

We may consider African marriage in three of its most important aspects. First, the marriage involves some modification or partial rupture of the relations between the bride and her immediate kin. This is least marked when the future husband comes to live with and work for his future parents-in-law while his betrothed is still a girl not old enough for marriage. It is most marked when, as in most African societies, the woman when she marries leaves her family and goes to live with her husband and his family. Her own family suffers a loss. It would be a gross error to think of this as an economic loss.[5] It is the loss of a person who has been a member of a group, a breach of the family solidarity. This aspect of marriage is frequently given symbolic expression in the simulated hostility between the two bodies of kin at the marriage ceremony, or by the pretense of taking the bride by force (the so-called "capture" of the bride). Either the bride herself or her kin, or both, are expected to make a show of resistance at her removal.

When this aspect of marriage is considered, the marriage payment can be regarded as an indemnity or compensation given by the bridegroom to the bride's kin for the loss of their daughter. This is, however, only one side of a many-sided institution and in some kinship systems is of minor importance. In societies in which the marriage payment is of considerable value, it is commonly used to replace the daughter by obtaining a wife for some other member of the family, usually a brother of the woman who has been lost. A daughter is replaced by a daughter-in-law, a sister by a wife or sister-in-law. The family is compensated for its loss.

A second important aspect of legal marriage is that it gives the husband and his kin certain rights in relation to his wife and the children she bears. The rights so acquired are different in different systems. Some of these are rights of the husband to the performance of duties by the wife (rights *in personam*) and he accepts corresponding duties towards her. He has, for example, rights to the services of his wife in his household. But the husband usually also acquires rights *in rem* over his wife. If anyone kills or injures her, or commits adultery with her, he may claim to be indemnified for the injury to his rights.

The rights obtained by a husband and his kin are different in some respects in different systems. The most important difference is in the matter of rights over the children the wife bears. An African marries because he wants children—*liberorum quaerendorum gratia.* The most important part of the "value" of a woman is her child-bearing capacity. Therefore, if the woman proves to be barren, in many tribes her kin either return the marriage payment or provide another woman to bear children.

In a system of father-right, such as the Roman *patria potestas,* the rights of the father and his kin over the children of a marriage are so preponderant as to be nearly absolute and exclude any rights on the part of the mother's kin. On the other hand, in a system of mother-right such as that formerly existing among the Nayars of southern India, the father has no legal rights at all: the children belong to the mother and her kin. This does not, of course, exclude a relationship of affection between father and child. Both father-right and mother-right are exceptional conditions; most societies have systems which come between these extremes and might be called systems of joint right or divided right. The system of division varies and there may be an approximation either to father-right or to mother-right.

Some societies in Sumatra and other parts of the Malay Archipelago have two kinds of marriage. If a full marriage payment is made, the children belong to the father; we may call this a father-right marriage. But if no payment is made, the children belong to the mother and her kin, the marriage being one of mother-right.

The same sort of thing is reported from some parts of Africa, for example from Brass in Southern Nigeria.[6] The father-right marriage, with a substantial marriage payment, is the usual form, but if only a small payment is made, the children belong to the mother's kin. The most definite example is from the Nyamwezi. In the *kukwa* form of marriage there is a payment (*nsabo*) made by the bridegroom to the father or guardian of the bride; children of such a marriage fall into the possession of the husband and his agnatic kin. In the *butende* form of marriage there is no payment and the children belong to the mother and her kin.

There is another aspect of marriage that must be taken into account. In Africa a marriage is not simply a union of a man and a woman; it is an alliance between two families or bodies of kin. We must consider the marriage payments in this connection also.

In so-called primitive societies the exchange of valuables is a common method of establishing or maintaining a friendly relation between separate groups or between individuals belonging to separate groups. Where material goods are exchanged, it is common to speak of gift-exchange. But the exchange may be of services, particularly those of a ritual character. There are societies in which there is an exchange of women, each group (family, lineage, or clan) providing a wife for a man of the other. The rule governing transactions of this kind is that for whatever is received a return must be made. By such exchanges, even by a single act of exchange, two persons or two groups are linked together in a more or less lasting relation of alliance.[7]

There are societies in some parts of the world in which the marriage payment and the counter-payment are equal or approximately equal in value. We may regard this as an exchange of gifts to establish friendship between two families, of which the son of one is to marry a daughter of the other. The kind, and to some extent the amount of the gifts is fixed by custom. But where the marriage payment is considerable in amount and there is a much smaller counter-payment, or none at all, we must interpret this as meaning that the bride's family is conferring a specific benefit on the bridegroom by giving him their daughter in marriage, a benefit that is shared by his kin, and that the marriage payment is a return for this. The transaction can still be regarded as a form of "gift-exchange" and as such establishes a relation (of alliance) between the parties.

It is characteristic of a transaction of purchase and sale that once it has been completed it leaves behind no obligations on either the buyer or the seller. (This does not, of course, exclude claims based on warranty.) In an African marriage, the position is very different. For one thing, the marriage payment may in certain circumstances have to be repaid. In some tribes where the payment consists of cattle, it is the same cattle with all their increase that should be returned. Further, in some African societies, the family that has made the marriage payment continues to have an interest in the cattle or other goods of which it consists. The payment received for a woman's marriage may be used to obtain a wife for a member of her family, usually her brother. This sets up a number of important relations between the persons involved.

It should be evident that the marriage payment is a complex institution having many varieties in form and function. In any given society, it has to be interpreted by reference to the whole system of which it is a part. Nevertheless, there are certain general statements that seem to be well grounded. In Africa, the marriage payment, whether it be small or large, is the objective instrument by which a "legal" marriage is established. In some instances, it is a compensation or indemnity to the woman's family for the loss of a member. This is particularly so where the marriage payment is considerable and is used to obtain a wife for the woman's brother. The payment may, in some instances, be regarded as part of an exchange of a kind that is used in many parts of the world to establish a friendly alliance between two groups. In some societies of South Africa and the Nilotic region, it is the derivation of the cattle used in the marriage payment that fixes the social position of the children born of the union. Where the same cattle or other goods are used in two or more successive marriages, this is, in some tribes, held to establish a special relation between the families thus formed. Where cattle are sacred in the sense that the cattle of a lineage are the material link between the living and their ancestors (having been received from those ancestors and being used for sacrifices to them), the use of cattle in marriage payments has a significance which a transfer of other goods would not have. This is not intended as a complete survey, which would be impossible within the limits of this essay. It is only an indication of how this institution, which is the procedure by which a husband acquires those rights which characterize a legal marriage (rights that vary in different societies), may be elaborated in different ways.

It has been said above that an African marriage has to be regarded as a developing process. One aspect of this is the development of the relation between the two allied families as children are born and grow up. We think of kinship only as a relation between two persons who have a common ancestor. But there is a kind of reverse kinship between persons who have a common descendant, and it is relationships of this kind that are created by the marriage conceived as a process.

African systems differ as to the rules concerning marriage between kin. In many, the general rule is that a man and a woman who are kin, or at any rate closely related, may not marry, and thus no bonds of kinship unite the two families before the marriage. On the other hand, there are many African societies in which it is thought very appropriate that a man should marry his cross-cousin, most usually the daughter of his mother's brother, or more rarely the daughter of his father's sister. In such marriages, the two families are already related before the marriage occurs. In marriage with the mother's brother's daughter, a connection between the families or lineages that has been formed in one generation is repeated in the next. There is also the very exceptional case of the Tswana, where a man may marry not only a mother's brother's daughter but such a near relative as the father's brother's daughter. We may expect that the social relations that result from a marriage alliance will differ in these different kinds of marriage, and a comparative study of the difference is desirable. It cannot be undertaken here. This section will deal only with certain features that characterize the relations of a man to his wife's relatives in a great number of African peoples and are also found among may other peoples in many parts of the world.

For seventy years, anthropologists have paid a good deal of attention to a custom found in many parts of the world and commonly referred to as "mother-in-law avoidance." This is a custom by which social contact between a husband and his wife's mother is limited in significant ways or in extreme cases entirely prohibited.

What is really the same custom varies from complete or nearly complete avoidance to the maintenance of social distance by a reciprocal atti tude of reserve and respect. Amongst the Ganda, "no man might see his mother-in-law or speak face to face with her."[8] Amongst the Galla, a man must not mention the name of his mother-in-law (actual or prospective), but he does not appear to be prohibited from speaking to her. But he may not drink milk from a cup she has used nor eat food of her cooking.[9] Thus, the custom has many varied forms.

It is not confined to a man's own mother-in-law. In some societies, a man must practice the same sort of avoidance towards the mother-in-law of his brother. In many, there is a similar avoidance of the sisters of the mother-in-law, and occasionally of the wife's grandmother. But a man must also avoid, or maintain a respectful distance from, some or his wife's male relatives, particularly her father, sometimes her father's brothers, and in some societies her mother's brothers. It is said that, amongst the Toro of Albert Nyanza, the avoidance between son- and father-in-law is even more rigid than that between son- and mother-in-law; and amongst the Lendu, another tribe in Uganda, the father-in-law can never visit his son-in-law except in the event of the serious illness of his daughter, whereas the mother-in-law may visit her son-in-law and his wife when two months have passed since the marriage.[10]

With this custom of maintaining a respectful distance between a man and his wife's parents and other relatives of the same generation, there is frequently associated a directly contrary relation between a man and his wife's brothers and sisters. This is the kind of relationship that is usually called the "joking relationship." It is fundamentally a relation expressed in disrespectful behavior. Persons between whom such a relationship exists are not merely permitted but are expected to speak and behave to one another in ways that would be insulting and offensive between persons not so related.[11]

As a first step towards the formation of a theory, we must bear in mind that in these relationships (both of "avoidance" and of "joking") behavior is highly conventionalized. In any society, the kinds of abusive speech or behavior that joking relatives may use are defined by custom. The rules that must be observed towards the wife's parents are similarly defined in detail, such as the Galla rule that a man must not drink milk from a cup that his wife's mother has used, while this does not apply to *dadi*, the intoxicating drink made from honey or from fruit of the Borassus palm, because this drink is "a thing of great kindness." A very widespread rule is that forbidding the uttering of the personal name of an avoidance relative. Thus, much of the behavior imposed in these relationships must be described as symbolic behavior and the rules are essentially similar to rules of etiquette. The acts and abstentions imposed by such rules are the conventionalized symbolic expression of the relative position of persons in a particular social relation or situation.

The view taken here is that the customs of "avoidance" and "joking"

have the same general social function. The differentiating principle between them is that by which, as a general rule (to which, as we have seen,
there are exceptions which require special explanation), behavior towards
relatives of the parents' generation should be respectful, while towards
relatives of one's own generation there is a nearer approach to equality
and familiarity. But within one's own generation there is often a differentiation of senior and junior, with a rule that the junior person must
show respect to the senior. So in some societies the rules of avoidance are
applied to the wife's elder sister as well as to the wife's mother, even where
there is a joking relationship with the wife's younger sister.

The "joking" relationship in its reciprocal form can be regarded as a
kind of friendliness expressed by a show of hostility. The mutual abusive
behavior would be simple hostility in other connections, but the joking relatives are required not to take offense but to respond in the same way.
The social separation of the man and his wife's relatives is symbolically
represented in the sham hostility, ruled by convention, and the friendliness is exhibited in the readiness not to take offense. This interpretation
applies to other instances of the reciprocal joking relationship that have
nothing to do with marriage.[12]

The joking relationship is clearly only appropriate between persons
who, in the general social structure, can treat each other as equals, and
this generally means persons of the same generation or those related as
"grandparent" and "grandchild." For the wife's parents and other relatives
of that generation, and sometimes for the wife's elder sister, an attitude of
respect is required. But it must be a different kind of respect from that
which a man shows in some African tribes to his father and in others
to his mother's brother as the person who is entitled to exercise authority
over him. This respect is totally incompatible with any open show of hostility. In a man's relations with his wife's parents, the social separation is
symbolically expressed in conventional rules such as the avoidance of the
utterance of their personal names or the Galla prohibition against eating
food cooked by the wife's mother. In the most extreme form of the custom,
there is complete avoidance of social contact with the wife's mother, to
whom a man may never speak and whom he may never meet face to
face, and there is sometimes a similar complete avoidance of the wife's
father.

There might be a temptation to regard this avoidance as a form of
hostility, since we tend to avoid persons with whom we do not get on
well. This would be a mistake. Among the Australian aborigines there
is complete avoidance of the wife's mother. When I asked a blackfellow
why he had to avoid his mother-in-law his reply was: "She is my best
friend in the world: she has given me my wife." Though this may seem
strange to our way of thinking, I think his answer was logical and adequate.
What disturbs or breaks a friendship is a quarrel. You cannot quarrel

with a person with whom you have no social contact, or with whom your contacts are strictly limited and regulated by convention.

A marriage produces a temporary disequilibrium situation. In the small and close-knit groups with which we are here concerned, any removal of a member results in disequilibrium. The event that most markedly produces this result is a death. But on a smaller scale the removal of a daughter by marriage is also a disturbance of equilibrium in her family. Moreover, the intrusion of a stranger into a group of kin is similarly a disturbance. Among the Nguni of South Africa, the bride, during the early period of her marriage, has to give presents to and perform services for the women of her husband's group and only after a lapse of time is she accepted as one of them. Any reconstruction of a disturbed equilibrium inevitably takes time—longer or shorter as the case may be.

The principal points of tension in the situation created by a marriage are between the wife and the husband's parents and between the husband and his wife's parents. In order to condense and simplify the argument, we are considering only the latter, but we must remember that the former is equally important. The point of maximum tension seems to be between the wife's mother, who is the person most closely and intimately connected with the wife before the marriage, and the son-in-law to whom have been transferred control and sexual rights over her daughter. This is, of course, what lies behind the vulgar English jokes about the mother-in-law.[13] The conventionally maintained "distance" between son-in-law and wife's mother does have the effect of avoiding conflict between them.

In some societies in Africa and elsewhere, the rules of avoidance are somewhat relaxed in the course of time, i.e., as the marriage develops through the birth of children. This is, for example, reported of the Kamba.[14] It is probably true of many other societies from which it has not been reported. This is easy to understand if we think of the marriage as a developing process. Whatever tensions or dangers of conflict there may be between the son-in-law and wife's parents are at a maximum in the early period of the marriage. The imposed "shyness" between them is functionally most significant immediately after the marriage.

A part of every kinship system is a set of regulations concerning marriage between persons related by kinship or through marriage. There are, in the first place, rules which prohibit marriage between persons who stand in certain relationships. An example is afforded by the list of prohibited degrees in the English Book of Common Prayer. The rules vary greatly from one system to another, and in a given society may vary from one period of its history to another. In many societies, there is what is called a rule of exogamy, by which a man is forbidden to take a wife from amongst the women of his own group (lineage, subclan, clan, or moiety).

On the other hand, in some systems there are certain relatives between whom marriage is not merely permitted but is regarded as desirable. The term "preferential marriage" is commonly applied to customs of this kind. The commonest examples are cross-cousin marriage (marriage with the daughter of the mother's brother or the father's sister) and marriage with the wife's sister or the wife's brother's daughter.

There are also rules relating to sexual intercourse outside marriage. Incest is the sin or crime of sexual intercourse between persons related either by kinship or through marriage within degrees defined by law or religion. Marriage and sexual intercourse outside marriage are not the same thing, and the rules relating to them must be separately considered. Most of the discussions about these rules have been vitiated by the failure to distinguish two distinct, though obviously related, problems.

There is, in most societies, a tendency to condemn sexual intercourse between persons who are forbidden to marry. But there are many instances in which a man and woman who may not marry may carry on a temporary affair without this being considered the grave offense to which we give the name of incest, and without being subjected to any legal or religious sanction.

Confining our attention to the regulation of marriage, however, there are certain requirements that must be met by a theory if it is to be worthy of any consideration. It must offer a general theory of the variations in these rules in different societies, and it must therefore deal not only with prohibited but also with preferred marriages. It must give some significant clue towards an understanding of why any given society has the rules it does. The test of a scientific theory is in its application to the explanation of particular instances. By this criterion, many of the speculative hypotheses that have been put forward are entirely useless and it would be a waste of time to discuss them. To anyone propounding a theory we might put the following question: how does the theory give us a clue to the understanding of why, amongst the Nkundo, a woman is forbidden to marry (in a second marriage) the husband's father's brother's son of her first husband's mother's brother's daughter; or why amongst the Hera of Mashonaland, a man may not marry a woman of the lineage of his wife's brother's wife, although he may marry his wife's sister or a woman of the lineage of his mother's brother's wife?

The theory here proposed is simply a special application of the general theory that the *raison d'être* of an institution or custom is to be found in its social function. The theory is that the rules or customs relating to prohibited or preferred marriages have for their social function to preserve, maintain, or continue an existing kinship structure as a system of institutional relations. Where a marriage between relatives would threaten to disrupt or throw into disorder the established system, it tends to be disapproved or forbidden, and the greater and more widespread the disturbance that would be caused by a marriage, the stronger tends to be the disapproval which it meets with. Inversely, preferential marriages are those which have for their effect to renew or reinforce the existing system.

The unity of the sibling group, with its implication of substitution of brother for brother and sister for sister, is a major principle of the Zulu system and a relatively minor feature in that of the Lozi. Following this, the Zulu system emphasizes the solidarity of the lineage group, and this can hardly be said to exist in Lozi. In sororal polygyny, one woman of a sibling group as part of a lineage supplements another; in the sororate she replaces her. Her duties are imposed on her by her lineage affiliation. To quarrel with her sister or neglect her sister's children is not simply a neglect of her marital duties; it is contrary to her obligations to her own closest kin. In the Zulu system, a marriage establishes a relation between a man and his brothers and the family of his wife, which should be permanent. Divorce is objected to because it is destructive of this permanence. If the man dies his wife passes to a brother. If the woman dies the relation can only be fully continued if she is replaced by a sister, unless she has borne children or is beyond the child-bearing age. In the very different Lozi system, the levirate and sororate could not possibly have the functions they have in the Zulu system.

Marriage with the wife's sister is, on the whole, more frequently found in association with the patrilineal lineage and what may be called father-right marriage, and it is in precisely such circumstances that it functions most effectively to maintain or strengthen the relationships set up by a marriage. In societies with matrilineal institutions there are variations. Thus, the Ashanti do not permit marriages of this kind. On the contrary, amongst the Bemba such marriages are approved, and the reason again lies in the social structure. By his first marriage a man becomes attached to the family of his wife, with whom, for at least some time, he must take up residence. Marriage with the wife's sister would strengthen this bond and introduce no new factor; whereas if, in a second marriage, he unites himself with a different family this must complicate and is likely to disturb the existing system of relations. Theoretically, one would expect that the Bemba should have given, at any rate in former times, a definite preference to marriage with the wife's sister.

In a number of African tribes, there is a custom by which a man is given his wife's brother's daughter as a wife. This is in a sense a variant of marriage with the younger sister of the wife. It exists in tribes in which the patrilineal lineage is a predominant feature of the social structure, and in such tribes a marriage of this sort renews by repetition the relationship set up by a first marriage between a man and the patrilineal lineage of his wife; he takes a second wife from the same lineage group, just as in the sororate he receives a second wife from the sibling group of the first wife. The second wife supplements or replaces, not her elder sister, but her father's sister. The structural principle involved is that of the unity of the lineage group.

In some African societies, a man is not permitted to marry the daughter of his mother's brother, and this rule is extended to the whole lineage to which she belongs, and sometimes to the clan. Other societies permit such marriages of cross-cousins, and in some they are given preference. (It must be noted that in a system of lineages or clans, whether patrilineal or matrilineal, cross-cousins belong to different groups.) There is no space available here for a general discussion of the reasons for this variation, as the subject is complex. Where the institutionalized relations of a man to his mother's brother (and his wife) are in important respects incompatible with his relations to his wife's father and mother, marriage with the mother's brother's daughter tends to be forbidden. Where there is no reason of this kind, then marriage of this sort renews in one generation a relation between families that was established in the preceding generation, and thus tends to be approved or preferred. A man takes a wife from a certain family or lineage and establishes a relation with her kinsfolk. His wife's brother becomes the mother's brothers of his children; if his son marries the daughter of this man there is a repetition of the previous connection.

There is a very important general difference in the regulation of marriage between societies that build their kinship system on cognatic relations traced equally through males and through females and those that adopt the unilineal principle. In a purely cognatic system, such as that of Anglo-Saxon England or ancient Wales, the prohibition against marriage applies to all cognates within a certain degree of kinship; marriage is forbidden between persons who have a common ancestor or ancestress within a certain number of generations. For example, two persons who have a common great-great-grandparent may be forbidden to marry. In a unilineal system, the primary rule is that two persons may not marry if they both belong to a socially recognized unilineal descent group. This may be a lineage, or it may be a clan. A rule of this kind is called "exogamy." Perhaps the most extreme example is the Chinese rule, not always, I believe, observed in these days, that two persons having the same surname may not marry, since such names are patrilineally inherited and therefore the two persons of one name may be supposed to have had an ancestor in common, though it may be three thousand years ago. There is no special problem about exogamy. The exogamy of a clan is the same thing as the exogamy of a lineage, with a wider recognition of kinship. The essence of the system of clans is that a man is required to recognize all the members of his own clan as his kin and to behave to them accordingly. The rule of exogamy, where it exists, is a way of giving institutional recognition to this bond of kinship. Like the classificatory system of terminology, which is frequently found associated with clans, exogamy is part of the machinery for establishing and maintaining a wide-range kinship system.

In unilineal systems, cognatic kinship outside the unilineal group may also be recognized. Thus, in ancient Indian law, a man might not marry a *sapinda,* a person descended patrilineally from one of his patrilineal ancestors within seven generations. He might also not marry certain cognatic kin, but the connection had to be a nearer one, within five, or in another system of law within three generations. There is also such a thing as lineal-cognatic kinship. In a system of patrilineal lineages or clans the rule of exogamy forbids marriage within the group; but there may also be a prohibition against marriage with a person of the mother's group. Inversely, in a system of matrilineal groups, a man may be forbidden to marry a woman of his father's group; the relationship is what is here called lineal-cognatic. It is evident from these remarks that in societies that make use of the unilineal principle there is an immense variety in the rules relating to marriage.

It is only possible here to deal very briefly with the subject of incest in its relation to the regulation of the marriage of kin. Incest is, properly speaking, the sin or crime of sexual intimacy between immediate relatives within the family, father and daughter, mother and son, brother and sister. In human societies generally, such conduct is regarded as unthinkable, something that could not possibly occur, and the idea of it arouses a strong emotional reaction of repugnance, disgust, or horror. It is characteristically conceived as an "unnatural" action, contrary not so much to law and morals as to human nature itself. It is this emotional reaction that we have to explain if we are to have a theory of incest. Another example of a kind of action frequently regarded as "unnatural" is parricide, the killing of a father or mother. The parallel between incest and parricide is illustrated in Greek drama.

Almost everywhere in human societies as we know them the first experience that any person has of society is in the parental family, the intimate domestic group of father, mother, and children. Certain emotional attitudes are developed in such a group with sufficient force to come to be thought of as "natural," in the sense of being part of human nature itself. The kind of emotional attitude existing in sexual intimacy, and the kinds of emotional attitude developed in the family towards the nearest kin, are felt to be violently contrary, incapable of being combined or reconciled. This is a matter of the logic of sentiments, not the logic of reason, and this is what is really meant when writers say that the repugnance to incest is instinctive, for there is a certain logic of the emotions which is the same in all human beings and is therefore inborn, not acquired. Individuals who behave contrary to this logic of sentiment, as by the murder of a mother, are behaving "unnaturally."

In Europe, in Christian times, incest, bestiality, homosexuality, witch-craft, as "unnatural" offenses, were quite logically regarded as offenses against the Creator, and therefore the concern of the Church. In Eng-land, it is only recently that incest has been treated as a crime to be dealt with by the secular courts. In many primitive societies, it is thought that incest will be punished by supernatural sanctions. These points are all significant for an understanding of the attitude towards incest. The family is normally regarded as something sacred; incest, like patricide or matricide, is sacrilege.

The attitude towards incest, in the narrow sense, may be extended to sexual intimacy between other relatives, but in different ways in different societies. In some primitive societies, sexual intimacy with the wife's mother is felt to be not less evil than with one's own mother. The cate-gories of relationship recognized in classificatory terminologies undoubt-edly have considerable effect. If a woman is to be called "mother" or "sis-ter" or "daughter," the relationship with her is thought of as being similar to that with one's own mother or sister or daughter, and it is obvious that this will very frequently be felt to forbid any sexual intimacy. It would be a sort of "symbolic" incest and as such objectionable; to have a sexual relation with a classificatory "mother" is a symbolic offense against one's own mother. Such symbolic incest, except ritually on specific occasions, is strongly reprobated among the Australian aborigines.

The whole theory of incest is one of social structure and of the nec-essary conditions of its stability and continuity. Incest, as here defined, is not merely disruptive of the social life of a single family, it is dis-ruptive of the whole system of moral and religious sentiments on which the social order rests. Prohibited marriages are for the most part simply those which would prevent the continuance of normal relations between the few persons who would be immediately affected. There are, however, instances in which a marriage between kin, not necessarily closely related, is felt to be an attack on the whole social order; this is so in the kinship systems of Australian aborigines. Such a marriage, if attempted, is a sort of crime against society and is likely to be treated as such.

One of the most famous pseudo-historical speculations of the anthro-pology of the last century was the idea that the earliest form of society was one based on "matriarchy" or "mother-right." One definition of this, given in the *Encyclopædia Britannica* of 1910, is "a term used to express a supposed earliest and lowest form of family life, typical of primitive societies, in which the promiscuous relations of the sexes result in the child's father being unknown." An alternative definition, frequently used, was a social condition in which kinship is reckoned through females only, and in which there would be no recognition of any social relationship of fatherhood. We have no knowledge of any societies of this kind in the present or in the past; it is, as Robertson remarked in his *History of America,* in the eighteenth century, a pure product of imagination.

But early anthropologists also applied the term "mother-right" to certain existing societies, McLennan to the Nayars of southern India, and Tylor to the Menangkabau Malays. These two societies provide us with a special type of system to which we may continue to apply the term "mother-right," and we may add to them the Khasi of Assam.

In the purest form of the "mother-right" system, a man does not acquire by marriage any rights of possession over his wife and her children. His relationship with them contains no jural element, but is one of mutual affection. He gives his wife gifts, but cannot transfer to her or to his children property which belongs to his lineage or over which the lineage members have a claim. There are some variations. Amongst the Khasi, a man did have certain rights over his wife since adultery was severely punished, and in this system there was an elaborate religious ceremony for marriage. The Khasi father occupies a position of respect and is revered by his children after his death. A widow may keep her deceased husband's bones for a time (thus keeping his spirit with her), but sooner or later the bones must go back to the man's lineage and clan. Yet divorce is common and may occur for a variety of reasons.

Mother-right is contrasted with "father-right" and the people chosen by anthropologists as affording a typical example of the latter were the ancient Romans, or rather one form of family that existed in Rome, characterized by *manus mariti* and *patria potestas*. There was a structure of patrilineal clans (*gentes*) and lineages. Possessive rights over a woman were ceremonially transferred from her father or guardian to her husband, and in the *coemptio* marriage, a payment was made to the woman's family in consideration of this transfer of rights. The wife thus passed under the power and authority of her husband; she transferred her allegiance from her own household deities and ancestral spirits to those of her husband. The father, the *paterfamilias,* had exclusive possessive rights over his children; they were under his power, the *patria potestas*. Over his sons he had the power of life and death, and might sell a son—the *jus vitae et necis et vendendi*. With this right, the law or the mother's relatives could not interfere, but in his exercise of his power the father had to observe the duties of religion, and for an abuse of power might receive censure from the members of his gens, or at one period perhaps from the Censors.

While in one sense mother-right and father-right are opposite types of system, there is another sense in which they are only contrasting varieties of a single type. What they have in common is the extreme emphasis on the lineage, matrilineal or patrilineal, and they both contrast strongly with systems based mainly on cognatic kinship; in both, the jural relations in kinship are rigidly confined to one lineage and clan. Possessive rights over the children belong entirely to the lineage, and inversely it is within the lineage that the individual has his most important duties and also his most significant rights, such as the right of support and rights of inheritance over property. In religion also (remembering that the Romans had patrilineal ancestor worship), it is the lineage or clan ancestors to whom one owes religious duties, and from whom one may ask for succor. The institutional complex of which mother-right and father-right are contrasting forms is, thus, one that can hardly make its appearance except at a relatively high stage of social development, where property and its transmission have become important, and where social continuity has come to be based on lineage.

Mother-rights, as represented by the Nayars, and father-rights, as represented by one form of marriage in Rome, give us useful points of reference for an attempt to establish a systematic typology of kinship systems. In both these types, the structure is one in which legal and jural relationships are as nearly as may be possible limited to the lineage and its connections. The contrary of this is to be found in what are here called cognatic systems, in which jural relations are based on cognatic kinship traced equally through males and females. Such systems, or close approximations, are found in some primitive societies such as the Andaman Islands, and in advanced societies such as Anglo-Saxon and modern England.

In Africa, a system that approximates fairly closely to the ideal type of a cognatic system is that of the Lozi, in which there is a minimal emphasis on unilineal kinship, so that lineages can hardly be said to exist as features of social structure. Professor Gluckman has brought out the marked contrast there is between the Lozi system and that of the Zulus which is a very close approximation to father-right. The Lozi system also contrasts with one of mother-right.

Relations of kinship involving rights and duties may also be traced through both male and female lines in a double lineage system in which the structure includes both patrilineal and matrilineal lineages or clans. Every individual has a well-defined set of relationships within his patrilineal lineage and clan, and another within his matrilineal lineage and clan.

Thus, we have four types of systems (ideal types based on empirical examples) to give us a framework within which to construct a typology: father-right, mother-right, purely cognatic systems, and double lineage systems.

In Africa, the nearest approach to pure mother-right is the system of Ashanti. The system is undergoing modification under European influences of various kinds, but it still retains some of its former features and illustrates what has in this discussion been held to be the basic structural feature of mother-right, the close and continued solidarity of the sibling group of brothers and sisters of one flesh and blood.

The system of certain tribes of Rhodesia and Nyasaland is a compromise formation in which the division of rights does not seem to be clearly defined, so that there are variations in practice not only from one tribe to another, but also within a tribe. This is connected with the local structure of this region, with its marked mobility by which persons move from one village to another, or establish new villages, so that the personnel of a particular village varies from time to time. The structural principle of mother-right appears in a contrary form to that of the Congo tribes, in the tendency for the group of sisters to continue living together, at any rate for some time. This is illustrated by the enlarged domestic group of the Bemba, consisting of a man and his wife and their married daughters with their husbands and children; the group breaks up when a man with his daughters forms a new domestic group of the same kind.

Both Professor Fortes and Dr. Richards draw attention to the existence of tensions and strains in the kinship systems of the Ashanti and the Bemba. But tensions and strains and possibilities of conflict exist in any system of rights and duties. The constraint of social obligations may often be felt as irksome. There is an unfortunate tendency for human beings in some circumstances to insist on their rights rather than to be punctilious in performance of duty. But it is obvious that a system based on compromise or on successive compromises is more likely to reveal tensions or conflicts than one in which jural relations are clearly defined and socially accepted. There is no reason why a system of mother-right should present more difficulties for individual adjustment than a system of father-right. But a system like the Bemba, with its division of rights and its occasions of rearrangement of structure, must obviously depend on the way in which individuals make personal adjustments with each other.

The Nguni peoples of South Africa, as represented by the Swazi and the Zulu, may be described as having father-right. Possession of children is determined by the marriage payment. "Cattle beget children" and "The children are where the cattle are not" is the way the people themselves express this. But during their infancy, the children belong to their mother. This is symbolically expressed in the custom by which she may protect them from sickness by making for them necklaces of hairs from the tail of her *ubulunga* cow, which belongs to the ancestral herd of her own lineage, and which she takes with her on her marriage, so that during the first period of her marriage she can drink the milk of her own lineage cattle. The *ubulunga* beast, cow for a woman and bull for a man, is a link between the individual and the *sacra* of his or her lineage, the cattle, the *kraal,* and the ancestral spirits. A woman, after her marriage, is entitled to the protection of the gods of her own family, and so also are her infant children who are attached to her more than to their father. It is at adolescence that a boy or girl becomes fully incorporated in the father's lineage. There is something similar in the Ashanti system, and still more definitely in the Congo systems, in the way in which a boy's relation with his mother's brothers becomes the preponderant fact in his life after adolescence.

This section illustrates the method of typological analysis applied to institutions of kinship. The procedure is to select certain types which can be used as standards with which to compare others. For the type of mother-right, it was necessary to go outside Africa, since even the Ashanti have only a qualified system of mother-right and, moreover, the Nayar and Menangkabau systems had been selected by anthropologists of the last century as best representing actual mother-right or matriarchy. It has also long been customary to take the ancient Romans as an example of father-right or patriarchy, though if we want an African example it might be possible to take the Zulu. It has been argued that the major structural principle of both father-right and mother-right is the maximum emphasis on the lineage as the source of jural and legal relations. The opposite type is therefore that of cognatic systems in which lineage has very little or no recognition. This gives three fixed points on what can be pictured as a chart on which systems could be given position by reference to these points.

In trying to classify kinship systems, a most important feature to consider is the way in which the relationship of a person to his mother's siblings and to his father's siblings is institutionally defined. In any system that approximates to the cognatic type, there is a tendency to treat the father's brother and the mother's brother as relatives of the same kind, and similarly with father's sister and mother's sister; but the assimilation may be less complete where there is some recognition, even though it be slight, of unilineal relationships. The degree of assimilation may sometimes be indicated in the terminology, as in the English use of "uncle" and "aunt." In classificatory terminologies, it may appear in the inclusion of the mother's brother under the term for "father" and of father's sister under the term for "mother." In the Lozi system, a man calls all the cognatic relatives of his mother in her generation (the children of her father's and mother's brothers and sisters) "mothers," male and female, and classifies as "fathers" all the cognatic relatives of his father. It is, therefore, not patrilineal or matrilineal lineage that is recognized in this terminology, but the Old English distinction amongst the cognates of a person between those on the "spear" side (through the father) and those on the "spindle" side (through the mother). It contrasts with the common Bantu custom of using "father" for the father's brothers an sisters and other persons of the father's lineage and generation, which is an application of the unilineal principle.

Cognatic systems are rare, not only in Africa but in the world at large. The reasons have already been indicated: it is difficult to establish and maintain a wide-range system on a purely cognatic basis; it is only a unilineal system that will permit the division of a society into separate organized kin-groups.

In a typological classification of unilineal systems, an important place must be given to those systems which recognize and attach importance to both matrilineal and patrilineal lineage relationships. This provides a special way of organizing a system of divided right by a cross-segmentation of the society.

Whether a kinship system functions well or not so well, as a mode of social integration, depends on the way it is constructed. Just as an architect in designing a building has to make a choice of structural principles which he will use, so, though in less deliberate fashion, in the construction of a kinship system there are a certain limited number of structural principles which can be used and combined in various ways. It is on the selection, method of use, and combination of these principles that the character of the structure depends. A structural analysis of a kinship system must therefore be in terms of structural principles and their application.

The unit of structure everywhere seems to be the group of full siblings —brothers and sisters. The group has its own internal structure by virtue of the distinction between the sexes and the order of birth. Its members, however, are of "one flesh and blood," and every system makes some use of this solidarity between siblings. This means that everywhere it is felt that brothers and sisters ought to exhibit affection and ought to co-operate and interact without serious conflict. Some of the ways in which the solidarity and unity of the sibling group is utilized in building wider structures have been illustrated in this Introduction.

Since in all societies the closest parental bond is that of children with their mother, the group of brothers and sisters with their mother constitutes a more extended unit of structure.

One of the most important questions to ask about a system is, in what way, if at all, it makes use of unilineal kinship as distinct from cognatic kinship.

A further important feature of the social structure of any people is the way in which the kinship system is connected with the territorial arrangement of persons. It is in the contact and co-operation of neighbors in a territorial group such as a village that relations of kinship have their most continuous influence on the social life.

African societies are undergoing revolutionary changes, as the result of European administrations, missions, and economic factors. In the past, the stability of social order in African societies has depended much more on the kinship system than on anything else. In the new conditions, kinship systems cannot remain unaffected. The first changes are inevitably destructive of the existing system of obligations. How far the disruption of the existing social order will go, and in what direction reconstruction will be attempted or possible, it is at present impossible to judge. The sanctions provided by the kinship systems for the control of conduct are being weakened. New sanctions, of which the agents are the policeman and the priest or minister of the church, are proving much less effective than those of which the agents were kinsmen speaking with the authority of the ancestors behind them.

19 Conjugal Roles and Social Networks

ELIZABETH BOTT

Propositions regarding the non-kin parts of family-community relationships seldom attain the rigor that propositions regarding kinship systems do. A notable exception is Dr. Bott's study of a series of London families. In her investigation she found a close correspondence between a structural feature of intrafamilial relationships and the nature of the network of friends of the spouses. In this selection from her book, Dr. Bott advances this proposition relating the extent of role differentiation between husband and wife and the extent of interconnectedness in their network of friends.

There was considerable variation in the way husbands and wives performed their conjugal roles. At one extreme, was a family in which the husband and wife carried out as many tasks as possible separately and independently of each other. There was a strict division of labor in the household, in which she had her tasks and he had his. He gave her a set amount of housekeeping money, and she had little idea of how much he earned or how he spent the money he kept for himself. In their leisure time, he went to cricket matches with his friends, whereas she visited her relatives or went to a cinema with a neighbor. With the exception of festivities with relatives, this husband and wife spent very little of their leisure time together. They did not consider that they were unusual in this respect. On the contrary, they felt their behavior was typical of their social circle. At the other extreme, was a family in which husband and wife shared as many activities and spent as much time together as possible. They stressed that husband and wife should be equals: all major decisions should be made together, and even in minor household matters they should help one another as much as possible. This norm was carried out in practice. In their division of labor, many tasks were shared or interchangeable. The husband often did the cooking and sometimes the washing and ironing. The wife did the gardening and often the household repairs as well. Much of their leisure time was spent together, and they shared similar interests in politics, music, literature, and in entertaining friends. Like the first couple, this husband and wife felt their behavior was typical of their social circle, except that they felt they carried the interchangeability of household tasks

Reprinted from *Family and Social Network* (London: Tavistock Publications, 1957), pp. 52–61, 92–96. Copyright 1957 by the Tavistock Institute of Human Relations and used with their kind permission and that of the author and publishers.

a little further than most people. One may sum up the differences between these two extremes by saying that the first family showed more segregation between husband and wife in their role-relationship than the second family. In between these two extremes there were many degrees of variation. This chapter attempts to interpret these differences in degree of segregation of conjugal roles.

The organization of familial activities can be classified in many ways. For the purposes of this research I find it useful to speak of "complementary," "independent," and "joint" organization. In *complementary organization,* the activities of husband and wife are different and separate but fitted together to form a whole. In *independent organization,* activities are carried out separately by husband and wife without reference to each other, in so far as this is possible. In *joint organization,* activities are carried out by husband and wife together, or the same activity is carried out by either partner at different times.

All three types of organization were found in all families. In fact, familial tasks could not be carried out if this were not so. But the relative amounts of each type of organization varied from one family to another. The phrase *segregated conjugal role-relationship* is here used for a relationship in which complementary and independent types of organization predominate. Husband and wife have a clear differentiation of tasks and a considerable number of separate interests and activities. They have a clearly defined division of labor into male tasks and female tasks. They expect to have different leisure pursuits, and the husband has his friends outside the home and the wife has hers. The phrase *joint conjugal role-relationship* is here used for a relationship in which joint organization is relatively predominant. Husband and wife expect to carry out many activities together with a minimum of task differentiation and separation of interests. They not only plan the affairs of the family together but also exchange many household tasks and spend much of their leisure time together.

Among the research couples, there were some general resemblances in the type of organization characteristically followed in a particular type of activity but, within these broad limits, there was a great deal of variation. Thus in all families there was a basic division of labor, by which the husband was primarily responsible for supporting the family financially and the wife was primarily responsible for housework and childcare; each partner made his own differentiated but complementary contribution to the welfare of the family as a whole. But within this general division of labor, there was considerable variation of detail. Some wives worked, others did not. Some families had a very flexible division of labor in housework and childcare by which many tasks were shared or interchangeable, whereas other families had a much stricter division into the wife's tasks and the husband's tasks.

Similarly, there were some activities, such as making important decisions that would affect the whole family, that tended to be carried out jointly by husband and wife. But here too there was considerable variation. Some husbands and wives placed great emphasis on joint decision, whereas others hardly mentioned it. Couples who stressed the importance of joint decisions also had many shared and interchangeable tasks in housework and childcare.

In activities such as recreation, including here entertaining and visiting people as well as hobbies, reading, going to the cinema, concerts, and so forth, there was so much variation that it is impossible to say that one form of organization was consistently dominant in all families.

Thus, although all three modes of organizing activities—complementary, independent, and joint—were found in all families, there were marked differences in the relative amounts of each, particularly in the amounts of joint and independent organization. I use the phrase *degree of segregation of conjugal roles* to compare the combination of the three modes of organization in different families. By degree of segregation of conjugal roles I mean the relative balance between complementary and independent activities on the one hand, and joint activities on the other. And, as noted above, a highly segregated conjugal role-relationship is defined as one in which husband and wife have a relatively large proportion of complementary and independent activities and a relatively small proportion of joint activities. In a joint conjugal role-relationship, the proportion of complementary and independent activities is relatively small and the proportion of joint activities is relatively large. These are differences of degree. Strictly speaking, it would be more correct to say that a conjugal relationship was "highly segregated relative to the other research couples" or "less segregated relative to the other research couples" or "intermediate in degree of segregation relative to the other research couples"; but in order to simplify the language I shall refer to them as "highly segregated," "joint," and "intermediate." If the hypothesis to be discussed in this chapter were to be tested quantitatively, it would be necessary to arrange the families on a scale according to degree of conjugal segregation. But the data on modes of organization, although detailed, were not collected with quantification in mind so that we did not make exactly the same observations or ask exactly the same questions of each couple. Rather than attempt a shaky quantitative analysis, I have left the definition in qualitative terms.

The research couples made it clear that there had been important changes in their degree of conjugal segregation during their married life. In the first phase, before they had children, all couples had had far more joint activities, especially in the form of shared recreation outside the home. After their children were born the activities of all couples had become more sharply differentiated and they had had to cut down on joint external recreation. Data from the group discussions with wives in the third phase, when the children were adolescent and leaving home, suggest that most husbands and wives do not return to the extensive joint organization of the first phase even when the necessity for differentiation produced by the presence of young children is no longer so great.

But the differences in degree of segregation of conjugal roles among the research families cannot be attributed to differences in phase of development, because all the families were in more or less the same phase. Early in the research, it seemed likely that these differences were related in some way or another to forces in the social environment of the families. In first attempts to explore these forces an effort was made to explain conjugal segregation in terms of social class. This attempt was not very successful. The husbands who had the most segregated role-relationships with their wives had manual occupations, and the husbands who had the most joint role-relationships with their wives were professional or semi-professional people; but there were several working-class families that had relatively little segregation, and there were professional families in which segregation was considerable. Having a working-class occupation is a necessary but not a sufficient cause of the most marked degree of conjugal segregation. An attempt was also made to relate degree of segregation to the type of local area in which the family lived, since the data suggested that the families with most segregation lived in homogeneous areas of low population turnover, whereas the families with predominantly joint role-relationships lived in heterogeneous areas of high population turnover. Once again, however, there were several exceptions.

But there was a more important difficulty. These attempts at rudimentary statistical correlation did not make clear how one factor affected another; it seemed impossible to explain exactly how the criteria for class position or the criteria for different types of local area were actually producing an effect on the internal role structure of the family. It therefore appeared that attempts to correlate segregation of conjugal roles with factors selected from the generalized social environment of the families would not yield a meaningful interpretation. This does not mean that social class is unimportant. But it does mean that mere correlation of social class with other factors is not very illuminating in itself. It is necessary to explain the correlation, to examine negative cases, to uncover the mechanisms by which social class and conjugal segregation are related to each other.

Because I could not understand the relationship between conjugal segregation, social class, and neighborhood composition, I put social class and neighborhood composition to one side for the time being and turned to look more closely at the immediate environment of the families, that is, at their actual external relationships with friends, neighbors, relatives, clubs, shops, places of work, and so forth. This approach proved more fruitful.

First, it appeared that the external social relationships of all families assumed the form of a *network* rather than the form of an organized group.[1] In an organized group, the component individuals make up a larger social whole with common aims, interdependent roles, and a distinctive subculture. In network formation, on the other hand, only some, not all, of the component individuals have social relationships with one another. For example, supposing that a family, X, maintains relationships with friends, neighbors, and relatives who may be designated as A, B, C, D, E, F . . . N, one will find that some but not all of these external persons know one another. They do not form an organized group in the sense defined above. B might know A and C but none of the others; D might know F without knowing A, B, or E. Furthermore, all of these persons will have friends, neighbors, and relatives of their own who are not known by family X. In a network the component external units do not make up a larger social whole; they are not surrounded by a common boundary.[2]

Second, although all the research families belonged to networks rather than to groups, there was considerable variation in the "*connectedness*" of their networks. By connectedness, I mean the extent to which the people known by a family know and meet one another independently of the family. I use the word "*close-knit*" to describe a network in which there are many relationships among the component units, and the word "*loose-knit*" to describe a network in which there are few such relationships. Strictly speaking, "close-knit" should read "close-knit relative to the networks of the other research families," and "loose-knit" should read "loose-knit relative to the networks of the other research families." The shorter terms are used to simplify the language, but it should be remembered that they are shorthand expressions of relative degrees of connectedness and that they are not intended to be conceived as polar opposites.

A qualitative examination of the research data suggests that the degree of segregation of conjugal roles is related to the degree of connectedness in the total network of the family. Those families that had a high degree of segregation in the role-relationship of husband and wife had a close-knit network; many of their friends, neighbors, and relatives knew one another. Families that had a relatively joint role-relationship between husband and wife had a loose-knit network; few of their relatives, neighbors, and friends knew one another. There were many degrees of variation between these two extremes. On the basis of our data, I should therefore like to put forward the following hypothesis: The degree of segregation in the role-relationship of husband and wife varies directly with the connectedness of the family's social network. The more connected the network, the greater the degree of segregation between the roles of husband and wife. The less connected the network, the smaller the degree of segregation between the roles of husband and wife.

At first sight this seems to be an odd relationship, for it is hard to see why the social relationship of other people with one another should affect the relationship of husband and wife. What seems to happen is this. When many of the people a person knows interact with one another—that is, when the person's network is close-knit—the members of his network tend to reach consensus on norms and they exert consistent informal pressure on one another to conform to the norms, to keep in touch with one another, and, if need be, to help one another. If both husband and wife come to marriage with such close-knit networks, and if conditions are such that the previous pattern of relationships is continued, the marriage will be superimposed on these pre-existing relationships, and both spouses will continue to be drawn into activities with people outside their own elementary family (family of procreation). Each will get some emotional satisfaction from these external relationships and will be likely to demand correspondingly less of the spouse. Rigid segregation of conjugal roles will be possible because each spouse can get help from people outside.

But when most of the people a person knows do not interact with one another, that is, when his network is loose-knit, more variation on norms is likely to develop in the network, and social control and mutual assistance will be more fragmented and less consistent. If husband and wife come to marriage with such loose-knit networks or if conditions are such that their networks become loose-knit after marriage, they must seek in each other some of the emotional satisfactions and help with familial tasks that couples in close-knit networks can get from outsiders. Joint organization becomes more necessary for the success of the family as an enterprise.

No claim is made here that connectedness of the family's network is the only factor affecting segregation of conjugal roles. Among the other variables affecting the way conjugal roles are performed, the personalities of husband and wife are of crucial importance. Most of this chapter will be devoted to a discussion of the effect of connectedness, however, because the importance of this variable has been insufficiently stressed in previous studies of family role structure. What I am trying to do is to make a comparative study of the relationship between conjugal role segregation and network-connectedness for each of the twenty families considered as a social system. In so doing, I have developed a hypothesis that, with further refinement of definition, preferably in quantifiable terms, might be tested on other families and might facilitate further and more systematic comparisons.

The analysis of social networks presented in this and the following chapter is only a first step. Before the analysis can become at all precise, it will be necessary to define degrees of intimacy and obligation of the various relationships. If possible, it would be advisable to interview several members of a network, following the links of interaction from one person to another, instead of relying on what each couple say about their network, as I have done. Precise definition of connectedness would require quantitative analysis of the total network, of the independent networks of husband and wife, of their joint network (the people with whom they have joint relationships), and of that part of the total network composed of kin, that composed of friends, and that composed of neighbors. But the data of the present research are not consistent or detailed enough to permit such quantitative analysis.

The nature of the relationship between conjugal segregation and network-connectedness may now be examined in general terms.

Close-knit networks are most likely to develop when husband and wife, together with their friends, neighbors, and relatives, have grown up in the same local area and have continued to live there after marriage. Many people know one another and have known one another since childhood. Women tend to associate with women and men with men. The only legitimate forms of heterosexual relationship are those between kin and between husband and wife. Friendship between a man and woman who are not kin is suspect.

In such a setting, husband and wife come to marriage each with his own close-knit network. Each partner makes a considerable emotional investment in relationships with the people in his network. Each is engaged in reciprocal exchanges of material and emotional support with them. Each is very sensitive to their opinions and values, not only because the relationships are intimate, but also because the people in the network know one another and share the same norms so that they are able to apply consistent informal sanctions to one another. The marriage is superimposed on these pre-existing relationships.

Although the networks of husband and wife are distinct, it is very likely, even at the time of marriage, that there will be overlapping between them. Judging by the Newbolts' account of their genealogy, one of the common ways for husband and wife to meet is through introduction by a person who is simultaneously a friend of one and a relative of the other. Male relatives of the wife are likely to be friends or colleagues of the husband, and, after a marriage has continued for some time, the husbands of a set of sisters are likely to become friends.

As long as the couple continues to live in the same area, and as long as their friends, neighbors, and relatives also continue to live within easy reach of the family and of one another, so long will the segregated networks of husband and wife continue, with minor changes. The husband is likely to stop seeing some friends of his youth, particularly those who work at a different place or go to different pubs and clubs. After children are born, the wife will see less of her former girl-friends and more of her mother and other female relatives. The wife becomes deeply embedded in activities with kin. Her children bring her into a new and even closer relationship with her own mother, who now becomes the children's grandmother. The husband is to some extent drawn into his wife's kinship circle, although he keeps in touch at least with his own mother. But more of his time is spent with colleagues and friends than with relatives. His life is centered on work and some form of recreation away from home; his wife's life is centered on her home, her children, and her relatives.

The data suggest that the woman's network of kin is likely to be more close-knit than the husband's network of friends, partly because relationships with kin are harder to break off, but also because kin have more mutual aid and material assistance to offer one another. Friends cannot use their resources, particularly their slender financial resources, to help one another when their first obligation is to look after their own wives and children and then their parents and more distant relatives. But this difference in degree of connectedness within the total network needs further and more precise study. It would be necessary to compare the type and degree of intimacy and obligation toward friends, neighbors, and relatives. It would also be necessary to quantify the connectedness not only of the total network, but also of that part of the network composed of kin, that composed of friends, and that composed of neighbors, and it would be advisable to compare the connectedness of the total network with that of the independent networks of husband and wife and with that of their joint network.

Apart from minor readjustments, then, husband and wife can carry on their old external relationships after marriage, and they continue to be influenced by them. In spite of the conjugal segregation in external relationships the overlapping of the networks of husband and wife tends to ensure that each partner learns about the other's activities. Although a wife may not know directly what a husband does when with his friends, one of the other men is likely to tell his wife or some female relative and the information is passed on. Similarly, any important activity of the wife is likely to be made known to her husband.

Because old relationships can be continued after marriage, both husband and wife can satisfy some personal needs outside the marriage, so that their emotional investment in the conjugal relationship need not be as intense as it is in other types of family. The wife, particularly, can get outside help with domestic tasks and with child care. A rigid division of labor between husband and wife is therefore possible. The segregation in external relationships can be carried over to activities within the family.

But although external people may help the elementary family, close-knit networks may also interfere with conjugal solidarity. A wife's loyalty to her mother may interfere with her relationship with her husband. Similarly, her relationship with her husband may interfere with her relationship with her mother. A man's loyalty to his friends may interfere with his obligations to his wife and vice versa.

Networks become loose-knit when people move from one place to another or when they make new relationships not connected with their old ones. If both husband and wife have moved considerably before marriage, each will bring an already loose-knit network to the marriage. Many of the husband's friends will not know one another; many of the wife's friends will not know one another. Although they will continue to see some old friends after marriage, they will meet new people too, who will not necessarily know the old friends or one another. In other words, their external relationships are relatively discontinuous both in space and in time. Such continuity as they possess lies in their relationship with each other rather than in their external relationships. In facing the external world they draw on each other, for their strongest emotional investment is made where there is continuity. Hence their high standards of conjugal compatibility, their stress on shared interests, on joint organization, on equality between husband and wife. They must get along well together, they must help one another in carrying out familial tasks, for there is no sure external source of material and emotional help. Since their friends and relatives are physically scattered and few of them know one another, the husband and wife are not stringently controlled by a solid body of public opinion. They are also unable to rely on consistent external support. Through their joint external relationships, they present a united front to the world and they reaffirm their joint relationship with each other. Joint relationships with friends give both husband and wife a source of emotional satisfaction outside the family without threatening their relationship with each other. Heterosexual relationships with non-kin are allowed, but they are controlled by being made into joint relationships.

Between these two extremes are the families with medium-knit and transitional networks. In the medium-knit type, husband and wife have moved a certain amount so that they seek continuity with each other and make their strongest emotional investment in the conjugal relationship. At the same time, they are able to have some segregated relationships outside the family and to rely on considerable casual help from people outside the family, so that a fairly clearly defined division of labor into male tasks and female tasks can be made.

The transitional families illustrate some of the factors involved in changing from one type of network to another. Husbands and wives who change from a close-knit to a loose-knit network find themselves suddenly thrust into a more joint relationship without the experience or the attitudes appropriate to it. The eventual outcome depends partly on the family and partly on the extent to which their new neighbors build up relationships with one another. An intermediate form of network-connectedness seems to be the most likely outcome. Similarly, in the case of families who change from a loose-knit to a more close-knit network, the first reaction is one of defensiveness over their privacy, but in time they tend to develop an intermediate degree of network-connectedness and conjugal segregation.

20 Community Status and Family Structure in British Guiana

RAYMOND T. SMITH

The interchanges between family and community are not always concrete; they may be symbolic as well. Status is a "commodity" which the family derives from the community. In his study of the Negro family in British Guiana, Dr. Smith describes the status system of the whole society. Families are oriented to this status system (indeed, contribute to it) and as a consequence develop a specific type of internal structure within the family. Smith's description of the Negro family in British Guiana is reminiscent of Frazier's account of the Negro family in the United States. In particular, we may note the important place that Smith gives to economic functions. Similarly, it is instructive to compare Smith's account of the shifts in the problems the need for economic support present with Riesman and Roseborough's account of the consumption career of the American family.

We maintain that the matri-focal system of domestic relations and household groupings, in the villages we have studied, can be regarded as the obverse of the marginal nature of the husband-father role. We further argue that there is a correlation between the nature of the husband-father role and the role of men in the economic system and in the system of social stratification in the total Guianese society. Men, in their role of husband-father, are placed in a position where neither their social status nor their access to, and command of, economic resources are of major importance in the functioning of the household group *at certain stages of its development.*

Such an argument requires a good deal of elaboration and we shall begin by attempting to summarize the main features of the status system and the family system as follows:—

Features of the Status System

A. There is a scale of color values at the extremes of which the "white" or European complex is given positive value and the "black" or Negro complex is given negative value, and this serves as a basis for the

From *The Negro Family in British Guiana*, pp. 221–28, 253–54, with the kind permission of the following: New York: Humanities Press; London: Routledge and Kegan Paul Ltd., in association with the Institute of Social and Economic Research, University College of the West Indies, 1956.

hierarchical ranking of persons and groups of persons, according to the color characteristics ascribed to them.

B. The other main basis of evaluation of a person's status is in terms of his performance in economic or occupational roles, thereby making it possible for a limited number of persons to achieve higher status than that which is initially ascribed to them on the basis of their color, though the ethnic component of a person's social character is never completely effaced as a factor in status placement. Achieved status is secondary to ascribed status, especially at the extreme ends of the color scale, but the evaluation of performance in jobs, educational attainment, etc., can serve as a basis for upward mobility especially in the middle zone of the color scale.

C. We may speak of a color-class system in so far as the internal differentiation of the social system allocates differential facilities and rewards largely on the basis of position on the scale of socially evaluated color differences, but the fact that performance criteria are taken into account keeps the system open to a degree where we can speak of classes which do not have an absolute one-to-one relation to ethnic factors.

D. Ethnic groups such as the Portuguese, Chinese, and East Indians, which do not fit readily into the color-class hierarchy, are able to infiltrate at all levels and to take over special functions where a relative lack of status-consciousness is an advantage, particularly in the retail and distributive trades. The development of a separate collectivity, primarily oriented towards a function implying the predominance of economic achievement, such as business enterprise, competition, and efficiency, really conflicts with ascribed membership of groups, and it would seem to have been fortuitous that these ethnic groups came from societies where there was already a tradition of trading, shopkeeping, money-lending, and so on. The market nexus of petty trading in British Guiana is interstitial to the ascriptively based social groupings, but it has not developed very far towards becoming organized or forming a primary focus of attention for the ordering of social relations; and in any case the larger scale marketing operations have been controlled by the higher-status ethnic groups. The very multiplicity of operators in the lowest level of the marketing system (especially vendors of garden produce, fruits, etc.) is an indication of the tendency to spread the functions and prevent specialization from developing to a point where it would conflict with the ascribed low status of the operators. One special feature of a differentiated group in market operations is the necessity for "affective neutrality," and this could most readily be found in the Chinese and Portuguese groups, where all other sections of the population did in fact regard them as being neutral in terms of the scale of color values and the symbolism connected with it.[1]

E. In the villages studied, the model of the total social system tends to repeat itself, but since the village is only a section of the total society, it does not have the same degree of internal differentiation. The village "upper class" is either occupationally or ethnically differentiated in the sense that its members are either non-Negroes or in high-status white-collar (usually government) jobs, and it shows its difference by means of "diacritical" signs such as dress, speech pattern, marriage pattern, etc.[2]

F. The main village group tends to be solidary vis-à-vis the rest of the society, and status differentiation within it is discouraged since this would conflict with the main status differentiations within the total social system. However, there are both non-hierarchical differentiations (segmentations) and minor differential prestige positions within it, as well as the inevitable age and sex differentiations which are not directly relevant to the present discussion.

G. There is a variation in the degree of internal differentiation as between the three villages.

Main Aspects of Family Structure

A. The household group tends to be matri-focal in the sense that a woman in the status of "mother" is usually the *de facto* leader of the group, and conversely the husband-father, although *de jure* head of the household group (if present), is usually marginal to the complex of internal relationships of the group. By "marginal" we mean that he associates relatively infrequently with the other members of the group and is on the fringe of the effective ties which bind the group together.

B. Household groups normally come into being when a man and a woman enter a conjugal union (legal or common-law marriage) and set up house together in a separate dwelling. Either or both partners may have children which were born prior to the establishment of an effective conjugal union.

C. During the period when the woman is bearing children, she will be most dependent on her spouse for economic support and most subject to his authority and control, but as her children grow older she becomes much more independent and acquires much greater security in her status as "mother."

D. Common-law marriage is a cultural characteristic of the lower class and can be regarded as a permissive deviation from the norms of the total social system. The nonlegal nature of the tie reflects the reluctance to establish a conclusive bond and is in accordance with the primary emphasis upon the mother-child relationship rather than the conjugal relationship.

E. There is a variation in the incidence of different types of conjugal union as between the three villages.

These two paradigms have been constructed in an attempt to compress into a more manageable form the relevant features of the two complexes we wish to correlate, and they are only intended as a brief summary of our previous descriptions.

It would seem that whereas biological relatedness is taken as a major focus of status ascription in the total social system, the unit of kinship which is emphasized in this respect is not the nuclear or extended family as such, but rather the widest possible kinship unit which is the ethnic group itself. Within this group, two other points of reference become foci of differentiation in descending order of importance (from this point of view). They are territorial affiliation (membership of the local community) and matri-filiation. Matri-filiation as a basis of status ascription has a long history in the West Indies, and under the slave regime it was taken as defining legal status. The child of a slave woman and a free man always took its mother's legal status and became a slave.[3] In the contemporary situation, the relation to the mother almost invariably determines the place of residence of the child, for it is the services rendered to the child by the mother, such as "care" in its broadest sense, which are among the main functions of the household group. In this respect it is significant that any woman will give any child a little food, and children quite often eat at their play-mates' homes or at the houses of kinsfolk if they happen to be there at meal times.

There is a sense in which we can take for granted the fact that the mother-child relationship will be a close one in any society, and the real problem then begins to center on the way in which masculine roles are integrated into the family system and the way in which the mother-child relationship is structured to fit in with the general structure including the masculine role pattern.[4]

In societies where kinship provides the basis for practically all the differentiation within the social system, the positions of prestige and control are almost invariably and totally vested in adult males, and no matter whether the system is patrilineal, matrilineal, or based on double unilineal descent, it is males in whom the principal rights over property and services are vested. The varying patterns of domestic organization may place these rights in different contexts, and even where the rights themselves are formally vested in women, as among the Hopi, it is still the males who control the exercise of these rights and who hold positions of primary managerial authority.[5]

It is clear from our discussions in previous chapters that the role of husband-father is by no means absent in lower-class Negro society in British Guiana, nor is it reduced to such insignificant proportions as we find in certain extreme matrilineal societies such as the traditional Nayar.[6]

Among the Nayar a woman resides in the joint household (*taravad*) of her matrilineage and is visited by a series of lovers with whom she has sexual relations. Her children remain with her in the *taravad* where they come under the authority of the eldest male member of the group, who may be the woman's brother, mother's brother, or even mother's mother's brother. The child's father, who is an outsider to the group (he may even belong to a different caste), has no economic, political, or ritual functions in relation to the *taravad* of his children. His relationship to his child is confined to presenting certain customary gifts at the time of the birth. The role of husband-father is not completely absent from the Nayar system, but it is reduced to extremely limited proportions.

However, men do have vital economic, political, status, and ritual functions in relation to their own *taravad,* and it is the existence of a tightly organized unilineal descent group, having strongly corporate functions, and laying stress upon the close interdependence of a set of brothers and sisters, that makes the Nayar system completely different from that with which we are dealing in British Guiana. The Nayar are able to reduce the husband-father role to minimal proportions precisely because male roles in relation to the *taravad* are so highly developed and the supportive activities of males in relation to women and children are embodied in the structure of the *taravad*. Virtually the only activities of men in relation to women which are left outside the sphere of the matrilineage are those concerned with sexual activity and procreation.

In the bilaterally organized kinship system of the villages with which we are dealing, men are essential providers of economic support for women and children. Women can, and do, engage in money-making activities, but they cannot be economically self-sufficient. The question then arises as to how men's supportive functions shall be tied in to the family system. There are thus two distinct problems to be considered. The first concerns the male role in society, and here we have indicated that men are expected to earn money to contribute to the support of women and children. We have described in some detail the difficulties which face men in a society where there is little prospect of steady employment, and we have also stressed the fact that there is little occupational differentiation and correspondingly little hierarchical status differentiation among the village men. The second problem concerns the direction in which men are to offer their economic support, and this is the main problem we are to consider here. Economic support for women and children is located in a series of statuses, the principal ones being those of son, husband and lover. It is not located in a group, for in a bilaterally organized kinship system there is no enduring kinship-group structure available. For any particular woman with children, the problem is to find a male in one of the above statuses to provide the necessary support. Chance factors inherent in the birth and death incidence render the likelihood of there being an individual always available to fill a given status somewhat uncertain, and therefore a situation such as the one in British Guiana has to be sufficiently fluid to permit a choice of alternative persons. This is particularly the case in bilateral systems of narrow range.

One way of resolving this difficulty is to vest the functions of economic support in a husband-father who is selected from a wide range of possible individuals, and this is precisely what happens in our case. However, the importance of the economic function of the husband-father becomes diminished as the woman passes her period of maximum dependence and becomes freed for economic activities of her own and as her sons begin to take over supportive functions. The reasons for this must be sought in the economic and stratification systems of the total social system.

In a society where the range of effective kinship ties is narrowed to a point where the nuclear family becomes a highly significant and relatively isolated unit, as in urban middle-class groups in the United States, then the position of the husband-father in the primary status-determining occupational system, rather than in an extended kinship system, is a crucial one. In such a situation, hierarchical mobility is normal, and the husband-father determines the social status of the whole unit by virtue of his position in the occupational system. He becomes the peg on which the whole unit hangs.

In British Guiana, the male member of the village groups neither has exclusive control over property and services, including the means of production for the livelihood of the household group, nor does he determine its status in the social system by virtue of his position in a graded occupational hierarchy, since this is already determined to a large extent by race or color, plus membership of the territorial unit which is the village. The important fact is that occupations are not hierarchically graded to any significant extent within the main Negro village groups, though the occupations of the Negro men are ranked low in the total occupational system in the same way that Negro men are ranked low in the color scale. The male's participation in the occupational system does not affect the status of the other members of the household group, which is already defined by their racial characteristics and territorial affiliation. This is a very broad statement and only holds good for the relatively undifferentiated lowest-status group. As soon as one approaches the upper fringe of this group, where prestige factors begin to operate, or get into the higher-status village group, then the occupation of the husband-father becomes significant, and there is a quite definite tendency for his position in the household group to be established and for him to become a reference point for the other members of the group. In the urban middle class certain other factors may intervene to tend to bring the focus of solidarity of the group back to the mother, particularly where the man marries a lighter-colored woman who then becomes a focus of attention for status placement on the color scale.[7] In the middle class there is always this interplay between occupational factors and color and/or cultural factors. In the lowest-status group, the only basis for male authority in the household unit is the husband-father's contribution to the economic foundation of the group, and where there is both insecurity in jobs where males are concerned and opportunities for women to engage in money-making activities, including farming, then there is likely to develop a situation where men's roles are structurally marginal in the complex of domestic relations. Concomitantly, the status of women as mothers is enhanced, and the natural importance of the mother role is left unimpeded.

Although we have had to present our argument rather forcefully in order to make it clear, there are certain reservations which must be entered. The analysis of family structure has shown quite clearly that the elementary family, consisting of a conjugal pair and their offspring, is not atypical in the groups we have been considering, but is in fact the normal unit of co-residence, particularly at the stage when a father-figure is important in the socialization of the children. It is not within our competence to discuss the psychological implications of this fact, but in any discussion of socialization it should be borne in mind that we are dealing with a social system where the *normal* unit of child-rearing is an elementary family unit. In particular cases of mental development it would be important to look for the deviations from this norm, and in discussing the psychological component of values it may be necessary to bear in mind the nature of the father-child and mother-child relationships. In the three villages we have been discussing it would not be justifiable to treat these questions as if the normal pattern were for children to grow up without any kind of relationship to a father or father-surrogate, and high illegitimacy rates are not an indication of these relationships.

In a variety of societies, we find a correlation between low social status in a stratified society and a type of family system in which men seem to lack importance as authoritarian figures in domestic relations. These are facts of social structure, and the arrangement of these structural elements is basically similar despite marked variations in their corresponding cultural complexes in different societies. We are really dealing with subsystems of the several societies, although certain aspects of the total societies are basically comparable. In all cases the subgroups with which we are most immediately concerned constitute relatively solidary groups, differentiated with respect to other groups in the society but internally relatively undifferentiated so far as status is concerned.

If our analysis is correct then it raises certain issues of general importance. It would suggest that there is a rewarding field for comparative study between Latin American and West Indian societies using a structural frame of reference. The relations of racial or ethnic groups become special cases of a general theory of social stratification, and "acculturation" has to be seen in the light of continuing social differentiations of a certain kind.

Cultural traditions of certain ethnic subgroups may be found to persist as indices of status differentiation rather than as a result of geographical isolation. Leach has graphically shown how even linguistic differences can persist between households in one local community provided there is a structural base for such cultural differentiation, and his conclusion that culture and structure appear to vary independently is borne out by our researches, though there is always the possibility that the independent variability is merely apparent at the particular level of abstraction at which we are working.[8]

21 *The Family and Peer Groups*

JESSE PITTS

*Another type of concrete group in which family members, particularly the young,
normally and regularly participate is the peer group. The peer group is widely considered
to be significant in the socialization of the child—for better or for worse. Available
accounts, however, leave the impression that the peer group influences only the individual involved, and that this is a one-way process. In this article, Dr. Pitts explores
more broadly the forms and functions of the mutual relationships between family and
peer group. For this article, Dr. Pitts draws upon his knowledge of French society, in
which he was reared, but also suggests some points of comparison with America.*

I. "May I Play with the Little Boy?"

Scene on a French beach: Toto, aged six, has been hard at
work making a mountain and using his bucket as the business end of the
steam shovel he is now impersonating. His mother is taking the sun, flat
on her back, her eyes sheltered by dark sunglasses. Another boy of about
the same age has been watching Toto. He moves closer. Toto goes on;
soon the other boy offers his help; two steam shovels could carve out a
hole big enough to accommodate a house, or at least a fire engine. . . . Toto
hesitates, turns back to his mother and asks: "Maman, may I play with
the little boy?" The mother sits up, one hand holding up the top of her
bathing suit, the other lifting her sunglasses. She blinks, looks over at the
"little boy." Her eyes search for the little boy's mother. If she cannot find
her, then the answer will be "no": a family *comme il faut* does not let
a six-year-old out of immediate range. If she finds the mother, she looks
at the clothing, the beach equipment, the general allure and concludes:
"Yes, you may, but stay here," or, "I'm afraid we do not have any more
time."[1]

To the American observer, such a scene is relatively strange. In this
country, little boys organize games without much of a "by your leave"
from the parent. Boys in France are different. They can play alone for long
periods of time. They find their playmates more frequently among their
siblings, each family living as a sort of separate society behind its high walls
and its closed shutters, a protection which it seems to take along wherever
it may go.

This article was specially prepared for this volume. It is partly based upon a chapter
from the author's Ph.D. thesis, "The French Bourgeois Family and Economic Retardation"
(Harvard University, 1957).

Very little spontaneity is allowed young French boys (and girls) in the choice of their playmates. Parents exercise strict supervision and do not hesitate, as would an American liberal, to tell the child he must not associate with an unsuitable companion. The child is made aware, very early, that he represents his family and that claims to fun are secondary to the requirements of propriety. The type of clothes the French bourgeois child wears on the playground is sufficient testimony to this fact.

The child will also realize that it is dangerous to make advances, and that it is the inferior, the weak, who make these advances because they need something which the other person possesses. Trying to originate social relations is an implicit avowal of some lack in one's family. The boy who is *réservé* (reserved) will be thought *bien élevé* (well brought up), and rewarded by his parents. Even if it means playing alone, the child will be discouraged from establishing random contacts which might compel his family to take notice of another family and expose them to possible rebuff. The play activity of the child, if it is unsupervised, may lead to difficult social situations where the desire to be human conflicts with the necessity of avoiding possible exposure to snubs. It must be realized that, in the intensely competitive atmosphere of French social life, the temptation is very great to snub whenever one has a chance, thus asserting a legitimate superiority over whoever seems to desire your company.[2] The French child lives in a world where, outside of the relationships ascribed by kinship, his social initiative is low. It is safer if his parents select his playmates. Cousins are, of course, preferred playmates, since any adult intervention in children's quarrels is colored by the ascribed benevolence of the uncle or aunt. Children of family friends are also highly suitable.

Relationships outside of the family and its friends are much more delicate, for parents are apt to interfere brutally if they deem the relationship a prestige deficit for the family. For that matter, they will interfere if they fall into a long quarrel with their friends or family members, and will compel their children to cease interacting with their erstwhile playmates. In the same vein, one of the first patterns of bourgeois behavior which the aspiring peasant, working-class or white-collar family will attempt to initiate, besides enforcing chastity on the daughter, is the restriction and planning of the children's *fréquentations* (contacts), even if it means shutting up the child in a two-room apartment for a whole Thursday.[3] This action shows a heightened sense of family pride which separates the family from its peers and marks it as having entered the mobility race.

Thus, the child is taught that his right to enter a relationship is limited by his obligation to bring satisfaction to the family, and that in any relationship which comes to his parents' attention, he must expect their control, and even their direction. Ideally speaking, he should need no playmates outside of those furnished by the family and its circle of well-established friends. To strike out for oneself is a sign of disloyalty and unfaithfulness, or even of foolishness, for the outside world is full of dangers, and one must not count on automatic good will.

In this paper, we shall try to show how the French bourgeois family fosters a certain type of peer-group membership, both consciously and through the unintended consequences of some of its socialization patterns. We shall end by showing how childhood and adolescent peer-group roles, in turn, create in the adult Frenchman certain types of membership capacities and incapacities. Though the French *bourgeoisie* includes only a small minority of the population, it is a model for the rest of the society. The consequences for social structure of certain general value patterns, transmitted to all French children by school and family, can be better perceived through the study of the *bourgeoisie* because this class has more means of implementation. The basic outlines of family and peer-group experience are relevant to all the urban-lower, middle, and upper classes.

We must now define what we mean by peer groups. It is difficult to define the peer group by its structure, precisely because it lacks the clear-cut structural features of formal organizations. It is easier to define it by its functions. The peer group is a social system, of two or more participants, which has pattern-maintenance and integrative functions for the society and the personality.

A. FUNCTIONS FOR SOCIETY

The pattern-maintenance functions of the peer group refer mainly to its capacity to provide formal organizations (economic, political, educational) with a steady supply of socialized motivation. By "socialized motivation" is meant a motivation which is not excessive or insufficient, in relation to the needs of the relevant social system, and that is "organization wise," i.e., it has learned the rhythm of work and the codes of communication that permit effective co-operation with others. The "steadiness" of the motivation supply refers to the fact that the peer group sets norms of achievement that are within the long range possibilities of its members, above which they become "eager beavers" or "apple polishers," and below which they are "gold bricks" or "goof offs." It defends the legitimacy of its performance norms against pressure from authority. This function is sometimes alluded to as the "conservation" of the peer group.

Taking into itself members who share a general commitment to values but whose individual motivations have varying intensity and content, it homogenizes motivation through the creation of a common denominator: loyalty to the peer group which draws upon early structures in the member's personality.

The integrative functions of the peer group refer mainly to its capacity for providing order, in spite of variations in the flow of the motivational and non-motivational facilities necessary for fulfilling group norms. Members will help one another through communication, and sometimes through special exertion, in order to cope with individual failures or un-expected resistances of the environment. Hence, the peer group represents the give and take which must take place if the expectations of formal organization are going to be realized; more abstractly put, it represents the homeostatic resiliency of roles in the face of constantly changing conditions.

B. FUNCTIONS FOR THE PERSONALITY

The peer group will reward the commitment to the level of value achievement embodied in membership through esteem: members are the "right sort." Once the individual is so defined, he will be given support regardless of temporary failures. The peer group is very permissive of the verbal expression of rebellion against the customers or outside judges of performance, because it defines failures as being due to circumstances beyond the control of the members. Thus the peer group acts as a source of nurturance, i.e., it grants gratification which is not conditional upon immediate performance. In fact, in relation to values not of immediate relevance to the peer group, the latter will tend to legitimize the member's definition of the situation as long as his attitudes remain compatible with his presumed commitment to the group norms. Thus, the peer group supports and protects the identity of its members. This is the core of its pattern-maintenance functions for the personality.

Its integrative functions center around the allocation of commitment to various role demands. Since the peer group represents a viable solution to the problem of order, conformity with the peer-group norms will imply the avoidance of excessive commitment to certain roles which would jeopardize performance in other capacities, or under-commitment which might expose one to societal sanctions.

Peer-group membership results in a sharper "reality perception," at least within the limits of the group's definition of the in-group–out-group situation. There is a higher awareness of the learning or performance gap, because the group allows the member's self a certain initial rebellion against the value demands put upon it. At the same time as the member perceives the problematical aspect of the environment, he also perceives the protective aspects of the peer group through the existence of other members who are pledged to co-operate with him in attaining his particular sub-goal. This is the origin of the feelings of warmth which members frequently feel for one another all the more as the out-group is defined as hostile or competing for scarce performance facilities. It is a form of identification, where regardless of alter's superiority, it is accepted by ego as available to himself, instead of consigning him to a general inferiority in terms of his own value commitments.

Performance demands which are made by an outside authority (parents, school, army officer, business organization) and which might raise a problem of identity, are transformed by the peer group into adjustive problems. It seems that, defined in this light, a very high level of learning can be assimilated by the individual, all the more since the peer group operates as a permanent public, permissive but omnipresent.

Because of these functions for both society and personality, the peer group operates as a bargaining agency between its members and the authority demanding performance. For instance, it will give adaptive compliance to orders requiring new levels of performance, only in return for assurance that its existence as peer group will not be threatened and that the costs in uncertainty will be minimized. It acts as the defender of personality and institutional requirements in relation to authorities bent only on economic or political rationality.

In this definition, we have dealt with an ideal-type description of a social system. In reality, all collectivities, all organizations, have peer-group dimensions which make up the bulk of what is called "informal organization," all concrete peer groups have some economic and political dimensions.

II. The French Bourgeois Family and Its Peer Groups

As he reaches school age, the French child discovers that the family is a complex social field with several circles of membership and a more complex hierarchy than he had realized at first. In the center is the nuclear family, composed of the mother, father, and the siblings. This is *la maison* or *chez nous*. It usually includes a servant, and in the more affluent circles a "demoiselle" in charge of the routine care of the children. Then there are the grandparents, the uncles and aunts, and the cousins. There may also be more distant relations. There are also the friends of the family, who are often addressed as "uncle" or "aunt," and their children, though not cousins, have a status that is similar. Beyond *chez nous,* roles cannot be simply ascribed on the basis of kinship terminology. There are complex systems of preferences, rivalries, hostilities, and of completely manipulative relationships where the child participates as a member of his nuclear family, but also in his own right. Blocked by his family from undertaking spontaneous relationships on the outside, the child is, by contrast, encouraged to develop relationships within the broad confines of the extended kin group. Here, what you give is not lost, it will return to you. Reciprocity can be expected within the family, even if it takes a long time to be realized—*cela reste dans la famille.* The nuclear family and the extended family are the vicars of God and motherland on this earth.

There is not, in the French extended family, a clear-cut allocation of power. There may be an elderly person, often a woman, who has a clear superiority by reason of age and fortune. The places below him (or her) are open to competitive struggles where few holds are barred, partly because the consequences of the struggle are rarely mortal: it is a question of relative ranking rather than a question of elimination.

Maiden aunts, bachelor uncles, childless couples have a special power position because the disposal of their property is largely at their discretion. Grandparents, though the civil code limits their testamentary freedom to one-quarter of their property, nevertheless have much freedom in deciding which family will receive the most cherished symbols of family continuity, such as the family homestead, the family souvenirs, or command posts in the family firm.

In a slow-moving economy, as France had prior to 1953, capital received very high returns as compared to the returns allocated to labor. Furthermore, old capital had much more prestige value than new capital. Hence, inheritance was, and still is, not merely a matter of a generalized facility—money, but is also a token of esteem and relative status within the extended family.

The areas of competitive achievement are the implementation of the family tradition, the contribution to the family's prestige in the outside world,[4] and the capacity to please the dispenser of favors. This is something more complex than sheer flattery, and it has a definite place in the French pantheon of virtues; for being able to give pleasure to someone is considered the feat of a culturally accomplished person.

In order to succeed in the competition, the nuclear family finds itself in a sort of permanent struggle both in relation to the outside world and within the frontiers of the extended family. Everyone has his part in this struggle—the father, the mother, the children. The division of labor is clear, the norms of performance for the child are exacting, the opportunities for relaxation are few. Being constantly evaluated in terms of his future adult status, the child has the problem of being loved for what he is now—incompetent and uncultured. The mother, highly involved in competitive representative activities which have a strategic importance for her family's standing, will not always be physically or even morally able to give the child the nurturance which the exacting nature of the family socialization demands would seem to make imperative. Where, then, will the child secure it? The answer is: through a network of family peer groups.

Given the fact that within the extended family and on the background of its common value system, the different styles represented by each nuclear family are constantly competing for supremacy, the child will have a strategic position. There will be competition for his allegiance. To the childless and the unmarried, he can offer the opportunity of fulfilling surrogate parent roles, which may often be formalized by godparenthood. With some relatives, the child can develop a standing independent of his parents, which he can use, literally, to bargain with them, because the parents believe that the private relationship of their children can bring benefits to the nuclear family. Access to these benefits, on the other hand, is largely through the child. In turn, the relationship with the relative can assume a peer dimension in this manner: the grandmother may define her relationship to her grandson partly as one of opposition to the child's parents, to her son-in-law in particular. She will support, in a covert fashion, resistance to the socializing pressure forthcoming from the father, and from his side of the family. By so doing, she gives a delinquent coloration to the relationship which topples her from her pedestal as the superior figure. The grandmother and the grandchild will share secrets. They are allies in a little war against the parents. In a real sense they are equals. More innocently, the grandmother may treat one of her grandchildren merely as her favorite. She breaks the rule of no discrimination and this is another secret which she shares with her grandchild, something they must jointly defend against the outside world including the rest of the family.

The child here finds a support which is forthcoming in spite of his reluctance or refusal to follow certain socialization pressures from his parents. He is finally loved for himself—as long as he remains faithful to his grandmother.

Once the grandmother appeals to her grandson to embrace the styles of her side of the family, she has put the child in a position to choose. The child, in order to conciliate her demands with those of his own nuclear family (which normally will have preference), transforms the cues for conformity into occasions of manipulation for his own interest and for his family's interests. He learns to show a semblance of conformity and to give to the grandmother what she wants to see or hear. In acting as representative of his *chez nous,* the dimensions of the role are still largely political— he acts under orders of his parents. The manipulation and exploitation of relatives to which the parents consent—if they do not promote it actively—is a delinquency shared with the parent. There too, the parental pedestal cracks—even if it does not topple: child and parent are partners in an unspoken crime. This is one of the few peer-group moments the French nuclear family will give the child until he or she reaches adolescence.

The consequences for the child's development are to give the seal of legitimacy to his own search for gratification. It is the difference which is respected—even if it needs to be hidden. The unique identity of the personality is entitled to its own satisfaction as long as its consequences are not destructive of the family.

The extended family exists as a sort of total society. The ties which bind it together are many: the competitive market, rather than being outside the extended family, is at least partly within it. Relationships based originally on love are limited by the relevance of their prestige and inheritance values. The homeostatic forces within the family are very strong and the introduction of a stranger is no small affair. The extended family, and the duty to foster the interests of the nuclear family, are a sort of built-in balance wheel for the search of individual pleasure. As long as one remains a good family member, one cannot do any wrong. On the other hand, one never knows how much one is loved and how much one is being exploited; how much one is respected or merely being adjusted to.

Thus, the French child learns the limits of value conformity and the complexity of life. Love, exploitation, complicity, respect, all mingle in relation to the same person. The meaning of action has to be secured through accepting apparent inconsistencies as part of the facts of life.

It would seem that the Oedipal and latency child learns the following definitions of the situation: the family is the source of all legitimate goodness, but all value pressures are tempered by the fact that adults seem to interpret them each in his own style. As a result, one can always find a relative for whom one's sin may be a minor poison and another for whom it may be the occasion for a secret bond. A delinquency shared is half-forgiven if it serves the family's interest or testifies to one's devotion to this interest.

The second major theme is that the relationships with the honored and powerful are more important and more complex than just being good: being really good is beyond the scope of all human beings. To be lovable is more accessible and more rewarding.

III. The Peer Group from Age Six to Puberty

It is in school that the child will, for the first time, escape some of the familial supervision over his life. This is an escape that parents anticipate with some foreboding. Frequently, in the more affluent *bourgeoisie* and upper classes, families delayed this moment either through the use of hired tutors or through the mother tutoring her children through the first years of schooling. By 1920, however, the use of the private school system run by Catholic orders, was the rule in this group. The Protestant *bourgeoisie* was more nearly content with the public school system.

The mood of the French school, like that of the home, is meticulous and formalistic. "Life is not made for fun" is what bourgeois families tell the child. The child soon feels obligated to bring back from school tokens of achievement that honor the training he has received at home. The school also sets the scene for competition between students for grades and prizes. There are no legitimate avenues of achievement outside of the curriculum. Children are rated on their trimestrial examinations from first to thirty-fifth (or whatever number corresponds to the last in the class). This competitive pressure is perceptible from the third grade onward, but even the first and second grades have their weekly medals for good behavior and their "good points" (stars) to initiate the competitive process.

Very few French families are immune from this "forcing" of the young intellect, and almost all are eager for those valuable diplomas that open the doors to a life as a civil servant or insure professional claims to income and prestige. The child often receives supplementary coaching at home or vacation assignments, so that he may one day pass the *bachot*, without which only an upper-class standing can remain secure.

The competitive work pressure exists, then, from the first to the twelfth grade, with anxiety mounting as one approaches the baccalaureate which 50 or 60 per cent of the students will fail on the first try; about one-third of those who fail in the first examination finally give up after several attempts.

Faced with such pressures, the child looks around for an avenue of escape or a source of support which does not depend upon academic performance. Though the child knows that his membership in the family does not depend on his grades, he knows that the latter influence strongly his standing in the eyes of his parents. He is compared with his brothers and his cousins; he is told that life will be difficult if grades are poor. His father, in particular, is the one who must be pleased. Academic performance is his affair, while the mother supervises training in manners. The French bourgeois father has relatively little contact with his small sons, except in academic matters. In fact, the best relationships that a boy may have with his father are those that are organized around some impromptu Rousseau-like[5] tutoring; botany on walks, visits to museums, historical lore while visiting ancient castles, or contemplating family souvenirs. It is the French equivalent of a good game of "catch" between father and son in America.

On entering school, the French child is torn from the security of his family and from the nurturance and support he derives from parental figures or parental surrogates. He is now thrown into a classroom where rewards are granted to performance competitively measured, and where the authority figure seems personally unconcerned about the fate of the pupil. No doubt in the early grades this change is cushioned by the maternal appearance of the female teacher. But by the third or fourth grade the universalistic pressure reaches its full force. In the face of such demands for performance, what is the nature of the child's ties to the school? What is there to cushion the impact of his socialization pressure?

The commitment of the child to the school is limited to the formal learning situation, since this is an obligation heavily reinforced by the family. The formal model of French culture must be learned. There is no other way of becoming a worthwhile person. On the other hand, as regards attachments to teachers, peer groups, or to the school as a general corporate body, the family generally takes a negative stand, as would be expected from our description of the family's control on the pre-school and extra-school social activities. We must not forget, in this context, that the ideal bourgeois pattern is for the family to train the latency child at home, and that the tutors, whom rich families gave to their male children, were considered little better than servants. Nor is there any school pride. The school exists as an independent entity that the child visits in order to get the necessary education. The family supports commitment to the *culture française* but none to the organization charged with teaching.

The child, however, is not quite ready for such functionally specific relations with an organization that is so important in his life, that gives him the culture without which he can never be secure out of his class, and that allocates rewards and punishments with no regard to his particular problems of achievement.

In the formal learning situation, the French child will recognize the leadership of the teacher, since it is recognized by his parents. However, he will defend his identity in the two ways he has learned and will continue to learn from his family: seduction of the teacher and rebellion.

French culture facilitates the use of seduction since it insists so much on style and the art of swaying an audience through the aesthetic arrangement of arguments, rather than through their intrinsic correctness. The insistence on orderly presentation is, above all, an insistence on easy communicability, and rhetoric is the art of persuading through pleasing the audience. The French student learns quickly the idiosyncracies of his teachers, his "pet peeves," his favorite authors and his stylistic preferences, and he tries to play on these sentiments to gain success.[6] In such a situation, the student learns to please, and the teacher rewards those who do it best.

Combined with the attempt at seduction, which can be successful only in the framework of basic compliance, the pupils will form a peer group which, as they grow in age, will challenge the teacher with increasing stubbornness.

Why is the French peer group so aggressively oriented? What are the motivational forces at the disposal of the peer group?

The motivational forces at the disposal of the French school peer group will be similar to those at the disposal of the school peer group of any nation, except for certain differences in emphasis.

First, there is the aggression, generated by parents and teachers through their socialization demands, which does not find a ready expression within the family or the French school room.

Second, there is the special reaction which is created by the pressures for competition mediated by the grading system. Thanks to this system, every peer is a potential frustrator. The peer group must cope with the aggression that each child will harbor against its competitors, and the likely result of this ambivalence is to turn the aggression against the outside authority who is defined as a greater frustration than any peer could ever be. In the American school, great efforts are made to avoid competition between pupils. The school attempts to promote the child's definition of the other, not as a potential depriver, but as co-operator for goals which can be shared rather than remain—like first place—the exclusive property of one. In the French case, aggression toward the teacher can cover the ambivalence; it cannot completely overcome it, and we shall see later a consequence of this ambivalence.

Finally, there is a paradoxical source of aggression, which is the family's ambivalence toward the school. On the one hand, the family wants absolute compliance with the cultural norms of the school; on the other hand, it does not recognize the legitimacy of the school as an organization competing with the family. The child faced with conflicting cues responds by compliance with the work demands, together with a constant challange to the rules of the organization.

The teacher who represents the school most immediately to the pupils, will thus be challenged in his efforts to enforce discipline. This rebellion of the student can be seen also as a demonstration of loyalty to his family. The parents cannot but give covert encouragement to this rebellion, not only out of jealousy but also because they share some of the child's anxiety: their child is judged by an outsider and through the child, and the value of the family's socialization efforts are also judged. The teacher holds in his hands a part of the family's prestige. This is a power the family will tolerate only out of necessity.

The punishments used by the schools, with their heavy reliance upon *retenue* and *consigne*,[7] tend to help the child to structure the school discipline as a conflict between school administration and family: the administration tries to separate the child from his family by compelling him to come to school during the Thursday and Sunday holidays.

The second motivational resource of the peer group will be the search for tension reduction and self-expression. Here again the French peer group is not unique in this respect. The difference lies in the matter of emphasis. French culture provides a model of *l'homme cultivé* which is most exacting and allows of no alternative goal patterns. In fact, there is no such thing as learning by trial and error—there is one right way to do everything in which the child must become thoroughly proficient before he is allowed to act on his own. There is no privacy officially granted to the child, as is the case in England, for instance. Children are constantly supervised lest they do something which would waste facilities, jeopardize their welfare and the family's standing. Because of this effort at supervision, the French family makes no effort to push the child into the peer group as the American family tries to do. As a result, the school peer group represents the one experience that neither family nor school can control because it remains *sub rosa*. Parents will rarely see the intimate friends that their child has made at school, nor will they be acquainted with the peer group. Visiting, and parties for school friends are practically unknown. As a paradoxical consequence, peer-group activities provide the one area of decision where the child is, more than in the United States, really free to be himself, unsupervised by adults and unimpressed by their values. *In America, the home is a great relaxation and freedom center; not so in France. On the other hand, the French peer group is, much more than the American peer group, a source of relaxation and defense of the member's identity.*

We have stated that all peer groups are based upon the commitment to a certain level of value achievement. Is the French peer group an exception? In one sense the peer group is bound to be delinquent, for there is no justification for not complying fully with the glorious tradition of French culture. Nevertheless, the French bourgeois child has learned, in the politics of his extended family, the importance of being loved for one's difference from others. He has also learned the legitimacy of pleasure so long as is does not jeopardize the nuclear family's interest position with the extended family, and the position of the latter within the community. In school, this pragmatic finding becomes universalized in a moral rule: French culture reveres individuality as long as it does not threaten order. This semi-Utopian wish is realized by the insistence on style: individuality expresses itself through expressive action which does not threaten the political and economic rationality of social structure. The individual is allowed, nay obligated, to secure as much sheer enjoyment out of life as he can. But he must not get into trouble. In case of open conflict, the needs of order must, of course, come first. Thus, we have the explanation of the semi-officious legitimacy of a peer group that is fundamentally delinquent.

The peer group, rather than being an organization for the pursuit of societal goals, or goals integrated to adult purposes, is a clearing house for individual interests. It strives to guarantee to each member the enjoyment of his own interests, which are mainly the freedom to express a delinquent motivation through fantasy or overt verbalization. First, there is the defense against the school authorities useful to all; then there are the *copains* (pals), who provide the supportive audience for spontaneity and the search for forbidden pleasure.

IV. Peer-group Activities and the Contract of Membership

Given the fact that all legitimate (officially legitimate) activities are monopolized by the family and the heavy school curriculum, there are few occasions where the peer group can engage in constructive activities along lines approved by adults, i.e., lines which embody a translation of adult values to the scale of children's physical and mental capabilities. Recreation time is scarce, and group games, which lack the seriousness of a sport, are insufficient media for the members' need for autonomy. A game is too easy, too ephemeral, in a word, too "childish."

The American peer group, recognized by both parents and administration, has the chance to engage in all sorts of activities: games are soon endowed with prestige, for they prepare the peer-group member for the serious sports of football and baseball, where he will carry the school colors. Games are serious business. The peer group also organizes entertainment, plays, collects money for charity drives, or delegates representatives to the school senate. It participates in sacred rituals, such as the pledge of allegiance to the flag. Furthermore, many aspects of the curriculum, instead of promoting competition and the isolation of the individual, tend to call upon the group for co-operative efforts: murals, music, and even "projects" that deal with civics, field trips, and the like.

The French peer group is barred from such opportunities. If we remember the high importance of aggression and its motivational resources, we should not be surprised to find the peer group engaging in systematic opposition to the administration's efforts to enforce universalistic rules in the rewarding of work, and trying to sabotage administration's efforts to maintain order. Where the administration encourages competition, the group will encourage co-operation and cribbing. Where the administration wants genuine performance, the peer group will cheat; where the former stresses proper form in speech and writing, the latter will try its utmost to create disorder and talk slang. Warfare against the administration, which includes the teachers and their classroom police function, will be the peer group's main activity as a united group. In this warfare, it will demonstrate great ingenuity and persistance as well as what appears to be, from the adult standpoint, a good deal of cruelty. Aggression here becomes a funnel for the expression of autonomy needs, an occasion to express one's difference and resistance to the tremendous pressures for conformity coming from school and family. Furthermore, aggression against the out-group is indispensible to solidify the solidarity of peers who are otherwise competitors and mutual frustrators.

To maintain order, the administration can only resort to the deployment of sufficient personnel so as to be able to bring overwhelming force at any one point.[8] This is especially true of the boarding schools which have been the experience of some 40 per cent of the upper and upper-middle class university students.[9]

The opportunities for victorious action by the peer group will be few and unexpected, except when it is a question of heckling a teacher or a *pion* (proctor) who is known to be defenseless. Hence the peer group's activities are mainly verbal, testifying to the existence of a community of delinquent motivation which might find expression at any propitious moment.

The teacher, faced with this coalition, can either try to dominate it through fear, or he may turn the tables on the peer group and "seduce" its members individually through his own charisma. Because of the ambivalence born of the competitiveness and of the official illegitimacy of the group, the French peer group is vulnerable to a seduction which dissolves its bonds. The successful teacher becomes exempt from heckling. On Christmas, he will receive a sizeable gift from the whole class.[10]

In view of the lack of constructive activities and the fact that warfare against the administration results in few frontal encounters, the organization of the peer group will remain rather elementary. While the American peer group sees its "regressive" components compensated and even neutralized by formal organization for the achievement of adult approved objectives, the French group remains mainly an undifferentiated audience.

The effective peer group is the ascriptive group of classmates. Other students of one's own age group or older are significant only peripherally, and are no more significant than other children met under circumstances where their complicity is required, either immediately or potentially.[11]

Leadership is often provided by the small clique of students unable to achieve satisfactory norms of performance along academic lines, and which provide the delinquent virtuosos. Leadership is temporary, and can be seized at any time by any peer member who wishes to indulge in some dramatic delinquency, whereby he becomes the symbolic representative of the peer group, which will reward him with prestige, and sympathy if he is caught.

Said one informant:

> The leaders of our class, insofar as you can talk of leaders, came from different "specialities," as one might say. When it was a question of *chahut* (hell raising) we had the clique of the good gymnasts who were also the poorest students. But we had also some smart boys who delighted in asking "iffy" questions of the teacher. When they succeeded in embarrassing the teacher, well, they had scored for us. . . . They were good students, and the teacher was quite defenseless in front of them, a little like: "Et tu, Brute. . . ."
>
> Many did not tolerate questions from students so that you must not think that this happened every day, nor would the questions attempt to show up the teacher as far as his knowledge was concerned. Rather, the questions were aimed at forcing the teacher to reveal his political opinions and thus bring him down to our level. As far as politics were concerned, we had our own opinions, that were as good as any man's. . . .
>
> Others aimed questions that were destined to sidetrack the teacher into some digression. This was a service to the group that the teacher's pets were well qualified to render. They might also ask him to read us some book instead of reviewing our French grammar. Then, of course, we had the "good" students who refused to belong. They came to class in order to learn and this is all. They were the *cuistres* (pedantic grinds).

They could get away with it if they were day students, and also if they were strong enough to defend themselves. If not, we sure gave them the business. . . . As La Fontaine said: "this age is without pity."

Access to the peer group is hard for a newcomer. Since the group is usually check-mated in its assaults against the administration, its hostility often will be vented against the *nouveau* (new student) who by his very intrusion challenges the ascriptive and closed character of the peer group.[12] Woe to the isolate who for some reason becomes the *souffre-douleur* (scapegoat) of a class. The peer group will persecute him with all the fury which comes from the deep fear of encountering his fate: the orphan, the child without support.

Another important factor of the peer group is its secrecy, not in an organized fashion as we meet it in American delinquent "clubs," but as an epiphenomenon of the complete isolation of peer-group activities from the rest of the child's world. Never in the peer group is there any mention of the members' families and vice versa.

Because the French peer group does not have a legitimate function in adult eyes, its emphasis upon the defense of each member's identity may interfere with the requirements of solidarity and loyalty, which are norms intrinsic to any peer group. Indeed, the French peer group scorns a moral posture as implying a level of conformity to rival organizations (school and family), which is incompatible with commitment to the peer group. If both these organizations state that "life is not made for fun," the peer group, on the contrary, is out to prove that they are wrong.

The consequence of the hedonistic orientation is that the peer group cannot expect the type of loyalty that the American or English peer group may claim. One rarely hears in France of loyalty to the school peer group pushed to heroic levels when the group comes into conflict with adult values.[13]

First there are the claims of the family which override everything else. Peer-group activities must not lead to such reprisals by the school activities as would reflect unfavorably both on one's standing in the family, and on the standing of the family in the community. The parents will not reward, as they do in America, loyalty to the peer group, even if it leads to difficulties.

Second, scorn for the moral posture militates against a heroic show of loyalty to the peer group. The group understands very well that the individual member will not prejudice his interest position for the sake of the peer group. The peer group is supposed to refrain from *cafarder* (snitching), but if the school administration starts pressuring an innocent, which it might well do purposely, the latter will not stand taking punishment for someone else very long. The delinquent "task force" will collapse, but this is not too important, for what matters is the preservation of the community of delinquent motivation. The latter does not depend on the attainment of a specific delinquent goal; it is the delinquent potentiality that counts.

Because the pressure from authority tend to create competition among the children, the ambivalence of peer-group members toward one another can easily break through, when the member sees an opportunity to secure official values.

The teacher can utilize this characteristic to increase his socialization pressure upon a child. If the child misbehaves according to his standards, for instance makes a very poor showing in his class work, the teacher will hold him up to ridicule. What happens is somewhat surprising by American or English standards: the peer group will side with the teacher. Instead of supporting its own, it will testify to its dedication *malgré tout* to the adult values and attack its hapless member.[14] By throwing the culprit to the administration wolves, the peer group secures a breathing spell. Perhaps in return, the teacher will read *The Three Musketeers* instead of doing the grammar lesson. The victim stands completely isolated. He has become an orphan. Few experiences can be more devastating to a child, and he will remember forever the great rule of French life: *Faut se méfier.* ("Be on your guard" is a better translation than "Don't trust anyone.") The family is still the only group which will fight for you whatever happens.[15]

Does this mean that peer group attachments will be brittle? On the contrary. The child has no illusions about the peer group. Being organized for the protection of its member's pleasure and interest position (and through the member, that of his family), occasions of greater gain elsewhere will result in a bit of betrayal here and there. There is no external goal which gives meaning and compensation for self-sacrifice. It is like the family—you must take people as they are. This does not mean that one betrays all the time. Far from it. Members through the years have learned the "economy" of each other's commitments. They know what to ask and what to expect. Wisdom consists in not asking too much and developing a fine antenna for what is possible. The burden of proof, on the other hand, is not on him who asks, it is more on him who refuses— lasting jeopardy of one's interest position is reason enough. To defend the group as an on-going protective organization, great loyalty can be mustered. The peer group functions best in immediate situations where the gains and costs are evident. It has very little resilience and capacity to absorb change. The commitment of the members is too hedonistically (nurturance) oriented: its reference is immediate. There is no commitment reserve, as it were. As a result, the opposition of the peer group to change is very strong, for this is one of the few issues where the group knows it can rely on automatic loyalty from its members. Hence, a certain mania for in-group–out-group opposition, which resolves the ambivalence of members toward one another.

V. Teen-age Peer Group

In the United States, the regressive aspect of the peer-group commitment will be partly dissipated and partly shifted, into other structures. The ascriptive group of classmates tends to be broken up by the intrusion of heterosexual interests through dating, as well as by the creation of hobby groups, or church groups, which sometimes assemble children from other schools. The peer group becomes strongly achievement oriented: one "makes the grade . . . ."

In France, heterosexual commitments, at, or after, puberty, are largely out of the question. What takes their place are intense friendships between peers of the same sex.[16]

The classroom peer group remains essentially the delinquent community. Outside of the development of intense intimate friendships, the two new phenomena which will impinge upon the nature of the peer group are (a) the development of political consciousness and (b) the Boy Scout movement.

Both of these developments put a brake on the elaboration of the delinquent pattern: the first by integrating the peer-group member to the wider society; the second, by giving the peer group an area for independent and adventurous action. The Boy Scout movement in France owed much of its success to the opportunities it gave for the types of action which are much more commonplace for the American peer group. As it was under confessional direction, it relieved the French family from the anxiety that any activity, not strictly controlled by the school and family, might lead the child to dishonor or disaster.

Boys Scouts in France are not so numerous as the politically conscious students.[17] The Scouts take a position that is exactly the reverse of the peer group; they are the "daily good deed" group. Parents find the Scouts very useful as a sublimation device during puberty, when there are no legitimate sexual outlets for the child. But the Scouts have the disability of not preparing the teen-ager for real life. They play in an atmosphere of Indian make-believe which, in fact, is more elaborate in France than it is in the American Scout movement. The parents want their child to be good, but not defenseless. The rugged life hides a naïve approach to society.

Politics, on the other hand, represents a new level of delinquency. It colors the revolt against authority with an ideological rejection of the present world as morally worthless. Thus, part of the rebellion no longer bears the onus of "immorality." It gives adult dignity to the rebellion, which includes teachers and parents under the symbol of the incompetent government.

The political rebellion also removes adolescent aggression from the family scene. Having asserted on an abstract and verbal level his rejection of the adult world, the student can let himself fall back, without remorse, on the delights of dependency upon his family, in a fashion that would be offensive to most American teen-agers.

VI. The Peer Group in Adult Life

It would be wrong to assume that the motivational structure which has been built during the primary and secondary school years is of little importance for the adult. On the contrary, the capacity to enter a *copain* (pal) relationship and to "trigger" such a relationship in another, is an essential asset to the properly socialized Frenchman. The *copain* motivational structure is essentially the capacity to form delinquent communities for the defense of a private interest against the encroachment of any outsider, particularly when this outsider is an official authority. Any interlocutor who can trigger off the "delinquent response" knows that he can count on the other for help in defeating the purpose of some universalistic rule presently working to his disadvantage. The condition, of course, will be that giving this help does not decrease the facilities available for ego's family. "Triggering the delinquent response" means essentially creating a climate in which a moral posture cannot be assumed.

This can be done best by alluding to a delinquency shared with the interlocutor—or if the word delinquency is too strong, to a common struggle against an outsider. And, as we know, all is fair in love and war. The allusion is not made directly, but through reference to the group in which the delinquency or the struggle took place. For that matter, no delinquency need have been committed or mentioned. It is enough that the group to which both parties belong refuses to condemn these delinquencies out of hand. Once the delinquent response has been triggered, then the solicitor is established as a *copain* entitled to immunity from injury to his interest position. The relevance of any universalistic rule which might justify the loss of alter's interest positions, in favor of a greater good, or a higher principle, has been "debunked." The only reason ego can offer for refusing to co-operate is to demonstrate the negative impact the co-operation might have on his own interest position, and the burden of proof is upon him.

Family connections, past school memories, regimental comradeship,[18] past membership in the Communist, Royalist, or Fascist youth organizations, are for Frenchmen in their forties a good reference point for the constitution of the delinquent community. Membership in the Free French or Resistance movements is a more recent reference. Furthermore, we must remember that, for much of the upper classes, the government (as differentiated from the ideal State-Motherland) has never had any "legitimacy."[19] Hence, any definition of the situation between two men as one of struggle against the government gives their respective interest position an automatic legitimacy. Against the government, "reasonable" delinquency is virtually a duty. Another excellent focus for the crystallization of the delinquent community will concern sexual desires for other people's wives.

Much *salon* activity, which assembles groups known as *coteries,* is devised to create and reinforce delinquent communities. These groups are characterized by extreme liberty of speech, lack of moral pose, and a strong fixation on a struggle against someone, or some other *coterie.* Members of a *coterie* participate in the debunking and polite slander of another. It becomes a blood bondage between members. The transmission of job and financial opportunities, especially when the latter involve advance notice of moves, and some "white-collar crimes" such as the violation of professional or state secrecy, are some of the outputs of these peer groups to the members. Another is the securing of protection for any one of their members who gets into trouble, or rather, who might get into trouble, for in these matters, an ounce of prevention is worth a pound of cure.

Another very important function of the *salon* is to pass on gossip about persons in positions of power. When the *salon* member comes into contact with the official and wants a favor, the knowledge of this gossip serves to trigger off the delinquent response in the official. In meeting a French official, a good deal of the time taken by the interview consists precisely in determining the peer membership of both solicitor and official, for with certain memberships goes the assumption of certain knowledge and certain attitudes. Another part of the preliminary discussion is designed to test how far the delinquent community is established, then the request of a solicitor is bound to be entertained favorably, or at least the arguments for refusing it will be different than they would be if this community did not exist. Perhaps the official needs a *quid pro quo.* In any event, both parties can do business, and are likely to arrive at a satisfactory arrangement.

Not all principles are removed from the transaction. What has happened is that both parties have decided that they will defend their joint interests against outsiders. Since their joint interests are those of their families, it is, finally, the principle of family and *camaraderie* which triumphs over the principle of government—one should add, the principle of the individual pitted against powers too big, too remote to be human.

The line is sometimes thin between the establishment of a delinquent community and blackmail. As always, these transactions demand a light touch (*doigté*).

The utilization of the delinquent community can become a means of government. France has been compared to an "eighteenth-century police state": eighteenth-century because of the antiquity of the filing system and the poor centralization of four different police systems working as much against one another as against their quarry.[20] The four police systems accumulate fantastic files on private citizens, next to which F.B.I. dossiers are child's play. These files are used to checkmate the activities of any citizen who tries too hard to rock the boat. The information collated from *concierges,* madames of bordellos, anonymous letters, disgruntled employees, rejected mistresses, and from reading the mail, can be used to cut the turbulent citizen down to size. It debunks his principles. The official will not use this knowledge to sound morally superior; the mere fact that he is using the knowledge makes him a partner in crime. Hence, *tout peut s'arranger* ("everything can be fixed"). The reformer has no zone of immunity which condemns his movement to stalemate. The *status quo,* once more, is saved.

This sort of checkmating is not limited to political affairs. In fact, the value against which the delinquent community will be most readily formed is the value of economic rationality, which often threatens the interest position of established family firms. Behavior where this delinquent community will be most apparent are coalitions in restraint of trade, price discrimination, nepotism, and the use of political power to block competitors. In this last case, the mechanisms mentioned above are highly relevant.

In conclusion, French peer groups, which appear frequently as delinquent or potentially delinquent communities,[21] will be strong. This, in turn, affects associational patterns in France. If we wish to answer the questions raised by Arnold Rose in his discussion of French voluntary organizations,[22] we could say that voluntary organizations are probably as numerous in France as in the United States, but it is their nature which is different. Formal voluntary organizations may be fewer and are certainly more expressively oriented and less instrumentally oriented than they are in the United States. Informal voluntary organizations are probably stronger than they are in the United States. The individual enters them with more difficulty and leaves them much more reluctantly than does the American. In maintaining his family's interest position, membership is more important to the Frenchman than it is to the American. On the other hand, the French peer groups will not support activities which might put into question the prevailing patterns of economics or political leadership, or require confidence in the benefits of long-term change. The contract which the peer group makes with the polity, for instance, will be much to the disadvantage of the latter: it will require much influence and security in return for a dubious compliance. No wonder political change in France appears as charismatic movements (the teacher seducing the students) sandwiched between long periods of well-tempered anarchy. The peer group must be bypassed rather than bargained with.

In discussing the French family and the peer group, we have described patterns that are not altogether unique to French society. Latin communities share them, certainly more than do Anglo-Saxon communities. Even the American will recognize, in our description of the French peer group, elements of his own school experiences—and the Southerner will recognize some features of the family life which can take place in any southern community. If these patterns are "French," it is more because of their concentration and primacy than because of their uniqueness. Furthermore, France itself is in a state of flux. This was written in the days of the Fourth Republic and a youth culture *à l'américaine* has been steadily developing. It remains to be seen how far economic growth will prove compatible with the importance of the delinquent community as a paradoxical mainstay of French order.

22 Kinship Relations and Relationships of Proximity* in French Working-Class Households

ANDREE VIELLE MICHEL

It is conventional to view city life as characterized by a decrease in the strength of kinship ties without replacement of them by comparable ties with others. Ties with others are seen as shallow and mechanical secondary-group relationships. Dr. Michel has studied† a group which does not fit this pattern. Parisian workers who live in furnished hotels, she finds, frequently develop ties with those who happen to be neighbors which have all the intensity and closeness of kinship ties. These relationships based on proximity rapidly become effective and full substitutes for kinship relationships.

The following observations were made during a study of working-class families living in furnished hotels in the *département* of the Seine. We have noticed that the relationships of proximity are particularly strong and often fulfill functions that, in other social strata, are confined solely to the family. The analysis of relationships of proximity, as seen in the place of residence, shows us the considerable importance that these relationships occupy in the daily life of these families and workers of the Parisian region.

This study was concerned with inhabitants of furnished hotels who have become permanent residents due to the housing crisis. They include families with children, women living alone as head of a household with or without children, and old workers. Single men form the mobile element of the population which is less easy to observe. In studying each category, we have noticed that the relationships of proximity very often take over, either in part or completely, the role played by kinship relationships in other social strata.

---

* The French is "voisinage." Literally this would be translated as neighborhood. For the French, however, the connotation is slightly different; "close neighborhood" would be more precise. We have chosen to translate the term as proximity, believing that term is closer to what Mme. Michel intended. Translator.

† Since this selection was made, Dr. Michel has published an extensive account of her research. See *Famille, Industrialisation, Logement* (Paris: Centre National de la Recherche Scientifique, 1959). Editors.

From Andrée Michel (née Vieille), "Relations parentales et relations de voisinage chez les ménages ouvriers de la Seine," *Cahiers Internationaux de Sociologie*, XVII (July–December, 1954), 140–46 and 151–53. Copyright by Cahiers Internationaux de Sociologie and used with the kind permission of the editor. Translated by John Brode.

Families with Children

In bourgeois or peasant families, the responsibility for the material care and upbringing of children and the protection and the education of minors are generally assumed by the parents or, occasionally, by the grandparents or other relatives who are living with the parents. The neighbors are only in exceptional cases given responsibility for children in the same apartment house. Despite the development of preschool institutions for children (family-aid services, nurseries, kindergartens, etc.), the parents are responsible in the eyes of the law for any failure to perform these duties.

In rural families, the home is large enough for grandparents to live with their children and grandchildren. Very often the grandparents care for the small children while their parents are in the fields.

In working-class families living in furnished hotels, such sharing of accommodations with relatives is generally impossible because of the restricted living space. Thus, the family unit is reduced to the parents and children. In addition, the physical distance from relatives who have stayed in the place of origin is an obstacle to maintaining frequent contacts with them. On the other hand, the closeness of the inhabitants in hotels, due to crowding, sharing the water supply, etc., leads the neighbors to participate more or less closely in the life of the family.

About 40 per cent of the parents in this study are obliged to send away one or more of their children because their living space is too small, and to place them in a household unrelated to the family.* Many parents find that the children become more deeply attached to the woman who is rearing them than to their own mother. It is not unusual to see a child pay more attention to his guardian, whom he sees every day, than to his mother, whose visits are irregular or rare. Sometimes the relationships established between the family of the child and that of the foster parents continue after the child has returned to his own family. This is not a true case of a relationship of proximity between inhabitants of the same hotel, but the daily contact of the child and his foster parent subsequently affects the mother-child relationship.

Relationships of proximity appear when the children live in the hotel with their parents. There, they are at first cared for by parents. However, the shared life in the furnished hotel soon extends the circle of adults who take care of the children. It is indeed rare that the birth of a child passes unnoticed by the neighbors; generally they offer the mother various little gifts to celebrate the occasion, while her relatives, who may

---

* Mme. Michel uses the term "nourrice," which translated literally is "wet-nurse." Though this function was included in some cases, clearly the meaning is more general. Translator.

be far away, never appear. If the child is baptized, the godparents are occasionally chosen from among the neighbors when no one related by blood or marriage is available. The baby-shower is attended by as many neighbors as relatives. All of these practices show that the parents seek for their children the good-will of the neighbors, with whom they have daily contacts, more than they seek that of rarely-seen relatives.

When the child takes his first steps in the courtyard of the hotel, he becomes, in part, the child of the little group that saw him come into the world and grow up. If his mother has left to go shopping or to attend to other things, he is taken care of by a neighbor until the mother returns. When he plays, it is rarely alone or in his family. Their living quarters are too small for children's horse play. Usually, he will play in the court-yard with the small group of neighborhood children. At five, when he goes to kindergarten, he will be cared for by the older children of the hotel, if he himself has no elder sibling. Rarely will he do his homework by himself but rather with a neighbor child who is in the same grade.

Thus, the child's life is not limited to his family circle, but encom-passes a larger sphere. As a result, the functions of protection, education, and surveillance of the child, normally assumed by the parents, are shared by those who come into contact with the child within the group environment of the hotel.

In some cases, the neighbors share with the parents the responsibility of feeding the child. For example, Mrs. D. lives in a hotel with her husband, a mechanic in the building industry, and her three children. Two other children are boarded with foster parents. The family has stayed in the same hotel as the parents of the husband ever since their home in Noisy-le-Sec was destroyed during the war. The wife, a native of Paris, has kept in touch with her mother, aunt, and godmother who live in the depart-ments of the Seine and of the Seine-et-Oise. As is common in working-class families, Mrs. D. handles the family budget. With her husband's pay and the family allowance, she must pay the rent, pay for the foster care of her two children, give her husband spending money, and cover her purchases at the local stores and the costs of housekeeping. When she runs short and is in need of money, she borrows from her neighbors and not from her in-laws or from her own family. Borrowing from one another is widespread in the hotels. Proximity creates relationships such that mutual assistance between neighbors is more frequent, more "familiar" one might say, than with even the closest parents.

Cases such as this are not infrequent. However, the participation of neighbors in the feeding and, generally, in all aspects of the life of the child is even more frequently seen when a child is being raised by a woman who lives alone, due to the death of her husband, divorce, or desertion.

Female Heads of Households

In the *code civil,* the husband, by marriage, contracts an obligation to support his wife and children. If and when he should desert them, his wife can demand support for herself and her children from him. Even if she is not married, the law enables her to prosecute the father of her children provided that she can establish paternity. But these possibilities provided for in the Code, are realized only if the wife brings the husband into court. The formalities, however, are long and expensive, especially for working-class women who are generally rather poorly paid. For many mothers, legal action seems pointless and they abandon it. If the father continues to evade his responsibilities, and the mother's family is not near, the neighbors frequently offer the help that the mother has neither hoped for nor solicited.

The following example illustrates the sort of spontaneous association that is formed between two young women, neighbors in a hotel. The first, Nadia, is a metal worker by profession, whose husband deserted her and their three-year-old child. She is currently unemployed since her health does not permit her to continue her previous, overly-strenuous job as a spray-gun painter. The second, Simone, also a metal-worker, is a young divorcée whose child is with a foster mother. How does the little association function that was spontaneously formed between the two women? Nadia takes care of the two rooms, does the shopping, and prepares the evening meal. Simone works all day in a factory. She furnishes Nadia with the money needed to run what can be called the household of the two young women. The dinners are prepared and served in Nadia's room. Their spare time in the evenings is spent together in playing cards and talking. Nadia's child has been more or less adopted by the neighbors in the hotel who show a paternal attitude toward him. Nadia's only relative is a brother whom she visits irregularly.

Here too, we observe that the relationships of proximity, based on residence in the same hotel, occupy a greater part in the life of the mother and child than kinship relationships. In effect, the neighbors render more support than do their family or relatives.

The second example that we have chosen is interesting as it shows who are picked to be the godparents of the orphan born in a hotel. The family is composed of five people: the mother, separated from her husband, and four children—Roger (18 years old), an apprentice plumber; Liliane (16), an apprentice hairdresser; Jacqueline (10); and Claude (5), in school. The family lives in a small room thirteen by ten feet. But the actual living space of the family has been enlarged, thanks to the neighbors. Meals are taken together in the single room, but some of the children sleep elsewhere: Liliane with an aunt who lives in the same building; Jacqueline with her godparent on another floor. Jacqueline's family and her godfather are not related. The choice of godparent was determined by the relationships of proximity the mother had with this working-class family. Similarly, the mother chose as godmother for her daughter another neighbor, a foreign immigrant, who was not related to them in any way. As a result, Jacqueline spends more of her free time with her godparents than with her mother. They feed, board, and clothe her. In addition, the family was able to use, for over a year, the room of neighbors on the same floor while they were absent. The analysis of these cases shows us that the kinship relationship was not involved in the choice of godparents for the child and that, on the contrary, the relationship of proximity was the determinant. The little group of neighbors shares with Jacqueline's mother and sister (in the absence of the husband who has not supported them since the separation) the responsibility for the education, feeding, and even lodging of the children.

The last child in the family, Claude, had been placed with a foster mother while the mother worked in a factory. As a result of the "proximity" of the family of the foster mother and the child, the daughter and son-in-law of the former became the godparents of Claude, even though there was no kin relationship between the families. The mother noticed with great bitterness that the child preferred her foster mother to herself. When she became unemployed she took Claude back, but the little girl kept up a relationship with her godparents which was said to be parental in nature. The child and her mother are invited to visit them during the holidays and school vacations just as though they were close relatives. This case demonstrates how relationships of proximity, formed from living in the same building, have been superimposed on other kin-like relationships. Whatever might be the nature of the proximity, it is, for the most part, the origin of profound social relationships between working-class people.

Old Working-class People

The study of this category of inhabitants confirms the importance of the relationships of proximity already brought out in the daily life of families and of women and children living in furnished hotels. Most of the aged workers in furnished hotels have lost track of their children, who often live far away from the old parents. Their meager resources are barely sufficient to pay the rent. Who, then, will help them, care for them when they are sick, provide for a funeral when they die?

In any of these circumstances, the group of neighbors will take on these tasks should the family fail. Very often, the adult inhabitants furnish these aged workers with small jobs that will help them to augment their incomes. More often, they share with them a part of the food that they have prepared for themselves. This practice is considered so natural that one does not even speak of it. Here again, when relatives are lacking, proximity produces a sort of tacit obligation, as far as care is concerned, toward these aged workers.

Another custom, equally prevalent, concerns the sick, the dying, and the dead. This custom is far removed from that which is traditional in bourgeois or peasant families. In such families, assistance to the sick and dying, arranging for the funeral, and the up-keep of the grave are generally taken on by the family or relatives. Often they will travel great distances in order to care for, or bury a relative, even one who is only distantly related to them. In these families, the neighbors only in exceptional circumstances take part in these affairs. In a furnished hotel or in a working-class building, sickness or death do not pass unnoticed, any more than a birth does, by the neighbors who usually will lend a helping hand.

We shall cite only one example. In a furnished hotel, Simone, a worker, died suddenly from a heart disease. Her husband, an Algerian worker, was absent at the time of her death; he was undergoing treatment in a sanatorium for pulmonary tuberculosis. Simone was an orphan and had no close relatives. One of Simone's neighbors, the oldest woman in the hotel, undertook the necessary arrangements. She notified the husband, sat up all night by the body, and took a collection among the residents of the hotel in order to pay the most urgent expenses. After the burial when the husband had returned to the sanatorium, she took charge of the grave, visiting it from time to time. Such an example is not at all exceptional. When the family is absent, the neighbors take care of the sick, aid the dying, and tend the graves.

We shall pass over the relationships among Algerian workers living in furnished hotels because these relationships may be influenced by kinship, in the case of their compatriots, or by their particular cultural attitudes, in the case of their European neighbors. Nevertheless, none of these factors interfere with the relationships of proximity of French and Algerian working-class people when the initiative is taken by the former. We have been able to observe several times that proximity creates a situation in which the relationships that develop between French and Algerian working-class people are completely devoid of any racial discrimination. For example, a mechanic in the Parisian Transport System was teaching his neighbor, an Algerian worker who was going to night school, to read French. Such actions are usually accompanied by explicit affirmations of the equality of Algerian workers with other workers. "They are just like the others," the French neighbors of Algerian workers assert. They do not realize that this opinion stems from the relationships that have been formed—often unconsciously—as a result of their living in the same building.

It might be asked if the conduct described above is peculiar to these inhabitants as a result of proximity. Often this proximity is over-bearing and borders on promiscuity. These ways survive, even though weakened, in the low-cost housing units. The children play together in the single courtyard, and relationships of proximity among the parents often exist between those living around the same stairwell or landing. Working-class housing, with its small quarters, large population, shared source of water, and common courtyard and laundry, is the setting in which relationships of proximity identical to those described in furnished hotels can develop.

One might ask if the behavior described above is not especially true for the nonworking part of the working-class population: mothers, children, unemployed, and old people. As a result of greater free time, are such people able to form relationships of proximity inside the furnished hotels more easily? Even though the participation of the nonworking element of the population seems to be more prominent in these relationships of proximity, it could also be demonstrated that they exist with the same frequency and with the same intensity among the members of the working part of the population.

The inhabitants in furnished hotels were never heard to justify the behavior patterns described in terms of the existence of customs. The population of furnished hotels is, as a matter of fact, a very recent one which has moved into these places only since 1945. Previously, the majority of the residents of these hotels were transients who soon moved on to ordinary housing. Thus, there was no possibility of customs arising among them. The behavior patterns that have been formed among the permanent residents did not have any heritage from the past. They are only the consequences of the conditions forced upon these inhabitants by the nature of their present existence. The practices of those who live in furnished hotels may be compared to those of the inmates of forced labor camps in Germany during World War II. The behavior patterns adopted in these camps stemmed from the conditions of existence imposed on the inmates and not from any pre-existing models.

Environment and custom are not mutually exclusive. In furnished hotels, the behavior patterns of the inhabitants resulting from the environment could become institutionalized if the housing crisis forced families to prolong their residence in these hotels.

As a result of this study, we are in a better position to analyze the interrelation of kinship and proximity in the life of the working class and to draw comparisons between the working-class family and bourgeois and peasant families.

In the bourgeois family, kinship relationships largely eclipse the relationships of proximity. The latter are virtually nonexistent at the neighborhood level. The relationships involved in work are often based on rivalry and competition. If solidarity is sometimes evident, intimacy is absent in professional relationships. The most stable relationships and the most frequent are those with relatives or in-laws, regardless of the degree of relatedness. In regard to these relatives, the law establishes obligations which are reinforced by custom and social approval.

In working-class families, relationship by blood and marriage diminishes or vanishes because of the living conditions imposed upon them. The smallness of the home often reduces the family unit to the parents and their children, while migration isolates the family from its relatives.

The most frequent, strongest, and most stable relationships are within the small groups based on proximity in the same building. These relationships generate new practices and obligations felt toward others than relatives. The worker takes this for granted, as one observer has already noticed.* When rural immigrants from Brittany or the center of France come to live in industrial cities and work in the factories, they form obligations to neighbors and work associates that were generally limited to relatives in the peasant families from which they came. The Parisian worker becomes accustomed to these practices from an early age, since from early childhood he has lived in an environment more extensive than just his family.

These obligations are not felt to be imposed from outside. They are born of the affective participation in the small group. Marx has already noted, in his *German Ideology,* the absence of all ideology (in the Marxist sense of the term) and of all feelings of separateness among the members of the working-class family. "Where the family is really broken up, as in the proletariat, the idea of the family is completely absent, though it is true that we can observe at times a tendency towards family life that is based upon real relationships." On the basis of this study, we may suggest that these characteristics of "real relationships" are also characteristics of relationships of proximity, and that these characteristics emanate from the nature of home life as well as from the work situation.

---

* P. Chombart de Lauwe, *Paris et l'agglomération parisienne* (Paris: Presses Universitaires de France, 1952), p. 106.

23 *Culture Configurations in the American Family*

JOHN SIRJAMAKI

In this paper, Professor Sirjamaki sets forth the basic value patterns which characterize families in American society. Although Sirjamaki is not concerned here with the process involved, such configurations guide and limit the behavior of families, establishing their goals and standards.

Most sociological studies of the family deal with it either as a social system or as a social institution. An important supplement to these approaches is the cultural analysis of the family in terms of its dominant configurations. When these can be specified for the family, it is possible to interpret the basic moral ideas which give the family its distinctive and identifying characteristics.

Culture configurations are the moral principles which comprise the social philosophy of a society. They are patterns of covert behavior; as such, they are the culturally approved rules or sentiments which motivate overt behavior and which integrate it into consistent patterns; and they can be deduced only from behavior. Such configurations exist on the level of the culture and arise in the context of everyday living. Members of a society comprehend the meaning of such precepts in the process of socialization, even when they are expressed tenuously or obscurely; and, indeed, configurations are difficult to state abstractly inasmuch as they generally operate below the level of awareness. Taken together, the configurations delineate the ethos of a culture.[1]

Configurations are thus the basic units of the value system of a society. They differ from the absolute ethics of religious or philosophical systems

Reprinted from "Culture Configurations in the American Family" by John Sirjamaki in the *American Journal of Sociology*, LIII (May, 1948), 464–70, with the kind permission of the author and the University of Chicago Press.

in that they are mundane, practical, this-worldly; having developed within the culture, they express the dominant values which are thought to be necessary for the continued functioning of the society. Ordinarily, configurational values are stigmatized by philosophers as base and inferior; Fromm has called them "socially immanent ethics" as contrasted to universal ethics.[2] For the social scientist, however, it is necessary to understand the configurations of a culture, since they motivate behavior much more continuously than do absolute ethical systems. The configurations will tend to support the total culture and to achieve an interrelatedness among themselves. As Sumner indicated, there is a strain for consistency in the mores.[3]

The concept of the configurations of the culture, and a knowledge of the manner in which these are expressed within an institution, illuminates the study of the family. Configurations reach into the most intimate areas of individual and family behavior; they furnish the meanings and determine right and wrong behavior in courting, in husband-wife and parent-child relationships, in heterosexual social activity, and in ideas about sex. Thus they supply the moral sentiments by which family members are influenced and make explicable the vagaries of their behavior.

At least four qualifications may be raised concerning the validity of applying culture configurations to the study of the American family. First, since such configurations are inferred by the investigator from the overt behavior of people, he must have available a considerable amount of observational data which, however, is currently lacking. Second, the use of such configurations should await an analysis of the total culture, and this has been attempted thus far in the most tentative manner.[4] The analysis of parts of the culture, however, will assist in the determination of the total culture ethos. Third, generalizations about American culture must be stated in the most broad terms and can attempt only to strike an average, since regional and ethnic subcultures obviously differ from the main pattern. To whom, it may be asked, do configurations apply? The answer is that configurations are generally valid, or will tend to become so, for the entire American society, in the sense that they represent the moral standards by which all behavior is evaluated and which exert a social pressure to secure some degree of conformance. Families of ethnic minorities thus quite apparently have patterns dissimilar to those of native-born families, but in time the American culture configurations come to influence the actions of at least the immigrant children and to bring their behavior into conformity with the general requirements of society. Finally, configurations are not easily amenable to quantification; they may seem to be accurately stated, but they are difficult to measure. There is no real answer to this objection other than to predicate the statement of configurations upon as careful objective analysis as is possible. A value system patently exists in every culture, and its appraisal should be sought by the social scientist.

The following configurations, among others, appear in the American family:

1. Marriage is a dominating life-goal, for men as well as for women.— It is felt that married life is the normal, desired condition for all adults, that it brings the greatest personal happiness and fulfillment, and that it permits the proper exercise of sex for the procreation of children and for individual satisfaction. The single adult life by contrast, according to this attitude, is empty and barren. That there is a considerable societal concern that women marry is generally recognized, but the greater courting and sexual initiative assumed by men has obscured the comparable pressure on them to marry, and adult men who postpone marriage into their thirties become objects of distress and conspiracy among friends and relatives. Most Americans marry in their twenties, and, for a considerable share of them, marriage at that age means a happy union of individual volition and social pressure.

Long ago, Professor E. A. Ross pointed out that Americans are the most marrying nation in western Christendom. United States census figures have shown that since 1890 they have married in steadily increasing proportions and at earlier ages.[5] About 92 per cent of adults will have been married at some time in their lives by the age of sixty-five,[6] and this is a sufficiently high number to suggest that nearly all persons marry who are physically and mentally capable of contracting marriage.

*2. The giving and taking in marriage should be based on personal affection and choice.—*Marriage is thought to be pre-eminently the linking of the lives of two young people drawn to each other by personal attraction. Arranged marriages, or those based on fraud or calculation, receive considerable disapprobation.

Dating is thought by many sociologists to precede serious courting and to be an educational process leading to it. Waller first analyzed it in terms of its distinctive cultural patterns.[7] In dating, the young woman undoubtedly receives the greatest cultural estimation of her personal qualities: merely to be a young, nubile female of attractive phenotype means that she is the object of considerable masculine attention and chivalry.[8] But, despite this high evaluation of young women, most men grow up in American society with the assumption, culturally derived, that the decision to marry rests with them; they expect in the fullness of time to lead some dear girl to the altar. Women, on the other hand, regardless of their personal qualities, can never be completely sure that they will receive a marriage proposal which they can consider seriously, or, more to the point, be asked to marry by the man upon whom they have fastened their desire.[9] The culture does not permit them to undertake active courting by themselves; to be a man-chaser is to suffer an ostracism which is enforced by the women themselves. Women are obviously not completely helpless in these sentimental matters, but they must use guile and finesse to bring the male to their side.

Since the biological fact of bisexuality predisposes women for the having and rearing of children, and therefore for the maintenance of a home, they are compelled to drive as good a bargain in the marriage market as they can. This they can manage only by a careful exploitation of the rules which specify correct maidenly deportment. Men, on the other hand, have greater volition in their marriage choices and are much more disposed as a result to manage their marital ventures in the bathos of culturally approved romance.

3. The criterion of successful marriage is the personal happiness of husband and wife.—Mutual compatibility is made the basis of marriage, and marital bliss becomes dependent upon the emotional sentiments, fluctuating and volatile as they may be, with which a couple regard their relationship. Ultimately their fullest felicity is believed to be achieved by having children, whose arrival and subsequent nurture are viewed as bringing satisfaction to basic biological and social needs. Childless couples are sometimes regarded as possessed of a selfishness which blights their union. Happiness in marriage is thus predicated upon a personal equation, the individual satisfaction and the opportunity for development of the couple.

The cultural accent upon happiness in marriage is of relatively recent origin. Marriages are ordinarily contracted and their success gauged by their contribution in the struggles of life. These may be the partnership co-operation of man and wife, the production of children, the social recognition of adult status, or the stability of marital status. Many such marriages may be buttressed by institutional supports, the most important of which is generally the exchange of property. The spouses may be selected for each other by the parents or other adults, after a careful scrutiny of their relative merits and upon some property agreement, in the belief that normal young people, once married, can fashion for themselves a successful marital life.[10]

A corollary of the American patterns of courtship and marriage, which is not always recognized, is the logical necessity of a relatively easy system of divorce. From a cultural viewpoint, if marriages are made on the basis of personal and inevitably shifting emotions, without the added support of other institutional devices, then they should be equally easy to dissolve. Persons marry to find happiness and, finding it not, turn to divorce as a way out. The present high divorce rate, therefore, is in this sense made explicable and partially condoned by the cultural rules of marriage.

4. The best years of life are those of youth, and its qualities are the most desirable.—A high evaluation is placed upon youth and early middle age in American society, while the old are sometimes treated with indifference and even callousness. Youth is regarded as a period of innocence, energy, and enthusiasm; it is inventive and pragmatic when faced with new experiences and is glad of change—qualities fondly believed to be typical of Americans in general.

Among the young, the unmarried girl, aged perhaps twenty, attractive of face and limb, is the center of attraction in thought and deed. In other societies young men, or old men, or mothers are variously regarded as ideal symbols;[11] in the United States it is the young, pretty girl. She therefore receives at this age the greatest gratification of her ego drives which will probably ever come to her. With men the ideal age is somewhere in the thirties; they need time in which to win occupational and social placement and need not depend so much upon chronological age for their acceptance.

From this high esteem on youth there derive important social consequences. Wherever the young are involved, whether it be in the conduct of schools, or juvenile delinquency, or maltreatment of children, or provision for their play opportunities, there is likely to be at least a quick emotional response to their needs.

Such sentiments as these do not, of course, arise in a social vacuum. They exist, rather, and become understandable in terms of American social history. Youth has received a high evaluation, precisely because its resourcefulness and resilience were valued qualities in the exploitation and development of the American continent. There have been, in addition, as compared to the age groups in European societies, relatively high proportions in the younger age categories in the American population; Americans have in this sense been a young people and correspondingly eager to admire the virtues of youth. The aged, on the other hand, have emerged as a significant social group only recently, and they are not yet favorably regarded.

Related to this cultural theme of youth is the existence of a considerable rift, not to say antagonism, between the generations. The conflict between the old and the young is common enough in human groups; what is significant is its intensity in American society. This is due, in large part, to the rapidity of social change in the United States and to the differing rates with which the generations have adjusted to those changes. Keller speaks somewhat nostalgically of the aged in primitive society as revered "repositories of wisdom";[12] in American society, they are unlikely to be regarded as possessors of a truth that has any relationship to their age.[13]

5. *Children should be reared in a child's world and shielded from too early participation in adult woes and tribulations.*—This configuration is obviously closely related to the high cultural esteem of youth. It is modified by social class: the sentiment is held most strongly by the upper levels of society, much less so by the lower, but even among the poor the social conditions of the American community prevent a too considerable precocity among the children.[14]

The cultural ideal is that children shall mature slowly in terms of their nature and age-sex grades in a prolonged child's world, which is characterized by a segregated class of children's activities.[15] In this juvenile social world they are allowed to grow, develop their abilities, indulge in play, and occasionally to perform such small and often artificial tasks as may be assigned them. Generally they are protected from the responsibilities of adults, and laws and customs prevent their too early gainful employment. In many American homes, particularly in the cities, there is actually not much useful work that children can perform even if they wish. Especially in middle-class families is the configuration most completely observed. The child is accepted as an individual, and his relationships with parents are often warm and affectionate.

Folsom has contrasted this pattern with that which prevails in certain western European families, in which the child is incorporated into the family of adults and in which he lives in their world rather than in a segregated youth society.[16] Moreover, unlike the American middle-class child who may become somewhat exhibitionist in his behavior because of the attention shown him, the European youth is often hastened along in the process of maturation and trained to deference and respect toward parents and elders in general.

Such training as the American child receives may start him off with a psychologically secure character structure,[17] but in other respects it prepares him inadequately for later life. Sometimes he has not broken the emotional ties with his parents or developed definite heterosexual interests; hence his fondness for "Mom."[18] During World War II, the British thought the American soldier adolescent.[19] James Graham Leyburn has pointed out that the American family is itself often at fault because of its inadequate integration with the larger community.[20] It may be unable, as a result, to prepare and to place its members into job, school, clique and class, association, and other social relationships in the society. Thus it delays the processes of maturation.

6. *The exercise of sex should be contained within wedlock.*—Prior to marriage, premarital intercourse is strongly condemned, and sex knowledge is kept hidden from children lest it be damaging to their moral character. After marriage, adultery is similarly proscribed. Sex may thus be legitimately expressed only within marriage, and the speaking of marriage vows makes highly moral sexual behavior which before then had been grossly immoral. The couple, previously prohibited from intercourse, may now embark upon an active, and socially approved, sex life. Sex, to speak figuratively, explodes upon marriage.

About sex there is considerable tension, preoccupation, frustration, shame, and deceit in American society. Judeo-Christian influences, and more immediately Puritanism, have given a sinful cast to sex and have condoned its expression in marriage only because of the grossly physical method of human reproduction. The tradition has particularly valued virginity, more especially in women, before marriage. But the strong interdictions upon sex have tended to heighten rather than to lessen the fascination with sex which exists among Americans. The furtiveness with which it is often approached and the numerous colloquialisms which refer to it indicate the uneasiness with which it is treated. Kinsey's exploration of the sex histories of American males has documented their actual performances.[21] These data indicate that the sex configuration is held with varying intensity at the several levels of society, apparently least so in the lower class. Even here, however, the materials re-emphasize the manner in which restrictive cultural attitudes condition and limit sexual outlets.

7. *Family roles of husband and wife should be based on a sexual division of labor, but with the male status being superior.*—According to this configuration, the husband is head of his family, its main economic support, and its representative in the larger community. Women, consigned to domesticity, are mothers and homemakers. These roles, biologically and culturally conditioned, provide for the structuring of all types of heterosexual relationships, in which the presumption of dominance generally rests with the males. Men are trained to develop the qualities necessary to fulfill their roles in economic, social, sexual, and other activities and to view themselves with self-respect when they have secured a competence in their performances. Women, too, are trained to their respective feminine roles, and these generally involve some degree of catering to men, somewhat as a complement to the expectation of greater male initiative. Terman's analysis of the desired pattern of sex typing in husband and in wife indicated how the cultural conception of the manly man and the womanly woman fall into the cultural mold.[22]

Women's behavior is governed by a double standard of morality which expects greater masculine enterprise not only in the sexual spheres but in many other areas of life. Women live, in male estimation, under a blanket of oppressive mores which restrains their ordinary, everyday movements. Where men have a relative freedom of action, women must cater to a public opinion of what is womanly behavior. In social life, women are under greater disapproval than men when they smoke or indulge in narcotics. On the job, they may encounter much male prejudice which affects their pay and possibilities of promotion. They are more protected by social legislation which governs their hours and conditions of employment.[23]

These cultural attitudes persist despite the social and economic events of modern times which have released women from the control of husbands and fathers. Before the law women have achieved a near-equality with men; they may seek gainful employment and retain their earnings; they have equal rights with men to education; they have all the freedoms necessary to live their own lives as they wish. Democratic sentiments further foster the desire that women develop as persons to enjoy the manifold blessings of American life and to have many of the privileges given men.

Women are thus caught in a process of social change, in which the cultural configuration restrains them to traditional roles, while new ones are proffered by economic and social forces. There is much confusion among them as a result. The young college girl, for example, may have difficulty in knowing to which force to respond: should she be content with the domestic role and look to the main chance of marriage, or should she seek outlets which include both marriage and other roles?[24] Apparently some urban upper-level women find the puzzle extremely hard to resolve and respond to it neurotically.[25]

Men, too, it must be pointed out, suffer in the realignment of roles, since they as much as women are conditioned to the status quo and may find it hard to accommodate themselves to change.

8. Individual, not familial, values are to be sought in family living.— The family is obviously affected by the considerable cultural affirmation of individualism, and the lack of a tradition of familism in American culture has further aided in the development of a configuration in which the family exists for the benefit of its members. The emphasis has been upon the individualization of all members of the family, the children as well as the parents, the wife as much as the husband. Obviously, the husband's prerogatives, nurtured in the bosom of the patriarchal family have had to be parceled out to the other members.

There are many important social consequences from the stress on individualism in the family. On the one hand, its promise is for the richer, fuller development of personality. On the other hand, it weakens the unity of the family. The stresses of American life, including industrialization, urbanization, internal migration, and social class, press hard against the frail shell of the family, attenuated as it is by the thinning of larger kin groups and often limited to its own resources in times of crisis. Further, since the family is not primarily important in placing its members into positions in the larger community, its members feel the strain of loyalties divided between the family and the outside affiliations.

If some of the configurations of the American family have been correctly stated, they indicate a social philosophy in which the values of individualism are paramount, or, more specifically, those which support the development of individual personality in the context of family and community relationships. A primary stress is placed on the family as a social group rather than on the functions which it performs for society. The family exists for its members rather than the members for the family. In this respect the family is in relatively close adjustment to the total culture, in which the democratic realization of the potentialities of all its members is an ideal.

But the family is pre-eminently an association based on antagonistic co-operation, and in times of hardship the antagonisms may predominate. The straining of family members for individualistic goals may blunt their sense of obligation to each other and to the larger society. When achievement of the desired values for which they grope seems far off and difficult, individualism may decay into gross egotism and selfishness. The family based on the chimera of personal values seems then faced with a dolorous future.

The American family, however, is not without resources. Contributing to its strength is the immense popularity of marriage, and through marriage the possibility of parenthood, both of them regarded as major life-goals. Staying power is also given the family by the affection and compatibility which draws two people into marriage, the warmth of relationships between parents and children, and the individualization of all members of the family. The structure of the family is such as to permit the desired nurturing of stable and democratic personalities.

In view of the ethos of the culture, the direction of evolutionary change in the family, and of desirable efforts at rational adjustments, is in the continued emphasis upon the social relationships within the family and upon the family as a social system through which fundamental life-purposes can be achieved.

24 *Variations in the Basic Values of Family Systems*

FLORENCE ROCKWOOD KLUCKHOHN

Dr. Florence Kluckhohn's paper also deals with the societal value systems which shape the form of the family. Although she deals at a very general level of value orientations, Dr. Kluckhohn does not conceive of the value system as unitary a system as does Sirjamaki. Rather, she advances the view that value systems always have preferred, permitted, and proscribed modes, with variation thus built into the value system. Kluckhohn is able to differentiate, with a single set of concepts, the values that underlie families of different ethnic backgrounds, and to account for the form and extent of conflict that families may develop.

For many years, my own interest has been centered on the variations of the quite universal institution commonly called The Family. And the still broader perspective has been the variations in basic value—value orientations—found both between cultures and within cultures. Therefore, it is from this point of view that I wish to approach the problems of diagnosing and treating disturbances in family relations.

Psychologically speaking, it is well known that the developing personalities of children are greatly affected by the kinds of relationships they have with a mother, a father, and siblings. Sometimes, but not very often, in the analyses of family patterns made in this country, the influences of grandparents and collateral relatives are considered. But even when these are considered, not much attention has been given to the differing effects of culturally variable family patterns upon the relationships themselves and the kinds of personalities which result from them.

One of the factors needing attention, then, is the cultural one, or—I would prefer to say—the value orientation factor. We are concerned with finding out both what kinds of strains are common to families and particular cultures or subcultures and what additional ones are to be expected when a family is in process of acculturation.

Basic values are not superficial phenomena. The value orientations (the term I prefer) of a people are deeply rooted, are mainly unconscious, and are also so pervasive that they markedly affect the patterns of behavior and thought of a people in all areas of activity. Let me quote a statement from Clyde Kluckhohn:

Reprinted from *Social Casework*, XXXIX (February–March, 1958), 63–72, where it appeared under the title, "Family Diagnosis: Variations in the Basic Values of Family Systems," with the kind permission of the author and publishers.

There is a "philosophy" behind the way of life of every individual and of every relatively homogeneous group at any given point in their histories. This gives, with varying degrees of explicitness or implicitness, some sense of coherence or unity to living both in cognitive and affective dimensions. Each personality gives to this "philosophy" an idiosyncratic coloring, and creative individuals will markedly reshape it. However, the main outlines of the fundamental values, existential assumptions, and basic abstractions have only exceptionally been created out of the stuff of unique biological heredity and peculiar life experience. The underlying principles arise out of, or are limited by, the givens of biological human nature and the universalities of social interaction. The specific formulation is ordinarily a cultural product. In the immediate sense, it is from the life-ways which constitute the designs for living of their community or tribe or region or socio-economic class or nation or civilization that most individuals derive their "mental-feeling outlook."[1]

The anthropologist, dealing with quite different cultures the world around, has concerned himself mostly with a demonstration of the often dramatic differences between cultures. What I wish now to present is a classification of values and some ideas about variation which allow us to analyze both this kind of difference and the other kind which I call intra cultural variation.

Three major assumptions underlie both the classification system of value orientations[2] and the conceptualization of aspects of variation in value orientations.

First, it is assumed that there is a limited number of common human problems for which all peoples at all times must find some solution. This is the universal aspect of value orientations because the common human problems to be treated arise inevitably out of the human situation.

But however universal the problems, the solutions found for them are not the same; hence the next consideration is the degree of relativity or, better, the range of variability. The second assumption is that while there is variability in solutions of all the problems, it is neither limitless nor random but is definitely variability within a range of possible solutions.

The third assumption, which provides the key to the later analysis of variation in value orientations, is that all variants of all solutions are in varying degrees present in all societies at all times. Thus, every society has, in addition to its dominant profile of value orientations, numerous variant or substitute profiles. And in both the dominant and the variant profiles, there is always a rank ordering of value orientations emphases rather than a single emphasis.

Five problems have been tentatively singled out as the crucial ones common to all human groups. These problems are stated here in the form of questions, and in each case there is a parenthetical designation of the name that will be used hereafter for the range of orientations relating to the question:

1. What is the character of innate human nature? (Human-Nature Orientation)

2. What is the relation of man to nature (supernature)? (Man-Nature Orientation)

3. What is the temporal focus of human life? (Time Orientation)

4. What is the modality of human activity? (Activity Orientation)

5. What is the modality of man's relationship to other men? (Relational Orientation)

The ranges of variability suggested as a testable conceptualization of the variation in the value orientations are given in Table 1.

1. Human Nature Orientation.—To the question of what innate human nature is, there are the three logical divisions of Evil, Good and Evil, and Good. Yet it may be argued that the category of Good *and* Evil is not one but two categories. There certainly is a significant difference between the view that human nature is simply neutral and the view of it as a mixture of the good and bad. Moreover, the subprinciples of mutability and immutability increase the basic threefold classification to six possibilities. Human nature can, for example, be conceived to be Evil and unalterable or Evil and perfectible; as Good and unalterable or Good and corruptible; as an invariant mixture of the Good and Evil or as a mixture subject to influence.

Few will disagree that the orientation inherited from Puritan ancestors and still strong among many Americans is that of a basically Evil but perfectible human nature. According to this view, constant control and discipline of the self are required if any real goodness is to be achieved, and the danger of regression is aways present. But some in the United States today, perhaps a growing number, incline to the view that human nature is a mixture of the Good and Evil. These would say that although control and effort are certainly needed, lapses can be understood and need not always be severely condemned. This latter definition of basic human nature would appear to be a more common one among peoples of the world, both literate and non-literate, than the one held to in the historical past of this country. Whether there are any total societies committed to the definition of human nature as immutably Good is to be doubted. Yet the position is a possible one, and it certainly is found as a variant definition within societies.

2. Man-Nature (-Supernature) Orientation.—The three-point range of variation in the man-nature orientation—Subjugation to Nature, Harmony with Nature, and Mastery over Nature—is too well known from the works of philosophers and culture historians to need much explanation. Mere illustrations will demonstrate the differences between the conceptions.

Spanish-American culture in the American Southwest gives us an example of a very definite Subjugation-to-Nature orientation. The typical Spanish-American sheep herder in a time as recent as fifteen years ago believed firmly that there was little or nothing a man could do to save or protect either land or flocks when damaging storms descended upon them. He simply accepted the inevitable. In Spanish-American attitudes toward illness and death one finds the same fatalism. "If it is the Lord's will that I die, I shall die," is the way they express it, and many a Spanish-American has refused the services of a doctor because of this attitude.

If the conceptualization of the man-nature relationship is that of Harmony, there is no real separation between man, nature, and supernature. One is simply an extension of the other, and the conception of wholeness derives from their unity. This orientation, little understood in this country since it is third order one, seems to have been the dominant one in many periods of Chinese history, and it is strongly evident in Japanese culture at the present time as well as historically. It is also the orientation attributed to the Navaho Indians by Clyde Kluckhohn.

The Mastery-over-Nature position is the first-order one of most Americans. Natural forces of all kinds are to be overcome and put to the use of human beings. Rivers everywhere are spanned with bridges; mountains have roads put through and around them; new lakes are built, sometimes in the heart of a desert; old lakes get partially filled in when additional land is needed for building sites, roads, or airports; the belief in man-made medical care for the control of illness and the lengthening of life is strong to an extreme; and all are told early in life that "the Lord helps those who help themselves." The view in general is that it is a part of man's duty to overcome obstacles; hence the great emphasis upon technology.

3. Time Orientation.—The possible cultural interpretations of the temporal focus of human life break easily into the three-point range of Past, Present, and Future. Far too little attention has been given to the full range of major variations in the time orientation.

Obviously, every society must deal with all the three time problems; each one has its conceptions of the past, the present, and the future. Where societies differ is in the rank order emphasis given to each; a very great deal can be told about the particular society or part of a society being studied, and much about the direction of change within it can be predicted, if one knows what the rank order emphasis is.

Illustrations of the variations in temporal focus are also easily found. Spanish-Americans, who have been described as taking the view that man is a victim of natural forces, are also a people who give a first order position to Present-Time. They pay little attention to what has happened in the past and regard the future as a vague and most unpredictable period. Planning for the future or hoping that the future will be better than either present or past simply is not their way of life.

Historic China was a society that gave first order value preference to Past-Time. Ancestor worship and a strong family tradition were both expressions of a Past-Time orientation. So also was the Chinese attitude that nothing new ever happened in the present or would happen in the future; it had all happened before in the far distant past.

Americans, more strongly than most peoples of the world, place an emphasis upon the future—a future that is anticipated as "bigger and better." This does not mean they have no regard for the past or thought of the present. But it certainly is true that no current generation of Americans ever wants to be called "old-fashioned." The ways of the past are not considered good just because they are past, and truly dominant Americans are seldom content with the present. This view results in a high evaluation of change, providing the change does not threaten the existing value order—the American way of life.

4. *Activity Orientation.*—The modality of human activity is the fourth of the common human problems giving rise to a value-orientation system. The range of variation in solutions suggested for it is the three-fold one of Being, Being-in-Becoming, and Doing.

In the Being orientation, the preference is for the kind of activity which is a spontaneous expression of what is conceived to be "given" in the human personality. In some sense, this orientation is a spontaneous expression in activity of impulses and desires; yet care must be taken not to make this interpretation a too literal one. In no society, as Clyde Kluckhohn has commented, does one ever find a one-to-one relationship between the desired and the desirable. The concrete behavior of individuals in complex situations and the moral codes governing that behavior usually reflect all the orientations simultaneously. A stress upon the "isness" of the personality and a spontaneous expression of that "isness" is not pure license, as we can easily see if we turn our attention to a society or segments of a society in which the Being orientation is the first order preference. Mexican society illustrates this preference well in its widely ramified patterning of *fiesta* activities. Yet never in the *fiesta,* with its emphasis on spontaneity, is there pure impulse gratification. The value demands of some of the other orientations make for codes which restrain the activities of the individuals in very definite ways.

The Being-in-Becoming orientation shares with the Being a great concern with what the human being is rather than what he can accomplish, but here the similarity ends. The idea of development, so little stressed in the Being orientation, is paramount in the Being-in-Becoming one. Erich Fromm's conception of "the spontaneous activity of the total integrated personality" is close to but not identical with the Being-in-Becoming mode.

The Doing orientation is so characteristically the dominant one in American society that there is little need for an extensive discussion of it. Its most distinguishing feature is a demand for the kind of activity that results in accomplishment achieved by acting upon persons, things, or situations. What the individual does, and what he can or will accomplish, are almost always the primary questions in the American's scale of appraisal of persons. "Getting things done" and "Let's *do* something about it" are stock American phrases.

Fromm also considers this orientation to be different from the one he defines in his concept of spontaneity, but he does not accord it an equally favored position. Instead, he actually condemns it as a fertile source of neurotically compulsive behavior. Although few would disagree that the Doing orientation of Americans makes for a competition with others which is often extreme and intense, it has not as yet been demonstrated that such competition customarily leads to or reflects compulsiveness in the technical sense of the term.

5. Relational Orientation.—The last of the common human problems to be treated is the definition of man's relation to other men. This orientation has three subdivisions: the Lineal, the Collateral, and the Individualistic.

Individual autonomy is always found even in the most extreme types of *gemeinschaft* societies—that is, folk societies. The like-mindedness and behavioral similarities of individuals in "homogeneous" groups have been overstressed. It is usually, if not always, the case that considerable leeway is permitted for individuality within the confines of the definitely fixed customs which *gemeinschaft* groups require for the ordering of human relationships. Individuality and individualism are both results of attention being given to the autonomy of the individual, but they are vastly different concepts, and significant nuances of meaning are lost when, as is so often the case, they are either confused or equated. There is actually less opportunity for a truly spontaneous individuality of expression in an individualistic society than in other more fixed and firmly regulated social orders. But, on the other hand, the man in an individualistic society need not remain in a fixed position and need not so often bow his head in acceptance of a dominating authority. He is much more "free to be like everyone else."

Collaterality also is found in all societies. The individual is not a human being except as he is a part of a social order, and one type of inevitable social grouping is that which results from laterally extended relationships. These are the more immediate relationships in time and space. Biologically, sibling relationships are the prototype of the Collateral relationship.

In addition, all societies must take into account the fact that individuals are biologically and culturally related to each other through time. There is, in other words, always a Lineal principle in relationships which is derived both from age and generational differences and from cultural continuity.

There will always be a variability, within systems and sub-systems as well as between them, in the primacy and the nature of goals which is in accord with variable stressing of the three principles. When the Individualistic principle is dominant, individual goals have primacy over the goals of specific Collateral or Lineal groups. This in no sense means that there is license for the individual to pursue selfishly his own interests and in so doing disregard the interests of others. It is simply that each individual's responsibility to the total society and his place in it are in terms of goals (and roles) which are defined and structured as autonomous ones in the sense of being independent of particular Lineal or Collateral groupings.

A dominant Collateral orientation calls for a primacy of the goals and welfare of the laterally extended group. The group in this case is always moderately independent of other similar groups, and the problem of a well-regulated continuity of group relationships through time is not highly critical. The Navaho extended families and the loosely articulated combinations of these in what Clyde Kluckhohn calls an "outfit" are illustrations of such groups. One also finds collaterality dominant in Italian culture. And although the individual Navaho or Italian always has some autonomous roles and some individualistic goals, and always also has some roles and goals that relate to a wider system viewed as continuous in time, the roles and goals that have primacy for him are those that are representative of his extended household group or "outfit."

If it is the Lineal principle that is dominant, it is again group goals that have primacy, but there is the additional factor that one of the most important of those group goals is continuity through time. *Continuity* of the group through time and ordered positional succession within the group are both crucial issues when Lineality dominates the relational system. Although other patterns are possible, it appears that the most successful means of maintaining a Lineal emphasis are either those based squarely upon hereditary factors such as primogeniture or those that are assimilated to a kinship structure.

To delineate the value-orientation profiles of the three groups included in the research monographs, histories, novels, and other sources were used. It is possible to test directly for the ranking of the orientations, but we have not as yet been able to do this for our sample.[3] These profiles are now given in Table 1, but given with the warning that "ethnic labels" can be dangerous. For example, some Italians and some Irish-Americans, most certainly variants in their homeland, were more attuned to dominant American middle-class values at the time they arrived in this country than are many Old Yankees after several hundred years of participation in United States culture. But we need the modal (typical) orientation profiles as a base line for the analysis of the difference between the problems expected and those found. Therefore, in the following table the modal profiles of the dominant Middle-class American, the Italian-American,

Table 1

CULTURE

Orientation	Middle-class American	Italian-American	Irish-American
Relational	Ind > Coll > Lin	Coll > Lin > Ind	Lin > Coll > Ind
Time	Fut > Pres > Past	Pres > Past > Fut	Pres > Past > Fut (but some indication of an earlier Past > Pres > Fut)
Man-Nature	Over > Subj > With	Subj > With > Over	Subj = With > Over (doubt about first order here and some doubt that there is a clear-cut first order preference)
Activity	Doing > Being > Being-in-Becoming	Being > Being-in-Becoming > Doing	Being > Being-in-Becoming > Doing
Human Nature	Evil > Mixed > Good Mixed Evil and Good > Evil > Good	Mixed Good and Evil predominantly	Most definitely an *Evil* basic nature with perfectibility desired but problematic.

and the Irish-American are drawn to the extent that we feel much certainty about them. For both the Italians and the Irish, the positions stated are those to which it is assumed a majority of the two groups held when they came to the United States.

As for the American middle-class case, I shall not take time to cite more than a few of the well-known facts. Parents are much concerned with the performance of their children, and training is ideally for independence of action and a show of initiative. Property gets classified as "mine and thine." Competitive behavior is rewarded and success acclaimed. The child is also quite typically the hope of the future for many families, most especially those where parents have not themselves gone as far as they had hoped to go. The family is quite individualized, and relations with relatives of the extended family, either Lineal or Collateral, are not usually strong. Extended relations certainly are not held to if the holding is regarded as detrimental to the social mobility of the particular nuclear family.

Of all known types of families, this one is probably the best suited to our highly rationalized economic system and other spheres of our national life. It does produce achievement-minded, independent, and future-oriented individuals who are largely free of ties that bind them in time and place. •

Critics of the American family all too often forget to consider the wider social system and the meshing of family and other institutions.

But the critics are correct in pointing to the numerous strains on individuals which are more or less endemic in such a family. There are many strains on women as wives and mothers, on men as husbands and fathers, and these, separately and in relation to each other, inevitably have effects upon developing children. Much has been written on all the strains and their effects. Erik Erikson, for one, has provided us with a most penetrating analysis in the chapter on "The American Identity" in his *Childhood and Society*.[4] Many books and articles have been devoted to the analysis of the American feminine role, to the American mother-child relationship, and some even to the roles men play as husbands and fathers.

In illustrating our use of the value-orientation theory for a diagnosis and interpretation of family relations, I shall first discuss some aspects of the Italian patterns. If one turns back to the table that lists the orientations of all three cultures, it is easily noted that there is a wide-range difference between the value preferences of the typical Italian and the middle-class American on all orientations. In each case, if the Italian is to become a thorough-going middle-class American in his basic values, he must move from his own first order preferences to what has been in the past his third order and least favored value choices. This is no easy move for any people to make and certainly not one that can be made quickly without creating problems. It has long been my contention that the assimilation process for peoples coming into this country will vary in accord with the degree of goodness of fit between the value orientations they brought with them and the dominant values of the society. When people have markedly different value preferences on all the orientations, the process will be slower and more fraught with difficulties than if there were agreement on some one or two. And the most difficult change of all is the radical shift to value positions that formerly had been the least favored of all.

All the Italian families of our sample are in process of movement away from typical Italian values to those of the dominant culture, but there are differences in both rate and kind of movement between the "sick" and "well" families. The most critical difference seems to be the order of change by orientation. In the "sick" families there has been, for one reason or another, a breakdown of the Collateral *relational* ties, whereas in the "well" families these ties are still quite strong. It is one thing to try to change from a non-planning Present-Time and Being oriented position when one has the "cushion" of ramified family ties to support and sustain one in case of failures, but quite another thing when these are lacking. The pacing of change and the cognitive grasp of the difference between goals and the means of attaining them and the relation of means to goals are the other striking criteria by which the two kinds of families can be differentiated.

In the Italian families defined as "sick" the Collateral ties have been

partially or wholly destroyed, and there is not as yet in any of them a sufficient understanding of an Individualistic relational orientation for them to
operate successfully as "isolated nuclear" families. They are stranded and
confused, virtually in a void as far as relations with others are concerned.
They also all show small ability to instrument their plans and desires for the
material things or other of the goals of middle-class culture which they have
come to consider important goals. The well families, in contrast, have maintained quite good Collateral ties on both sides of the family—and relative
both to goals set and the means of attaining them, they are far more
"realistic."

All these families have problems, many of them very similar in origin,
in nature, and in degree. It is the handling of them which varies so greatly.
In the well families there is, in addition to the more realistic grasp of the
relation of means to ends, a greater ability on the part of the parents to
look problems in the face and communicate with each other about them.
The parents in the sick families have poor communication with each other,
and they characteristically deny that there are tensions between them or
that they are in any way to blame for the problems they face. They project
onto the outside world, but more important still they also have found a
focus for projection within the family itself—a particular child.

Let me illustrate from two cases ever so briefly. In one of these—one
where we have had little success in the treatment of the family—the father
and mother have both had troubles with their extended families, and they
feel that in no way can they count on the relatives to help them out; they
also, partly because of these same relatives, are a "looked down upon"
family in the community (largely Italian) in which they live. There is a
great deal of friction between themselves which scarcely ever comes out
into the open. In fact, one of the main reasons for the failure of therapy
in this family was that, every time the therapist of the father or the mother
came close to bringing to the fore the problems between them, there was a
withdrawal on the part of one or both. The father in particular was extremely reluctant to co-operate if co-operation meant any discussion of
himself or his relationships.

Teachers of their children, the doctors whom they sought out in great
variety, employers, and neighbors whom they accused of spying upon them
were frequent targets for their feelings of failure and frustration. But it
was their first child, a little girl of ten years with a low level of intelligence,
who was the main target for the projection of their problems. They constantly assigned to this child the implicit and informal roles of "the bad
girl," "the girl who was and would always be a disgrace to them," "the
child who was a cross to bear." The child is, indeed, a difficult case. Not
only is her intelligence low, but she is the closest to being an atypical child
of any that we had in our sample. But one may, and we did, question how
much of her most bizarre behavior and her lack of ability to perform in

school were effects of the roles that both the father and mother have assigned to her. Certainly it is a fact that the parents have been (1) strongly resistant to facing the possibility that the main problems are in themselves rather than in this one child and (2) almost equally resistant to agreeing to anything that might really help the child. In other words, her aberrant behavior, which they certainly in some part induce, seems to be necessary for the maintenance of what family equilibrium does exist.

In another case, not dissimilar in general outline, we were more successful in treatment but only after a very long period of time. This family, too, was cut off from ties with the extended families of both father and mother, and there was an even greater feeling of isolation relative to the community in which they lived. Here the child singled out as a problem child upon whom many kinds of frustrations and anxieties could be projected was a little girl, the second of the family, who again was less bright than her siblings. But another factor in the focusing of attention upon this particular child was that after a long siege of rheumatic fever that she had had, her doctors, all middle-class Americans, had insisted that special attention be accorded her. She was to have a room to herself, a special kind of bed, and other attentions that did not fit in at all well with the Collateral patterning of Italian families. This special treatment increased resentment toward her and made her the better target for all kinds of tensions. And here again the informal and implicit roles assigned to her were that she was untrustworthy, irresponsible, and would always be a probable source of disgrace to the family in the wider community. The additional one was that she was demanding in a way "good" Italian children should not be.

Obviously, in these and all our other cases, the factor of value conflict is only one of many to be considered. But its importance becomes most apparent when one compares families that are so very similar in many ways but very different in the degree to which acculturation is a problem for family equilibrium.

The significance of the value factor is made even more obvious when the acculturation processes of different groups are compared. In the Irish-American group, for example, one finds different problems because the shifts in value positions which the Irish have had to make, if and when they become assimilated, are different from those Italians must make.

But rather than give the details of this comparison, I wish to illustrate from the Irish-American case another use of the value-orientation theory in the analysis of family problems. This use is the prediction of the kinds of strains one is likely to find common in a system because of the particular combination of basic values adhered to in a culture and the further strains that are produced when acculturation occurs.

In our analysis of the culture of rural Irish, we were especially struck by the possibilities for much intracultural strain because of the juxtaposition in the total value system of a very strong first order Lineal relational orientation[5] and a dominant human-nature orientation which is a more extreme version of the Evil but perfectible position than even that adhered to by New England Puritans. This particular combination of value orientations requires on the one hand a training of persons for dependent behavior and a low degree of individual responsibility, but on the other keeps them ever conscious of an evil nature which they *themselves* must control. The Yankee Puritan whose dominant relational orientation was Individualism was not caught in this dilemma of contradictions. Thus, we expected to find, fairly typically, in the Irish group strong denial and escape mechanisms. More concretely, we predicted that members of the group would commonly deny responsibility for happenings, including consequences of their acts, but that they also would have intensive guilt feelings. It was further predicted that escape patterns would be prevalent—most especially in cases where men in their occupational roles had been thrown too much and too soon into situations demanding much individual responsibility and quite independent action. Conversely, it was expected that there would be fewer instances of either of these defense mechanisms in cases where men had found employment in organizations, governmental or otherwise, which were quite Lineal in character. It was also expected that sexuality would be a source of great anxiety to this group.

On the whole, our findings have accorded well with our expectations. The prevalence of the denial and escape defense mechanisms has been striking indeed. Treatment of the "sick" Irish-American families has been greatly handicapped because issues and problems are so often and so strongly denied. Moreover, it has been our experience that it is difficult to keep Irish-American families in treatment.

These few illustrations must serve to indicate how we have found the factor of basic values—value orientations—critical to the analysis of family relations.

25   *Pressures to Remarry: Institutionalized Patterns Affecting the Divorced*

WILLIAM GOODE

The divorced person, especially the divorced woman, Professor Goode argues, has an equivocal position in American society. Such persons do not have the "standard package" of ties, obligations, and identity which are expected of adults and which render it easy for others to relate to them. This situation, Goode suggests, evokes pressure on the divorced to remarry, to conform once again to the accepted patterns and thereby reinforce them.

What kinds of institutional patterns and pressures (indirect or direct) must exist, if a high divorce rate is to continue without creating major disruptive forces in the society? We cannot answer this question in such general terms, but we can begin to answer it for our own society.[1] We must also leave aside just how high, under any conceivable postdivorce institutional arrangements, the divorce rate could become without disrupting the kinship institutions.[2] We are only asking what are the institutional patterns, whether we call them quasi-institutions or indirect institutions, that serve to minimize the disruption stemming from a failure to define clearly the role of the divorcee. We do not believe that our high rate of divorce creates great *societal* disorganization. That it creates considerable personal disorganization can be easily documented. Is it, then, possible, that there are various structuring factors which serve to keep the kinship institutions functioning in our society, even with a high divorce rate and a failure to define appropriate role behavior for the divorcee?

We start with the fundamental fact that there is at least apparent structuring. There is a great regularity in the behavior pattern of most divorcees: they are reassimilated to the status of "married." Indeed, their remarriage rate is even higher than the marriage rate for single people in the ages beginning with the late twenties. Apparently about 94 per cent of women divorcing at age 30 will eventually remarry.[3] Although we cannot give so precise a figure for our own sample, since we did not follow them over a period of years, 54 per cent of these divorced mothers aged 20–38 at the time of the divorce had remarried in our Time Group IV (interviewed 26 months after the divorce), and 50 per cent of the rest have a steady date. Moreover, as we shall note later, the "rate" of remarriage actually seems

---

Reprinted from *After Divorce*, pp. 206–16. Copyright 1956 by The Free Press of Glencoe, Illinois.

to be higher when there are more rather than fewer children. And, for reasons we shall present in this chapter, we are rather convinced that the remarriage rate of divorced mothers is not much lower than that of female divorcees generally.

Much of our analysis of kinship institutions documents the structural importance of children. The theoretical notions underlying this focus are to be found in the existing literature on the family.[4] The nub of these considerations is that the focus of kinship institutions is the status and care of the child, specifically, the procreation, maintenance, status placement, and socialization of the child. The infrequency of generalized sexual chastity as an ideal demonstrates that kinship institutions do not have the "control of sex" as their primary function. Most prohibitions and injunctions that deal with the spouses also serve to define the proper care of the child and to fix responsibility for such tasks. Finally, it is an obvious theoretical proposition, and not a paradox, that this apparent concentration on the child must be interpreted as a real concentration on the adult world: it is by fixing the place, role, tasks, destiny, and relationships of the child that such matters are also determined for the adults, who are connected by the biological and social fact of the child. It is because the child creates these connections of responsibility—role obligations and rights, i.e., institutional relationships—between adults, and families of adults, that the kinship institutions concentrate upon the child. Consequently, our concentration on the "indirect postdivorce institutions" that relate the child to the parents is not due to our having only divorced mothers in our study; it is due to the great theoretical importance of these relationships in any analysis of kinship institutions.

In our own society the structural disruptions created by a high divorce rate without explicit postdivorce institutions are accentuated by (1) the fairly general disapproval of divorce, particularly when children are involved; and (2) the perhaps increasing structural importance of the nuclear family as the primary kinship unit, that is, the family composed of parents and children and with few strong ties with further generations or collateral relatives.

Now, the divorcee is not entirely without normative guides, even if for the most part these do not refer to the status of divorcee. Some of these guides are to be found in the extensive body of marriage and divorce laws of the states. Within each state the law undertakes to define the legal responsibilities of the husband for the care, if any, of the wife, care of the child, and sometimes, reciprocally, the responsibilities of the wife for the husband. In addition, of course, the law defines her responsibilities toward the children, if there are any. Finally, there are rather elaborate laws relating to property ownership within the family, including inherited property, as well as gifts and purchases. Since the family is a major institutional focus for the inheritance and enjoyment of property, the corpus of family law overlaps considerably with other bodies of law.

In general, these legal prescriptions are attempts to enforce or to define in some detail the statuses and roles of husband and wife, and of father and mother, but not usually those of divorcee. Often the problems of legal specification become so involved that it is difficult to find a clear foundation or origin for them in the normative prescriptions of the kinship structure, as seen and understood by the average adult. Nevertheless, it is safe to say that few, if any, legal prescriptions relating to the family are without some such foundation and origin.

Both the legal and the social definitions of the status of divorcee are somewhat ambiguous. However, the legal and social definitions of parent (divorced or not) are much clearer. Indeed, one must find very particular circumstances in order to locate exceptions to the general clarity of duties and rights of parents. Such exceptions might be the situation in which a child becomes a serious juvenile delinquent or exhibits symptoms of psychosis or severe mental retardation. In such cases, just what the parent is supposed to do is not clearly prescribed by the norms of the society (although the legal rules are relatively clear). And, of course, it is hardly necessary to comment that there are many details of these rights and duties about which there is much argument in our time. Thus, for example, whether the parents have much, if any, right to interfere in the choice of spouse by the children; just how late the children may stay up; and even the control over comic books, television, etc., are highly specific points about which there is great argument within parental circles. It is perhaps true, then, that the *rights* of parents are often unclear, at least in contemporary society. Nevertheless, we believe that, in general, the *duties* of parents are fairly clear.

The ambiguity of role is reduced even more if we turn from the general role of "parent" to that of "mother." Although we have few survey data with respect to the behavior of mothers, and only isolated bits of knowledge about variations in the attitudes held by the population with respect to maternal behavior, the ideal institutional pattern can be formulated in at least rough terms. The commercialization of this ideal, as seen in such manifestations as Mother's Day, would not be possible if there were not a substantial and relatively univalent set of ideals about the approved role behavior of the mother. It is not useful or relevant here to analyze in any detail the sometimes amusing journalistic notions regarding the "mother-complex" in this country. It is sufficient to note that the ideal behavior of mother has its mirror image in a set of ideal expectations as to children's responses to the maternal behavior. For example, sons are supposed to revere their mothers, protect them, etc. This set of complementary role expectations is fairly well defined. The position of mother in our society is complex. Without denying that complexity, we would nevertheless assert that "mother" is a "primary" status and contains less ambiguity of role expectations than even the status of father. This "primary" character may be seen in several socio-structural nexuses. One connection is with the egalitarian tendencies of the movement for the emancipation of women. Here it is sufficient to note that the attitudes toward a single woman's being in the job market are relatively permissive, and are less so for the married woman without children. However, the attitudes against the mother's working are much stronger.[5] Furthermore, much of the verbal approval of the mother's working is likely to be hollow in actuality. That is to say, within almost every social group the working mother is under strong pressures to take care of her children and to leave the job market. Her claim that the extra salary is absolutely needed for survival is viewed with considerable skepticism, even when the claim is not openly rejected. This general disapproval becomes relatively strong in precisely those middle-class strata where the egalitarian notions are held most strongly, because in such strata and groups the recent psychodynamic justifications for child freedom, child affection, breast feeding, security in mother love, etc. have become most fully accepted.

The primary character of the status may be viewed in another way: all other role obligations are residual, compared to this, and must wait until those of mother are satisfied. Everyone occupies several statuses. One may be father, physician, friend, cousin, neighbor, member of the board of education. Thus, he has other roles to play and responsibilities to meet than paternal ones. This is true for the mother as well. However, compared with other major statuses, that of mother is more likely to be viewed as exclusive, and other roles as residual. The maternal obligations have first call on her energies. The legitimacy of *non*-maternal responsibilities is questioned unless it can be shown that the maternal responsibilities themselves are being properly met; and the clarity and moral force of this prescription are greater than for her other statuses.

We may phrase the situation in a slightly different fashion. We are all more surprised in our "anonymous" urban society when a woman fails to let us know that she is a mother, than when she does not tell us she is *married*. We accept the fact that she may wish to be considered single or may feel herself to be unmarried in all but legal senses. We suspect, however, that she has rather basic personality problems if she attempts in any way to hide her motherhood.

This greater definiteness and weight of the motherhood role is apparently not confined to contemporary society or even to Western society. There are many psychodynamic and socio-structural factors which make the pattern a cultural universal. We are not concerned with those at the present time. We need only note the basic fact that the status is primary and unambiguous, in several senses and with respect to most areas of behavior.

One may differentiate further and suggest that there is least ambiguity of status with respect to (1) widow-mother; while (2) wife-mother and (3) divorcee-mother follow in order of increasing ambiguity. This further differentiation does not undermine the essentially greater clarity of the basic mother status as against that of other kinship statuses.

Now, in spite of the general failure of the society to define closely the appropriate differences in behavior for the divorcee or for the divorcee-mother as against that of the nondivorcee-mother, there are some differences in the social attitudes toward the three categories of widow-mother, wife-mother, and divorcee-mother, and very great differences in their positions in the social structure. Only the second of these continues to act in a complete family. The wife-mother is related to a husband-father, and the two form a couple, in various senses and with respect to an immense network of relationships and social definitions. This cannot, of course, be the situation of either the widow-mother or the divorcee-mother. As several analysts have pointed out, various structural factors in the social positions of the spouse are similar for the widowed and the divorced. On the other hand, the widow enjoys considerably greater sympathy, unquestioned help, rallying of friends and kin, etc.[6]

Thus the widow has a completely unambiguous status, and her corresponding role expectations are relatively clear. This is true for the ideal case, and the complexities of daily living simply redefine this ideal pattern without changing it greatly. For example, the widow may actually have to be a worker in addition to being mother because of financial problems, but this qualification is already envisioned in the fuller statements of the ideal widow-mother.

Now, both the lesser approval enjoyed by the divorcee-mother and the greater amount of status ambiguity press in the same direction: toward remarriage.

There are few solutions to the institutional ambiguity, and all these are only partial solutions. The mother may rid herself of her children by giving custody to some member of her family. This presents legal complications in some cases, and women are socialized to find this solution rather unacceptable. The mother may instead attempt to work out an unambiguous role in a bohemian group or in a relatively anonymous urban situation. Anonymity is almost impossible when there are children. The bohemian solution is difficult for the majority of mothers and in most cases will be only a temporary solution.[7]

The most frequent solution, and the one that is institutionally clearest, is to marry again. The greater clarity of role definition that results is easily seen. So far as strangers are concerned, there is no particular reason to question the new marriage. There is a father for the children and a common domicile. The mother is once more wife-mother, and the lesser events, problems, solutions, etc., of daily life are very similar to those in families where there has been no history of divorce. The social position is somewhat more complex when there are visiting rights and custodial battles. However, both visits and battles decrease in importance as time goes on. And, in any event, they are only intermittent in all but a very small proportion of cases.

Finally, the reconstitution of a full household gives the woman a strong hand in dealing with her ex-husband. She usually has custody by law and now offers her children a home that is apparently normal to the outside eye. Both children and mother are likely to be sensitive to this social aspect of the situation, and thus the mother is better able to resist the otherwise potential power of the husband to divide the children's loyalties in some substantial manner.

We have emphasized the factor of status ambiguity in the pressures toward remarriage. Common-sense factors press equally in the same direction. Nevertheless, even some of these can be grouped under the general category of institutional ambiguity. The most important common-sense factor is, naturally, that of money. The female earns less money than the male in our society for the same type of job. Even without listing other aspects of the problem of the female divorcee's income, it is clear that she is in a precarious financial situation after the divorce. It is true, of course, that she may have been in a disadvantaged financial condition prior to the divorce also, but she could do very little about the problem at that time. Once she is divorced, she has a further alternative, that of remarriage. Even remarriage with a husband at the same job level as her own allows her greater financial security. There are then no added expenses for child care.

The same kinds of comments may be made with respect to the general problem of energy allocation in the care of children. It is difficult for one person alone to take care of children. Not only are there many occasions when the adult must be absent for such activities as shopping, but illness of the adult or of one child may disrupt even the most cleverly organized routines and schedules. At such times, the presence of another adult to share the time and energy burdens is of very great importance. In addition, the psychic strain of caring for children, whose energy and energy-recovery are likely to be greater than that of the adult, requires help at various times from another adult. Institutional prescriptions do not define clearly how the divorcee-mother is to solve this problem, but other people are not morally required to help her. Our kinship system permits divorce, but does not provide for its consequences.

The only institutionally sanctioned solution for this problem is marriage, although various other social arrangements or speculative possibilities exist—for example, co-operative arrangements among widowed and divorced mothers, the use of extended kinship networks with or without remarriage, or various forms of polygamy.

In addition to these pressures that are intrinsic to the situation once the primary role responsibility of the mother is accepted, there are *direct* social pressures toward marriage which vary in intensity and explicitness. Some of these pressures occur as direct criticism and advice. Most of them occur, as is so often true for many powerful social pressures, in relatively minor, but recurrent and insistent, experiences of friction and incongruence between the demands of any given social circle and the needs or possible behavior of the divorced mother. These are, then, further elements in institutional integration. For example, adult informal groups are made up of couple relationships. Almost everyone in our society gets married, and even the unisexual social groups of neighborhood and work, such as sewing circles, or office bowling groups, may rest in part upon additional ties between couples. When they do not have such a basis, they are likely to be compartmentalized as to time, place, and importance. The unmarried person, whether divorced or single, finds as he becomes older that he simply does not fit into his social circle well, unless he brings along a person of the opposite sex as his partner. The adult couple planning to invite friends over finds it a nuisance if they must find a date for an unmarried friend. When the unmarried person is engaged, the problem is partially solved, and this is the case only because such a couple is assimilated to the general married-couple pattern. Thus, the kinship institutions press the divorcee toward remarriage by making her unmarried status inconvenient.

Furthermore, married couples spend some time and energy in attempting to see to it that their unmarried friends get married, and this pressure increases with increasing age. Some cynics have remarked that these pressures are simply an effort on the part of the married to force others to assume the burdens and troubles of the married. The matter is of course more fundamental in character. All couples spend much of their time together in discussing matters of common interest. To the extent that an individual or individuals are still dating, or for any reason simply do not have the ordinary marital experiences about which conversation turns, the individual will feel somewhat isolated, and cannot contribute adequately to the gossip, or even enjoy it. Alternatively, the couples will generally not be so interested in things outside marriage, and thus the activities of the unmarried are of less concern to them.

This difference becomes greater when there are children, since a major part of couple conversation relates to the activities of children and the problems created by children.

To some extent, it is also doubtless true that the unmarried, whether divorced or single, are viewed by spouses as potential threats. The divorced particularly represent *symbolic* threats, in that their existence demonstrates the possibility of ending existing marriages. They represent an *actual* threat to the extent that they are a potential alternate spouse for someone already married. Doubtless one can exaggerate the sexual mythology of the divorcees, and especially of the female divorcee, but this factor is certainly of some importance.

Finally, there is a rather strong feeling, as we have noted before, that children "need both parents." The divorcee-mother is under constant criticism or advice relating to the importance of her acquiring a husband as surrogate father for the children.

It will be noted that in these comments we have laid no emphasis at all upon the romantic complex or the importance of love. We do this, not because there is no residue of romanticism in divorcees, but because the minor and recurring pressures toward remarriage do not generally take this form. The main pressures relate to the moral responsibility of the mother, the status ambiguity of the divorcee, the needs or requirements of social groupings composed of couples, and the problem of allocating money, time, and energy—that is, factors that are mainly the *indirect* effects of the *explicit* kinship institutions.

We might add here, although we have no data on this point, that children also make demands upon their parents to remarry. Children of divorcees are aware of their own status ambiguity and usually desire to "be like other children." We do not in this connection discount Oedipal ties or the more general possessiveness of children in postdivorce situations of instability and divided loyalty. Nevertheless, there is romanticism in children as well and a perception of kinship structures, and we would speculate that a majority of children sooner or later suggest to their divorced mother that she remarry. We are not certain that this would be the case for divorced fathers, but children's contacts with their fathers are intermittent and of short duration for the most part.

One final pressure beyond the above is mentioned often in common-sense discussions. It is the inconvenience of sexual pleasure outside of marriage. Divorced adults of either sex, unless disadvantaged to an extreme degree by physical handicap or psychic disturbances, find it possible in contemporary American society to locate sexual partners outside marriage. This is the case for a variety of reasons that are not relevant to our discussion. However, such relationships involve far more complications and difficulties than the innocent and the morally strict, with their notions about the "freedom" of the less strict, can possibly believe. Individual cut-and-run sexual episodes may remain undetected; but it is almost impossible for any continued sexual relationship to remain unknown to the social circles of both partners. Any arrangement short of continual and free access to one another is also likely to fall short of satisfying the relatively unchanging sexual demands of the adult, so that the liaison will become well known. It may even approach a quasi-marriage, and thereupon the pressures to legalize the relationship can become strong. This is particularly the case when children are involved, since most adult friends of the sexual partners believe that parents should be more moral than non-parent adults.[8]

Furthermore, in our society the woman in particular is conditioned to respond less fully and adequately in a sexual relationship if it is defined as purely for sexual pleasure. It is the statistically rare case when the woman feels as comfortable in such a relationship, without a close approximation to a love pattern, as she does in marriage. The man is not quite so inhibited, but for most occupational strata some approximation to sexual probity is asked and may even be demanded. Furthermore, the problems of time and place make a continuity of sexual outlet fairly inconvenient. Putting the matter in the most awkward way possible, given the boudoir facilities, working hours, and social relationships within any given clique or circle, a couple must carry out detailed and clever plans if they wish to continue a sexual relationship without eventual marriage. The divorcee consequently finds any given sexual arrangements short of marriage increasingly inconvenient.

In the most general formulation, the institutional arrangements with reference to kinship in our society allow little room for the adult non-married, divorced or single. The patterns of action, the expectations, the types of invitations and conversations, increasingly center (with increasing age) on households and children. The non-married, and especially the divorced mothers, find many difficulties in the way of simple living patterns outside marriage. We phrase this negatively, since the participant experiences the situation in terms of difficulties and problems rather than in terms of explicit institutional definitions of the divorcee status. Nevertheless, the principle would seem to be that most of the social actions of the non-married with children are made socially difficult within the contemporary American kinship system (and most others as well).

We may phrase the matter differently by noting that with reference to kinship roles most of us have been socialized to feel most comfortable, and to respond without thought most easily, in the married status. Thus, almost all roads for the divorcee, even when not so labeled by institutional prescriptions, lead to remarriage.[9]

In this way, then, the institutional problem is solved. The divorcees, male and female, do move to a defined status, in which the role expectations are more clearly defined. We have emphasized the informal and non-explicit pressures, since we are convinced at this stage of thinking that these play a far more important role than any overt threats, promises, rational compromises, etc. We need hardly comment that this is merely a specific instance of a much broader social theorem, the general proposition that not only does the society socialize its members to feel more comfortable in the statuses that are already defined, but the social structure makes deviant behavior difficult and inconvenient, even when it is not explicitly punished.

We may further comment that the movement toward a new marriage (a) sets in train and (b) is accompanied by other adjustmental processes. Entering the courtship phase is at once an index of adjustment and a cause of it. The same proposition may be made with reference to the new marriage itself. That is, the complex pattern of pressures we have just outlined causes the male or female divorcee to go into the behavior of dating, even when the individual does not really feel emotionally free of the former spouse. The individual may thus be forced into what is suggested as "appropriate" behavior even before the emotional freedom supposedly expressed by dating has been adequately achieved. On the other hand, the behavior itself helps the individual to free himself or herself emotionally of the former spouse. That is to say, in the dating situation the individual is given some emotional response, is treated as an attractive person, etc., and this may help to some degree in assuaging old psychic hurts.

More important is the fact that this behavior creates a redefinition of status for the individual. She begins to see herself as "eligible," as an individual. The divorcee no longer needs to look at herself as "wife" or "ex-wife," but as "divorced," or even "not married"—in any event, as a potential spouse or as open to romantic interest or involvement. The individual must begin to see herself as separated from the previous relationship, and the new behavior itself offers her the opportunity of seeing this new definition in the eyes of others, whom she dates or sees frequently. To a lesser extent this is the case for male divorcees, as well.

Similarly, although economic problems are difficult to solve, the action of taking a job and working at a job sets in motion various factors that define the woman's primary status (at least on the job) as worker. Even when her primary status is mother, and a secondary status is that of worker, neither of these definitions refers to any great degree to her status as "ex-wife."

The same proposition may be made with respect to other kinds of activities. In other role behavior away from the primary demands of motherhood, the individual divorcee is gradually seen and judged in other contexts. She is defined as "girl," divorcee, mother, worker, club member, etc., but she is less and less defined as anybody's "ex." Ultimately, even the "status" of divorcee may at worst become a general status not tied to any particular male.

These complex factors emphasize, therefore, (1) the finality of the divorce and (2) the possibilities of a new status. With reference to this second emphasis, the possibility of new marriage is emphasized increasingly as something that is desirable or important. Thus the new activities and behavior change the divorcee's focus, from the past and direct it toward the present and future as an individual rather than as a person with a historical connection with a particular man.

Divorcees, therefore, like all of us, are engaged in daily tasks of planning, buying, voting, or working, and in their social contacts, they find that far fewer people care about their personal traumas and difficulties than they could have believed. Alternatively, most coworkers and the people in her friendship circles offer her less and less opportunity to remember that there was a spouse. This is so whether the spouse is dead or merely divorced. These circles and networks of acquaintances will not be greatly concerned with someone who is socially not there. For the former spouse is socially there only derivately. He is there only through the behavior and attitudes of his ex-wife. Since her own circles wish to anticipate her actions and behavior (because they are in continual interaction with her and can mesh their lives with hers only by such social prediction), the former spouse becomes from their point of view only an intrusion, to be combatted by pressures on her to build a new life independently of this former relationship.

The kinship institutions do not, then, make provision for the consequences of divorce, within its structure. But, by the very fact that there are no such provisions, no set of status privileges and stigmata, which would allow the divorcee to play easily the mother role outside marriage, the institutional patterns create pressures toward new marriages, while offering some positive inducements in the same direction. There is thus as yet little direct institutionalization of postdivorce adjustment. But the larger kinship patterns nevertheless force very similar behavior on divorcees, by making difficult or inconvenient any other status than that of married mother.

It is thus that our society has been able to bear such a high rate of divorce without specific, direct kinship prescriptions for handling the problems that are created by the dissolution of a marriage. Although the rate of divorce is high, the existing kinship institutions indirectly move both child and mother back into relatively well-defined statuses, thus fixing responsibility for maintenance, status placement, and socialization of the child. Whatever the degree of personal tragedy in these experiences, for both parents and children, most of these individuals move forward into definite, new kinship units. As a consequence, there is little evidence that our high divorce rate is undermining the larger social structure. Moreover, we see in this extended theoretical analysis an implicit broader generalization: That under most structural arrangements, a high divorce rate in any culture will be accompanied by a high remarriage rate.

PART III

Internal Processes of the Family

26   *Role Differentiation in the Nuclear Family: A Comparative Study*

MORRIS ZELDITCH, JR.

Some early anthropological evidence suggested that there was unlimited variation in where the line between husband and wife activities was drawn. Professor Zelditch was led by theoretical considerations to predict the oppositie: that despite variation in specific activities, there would be a general principle of differentiation of function between the sexes. In this selection, Zelditch reports the results of his test of this hypothesis on a carefully selected sample of 56 societies. The weight of the evidence, he finds, is strongly in support of the hypothesis.

The analysis of our own nuclear family structure reveals certain patterns of differentiation that we also see in other societies if we clearly distinguish the nuclear family from the extended kinship groupings in which, in a great many societies, they are incorporated. Parsons has pointed out that in this particular instance it is fruitful to begin analysis with the more highly differentiated social system of the United States, rather than the so-called "simple" non-literate societies, because in our society the nuclear family is structurally isolated from extended kin solidarities and functionally differentiated from other systems. But the nuclear family is not something characteristic only of our society. Murdock, for instance, has stated flatly that it is a discernible functioning group in all societies entering his sample; and there have been only one or two exceptions reported in the entire anthropological literature.[1]

In our system, the marriage pair is given precedence as a solidary unit over any link with the parents of either member of the pair. The so-called simple non-literate societies, on the other hand, often give precedence to solidarities with the family of orientation of one of the pair, or, in more complex forms, strong though differentiated obligations to

Reprinted from Talcott Parsons and Robert F. Bales, *Family, Socialization and Interaction Process,* pp. 307–15, 338–42. Copyright 1955 by The Free Press of Glencoe, Illinois.

both parental families. Even in the bilateral cases most closely approaching our own, the isolation of the nuclear family is not the distinguishing structural characteristic; rather a bilateral system generally functions to incorporate the nuclear family in a kin-oriented group, but one in which membership is fluidly structured from generation to generation.

Nevertheless, the nuclear family ordinarily *can* be distinguished, and does function as a significant group. This particular point, in fact, is responsible for a good many of the issues in the interpretation of matrilineal systems, which we will consider later, and a failure to distinguish the nuclear family from other kinship units in which it is incorporated is likely to confuse any sort of analysis of concrete kinship behavior.

The nuclear family in our society has a particular pattern of roles which we now suggest has a generic significance. There is, in other words, an underlying structural uniformity which gives a baseline for the analysis of the range of variation usually noted.

A statement of this sort, of course, can be only hypothetical at this point. It is the purpose of this paper, however, to indicate that it is not *only* hypothetical. On what basis can we argue that this uniformity occurs? A reference to Bales's and Slater's discussion[2] provides at least part of the answer. We argue, for instance, that it is essentially fruitful to consider the nuclear family as a special case of a small group, and that the mode of differentiation observed in small groups has a generic significance which extends to any of its special cases. The fact that Bales's experimental groups are ephemeral compared to nuclear families (even those which are terminated after only a few months of existence) does not imply that the conclusions reached from these groups are ephemeral.

More generally, a nuclear family is a social system, and the peculiar attributes which distinguish it from other systems (its particular age-sex structure and primary function, for instance) should be examined within this more general context. All groups are subject to certain imposed conditions of existence: not that all groups exist, but that all groups that do exist meet these conditions.[3] If we assume the existence of a nuclear family, therefore, we must inquire into the conditions of its existence. And certain of these conditions are common to all groups, appearing in such diverse forms as Bales's experimental groups and the family pattern of peasant Ireland.

Among the conditions of a system's existence is at least a certain degree of differentiation along lines imposed by the orbits of the system's movement. Consider first the general pattern of differentiation which in broad outline appears from the experimental small group. There is a tendency for a *task leader* and a *sociometric star* to appear. Although there is some problem in clearly isolating the complex factors defining the task leader, he seems to be associated with certain *behaviors* (in general terms, "task" behaviors; more specifically in giving suggestions, directions, opinions), and certain *attitudes* (involving, apparently, an inhibition of emotions and the ability to accept hostile reactions from others in the process of pressing a point, etc.). There are also, of course, reciprocal behaviors and attitudes on the part of other system-members toward the task leader. The sociometric star, although the term originally derives from attitudes taken toward ego by alters, also tends to show a certain pattern of behaviors and attitudes; namely, the *expression* of emotions, supportive behavior to others, the desire to please and be liked, and a more generalized liking for other members. The star may, of course, express negative reactions as well as positive supports; typically, these are significant in releasing negative reactions (often through humor) of the group as a whole, reducing, in consequence, the general tension level. (The difference between a "leader," here, and one who fails to become a leader may very well lie, in part, in the capacity to express reactions felt by the group as a *whole*.)

From a general theoretical point of view, this is *not* a fortuitous pattern of differentiation; it defines, in fact, the two basic conditions of the existence of a social system. In order to clarify and illustrate what we mean by this, we may take the nuclear family as a specific case; and it may be useful at the same time to begin with a differentiation logically prior to role differentiation itself.

Assume a time T_1 in which members of the nuclear family are dispersed somewhere in the external situation involved in devotion to the "task," or what we call "instrumental" activities. By either of these terms we mean here the manipulation of the object-world in order to provide facilities for the achievement of goals defined within the system. In our society, for instance, the husband typically goes to work in the morning, the mother shops or cleans up, the children go to school if they are old enough. In many other societies a similar dispersal, involving a departure of at least the husband-father (out hunting, or farming), often occurs. Now clearly, if there is no second occasion, T_2, during which the members of the system are *reunited,* the system will tend to disappear. It will no longer be identifiable as a system.

There is then, a most primitive level of differentiation here in the simple presence or absence of members on two different occasions. From this, it is clear that one imperative of all social systems is integration, a coming together, which of course Durkheim emphasized a considerable time ago.

The other side of the coin, involving here a dispersal of members, introduces a more complex level of analysis. Although dispersal of system members is common during instrumental activities,[4] it is not necessary to define what we are talking about. We merely suggest this as a first point of purchase on the type of analysis involved. Typically, in fact, the mother and children remain at some location symbolically associated with the system's existence—the home is the crucial symbol, of course—and there is always a *latent* existence to the system (if it is to reappear). This function of symbols, in giving latent existence to systems, is of obvious importance as a basis for their physical reintegration.

What is significant in the differentiation of these two occasions, however, is not the states of spatial dispersion and integration, physically, but the difference in behavior and attitudes involved. The system may in fact always act in concert from the present point of view, and still show the differentiation we are here concerned with.

Reverting to our time period T_1, then, assume that all members are physically adjacent but devoted to instrumental or task activities. The entire family, say, is out farming in the fields. These instrumental activities involve, in gross terms, the manipulation of objects (plows, or hoes, etc.), and an attitude composed of Parsons' pattern variables "specific, affectively neutral, universalistic, achievement-oriented," or in more gross terms a "rational" attitude toward the external situation, and an *inhibition* of emotions toward other members of the system. *In order for the system to continue as a system,* we now say, there must at some point be a *change* in attitude and behavior to integrative-expressive activities—to laughing, playing, release of inhibited emotions, the expression of affection for each other, a warmth and a symbolization of common membership through supportive, accepting behavior.

If we reverse our assumptions, we arrive at the same basic conclusion, something we were not able to do when we considered only physical presence or absence (we were not, that is, able to show why dispersion *had* to occur). Assume the time period T_2 in which all members are affectionate, responsive, emotionally warm and attached to each other, often symbolized in the meal-time break. The system *cannot* continue in this state forever. It must, at some point, change to the necessary activities—and the associated attitudes—involved in manipulating the facilities of the object world so that the family has the food, shelter, fire, etc., which the external situation can provide. The family then becomes reinvolved in the *task,* which, no matter how much integrative behavior there was before or will be after—and perhaps also at breaks during the task—must concentrate on *getting the job done.* It must, that is, at least for the time being, devote its attention to instrumental acts.

A considerable refinement is involved in the further differentiation of the structure of *roles* in the system. One clue, perhaps, is suggested by the earlier peripheral comment that while husband-father is away at work or in the fields, the mother very often stays at home symbolizing the integrative focus of the system (even though her activities may be primarily instrumental during this phase of family activity). The fact that it is the mother who stays home is not, for the present, significant although shortly it will become so. What *is* significant, is that *someone* stayed, and that someone is in fact *more* responsible for integrative-expressive behavior than the person who went off to work.

Why after all, are *two* parents necessary? For one thing, to be a stable focus of integration, the integrative-expressive "leader" can't be off on adaptive-instrumental errands all the time. For another, a stable, secure attitude of members depends, it can be assumed, on a *clear* structure being given to the situation so that an *uncertain* responsibility for emotional warmth, for instance, raises significant problems for the stability of the system. And an uncertain managerial responsibility, an unclear definition of authority for decisions and for getting things done, is also clearly a threat to the stability of the system.

We can say, then, that the system must differentiate behaviors and attitudes in order to continue to exist as a system;[5] and that a further condition of stability is also that some specialization occur in responsibility for the attitudes and behaviors involved.

We actually want to examine two things in this paper. One is related to the generic significance of a certain pattern of differentiation. The relevant role-system, however, is indeterminate with respect to allocation when taken at this level. It is necessary to consider the nuclear family as a type of group peculiarly structured around age-sex differences in order to arrive at a hypothesis concerning who plays the instrumental and expressive roles.

Now any system, it should be noticed first, has a problem often considered peculiar to families, that is, the processing of new recruits. While the "barbarian invasion" may be considered of special significance for the family, and thus to impose special conditions on its existence, the problem is in fact generic to all systems. Thus the family resembles other groups in this respect as well as in the more general terms discussed so far. What differs, and the difference is of crucial structural significance, is the age-sex matrix of the family, and with it the situational reference points for the allocation of *facilities* in the performance of roles. At the grossest level of analysis, for instance, the father is stronger than the son, so that he, rather than the son, is allocated to leadership roles in instrumental activities (with the possible, and amusing, exception of the polyandrous Marquesas).

At least one fundamental feature of the external situation of social systems—here a feature of the physiological organism—is a crucial reference point for differentiation in the family. This lies in the division of organisms into lactating and nonlactating classes. Only in our own society (so far as I know, that is) have we managed to invent successful bottle-feeding, and this is undoubtedly of importance for our social structure. In other societies necessarily—and in our own for structural reasons which have *not* disappeared with the advent of the bottle—the initial core relation of a family with children is the mother-child attachment. And it follows from the principles of learning that the gradient of generalization should establish "mother" as the focus of gratification in a diffuse sense, as the source of "security" and "comfort." She is the focus of warmth and stability. Thus, because of her special initial relation to the child, "mother" is the more likely expressive focus of the system as a whole.

The allocation of the instrumental leadership to the husband-father rests on two aspects of this role. The role involves, first, a manipulation of the external environment, and consequently a good deal of physical mobility. The concentration of the mother on the child precludes a primacy of her attention in this direction although she always performs some instrumental tasks. In addition to the managerial aspects of the role, there are certain discipline and control functions of the father role. Consider, again, why *two* parents are necessary at all. The initial mother-child subsystem can do without the father (except that he provides food, shelter, etc., for this subsystem so that it need not split up to perform many of its own instrumental tasks). But some significant member of the nuclear family must "pry the child loose" from the mother-dependency so that it may "grow up" and accept its responsibilities as an "adult." There is necessarily a coalition of father and mother in this, or no stable socialization pattern develops. But the mother, by her special initial relation to the child is relatively more susceptible to seduction out of the coalition. We may note, for instance, that one of the pathologies of family dynamics may arise because the father tends to be susceptible to seduction by daughters; and the very fact of his relative power in the coalition makes this more of a threat to the family as a system. The problem of the "weak, ineffectual" father is more significant than that of the "weak, ineffectual" mother. (Conversely, of course, and quite as significant, the problem of the "cold, unyielding" mother is more of a problem than the "cold, unyielding" father.) If, therefore, the female is allocated the integrative-supportive role, there must necessarily be an allocation of authority for discipline and relatively "neutral" judgment to the husband-father.

We may summarize the hypothesis we have stated then, in this way. Because the nuclear family is a special case of the more general class of social systems, and because it must meet certain conditions of existence common to all social systems, we suggest that:

1. If the nuclear family constitutes a social system stable over time, it will differentiate roles such that instrumental leadership and expressive leadership of the system are discriminated.

Because the nuclear family, on the other hand, has certain peculiar features not common to all systems, we are further able to state a certain hypothesis about the allocation of these roles to system-members. This peculiar feature is the age-sex matrix of the nuclear family and the differential distribution of facilities for the performance of the fundamental roles. We suggest that:

2. If the nuclear family consists in a defined "normal" complement of the male adult, female adult and their immediate children, the male adult will play the role of instrumental leader and the female adult will play the role of expressive leader.

Summary and Conclusions

These hypotheses were tested on a sample of 56 societies drawn from a larger list of 75. An attempt was made to judge these societies by specific criteria but variations in the ethnographic materials made this difficult. While rather significant conclusions can be drawn, the crudeness of the method of verifying them makes them rather difficult to evaluate. This should be carefully considered in accepting the conclusions of the tests. In at least half of the cases, for instance, if "respect" and "affection" do not in fact indicate instrumental and expressive leadership (i.e., as defined in terms of actions of ego), then the hypotheses cannot be legitimately considered "proved" or "disproved." This chance was taken on the grounds that, having sacrificed the method of intensive analysis in the original conditions of the design, extensive replication was necessary. This demands numbers; and the number of monographs which provide evidence on the basis of direct designation rules is limited. Differences in rating might also be considered; although it may fairly be said for the differentiation hypothesis, at least, that the number of negative cases could have been increased by the equivocal cases finally judged positive and the hypothesis would still have held. The chief equivocal cases were the Lozi and the American middle-class family, which some raters might have treated as negative.

We may, as a matter of fact, consider the American middle-class case in reviewing the definitions we have given to instrumental and expressive leadership. From certain points of view, the American middle-class family approaches most clearly to equal allocation (or "no allocation") of instrumental and expressive activities. The universalistic value schema (in which women are "just as good as" men) coupled with the general attitude toward the explicit expression of authority ("I'm agin it") apparently constitutes the limiting case of no differentiation at all. Underlying this broad value-schema, however, a rather clear differentiation occurs.

In the distribution of instrumental tasks, the American family maintains a more flexible pattern than most societies. Father helps mother with the dishes. He sets the table. He makes formula for the baby. Mother can supplement the income of the family by working outside. Nevertheless, the American male, by definition, must "provide" for his family. He is *responsible* for the support of his wife and children. His primary area of performance is the occupational role, in which his status fundamentally inheres; and his primary function in the family is to supply an income, to be the breadwinner. There is simply something wrong with the American adult male who doesn't have a "job." American women, on the other hand, tend to hold jobs *before* they are married and to quit when "the day" comes; or to continue in jobs of a lower status than their husbands. And not only is the mother the focus of emotional support for the American middle-class child, but much more exclusively so than in most societies (as Margaret Mead has pointed out in her treatment of adolescent problems). The cult of the warm, giving "Mom" stands in contrast to the "capable," "competent," "go-getting" male. The more expressive type of male, as a matter of fact, is regarded as "effeminate," and has too much fat on the inner side of his thigh.

The distribution of authority is legitimized on a different basis in the "democratic" family than in the so-called "traditional" one; but the father is "supposed" to remain the primary executive member. The image of the "henpecked" husband makes sense only on this premise. His "commands" are validated on the basis of "good judgment," rather than general obedience due to a person in authority. But when the mother's efforts at "disciplining" fail, she traditionally tells the errant child, "Wait till Daddy gets home."

In generalizing this pattern, of instrumental leadership focused on the achievement of tasks and expressive leadership focused on emotionally-supportive behaviors, the most difficult problem of interpretation lies in clearly distinguishing the nuclear family from the descent groups which in some cases took precedence as solidarities over them. This may be discussed in terms of two rather unique cases. The Nayar (who do not appear in this sample) so completely incorporate the mother-child system in the matrilineage that no husband-father status exists in the sense usually given to this term. The males of the matrilineage take over the husband-father's functions, and to all intents and purposes *no nuclear family exists.* This is the limiting case in the incorporation of nuclear families in larger descent groups. It is, in a sense, the mirror opposite of the American isolated conjugal family; the same principle, applied in different ways is at stake. The question is simply the relative solidarity of two cross-cutting systems. In our society, the nuclear family is clearly a stronger solidarity than any other kinship based group and no corporate descent group exists. Among the Nayar, the matrilineage was the clearly dominant solidarity to the unusual extent of destroying the nuclear family as a continuously functioning group entirely. Somewhere in between these poles lie most of the cases known. The Trobriands approach the uniqueness of the Nayar, however, in giving the mother's brother more extensive obligations to and responsibility over the nuclear family of his sister than is common even in matrilineal societies. (It may some day turn out that many of these obligations are primarily symbolic and do not in fact take up as much of the mother's brother's productive activity as has been supposed.) The effect of this is to reduce the husband-father's role in the nuclear family, since he is a mother's brother in someone else's nuclear family and is occupied in task-functions outside his own nuclear family. Again, the basis of this is clearly the relative emphasis on the lineage as a solidarity.

Ordinarily, however, the solidarity of the lineage does not completely obscure the husband-father's instrumental role in his own nuclear family. The Trobriands, that is, is not the paradigmatic matrilineal case, any more than the Nayar is. And where the husband-father spends any time at all in his own nuclear family even in the matrilineal case he takes on significant de facto instrumental authority. To the extent, that is, that the nuclear family does function as a system, it differentiates in the direction expected.

In dealing with the allocation problem, it is apparent that the initial relation of mother and child is sufficiently important so that the mother's expressive role in the family is largely not problematical. It is particularly important to note that apparently no systematic principle, such as the impingement of descent groupings, tends to reverse her role, unless the Mundugomor can be taken as an instance. (It is likely that the problems of the Mundugomor arise because of the cross-cutting solidarities within the household group, and that it can best be described, not from the point of view of aggressive, dominant roles defined for the mother and father, but rather as a system subject to great tensions which are revealed in mutual hostilities.)

The allocation of instrumental leadership to the father, on the other hand, is only problematic in the sense that the interrelation of the nuclear family and the descent group may, in one class of cases, obscure the husband-father's role. And this we have already discussed. In the patrilineal cases, in which this particular problem raises fewer interpretative issues in concrete systems (except that, of course, there are important problems in the relation of a husband-father to *his* father), the role is reasonably clear. This is true also for bilateral systems.

On the whole, therefore, when the nuclear family can be clearly distinguished from incorporating solidarities, it differentiates in the direction expected and allocates the relevant roles to the persons expected. And the problems which are raised in interpreting the data do not arise so much from whether or not this is true, but rather from what effect the precedence of obligations to corporate descent groups may have. This becomes, stated in a general form, a problem of the relative authority of the husband-father compared to that of some person in the superordinate descent group; where this descent group is matrilineal, the problem is one of the relative authority of father vs. mother's brother. The effect on patrilineal systems is to confine the difficulties in this relationship within the corporate descent group; and eventually the husband-father achieves a role of dominance in the descent group as well as the nuclear family. The effect in matrilineal systems is different, since the father can never become a member of the matrilineage. He must validate his position through his contribution to the everyday life of the household group, and his position is much less stable. In a great many cases, nevertheless, he does become the significant instrumental figure in the household group; and always, relative to mother this is the case. From the point of view of his legal status in the system, he is at the same time freed from certain obligations to his own family and denied certain rights in control of his own family; from the point of view of the general conditions for the existence of social systems as systems, however, he must accept some of these obligations and be allowed certain of these rights.

27 *Task Differentiation of Husband and Wife in Family Activities*

P. G. HERBST

In conjunction with a broad study of personality and social structure in an urban setting, P. G. Herbst studied the patterning of activities and decision-making in nearly 100 families in Melbourne, Australia. Herbst finds a pattern of differentiation between husbands and wives that fits Zelditch's general hypothesis. Herbst's data show, in addition, some of the dynamic properties of the "field" of activities. Not only are there clearly demarcated "regions" but there are definite "paths" along which individuals move as their participation in family activities increases or decreases.

In the course of the UNESCO[1] studies of the Australian culture, a special study was made of the relationships within the family between husband and wife. While data on most other relevant aspects of social living were obtained, finding out what goes on within the family presented a number of difficulties. Without, however, some reliable and, if possible, quantitative data on the family, which represents a basic and primary institution within society, an integration of the data on social stratification, child development and adjustment, and other aspects of the culture would have been greatly handicapped.

In making an attempt to determine the structure of the family, there were two major problems that had to be solved. The first was one of fundamental theory, namely, which variables had to be measured in order to determine the possible behavioral relationships that may exist between two individuals, in this instance the husband and wife. The second problem, a more practical one, was how the necessary data were to be obtained.

The theoretical analysis made of this problem is based on Lewin's concept of a psychological field. While, however, the "life space" of the individual represents the subjective aspects of the situation as the individual perceives it, the "behavioral field" that will be discussed represents the objective characteristic of the behavioral world in which he acts. Although he may be unaware of its structure, this behavioral world will determine tensions which he experiences and which both limit and determine the type of behavior he can engage in to reduce tension within his field.

Adapted from "The Measurement of Family Relationships" *Human Relations,* V, No. 1 (1952), 3–35, *passim,* with the kind permission of the author and Tavistock Publications, Ltd., publishers.

The "behavioral field" of an individual will, thus, consist of *all* the various activities that he is found to engage in. Similarly the "group field" consists of all activities engaged in by the members of the group. Each activity will be co-ordinated to part of a region within the field, so that regions will be found to have topological relationships to one another, that is, some regions will have a common boundary and some will not.

The behavioral field of the family is differentiated into the following four regions covering the various activities within the family:

1) Household Duties (H)
2) Child Control and Care (C)
3) Social Activities (S)
4) Economic Activities (E)

For each area of activity within the family field three possibilities exist:

H_a = The husband does the activity by himself
W_a = The wife does the activity by herself
B_a = They do it together

The number of activities that falls into one of these categories determines the relative size of the husband's and the wife's activity field and the relationship between them.

The degree and direction of power relationships define the extent to which the structure of one field is determined by that of the other. For each area of activity three possibilities exist, as before:

H_d = The husband decides it by himself
W_d = The wife decides it by herself
B_d = They decide about it together

The number of activities falling into either one of these categories determines the size of the respective power fields, and the size of the overlapping region within which no asymmetrical power relationship exists. The power relationship, however, cannot be defined separately from the activity relationship. It is clearly not sufficient merely to know who makes the decisions within a certain area of activity, without also knowing the direction of the power relationship, that is, whose behavior is being decided on. It will thus be necessary to co-ordinate the power dimension to the activity dimension, which jointly determine the structure of the group.

Derivation of Interaction Patterns

In the following table the *activity variable* is given by the horizontal axis. The resulting combinations between these two variables gives us the possible number of interaction patterns. This table will be used as the basis of the scoring system for the determination of family structures.

Table 1

		Activity	
	H_aH_d	B_aH_d	W_aH_d
Decision	H_aB_d	B_aB_d	W_aB_d
	H_aW_d	B_aW_d	W_aW_d

The meaning of these interaction patterns can be tabulated as follows:

Table 2

Symbol	Description	Designation
H_aH_d	The husband does and decides about the activity by himself	Husband Autonomy
W_aW_d	The wife does and decides about the activity by herself	Wife Autonomy
B_aH_d	They do it together, the husband decides	Husband Leadership
B_aW_d	They do it together, the wife decides	Wife Leadership
W_aH_d	The wife does it, the husband decides	Husband Autocracy
H_aW_d	The husband does it, the wife decides	Wife Autocracy
B_aB_d	They do and decide about it together	Syncratic Co-operation
H_aB_d	The husband does it and both decide ⎫	Syncratic Division of
W_aB_d	The wife does it and both decide ⎭	Functions

From the above, a number of basic types of patterns can be defined by summing in terms of similar power relationships.

The Autonomic Pattern.—This is given by the sum of areas of autonomous activities, $(H_aH_d + W_aW_d)$. If the sample of activities is sufficiently large, the relative sizes of autonomous areas can also be determined. There is, of course, a point beyond which this pattern cannot increase without destroying the family group. This point will later be experimentally determined for both husband and wife.

The Husband-dominance Pattern.—This is given by the summation of areas of husband leadership and autocracy $(B_aH_d + W_aH_d)$, and thus gives the size of the husband's power field within the family. If the size of the husband's power field increased beyond a certain point, to be defined by the data, the type of family structure that ensues can be referred to as husband-autocratic.

The Wife-dominance Pattern.—This is similarly defined by the sum $(B_aW_d + H_aW_d)$, and serves as a measure of the wife's power field. The wife-autocratic family will be defined in terms of the size of the wife's power field.

The Syncratic Pattern.—This includes primarily the syncratic co-operative pattern (B_aB_d), and normally includes the areas with a syncratic division of functions. In this survey, the frequencies obtained for the latter type of behavioral interaction were too small to be taken into consideration, so that in the presentation of results the term syncratic will refer to the syncratic co-operative pattern only.

The other problems are methodological. It will be clearly impossible to find out all activities engaged in by the family. It was, therefore, necessary to devise some method of obtaining a representative sample of family activities. An attempt to obtain a representative activity sample was made by the selection of activities from each family region and by covering, insofar as possible, every phase in time from morning till night of an ordinary day at home. A list of 31 everyday activities was finally selected.

Also, there is the problem of the source of information, and which would be the most reliable method to use in obtaining it. A short period of observation would be insufficient even if full co-operation were obtained. A deeper functional penetration would distort existing family relationships, quite apart from its being uneconomical of time. On the other hand, an interview of the husband and wife might be expected to yield some biased or stereotyped replies.

It was decided to use the group of children from 10 to 12 years of age who had already been studied during the UNESCO project. A number of group administrations of a questionnaire was made which consisted of closed questions. The children were told that the investigators were interested in finding out something about the kind of things they did at home, and in the second part who decided about them.

Composition of the Sample

Three separate Group Administrations were made to 96 children in the sixth grades of two Melbourne State Schools. The age range of the children was 10–12 years. Forty-eight per cent were boys and 52 per cent were girls. Their average I.Q. on the Otis Intermediate was 108.

Eight months earlier, the children had been among those who, during the UNESCO studies, had been interviewed for four hours each, including sociometric testing. Intelligence, achievement, and various projective tests had also been given. In addition an interview study of their parents had been made and data on the children obtained from their teachers.

The results for 10 children who came from broken homes had to be treated separately.

The *class composition* of the sample for which full data on family structure were obtained is as follows:

Semi-skilled	26
Skilled	26
White Collar	17
Employers and Self-employed	17

The sample can, on the whole, be regarded as representative of the Melbourne city population[2] with the following provisos: Almost all the children came from Protestant homes. (Catholics are approximately 24 per cent of the population.) The sample excludes the lower-lower and the upper strata of society. These, however, would not constitute more than about 5 per cent of the population as a whole.

Regions

On analysing the results in terms of the percentage frequencies of the nine types of interaction patterns, it was found that, with minor deviations, items in each region have a similar distribution of frequencies of interaction patterns. Table 3 shows the percentage distribution for a typical item in each region.

The region of household duties was found to be predominantly autonomic in structure. On the basis of the data, a further subgrouping was made:

   i) Husband's Household Duties
  ii) Wife's Household Duties
 iii) Common Household Duties

The first consists of activities which fall into the husband's autonomous area (i.e., activities he does and decides about by himself); the second, of activities which fall into the wife's autonomous area. The third region consists of activities in which both parents, as well as other members of the family, participate frequently and which is characterized by a wife leadership in addition to a wife autonomous pattern.

The region of child control is characterized by a wife leadership pattern, i.e., both parents look after the children, but decisions rest with the wife. It can in a sense be regarded as a transition region between that of household duties, with their marked autonomic characteristics, and the syncratic co-operative pattern of the social and economic region.

The item analysis shows that these regions can be presented in terms of a scale from the wife's autonomous pattern across to the husband's autonomous pattern, with the extreme ends of the scale consisting of activities rigidly defined in terms of sex roles, and the center consisting of activities which are engaged in and decided about jointly, and which are thus independent of sex roles.

Table 3. Percentage Frequency of Interaction Patterns for a Typical Item in Each Region

Item No.	Item	Region	H_a			B_a			W_a			No. of Items within Region
			H_d	B_d	W_d	H_d	B_d	W_d	H_d	B_d	W_d	
10	Ironing	Wife's household duties	—	—	—	—	1.3	18.7	—	—	80.0	7, 9, 10, 14
19	Do the dishes	Common household duties	—	—	4.2	7.0	13.9	41.7	4.2	2.8	26.4	8, 15, 18, 19
16	Table manners	Child control and care	—	1.3	—	6.3	46.3	38.8	—	1.3	6.3	1, 4, 16, 17, 20, 31
24	Invite visitors	Social	—	—	—	1.3	74.4	12.8	—	5.1	6.4	23, 24, 25, 26, 27, 28
29	Pay for holidays	Economic	4.3	7.2	7.2	13.0	44.9	18.8	—	—	4.3	(5, 6), 22, 29, 30
12	Mow the lawn	Husband's household duties	64.3	7.1	8.9	5.4	5.4	7.1	1.8	—	—	11, 12, 13

Relationship between Regions

Given that a member of the family participates in A, in what way will this determine whether he will or will not participate in regions B, C, etc.? If the various behavioral activities are independent of one another, then any member of the family would be free to choose or reject participation in any of the family's various activities, and his participation or nonparticipation in any one region would in no way affect his possibility of participating in any of the other regions. If, on the other hand, a definite relationship of that kind is found to exist, then this would serve as an additional validation of the basic hypothesis on which the present method is based, namely, that the family has a field structure and can be treated as an interdependent whole.

The investigation of this problem was made possible by means of a participation scale devised by S. B. Hammond.

Doing an item "always" was given a score of 2; helping, or doing an item "sometimes," was given a score of 1; and "never" doing an item a score of −2. A total was then obtained for each region. An individual was said to participate in a region if his total score for that region was zero or above, or in other words the degree to which he participated had to be equal to, or greater than, the degree to which he did not participate.

The following six regions were used:

   i) Wife's Household Duties (*HW*)
  ii) Common Household Duties (*HB*)
 iii) Husband's Household Duties (*HH*)
  iv) Child Control and Care (*Ch*)
   v) Economic Activities (*E*)
  vi) Social Activities (*S*)

To test the hypothesis, the results for each member of the family were arranged in terms of the number of regions in which he or she did not participate, according to the evidence of the children in our sample.

We find that 16 of the husbands in this sample participated in all 6 regions. Out of the 18 who failed to participate in one region, 16 did so in the Wife's Household Duties. Out of the 26 who failed to participate in two regions, 23 did so in the Wife's and the Common Household Duties, and so on. The order in which the husband relinquishes family activities is seen to be: first, the Wife's Household Duties, followed by the Common Household Duties, Child Care and Control, the Husband's Household Duties, and then Social Activities. Similarly, the opposite order of regions would have to be traversed if he were to increase participation.

Even the relatively few discrepancies follow the basic pattern. Thus, given the number of regions in which the husband participates in the family's activities, one can predict in which of the six regions he will or will not participate. The prediction will be correct in 83 per cent of all cases, and not be out by more than one region in the remaining cases.[3]

As his degree of participation increases, he will first engage in his Household Duties, then in Child Control and Care, then in Common Household Duties, and finally in his Wife's Household Activities—he could not normally, for instance, help with the Control of Children without also doing his Household Activities, and of course without also participating in the Social and Economic Activities of the family.

In the case of the husband:

   a) Given the degree to which he participates in the family's activities, the regions in which he will and in which he will not participate are largely determined.
   b) His choice of regions in which he will participate is limited by the

fact that, in so far as he remains a member of the family, he has to participate minimally in its Social and Economic Activities. Within the range of the remaining four regions, he is most likely to participate up to the level of Child Control, and an increase or decrease of his degree of participation becomes increasingly difficult with increasing distance from the optimum position.

c) Given that the husband participates up to the level of Husband's Household Duties, and he needs to move in the direction of the region of his Wife's Household Duties, then he must approach that region by participating in the intervening activities—the Control of Children, and Common Household Duties.

It is thus seen that social space, in this instance the husband's path field, has a definite structure which can be objectively determined, and which both limits and determines the behavior of the individual.

The same kind of analysis was made for the wife, and for children of various ages and both sexes. *For each of these, a definite but different path field was found to exist.* In the case of the wife, 95 per cent conform entirely to the pattern, 5 per cent deviate by one region, and none by two or more.

For the total of 343 individuals, on whom data were available from the subjects, path fields were obtained for the husband and wife, and boys and girls respectively for the age ranges of 4–8 years, 10–12 years, and 14 years and over.

In the case of the wife, no instance was found in which she did not participate in her Household Duties, the Care and Control of Children, and Social Activities, so that an absolute level exists between which her participation does not normally fall.

However, only 4 per cent of the sample engaged in none but these activities. The next region she may enter is that of Common Household Duties. If she increases her degree of participation beyond this, she is about five times more likely to move into the economic region than into that of the Husband's Household Duties. The extent to which the path field forms a consecutive hierarchical pattern can be taken as a measure of the extent to which it is stabilized and structured. In the case of the wife, the field appears to be in a stage of transition: the economic region is coming to be increasingly within her normal range of participation.

By the age of about four years, children normally participate in the various Social Activities of the family. Up to the age of about eight years, however, there are regions in which they have no regular participation. For both boys and girls, these consist of the economic and child-control region together with the Husband's Household Duties, in the case of the girls, and the Wife's Household Duties, in the case of the boys. Complete role differentiation by sex has thus already taken place at that age.

28 Illness, Therapy, and the Modern Urban American Family

TALCOTT PARSONS and RENEE C. FOX

One of the problems the family faces is the physical and psychological condition of the members; when one person is sick he must be cared for. This requires the mobilization and utilization of various resources. Professor Parsons and Dr. Fox explore some of the structural correlates of changing patterns in the care of the sick. They suggest that the growing tendency for the care of the sick to be carried on outside the family is intimately related to the increasing specialization of the family and its structural isolation. Parsons and Fox see the current patterns of care as well geared to the resources of the family and to the strains inherent in the family.

The primary purpose of this paper is to show that the relations between illness and the family are to be understood only through combining sociological analysis of the structure of role-systems with psychodynamic analysis of certain processes in personalities. For we regard illness as both a psychological disturbance and a deviant social role.[1]

Doctor-Patient and Parent-Child: Some Analogies

We begin our analysis by suggesting that there are intimate psychodynamic relationships between the processes which occur in the normal system of family interaction, and those which obtain both in the doctor-patient relationship and in such more elaborately differentiated health-care institutions as the hospital. At the same time, we propose that the emergence of the medical profession and of the hospitals into their strategic position in contemporary society is not solely attributable to the accumulation of technical medical knowledge and its application in technological processes. Rather, it is our paramount thesis that the doctor and the hospital provide a set of institutionalized mechanisms for handling certain of the motivational problems of personality adjustment: mechanisms which, in certain respects, are functionally alternative to those of the family. Thus, the family and therapeutic institutions resemble each other; if this were not true, the kind of functional relationship between them which we wish to analyze could not.exist. At the same time, they also differ in fundamental

Reprinted from *Journal of Social Issues*, XIII, 4 (1952), 31–44, with the kind permission of the authors and publisher.

respects; if this were not the case, there would be far less reason either for the existence or for the effectiveness of these institutions.

The elements of correspondence are perhaps best approached in terms of two analogies: on the one hand, the similarity between illness and the status of the child in the family; on the other hand, the overlap between the physician's role and that of the parent. The common point of reference for the first analogy is the status of the non-sick adult member of society. Both child and sick person differ from this norm in two primary respects. The first is capacity to perform the usual functions of an adult in everyday life. The child is not yet able to do this; partly because biological maturation has not gone far enough, partly because his socialization is still incomplete. Similarly, one of our main criteria of illness is that the sick person is "incapacitated." In the usual case, he has been capable of normal functioning, but his illness, in some degree, makes him unable to carry on. The second respect in which the child and the sick actor are similar is that they are both dependent: needing and expecting to be taken care of by stronger, more "adequate" persons. Thus, in these two senses, illness is not unlike more or less complete reversion to childhood.

The analogy of physician (and other hospital personnel) and parents in part is simple and obvious. These are the stronger and more adequate persons on whom the sick person and the child respectively, are made to rely; they are the ones to whom he must turn to have those of his needs fulfilled which he is incapable of meeting through his own resources. As we shall maintain, these analogies must not be pressed too far. But they do constitute a convenient jumping off place for our analysis.

Illness, so far as it is motivated, is a form of deviant behavior, and, as such, may be subjected to a standard sociological analysis of deviance. Compared with other types of nonconformist behavior, sickness characteristically entails passive withdrawal from normal activities and responsibilities. As such, it should be distinguished from active rebellion against the normal social expectations, and from the types of deviance characterized by compulsive conformity.[2] For it is an escape from the pressures of ordinary life. In a society such as our own, illness is a very strategic expression of deviance: first, because our culture enforces an unusually high level of activity, independence, and responsibility on the average individual; and second, because it connects so closely with the residua of childhood dependency (which, we may suggest, are more intense in our society than in many others, because of the particular structure of our urban family[3]). From the point of view of the stability of the social system, therefore, too frequent resort to this avenue of escape presents a serious danger. This is the primary context in which we think of illness as an institutionalized role and its relation to therapy as an important mechanism of social control.

It should be pointed out that as a role the state of illness is partially and conditionally legitimized. That is, if a person is defined as sick, his failure to perform his normal functions is "not his fault," and he is accorded the right to exemption and to care. At one and the same time, however, the sick person is enjoined to accept the definition of his state as undesirable and the obligation to get well as expeditiously as possible.

Similarly, childhood is more than a condition. Like illness, it also is a conditionally legitimized social role. The child is permitted to be childish only temporarily. He accepts the obligation to grow up, even though at times it is very painful, and to co-operate with his parents in helping him to achieve maturity.

We feel it is largely because of this close correspondence between the status of the child and of the sick person that it is important to have the major part of illness in our society tended outside the family. However, since the family has been the principal refuge for the sick in most societies, the question arises as to why in our society we are so ready to send our sick outside the family to special medical institutions. The importance of the technological factors we grant; but, as already indicated, we feel that there is more to it than that.

Some Vulnerabilities of the American Family

The primary psychodynamically relevant reasons we find in the special character of the American urban family, which is extremely vulnerable to certain types of strain. Mechanisms have developed which relieve the family of the additional stresses which would be imposed upon it by making the care of the sick one of its principal functions. At the same time, most cases of illness with psychological components are probably more effectively cared for in the special circumstances of our society by professionalized agencies than they would be in families.

When ranged alongside the kinship groups of other social orders, the most striking features of our family system are: its small size; the isolation of the principal unit, the conjugal family, from other sectors of the kinship system; and the modern family's apparent functionlessness. With respect to its loss of function, the urban family has, above all, ceased to be an agency of economic production—by obvious contrast, for instance, with peasant families the world over. Furthermore, even in the close-knit setting of the immediate community, little political responsibility is taken by families as units.

We interpret this to mean that the influence of the family in our society has become highly *indirect*. In fact, as we see it, the contemporary American family derives its functional import almost exclusively from the effect it has upon its members as personalities. For us, the primary significance of this family type resides in the fact that it insures per- petuation of cultural patterns essential to the society (above all, its values) by motivating the actor to carry out these major patterns. With respect to adult family members this is primarily a "maintenance" or regulatory function: a matter of absorbing, easing, and dealing with the consequences of various kinds of strain arising out of their life situations. For children, on the other hand, it involves the powerful process of social-ization.[4]

The American family is well adapted to the exigencies of a modern industrial society. But it is also highly susceptible to many grave strains. For, though the wife-mother bears the major socio-emotional responsi-bilities within the family, she is largely excluded from those occupational roles which are the source of family status and socio-economic sustenance. Further, whatever her activities outside the home may be, they tend on the whole to be "representative" ones undertaken in the name of the family.

On the other hand, the husband-father as the provider and primary status bearer of the family is exposed during all the working hours of his existence to the distinctive rigors of the marketplace, wherein he carries the heavy load of responsibility for the family. In addition, he is classically a "scapegoat": the symbolic target at which the child primarily aims the hostile-aggressive impulses aroused in him as he undergoes the stressful process of socialization. It is the specialized function of the wife-mother to act as skillful mediator of the child-father relationship and thereby to assure both the perpetuation of family solidarity and the emo-tional security of the child.

The roles of the wife-mother and the husband-father, then, are char-acteristically subject to a complex of structural strains, as is the child in his role of socializee, particularly when sibling rivalry intervenes. Finally, in our society, the advent of old age brings still another set of problems in its wake; forced retirement from the occupational sphere so crucial to the male actor's sense of worth, and to the woman's status and security systems; and overwhelming socio-psychological isolation.

As a response to any one of these family-based or focused social pressures, illness could provide a tantalizingly attractive "solution." For the sick role is a semilegitimate channel of withdrawal—exempting the social actor from adult responsibilities and enjoining him to allow himself to be taken care of by others. As we have already emphasized, illness is very often motivational in origin. Even in those instances where the etiology of the disorder is primarily physico-chemical, the nature and severity of symptoms and the rate of recuperation are almost invariably influenced by the attitudes of the patient.

It is easy to see, therefore, how the wife-mother, for example, might "choose" the sick role as an institutionalized way out of her heavy "human relations management" responsibilities in the family; or how she might seize upon illness as a compulsively feministic way of reacting to her exclusion from the life open to a man. Similarly, the passive-dependent role of illness offers the husband-father semi-institutionalized respite from the discipline and autonomy which his occupation demands of him.

As for the child, we have already indicated that he is being pushed and pulled along a tension-ridden path which points toward adulthood. It is almost a foregone conclusion, then, that at any point along this sociali-zation continuum, illness can provide him with a method of escape from progressively more exacting obligations to behave in a mature fashion. For sickness not only allows the child to be nurtured and cared for as the infant that he still yearns, in part, to be; but, in becoming the central focus of family solicitude and concern, the sick child also achieves tem-porary victory in the competition with his siblings for a lion's share of parental attention. Coming around full circle in the family's life span, we can easily see how illness might serve not only the child, and the young and middle-aged adult, but the elderly person as well. The aged individual, occupationless, and with no traditionally assured place in the families es-tablished by his daughters and sons, through illness may once again become an integral member of a meaningful social group, cared for either by his grown children or by a medical community of some sort.

Family Care of the Sick: A Functional Analysis of Liabilities

We turn now to consider the problem of the resources available to the family for dealing with these tendencies to make psychological use of illness. What are the probable consequences of attempting to cope with the psychological impact of serious illness within the American family— both upon the sick person himself, and upon other members of the family?

First, we note the probability that handling sickness outside the fam-ily serves to discourage falling ill in the first place. It is a method of preventing a person from "eating his cake and having it too." Care of the sick places upon those who assume the responsibility the obligation to accept the sick person in his state of illness. If this component of accept-ance, therefore, were combined with the supportive features of the normal familial role, there would be a double reinforcement of the motivation to illness. The sick person could then enjoy good standing in the family—in the psychological sense, "all the comforts of home"—without paying the normal price for such familial acceptance: the fulfillment of role-obliga-tions. In this respect, then, the family has an inherent tendency to set a "vicious circle" kind of interaction into motion: driving the sick actor deeper and deeper into his illness, rather than reducing his psychological investment in his disorder.

Next, what of the position of the members of the family who are not sick: what resources do they have to meet the impact of illness? We suggest that these resources are relatively weak; that consequently, the inherent social control patterns of our family would be seriously jeopardized by the strain of caring for illness. In the first place, the American family apparently operates at high levels of emotional intensity—with relatively little margin for "shock-absorption." In the second place, the specific direction of pressures from the demands of the sick strike it at what appears to be a vulnerable point. We wish to discuss each of these aspects of the problem in turn.

What we have called the isolation of the conjugal family, combined with the impersonal character of so many of our social relationships outside the family, means that we place a very large proportion of our emotional eggs in the one basket of the family. Each relationship within this small group, then, becomes critically important, both to the stability of the family itself and to each of the participants as a personality. The focal problems, in turn, center at two points: the marriage relationship and the parent-child relationship, particularly that of the mother to her children.

The constitution of our family means that there are ordinarily only two adults to take the roles of major responsibility. Further, there are no clear-cut stipulations as to which of the two is really "boss." Rather, the husband-wife relationship in the American family is defined to a very high degree in terms of equality and spontaneous emotional mutual attraction.

There are many indications that the load placed upon the marriage relationship in our family system comes closer to the maximum it can stand than is true for most other systems. We have long felt, for example, that the high American divorce rate is not an index of the "withering away" or disorganization of the family, as it is sometimes supposed. Quite to the contrary, it is our conviction that the oft-cited increase of divorce derives from the unique intensity and emotional import of the husband-wife relationship in our society, and from the heavy burden that such heightened affectivity imposes upon marriage. Similar things can be said about the parent-child relationship. How, then, does illness play into this precariously balanced, emotionally highly-charged system? This question can best be answered by following out the consequences of the serious illness of family members, one by one.

Take first the case of the husband-father. Although the exemption from adult masculine responsibilities granted him by the sick role worsens the position of the family and makes its adaptive problems more difficult, it is the husband-father's claim to be taken care of which has the more immediately disruptive impact on the family's internal situation. The wife, of course, is the primary sick-room attendant. The most obvious consequences of her ministrations is the withdrawal of her full quota of attention from the children. The presence of the husband-father in the home at unaccustomed times is relevant here; but far more important are his greatly enhanced physical and emotional needs. The intricately balanced way in which the wife-mother normally distributes her attention between husband and children is upset, for the children are called upon to sacrifice part of their maternal support to the father.[5]

The illness of a child, on the other hand, tends to disturb family equilibrium by making it more difficult for the mother to meet the needs of the father. What is more, the mother also runs the risk of making sibling rivalries more acute.

Finally, illness of the mother herself is clearly the most disturbing of all—and this may well be the nub of the whole matter. For, in the normal course of events, the mother is the primary agent of supportive strength for the entire family unit. Her illness, therefore, subjects husband and children alike to a condition of under-support, at a time when they are suddenly being asked to meet unexpected demands of major proportions. In the light of this, a mother-wife who is motivationally inclined to cast herself in the sick role may very well constitute the greatest single source of danger that illness can inflict on the family.

To all these foregoing considerations, a more general point should be appended: the insidious effects the claims of the sick person are liable to have on the healthy members of his family—regardless of whether the stricken actor is mother, father, or child. For, if we are justified in our supposition that latent dependency needs are present in almost all normal people in our society, it follows that most individuals will also have a tendency to develop defense mechanisms against those needs. As a result, there is a high probability that our families will be inclined to *over*-react to the passive-dependent nature of illness, in either of two ways. On the one hand, family members may tend to be *more* sympathetic and supportive of the sick person than they ought: bolstering their own defense against a desire to be taken care of by projecting this need onto the sick person. Through their indulgent attitude toward the ill actor (over-emphasis on the positive, supportive aspect of the treatment; under-emphasis on the disciplinary aspect), the family may invite him to perpetuate his illness. On the other hand, the family may display an excessive intolerance with respect to the debilitating features of illness—regarding them as a sign of weakness—and impose overly harsh disciplinary sanctions on the sick member. Such hyperseverity, of course, is as unfavorable to full and rapid recovery as over-permissiveness.[6]

In other words, what we are suggesting here is that the optimal balance between permissive-supportive and disciplinary facets of treating illness is peculiarly difficult to maintain in the kind of situation presented by the American family. Medico-technical advances notwithstanding, therefore, therapy is more easily effected in a professional milieu, where there is not the same order of intensive emotional involvement so characteristic of family relationships.

This, of course, is a functional argument, and as such does not explain how the segregation arose in the first place. Very broadly, however, we may suggest that technological developments provided the opportunity to treat illness outside the family, while the kinds of strains we have out-lined have predisposed people to take advantage of the services of medical personnel. The further we have gone in our discussion of the American family, the more apparent have become the dynamic interdependence of illness, the family, the physician; deviance, socialization, and social con-trol.

The Doctor-Patient Relationship and the Roles of the Ill

When the sick actor and his family join forces with the doctor, a therapeutic subsystem is established which, ideally speaking, should facilitate the actor's recovery from illness. At this meeting place, where the disabled individual contracts technically competent help with whom he agrees to co-operate in a concerted effort to get well, the sick role evolves into the patient role.

In spite of the fact that illness is often highly motivated, it should not be supposed that passage from health, to sickness, to the status of patient, is easily effected. From whatever socio-psychological baseline the actor enters the sick role, adherence to the institutionalized dictates of this role is attained only by virtue of a learning process: a socialization experience not without its special problems. In the words of one patient: "It some-times takes a long time to learn the things we have to learn. . . ."

Even for a passive-dependent personality, the so-called exemptions of sickness usually present certain real difficulties. Since the sick individual is called upon to acknowledge the authority of medical personnages over himself, the obligations of the role of the patient imply temporary re-linquishment of the rights as well as the duties, of normal adulthood. For any socialized actor, then, acceptance of this child-like status, with its attributes of inferior status and its socio-emotional skewing, entails con-siderable adjustment; a sort of "de-socialization" process is necessary. In the light of the motivational challenge which this unlearning entails, it would seem that the structuring of the doctor's role serves a cushioning and delimiting kind of function. For, were the doctor to treat his patient exactly as the mother and father are enjoined to treat their child, in most instances, he would be overtaxing the adult actor's capacity to tolerate dependency.[7]

It is not merely on dependency grounds alone, however, that the sick patient role involves an affect-laden learning sequence. There is also the fact that an individual in our society, when befallen with a relatively acute or severe malady, is likely to be wrenched from the reassuring familiarity of his home, his job, and his friends, and placed in a totally strange hospital bed. Illness sets him down in a new, medical-scientific world to which he must become acclimatized. And this transplantation is by no means an easy one to undergo. Though the hospital community in which he finds himself is supposedly geared to returning the patient to his full participation in life outside, it is nevertheless true that the distance between this newly-inherited sick world and the well world which he has temporarily left behind is vast indeed. As one patient phrases the dichotomy between these two universes: "when you're outside on the sidewalk there, you know there's sick people in there in the hospital. But that's breezed right through your mind. You don't know what's going on in there. Furthermore, you don't really care. Because you're out. You're walking on the street. . . ."

The sharpness of this cleavage between sickness and wellness in our society, so problematic to the new patient, is a function of the physical and psychical separation of the hospital from the sites and activities of normal adult existence. We have already discussed some of the multiple reasons for which our society has seen fit to isolate the seriously ill patient from his family and the ranks of the non-sick in general. Most obvious among these is the phenomenal growth of scientific medicine in modern Western society—rendering the traditional home-remedy type of medical care obsolete by bringing in its wake teams of white-coated specialists, manifold test-tube procedures, an elaboration of machinery, and formal professionalized psychotherapy. Less apparent than these technological determinants, but fully as significant, are the socio-psychological reasons for which we have erected brick walls between the sick and the healthy: the special appropriateness of illness as a deviant expression in our society (hence, the dangers of exposing the non-sick to bio-psychical "infection"), and the unique defenselessness of the American urban family when faced with the illness of one of its members.

The insulation of the sick, however, not only serves passively to protect our family system and our society at large from "contamination." Rather, it is one of the potent mechanisms which launches the patient on his recovery-directed efforts, by involving him in a complementary role-relationship with therapeutic agents. If the therapy to which he becomes subject is truly successful, the getting-well process which the patient undergoes will entail meaningful attitudinal changes as well as biochemical ones.

The Doctor's Role in the Therapeutic Process

Sociological analysis of the therapeutic process has brought out sharply certain broad conditions of effective therapy, yielding a list of its major components and the temporal order of their utilization. Looked at from the point of view of the attitudes and manipulations of the physician,[8] therapy involves four primary aspects.

In the first place, there must be *permissiveness:* allowing, even encouraging the patient to express deviant ideas, wishes, and fantasies. The mere privilege of being treated as sick belongs in this category, but presumably is not enough. In other words, the fact of deviant motivation must be accepted by the therapist, assuring the patient thereby that he is, in this sense, taken seriously.

The second therapeutic component is what psychiatrists often call *support:* a more holistic kind of acceptance. This is not so much a matter of respecting the details of the patient's troubles. Rather, it consists in valuing the sick actor as a person in his role: accepting him as a bona fide member of the therapeutic system because he is deemed worth helping. From one point of view, this is the sick person's immediate reward for trying to be a good patient.

In the light of the above analysis, it is clear that these features of the therapeutic role help to minimize inhibitions about giving way to dependency needs. In fact, through transference, the patient develops a powerful attachment to the therapist, the ingredients of which draw heavily on residua of unresolved childhood motivational structures. Thus, it becomes doubly necessary that the permissive-supportive aspects of the therapeutic process should not stand alone, if the leverage gained over the patient's motivational system is to transform, rather than confirm, his deviant motivational orientations.

The therapist applies this leverage in two primary ways. In the first place, the permissive-supportive aspects of the situation arouses the patient's expectations of positive deviant wish-fulfillment, and emboldens him to express them. The therapist must frustrate these desires by refusing the looked-for reciprocation. That is, though the patient will treat him as a parent-figure, a close friend, a lover (or, often, as a personal enemy), the therapist *will adhere scrupulously to a professional attitude.* Stated differently, he avoids reciprocating the patient's transference with countertransference of his own. This creates a conflict between the expectations of the patient which are encouraged in the permissive-supportive phases of therapy, and the disciplining of overt wishes that the therapist later demands of him. A secondary tension is thereby set up—which is easier for the patient to analyze than primary ones.

Concomitantly or increasingly, the therapist *introduces conditional rewards* (of which his approval is probably the most important) for the patient's good work in the therapeutic situation. Above all, he approves the patient for gaining insight into the character and motives of his own behavior. Thus, through the therapist's denial of reciprocity and his wielding of conditional rewards, the patient is pushed out of his pathological dependency. At the same time, dependency is positively utilized to sensitize him to the meaning of the refusal of the therapist to reciprocate, and to heighten the significance of rewards coming from that source. We may say, then, that a situation is created where conforming with the wishes of the therapist—gaining his approval for adult behavior—comes to outbalance the secondary gain of the pathological state itself. Ideally speaking, the patient gradually gives up his deviant orientation and comes to embrace maturity in its stead.

Though the basic components we have just reviewed for the case of psychotherapy are also the focus of child socialization, the differences between these two processes must be underscored. First, "classical" psychotherapy occurs in a two-person system, with one patient and one therapist. Socialization, on the other hand, entails two parents and a child, at the very least. Secondly, whereas the family milieu is a deeply affective one, the therapeutic setting is more neutrally-toned. Both these distinctions point up the fact that for all their striking similarity, the doctor-patient and parent-child relationships are not identical. Whereas the patient is a partially socialized adult who must be taught to reassume his role-obligations, the child is learning his obligations for the first time. Because child socialization has much farther to go than the therapeutic process, rearing the child has been delegated to two adults: the primarily supportive mother, and the more disciplinary father. This division of labor lightens the parental load, and assures that both aspects of socialization will have balanced attention given them. The general protectiveness of the family, on the other hand, serves a bolstering function: endowing the child with the psychical fortitude he needs to cope autonomously with the outside world.

Family Care vs. Professional Care

These facts give us a baseline from which to point out some of the main reasons why too great a predominance of family-managed treatment might not only threaten the ongoing of the family itself but also impede the recovery of the sick person as well. First, in some cases, the power of a familial therapist (e.g., the wife-mother, when either the husband-father or the child falls ill) could easily overactivate the sick person's dependency, bringing about a regression to childhood level. Extra-familial therapeutic agents have better-developed safeguards against such an eventuality. For example, contact with the therapist is restricted to stated appointments under carefully regulated conditions; and the impersonal professional character of the hospital seems to have a similar function. Even so, evidence shows that particularly in cases of severe illness, it is relatively easy for the patient to acquire a very deep-seated investment in his sick role, either in the form of dependency on an individual therapist or in that of attachment to a hospital situation.[9] Though the process of desocialization in learning to become a good patient is an essential prerequisite of successful recovery in most cases, it is therefore equally important that it should not go too far;[10]

and the condition under which it takes place should be carefully controlled. The American urban family, we suggest, has a strong tendency to permit desocialization excesses.[11]

Secondly, since our family is essentially non-authoritarian in nature, and the motivation to illness is so deep-rooted in our society, the American family is a relatively weak counteractant of sickness. The professional therapist, in contrast, derives his potency from two sources. For one thing, his role is integrated with the adult world in a way that the family member in his kinship status is not.[12]

If the sick person is to be healed, then, and the well-being of our kinship system is to be assured, the modern American family cannot undertake major responsibility for care of the sick. That the doctor may easily err in the direction of under-support, however, if he too drastically extrudes the family from his sphere of operation, is cogently suggested by certain recent developments in the modern hospital. Of late, hospitals throughout the country have been experimenting with such plans as allowing the mother and her newborn infant to room together, permitting the mother to stay overnight with her hospitalized child, and extending visiting hours for all categories of patients. Since all these trial developments invite the more full-blown participation of family members in the hospital community, it appears to us that they may express a felt need for the greater inclusion of the family's permissive-supportive concern in current medical therapy.[13]

Our analysis of these particular empirical occurrences may be speculative. But the larger theoretical point it is intended to illustrate is much less challengeable: Making the sick individual better calls for the well-timed, well-chosen, well-balanced exercise of the supportive *and* the disciplinary components of the therapeutic process; and the ministrations of *both* the doctor and the family.

Our sick actor now stands poised on the threshold of recovery; there is a deep motivational sense in which he may not be the "same" person who originally fell ill. Evidence for this hypothesis is the sizeable body of literature penned by former patients: subjective assertions of the fact that the sick role and successful emergence from it may effect a far-reaching socialization process in the recovering actor. For all the socio-psychological reasons we have been attempting to outline in this paper, it is highly probable that illness might bring an intensive learning experience in its wake. Incapacitated and emotionally disturbed; relieved of the weighty responsibilities of the well world; removed in large part from the custodianship of his family and other significant actors who would be likely to reinforce or exacerbate his psychosomatic withdrawal—the ill individual comes to live for a while in a medical-dominated sphere. Here, he is granted nurture and sustenance; but never so much as to balance out the heavy impress of deprivation, subordination, and loneliness to which he is also subject. These are the penalties which give impetus to the patient's desire to re-achieve wellness: the challenges to which he responds (ideally-speaking) by re-embracing the world of health.[14]

Conclusion

We have given evidence which, we feel, indicates that the development of specialized professional health-care agencies, and the consequent removal of much of the treatment of illness from the family, is attributable to something more than the technological developments of modern medicine. We have tried to show that it is highly probable that certain features of the American urban family, in their impact on the personalities of its members, have tended to push the sick person out of the home. And we have argued that, on the whole, extrafamilial care of the sick is positively functional for American society in at least three respects. The first is protection of the family against the disruptive effects of the illness of its members. The second is the preservation of some of the positive functions of the sick role as a mechanism of social control—primarily, by directing the passive deviance of illness into closely supervised medical channels where it finds expression, but cannot easily spread. The third is facilitation of the therapeutic process—not only technologically, but in a *motivational* sense as well.

We wish to point out that such new insights as we have been able to gain into these matters are only possible because of certain rather recent developments in the sciences of human action: above all, the possibility of bringing sociological and psychological analysis to bear upon the same set of problems in a complementary way. A simple sociological analysis of family structure and of the therapeutic system would not have helped us very much; nor, we feel, would a purist personality theory approach have proven especially enlightening. And yet when the two are put together a quite new order of understanding emerges.

We have deliberately kept our discussion on a theoretical level, without attempting to work out its possible practical import; for, within the scope of a single article, it would not have been possible to do justice to both. In conclusion, however, we would like to suggest that the potential implications of our analysis for practice ramify in several directions. For example, we think that perhaps we can aid physicians and hospital administrators in their search for effective ways of dealing with the family members of their patients. Further, our material also seems relevant to the question of how visiting privileges and other forms of association with hospital patients accorded to families could be more optimally managed.

It is our belief, however, that most important and far-reaching of all is the fact that both theoretically and empirically, the social and psychological sciences are now highly enough evolved to make "illness, therapy, and the family" a fruitful field of action research.

29 *The Resolution of Role Conflict within the Family*

JOHN P. SPIEGEL

In its internal dynamics, the family must include activities which lead and co-ordinate the various members into some coherent pattern of movement toward goals. This functional requirement exists even when—perhaps especially when—integrative problems exist. In this paper, a psychoanalyst with broad acquaintance in the social sciences presents a classification of the modes of resolving various types of role conflict within the nuclear family. Although Dr. Spiegel's paper focuses upon resolving conflicts, it is included here to suggest the processes involved in the working out of the co-ordinative problems which exist for all families.

In an investigation of the relation between cultural-value conflict, family conflict, and the emotional adjustment of the person, in which I am participating with Florence R. Kluckhohn and a number of co-workers, the concept of social role is being used to observe and analyze the details of behavior which is functional or dysfunctional for the family as a whole. The social role[1] concept is useful for this purpose because it facilitates observation of the way the individual members of the family become involved in the family as a superordinate system of behavior. It helps to describe not only the interaction of two members as they adjust to each other, but also the transactions[2] of a plurality of members as they interweave in the special type of compulsiveness or control which a going system always imposes on its members. Since the uniquely compulsive elements of the family system leave a characteristic stamp upon the personality development of the child, it is important to have a way of teasing apart the rather subtle elements of which it is composed.

In studying a group of families of emotionally disturbed children and

Reprinted from Milton Greenblatt, Daniel J. Levinson, and Richard H. Williams, *The Patient and the Mental Hospital*, 545–64. Copyright 1957 by The Free Press of Glencoe, Illinois.

comparing them with families in which the children are free of clinically manifest disturbance, we have found evidence of what promises to be a consistent difference between the two groups. In the first group the children inevitably become involved in a conflict or disequilibrium situation which exists between the parents. Most frequently, neither the child nor the parents are aware of this fact, nor are they aware of the ways in which it comes about. In the second group of families, although there may be sources of tension between the parents, the children are minimally involved in them. In order to avoid excessive variability in our two sets of families, we have kept them similar with respect to size and with respect to ethnic, regional, and class variables. Nevertheless, the sources of tension can be related in every case to differences and incompatibilities in cultural-value orientations and, as a corollary, in definitions of social-role expectations. These incompatibilities have a pronounced bearing upon the object relations and unconscious psychodynamics of the transacting members of the family. However, I shall not deal here with the origin of the cultural-value conflict or its direct relation to the intrapsychic process. In this paper, the cultural-value conflict will be assumed to underlie the role conflict in the family, and attention will be centered rather on the ways in which the role conflict[3] is handled.

While we were studying the ways in which parents unwittingly involve one or more children in their own conflicts, it became clear that this process, so ably reported by Adelaide Johnson and her co-workers,[4] could be described in the usual psychodynamic terms. Through identification with the unconscious wishes of the parent, the child acts out the parent's unconscious emotional conflict. The acting-out serves as a "defense" for the parent, making it unnecessary for him to face his own conflicts. This vocabulary is adequate for most purposes and, besides, confers a kind of credibility upon the description because of long usage and ready acceptance in the mind of the user. Nevertheless, it left us unsatisfied. Even with the qualification of the term "unconscious," the description sounds too planned and too much under the control of one or more persons. A constant observer of the family—or of any other persistent group process— has a somewhat contrary impression that much of what occurs in the way of behavior is not under the control of any one person or even a set of persons, but is rather the upshot of complicated processes beyond the ken of anyone involved. Something in the group process itself takes over as a steering mechanism and brings about results which no one anticipates, or wants, whether consciously or unconsciously. Or the steering mechanism may bring about a completely unexpected pleasant effect. On the basis of numerous observations, we were struck with the fact that so often what is functional for one member of the family group may be dysfunctional for the family as a whole. The opposite also holds: what is functional for the family as a whole may have very harmful effects on one person. These phenomena take place unwittingly, not only because of the unconscious dynamics within each person, but also because of the operations of the system of relations in which the members of the family are involved.

To describe accurately the characteristics of a system of relations within a group over a considerable span of time is no small task. The most successful attempt to do this known to us is the method of interaction process analysis devised by Parsons and Bales.[5] However, the categories of interaction used by these workers is at too high a level of abstraction for our purposes. We decided, therefore, to use their basic concepts of behavior occurring within role systems of ego and alter or any number of alters, but to devise our own set of categories for observing the roles involved. Thus, the basic concept used in analyzing the family as a system consists of describing the behavior of any one member, in terms of his role, in transaction with a role partner or partners. A role is defined as a goal-directed pattern or sequence of acts tailored by the cultural process for the transactions a person may carry out in a social group or situation. It is conceived that no role exists in isolation but is always patterned to gear in with the complementary or reciprocal role of a role partner (alter). Thus, all roles have to be learned by the persons who wish to occupy them in accordance with the cultural (or subcultural) values of the society in which they exist. If that society is fairly homogeneous and well integrated, then the roles will be patterned in such a way that their complementary structure is obvious and stable.

The roles pertinent to the family as a system consist of husband and wife, mother and father, son and daughter, brother and sister. This is not an exhaustive list, and refers to the nuclear rather than the extended family. But if one compares these roles on any axis of variation, such as ethnic or class affiliation, it is apparent that they are defined differently, and their complementary structure varies according to the particular mode of family organization characteristic of that class or ethnic group. It is true that even within a class or ethnic group there is considerable variation of pattern. Nevertheless, one mode of organization tends to be typical or dominant compared to the others. For example, an American middle-class wife tends to expect her husband to treat her as an equal. She expects of her husband a good deal of independence, initiative, and planning for future success in his occupation, but in his relations with her and with the children, she expects co-operation, sharing of responsibility, and individual consideration. Reciprocally, the husband expects his wife to help in his plans for future economic and social success, notably by putting his success goals above any personal career or occupational goals of her own, and by developing the social and domestic skills suitable to his particular occupational status. There is evidence that these complementary role expectations may not be precisely reciprocal—that is, there may be some built-in strain—but on the whole they fit with each other fairly well.

By way of comparison, it is illuminating to select some of the complementary role patterns in the lower-class family of Italian origin. Here the wife has no wish that her husband spend a great deal of time thinking or planning about occupational success. She expects her husband to work steadily and do his best to bring in enough money to satisfy the needs of the family, but she does not expect his economic or social status to change. She expects rather to have a large number of children who will soon join the husband in trying to increase the economic intake of the family, but in the meantime there is always help to be expected from relatives and friends if there is real need. On the other hand, she does expect him to spend a lot of time keeping up contacts with the extended and complicated networks of relatives and friends in order to keep the family's own position secure. At home, she does not expect to be treated as an equal. Rather she expects him to make the chief decisions, relieving her of responsibility so that she can tend to the needs of the large brood of children. For his part, the husband expects submission but also a good deal of nurturant care from his wife. He wants her to be chiefly concerned with his children. Everything else is secondary. For both of them there is an accent on enjoyment and a sense of festivity in family life which is of greater importance than hard work and planning for the sake of social ambition. Again, although definite strains can be noted here and there, the roles of the family members vis-à-vis each other are characterized by a complementarity of expectations which fit each other in fairly smooth and systematic ways.

The Equilibrium-Disequilibrium Balance

I hope that these all-too-brief examples of contrasting husband-wife role patterns illustrate how complementarity can be maintained in spite of variation in goals, values, and concrete sequences of acts within the role systems. The principle of complementarity is of the greatest significance because it is chiefly responsible for that degree of harmony and stability which occurs in interpersonal relations. Because so many of the roles in which any one person is involved are triggered off by cultural cues in a completely complementary fashion, he tends not to be aware of them. He enacts them automatically, and all goes well. This automatic function of role systems has significance for psychological economy of effort. The person is spared the necessity of coming to decisions about most of the acts he performs, because he knows his parts so well. This saves his efforts for those acts which occur in less stabilized role systems. In this way, role reciprocity confers spontaneity upon human behavior. Self-consciousness and self-guarding enter the scene along with role conflict, which sharply raises the number of decisions which have to be made with respect to any sequence of acts. As long as complementarity is maintained at high levels of equilibrium,[6] decisions are decentralized, so to speak. They are taken care of by the system of role relations rather than by the person's acting in a self-conscious manner.

However, it is a part of the human condition that high levels of equilibrium, figured by precise complementarity of roles, are seldom maintained for long. Sooner or later, disharmony enters the picture. Complementarity fails; the role systems characterizing the interpersonal relations move toward disequilibrium. The role partners disappoint each other's expectations. The failure of complementarity feeds back into the awareness of the participants in the form of tension, anxiety or hostility, and self-consciousness. If the process continues without change, it will end in the disruption of the system. This process is so familiar and inevitable that it seems to merit no further comment. Yet it may contain some general elements which, if subjected to critical scrutiny, could throw light on family behavior. The key to its analysis would consist of a study of the conditions leading to the break-down of complementarity and to its subsequent restoration. Although this study has not been carried as far as I would like, our current experience indicates that there are at least five causes for failure of complementarity in role systems within the family. I shall review them here very briefly, without the extended discussion and illustration which they deserve.

1) Cognitive Discrepancy.—One or both persons involved in the role system may not know or have sufficient familiarity with the required roles. This is especially likely to occur with respect to age roles, and therefore frequently characterizes sources of disequilibrium between parents and children. When the pattern of acts constituting the role is not clearly mastered or not cognitively mapped or internalized, complementarity can be maintained only with difficulty. Cues are misinterpreted, and misunderstanding reduces complementarity of expectations. Both participants must have a relatively high tolerance for frustration and failure, and both must assume informally the roles of teacher and learner alternately. This alternation and reversal of roles will be discussed later in connection with the mechanisms of restoration of complementarity. In this culture, cognitive discrepancy is a characteristic problem between adolescents and the adult world. It also occurs between husband and wife at various developmental crises, or with respect to any sudden, new situation. For example, the wedding and immediate postnuptial situation require much new learning of roles. So does the birth of the first child, the first severe illness, and so forth.

2) Discrepancy of Goals.—Roles are patterns of acts directed toward immediate or ultimate goals. The goal of ego, interlocking with the goal of alter, determines the motivational principle behind the person's taking of the role. Some goals serve the purpose of gratification, while others are chosen for the sake of defense. The same goal may serve either purpose, but if there is a shift in motivation, there is usually a shift in the definition of the role. For example, in one of the "sick" families studied—a family of Italian extraction whom I shall call the Bonellis—an eleven-year-old daughter, Joanne, the middle one of three girls, repeatedly made demands upon her father for gifts of all sorts. Her motive was originally desire for gratification, but it was mixed with a defensive need to test whether she was being rejected or not. At first the father gratified her demands intermittently and inconsistently. He gave when he felt like it and at other times refused. Both giving and refusing represented satisfactions for him, and he included rewarding and withholding as legitimate goals in his conception of the father's role. However, the daughter gradually defined his withholding as confirmation of her fear of rejection and tested more intensively by increasing her demands. The father defined this as "pestering" and responded with increased withholding and disapproval, while claiming that he was trying his best to satisfy her. This claim was not true, since he consistently rewarded Rosemarie, the older sister, more than Joanne. But now the goal of withholding had become defensive against the implied meaning of her demands—that he actually preferred the older sister. In this complicated transaction, the defense was accomplished on the father's side through defining the daughter's motivation as coercive and assigning to her the informal role of pest, while giving himself the informal role of victim. Although a tenuous complementarity was maintained by the defensive establishment of the informal pest-victim relation, actually their goals became more and more discrepant. This discrepancy of goals was one of the chief reasons why the family brought the girl into the psychiatric clinic for treatment. The parents verbalized the failure of complementarity by characterizing the girl to our interviewers as a bad and disobedient daughter. They had tried their best to teach her "right from wrong," but she was unable to "learn." It is significant of the defensive problem in this family that her behavior was ascribed to a cognitive and value discrepancy —that she couldn't "learn" the correct behavior—when actually it was due to a motivational problem concerning unavowed goals.

Another source of discrepancy in goals is biologically determined, rather than of motivational origin. Fatigue, illness, and lack of maturation are accompanied by a *restricted capacity for goal attainment*. Other biological limitations, such as deficiency of intelligence, have the same effect. Such limitations produce disequilibrium when one of the role partners is unable to accommodate through a change in level of expectancy regarding goals to be attained, which he looks upon as rewards, as in the example of the parent who cannot accept the limited intelligence of his child.

3) *Allocative Discrepancy.*—In any particular social situation there is a question of the person's right to the role he wishes to occupy. There are four principal ways in which roles are sorted out among those who contend for them.

(a) Some roles, such as age and sex roles, are *ascribed.*[7] This means that they are universally expected and the person has practically no leeway: he is not free to decide to change his sex or age role. If a man tries to change his sex role, as in transvestitism, he is likely to invoke intense criticism. The same is true, although to a lesser extent, of age roles. The child who tries to act like an adult usually produces a critical response, and the same holds for the reverse situation.

(b) Some roles, such as occupational and certain domestic roles, have to be *achieved.*[8] As an allocative principle, achievement involves effort, the satisfaction of prerequisites, and some form of ceremonial recognition such as licensure, contract, conferring of a diploma, appointment, and so forth. There is more leeway than in the case of ascribed roles, but strong sanctions will be invoked if an achieved role is simply taken without observing the required formalities.

(c) Some roles, in the main of an informal character, can be taken simply through *adoption.* No one has to ask permission to take an adopted role, although there may not always be approval of it. For example, the father in the Bonelli family adopted the role of victim. He could have responded to his daughter's demands with some other role activity. He could have treated them as childish antics and laughed them off in the role of amused spectator—this was actually a tack he frequently took when his feelings were not intensely involved. By adopting the role of victim, however, he *assigned* her the complementary role of pest. The assignment was implicit rather than explicit. That is, it was concealed or masked, and on the whole he treated her as if she had spontaneously adopted the role of pest toward him. Thus, adoption-assignment describes for role transactions what is denoted for the person by the concepts of introjection-protection. If he had been able to laugh off her demands, he would have treated her behavior as essentially playful.

(d) Playfulness is the sign of the last allocative principle, which is based on *assumption.* Assumed roles are not serious. They are taken in games or play, and are held to be at some distance from "reality." The child who plays mother is not really confusing herself with her mother. Thus, there are no sanctions invoked for assumed roles, provided the person has emitted the culturally appropriate cue indicating the assumption of a role. The facial configuration referred to in the expression, "Smile when you say that," is such a cue. It is obvious that assumed roles are of the greatest importance to the development and socialization of the child. But they are of equal importance to adults, not only for the sake of recreation and informality, but also as a means of escape from a disequilibrium situation. The formula, "I was only kidding," changes an adopted or achieved role into an assumed one, and thus establishes a new type of complementarity when the old one was threatened with failure. In this connection, withholding a cue indicating whether a role is adopted or assumed is a frequently used method of concealing or masking motivation. Alter is left in the dark and does not know whether ego was serious or not.

The most common sources of allocative discrepancy leading to a failure of complementarity are, first, use of a culturally invalid or inappropriate allocative principle; second, withholding of a cue indicating the allocative principle being used; and, third, emission of a misleading cue which gives alter the impression that one allocative principle is in use when in fact another one is actually present. For example, in the Bonelli family, the mother was angry about the favoritism and excessive attention which the father showed toward their oldest daughter. In her eyes his behavior was largely seductive. At the same time she was ambivalent about his behavior, and unable to express the full range of her feelings. She preferred to attack him on the ground of not being a typical American Daddy. So she reproached him for showing too much favoritism and for being unfair to the other children, saying nothing about the competitive feelings toward her daughter which his behavior stimulated in her. His response was to deny anything inappropriate in his behavior toward his daughter, and to accuse his wife of being irritable and unduly apprehensive in this situation. Actually neither of them wanted to push the situation to the full extent of their feelings. There was an implicit agreement to avoid it and to substitute in its place their co-operative concern with the excessive demands and "disobedience" of the middle daughter.

An analysis of the allocative principles involved in this source of disequilibrium between the parents reveals, first, that the mother defines the father's role as invalid. In her eyes he acts like a lover to his daughter, and this is doubly inappropriate. It is not a part of his ascribed role as a father, or of his achieved role as a husband. He has no right to this role. Second, the father agrees with the mother's view of the allocative principles but denies that he has taken a lover's role. But since both the accusation and the denial are implicit—that is, they are only hinted at, not directly verbalized—it is necessary to look for the operations through which the potentially explosive aspects of this situation are avoided. This occurs by a mutually unconscious shift of the dispute to the ground of a cultural value discrepancy—the father's failure to be a typical American rather than a misguided Italian Daddy. At the same time, according to the observations of the interviewers who are studying the family, there is an ill-defined but quite intense intimacy between the father and daughter. It is hard to decide whether it is merely a playful aspect of filial attention and devotion, or whether it is something more than this. At times, the daughter seems actually to take the mother's role toward the father. The cue which would distinguish whether this was an assumed, adopted, achieved, or ascribed role is missing. But the father's direct description of his activity—his own perception of his behavior—on being questioned is that it is merely a part of his generally ascribed role as father. He even goes so far as to deny to the interviewer that he shows any favoritism, claiming that he treats all his children alike.

Withholding allocative clues or emitting misleading cues are in part attempts to avert the full denouement of failure of complementarity with its accompanying intense disequilibrium. Insofar as they have this function, they will be discussed below in connection with that step in the restoration of equilibrium for which I shall propose the term *masking*. It is probably obvious that these are general processes occurring in transactions at all levels of the social system. Withholding allocative cues universally produces a masked or ambiguous situation favorable for the reading-in or projection of intentions. Emitting misleading cues is also a familiar device, whether in the hands of spies at the international level, or confidence men on home territory. Be that as it may, their connection with failure of complementarity is this: at the point at which the situation becomes unmasked, the allocative discrepancy is revealed in all its starkness. The disequilibrium is characterized by disillusionment ("You deceived me!"), protest ("You have no right to do what you did!"), alarm ("I've been robbed!"), and various similar phrasings in the vocabulary of victimization.

4) Instrumental Discrepancy.—A review of the origins of failure to maintain complementarity in role relations cannot neglect the fact that non-human events and objects form part of the context of all behavior. Insofar as role activities require technical instruments, equipment, furniture, props, costumes, climate, and other appropriate physical facilities (including money!), a deprivation or insufficiency of these instrumental perrequisites interferes with role transactions. The point is so obvious that it is represented in various traditional and contemporary maxims, of somewhat dubious accuracy. When equestrian skills were at a premium, instrumental discrepancy was pictured as, "For want of a nail, the shoe was lost/For want of a shoe, the horse was lost/For want of a horse, the battle was lost. . . ." Today, in a less heroic cultural climate, one frequently hears, "There's nothing wrong with him that money won't cure!"

Despite the therapeutic oversimplification, such sentiments underscore the potential for severe frustration inherent in instrumental discrepancy. In addition to legitimate and actual deprivation, instrumental discrepancy easily assumes displaced or symbolic functions. For example, in the Bonelli family, the father complained that he did not have the money to buy the things that his family demanded. Actually, he tried desperately to earn more money by taking extra jobs in addition to his main employment. These frenzied efforts defined him as a failure in the dominant American cultural pattern of occupational and economic success, because he was unable to plan, budget, or save any money. On the other hand, this strenuous activity relieved him of the potential accusation of neglect—of not caring for his family's welfare. Yet the need to neglect underlay much of his overcompensatory striving. Unconsciously he resented having to take the role of the father, the provider, and would have preferred to compete with his children as the recipient of parental care and concern. This source of role discrepancy, however, had to be hidden from his conscious awareness, and its energy had to be partly displaced into other types of activity or passive avoidance of activity.

Unconsciously contrived instrumental deficiency admirably served this purpose. The family suffered from protean forms of equipment failure. The screens had holes, the cellar frequently flooded, the car broke down, the icebox was constantly in need of repair, fuses blew, pipes broke, paint peeled. In the midst of this chaos, the father gave the impression of much activity, rushing about to attend to the latest crisis, accompanied by strident advice from his wife. Actually, he neglected repairing obvious defects until it was too late. The result of the neglect was painful to the wife, who had high standards of housekeeping. He met all criticism from her with the attitude, "What can I do? I'm doing my best!"

From this description, it is apparent that instrumental discrepancy can be consciously or unconsciously motivated. To the extent that this is true, it is closely related to goal discrepancy. It must be kept in mind, however, that it can occur quite fortuitously, as in the case of accidental loss or deprivation by fire, robbery, or some other external agent.

5) Discrepancy in Cultural Value Orientations.—As was said before, roles are patterned in accordance with the value orientations of a culture or subculture. In mixed marriages, in families that have moved suddenly from one culture to another as in emigration, and in families that are moving up or down the social class ladder, the possibilities of confusion or outright conflict in cultural values are very great. However, even in families not involved in such dramatic transitions, there is a possibility of discrepancy of cultural value orientations. This is especially true in the United States, because of the extreme mixture of values beneath the surface layers of apparent uniformity of the social system. In this country, cultural traditions are so various and so frequently at odds with each other that almost any person will have internalized some degree of cultural conflict.

In our project we are using the scheme of variation in cultural value orientations proposed by Florence Kluckhohn[9] to keep track of the cultural attitudes which can give rise to conflict. This has proved very useful, but it is too detailed and involved to set forth here. However, the way in which cultural value discrepancies can give rise to disequilibrium can be illustrated again in the case of the Bonelli family. The mother was born in this country of Italian-born parents. The father was born in Italy and did not come to the United States until he was eight years old. Consequently, the mother considers herself, correctly, to be more Americanized than the father. In both of them there is a great deal of conflict and confusion over the transition to the American patterns, but on any specific issue between them, she is always closer to the American middle-class cultural orientation. She would like to cook only American food, but he insists on Italian dishes. She would like to get away from the home, visit with friends, and ultimately obtain a job, but he insists that she constantly stay home and care for the children. She would like her husband to show more initiative and independence, although she has the capacity for making decisions and solving problems. He backs away from responsibility and is unable to discipline the children. She would like to plan for their own future and that of the children, but he is so occupied with present concerns that he cannot get his eyes on the future as a good American would.

These discrepancies in cultural values are associated with incompatible definitions of their roles as husband and wife, mother and father. Thus, the complementarity of their role relations is always somewhat strained. The strain would be reduced if the father were moving, culturally, in the direction the mother wants to go. But her activity toward him makes it impossible for him to utilize what potentials for movement he possesses, since he is continuously defined as a failure in terms of the American patterns. He defends himself by pleading incapacity, by claiming that he is "trying" as hard as he can, and by asking that she accept as culturally adequate substitutes other informal roles. One of these is the role of comedian which he plays with great skill, offering entertainment in the place of successful performance. However, his position vis-à-vis the value discrepancy is essentially destructive to his self-esteem. He takes his revenge on his wife through his seductive relations with his oldest daughter. In this way a value discrepancy, in which he is the loser, is compensated by an allocative and goal discrepancy in which he is the victor. Since these complicated transactions represent attempts to stabilize or restore equilibrium through *masking* and *compromise,* their further discussion will be postponed until I take up the discussion of these processes.

It is apparent that, in discussing the varieties of failure of complementarity in any concrete empirical focus, it is virtually impossible to avoid discussing simultaneously the efforts occurring in the system of transactions to compensate or re-establish equilibrium. Failure of complementarity is so disruptive that it is almost always accompanied by processes of restoration for which I would like to use the term *re-equilibration.* In any ongoing system of relations such as a family, then, one can observe re-equilibration occurring whenever the balance of equilibrium to disequilibrium in the state of the system moves too close to the disequilibrium pole. It seems to me that it is the empirical admixture of these three processes—that is, of equilibrium (high complementarity), disequilibrium (low complementarity), and re-equilibration—that has made the processes involved in the stabilization or healthy internal adjustment of the system so difficult to recognize.

Re-equilibration

The restoration of equilibrium, once complementarity is threatened with failure, is itself an extremely complicated process. I have distinguished eleven steps in the process which I will here describe briefly. I believe these steps have a temporal order and that this order has a kind of internal logic. Unfortunately, I am unable to discern the basis of the order and must therefore leave the presentation in an excessively descriptive and *ad hoc* condition. The description has heuristic value, though it will not leave the reader free of the suspicion that it is arbitrary and incomplete. I am myself dissatisfied with it, but at least it is a method of systematically noting processes in the family which are subtle and difficult to observe.

With respect to the problem of internal logic or the underlying process connecting the various categories, one thing can be said. The eleven categories fall into two groups which are basically different. The first five categories belong together, as do the last five. The sixth forms a connecting link between the two groups. The difference between the two groups is concerned with the method by which the role conflict is handled and the equilibrium restored. In the first group, the resolution is effected by means of a unilateral decision. Ego resolves the discrepancy by giving in to alter, or vice versa. One or the other parties to the conflict agrees, submits, goes along with, becomes convinced, or is persuaded in some way. For this group, therefore, I would propose the term, *role induction.*[10] The net effect, whatever the particular step may be, is that alter is induced to take the complementary role which will restore the equilibrium with ego. Ego's role, on the other hand, does not essentially change. The techniques of induction have been dealt with in the classical tradition of rhetoric and have been given a contemporary analysis by Kenneth Burke.[11] They have also been considered in contemporary studies of propaganda devices. I am very much indebted to Burke for his detailed and illuminating studies of the relation between persuasion and discrepancy.

In the second group of categories, re-equilibration is accomplished through a change in roles of both ego and alter. Complementarity is re-established on a mutually new basis. Because of the novel solution of the conflict, I suggest for this group the term, *role modification.* The change in role expectations is bilateral, and the modification techniques are based on interchanges and mutual identifications of ego with alter. Although the distinction may be somewhat vague, induction techniques are founded on manipulative and instrumental procedures, while modification techniques are based on insight and communicative procedures.

Role Induction.—(1) *Coercing* holds first place as the most universally available induction technique. It may hold its primacy either on biological or cultural grounds or both. It can be defined as the manipulation of present and future punishments. Thus it ranges from overt attack to threats of attack in the future, and from verbal commands to physical force. It varies in intensity from mildly aversive manipulations to cruel and unusual torture. It owes its universality to its connection with the hostile-aggressive patterns of behavior within the person. The reverse is, of course, also true. This is to say, that the hostile-aggressive behavior would have no biologically useful function if coercion did not exist as a culturally patterned mode of settling role conflicts. It exists in every family we have studied, and it is probably safe to say that it is present in every enduring social system, no matter how much it may be veiled. If it is successful, the role conflict is settled through submission, in which ego accepts the complementary role enforced by alter. However, none of the induction techniques can guarantee success. They may all be met in one of two ways: either by a specific neutralizing technique or by a counterinduction. The specific neutralizing technique for coercing is *defying*. The counterinductions may vary from retaliatory coercion to any of the other reequilibration categories.

(2) *Coaxing* is in second place, not because it is less universal than coercing, but because it seems somewhat less readily available as an induction technique. It is probably not the best term for this category, although it specifies the basic principle involved in it. Coaxing can be defined as the manipulation of present and future rewards. Thus, it includes asking, promising, pleading, begging, and tempting. Ego accedes to alter's request in order to gain alter's reward, just as in coercing ego submits in order to escape alter's punishment. The child who says, "Please!" by word or gesture, rewards his mother with love or compliance when she gratifies his request. In tempting, bribing, or seducing, alter's rewards are likely to be more concrete! However, in seduction, the behavior is invaded by masking—insofar as the seducer conceals his actual motives— and consequently this is probably not a pure case.

Coaxing owes its universality—and its irresistibility—to the fact that it expresses ego's wish for gratification and stimulates a wish to gratify an alter. It epitomizes desire. In spite of its power, it is no guarantee of success in resolving role conflict. As with the other induction techniques, it can misfire if ego responds with a specific neutralizing technique or a counterinduction. The specific neutralization for coaxing is *refusing* or *withholding*. All specific neutralizing techniques are essentially without affect. The affective neutrality occurs because the response is simply a technical way of meeting a persuasion. However, the neutrality may be hard to maintain, and some degree of affective response may creep into it. To the extent that this happens, the response becomes transformed into a counterinduction. For example, defying is simply a holding-out against threat and is not in itself affectively toned. But if ego feels anxiety over the success of defying as a way of warding off threat, then he is likely either to submit, or to become hostile and respond with counter-coercion. Similarly, refusing is merely a way of warding off the pressure of coaxing, but if ego is anxious about its effect—for example, if he feels guilty—he may respond by coercing or postponing, or some other induction.

(3) *Evaluating* operates upon the role conflict in a somewhat more derived way than coercing and coaxing. In the usual case it follows upon them, and therefore is likely to be a counterinduction, although this is not necessary or inevitable. In evaluating, alter responds to ego's behavior by identifying or categorizing it in a value context. Thus, it includes such activities as praising, blaming, shaming, approving, and disapproving. For example, if alter tries to resolve the role conflict through coercion, ego may evaluate his behavior by saying, "Stop behaving like a fool!" or "Quit trying to act like a little Hitler!" The *stop* and *quit* signal defiance, but ego clearly is responding as if defiance were not enough either to express the degree of affect mobilized in him or to neutralize the degree of coercion emitted by alter.

The effect of this kind of induction is based upon the manipulation of reward and punishment. It differs from coercing and coaxing in that the reward or punishment is generalized, categorized, and thus placed in a class of value judgments—either positive or negative—linked by verbal and visual imagery to the category. When ego says that alter is "acting like a fool," he is linking alter's behavior to a class of punished or devalued activities symbolized by the figure of the fool. He establishes an identity between alter and all other fools. If alter accepts the identity, then he will define his having coerced as punishable or noneffective and will terminate or extinguish his coercive activity. He may then substitute some other induction, such as coaxing, to resolve the role conflict. However, he may not accept the identity employed in the evaluation, and if so, he may use the specific neutralizing technique to be employed against evaluation. This is *denying*. For example, alter may respond to ego's evaluating by saying, "I am *not* behaving like a fool, and if you don't do what I've asked you to do, you'll have to suffer the consequences!" After denying, ego returns to coercing, showing the circular pattern characteristic of any protracted quarrel.

The same mechanisms hold true for positive evaluating such as praising. Of course, positive evaluating is more likely to be accepted, since it is a reward, although it may not be so interpreted, as in the case of what is held to be unwarranted flattery. The case of flattery, however, is another example of a compound induction because it is likely to be mixed with various degrees of masking. Alter is apt to perceive ego's flattering as concealing a hidden motive. Apart from masking, there are still good reasons for denying positive evaluating. Since the motive behind ego's positive evaluation is to induce alter to take the complementary role which will restore equilibrium, alter may deny in order to ward off this outcome. This certainly happens in the case of praise, encouragement, or support, when alter is resisting the induction process. A mother, attempting to encourage her reluctant son to go to school for the first time, may say, "Johnny, I'm sure you'll enjoy school. You'll have a good time, and Mommy will be proud of you, just like she is of Freddy [an older brother]." First the mother coaxes by holding out the promise of future reward (enjoyment), and then she reinforces with a positive evaluation, putting Johnny with Freddy in a class of rewarded objects (pride). Such an inducement can easily backfire. Johnny bursts into tears and says, "No! I don't wanna go. I won't have a good time." (Refusal of coaxing.) "And I don't care about Freddy. I'm not *like* him!" (Denial of identity and of evaluation.) This leaves the discrepancy of goals about where it started, at high disequilibrium, and the mother may now try coercing, or she may postpone the settlement of the conflict until Daddy comes home, or until tomorrow when Johnny's resistance may be lowered.

(4) *Masking* is another universal induction technique, more indirect than the three discussed so far. It may be defined as the withholding of correct information or the substitution of incorrect information pertinent to the settlement of the conflict. It includes such behavior as pretending, evading, censoring, distorting, lying, hoaxing, deceiving, and so on. These words are taken from ordinary usage and are apt to have a negative connotation. However, it is not my intention to give masking—or any other induction technique—either a positive or negative value. It occurs universally in the course of organism-environment transactions, and has its biological and cultural aspects. The tiger stalking its prey is masking, as is the camouflaged bird sitting on its nest. Every culture has its patterned ways of concealing information and its criteria for determining what information may or may not be revealed, with or without distortion. In studying masking, my intention is merely to determine its *function* for the way the system is working. I believe it is as significant to the function of the social system, large or small, as is *repression* to the function of the personality as a system. Repression is universal as an intrapsychic process, and it means that information available to certain components of the personality is either completely unavailable to another component or reaches it only in disguised form. Repression has a biological basis in the function of the organism, but the content of what is repressed is related to the content of what is masked in the social system. This is a point which Sullivan[12] repeatedly stressed in calling attention to the significance of

interpersonal relations to the function of the personality. However, Sullivan tended to see only the negative side of masking. He noted how it produces obstacles to successful communication which the person internalizes, but he was not interested in its function for the social system itself.

Masking is so complex and so intrinsic to re-equilibrating processes in the family that it is impossible to discuss it adequately in this small compass. Little white lies and minor disguises of motives take place so automatically that they are scarcely noticeable. For example, displacement and substitution of roles between parent and child are ubiquitous. A child bumps himself on a chair, and the mother says, "Naughty chair!," assigning the chair a human activity and then evaluating that activity as if it were part of a coercive induction. Why does she do this? Pain produces anger and in order to avoid the potential role conflict which may be precipitated between herself and her child, she involves the child in a make-believe conflict with the chair, with herself in the role of referee. Furthermore, she denies the potential negative evaluation of herself as insufficiently protective of the child, by displacing the carelessness to the chair. This preserves equilibrium between herself and the child and thus is functional for their role system. But one can ask whether what is functional for their role system may not be dysfunctional for the child's ability to test reality. She conceals the important information that pain and accidents can occur without motive and need to be endured in the inevitable process of maturation and acquisition of autonomy by the child. Thus her masking ties the child to her in a dependent relation in which she plays the role of protector. She conceals both from herself and her child information about her resentment at the growing independence of the child, which, if it were available as a message, would read, "If you're going to act so independently, you ought to be punished. But I don't want you to know that I think this, so I'll pretend that it's not your behavior I resent but the chair's. You will understand that the world is full of hostile chairs, and you need me to protect you from them." If the child does not see through this masking, he will take the complementary dependent role which his mother desires for him.

In studying the family, it is often difficult to disentangle the significance of minor masking, as in the example just discussed, from major transactions in which the masking is very dramatic. For example, in the Bonelli family both the cultural value discrepancy and the sexual goal discrepancy between the parents were masked and the role conflict displaced to the middle daughter who was explicitly defined by both parents as the major source of all their difficulties. The test of significance is to discover what happens when the induction technique is unmasked. *Unmasking* is the specific neutralizing technique for masking. The role partners confront each other with what has been concealed or disguised. Where the masking has averted a major disequilibrium, unmasking can be extremely explosive. As a result of therapy with the mother, father, and middle child in this family, the mother began to displace less of her role conflict to the middle child and to pay more attention to the father's relation to the oldest daughter. The change was registered in a violent scene in which the mother openly voiced her resentment to the father, who then lost his temper and threw a lighted cigarette at her, denying all the while the truth of her accusation. This unmasked the sexual situation but left the cultural discrepancy still concealed—that is, not directly stated as a source of role conflict between the parents. It is our hunch that when this conflict opens up, the violence in their feelings will be even greater.

(5) *Postponing* may seem to fit uneasily as an induction technique since it appears to be merely a negative or passive way of dealing with role conflict. Nevertheless, it is undertaken with the expectation in both ego and alter that "in the interval he will change his mind." The process by which the conflict is to be settled is deferred in the hope of change of attitude. Indeed, this is very likely to be successful since the intrapsychic process always tends to work toward a resolution of conflict. The implied instruction, "Think it over," or the promise, "I'll sleep on it," often achieves the desired effect. Most role conflicts in the family are not settled at the moment, but are deferred and taken up afresh, time and time again. From the point of view of persuasion, the question between ego and alter is, Who has the most to gain from postponing? If ego considers that he has very little to gain, he may attempt the specific neutralizing technique when alter attempts to postpone. This is *provoking*. If ego is afraid of postponement, he may provoke or incite the conflict to appear in full force.

(6) *Role reversal*[13] is a transitional re-equilibration midway between role induction and role modification. It can be defined in G. H. Mead's sense as the process of taking the role of alter.[14] Ego proposes that alter put himself in ego's shoes, trying to see things through his eyes. Or ego initiates the reversal, hoping that alter will do the same. Ego may say, "Well, I think I'm beginning to see your point, but. . . ." Or, "It doesn't make too much sense to me, but I think I see what you mean." Insofar as this is a nonmanipulative approach, it cannot be classified as an induction, and it therefore requires no specific neutralizing technique. On the one hand, if alter responds to role reversal with an induction, then ego may give up the attempt to reverse roles, and the whole process will revert to inductive and counterinductive maneuvers. On the other hand, the role reversal may well kick the process of re-equilibration toward role modification and a novel resolution. It is this ambivalent position that makes it impossible to classify role reversal as belonging to either group; it is really transitional between both of them.

Whether role reversal is effective or not depends in large part on the intensity of masking procedures in the family relations. The more energy in disequilibrium is being defended by masking, the less likely is role reversal to take effect. In the Bonelli family, the interviewers seeing the parents tried repeatedly to test their ability to reverse roles with Joanne, the middle daughter. For example, the mother's interviewer would say, "Do you think Joanne is sort of feeling left out in the family? Maybe she feels she isn't getting enough attention." To this sort of approach, the mother, for a long time, would respond with the statement, "But how could she? We try so hard to treat them all the same!" The same sort of thing tended to happen with respect to Joanne's stealing. Joanne was not given an allowance or permitted to baby-sit in order to earn some money. This was always defended on the basis of the evaluative induction: Joanne steals. She's not reliable. We can't trust her, and so on. The interviewer asked how Joanne could ever learn to take responsibility if she were not given some. After a while this role reversal "took" with the mother, who started to treat Joanne as if she were not an irretrievably deviant daughter. This coincided with an intensive role reversal program between the interviewer and the mother, in which the interviewer tried continuously to understand how the mother was feeling. The double-barreled procedure moved Joanne out of the masking process in which she had been held as if in a vise. In turn, this led to the unmasking of the sexual conflict between the mother and father with respect to Rosemarie, the oldest daughter.

Role Modification.—(7) *Joking* is an outgrowth of role reversal. It is the first sign that role modification is in progress. The role partners, having successfully exchanged places with each other and thus having obtained some insight into each other's feelings and perceptions, are now able to achieve some distance from their previous intense involvement in the conflict. They are able to laugh at themselves and each other. The laughing proceeds in part, as Freud pointed out, from the saving of psychic energy coincident with the partial solution of the conflict. The jokes also permit the expression in sublimated form of some of the induction techniques which are about to be relinquished—such as coercing and evaluating. The joking process moves the allocative base of the transaction to a whole set of assumed roles, and thus introduces playfulness into what was previously a tense set of achieved or adopted roles. In play, the role partners try on for size a series of weird or impossible solutions, out of which is gradually fabricated the substance of the possible solution.

(8) *Referral to a third party.* Role reversal and joking may not of themselves create a role modification. They are helpful but not necessarily sufficient for this type of re-equilibration. Therefore, ego or alter, or both, may refer the conflict to a third person—perhaps another member of the family, a friend, or an organization—for help in its solution. The assumption is that the third party is less intensely involved in the conflict and has information or skills not available to ego or alter. Thus he can

visualize a solution with greater ease. There are two difficulties which may arise from this re-equilibrating procedure. First, the third party chosen may steer the process back to a manipulative procedure and thereby restimulate the induction process. Secondly, and coincidental with this, the third person may form a coalition with ego against alter, or vice versa. If the third person is within the family, the attempted solution through referral frequently gets grounded on the rocks of such a coalition. This triadic situation has been studied by Simmel,[15] and more recently by Mills[16] in artificially composed groups. However, the process involved in it needs much more extensive investigation. In the Bonelli family, third-party referral within the family always seemed to end in a coalition. At the outset the parents were allied against Joanne. As unmasking proceeded, the father and Rosemarie were revealed in a coalition against the mother. There was evidence that the youngest child and the mother were in alliance against the father. These shifting triadic relations are among the most difficult transactions to unearth and keep track of in the family. Yet they are of the greatest importance to the dynamics of role conflict and thus to the way in which the family system is organized and functions.

Referral is invoked whenever a family comes to a community agency for help and is inevitably associated with the role of the psychiatrist or other mental health worker. Implicitly or explicitly, the helper is asked to judge, referee, or take sides. The interviewers seeing our families are inevitably pitted against each other in a semicoalition with the particular member of the family they are seeing. This process is neutralized by our team approach in which the interviewers exchange information continuously with each other, permitting all of them to obtain a balanced view of the over-all family process. If there is delay in the collaborative interchange between interviewers, then the coalitions are apt to get out of hand. It seems a good working rule that the more information available to the person taking the role of the third party, the easier it is for him to avoid getting entangled in a coalition. As a corollary to this proposition, the more information available to the third person, the easier it is for him to help the role partners to a novel solution and to avoid a manipulated solution of the conflict.

(9) *Exploring* is the next step in role modification. Ego and alter probe and test each other's capacity to establish a novel solution. This process was already initiated in the joking phase, but now it is undertaken more seriously. If a third party has been able to avoid becoming entangled in a coalition, he can be of great help in promoting exploration. To a considerable extent, this describes the activity of the psychiatrist, case worker, nurse, or whoever is involved in the solution of a family problem. It is almost always accompanied by temporary relapses to an induction procedure, but once initiated, it tends to be self-steering. Ego and alter propose and reject possible solutions. This is accomplished not so much

through verbal formulations as through actual behavior, although both paths toward the solution are probably necessary.

(10) *Compromising.* After a sufficient amount of exploration, ego and alter come to see that restoration of equilibrium involves some change in the goals each desired or in the values by which they were guided. Thus they must settle for somewhat different complementary roles than those with which they started. If the process of re-equilibration has involved a successful referral, the third person takes very little part in the actual compromise solution. His role has accomplished its function when exploration moves re-equilibration to the threshold of compromise.

(11) *Consolidating* is the last step. It is required because the compromise solution is characterized by novelty, and cognitive strain is still present. Even though ego and alter establish a compromise, they must still learn how to make it work. To put the matter somewhat differently, compromise can be defined as the adjustment and redistribution of goals. Then consolidating is associated with the adjustment and redistribution of rewards. The roles are modified through the redistribution of goals. The new roles still have to be worked through and internalized by ego and alter as they discover how to reward each other in playing the new roles.

Conclusion

The study of how the family functions and maintains itself as a going system is greatly facilitated by the observation of role transactions concerned with equilibrium (high complementarity of roles), disequilibrium (low complementarity of roles), and re-equilibration (restoration of complementarity). I suspect that these same processes occur in other small-scale social systems, such as a factory or a mental hospital. To what extent they can be detected in large-scale social systems, such as a total society, I do not know. In a small-scale system such as the family, most of the process which can be seen by the observer is concerned with equilibrium. Complementarity of roles is high, decision-making is low, and most events take place automatically, leaving a considerable degree of spontaneity to the persons in transaction with each other. This is the routine, the way the system usually works. However, there are inevitable strains in any such system, and these give rise to disequilibrium. The strains can be analyzed in terms of the cognitive, goal, allocative, instrumental, and value structures of the roles. A strain represents a discrepancy in the expectations of any ego and alter with respect to these role structures. Thus it can be described in terms of role conflict. Strain gives rise to anxiety because, if left unchecked it will lead to a rupture of the role relations, and thus to a disruption of the system. Without a discussion of the origin of this anxiety in the basic structure and function of the intrapsychic process, it can be said that the role conflict gives rise to defensive processes both in the person and in the family system. For the family system, this reactive process can be described as an attempt to restore the complementarity of roles. The process itself can be called re-equilibration, since its effect is to restore the equilibrium which has been shattered.

Re-equilibration can be analyzed as an eleven-step process. The first five of these steps are manipulative. Ego attempts by persuasion or by some other means to get alter to comply with his expectations. If compliance is achieved and alter takes the necessary complementary role, then equilibrium is restored. For this reason, these steps are grouped together as a process called role induction. The last five steps are based on mutual insight rather than manipulation. They lead to a novel solution of the role conflict underlying the disequilibrium. These steps are grouped together in a process called role modification. The sixth step is intermediate between the two groups, since it can lead either to induction or modification.

If modification is successful, then the new solution of the role conflict sinks into the normal routine of the family. The "problem" has disappeared. In this way modification differs from induction. Induction is primarily defensive. The disequilibrium is warded off, but it is always likely to crop up again. It is an unsettled problem to the system, and the resolution of the strain is more apparent than real. In this way the role conflict becomes internalized by the members of the family and is likely to be productive either of a neurotic symptom or of difficulties in interpersonal relations. In dealing with emotionally disturbed persons, whether in office practice or in a mental institution, one observes the appearance of new versions of the old, unsettled family role conflict. Therefore, it is fruitful to examine the role systems which the patient recreates in these settings to see in what way they reproduce the defensive, inductive procedures which were experienced in the family. Also it is necessary to discover in what way the new institutional settings may have elaborated role conflicts and inductive re-equilibrations—because of their own internal organization—which resemble the original strain in the family.

30 The Emotionally Disturbed Child as the Family Scapegoat

EZRA F. VOGEL and NORMAN W. BELL

Continuing the same line of thought presented in the previous paper by Spiegel, the editors here present a research report on their work with families of disturbed children. This paper is concerned with why the child is assigned a particular role in the family and how he is induced to take that role and to stay in it. Although this sort of role assignment and induction is deleterious for the child's development, it is a type of leadership, and it reduces the integrative problems faced by the family. Once again processes which are presumably universal are highlighted in abnormal cases. Since this paper attempts to account for the development of a particular type of personality state in terms of family processes, it is also relevant to Part IV of this book, which deals with the interrelationships of family and personality systems.

The phenomenon of scapegoating is as old as human society. Sir James Frazer records, in *The Golden Bough*,[1] numerous instances, reaching back to antiquity, of public scapegoats, human and other. He views the process of scapegoating as one in which ". . . the evil influences are embodied in a visible form or are at least supposed to be loaded upon a material medium, which acts as a vehicle to draw them off from the people, village, or town."[2] The scapegoat's function ". . . is simply to effect a total clearance of all the ills that have been infesting a people."[3] Frazer was dealing with the phenomenon at the level of a society, tribe, village, or town. It is the purpose of this paper to examine the same phenomenon within families, by viewing an emotionally disturbed child as an embodiment of certain types of conflicts between parents. This pattern is a special case of a common phenomenon, the achievement of group unity through the scapegoating of a particular member. It is, perhaps, more widely known that a group may achieve unity through projection of hostilities to the outside,[4] but there are also a large number of cases where members of a particular group are able to achieve unity through scapegoating a particular member of that group. Thus, the deviant within the group may perform a valuable function for the group, by channeling group tensions and providing a basis for solidarity.

The notion that the family is in large part responsible for the emotional health of the child is a compelling one in contemporary behavioral science.

Specially prepared for this volume on the basis of work done by the authors in connection with a broader research project, "Cultural Values, Family Roles, and the Mental Health or Illness of the Individual." The research was directed by Drs. John P. Spiegel and Florence R. Kluckhohn and supported by the National Institute of Mental Health and the Pauline and Louis G. Cowan Foundation.

By and large, however, the research has focused largely on the mother-child relationship, and the independent variable by which the mother-child relationship and the child-rearing practices are usually explained is the personality and developmental history of the mother. Recently, an attempt has also been made to treat the father-child relationship, again largely in terms of the personality and developmental history of the father. While in clinical practice there is some awareness of family dynamics, in the literature, the family has largely been treated simply as a collection of personalities, and the child's personality development has been seen almost exclusively as a direct result of the separate personalities of his parents.[5] Rarely is the interaction of parents treated as a significant independent variable influencing childhood development. Even when broader cultural patterns have been considered, childhood development has been related to child-rearing practices and socialization into the culture, with little consideration of the family as the mediating unit.

Data for this paper are derived from the intensive study[6] of a small group of "disturbed" families, each with an emotionally disturbed child, and a matched group of "well" families without clinically manifest disturbance in any child. Of the nine families in each group, three were Irish-American, three Italian-American, and three old-American. The families were seen by a team including psychiatrists, social workers, psychologists, and social scientists. The disturbed families, on which this paper is based, were seen weekly in the offices of a psychiatric clinic and in their homes over periods ranging from one to four years. Detailed information was gathered about the members' developmental histories and character structure, but even more specific data were obtained about current processes.

The present paper is concerned with how a child in the family, the emotionally disturbed child, was used as a scapegoat for the conflicts between parents and what the functions and dysfunctions of this scapegoating are for the family.

In all the disturbed families it was found that a particular child had become involved in tensions existing between the parents.[7] In the "well" families used for control purposes, either the tensions between the parents were not so severe or else the tensions were handled in such a way that the children did not become pathologically involved. In general, both parents of the emotionally disturbed child had many of the same underlying conflicts, but in relationship to each other, they felt themselves to be at opposite poles, so that one spouse would act out one side of the conflict and the other would act out the other side of the conflict. They had developed an equilibrium in which they minimized contact with each other and minimized expressions of affect, particularly hostility, which they strongly felt for each other, and this made it possible for them to live with each other.[8] But this equilibrium had many difficulties, the most serious of which was the scapegoating of a child.

1. Sources of Tension That Lead to Scapegoating

It is our contention that scapegoating is produced by the existence of tensions between parents which have not been satisfactorily resolved in other ways. The spouses in the disturbed families had deep fears about their marital relationship and about the partner's behavior. They did not feel they could predict accurately how the other would respond to their own behavior. Yet, the other's response was of very great importance and was thought to be potentially very damaging. The partners did not feel they could deal with the situation by direct communication, because this might be too dangerous, and they resorted to manipulations of masking, evading, and the like. This atmosphere of tension has several sources. One of the sources was the personality problems of each spouse, but in the present analysis the focus will be on the group sources of the tension. These tensions usually have several sources. At a very general level, one of the main sources of tension was conflict in cultural value orientations.[9] Value orientations are abstract, general conceptions of the nature of human nature and man's relationship to it, of man's relation to man, of the most significant time dimension, and of the most valued type of activity. All societies have preferences and alternative preferences to these basic dimensions; these preferences are expressed within a wide range of phenomena. In complex ways, they are related to personality and social structure and to more specific values. When people are in the process of acculturation, as was the case with the families of Irish and Italian backgrounds, many possibilities for value-orientation conflict arise. Any one individual may have been socialized into conflicting or confused patterns, and be unsuccessful in bridging the gap. Marriage partners may have been socialized into different patterns and be working on different assumptions. All our disturbed families had problems of these sorts. Some were trying to shift quickly to a set of orientations they had not thoroughly internalized, and without having neutralized previous orientations. Others were trying to live by conflicting orientations.[10]

A common example of the cultural value conflicts was the conflict centered around the problems of individual performance. There were considerable pulls toward the American middle-class achievement patterns. In families which had partially internalized both sets of value orientations, it was impossible to live up to both sets of values, and whichever the family chose, this meant that certain conflicts would result.

Another source of tension was the relations of the family and the larger community. Disturbed families usually had problems in this area, rejecting and/or being rejected by the community. In some cases, a family had very severe disapproval of a very close-knit ethnic neighborhood directed at them. In other cases, families had moved from ethnic neighborhoods to more fashionable suburbs and suffered in their own eyes by comparison to their new neighbors. Consequently, their social relationships with these neighbors were often minimal; when they did exist, they were usually strained or else one spouse had fairly good relationships with some friends and the partner had poor relationships with these friends. All families, to a greater or lesser extent, had problems in their relationships with families of orientation. Typically, the wife was strongly attached to her parents and antagonistic towards her husband's family, while the husband was attached to his parents and antagonistic to his wife's family. If either spouse was critical of his in-laws, the partner typically defended his own parents and became more critical of his in-laws. If one spouse was critical of his own parents, the partner was often friendly to them. The unbalanced attachments to parents and parents-in-law was not resolved. Changes usually produced more tension, but the basic sources of strain remained unchanged.[11]

2. The Selection of the Scapegoat

The tensions produced by unresolved conflicts were so severe that they could not be contained without some discharge. It is not surprising that some appropriate object was chosen to symbolize the conflicts and draw off the tension. Conceivably, some person or group outside the family could serve in this capacity. However, in these disturbed families, the parents had by and large internalized the standards of the surrounding community sufficiently so that they had great difficulty in finding a legitimate basis for scapegoating outsiders. In addition, most of these families had very tenuous ties with the community, and since they were very concerned about being accepted, they could not afford to antagonize their associates. While some of the families did, at times, have strong feelings of antagonism toward various members of the community in which they lived, they could rarely express this antagonism directly. Even if at times they were able to manifest their antagonism, this usually led to many additional complications, and the family preferred to scapegoat its own child.[12]

Channeling the tensions within the family did not lead to difficulties with the outside, but usually the latent hostilities between the husband and wife made it very difficult to deal with problems openly between them. There was always danger the partner might become too angry, which would lead to severe and immediate difficulties. A number of factors made a child the most appropriate object through which to deal with family tensions. First of all, the child was in a relatively powerless position compared to the parents. While he was dependent on the parents and could not leave the family, he was not able effectively to counter the parents' superior power. Although the parents' defenses were fairly brittle in comparison with those of well parents, still their defenses were much stronger than those of their children. Because the child's personality is still very flexible, he can be molded to adopt the particular role which the family assigns to him. When the child does take on many of the characteristics which the parents dislike in themselves and each other, he becomes a symbolically appropriate object on which to focus their own anxieties. Since the person scapegoated often develops such severe tensions that he is unable to perform his usual task roles, it is important that those family members performing essential, irreplaceable functions for the family not be scapegoated. The child has relatively few tasks to perform in the family, compared to the parents or other elders, and his disturbance does not ordinarily interfere with the successful performance of the necessary family tasks. The "cost" in dysfunction of the child is low relative to the functional gains for the whole family.

In all cases, with partial exception of one family, a particular child was chosen as the scapegoat, while other children were relatively free of pathology. The selecting of a particular child is not a random matter; one child is the best symbol. Just as a dream condenses a variety of past and present experiences and a variety of emotional feelings, the scapegoat condenses a variety of social and psychological problems impinging on the family.

Who is selected as the scapegoat is intimately related to the sources of tension. Where value-orientation conflicts existed, the child chosen was the one who best symbolized these conflicts. For example, if the conflicts revolved about achievement, a child who failed to achieve according to expectations could become the symbol of failure. Alternatively, a child might be an appropriate object because he was achieving independently and thus violating norms of loyalty to the group.

The position of the child in the sibling group frequently became a focus for the unresolved childhood problems of the parents. If the parents' most serious unresolved problems were with male figures, the child chosen to represent the family conflict was usually a male child. Similarly, sibling order could be a strong factor. If one or both parents had difficulties with older brothers, an older boy in the family might become the scapegoat.

In two cases, the sex or sibling position of the child seemed to be particularly important in the selection of a particular child as the family scapegoat. In one of these cases, the mother was the oldest of three siblings and had considerable feelings of rivalry with her next younger sister which had never been effectively resolved. Although the father had two older siblings, they were so much older that to him they were a separate family. In his effective family environment, he was the older of two children and had considerable feelings of rivalry toward a younger brother who displaced him and for whom he subsequently had to care. This couple has three children, and there was an unusual amount of rivalry between the oldest and the second sibling. Both the parents sided very strongly with the oldest child. They were continuously conscious of the middle child bothering the older, for which they severely criticized this middle child. There are many striking parallels, even to small details, in the relationship between the parents and their next younger siblings and the relationship between their oldest child and the next younger sibling.

Another pattern revolved about the identification of a child with a parent whom he resembled. This was found in all families, sick and well, in one form or another; but in the disturbed families, the child was seen as possessing very undesirable traits, and although the parent actually possessed the same traits, the focus of attention was the child and not the parent. In one family, in particular, this pattern was striking. The father and the eldest son had very similar physical characteristics; not only did they have the same first name but both were called by the same diminutive name by the mother. At times, the social worker seeing the mother was not certain whether the mother was talking about her husband or her son. The wife's concerns about the husband's occupational adequacy were not dealt with directly, but the focus for her affect was the child and his school performance. In fact, the son was criticized by his mother for all the characteristics which she disliked in her husband, but she was unable to criticize her husband directly for these characteristics. She channeled all her feelings, especially anxiety and hostility, to the child, although her husband had similar problems. Furthermore, in order to control her feelings toward her husband, she remained very aloof and distant and was not able to express to him her positive or negative feelings. While she channeled many criticisms and anxieties through the child, she also expressed many of her positive feelings to the child, thereby leading to severe Oedipal conflicts. The husband was not happy about his wife being so aloof from him, but on the other hand he found that by co-operating with his wife in criticizing the child, he was able to keep the burden of problems away from himself. He thus joined with the wife in projecting his own difficulties and problems onto the child and in dealing with them as the child's problems rather than as his own.

In three of the families, the scapegoat had considerably lower intelligence than did the other children in the family. In all these families, there were serious conflicts about the value of achievement, and the parents had great difficulty themselves in living up to their own achievement aspirations. In all these three cases, the parents were unable to accept the fact that their children had limited abilities, and they continually held up impossible standards for these children. Although all three children had I.Q.'s in the 80's or below and had failed one grade or more, all three mothers stated that they intended that their children should go to college. At the beginning of therapy, one of the mothers hoped her son would attend medical school and become a doctor; another had begun to put away a small amount of money from a very tight budget for her daughter's college education, even though the daughter's intelligence was that of a moron. At the beginning of therapy, none of the parents was able to deal directly with his own difficulties in achievement. In contrast, in one of the families, there were two children in the family who had very low intelligence, one of whom had failed a grade in school, but the family scapegoat was a boy who had normal intelligence. In this case, the parents, who had average intelligence, had resolved their conflicts about achievement by denying that they were interested in achievement and accepting their social position. This child of slightly higher intelligence and greater physical activity was seen by them as a very aggressive child who was always doing too much, and the parents were continually worried that he was "too smart."[13]

In a number of cases, the disturbed child either had a serious physical disease when he was young or a striking physical abnormality such as a hare lip, bald spots in the hair, or unusually unattractive facial features. The mere existence of some such abnormality seemed to draw attention to one particular child, so that if there were some sorts of anxieties or problems in the family at all, the child with the physical peculiarities seemed to become the focus of the family problems. Here again, however, it was not the mere existence of a physical defect but its meaning[14] in the life of the family which gave it its significance. For example, in some families there was a feeling that they had committed certain sins by not living up to their ideals, for instance by using contraceptives. This was a very common problem, since many families could not possibly live up to the two opposing sets of ideals which they had at least partially internalized. The child's physical abnormality became a symbol of the family's sin of not having lived up to some partially-internalized values, and the malformed child was seen as a sinful child who was not living up to the standards of the group. Since the family's relationship with the community was often tenuous, the fact that one of their children had physical abnormalities that made the child the focus of neighborhood ridicule, served to make the parents increasingly ashamed of the child's physical characteristics and to focus increasingly more attention on this child. For example, one of the main concerns of the family with the unusually ugly child was that other children were continually teasing her about her appearance. However, the concern was less for the child herself, and more for the whole family. Her problems symbolized the parents' past and present problems with the neighborhood; rather than sympathize with the child, they abused her all the more. In another case in which a female child's physical illness became a focus of the family's problems, the parents were extremely concerned about her safety, which was again related in part to the potential dangers in social relationships with the outside world. As a result of the girl's illness, the family became much more cautious than was necessary, and on some occasions they were even reluctant to accept medical advice that she could participate in certain activities without danger to her health. The continual contacts that the child had with middle-class professional personnel through hospitalization and clinic visits led her to accept certain middle-class American values more than did the rest of the family, and the family was continually expressing the feeling that she had different attitudes after hospitalization and contact with hospital personnel. The disliked attitudes ascribed to the child were in general those of middle-class American culture.[15] Not only abnormalities but general body type could become the symbol to call forth scapegoating. In two families, the spouses had many problems in their sexual life. Rather than face these maladjustments directly, the problems were expressed through concern about the masculinity and normality of a slender, graceful son.

While the general process of symbolization of a scapegoat is very similar to the dream symbolization, there is one problem in the family selection of a scapegoat which is not met in the selection of a dream symbol, and that is the problem of availability. While in dreams, any symbolic representation is open to the dreamer, in the family only a very small number of children are available as the potential scapegoats. Hence, when there is a serious family problem and no child is an appropriate symbol of the problem, there must be considerable cognitive distortion in order to permit the most appropriate one available to be used as a scapegoat. For example, in one family which was very concerned about the problems of achievement, the focus of the family's problems was the eldest son. Although he was receiving passing grades in school, whereas the parents had had very poor school records, the parents were very critical of his school performance. Because of this pressure, the child worked hard and was able to get somewhat better marks on his next report card. However, the mother stoutly maintained that her son didn't deserve those grades, that he must have cheated, and she continued to criticize him for his school performance.

The other aspect of the problem of availability resulted from the fact that the parents apparently have had tensions since early in marriage. As nearly as it was possible to reconstruct the marital history, it appeared that the spouses had selected each other partly on the basis of the fact that they shared many of the same conflicts and understood each other quite well. Not long after marriage, however, they seemed to have become polarized in their conflicts, so that one parent represented one side of the conflict and the other represented the other side. This seems to have given each of the spouses a way of handling his own conflicts and allowed each to remain fairly consistent and well integrated by projecting difficulties onto the partner. However, it also led to very severe difficulties in the marital relationship and created many tensions which were quickly displaced onto the first available and appropriate object, very often the first child. Since the eldest child was the first one available for scapegoating, he often seems to have been assigned this role and, once assigned, has continued in it. Perhaps because of his prior availability and his closer involvement in the adult world, he is a more appropriate object for the scapegoating.[16] In the one case in which a child was able to escape the scapegoat role by decreasing his attachment to the home, the next most appropriate child was used in the scapegoat role.

3. Induction of the Child into the Scapegoat Role

If the child is to be a "satisfactory" scapegoat, he must carry out his role as a "problem child." The problem behavior must be reinforced strongly enough so that it will continue in spite of the hostility and anxiety it produces in the child. This delicate balance is possible only because the parents have superior sanction power over the child, can define what he should or should not do, and control what he does or does not do. This balance necessarily requires a large amount of inconsistency in the ways parents handle the child.

The most common inconsistency was between the implicit (or unconscious) and the explicit role induction.[17] In all cases, certain behavior of the child violated recognized social norms. In some instances stealing, fire-setting, expressions of hostility, or unco-operativeness affected the child's relationships with people outside the family. In other instances, bed-wetting, resistance to parental orders, or expression of aggression to siblings affected relationships in the family. But in all instances, while the parents explicitly criticized the child and at times even punished him, they supported in some way, usually implicitly, the persistence of the very behavior which they criticized. This permission took various forms: failure to follow through on threats, delayed punishment, indifference to and acceptance of the symptom, unusual interest in the child's symptom, or considerable secondary gratification offered to the child because of his symptom. The secondary gratification usually took the form of special attention and exemption from certain responsibilities. While the parents had internalized social norms sufficiently to refrain from violating the norms themselves, they had not sufficiently internalized them to prevent giving encouragement to their children for acting out their own repressed wishes. The wish to violate these norms was transferred to the child, but the defenses against this wish were never as strong in the child.[18]

Another type of inconsistency seen was that one parent would encourage one type of behavior, but the other parent would encourage an opposing type of behavior. The result again was that the child was caught in the conflict. This also permitted one spouse to express annoyance to the other indirectly without endangering the marital relationship. For example, in one case, the father objected to the son's leaving toys lying around and would violently explode at the child for such behavior, implying that the mother was wrong in permitting him to do this. The mother realized that the father exploded at such behavior and did not stop the father since she "knew he was right." Nevertheless, she often indicated that the child need not bother picking up the toys, since she felt that he was too young to have to do such things by himself and that the father was too strict. If the mother's encouragement of the behavior annoying to the father was explicit, there would be danger that the father's hostility would be directed at the mother rather than the child. By keeping the encouragement implicit the mother was able to deny that she had encouraged the child. The father was usually willing to accept this denial, even if he did not believe it, rather than risk an explosion with his wife. In some instances, however, the other spouse was angered or felt compelled to criticize the other for not handling the child properly. Then the encouragement of the child to behave in a certain way would have to become more subtle to avoid criticism of the other spouse, another delicate balance to maintain. A parent had to give sufficient encouragement to the child to perform the act, without making it so obvious that his spouse felt obliged to criticize him.

In addition to the inconsistent pressures resulting from the difference between explicit and implicit expectations and from the differences between the expectations of the two parents, the child also had to deal with changes in each parent's expectations. From the parent's conscious point of view, this inconsistency resulted from an attempt to reconcile two conflicting desires: teaching the child to behave properly and not being "too hard on the child." When a parent was consciously attempting to teach the child proper behavior, he was extremely aggressive and critical.[19] At other times, the parent felt he had been too critical of the child and permitted him to behave in the same way without punishment, and would be extremely affectionate and supportive. While the explanation given for this inconsistency was that he wanted to teach the desired behavior without being "too hard on the child," its latent function was to prevent the child from consistently living up to the ostensibly desired behavior and to preserve the disliked behavior. The period of not being "too hard on the child" served to reinforce the disapproved behavior and the period of "being firm" permitted the parents to express their anxieties and hostility. This balance was also very delicate since it was always possible that negative sanctions would become so severe that the child would refuse to behave in such a way that parents felt he could legitimately be punished.

The delicacy of this balance was perhaps best exemplified by the problem of bed-wetting. Parents complained about bed-wetting, but at the same time they could not bring themselves to do anything to alter the child's behavior. If the therapists could get both parents to be firm at the same time, the child would usually stop bed-wetting. Very soon, however, by putting a rubber sheet on the bed, or buying special night clothes "just in case he wets," the child was encouraged again to wet. One mother succeeded several times in finding methods to stop her son's wetting, but immediately stopped using them "since he's stopped now." In several cases, the parents would alternate in being concerned and trying to be firm and being unconcerned and implicitly encouraging the behavior, at all times remaining inconsistent, one with the other. It seemed clear that whether or not the child wet his bed was a relatively sensitive index of just where the balance of rewards from the parents lay. In general, however, the implicit demands carried the greater sanction power and the child continued with the behavior of which the parents unconsciously approved and consciously disapproved. Presumably, the sanctions of the parents against bed-wetting would increase as the child grew older, and the balance would become delicate only at that later time.

Since these conflicting expectations existed over a long period of time, it is not surprising that the child internalized these conflicts. Once a child was selected as a deviant, there was a circular reaction which tended to perpetuate this role assignment. Once he had responded to his parents' implicit wishes and acted in a somewhat disturbed manner, the parents could treat him as if he really were a problem. The child would respond to these expectations and the vicious cycle was set in motion. Both the child and the parents, then, had complementary expectations. The particular role assigned to the child was appropriately rewarded. It is difficult, if not impossible, to distinguish just at what point the parents began treating the child as if he were a problem and at what point the child actually did have internalized problems. There does not seem to be any sudden development of the child's problems; rather, it is a process occurring over a period of time. By the time the family was seen in the clinic, the vicious cycle was well established, and the child had internalized his disturbed role to such an extent that it was difficult to effect change only by removing external pressures. This was, of course, particularly true for older and more disturbed children. The fact that the child becomes disturbed adds stability to the role system, so that once set in motion, scapegoating did not easily pass from one child to another. In the well families, when scapegoating did take place, it was less severe and did not become stabilized with one child as a continual scapegoat.

4. The Rationalization of Scapegoating

When a scapegoating situation was established, a relatively stable equilibrium of the family was achieved. However, there were difficulties in maintaining the equilibrium. Parents had considerable guilt about the way they treated the child, and when the child was identified as disturbed by neighbors, teachers, doctors, or other outside agencies, pressure was brought to bear for some action to be taken. When called upon to explain, parents did not have much difficulty in explaining why they were so concerned about the child, but they did have great difficulty in rationalizing their aggressive and libidinal expressions to the children.

One way in which the parents rationalized their behavior was to define themselves, rather than the children, as victims. They stressed how much difficulty there was coping with all the problems posed by their child. For example, mothers of bed-wetters complained about the problems of keeping sheets clean and the impossibility of the child staying overnight at friends' or relatives' homes. Such rationalizations seemed to relieve some of the guilt for victimizing the children and served as a justification for continued expressions of annoyance toward the children.

Another way was to emphasize how fortunate their children really were. For most of these parents, the standard of living provided for their children was much higher than the standard of living they enjoyed when they were children. One of the central complaints of these parents, particularly the fathers, was that the children wanted too much and got much more than the parents ever got when they were children. This was seen by the parents as a legitimate excuse for depriving their children of the toys, privileges, and other things they wanted, and for refusing to recognize the children's complaints that they were not getting things. A closely related type of rationalization stems from the change of child-rearing practices over the past generation. The parents felt that their parents were much stricter than they were with their children and that children nowadays "get away with murder." Many of the parents had acute conflicts about how strict to be with children, and when the parents did express aggression to the children, they often defined it as beneficial strictness and "giving the child a lesson." Since their own parents were much more severe with them, their own children don't realize "how good they have it."

The parents also used various specific norms to justify their behavior. Even though the parents may be giving implicit encouragement to break these norms, the fact that these social norms are explicitly recognized gives the parents a legitimate basis for punishing the children. As long as the permission for disobeying the sanctions is implicit, it is always possible for the parents to deny that they are really giving it. In general, these parents were reluctant to admit that their child had an emotional disturbance or that he was behaving the way he was because of certain inner problems. They generally interpreted the disturbed child's behavior as willful badness. They felt that the child could behave differently if he really wanted to. Hence, what was needed, in their view, was not consideration, advice, and help, but a "lesson" in how to behave, i.e., severe reprimands and punishment; but even this they could not give. At times, the parents attempted to deny completely that they were scape-goating this particular child. They insisted very rigidly that "we treat all the children just the same." At other times, the parents insisted that this one particular child was just different from all others, implying that this child deserved punishment and that they were good parents since their other children have turned out so well.

Frequently, the mothers expressed, although inconsistently, unusually strong affection for a son. They justified this almost invariably in the same way: the child had problems and difficulties and thus needed more help and care than the other children. However, what they considered care and protection far exceeded the usual limits. This can be seen for example, in the mother who carried her twelve-year-old son from the bed to the bathroom so that he could avoid bed-wetting, in the mother who con-tinually fondled her adolescent son and called him "lovie," and in the frequent slips of the tongues by a variety of family members which identified the mother and son as spouses. Fathers, on the other hand, often had special attachments to, and fondness for, daughters.

All these attempts of the parents to rationalize their behavior had a very defensive quality and showed the difficulty these parents had in reconciling their own behavior with general social norms about child-rearing. In the more severely disturbed families, the pressing nature of their problems required serious distortion of social norms, but in the mildly disturbed families, more attention was given to the social norms, and attempts were made to express emotions in more acceptable ways. In any event, much energy was required to keep the balance stable, a state which required co-ordination of many subtle and inconsistent feelings and behaviors. It was, in effect, an "armed truce," and the danger of an explosion was constantly present.

5. Functions and Dysfunctions of Scapegoating

a) Functions.—Although the present paper has been concerned with the dynamics of the family as a group in relation to an emotionally dis-turbed child, some comments should be made on the functions that scapegoating serves for the parents individually and for external social systems. For the parents, scapegoating served as a personality-stabilizing process. While the parents of these children did have serious internal conflicts, the projection of these difficulties onto the children served to minimize and control them. Thus, in spite of their personality difficulties, the parents were able to live up to their commitments to the wider society, expressing a minimum of their difficulties in the external economic and political systems. Most of the parents were able to maintain positions as steady workers and relatively respectable community members.

While the scapegoating of the child helped the parents live up to their obligations to the community, often they did not live up to their obligations as adequately as other families, and the whole family became a scapegoat for the community. Then the same mechanisms existed between the outer community and the family as between parents and child. The families, like their children, seldom fought back effectively; instead they channeled their additional frustrations and tensions through the child. Once established, many forces may play into the scapegoating situation. Though the child suffered additional burdens, through the medium of the family, he helped drain off the tension of the broader community in relation to a particular family.

From the point of view of the family, the primary function of scapegoating is that it permits the family to maintain its solidarity. In all the disturbed families, there were very severe strains which continually threatened to disrupt the family.[20] In all the disturbed families, very serious dissatisfactions between spouses came to light during the course of therapy, which were much more severe than those found in the well families. In the two families with the most severely disturbed children, when the scapegoating of the child eased up during therapy, the explosions between parents became so severe that there was serious fear that the family might break up. In the one case in which the problems between spouses remained relatively latent throughout therapy, marital problems emerged more clearly after the termination of therapy, and this led to serious anxiety attacks of the father. Yet, considering these internal strains, all of these families have shown surprising stability. Only in one family had there been a brief period of voluntary separation between the parents, and it had occurred before their first child was born. By focusing on one particular child, the families were able to encapsulate problems and anxieties which could potentially disrupt various family processes. There seemed to be an added solidarity between the parents who stood united against the problem child. The fact that it is a child who is disturbed permits the parents to continue to perform the tasks necessary for household maintenance with relative stability. Since the child is in a dependent position and contibutes relatively little to family task activities, his malfunctioning does not seriously interfere with family stability.

b) Dysfunctions.—While the scapegoating of a child is effective in controlling major sources of tensions within the family, when a child becomes emotionally disturbed, this leads to disturbing secondary complications which are, however, generally less severe than the original tensions. One dysfunction is that certain realistic problems and extra tasks are created for the family. The child does require special care and attention. If, for example, the child is a bed-wetter, then the family must either wake him up regularly, or wash many sheets and take other pre-cautions. This becomes particularly acute when traveling, visiting, or attending camp. Often the child cannot be left alone, and someone must continually look after him. If the child is to receive treatment, then the parents must expend time and money in providing this.

In addition, while the child is responsive to the implicit sanctions of his parents, he, too, may develop mechanisms of fighting back and punishing his parents for the way they treat him. Often the child becomes very skilled in arousing his parents' anxieties or in consciously bungling something his parents want him to do. Of course, the mother, being present during most of the day, experiences more of this counteraggression, and this in part accounts for her readiness to bring the child in for treatment. In most of these families it was the mother who took the initiative in seeking treatment. It would appear that as long as she can carefully control the amount of hostility the child expresses to her, she can tolerate this dysfunction, but when hostility rises above a certain point she is willing to seek outside help.

While the functions of the scapegoat within the nuclear family clearly outweigh his dysfunctions, this is typically not the case with the child's relationship outside the nuclear family. While the family gives the child sufficient support to maintain his role in the family, the use of him as a scapegoat is often incompatible with equipping him to maintain an adjustment outside the nuclear family. This problem becomes particularly acute when the child begins important associations outside the nuclear family in relationship with peers and his teachers at school.[21] It is at this time that many referrals to psychiatric clinics are made.[22] While the child's behavior was perfectly tolerable to the parents before, his behavior suddenly becomes intolerable. While he may still be performing the role the family wants him to play in order to be a scapegoat, this comes into conflict with his role as a representative of the family. The family is thus in conflict between using the child as a scapegoat and identifying with the child because of his role as family representative to the outside. Both sides of this conflict are revealed most clearly in the one family which carried on a feud with the outside and alternated between punishing the daughter for her poor school behavior and criticizing the teachers and children in school for causing problems for their daughter. In nearly all of these disturbed families, school difficulty was a crucial factor in the decision to refer the child for psychiatric treatment. While the child's behavior was rewarded at home, it was not rewarded at school, and while the family could tolerate the child's maladaptive behavior at home, when the school took special note of the child's behavior, this proved embarrassing and troubling to the parents.

This problem in relation to the outside world is perhaps most striking in the case of the school, but it is also true, for example, in relationships with neighbors and relatives. Neighbors and relatives are likely to be very critical of the family for the child's disturbed behavior, and it is often at such times that the family makes the greatest effort to get rid of the child's maladaptive behavior. In those families which alternated between punishing and rewarding the child's behavior, difficulty with the outside was often a cue to the family to move into the stage of punishing and criticizing the child's behavior.

While, as a whole, the child's disturbance served to relieve family tensions, it often led to further family tensions. To the extent that outside norms or standards, by which the child does not abide, are considered legitimate, inevitable frustrations arise. While the parents made strenuous efforts to interpret this as a result of the child's behavior and not of their own behavior, this effort was never completely successful. In accordance with modern child rearing theory to which they are at least exposed, they consider themselves at least partly responsible for the disturbance of the child, and this seems to have been particularly true at the time of therapy. Thus, the child's disturbance feeds back into the problems which must be faced by the parents, and the marital pair often project the responsibility for the child's disturbance onto each other. The mother will say, for example, that the father doesn't spend enough time with the children, and the father will say that the mother doesn't manage the children properly. While this was thus dysfunctional to the marital relationship, it never became so prominent that the parents ceased using the child as a scapegoat. The predominant direction of aggression was still toward the badly behaved child rather than toward the other spouse.

While the disturbed behavior leads to some dysfunctions for the family, it is the personality of the child which suffers most as a result of the scapegoating. Any deviant or scapegoat within a group feels strong group pressure which creates considerable conflicts for him.[23] While other groups may also maintain their integration at the expense of the deviant, in the nuclear family this can be stabilized for a long period of time and result in far more serious personality impairment of the child assigned to the deviant role. The development of the emotional disturbance is simply part of the process of internalizing the conflicting demands placed upon him by his parents. While in the short run the child receives more rewards from the family for playing this role than for not playing this role, in the long run this leads to serious personality impairment. In short, the scapegoating mechanism is functional for the family as a group but dysfunctional for the emotional health of the child and for his adjustment outside the family of orientation.

31   *Legitimacy and the Incest Taboo*

KINGSLEY DAVIS

A primary group, such as the family, implies intense emotional ties among its members. The family is unique in that it has to incorporate both the permission of sexual access leading to procreation between some members (the spouses) and the prohibition of such contact between other members (siblings and parent-child pairs). The latter, the incest taboos, are universal on a society-wide basis and are among the strictest of prohibitions that exist. At the same time, as Professor Davis points out, there are the problems of binding the father to the mother and offspring and of legitimizing those offspring. In the accompanying selection, Davis defines the "principle of legitimacy" and shows why incest taboos are necessary to preserve an integration of the family which allows it to carry out the tasks it is assigned.

The structure of the human family is rooted not in biology but in the folkways and mores. This is why the exact form of the family varies significantly from one culture to another. Since the functions of the family are centered on reproduction, the institutional organization must utilize biological principles, and these set certain limits on the amount of cultural variation. The mores cannot require that men become pregnant or that women have fifty children each. But within limits the cultural organization can emphasize and suppress, add and subtract, guide and control, until it has created a family system that is functionally and structurally related to the rest of the social order. Without an institutional system for the performance of the family functions, these functions would not be performed. We have already seen that man as a species can survive only in a cultural milieu. There is nothing about the family, including sexual intercourse and the handling of the newborn child, that does not have to be learned. There is nothing about it that does not involve social definition and mutual rights and obligations. It is necessary, therefore, to examine some of the basic mores which support the structure of the family and

From Kingsley Davis, *Human Society* (New York: The Macmillan Co., 1949), pp. 399–405. Copyright 1949 by The Macmillan Co. and used with their kind permission.

which are as ubiquitous as the family itself. The first of these is what may be called the principle of legitimacy.

The weak link in the family group is the father-child bond. There is no necessary association and no easy means of identification between these two as there is between mother and child. In the reproductive groups of monkeys and apes, the male parent is held in the group, not by any interest in the offspring, but by his interest in the female. Among human beings, a bond is created between the father and his children by a complex set of folkways, mores, and laws. Similarly, a durable relation is created between him and the mother. The mother's relation to the child is also socially regulated, but in this case the bond is more easily established and maintained.

The social definition of fatherhood we may call, following Malinowski,[1] the "principle of legitimacy"—the universal social rule that "no child should be brought into the world without a man—and one man at that—assuming the role of sociological father, that is, guardian and protector, the male link between the child and the rest of the community."[2] Without this general rule, to which many others are subsidiary, there would be no family; hence it is as universal and fundamental as the familial institution itself. It prevails no matter what other conditions prevail. Children may be an asset or a liability, prenuptial and extramarital intercourse may be forbidden or sanctioned, still the rule runs that a father is indispensable for the full social status of the child and its mother. Otherwise, the child is illegitimate and the mother disesteemed.

Obviously the principle of legitimacy implies to some extent the control of sexual relations, since sex relations are a necessary condition of procreation. But all communities make distinctions between the various links in the procreative process. Most societies, for example, dissociate coitus and parenthood. "Broadly speaking, it may be said that freedom of intercourse though not universally is yet generally prevalent in human societies. Freedom of conception outside marriage is, however, never allowed, or at least in extremely few communities and under very exceptional circumstances";[3] and if allowed it is likely to be interrupted with abortion or the resulting offspring may be eliminated through infanticide. In those societies where prenuptial intercourse is regarded as perfectly legitimate, marriage is yet a *conditio sine qua non* of legitimate children. Persons having free intercourse in such societies either escape pregnancy or parenthood by one means or another, or they marry when pregnancy occurs. Liberty of sexual intercourse is therefore *not* identical with liberty of parenthood. "Marriage cannot be defined as the licensing of sexual intercourse, but rather as the licensing of parenthood."[4] The early anthropologists, who were so interested in the question of whether or not extramarital intercourse was permitted in the tribes they studied, would have done better to ask the more profound question of whether or not unmarried parenthood was allowed. A positive answer to the second question would have unhinged our notion of social organization far more than a positive answer to the first question.

There are various ways in which the principle of legitimacy may be violated. The offense is simple when the man and woman are unmarried to anyone, because by subsequently getting married to each other they may legitimize their illicit offspring. But if either of them is already married to another party, the illegitimacy is adulterous and may be defined as either unimportant or exceptionally bad, depending on how much importance the culture attaches to physiological paternity as against sociological fatherhood. If the two parties are closely kin to each other (members of the same family), the illegitimacy is incestuous and is everywhere (except in ancient Egypt and in certain royal lines) considered horrible.[5] Obviously if a society is to have a family institution it must condemn illegitimacy, but why is incestuous illegitimacy or simply incestuous intercourse an object of such special condemnation? Why, in other words, do incest taboos exist? No one can claim a scientific understanding of the family, or indeed of society, without an answer to this question.

The family is an *organized* group. Its members occupy a definite set of mutual statuses, interact according to definite behavior patterns, and are motivated by reciprocal attitudes and sentiments. Without this institutional organization, the family's performance of the four main functions mentioned above could not be accomplished. Sheer animal mating alone would not produce a new generation—not even in the physical sense, much less in the social sense. It is through the institutional organization that the sexual urge is harnessed to the work of creating a new generation, that the procreators are held responsible for the welfare and socialization of the young. Through this organization, the offspring are provided with a peaceful and protected milieu in which they safely reach maturity and from which they are well launched into the competition of the larger society. Should the different statuses and relationships in the family become confused, the organization and functional efficiency of the family would be lost. The incest taboos confine sexual relations and sentiments to the married pair alone, excluding such things from the relation of parent and child, brother and sister. In this way confusion is prevented and family organization is maintained. The incest taboos, therefore, exist because they are essential to and form part of the family structure.

Suppose that brothers and sisters were allowed to violate the incest taboos. Consider first the effect of the sexual rivalry which would develop between brothers and between sisters. If, for example, there were two brothers and only one sister in the family, sexual jealousy would probably destroy the brotherly attitudes supposed to prevail; the conflictful situation that would result would not be sufficiently peaceful for satisfactory socialization. Since siblings are generally reared in the same household, such rivalry would be stimulated very early and would be very intense. Moreover, since the number and sex distribution of siblings in different families is impossible to control, no standard institutional pattern could be worked out so that jealousy would be a support rather than a menace. Consider next the confusion that would result when children were born of such brother-sister relations. The brother would be not only his child's "father" but also his "uncle"; the sister would be not only her child's "mother" but also his "aunt." In addition, there would arise a family within a family, a cancerous growth upsetting the original group and leading to an extreme concentration of each family within itself.

If sexual relations between parent and child were permitted, sexual rivalry between mother and daughter and between father and son would almost surely arise, and this rivalry would be incompatible with the sentiments necessary between the two. Should children be born the confusion of statuses would be phenomenal. The incestuous child of a father-daughter union, for example, would be a brother of his own mother, i.e. the son of his own sister; a stepson of his own grandmother; possibly a brother of his own uncle; and certainly a grandson of his own father. This confusion of generations would be contrary to the authoritarian relations so essential to the fulfillment of parental duties. The daughter receiving attention from her father, furthermore, would be in a weak position. Whereas sexual relations usually connote equality of status between the parties, father-daughter incest would put the daughter in a position of subordination. While she was still immature the father could use his power to take advantage of her.[6] Her position vis-à-vis the parent is one of dependence and submissiveness. Legitimate sexual relations ordinarily involve a certain amount of reciprocity. Sex is exchanged for something equally valuable, not squandered or extorted. A woman is expected to use her attractiveness to gain certain legitimate ends such as recognition, status, and a husband. The family stands back of her and helps her to make a respectable bargain. Monopoly by the father and his jealous resentment of outsiders would jeopardize the girl's opportunity. The child must be protected from parental aggression during her immaturity and enabled to make use of her status as a female upon something like equal terms. But such protection is not easy, because the temptation presented by a young and attractive member of the opposite sex in the same household is very strong. Only the most stringent taboos can restrain the parent from the thought and the deed. The taboo on incest is one of the strongest mores in existence.

When we think of the family's functions, its peculiar structure, and its reciprocal sentiments and roles, we can understand why the prohibition of incest is absolutely indispensable to its existence as a part of social

organization. Since no society can get along without an efficient reproductive unit, we find that incest taboos are everywhere imposed, their violation viewed with a horror so profound that some observers have mistakenly judged it to be instinctive.[7]

32   *The Failure of Solidarity*

ALBERT N. COUSINS

In a sense, the family contains built-in problems of solidarity in that children have to be socialized for independent existence outside the family. In American society, it is expected that a considerable degree of independence will be achieved, and this relatively early in life. The problems for the family of maintaining its integration and the loyalty of its junior members are concomitantly great. Professor Cousins investigated these problems and how families responded to them in a group of stable middle- and upper-class families. In this selection from his longer work, he specifies what the problem of solidarity is, shows how it impinges on families of different class levels, and formulates the types of responses that families make in order to remain stable.

It will be the object of this chapter to inquire into the problem of the child's solidarity with the other members of the family group.

Solidarity Defined

The concept of *solidarity,* as understood here in reference to the nuclear family as a social system, consists of the relative preponderance of favorable over hostile affects, and a similar balance of moral respect (as over against moral condemnation), among the coparticipants in the concrete group acting out the system. From the standpoint of action, family solidarity may be said to subsume those voluntary and morally obligatory patterns of co-operative interaction among the incumbents of the several institutionally defined statuses, to the total or partial exclusion of nonparticipants.

Analytically, solidarity has two distinct aspects. As an instrumental condition of action, on the one hand, it is a functional imperative for the attainment of satisfactions, for in activities requiring joint activity it assures a dependability of favorable response. On the other hand, as a resultant of interaction, solidarity is a reflection of "the common orientation of the actors in the social system to a common choice of ends, particularly ultimate ends and the means, particularly in the field of influencing the action of others, as well as making a consistent and common scale of relative evaluation of the different individuals possible."[1]

From "The Stable Family: A Study in Group Control" (Unpublished Ph.D. dissertation, Harvard University, 1950), pp. 313–402, with the kind permission of the author.

In the absence of extended, or consanguineous, loyalties, the nuclear family is today institutionalized as the effective solidary unit in the American kinship system. The conjugal family comprises the domiciliary group under the neo-local pattern of residence, functions as the unit of subsistence, is pre-eminently the locus of the socialization of the young, and in that it includes the procreative pair, permits the only legitimate exercise of the sex impulse.

The effectiveness of the nuclear family as the normal solidary kinship unit may be seen in certain illustrative patterns which underscore the priority of obligations of members to each other, in contrast with obligations to others. Accordingly, in his capacity as husband and father, it is no less morally (that is, carrying informal sanctions as well as involving positive and disinterested motives to conformity) than legally (bearing formal sanctions applied by the agents of the political structure) the man's responsibility to provide his wife and dependent children with subsistence in preference to doing so for other individuals. In the same way, in response to the expectations defining her role as mother, the woman is obliged to satisfy, either herself or by delegation, the demands for care made upon her by her immature children, who have a clearly recognized claim to such services prior to those made by others. Again, although the law leaves it to the pressure of opinion to enforce, it is a leading norm in the culture, religiously and traditionally sanctioned, that dependent children render respect and deference to their social parents in contradistinction to such attitudes to others, say, among the fringe of "relatives." In the American kinship system, as Linton says, it is the nuclear unit which "is expected to be the primary focus of its members' interests and loyalties."[2]

The solidarity of the nuclear family is subject to strain today: first, by certain considerations, centering on the articulation of the family as a system with the system of stratification of the larger society; and, second, in consequence of certain incompatibilities of ideology to which the family group is situationally exposed. This strain is focused on the performer of the filial role, particularly on the boy, although also on the girl, for it would be erroneous to suggest that only the son comprises the nexus by which this strain is mediated to the family.[3] The incumbent of the masculine filial status tends to be distinguished here principally for heuristic purposes in keeping with the aims of this study, although in fact he is implicated in this particular functional problems perhaps more conspicuously than in his feminine counterpart.

Our first task is to present the several aspects of the problem from the subjective standpoint of the incumbent of the masculine filial status to show the forces which interfere with the maintenance of solidarity between him and the other members of the group.

Solidarity as a Functional Problem

The family as a social system serves to transmit the social heritage to the new generation and thereby facilitates its absorption into the larger society as the bearer of a particular culture. This process consists essentially in training the child to perform the generalized roles appropriate to him as a member of the society by inculcating in him the generalized orientations current in it.

On the basis of certain external characteristics—notably, age and sex—which are independent of the particular capacities of the individual, the training of the child proceeds in differential fashion. Age grading, for instance, tends to give the older child a certain range of duties and privileges which enable him to develop free from the hampering condition of an unmitigated struggle with those above as well as below him in the scale of ages. Similarly, the development of traits deemed proper to the child's sex is facilitated by differential treatment. From the time of the child's birth, a subtle but unremitting process is set into motion, its result being the inculcation of attitudes and the evocation of certain potentialities at the expense of others, which thus establish positive motives to conformity with generalized patterns of action.

The imperative process of socialization is carried on in American society largely by the child's biological parents. Kinship thus operates as a selective principle in that consanguinity serves as the basis upon which certain adults are singled out as the representatives of the culture who will stand in closest proximity to him and, therefore, will act as mediators in whom he can find the essential clues for modeling his behavior and sentiments. By virtue of their kinship status, parents are invested with the powers of exercising sanctions over the child in order to restrain tendencies toward deviance. They also bear the obligation of furnishing rewards for the promotion of action and the internalization of states of mind valued in the culture.

Assimilating socialization to the kinship bond is accompanied by the ascription of the parents' generalized status to the child. First, by virtue of ascription the child occupies a position in the scale of stratification that is recognized as co-ordinate with that of his parents. Second, in terms of accessibility to rational and nonrational advantages—power, wealth, and prized personal attributes—the child is also on an equal footing with his parents through the nexuses of inheritance and socialization. The initial ascription of status, together with reliance on the biological parents as the chief source of cultural traits, thus may constitute a limiting factor for the child, in view of his eventual participation as an adult in a society committed in crucial respects to the principle of status achievement as well as differential rewards competitively allocated.

The ascription of status is incompatible with status achievement most notably in relation to the child's identification with parents in a subordinate class position or affiliated with a disprized ethnic group. In that kinship identifies the child with such inferior categories, it constitutes a liability in his competition for self-validation and aggrandizement. The importance of these for the individual's self-esteem and his real gains runs counter to the claims made on the child that he be solidary with the members of his family of orientation. Although involving the filial roles of both sexes, this problem appears to weigh more heavily upon the boy by virtue of the asymmetry of adult sex roles, which places a greater premium upon masculine attainments and a larger measure of obloquy upon masculine failure.[4]

A second source of strain lies in the existence of mutually exclusive rationales justifying interindividual influence in controlling action. Kinship interaction is pre-eminently the locus of what Piaget has termed the "morality of constraint."[5] Prescriptions given by the parent for the control of the child in this respect are deemed imperative and absolute, the parents being conceived as agencies of an immutable, traditional order. This is the sacred aura carried by the parental role through its identification with a suprarational, nonempirical sphere of reference as well as the child's dependency. On the other hand, in the progressive secularization of the culture,[6] with its emphasis upon the rational justification of beliefs and practices, pragmatic self-interest has come to challenge the unequivocal acceptance of parental control and of traditionalism in general.

This rationale is much in evidence in the interaction of the child in the peer-culture groups, a relationship which, in the present context, is perhaps best described as expressing one aspect of the strain on family solidarity introduced through the secularization trend, namely, the incompatibility between the family as the chief exponent of Christian virtues and metaphysically based subservience to the common good, and the peer society as the training ground for the child's entrance into the somatotonically oriented, rationally self-interested society.[7] The growing child, especially the boy, tends to be influenced in a great many ways which are inconsistent with the values inculcated in the home.[8] He learns direct aggressiveness and combativeness, engages in hazardous exploits, steals, lies, and experiments sexually; and in numerous other ways, which are of positive significance for his eventual adjustment, he repudiates the values he has learned to prize from his parents' teaching.

It so far as the Christian tradition is viable, it is transmitted to the child directly by his parents or indirectly through their introducing him to the religious faith as mediated by the church. This tradition, as a creed, subsumes the tenets of humility, tolerance, submissiveness, magnanimity, altruism, and the superiority of post-mortem over mundane rewards. These values, moreover, are precisely the ones most fully expressed in kinship interaction, in which persons are valued as ends. In spite of the recession of theologically posited goals, the belief that worldly failure is a claim upon eventual self-realization remains deeply imbedded in the ethos, but not so deeply as does the value of mutual service and altruism, on which family relationships are based, and which are perhaps the prototype for the Christian ethic. With the relationalization of life, personal striving for material and prestige goals —translatable into power, enjoyment, and relief from anxiety as to the future and one's intrinsic value—has assumed more crucial significance for the individual. The result is that even at a relatively early age the child's orientation, thus fostered, leads to his questioning the diffuse obligations presupposed by virtue of kinship and the nonrational justifications underlying kinship interaction.

To secure the approval of the peer group, in which he participates as a novitiate to the larger society, the child is obliged to demonstrate a highly developed capacity for self-reliance, which means he must repudiate his parents' beliefs and conform closely to the deviant norms that the group formulates. Further motivation for this is supplied from still another source: in view of the prominent influence of the mother (and the female school teacher) in the process of socialization and the relative absence of tangible male models in the boy's situation in the type case, the ambiguity of temperament which is formed under the influence of genteel ideals received from women promotes an overreactive identification with the peer group, particularly during adolescence. It might also be added that these pressures motivating the renunciation of parental control may at second remove, so to speak, undermine solidarity in the family by carrying over into agnosticism—the repudiation of religious authority in consequence of the repudiation of parental authority, where a structural flaw already exists, as we have seen— thereby weakening the suprarational foundations on which family structure rests.

We have here singled out two configurations as sources of strain for the solidarity of the incumbent of the filial status with the other members of the nuclear unit. These are (1) ascribing status on the basis of kinship which may limit the achievement of status, and (2) the incompatibility between the value system exemplified in familial interaction and that expressed in the larger society. Finally, attention has been directed to certain considerations involved in the child's participation in the peer group, which has resulted in practices deviating from those valued in the context of the family.

We may observe that given the situation in which the child is exposed to mutually exclusive obligations, and the parent, correspondingly, to the situation in which his duty to socialize the child fails to be discharged, either or both parent and child may convert this discrepancy into a condition of the situation, while still retaining the culturally imposed criteria of adequate socialization. In this mode of symbolic response, the actor attributes responsibility for the undesirable state of affairs to forces beyond his control. This is facilitated by the culturally implicit conception of the child as innately depraved. The discrepancy is thus held to be "natural," "inevitable," "inescapable," or the like.

This symbolic mode of response has the capacity of reducing tension as well as averting conflict between family members generated by the fact that the parent has failed to achieve the ends of socialization and the exercise of moral authority, and the child has failed to act in the manner prescribed in the culture and enunciated by the incumbent of the parental status. Attributing this disparity to an order of nature makes intervention futile, but it also absolves the person's failure and obviates recrimination. In short, nothing can be done about it; hence failure is transcended. Secondly, seeing the unsanctioned behavior of the child as conducive to certain desired ends results in making overt action undesirable, while allaying condemnation of the self and the other participants in the relationship. Finally, voiding the parental authority has the function of alleviating tension through the denial of responsibility, thus also, in turn, of averting conflict between the coparticipants in the family unit.

In this mode of symbolic response the problem of the instability of solidarity is resolved on both the level of the individual and that of the family. Symbolic responses, however, do not exhaust the methods which are found in coping with this particular problem. To present the others it is necessary to deal with responses of overt action.

Overt Functional Responses

By an overt response may be understood a pattern of intervention in the situation, in which one member exercises influence over another participant, either by affecting the latter's state of mind or the objective aspects of the situation, and which tends to reduce personal tension and social malintegration within the family.

The first pattern of responsive intervention which may be inferred is what is perhaps best termed as that of *continuity*. Here the parent recognizes the normative goals of socialization and in his actions attempts to enforce them upon the child by, first, imposing sanctions (rewards or punishments) which have the capacity of inducing the child to attempt to attain those goals, and, second, by effectuating the child's withdrawal from the situation which is deemed to evoke the culturally deviant behavior. In the former, the child is an active element in the sense that, in the parent's manipulation of either subjective or objective factors, the child figures as a goal-directed entity, with the parent hindering his attainment of his goals either by depriving him of the necessary means, by persuading the child to reintegrate his ends, by facilitating his attainment of other goals contingent upon his abandonment of unsanctioned ends, or by inducing unintended deleterious consequences. In the latter, on the other hand, the child plays a passive role in the sense that, although the deprivation of means may be involved to a greater or less degree, the attempt that is made by the parent in manipulating the situation is aimed at averting the child's entertaining deviant goals, thus obviating the parent's exercise of any expiatory, or punitive, types of influence.

This pattern of overt action on the part of the parent needs little concrete exposition. Physical chastisement, denial of money or other means such as the use of an automobile, time, and the like, the withdrawal of affection, the exercise of condemnation, threats of dire consequences, and others are obvious ways employed by the parent to reduce the child's acceptance of the outlawed ways of behaving. The variety of ways parents have of concretely applying negative sanctions are many. So, too, in the matter of rewarding conformity, which inhibits deviance, the range of specific practices is wide.

Middle-class and upper-class parents are both observed to utilize patterned, as distinct from idomatic, isolation to avert the child's adoption of deviant goals and practices. These, furthermore, exhibit distinct class differences. Whereas the middle-class parent, in coping with the problem of the child's solidarity with the members of his family, makes use of lateral isolation, the upper-class parent, on the other hand, tends to adopt vertical isolation. Lateral isolation is the restriction of the child's range of interaction to a plurality of persons with a more or less circumscribed territorial base. This concept makes meaningful the many statements of middle-class parents to the effect that they chose the location of their residences with regard to the "character" of the local community. "This is a very good community to bring up children in," a middle-class mother will say apropos of the conditioning influence of "natural areas" upon the value organization of children. To the extent that such isolation deprives the child of contact with realistically motivated delinquent behavior, such as rational theft committed by the underprivileged, it is a pattern which *ceteris paribus* enhances the child's solidarity with his family. To the extent, however, that the peer group serves the end of developing orientations and definitions of the situation which are of functional value for the individual's adaptation to the larger society, and whose inculcation and active rehearsal are precluded within the scope of familial interaction, its effectiveness as a responsible mechanism must, accordingly, be qualified.

The upper-class parent typically commands resources which are not at the disposal of his middle-class counterpart. These are manifested in his utilization of the pattern of vertical isolation which certain writers have termed "functional isolation." Here the child is pressured to restrict his associational activities to interaction with individuals of at least co-ordinate status, within limits regardless of their spatial location. The availability of transportation and such other facilities—for example, over-night or longer-term accommodations—makes such a practice feasible.

It is apparent, of course, that this arrangement is conducive to socialization in upper-class terms. If the child is not exposed to con-tradictory goals and practices, he is then, as a result of re-enforcement, more apt to be receptive to those accepted by his parents. The ways in which such isolation promotes the child's solidarity with his family group, however, apart from these general ones may be suggested by calling attention to the prevalence of chaperonage in the upper class. Although chaperonage, in the traditional sense of the word, may not be said to be as extensively practiced as it was in the not-too-distant past, it tends to persist in certain analogous forms. For instance, the viability of humanistic values among the upper class, together with the realistic appraisal of the child's capacities, tends to issue in the practice of mixing ages in common leisure practices, notably in travel, the cultivation of artistic activities, and in sports. The adult persons involved in such activities tend to serve as chaperones, that is, as status incumbents of the age group of the child's parents, or as surrogate parents. It is perhaps not unreasonable to con-clude that a greater part of the activity of the upper-class child comes under the purview of adults—kin, functionaries, and others—than is true of the middle-class child.

The second conspicuous way in which isolation operates to preclude the upper-class child's orientation to outlaw peer-group goals lies in the effects of the parent's deliberate restriction of the child's interaction within the circle of extended kin. In this connection, not only are diffuse obliga-tions and psychotonic values strengthened, but the child's tendency to adopt deviant practices is discouraged in other ways too. The presence of a related child tends to redintegrate the whole complex of kinship loyalties and pesssures to conformity, thereby counteracting tendencies on the part of the child to engage in unsanctioned behavior. It is per-haps in relation to sexual expression that the presence of peers who are also kin plays its most strikingly inhibiting role. The operation of the incest taboo militates against overt sexuality, particularly against the as-similation to sex of such non-intrinsic factors as defiance of authority, the acquisition of power, exploitation, and the like. In these respects, vertical isolation as practiced among the upper class serves the need of re-enforcing the child's solidarity with the other family members, in addition to implementing the general socialization process.

Elements of conformity are, of course, freely encountered in the available protocols of children. Another form of response, however, is the expression of a distinct segregation of role. The child's utilizing a segregation of role consists of his synchronously displaying the different forms of behavior which, on the one hand, are approved by his parents, and, on the other, are approved by his peers. Thus, the child withholds information from his parents concerning his participation in outlawed activities. Or he practices duality, that is, refrains from performing certain acts when in their presence. Again, the child may perform his filial role so well that he takes advantage of the favorable affects so created to give him greater leeway to engage in unsanctioned, and un-revealed, activities. For example, scholastic achievement may be utilized as a means of wringing concessions from parents. This appears to be more characteristic of middle-class families than of those in the upper class. Among the latter, performance in regard to approved punctilio and ritual and spontaneity in regard to the discharge of obligations to extended kin, such as in hospitality, seem to be functional equivalents of scholastic achievement.

In regard to the parents, the pattern of *canalization* is to be understood as the child's acceptance of the goal-ideals of socialization which are here in question and, in addition, of his attempts to associate the demands that are imposed upon the child by the peer group with groups that participate in the legitimate process of socialization. Canalization repre-sents the parent's effort to inhibit both the child's orientation to outlaw goals and his display or unsanctioned behavior, through the medium of directing the activities of the child into situations where presumably the child's role as a member of a kinship group will come into play, with all that this implies for status preservation. On the part of the child, canalization consists of the adoption of socially approved forms of be-havior in terms of which he can continue to orient himself to the values which are fostered in the peer group.

So it is that middle-class parents, for example, attempt to direct children's activities into the framework of the school, the church, the Boy Scouts, and various youth affiliates of adult associations. The ap-proval which the middle-class parent gives his child's participation in these activities may be gathered from the following statement of the mother of two children. The informant reported that the children occa-sionally "do things around the house. But in general, we try, I guess, to have them do what they do with least resistance. Anyway, they have many activities. They're both very busy children. They're both in the young people's group at the church. We have a forum there. And then, of course, there are their school activities, like dramatics, athletics, and all that sort of thing. They also touch a little on social work at church."

This particular informant went on to relate, with patent satisfaction, that the children had both participated in a visit to the United Nations headquarters in conjunction with the young people's group sponsored by the church with which the family is affiliated. How the child makes use of such legitimate situations to engage in activities which are not germane to them, but rather are responsive to peer-group expectations may be suggested by noting that the informant's son disclosed to the investigator that in the course of the trip many of the boys and girls petted on the bus and some seized upon the opportunity to use liquor. The fact that such behavior is not entirely attributable to intrinsic, or organic desires was discussed earlier and need only be noted at this point.

Organized athletics, typically structured about the school in the middle class, is particularly apt to be approved by the parent as a mode of canalization. Athletics not only caters to the avoidance of sex by the child but also to the denial of other impulses which lend themselves to capitalization within peer relationships, such as the use of tobacco and alcohol. Moreover, athletic participation permits organization by persons of the parent's generation. For the child, athletics is a desirable pattern in which aggression may be legitimately displayed, which is a potent source of status among peers, and whose accompanying denial has the capacity of relieving guilt generated in various contexts.

Instrumentalities of canalization particular to the upper class include such agencies as the Junior League—which is directed by individuals of the parent's age group and wherein membership is contingent upon the satisfaction of certain standards of decorous conduct and social welfare work—exclusive clubs, and the employment of special functionaries to teach dancing, sports, and other skills. These agencies constitute fields of force pressing upon the individual child to act in terms of his kinship-defined role, by virtue of the fact that he tends to participate in them as an incumbent of his established status.

Turning now to the third overt functional response to the problem of the child's solidarity with the nuclear unit, when the parent rejects the inviolability of the goals of socialization or relinquishes the parental status as the locus of their implementation, the mechanism of group control that is thus utilized may be termed *discontinuity*. As a tentative generalization, it may be stated that in the upper class the reduction of faith in the goals of socialization is conspicuous in the presence of adherence to the received definition of the parental role. In the middle-class family, on the other hand, a reversal of this pattern is apparent. The middle-class parent continues to uphold the culturally sanctioned ends of socialization while at the same time denying the parental status its nonrational powers of attaining them. The following illustration may well begin the discussion of how the upper-class parent tolerates the child's display of culturally interdicted behavior, provided it is restricted to interaction with the child's peers. The informant, an upper-class mother whose lineage is of wide repute, said: "Of course, the boys know bad words. Frank came out with a four-letter word just recently. I suppose he expected me to fall off my chair. What he said had just slipped out, and he stood there waiting for the lightning to strike. I said, 'I supposed you knew that word, but it certainly was stupid to use it in front of me.' That's all. . . . I haven't had any trouble with the children's being dirty-minded. That's different from using profanity. Yet I'm sure they are. I know, because I've heard them. I remember they were chattering away in John's room once. They were reciting that dirty limerick. But I'm not going to do anything as long as they keep it to themselves and don't use it in front of others."

Another upper-class mother revealed: "Like bathroom language—I tell them it's best to do it alone in their room behind closed doors. We're trying to bring up the children to be individuals who understand that they have to live in a world with other people. I feel that it's never too early to give children adult versions of things. I firmly believe in and practice that. . . . I must say though that their language doesn't bother me . . . It doesn't offend me basically."

Although such a sanctioned segregation of role as appears above in regard to use of improper speech cannot be said to apply to the child's overt sex behavior, judging from the available case materials, by inferring from the permissiveness shown his symbolic sex expression, the child may easily extend this attitude of the parent to cover his tendencies to accede to the peer-group's expectations concerning sexual activities. Smoking too, among upper-class children, is apt not to be combatted by the parent so much as condoned, provided it is restricted to times and places where it constitutes a strictly peer-group practice.

Assuming the data are adequate and reliable, the crucial determining fact for the scarcity of indications that the middle-class parent deliberately stimulates a segregation of role on the part of the child would appear to be that moral superiority, in the sense of conformity to respectable standards of conduct, constitutes the middle-class person's chief claim to social position that is wholly dependent upon his own efforts and not upon situational circumstances, such as access to economic opportunity. Hence "respectability" is of crucial importance as a means of self-validation. Further evidence for the conclusion that in the middle class the parent is less apt to sanction the child's segregation of role lies in the greater frequency with which upper-class children confide in their parents, along sex lines, about their conduct that from the standpoint of the culture is deviant. Middle-class children seem more likely to confide in neither parent about their delinquencies, but rather simply to practice deception and duality, or an unacknowledged segregation of role. The middle-class parent may recognize this situation but does not openly disclose this to the child.

The second component of the functional response of discontinuity to the problem of filial solidarity is the condition in which the individual can be observed to void his status as parent. This consists of the loss of affective and moral backing for the discharge of the obligations of the role as well as for the claiming of the rights which correspond to them. In short, the parent exhibits a loss of conviction and feeling of responsibility in regard to the patterns of action that are subsumed under the social position of parent. He shows a loss of subjective identity with his role.

However, the culturally enjoined ends of socialization are not renounced. They continue to receive the parent's support. It is simply that the parent does not regard them as goals that he himself has determined. They are rather ends which he feels are required—rationally or as a matter of social fiat. In exacting conformity to them by the child, the parent tends, therefore, to justify them as externally imposed requirements with which he is himself not intrinsically identified. The parent tends to be self-conscious in regard to his role. Rather than react with an affectively charged display of will to the child's recalcitrance, the parent appeals to some pragmatic test, such as a rational standard or the criterion of majority determination, and the like.

The insistence by certain parents, particularly upper-class, on the recognition of their absolute status vis-à-vis their children is in striking contrast with his condition of status voidance. "The children have told me often that I'm not fair," said an upper-class mother. "That's mostly based on what other children are allowed to do. I? I've been very disagreeable about that: I've simply told them that while they live here, I'm the boss and they ought to get used to it." This tenor is fairly frequent among upper-class parents, more so than among middle-class parents.

To illustrate the operation of appealing to some objective standard in preference to precipitating a contest of wills between parent and child, the question of clothing, together with its implications for the child's mind in regard to being a "sissy"—that is, showing oneself less hardy, vigorous, and daring than the standard prevailing in the peer group—suggests itself. Here the parent may be seen to respond to the conflict of values to which the child is subject by shifting the onus for the determination of the child's conduct in this situation from himself to an objective aspect of the situation, namely, the temperature. "We had frequent rubs over that sort of thing," a mother told the investigator. "So we've set up a temperature schedule. We've agreed that when it's under 40 degrees they both are to wear leggings. Between 40 and 50 it's overalls. When it's above 50 they may wear just a skirt and jacket. That arrangement has proved to be perfectly satisfactory."

Voidance of the parental status may also be observed in terms of a retreat from heteronomy, in which the parent abandons his reliance on the child's voluntarily accepting the definition of the situation presented to him arbitrarily, and replaces this mode of influence with an appeal to rational considerations, albeit within a non-rational framework of ends. For example, a mother stated that although she forbade her daughters to wear dungarees to school, they continued to do so. She then adopted the tactic of pointing out to them that the "nicer" people in the community disapproved of such apparel.

The parent may, furthermore, abridge the culturally defined prerogatives of his role by co-opting the child, so that the child comes to exercise a measure of freedom in determining the regulations under which socialization is to occur. A mother was telling the investigator that her children occasionally are subject to conflicting requirements established by the peer group and by their parents. "We have some disagreement about their bed hour. That's something they get from their friends at school. Each year we state their official bed hour. It's about the same as their contemporaries. So there isn't much trouble about that." Instead of sharing the power of determination with the child indirectly, as in this fashion taking the prevailing peer standards into account, the parent may directly call on the child to establish norms for himself on the basis of approximating equalitarian rule. Thus a child declared: "They usually decide on a plan that we have to keep and do. If one of us doesn't do her practicing, they make us decide on a plan to do it. Or they decide one for us. But we like to make our own plan."

Finally, status voidance may correspond to the condition in which the parent views his social position in the family as depending upon the development of special competence. In this event the parent attempts to establish his position vis-à-vis that of the child on the basis of his acquiring attributes that will command the child's respect, and hence will be conducive to his exercise of influence. This achievement of status by the parent may be illustrated by the statement made to the investigator by one middle-class father. Nowadays, he said, there is "a pressure on parents, because parents have to win leadership. It's unusually difficult too for a parent who is unable to win leadership or where the vicissitudes of circumstances defeat him. . . . For instance, some time ago I won a point with Clarence. He didn't understand Browning. He asked me about him and I didn't know. I had to study up on it. Then I explained it to him. That won me a lot of prestige. In our house the problem is different from most. My wife was raised in Germany and I studied languages. I like Math. My wife is good in English. So when we're cornered we can keep a little ahead of them. It must be very difficult with people without training. And then there's something else. You have to be careful not to compete with children where you know they can beat you. Physical strength. I simply tell Clarence, 'You're stronger than I am now. You lift this rock. I'm getting old.' He likes that."

The substitution of achievement for ascription in regard to parental status may, on the other hand, as this informant suggests, be negative.

That is, the parent will strive not so much to enhance his prestige in the eyes of the child as not to expose his fallibility. "We don't bring up anything controversial in front of the children. When we do, we just don't take any definite stand, so that they won't go wrong later. . . . That way there's no dogma in what we tell them. We don't tell them anything is absolutely right or absolutely wrong. There's good and bad in everything. We tell them some things are right one time and wrong another. . . . We don't hold ourselves up as shining examples."

These three modes of response—generalized from the available materials and what we have chosen to term the patterns or processes of *continuity, canalization,* and *discontinuity*—comprise the overt efforts made by family members in coping with the problem of the child's solidarity with the other members of his family of orientation. These supplement the symbolic modes of response presented earlier. They consist in common of the exercise of inter-individual influence and are functional in accordance with the fact that they appear to contribute to the maintenance of the nuclear unit as an integrated and adaptable social system.

33   Some Problems in the Study of Hostility
and Aggression in Middle-Class
American Families

KASPAR D. NAEGELE

As the psychoanalyst Flugel pointed out many years ago (in The Psychoanalytic Study of the Family), the family has to integrate the hostility and aggression of its members quite as much as their love and affection. In middle-class families, where violence tends to be abhorred and harmony approved of, there may be many problems in handling the impulses and behavior that are disapproved of. This can be especially true as regards children, who have not fully acquired the standards of the adult world. Professor Naegele has studied this problem intensively in a contemporary suburban community. Here he reports on the nature of the problems families encounter and how they deal with them.

This paper is primarily an impressionistic sketch of an on-going piece of family research. No conclusions can as yet be offered. Instead, I intend briefly to suggest a frame of reference for the study of family hostility[1] as well as enumerate some of the procedures of field work used in the present project.

Much has been written about the family by many sociologists of various persuasions. Yet a large part of this phase of sociological effort leaves one dissatisfied. Admittedly, data on our own types of family structure are hidden from clear view precisely because of their familiarity as well as their privacy. But this fact is not sufficient to account for the disparity between the experienced complexity of family life and the sparsity of published details made significant by a sustained and incisive theoretic orientation. Headway could be made by the use of a frame of reference which combines sociological with psychological considerations, without confusing them, and which draws its vitality from the impassioned analyses of the structure of large-scale social systems and of individual character as begun by Weber and Freud. At the present time, family research seems, on the whole, to have made little consistent use of the leads of kinship analysis and to have by-passed a cumulative effort at spelling out the empirical details of the social structure of various types of American families. As it is, we hear much about the family as a "unity of interacting personalities," about processes of accommodation or conflict, or about

Reprinted from the *Canadian Journal of Economics and Political Science*, XVII (February, 1951), 65–75, with the kind permission of the author and the publisher.

the kinds of valuation that marital partners place upon one another; yet we hear little of the intervening details which, in their fullness, would give us a sense of how indeed a family as an on-going concern functions, and how the inherent or emergent demands of its social structure are met, how the social structure of a family is related meaningfully or functionally to the rest of the social system, and how any given family of orientation dissolves into successive families of procreation.

Family research appears to be the victim of an inhibiting disjuncture of perceptual and conceptual vision. We can read variously fascinating case material of specific personalities or more or less global descriptions of the American social system and of the American family. True enough, the latter are differentiated along class, ethnic, religious, and regional lines. Yet such differentiations seldom actually meet clinical accounts. It is as though the clinician suffered from short-sightedness and the sociologist from its opposite. The mere summation of these maladies does not, of course, bring a given phenomenon into clear focus. If we looked instead at *variations* in family structure within the established differences of class or ethnic context, idiosyncratic personal facts might enlarge their significance—especially if they were ordered simultaneously to personality as a unit of analysis and to a particular position in a system of changing relationships. Given variations in the structure of middle-class American families, for instance, what is the pattern of sibling rivalry? Are there characteristic differences in the experiences for the oldest, the middle, and the youngest child? What are the sibling alignments and rivalries in families of three, four, or five children of varying age differences? In what directions are identifications likely to develop among younger brothers who have older brothers rather than older sisters? Who will be the beneficiaries of sympathy and targets of hostility in families of different age and sex composition? Despite all the books on the family, at the moment there are no published explorations into the personalities of all members of a single family which has also been described in sociological detail. It is, therefore, not surprising that current research omits consideration of the subtler and more elusive aspects of family life, even though, as one consequence of the paucity of sustained theory, publications on the family tend to be voraciously inclusive on a descriptive level. Everything from eugenics to budgets is *somehow* included. Yet one searches in vain for imaginative and systematic accounts of the way in which families achieve their specific solidarities, allow or do not allow for privacy or even secretiveness, allot time for sharing information on the day's event, sustain or combat gaps of communication between various members of the family, casually welcome outsiders or keep them remote, encourage dependency or loneliness, or adjust to a name that once meant less or more than now.

Of course, many important problems *are* being studied: the predictable elements of marital adjustment, socialization differences among classes and ethnic groups, the effects of a depression or "troubles" on family stability, the intricacies of courtship practices, differential fertility, the family cycle, or time required for various phases of marital adjustment. Besides, there is no area in the social sciences where it is not easy to make self-righteous claims of gaps or omissions. To fill these is usually hard. However, in the case of the family, the need is especially great to begin with a conception of the family as a social structure, in the context of which an on-going process of socialization strongly affects the character formation of the young and re-creates in diverse and usually unwitting forms the earlier family experiences of the old. Moreover, the dynamic connection between families of orientation and procreation is compounded by equally important relations between family structure and the rest of the social system. This means that the generic and specific features of the family as a social system ought to be seen steadily and as a whole so that the specialized accounts of marital adjustment or socialization differences, to take two examples at random, do not merely become atomistic reports but instead add to a systematic knowledge of the sociology of primary groups and the psychology of its sustaining personalities.

Details of the social structure of middle-class American families have been described most preceptively by Talcott Parsons[2] and Kingsley Davis.[3] Marion J. Levy[4] in similar terms has given an account of the Chinese family. The present paper owes very much to these analyses. As I understand them, they all assume, though under different names, that all social systems must, by definition, meet certain "functional requirements" or involve specific "functional foci" and that in addition a family, by virtue of its specific functions (taking place in a specific social system) and its implication (usually) in sexual and reproductive processes, evolves a specific and characteristic structure. This structure has determinate aspects —Levy, for one, has distinguished these as role differentiation, solidarity, economic provision, distribution of power and authority, and patterns of integration—which vary in their concrete details between cultures or classes and probably also within these. Certain "problems," in other words, must be "solved." As yet we have no unanimous phrasing or listing of these. The comparative analysis of family structure—as well as its psychological elucidation—would, however, be well advanced if we began with the perhaps "obvious" notions[5] that the family to maintain itself must, among other matters, establish modes of communication, sustain shared cognitive as well as normative orientations, regulate affective expression, socialize the young, and manage disruptive elements in its interactive processes or, to use different language, define the rights and obligations of its various members, establish a division of labor, maintain solidarity, distribute prestige, and foster integrative mechanisms. There are, as was said, invariant problems, and their *solution* varies, but not at random. Any given social system requires its own type of family structure and provides for limits within which, but not outside of which, variation is possible or at least permissible. The use and revision of such a point of view ought, eventually, to allow one to remain sensitive to the many subtle details of family life and yet gather such details for the sake of a systematic exposition rather than as illustrations of purely idiosyncratic constellations of people or events. Surely there is a sociology of everyday life and not only a psychopathology of it. The richness of the latter holds promise for the potentialities of the former.

I do not want to suggest, of course, that research on the family would cease to be as dissatisfying as it is now if we merely heightened our sensibility and diligently recorded imaginatively perceived details of domestic tranquillity and stress. There must be a theoretic orientation in terms of which findings can be cumulative. There is, indeed, a whole disharmonious symphony of such orientations in existence. The present paper favors one of these especially the one that has come to be called structural-functional analysis. An evaluation of the alternatives to this perspective would go far beyond the set limits of this paper. The consistent use of a sensitive theoretic orientation ought also to reintroduce into our published accounts some of the experienced details of family living—the rituals, for instance, associated with the father's leaving in the morning or returning in the evening, rituals by which the "contraction" and "expansion," as it were, of the family orbit are smoothly maneuvered. Empathy, as a psychological mechanism for the maintenance of valued family solidarity, is another problem area for investigation. How, for instance, do children learn to become, as some mothers put it, diplomatic, to respond to the moods of their parents; or how do parents value or disregard emotional displays in front of their children? Perhaps one might almost go so far as to suggest that what Thomas Mann did for the Buddenbrooks, social scientists, with different limitations and language, ought to do for a whole series of families.

These, and other considerations, encouraged me to begin a joint piece of research with Dr. David F. Aberle which is now in progress, and which, within recent months, has kept me busy interviewing twenty-five mothers for about six hours each in their own homes in a well-to-do suburb of a large city on the eastern seaboard. A project in mental health had been set up in that suburb in 1948. This project is staffed by psychiatrists, clinical psychologists, a psychiatric social worker, and social scientists. Its aim, broadly speaking, is to develop methods for assessing case loads of this community. Its aim, too, is to do research in the areas relevant to problems of mental health. The clinical staff of the project has offered free short-term psychotherapy to any member, old or young, of the community who wishes to avail himself of its services. In return, it hopes to be able to do research in the community. This is not the place to discuss the advantages and disadvantages of such a *quid pro quo* or to analyze in any detail the intricacies involved in the co-operation between psychiatrists and social scientists. Suffice it to say that in the autumn of 1949 a group of families— about twenty-five in number—offered themselves for study after having been addressed by the director of the mental health project at one of their meetings. It had been a practice that the members of the project staff would speak at various P.T.A. and other meetings throughout the com- munity. It had further been a theoretically argued aim of the whole project not to confine its therapy and diagnostic activities to the one member of a particular family that might come to it, but to include as far as possible an evaluation of all the family members involved, and thus to think of people as systematically living in a certain "orbit" of relationships. At first sight, such a perspective may be obvious enough, but translated into actual psy- chiatric practice it is difficult and is not often found. At any rate, the group that offered itself for study is not primarily a cross-section of the com- munity's population; rather it is a special group of well-to-do families who live in their own homes, run their own cars, earn anywhere between $5,000 and $20,000 a year, and facilitate their life with the various technological advantages of middle- and upper-middle-class living, such as automatic stoves, dishwashers and other gadgets. For some years now they have organized a nursery school for which they have hired two full-time teachers with whom are associated teachers in training. The school meets throughout the school year five mornings a week and uses the facilities of a church. Each family pays quite a sizeable fee; in addition, each mother puts in one morning a month helping out with getting the children dressed and un- dressed, giving them juice, and performing other chores. I should perhaps say at this point that the rest of this paper will inevitably be an incon- gruous mixture of anecdotal material and theoretic speculation. One reason for this is that my material has as yet not been analyzed; another is that I have come to feel that social research involves looking after so many untidy details which, were they ever fully reported—and unfortu- nately they never are—would in themselves yield additional insights that are now left unrecorded and often left untaught.

Dr. Aberle's and my study got under way when the whole nursery school group met in a large living room of one of the families and was addressed there by the director of the mental health project, and by Dr. Aberle and myself. It is, I think, useful to note here that, although Dr. Aberle and myself were all along associated with this project, we made it verbally quite clear that we were concerned with research, not with therapy, that any family which in the course of contact with us might wish to discuss a problem further should then come to see our clinical staff in our quarters, that our clinical facilities were available but that Dr. Aberle and myself were by no means therapists. The fact that Dr. Aberle and I went into the homes of these mothers further symbolized, I believe, the difference between us as researchers and the other staff members as therapists. Let me hasten to add that this does not mean that many mothers did not ask for advice, did not talk over with us the advisability of having further contact with our service, or did not feel that even the conversations they had with us helped them—at least in some instances—to reassess their own anxieties or the manner in which until then they had defined what seemed to be problems.

The line between therapy and research is thin. This is a problem area about which, again, there is no time to go into detail. Crucial facts about the display of aggression within a family, for instance, usually are not reliably reported by a respondent until as a result of accepted and sustained contact at least some transference has taken place. But then, is it right for a researcher, who is liable to disappear again after three or four meetings, to allow such transfer to develop? By the same token, one could easily phrase a problem the other way around—for the psychiatrists, who supposedly do enjoy good transference on the part of their patients and thus might presumably be in a strategic position to gather intimate and useful facts, frequently argue that demands of therapy run counter to the demands of research and that the facts needed by their social science colleagues will just have to await collection until the patient brings them up spontaneously. Or else with much, though partial, truth, he accuses the social scientist of frequently doing research that arouses more anxiety than is justifiable and of collecting facts by quickly tearing them loose from their emotional moorings and losing half of their actual meaning. It is quite clear that if, indeed, we want to integrate an analysis of social systems with an analysis of character structure and to add to both a dimension of depth which increasingly we have come to expect, then these and many other practical problems of research will have to be solved.

Meanwhile, Dr. Aberle and I interviewed fathers and mothers as best we could and found that all parties to the interview *enjoyed* themselves greatly. This fact, again, is usually not mentioned in scientific publications yet surely without it much research would not be possible. Besides, for some curious reason, the more positive aspects of social interaction seem quite refractory when it comes to analyzing them, so that our extant analyses seem all weighted towards the "problematic or pathological" as though it were easier to spell out the liabilities of any given situation than it is to account for the assets. True to form, then, I set myself as the problem to be studied what people ordinarily do regard as liabilities, namely aggressiveness within a family. A theoretical starting point for such an analysis is provided by the suggestive essays on middle-class family structure to be found in the writings of Talcott Parsons and Kingsley Davis. I shall take their description of the stresses and strains of middle-class American family life for granted here. For my part, I wanted to see how indeed aggression is defined within the nursery school families, what forms it takes, against whom it is directed and with what intensity, and what responses its expression arouses. I had, of course, to limit myself. Accordingly it was decided that I would interview mothers only and that, in addition to Dr. Aberle's interviewing the fathers, someone else would later study the children so that eventually we would have a relatively reliable picture of the structure and dynamics of the families.

My problem, therefore, became one of finding out from mothers what they mean by aggression, how children and parents express their aggression and with what result from the other members of a family, how mothers especially handle not only the aggressiveness of their children but also their own aggressiveness and hostility toward children and husband. Beyond that, however, I hoped at the time to relate findings on this score to findings about differences in family structure. I assumed, before starting out, that it was possible to describe all these families as instances of a general middle-class type but that there would probably be variations which for present purposes could be utilized. I hoped to order these variations along three lines: solidarity, division of labor, and authority. To what extent this point of view is a useful or a mistaken one remains to be seen. For the more formal definitions of these terms, I looked especially to the work of Levy on the Chinese family and therefore also to his sources of inspiration. As far as the interviews were concerned, under "authority" I included questions on how parents justify their commands, how decisions were formed, how power was distributed and responsibility allocated, to what extent parents saw to it that their children could or could not appeal from one to the other, how they felt about differences in degrees of strictness between fathers and mothers, and how they disciplined their children. With regard to "solidarity," I wanted to know whether mothers considered the family a close one, whether the family kept much to itself or had many contacts with outsiders including relatives, whether privacy was or was not valued and how it was maintained, whether a mother felt that her children or her husband shared or did not share their concerns with her, how a mother compared her present family with her family of orientation, and to what extent doing things as a family, as it were, was a valued activity and how parents saw to it that they would have time for themselves without the children or even time entirely alone without the other marital partner and the children. Under "division of labor" I included questions on the allocation of tasks, flexibility or rigidity of household routine, the importance placed on routine versus spontaneous activity or on housework versus other matters such as reading, going out, playing with the children. I realized from the very beginning that a family's style of establishing routine or authority or solidarity is anything but stationary. It is subject to many changes resulting from changes in the age, size, and degree of socialization of its members. Ideally the study of the family is a long-term project which includes reference to all the stages of the family cycle.

Before I began, I had one other set of speculations in the back of my mind. I assumed that by and large aggression was defined "negatively," the more so when it was expressed on the part of family members, including parents, who are old enough, as common sense has it, "to know better." Ironically enough, I did not take this assumption seriously enough, for it implies, actually, that aggression is a topic which middle-class families at any rate tend to avoid discussing in any detail with outsiders. On the whole, the display of aggression is not defined as one aspect inevitable in any form of sustained and intimate social interaction, which can, if properly handled, even add to the unity of the relationship of which it seems a disturbing expression. I assumed that, by virtue of their arrangement, middle-class families would be marked by stresses and strains that might provide a fertile soil for the development of aggression and hostility. At the same time, however, the middle-class family becomes defined as one in which it is appropriate both for all members to love one another and for all of them to express themselves as "they really are." This tends to set up a conflict, especially if any anger and hate expressed as a result of this formula is seen as an entirely unproductive and detractive phenomenon. The situation becomes all the more confusing since the norms governing appropriate and inappropriate expression of aggression and hostility lack the requisite specificity so that children do not quite know what they are allowed to do nor adults what they should allow them. In addition, many of the mothers interviewed viewed their own strict upbringing in the light of rationally acquired contemporary psychological descriptions, provided their children with a certain permissiveness and an opportunity to act out, as it were, their own previously suppressed id, then found themselves unable to discipline the children and, consequently, beset by a mixture of helplessness and envy for the freedom of their children, frequently questioned whether indeed they were "good mothers." There are other strains, too. How can one love one's children and still have due regard for the needs of one's self, how can one be a good mother and lead a full life, or a successful man and be a good father, how indeed can one love all one's children equally despite experienced preference for one, how can one express hostility without reinforcing it with guilt and shame?

An attempt was made to include in interviews with the mothers data on some or all of these matters. The first forty minutes of the first interview, moreover, were spent on filling out a face sheet concerning basic information about education, age, family structure of the mother, a few details on the grandparents, and the like. The rest of the interview was a compromise in trying to cover certain areas and at the same time letting the mother take the lead and follow her own associations. There was also a compromise in discussing intimate and more superficial aspects of her life. Meanwhile, Dr. Aberle investigated the fathers' contentment or discontent with their jobs and the relationship between satisfactions derived on the job and behavior displayed at home towards wives and children. We pooled our information as far as we could, shared our impressions, and each tried to get information helpful to the other. By visiting our subjects at their homes, we could also get some impression of the neighborhood in which they lived, of their taste, of the way in which mothers might handle interfering children, and generally we could observe our subjects in their home setting. Frequently the interviews were completed, in the case of the husbands, with alcohol; or, in the case of the mothers, with coffee or tea. We were, in other words, treated as guests, at times shown pictures of the children when they were younger, and generally exposed to the household; something which, in that form, would never have been possible had we interviewed our subjects in our own quarters.

The data, as I have said, are not yet analyzed and will, as usual, shrink under inspection. Some highly tentative impressions, though, might be worth mentioning at the risk of later invalidation. The richness of information tends to vary considerably from family to family. This is a result of differences in rapport between interviewer and subject, and these differences in turn are related to the time of interviewing (evenings being more productive than mornings), the personality of the subject in relation to the personality of the interviewer, the amount of interruption from children, phone calls, tradesmen, and so on in the case of mothers, of the tiredness after work in the case of fathers, and so forth. Nevertheless, with one exception, we were never refused an interview and though at one or two points we were called impertinent, mostly our subjects talked freely and enjoyed talking. The mothers, especially, found talking about their children a self-rewarding activity and, thus, asked about the scientific value of our effort less frequently than the fathers. Frequently, though, we were asked the embarrassing and natural question, "How indeed are you going to make sense of all the things that I am telling you?" We promised to let them know at a later date and, in return for their hospitality, planned to entertain all twenty-five families in our own quarters sometime during the autumn and at that time give them some tentative impressions without giving away confidential information. We thus hoped to reward them in some measure for their past help and perhaps secure from them further co-operation.

By the indices of education, income, residential area, and type of house, it would seem that our families occupy *similar* social statuses. The families, though, show that there is considerable *variation* with respect to authority, division of labor, and solidarity. All parents affirm that they "stick together" when it comes to enforcing rules and making demands. They also admit that they usually are not equally strict. In some households, husbands are ready to take over any of the household chores if necessary; in others husbands draw definite lines. In all, of course, there is some sexual division of labor. As a rule, most of the mothers interviewed felt that their children obey their husbands better than they obey themselves. They rationalize this on the basis of the fact that the children are with the mothers so much more, can wear down mothers more frequently, and are, perhaps, a little more afraid of their fathers than they are of their mothers. At the same time, some mothers complain that their husbands are too demanding and will not give their children sufficient reasons for their commands or listen to the reasons children offer for their own demands. In almost every family, at least one child is an object of concern either because he or she is too aggressive or too withdrawn or passive. Mothers, though, tend to object to aggression as something that interferes with the smooth running of a household routine, while fathers object to it more as indicative of undesirable "character traits." As might be expected, mothers are more frequent targets of aggression on the part of children than are fathers. But perhaps, too, in this group, children are less afraid of their mothers. Besides, the mother is more understanding if a child hits her or explains that it hates her than the father might be in similar situations. In their description of their children's aggression and hostility, mothers mention all extremes—from a note they might find in a desk which says, "I hate my mummy," to the description of one little boy who invariably hits his father when the latter arrives home in the evening. Spontaneously, though, all these mothers assure me that their children are not malicious or mean. One gets the impression they would be greatly upset were this not so. One hears a lot about squabbles among siblings; and one hears a lot, too, about how "little things" always set these things off. There seems to be no great awareness that "little things" can have large symbolic significance.

Though there is the claim in most families that there is little if any marital discord, all mothers admit to getting angry with the children. They admit, too, that they displace aggression against their children. There is much shame associated with the display of this aggression but, if one probes for guilt, one finds mothers admitting to it in only about half the cases. Yet most of the mothers wonder with some concern whether other mothers, too, get angry and especially how their "calm neighbors manage to be so calm." It is almost as if middle-class standards generate a public morality to which private reality does not correspond and which aids in maintaining a gap between neighbors and friends. No one quite knows what the other is really like, and all compare their private selves with the public appearance of others—unless, of course, children in the back yard report to each other on the true disposition of their parents within hearing of at least one of the mothers concerned. How, incidentally, do children learn to be quiet outside their homes about some of the things they see and hear and feel within their homes? It is not too difficult to get mothers to verbalize incidents about how their children annoy them and how they might take their anger out on their children, how they "blow up" on occasion. It is, however, very difficult to get these mothers to admit the same behavior vis-à-vis their husbands. It may well be true that, as they report, they never have arguments. But, unfortunately, they then do not go on to confirm or deny what form the unspoken tensions take, how they are resolved or displaced, exhibited to the children or hidden from them.

It is gratifying, indeed, that the majority of these twenty-five families are proud of their harmony and can, therefore, provide needed non-pathological case material. But, since the difference between the pathological and the normal is not one of the absence of problems in the latter and their presence in the former, but the absence of certain solutions and techniques in the former, it is unfortunate that precisely the so-called normal families tend to be unaware, for the most part, of the details of their techniques of solving the recurrent problems of daily life. Still, where there is less harmony, one can distinguish at least three types of pervasive atmosphere. Let me call them those of the bristling, the sulking, and the explosive family. In the first, one can feel much tension, hostility, and anger, none of them expressed directly and all of them expressed indirectly through nasty remarks with a "dear" in front. In the second, anger is expressed indirectly by silence which lasts. In the last, there are scenes which pass quickly and usually clear the air though they may leave bitter residues. In some of the families, by the way, it is the second, rather than the first child who is the difficult one. It may well be, of course, that the stereotype of the first child who is difficult is wrong in the first place and that therefore we are not dealing here with any problem of significance. Perhaps we are dealing mainly with the effect of changing fashions of childraising, though the age range of the children of this group is not too large. Most of the first-born were born during the war, none of the children is older than twelve, the majority of the families have no more than two or three children, and all of the mothers—with one exception—are in their early thirties. I have to add that all of the mothers interviewed admit that their handling of the children is subject to changes in mood. These changes they explain partly on physiological grounds and mostly leave unexplained. They explain aggressive or hostile conduct very frequently on the basis of tiredness and then stop there. Tiredness and sickness, it would seem, are pushed aside as states in which one is not quite one's self and during which, therefore, one is not entirely responsible for what one does. The other point of view, that perhaps one is then really one's self, shorn of some of the more superficial self-controls, otherwise made possible by abundant energy, is not taken.

In conclusion, I might say, mothers often talk with annoyed bewilderment about the contrast between their children's good behavior in school and bad behavior at home. In these cases, the children are especially troublesome immediately after returning from school. Lunch then becomes a battleground unless the food is ready on the table and mother can direct her attention to controlling the children who are only too ready to unload tensions accumulated during the morning on a mother who, after all, asked them to behave well on the outside. If one asks the mother then whether she would prefer the situation the other way around, she protests vehemently and assures one that, if at all, she would rather have her children bad at home than outside.

To be sure, these are haphazard impressions. Perhaps they will eventually provide leads for more systematic conclusions.

34   *Family Ritual and Family Integration*

JAMES H. S. BOSSARD

and ELEANOR S. BOLL

Integration is maintained not only by the solution of specific problems such as Cousins and Naegele discuss and general problems such as Davis assays. Very significant contributions to integration are made by symbolic means of expressing the unity and problem solutions that exist. The expressions, by making concrete and dramatic the identity of the family, reinforce integration. Professor Bossard and Dr. Boll have attended, as few others have, to the ritualization of activities, even simple daily activities, in families. In this selection they present some conclusions about the contributions which rituals and routines make to the integration of the family.

In analyzing family life from within, our attention came to focus early in our studies upon certain forms of family behavior so recurrent as to suggest the term "habit," and yet having about them aspects of conscious rigidity and a sense of rightness and inevitably not generally associated with mere habits. They were habitual forms of family behavior, but with added features that made them more than habits. We came ultimately to think of these as family rituals. We shall speak of ritual here as meaning a pattern of prescribed formal behavior, pertaining to some specific event, occasion, or situation, which tends to be repeated over and over again. As it develops, it tends to demand relatively punctilious observance, admitting of no, or at least very few, exceptions or deviations. As time goes on, it often becomes ceremonious, and sometimes solemn. Ritual is something to be done, not something to be thought out.

Ritual may arise about, and develop in respect to, any aspect of family life. In an earlier day, many families held devotional services in which the father was the leader but in which everyone was expected to participate. This practice still continues, particularly in certain parts of this country, although its over-all prevalence has undoubtedly declined. Because of the older tendency to restrict the use of the term "ritual" to religious ceremonials, family rituals may be thought of by some contemporary readers as confined to such and similar practices and, since these have declined in frequency, may tend to think that the subject is of declining importance. As our study will show, this is far from the truth.

Reprinted from *Ritual in Family Living* (Philadelphia: University of Pennsylvania Press, 1950), pp. 9–11, 199–203, with the kind permission of the publisher.

In many families the meal is highly ritualized, with a ceremony of carving and serving, of seating arrangements (such as no one sitting down until Mother is seated). Many of the rituals of family life have to do with etiquette; others, with the attitude of children toward parents. Or they develop as a part of the routine of child care. One who takes a child for a walk on Sunday afternoon, or reads the comic strips on Sunday morning, or reads a fairy tale before bedtime, and repeats the event several times, is very apt to discover that subsequent developments turn these practices into rituals. Again, many rituals center around holidays, such as Hallowe'en, Thanksgiving, Christmas, New Year's Day, and the Fourth of July. In all these instances, a pattern of social behavior develops within the family, which each member of the group is expected to observe as a part of the group functioning.

Ritual obviously, then, comprises much of the behavior of which a family is proud and of which its members definitely approve. As a phase of family life, it is what the family sees about itself that it likes and wants formally to continue. Thus it seems essential for an understanding of family life that we study this: it may be highly important for the happiness of families that we seek to encourage and promote it. It may be that if mates agree on what they want thus consciously to promote in family life, and how to promote it, that we have identified an agency and area of family rapport. Possibly family tension and discord may be the inevitable price of differentials in ritualistic experiences and loyalties in the respective family backgrounds of the mates. Other studies of family failure and success have shown how significant such differences is background may be.[1] Ritual has been referred to as the core and essence of culture; we are inclined to think of family rituals as the hard core in a cultural approach to the study of the family. In fact, the longer our studies of the inside of family life have continued, the more we have come to wonder if ritual may not be the best one starting point for the study of family life, just as it has long been recognized as the best one for the study of religion. The first analytical comprehensions of religious phenomena were based on the observations of the ceremonies of believers.

At any rate, we are presenting herewith a pioneer study of ritual in family living. It is based on data gathered from more than four hundred families. Consideration of the theoretic bases, and of the details of this study, have occupied our attention over a number of years. This study is, so far as we know, the first systematic one of the subject. It is bound, therefore, to reveal many of the defects of a pioneering study. Obviously, it leaves unconsidered many problems arising in connection with family rituals, particularly in their relation to associated phenomena. Of many of these we are fully aware; and some of them, at least, we hope to deal with more adequately in future publications.

Family Ritual and Family Integration

"The family," write Burgess and Locke, "like all organisms, is in a process of constant accommodation to environing and to internal forces. Perhaps more than any other social group, it is a demonstration or an experiment in the integration of heterogeneous elements; heterogeneous in age, sex and temperament, and often also in social experience, economic activities, and cultural background."[2]

Perhaps the over-all conclusion that emerges from the assemblage of our material is that ritual is a relatively reliable index of family integration. What do we mean by family integration? Does it mean absence of discord? Obviously this is an aspect or index of it, even if negative in character. Is it ability to withstand shock or stress or strain? Possibly, but this would seem to be somewhat a matter of accepted values, and character traits of the constituent members rather than an interactive product or structural strength. The word "integrate" means to bring together and to make into a whole, and we use the term "family integration" to mean the welding or unification of its diverse elements into a complex whole or harmonious relationship. An integrated family means to us a well-knit family, one bound together with strong and continuing ties, and functioning smoothly as a unit.

If one conceives of family integration in generic terms, there are many indexes which may be utilized to identify it. These include the effective meeting of common problems, the ability to resist major crises, smoothness of operation, lack of tension or conflict, evidences of family pride, criteria of family co-operation and continuity, and continuity of family planning. Thinking in terms of process, family integration is unrelated to moral purposes or cultural values. A well-integrated family may evidence it in recurrent feuding with another family, in packing boxes for shipment to displaced persons, in periodic outbursts of drunkenness, or long-range planning for the successive education of the children in a large family.

Ritual indicates many things and serves many purposes in the life of a family. The existence of well-established ritual implies, for example, a considerable amount of likemindedness among the members of a family. Take such a simple yet basic fact as a common interest in family life. The development of a ritual by a family is an index of the common interest of its members in the family as a group. Parents who are conscious of the family as a group, who wish to make a success of family living, who think of their family as a continuing and permanent arrangement, are the ones most likely to initiate and continue the co-operative procedure which yields as a ritual. One can detect, therefore, at the very beginning, a selective process between those family members who develop and utilize ritual, and those who do not. One must be interested in his family, want to make a go of it, and think of it as a permanent relationship, to look forward to the establishment of family rituals and traditions.

Again, rituals are developed co-operatively. This gives and stimulates a sense of group participation, a further sharing of intimacies, and a sense of lively satisfaction. As Adams pointed out years ago, the feelings of satisfaction that accompany the performance of ritual, and the "pause of satisfaction" that follows the achievement of ends in mind, constitute the essence of the aesthetic experience. In other words, the aesthetic experience is a concomitant of successful participation in the ritualistic act.[3] "The rite is performed; control is achieved; the participants rest satisfied."[4]

Third, common participation is a ceremony that carries with it a sense of rightness that makes for family pride. One senses this feeling of pride in almost all of our case records. Even if there was a sort of playful apology, or grumbling pose of feminine coyness in the lines of the case record, it was easy to detect the shades of smug satisfaction between the lines which described the family rituals. The eager willingness with which so many persons co-operated in this study has already been mentioned. Apparently family pride makes for ritual, ritual makes for family pride.

Next, many of our rituals involve refinements of living, and adherence to them implies, and stimulates, a common interest in such refinements. Ritual necessitates a certain formality in social relations, and complementary to this are consideration for the rights of others and the discipline of self, all of which makes for good group relations. It is obvious from our material that ritualism and formalism in family relations make for predictability of behavior response, and this tends to reduce strain and disorder.

The limitations of space permit the mention of but one other role of ritual in family life, and that is its frequent service as a means of controlling the behavior of its members. L. L. Bernard speaks of this aspect of ritual in his *Social Control,*[5] and we have found many instances of this role in our material. Most of our cases have to do with its use to control the behavior of younger members of the household, to regiment and standardize their conduct. Some technique proves to be successful, always produces the same result, and thus comes to be ritualized. But not all cases deal with the control of children. Mother is not above the utilization of ritual to regiment a not completely reliable husband, and at least one husband and his children, in view of Mother's immunity to the inexorableness of the clock, copy a page from the late King Edward VII whenever the family is invited to any occasion. (Edward VII had all clocks in his home set one hour ahead, to enable him more nearly to meet engagements on scheduled time.)

In emphasizing ritual as a significant index of family integration and conserver of family values, we run a certain risk of being misunderstood.

Some cynical soul, in looking over our detailed material, might notice, for example, a ritual in which the entire family gather nightly to drink grape juice before retiring, and rush to interpret us to say: "Drink grape juice before going to bed and have a happy family life." Some of the criticism of the Burgess-Cottrell study comes very close to being of this sort.

This, however, is far from the point we wish to emphasize here. The evening drink and the grape juice are wholly incidental and trivial. What is significant is that the family gathers nightly, engages in a common experience, relaxes together, and exchanges comments before retiring. In thus participating in a recurrent event, which involves some degree of co-operation, the members of the family promote their common life and group rapport. One final word of anticipatory defense. For every conclusion presented, there is case material to support and illustrate it. But for virtually each of our findings, there are also contrary cases. Just as there are speculators who play the stock market on the theory of *Contrary Opinion,* i.e., bucking the majority trends, so there are persons and families who behave "the other way." We not only admit these cases, but we are trying also to understand them. The exception as well as the rule is grist for the mills of the scientists, and the gods as well.

Basically, what we have been trying to show is that ritualizing is a process of family interaction and culture transmission, and that its role depends upon its content and the manner of its utilization. A ritual, appealing in content and manipulated wisely, becomes a powerful and constructive weapon in the integration of a family; and an ill-adapted ritual or a good ritual misused may become an agent in its disintegration. This, perhaps, will serve to explain both our generalizations and the exceptions to them.

Summary

1. A recapitulation of earlier emphases shows that writers of autobiographies largely picture their childhood family experiences in terms of family rituals; that the comments of university students emphasize rituals as easing stress and strain in group living as well as serving to condition the behavior of younger family members; that rituals are an integral part of the family culture varying definitely from one class level to another; and that while the rituals of a family vary from one stage of its development to another, some persist through the years from one generation to another.

2. Rituals regularize personal relations, both of the family as a whole, and between individual members. Particularly significant is the regularization of relations between husband and wife, and parent and child.

3. Ritual is suggested as the best starting point for the study of family culture patterns. Family rituals are the core of the family culture.

4. Passage from the life in one family to that in another calls for ritualistic readjustments. Marriage brings together persons of different ritualistic backgrounds. Earlier family experiences with rituals may result in fixations and resultant regressions in the married life of the individual.

5. The over-all conclusion that emerges from the assemblage of our material is that ritual is a relatively reliable index of family integration.

6. Exceptions to the conclusions presented in this volume are admitted freely, and supported by case material. These exceptions are recognized as fruitful leads for further study.

35   *Norms and Ideology:*
The Normal Family

ELIZABETH BOTT

Based again upon her detailed study of London families, Dr. Bott here expounds the nature of the specific norms which regulate and regularize life in normal families. She puts these norms within the context of the ideology from which they derive, and which, as they are lived up to, they reinforce.

There was not complete consensus among the research couples about what constitutes a normal family. Their concepts varied according to individual experience. An attempt is made to account for the variations and to discuss the way in which norms are arrived at.

In any group discussion, lay or technical, of family life, people are quick to agree that there is no such thing as a "normal" family. No one, they argue, is perfect and no family is perfect either. But at some later point the phrase usually creeps back into the discussion, though its meaning may have changed slightly; from being the "perfect" family it has become the "average" family. The label may be changed too; words like "average" or "ordinary"—our own choice—may be used instead of "normal." In common-sense usage the word "normal" and its various substitutes are thus very ambiguous. They may mean perfect, average, or customary, according to context. But it is impossible to get away from using the idea of normality. One must have some sort of base line, some standard against which variations can be compared. So the concept of the normal family continues to be used in spite of its ambiguity. And, in fact, its very ambiguity is useful in casual discussions; the same word and the same basic idea can be used with different meanings according to the context of comparison.

Reprinted from *Family and Social Network* (London: Tavistock Publications Ltd., 1957), pp. 192–215. Copyright by the Tavistock Institute of Human Relations and used with their kind permission and that of the author and publishers.

In technical discussions it is still necessary to have a yardstick, a standard of comparison. People who study grossly abnormal families are particularly in need of some understanding of the "normal" family so that they may know how and to what degree the abnormal families they study are deviant. But in technical work the ambiguity of the term "normal" leads to confusion. It ceases to be convenient. It is therefore necessary to distinguish verbally between the various meanings of "normal" and "norms," and to relate them to one another. In some work, as I suggest later in this chapter, it is most useful to compare families against two or more different standards of normality.

First, there is normal in the sense of "clinically ideal." This is the meaning that most clinical psychologists and psychoanalysts use. The exact content of the ideal varies according to the psychological theory employed, but "normal" in this sense is always an ideal which may be approached but never fully realized in practice.

Second, "normal" may mean statistically average behavior. For this I suggest the term "behavioral mode."

Third, "normal" may mean behavior that the informants themselves think is morally right or at least expected and customary. This is the usage with which I am chiefly concerned in this chapter.

Fourth, sociologists and anthropologists sometimes use the term "norm" to mean a typical pattern, a sort of generalized model of conduct, which they abstract from informants' behavior as well as from their stated ideals and expectations.[1] I do not use the term in this sense. Of all the various usages, I find this the most vague and confusing, for its precise empirical referents are seldom made clear.

In this chapter I chiefly discuss norms in the third sense, that is, people's ideas about what behavior is customary and what behavior is right and proper in their social circle. These norms are social. They are views that informants assume they share with the other members of their social circle. They are not views that informants think are personal attitudes of their own. If expected behavior is not felt to be ideal, or if ideal behavior is not expected, I make a distinction between *ideal norms* and *norms of expectation*. If the expected and the ideal coincide, I do not use a qualifying adjective.

It is often assumed that there is a large measure of agreement on the social norms of family life in the society as a whole, and that these norms are embodied in the teachings of churches and the rulings of courts of law. Such a view implies that given individuals will recognize that these agreed-upon external standards exist and that they will be able to make the norms explicit without difficulty. It seems to me that this view of social norms is much more appropriate to a small-scale homogeneous society than to a large-scale society with a complex division of labor. In a small-scale society, where many people know one another, where there are few strangers, and most relationships serve many interests, agreement on familial norms develops out of constant interaction, and individuals know what the norms are. Most anthropologists report that their informants have little difficulty in making explicit the approved and customary rules of conduct between members of elementary families and between more distant kinsmen. Behavior does not always conform to norms, but at least people know what the norms are and when they are deviating from them. If such societies have courts of law, most laymen are familiar with court procedure and know the norms on which the court will draw to make judgments. Similarly, everyone will know what norms of familial conduct are embodied in religion. But recent work shows that even in primitive societies norms should not be regarded as a precise, consistent set of rules. Gluckman points out that the Lozi have some very precise rules ("a husband must not go to his wife's granary") but that others are vague ("a husband should treat his wife properly").[2] This very vagueness leaves room for flexible adjustment to varying circumstances. Similarly, norms may contradict one another, which permits selection to suit personal and social convenience. Although there is a fairly high degree of consensus on what the norms are, they are rarely made explicit in times of conflict or crisis, when people use them to justify their own behavior or to pass judgment on that of others.

Even in a small-scale society, then, norms are not precise and consistent. But in a large-scale society the situation is much more complicated, especially where familial norms are concerned. How much agreement on the social norms of family life one would find if one interviewed a representative sample of the general population I cannot say, for I have not been engaged in that kind of study. Among the research couples, there were some points of agreement; most of these were very vague and general and did not give a precise blueprint for action. On many points there was considerable variation from one couple to another. Furthermore, not only was there variation among the families interviewed, but several couples also drew attention to the fact that there was variation among the people they knew personally. Two couples also pointed out that there must be variation in the society at large, if one could believe the wireless, television, newspapers, books, and so forth. But most couples did not even mention such sources of information. They discussed only their own little world of the people they knew personally or had known in the past.

Another fact emerged clearly in our interviews: informants found it very difficult to make familial norms explicit at all. There were several reasons for this, which are discussed below, but in the present connection the relevant point is that inability to make norms explicit was closely associated with awareness of variation. It was the couples who drew attention to variation who said they could not make generalizations about customary and proper ways of familial behavior. Difficulty in generalizing depended also on the context and the situation. People were reluctant to generalize when asked direct questions about norms, although they made many implicit generalizations when talking spontaneously.

In this chapter I attempt to interpret these two findings: first, that there was less consensus on familial norms than is commonly assumed, and second, that many informants found it difficult to state norms explicitly. Perhaps one should not speak of social norms at all in this situation. If consensus is made essential to the definition of social norms, then the research families had only a few very general social norms concerning familial roles. Most of their views on the subject would have to be described as personal opinions. But the data suggest that there is an intermediate stage between complete consensus and random variation. Informants *thought* there was agreement even when there was not. Or, to be more accurate, in some contexts they thought there was agreement and in other contexts they thought there was variation.

Some refinement of terminology is necessary. In ordinary usage, the term "social norms" has a double connotation. It means norms that are in fact agreed on by some group or category of persons; it also means norms that individuals think are current in some group or category. I find it necessary to distinguish these two aspects. I use the term *social norms* to refer to the norms people think are current in some group or category. I suggest the term *norms of common consent* for norms on which there is in fact consensus. I use the term *personal norms* for those ideals and expectations that informants think are their own private standards, different from those they attribute to other people.

Discussion of Field Material

For the first eight or ten interviews, we did not ask any direct questions about the norms of conjugal roles. Such questions were left until the last two or three interviews. In the course of the earlier interviews, it became clear that each couple had a fairly consistent set of standards by which they were judging their own and other people's performance as husbands and wives. The field workers picked up these codes very quickly almost without being aware of doing so. Indeed, I was so convinced that such standards existed that I thought informants had made explicit statements about how husbands and wives should behave. It was only when I went carefully over the field notes again that I realized nothing had been said directly; everything was conveyed by implication, by complimentary or derogatory remarks about friends, neighbors, and relatives. Very few general comments were made until direct questions were asked, and even then, many couples were reluctant to make any generalizations.

VARIATIONS IN CONTENT OF NORMS

On the basis of their spontaneous statements and replies to direct questions, it is possible to summarize the norms the couples adhered to.

There were a few general points of agreement, that is, there were a few norms of common consent. All the couples took it for granted that each elementary family should be financially independent of relatives and friends and should have its own dwelling. All couples took it for granted that there should be a basic division of labor between husband and wife in which the husband was primarily responsible for supporting the family financially and the wife was primarily responsible for looking after the children and seeing that housework and cooking were done. The world would be upside down if the woman went out to work and the husband stayed home to care for the house and the children, although it was recognized, with varying degrees of disapproval and approval, that husbands sometimes helped with child care and housework and wives sometimes went to work. All couples took it for granted that adultery was a serious offense. It was assumed that parents were obliged to care for their children until they could look after themselves, although the standards of good care differed from one family to another.

These norms were not explicitly stated in so many words. They were simply taken for granted. I think one may say that these general points of agreement arise from similarities in familial tasks and *general* similarity of social environment. Most of these norms of common consent were very vague and general so that a considerable variety of behavior could be encompassed within the bounds of conformity.

Many norms varied according to network connectedness. Variations in content have been discussed above and need be only briefly summarized here. Couples in close-knit networks expected husbands and wives to have a rigid division of labor. There was little stress on the importance of shared interests and joint recreation. It was expected that wives would have many relationships with their relatives, and husbands with their friends. Both partners could get help from people outside the family, which made the rigid division of labor between husband and wife possible. Successful sexual relations were not considered essential to a happy marriage.

In contrast, families in loose-knit networks had a less rigid division of labor, stressed the importance of shared interests and joint recreation, and placed a good deal of emphasis on the importance of successful sexual relations. They were more self-conscious about how to bring up their children than couples in close-knit networks. They were aware that the people they knew had a great variety of opinions on this subject and they were worried about which course they themselves should follow.

In addition to these variations according to connectedness of the family's network, there were many idiosyncratic variations. One couple carried the idea of joint sharing of tasks to a point that almost denied the basic division of labor between husband and wife. They stated their views more strongly on some occasions than others. In the most emphatic statement they said wives and mothers should be able to work if they wanted and that it was quite all right for women to work in the same field as their husbands, to be better at their jobs, and to earn more. They implied that this view was generally accepted in their social circle. Another couple with a similar sort of loose-knit network had very different norms on the role of the mother. They said that people in their social circle thought mothers of small children should not work, although in some cases they had to. Each couple recognized that the issue of whether mothers should work or not was highly controversial, but each regarded his own solution as the right course of action and indicated that the other people in their social circle held similar views although they did not always adhere to them in practice.

There were other more subtle variations. Couples with loose-knit networks, for example, generally stressed the importance of joint decision-making by husband and wife. But one wife implied that men were generally more dominant in fact, although not in theory, whereas another wife implied that men were more dominant in theory, although not in fact. Each was attributing to other people what was in fact the case in her own household. Again, a wife suggested indirectly that women in general were more sensitive than men and better at dealing with children and smoothing over difficulties between people. Here she seems to have been attributing to people in general not what was actually the case in her own family but what she would have liked to have been the case. In our judgment, her husband was more skillful at handling interpersonal relations than she was. In another case a wife made a similar statement, but here it seemed that she was in fact generalizing from her own behavior. In another case a husband maintained, in the face of protests from his wife, that his handling of the family finances was the usual and the right procedure among his friends and among families in general.

In brief, there was a tendency for people to treat their own behavior and standards as the norm for other people as well as for themselves. In some cases people implied that the exact opposite of their own behavior was the general norm—a sort of wish-fulfilment about their own behavior. It seems from these cases that people sometimes treat their personal views as social norms. Ideally, of course, one should interview the people with whom the couple identify themselves to see if they would acknowledge the conjugal standards attributed to them—to see whether the social norms of the couple are in fact norms of common consent. In practice, this is very difficult when couples live in networks. And in some cases it would be impossible because, as I describe below, some couples identify themselves with abstract categories of person. But from statements made by the couples in other contexts, it often appeared that there was a good deal of variation among the members of their networks, not only in behavior but also in norms, so that in setting up one sort of behavior as the norm, the couple were making a considerable over-simplification. In consideration of these cases of displacement and projection of one's own norms on to other people, I have come to the conclusion that the usual sharp separation of personal attitudes from social norms does not do justice to the facts of the situation. The research couples assumed they shared certain standards of conjugal behavior with other people, but some of these social norms were partly a thing of their own creation. Doubtless they had assimilated norms from experience with other people. But they also seemed to have selected some expectations and ideals rather than others, and they sometimes attributed their own personal version of norms to people in general or to some group or category of their own choosing without being aware of doing so.

HOW NORMS WERE EXPRESSED

a. *The Difficulty Experienced by Informants in Making Norms Explicit.*—I have mentioned above that although informants continually expressed norms indirectly in spontaneous discussion, they made very few explicit generalizing statements. In the last two or three interviews we asked several direct questions that were intended to get people to talk about norms more directly. We found many of these questions difficult to ask and informants found them difficult to answer so that certain questions were often left out. The questions were these:

1. What do you think the main changes in the family have been in the last fifty years or so? The aim of this question was to find out not only what people thought about social change, but also how they would characterize modern families in general.
2. How would you describe the rights and duties of husband and wife?
3. How would you describe the ideal husband, the ideal wife, the ideal child?
4. How do you feel your own ideas on how to run a family resemble those of people you know, or are different from them?
5. When you got married, did you have a clear idea of what family life would be like? Have your ideas changed?
6. What do you feel are the important things in keeping a family ticking over? What things make it difficult?

Couples found all of these questions, except the first, difficult to answer. Couples with loose-knit networks seemed to find the second question particularly difficult. Their usual reaction was either a prolonged uncomfortable silence—two minutes in one case—or an immediate reply to the effect that there was so much variation one could not generalize. Couples with more close-knit networks found the questions a little easier, although even they often remarked that no two people would agree on how husbands and wives should behave or customarily did behave.

I think there are several reasons for the difficulty people experienced in answering these questions. First, since the field workers belonged to the same society, more or less, informants may have felt that we had some ulterior motive for asking the questions. Otherwise why should we ask questions to which we must have answers of our own? We never became very successful in allaying this sort of anxiety or in asking direct questions skillfully. The question about ideal husbands and wives and children was particularly upsetting. Because we interviewed husband and wife together, it was interpreted as an invitation to comment on the other partner's conjugal deficiencies in his and the field worker's presence. This question did not produce much useful information on norms, but we kept asking it because it was useful to compare how people coped with the slight awkwardness of the situation. But although we did not fully realize it at the time, this question upset the atmosphere of the interview so much that people did not give their full attention to the questions that followed it. If we were asking direct questions about norms again, we should omit this question or put it at the end.

But our awkwardness in asking questions about norms cannot be the only factor, because however stupidly we asked about occupational roles, we always got straightforward answers. Occupational roles are specific and easy to describe. Familial roles are diffuse; they cover many different activities, the organization of which is left to the discretion of the individuals concerned. People become so involved emotionally in familial roles that it is very difficult for them to separate themselves from the roles conceptually.

Another factor affecting difficulty in stating norms explicitly may have been the absence of overt crisis in the families. Norms are usually brought forth only in times of crisis and conflict, when they are used to justify one's own behavior and to pass judgment on that of other people. When nothing much is going wrong, there is no need to state what the norms are.

The fact that couples in close-knit networks found the questions easier to answer suggests another factor. Many of the people they knew were known to one another, so that out of their constant interaction a general measure of consensus had been reached. The family knew, more or less, what the agreed standards were and could make them explicit. Couples in loose-knit networks were more aware of variation. Since many of the people they knew were not acquainted with one another, there were fewer norms of common consent. It was impossible for such couples to reply to the questions without making gross over-simplifications. Perhaps some of their discomfort and hesitation when asked direct questions sprang from a realization that they made such generalizations implicitly in spontaneous discussion all the time, but that their generalizations were not very accurate.

b. References to Individuals, Groups, and Categories.—Most spontaneous expressions of norms took the form of comments on friends, neighbors, and relatives. Very occasionally couples also referred spontaneously to groups or categories of person, although these more general references were made much more frequently in replies to direct questions about norms.

No one referred to religious teaching on the family and no one mentioned legal rules. Indeed, although we did not ask enough questions on this point, it was our impression that most of the research couples were almost totally ignorant of their legal rights and obligations as members of a family. Some expressed surprise at the strange rules of familial behavior the courts enforced. Unless informants had had direct experience of the law, they thought it was something they did not need to know about, something very far removed from their everyday life. Similarly there were very few references to reports of family life in newspapers and other media of mass communication, and none of the couples expressed the anxiety shown in public statements about divorce, delinquency, the decline of religion, and the moral decay of the family. Of course, the fact that there were so few explicit references to religion, law, and the media of mass communication in spontaneous discussion or in reply to our direct questions about norms does not mean that people's conceptions were entirely unaffected by such institutionalized expressions of norms. Our data were not collected to show how public expressions of norms influence people's own views, but it does seem likely that they are highly selective in assimilating such information, taking in what fits in with their own personal experience and ignoring or reworking most of the rest. Similarly, it seems very likely that expression of norms varies according to the social situation and the research technique used. The norms expressed in the group discussions we attended were much closer to those of newspapers and the church than to those expressed by the research couples in interviews. If we had used questionnaires or highly structured interviews with the research families, we should probably have been given a rather different view of familial norms. I would suggest that there is no single correct way of getting at the truth about norms. Different techniques will reveal different aspects of it.[3]

In spontaneous discussion, all couples made indirect expressions of norms in talking about particular individuals they knew. Of all these specific individuals, parents were the most important referents. Parents provided the basic models of family life that the couples we were interviewing were trying to emulate or improve on. There were also many references, usually negative, to friends, neighbors, and other relatives besides parents. A wife, for example, remarked that her brother-in-law was a good bread-winner but neglected his wife and children so that his was not a happy family. Implicitly she was drawing a contrast with her own husband, who was not a great success at his job but did enjoy the company of his wife and children. Or again, a wife remarked that one of the neighbors had ridiculed her own husband in public, with the clear implication that such behavior was very disloyal and ill-mannered. One husband, in the midst of an argument with his wife, went straight through a list of all his friends to show her that all men were difficult to live with and that she was expecting far too much of him. As we got to know families better, we began to be told their gossip. Gossip is one of the chief means by which norms are stated and reaffirmed.

Informants referred to groups or categories of person as well as to specific individuals, especially when replying to our direct questions about norms. Many different reference groups were selected. There was no one group or category that everyone chose as a matter of course. This contrasts with the situation in a small-scale society, in which the group referent is clear; the norms apply to everyone in the society, or at least to everyone in a clearly defined subgroup within the society. When a family is not contained in an organized group, but only in a network, especially a loose-knit network, the referent of the norms becomes much less predictable and more complicated.

When informants were trying to generalize about standards of conjugal behavior, I think most of them were considering primarily their own personal experience, their informal social network of friends, neighbors, and relatives. But no one referred to this set of people as such, presumably because it is difficult to conceptualize a network, since it has no beginning and no end. Some couples referred to local areas. Others tended to choose sets of friends or some kind of abstract category such as "people like us" or "our social circle" or "our kind." Such choice depended partly on the connectedness of the family's network. If a couple had a close-knit network, they usually talked about local areas, although they sometimes also referred to the conjugal practices of other generations or social classes. If they had a loose-knit network, they referred primarily to sets of friends or to abstract categories. Previously it was noted that the most close-knit networks were found where most of a family's friends and relatives were living in the same local area as the family itself. It is hardly surprising that such families conceptualized their network as the local area in which most of the members lived. Families with loose-knit networks did not choose a local area as a reference group, for their relatives and friends were scattered all over England. The closest they could come to a concrete reference group was a set of friends. When they were trying to generalize more broadly they referred to more abstract categories such as "people like us" and "our social circle." In the cases where we thought to ask whom informants were thinking of when they used such phrases, it was clear that the meaning shifted according to context. Sometimes it meant "people of our general class and style of life"; sometimes it meant "people of our age and style of life"; sometimes it meant "our friends" or "potential friends." People who used such words shifted imperceptibly from one meaning to another, and often reference to the category was followed by references to specific individuals who came within it.

People also referred to groups and categories in which they did not place themselves. Families who had had experience of close-knit networks in the past often referred to the local areas in which they had formerly lived. Families with loose-knit networks usually referred not to local areas but to other classes and generations. All couples contrasted their own conjugal standards occasionally with those of the older generation and "Victorian families."

The patterns of selection described above were only general tendencies. Couples varied greatly in choice of reference groups and in feelings toward them. Thus, one couple identified themselves with the local area in which they lived and subscribed almost completely to the standards of conjugal behavior they attributed to the people in it. They contrasted it favorably with conjugal behavior in other areas. Another couple of similar occupational status and general background (but a more loose-knit network) said they liked their local area and would never leave it, although they did not approve of all the local standards of conjugal behavior. They said it was terrible the way the wives gossiped about their husbands and the way husbands never spent any time at home. They felt they themselves had personal standards that were different and better. At the same time, they condemned the conjugal practices of other areas and other classes.

Many couples used several different reference groups. Thus, the plumber and his wife contrasted the confused and variable conjugal standards of their present local area with those of the areas in which they had been brought up. They also contrasted themselves with the households that the husband encountered in the course of his work. Their evaluation of themselves varied according to the context of comparison. Some couples rejected almost completely the norms they attributed to the group with which they identified themselves. Thus one couple acknowledged that they were similar in occupation to their neighbors and relatives but said they had a totally different outlook. They criticized their neighbors and relatives and identified themselves with an abstract category of nice people who had high standards of cleanliness, orderliness, and good manners. At the same time, in the course of spontaneous discussion they revealed that they visited their relatives and neighbors more than this sweeping condemnation implied. Some other couples who rejected the standards they attributed to their local area or friends did not bother to identify themselves positively with some other group or category. They were content to present themselves as deviants above the norms of the category in which they placed themselves. But not all couples selected reference groups in such a way as to make themselves appear in the best light. A few couples went to some trouble to make themselves appear average—that is, they chose categories in which they were placed in the middle when they might easily have chosen categories of such a kind that they would have been at the top.

I do not mean to suggest here that the couples we interviewed were deliberately distorting the norms of sets or categories of people. In nearly all cases, we felt their descriptions were consistent and probably reasonably accurate when they were describing concrete individuals with whom they had had direct experience. Of course we cannot be sure of this because we could not interview all their friends, neighbors, and relatives. But when they were asked to generalize about norms, oversimplification and distortion were inevitable. Families with loose-knit networks had a particularly difficult time here, since the variation among the members of their networks was greater. In brief, when families live only in networks, when there is no organized group that they must almost inevitably use as a reference group, they must construct reference groups. They must generalize from their varied social experience to reach some simplified description, which is inevitably distorted. If they choose, they can identify themselves or contrast themselves with categories that show off their own behavior and standards in a favorable light. If they choose, they may select categories that will make them seem average. If they have a close-knit network, they will probably choose categories that are fairly close to their everyday experiences with friends, neighbors, and relatives, although they are not compelled to do so. If they have a loose-knit network, their categories are likely to be more abstract and generalized. And the more remote the reference group from their everyday experience, the greater is the opportunity for unfettered exercise of imagination.

Expression of norms thus varied according to the context and the particular individual or group that was being evaluated and compared with the couple's own standards of behavior. Couples had a considerable range of choice in selecting the group or category with which they identified or compared themselves. This ability to choose one reference group rather than another makes it easy for informants to treat personal norms as social norms, for it is not difficult to find or construct some abstract category of person who shares one's own views.

DEVIANCE AND CONFORMITY

Variation and flexibility of norms make it difficult to say what is deviance and what is conformity. In the course of the research I have come to the conclusion that it is impossible to make general, universally applicable assessments of levels of family functioning, which is a major aim of much research on the family. Such an aim assumes that there are many norms of common consent about familial roles. Too often, the norms selected as the standard are those that the research worker thinks are current in his own social circle. Even if they are accurate for this category of person, they may be quite inappropriate for other types of family. I am not asserting here that families must never be measured against some standard, only that one should realize that the standard is arbitrary and that many families will not subscribe to it.

I think it is necessary to distinguish between *felt deviance* and *externally defined deviance,* felt deviance being lack of correspondence between the family's behavior and their own social norms, externally defined deviance being lack of correspondence between their behavior and some standard chosen by the research worker. It is very difficult to determine felt deviance, partly because people have trouble in conceptualizing norms, partly because they do not like to talk about deviance unless they think they are above their norm rather than below it, partly because they often use several different reference groups, and partly because they may be at or above their norms in some respects and below in others.

At the risk of considerable oversimplification, I have tried to infer felt deviance for the research families, with the following results. Seven families conformed in most respects to the norms they attributed to their most frequently used reference group. Seven thought they were better in some respects. Three thought they were worse in some respects. Three thought they were different without being better or worse. There were only two cases in which internal inconsistencies suggested that the couple were seriously misrepresenting their own behavior and that of the people in their most frequently used reference group. Both these couple placed themselves above their norm.

Felt deviance can be compared with various types of externally defined deviance. If one takes conformity to the very general norms agreed on by all families, the norms of common consent, only two families were below these norms and even these families were below only in some respects, not in all. Both families tacitly acknowledged their deviance in the relevant respects.

If the norms of each set of families with similar degrees of network-connectedness are taken as the standards, there were fourteen cases in which felt deviance (or conformity) and externally defined deviance (or conformity) coincided, and six cases in which they did not agree. These six cases include the two couples mentioned above who probably misrepresented their own behavior and the norms of their reference groups. In the other four cases, the social norms of the families were slightly different from those of other families with similar types of network.

If one uses Burgess' "companionship" family as the standard,[4] only nine families conformed. Of the eleven deviant ones, the behavior of two was at their own norm, six were above, one was below, and two were different without being above or below.

In brief, if one uses different standards, one gets different measures of deviance. Perhaps in situations in which there are only a few norms of common consent, it would be convenient to determine what might be called *average norms*. These would consist of a quantitatively determined mean of the social norms expressed by the members of some category or set of persons selected by the research worker. Such an average measure would permit comparison of particular informants' social norms against a general standard, admittedly an artificial one, even when there were few norms of common consent.

If one must evaluate families, I do not think it matters greatly what standard is used, provided it is relevant for the immediate problem and provided one bears in mind that there is not likely to be consensus on this standard among one's informants. But in almost any evaluative study, I should think it would be instructive to compare felt deviance with externally defined deviance. This permits one to do justice to the families' own standards and to the fact that their ideas of right and wrong, of the customary and the unusual, may be quite different from those of the research worker. But at the same time, it allows the research worker to use a fixed standard against which all variations, both in norms and in behavior, can be compared.

CONFLICTS OF NORMS

Among the research families there were many examples of inconsistencies between norms. A wife should be able to work; a wife should stay home to look after her children. Among the families with comparatively close-knit networks, there was a conflict for the wives between obligations to the mother and obligations to the husband. In several cases, ideal norms and norms of expectation conflicted with each other. Couples in close-knit networks said that husbands ought to give their wives a liberal housekeeping allowance, but they did not really expect such generosity. One wife complained about her husband's stinginess, and another wife constantly stressed how fortunate she was in having a generous husband. The first wife thought most other women suffered as she did, whereas the second thought her husband was most unusual, but in both cases it was clear that the norm of expectation was that husbands would not give enough.

It is sometimes assumed that discrepancies and conflicts of norms are a sign of social change—an assertion that assumes the "normal" state of social systems to be one of harmony and consistency. But, as I have stated above, norms are seldom consistent even in small-scale societies that are changing slowly, and it seems likely that certain types of conflict are endemic in a social system. It is difficult to imagine that conflict of norms about loyalty to one's mother and to one's husband could be eliminated from families with close-knit networks. It may disappear if the family moves, but then the whole organization of external and internal relationships is altered.

Conflicts between norms need not, as is sometimes suggested, lead to personal and social conflict. In favorable circumstances people may be able to reconcile the requirements of conflicting norms. Thus, one of the wives with a close-knit network was able to fulfill her obligations both to her husband and to her mother, partly because of her own skill and tact, but also because her husband and her mother got along well together. In other cases, wives were both working and fulfilling their obligations to their children, to their own and their husbands' satisfaction. Individuals may also cope with discrepancies of norms by constructing their own solution as an ideal norm and projecting it on to their social circle or some other reference group of their own choosing. This does not solve the problem on a social level but it does sort things out for the individual.

As I have stated above, people do not usually make norms explicit spontaneously except in situations of interpersonal conflict, and we were not able to witness many such disputes. The research families knew they were being studied as "ordinary" families, so that it is not surprising that they did not display their conflicts before us. After the first few interviews, when they had lost much of their uneasiness about revealing the fact that they did not always get along well together, they would describe rows they had had in the past or might have in the future. But only one couple had a row in the presence of one of the field workers. In this case each partner asserted that he was behaving correctly and that the other was in the wrong. Each proclaimed different norms and tried to show that his own view was generally accepted in their social circle. It did not happen, as it often does in small-scale societies, that the disputants agreed about the norms in principle but disagreed over whether and how they had conformed to them.

Concluding Discussion

In this chapter I have reported more variation in the norms of familial roles than is commonly assumed, and I have also shown that many of the people we interviewed found great difficulty in making norms explicit. I have suggested that both facts can be interpreted in terms of the immediate social environment in which the research families lived. The argument may be most clearly summarized by contrasting the position of families that are encapsulated within organized groups with those in close-knit networks and those in loose-knit networks.

In an organized group in which members are in constant interaction, one is likely to find a large number of norms of common consent. Constant interaction corrects individual idiosyncrasies of ideology. The norms I have defined as social norms, that is, the norms people attribute to the group with which they identify themselves, are likely to be more or less the same as the norms of common consent. In other words, there is little variation in the norms various members of the group attribute to it. Members of the group will find it easy to make norms explicit. Almost inevitably, members will use the group itself as a reference group when discussing familial norms. Individual members may of course have discordant personal views, but they will be aware of the discrepancy between their own views and those of other members of the group, just as they will soon find out if their own behavior is deviant. Opportunities for treating personal norms as social norms are reduced to a minimum. This does not mean, of course, that group norms never change. They may change in response to changed external conditions and through internal upheavals in which the personal views of individual members may play an important part.

In a close-knit network, the group situation is approached, but there is more variation in norms, since not all members of the network interact with one another. If one could interview all the members of a close-knit network, I should predict that one would find a fairly large number of norms of common consent: the social norms of the various members would be in fairly close agreement with one another. There would be more variation than in a group, less than in a loose-knit network. People in close-knit networks are likely to be intermediate in ability to state norms explicitly; they will have more difficulty than people in organized groups, less difficulty than people in loose-knit networks. People in close-knit networks are likely to use their networks as reference groups, although they conceptualize them as local areas. But they are not compelled to make this selection. They may also choose abstract categories or groups of which they have no direct experience. In such a situation, people have some opportunity to treat their personal norms as social norms, but if they are in constant interaction with the members of their network, and if the members of their network are in constant interaction with one another, they are likely to be made aware that their social norms are not norms of common consent.

In a loose-knit network, fewer members know one another and there is less interaction. More variation in norms is likely to develop. There will be fewer norms of common consent, more variation in social norms from one member of the network to another. Informants find it difficult to make norms explicit, especially when their attention is focused on variation by direct questions. But, at the same time, they do assume implicitly that they share their standards of conjugal behavior with other people. By my definition they have social norms, although there are few norms of common consent. People in loose-knit networks have considerable opportunity to treat personal norms as social norms, to assert that the standards they follow are those that are current in their social circle or in some other similar reference group. The referent of their social norms, although derived from experience with their friends, neighbors, and relatives, is likely to be an abstract category. Because they have so much experience of different standards among the people they know, their reference groups must be generalized and over-simplified, and they have a considerable range of potential reference groups to choose from.

The suggestion that personal norms may unwittingly be treated as social norms raises the question of how norms are acquired by individuals. The psychological mechanisms of this process are very complex, and I shall do no more here than suggest some points that merit further reflection and inquiry.

In the literature of social psychology, much stress is placed on the internalization of norms through interaction with other people.[5] This interpretation of the individual as a passive recipient of external norms is too simple for the data I have reported here. When individuals and families live in networks rather than in groups, the process of norm formation becomes more complicated. I would suggest that individuals internalize other people's standards from their experiences with them, but that this is not the end of the matter. If the internalized standards agree with one another, which tends to happen in organized groups and in close-knit networks, there is little necessity for selection and internal rearrangement. If many different and contradictory norms are internalized, individuals select some rather than others and construct their own version in accordance with their personal needs. They may attribute this personal version, or certain aspects of it, to other people besides themselves, and they have a wide range of reference groups or categories from which to choose the recipient of their norms. In brief, projection and displacement play as important a part as internalization in the acquisition of norms.

I would suggest, then, that both psychological mechanisms, introjection (internalization) and projection, are always involved in the acquisition of norms. Indeed, recent findings of psychoanalysis explicitly stress the importance of projection as well as introjection in all learning processes.[6] This view is also implicit in the work of George Herbert Mead.[7] In the case of couples in loose-knit networks, the separate effects of the two mechanisms are comparatively easily distinguished. In close-knit networks or organized groups it is much more difficult to separate the two mechanisms. Errors of projection and of introjection are more rapidly corrected by constant interaction, so that a common standard is reached both internally and externally.

36 *Differentiation of Values in a Modern Community*

JOHN R. SEELEY, R. ALEXANDER SIM,
and ELIZABETH W. LOOSLEY

In previous selections, evidence was presenetd regarding the differentiation of activities within the family, a differentiation which evidently has a basic, universal principle. One would expect that such differentiation would not persist unless supported by, and support- ing, some differentiation in values. This excerpt, from a community study by Seeley and co-workers, examines the differential patterns of values held by men and women in this middle-class setting and suggests some of the far-reaching effects of this differentia- tion.

The deepest cleavage[1] in the belief system of Crestwood Heights—more basic and deeper (we feel) than differences in age, ethnic group, or status—is created by the striking divergence in the belief systems of men and of women.[2] The differences, the polarities, the selective, un- like, and emphatic emphases exist not merely at the level of detail, but, more important, at the very core of belief.

This cleavage, which seems on the basis of our experience to appear in connection with virtually every important conviction, is obscured and covered over by another difference between men and women: as to whether, indeed, such important differences between them exist. Perhaps as a function of the conflict involved in the progressive emancipation of women in the last century or half-century, perhaps for other reasons,[3] the ideology of the women tends to minimize the differences between the sexes. The "without regard to race, creed or color" pronouncement, the "people are people" view, the individualistic approach which tends to regard any categorization of people as wicked: these are used with perhaps even greater warmth and emphasis to play down or deny differences be- tween men and women, other than those unblinkably given by anatomy.[4] The women are thus—and here again they are in league with the experts— the promoters of an ideology of identity at the ideological level: men and women should, they feel, and would, except for irrational accidents of

From *Crestwood Heights,* by John R. Seeley, R. Alexander Sim, and Elizabeth W. Loosley. Copyright 1956 by the University of Toronto Press; Basic Books, Inc., the Amer- ican publishers; and Constable and Company, the English publishers; and used with their kind permission.

history, share a single value-system: the "maturity," individual-oriented values for which they themselves stand.

The men, on the contrary, tend to exaggerate the cleavage, and even, ideologically, to regard it as an impassable gulf to be accepted with good-humored tolerance. "Weaker sex," "inferior species" is now forbidden terminology, but the classification of "women and children" is more than a separation of convenience. Women are alleged to be unalterably senti-mental, non-logical, and incapable of the heroic efforts needed for sub-stantial accomplishment. This is supposed to be so much the case that the case cannot—in spite of all the evidence—be demonstrated to women. They must be "handled," like children, with careful concealment of the definition by which they are defined.

That the differences in ideology exist would be denied by one side (the women); that they ought to be examined as having validity, as possessing equal biological and social importance, as being complementary and mu-tually necessary in the division of labor, social and evolutionary, would be denied by the other side (the men).

An exhaustive treatment is not possible here, but some illustrations of such differences may be useful.

Ideology and Action

1. Individual and Group.—One such striking difference, perhaps the most important in its effects on the formation of character and on human relations, is found in the estimate of the moral value and operational im-portance of "the individual" and "the group." For the women (and their allies among the experts, male and female), the supreme value is the happiness and well-being of the individual, which taken in its immediacy determines day-to-day policy. Does a general rule press heavily on a given child? Then the child ought to have special support, or an exception to the rule should be made, or the rule should be amended or abolished. The particular, the unique, the special, the case, the individual is both the focus of concern and the touchstone of policy. The institutional regularities are seen rather as obstacles than as aids to the achievement of the good life. Mores, folkways, laws, norms are considered to function as obstructions to the development of those unique characteristics, configurations, and activities which are the height of value, if not its very meaning. Individuals so reared and freed will, it is felt, produce the minimum of order which may be required—if any is—for concerted action where that is necessary.

The men have a firm hold on the other horn of what is cast by both sides as a dilemma. For them generally, the organization, the business, the institution, the activity, the group, the club, the rules, the law are the focus of loyalty. True, they have a supplementary or supporting belief, that the stability and persistence of the group accrue to the good of the individual; but the "army" comes clearly before "the soldier" and indeed without it there will be no soldier. If the individual will learn to fit into the going institutions, he will find therein whatever field of expression and achievement it is proper and permissible for him to have.

This polarity implies other polarities, reaching perhaps even deeper. For the man (say, a father), a given act (say, his child's) is one of a series of acts classified, according to its formal, quasi-legal properties, with other acts having similar external consequences—particularly, naturally, for government, authority, and the maintenance of norms and practices. For the woman (say, a mother), the same act is seen chiefly as embedded in its immediate context of meaning and emotion, with roots reaching back to previous, perhaps formally dissimilar acts, in that particular child's emotional history. The man's first step in the analysis of a problem is analytic and categorical; the woman's is synthetic and contextual. The man has the "play" as the frame of reference for the act; the woman has the "actor." The "universe of acts" of which the given act is a sample is, for the man, the universe of acts (regardless of agent) that have similar effects; for the woman, the universe of acts of which this is a sample is the universe of that particular actor's acts.[5] For the man, effect and achievement are the paramount dimensions of classification; for the woman, motive, intent, and feeling.[6]

These primary orientations which lie at the level of thought and feeling and expression, are, curiously, contradicted by each sex in its role as "operator." The men, who allege the supremacy of the organization, the collective, are the practitioners of skills which rest, consciously or not, upon contrary beliefs. They bring to rare perfection and are secretly (within or between themselves) proud of those arts of interpersonal manipulation that are intended to make the organization work to the benefit of a particular individual. They have the "know-how": they know "who's who" and "what's what." Business is thus chiefly an interpersonal operation in which the ostensibly worshipped collective and its norms are *felt* to function (as the women *say* they do) as obstacles to be dealt with or circumvented as far as prudence will permit. The appeal is taken by the individual to the individual for the sake of the individual, although the best cover for action is reference back to the welfare of the organization as the apparent ground.

The women, on the contrary, who allege the supremacy of the individual notably act in groups to persuade or coerce individuals into making changes in the conditions of group life, for example, a change in a norm system or activity. It is they who, instead of taking direct individual-to-individual action, organize, work in concert, know and use the techniques of group pressure, and so secure alteration in the circumstances of the group.

It should perhaps be re-emphasized that these contradictions within the sex groups and oppositions of orientations between them are genuine, and not, as might be supposed, mere fronts or deceptive devices. For the women, the preoccupation with the good of the individual in all its immediacy is indeed paramount; it organizes thought and feeling and perception. No less genuine is the male attachment to the welfare of the organization. It is only that each sex, in action, moves as it would logically be expected to move if it held the ideology of the other.[7] What might be said, summarily, after due allowance for exceptional individuals or for ordinary individuals acting under exceptional circumstances, is that men tend to use a psychology of individual differences in the name of the institutions, quite commonly for an individual, competitive object; the women tend to use a social psychology in the name of individual autonomy, quite frequently to secure collective and co-operative alteration in the ways of groups.

2. *Voluntarism and Determinism.*—Logically subordinate, perhaps, but psychologically prior to the individual-group polarity is a polarity that, for want of a better name, might perhaps be called "voluntaristic-deterministic."

Ideologically, the women are great determinists of various schools of determinism, particularly, but not exclusively, psychological.[8] For them, the school psychologist's reiterated statement that "we should remember that behavior is caused" has the ring of the self-evident as well as sufficient statement. They, together with the majority of the experts, are concerned with the discovery of just those regularities in human behavior which will permit an expanding science of known laws or determinacies in reference to it.

The men, ideologically, find themselves very nearly at the opposite pole. They tend toward a Great Man theory of history, both ancient and everyday. They see and feel an active agency; the underlying theory of the free will is dominant; they are great voluntarists and, therefore, moralists. What a man can do depends largely on the strength of his desire or his will to do it, and the success stories which they admire demonstrate the soundness of this view very nearly as well as the success stories which they *are*.

What is true for each sex as a routine of thought and feeling is again contradicted for each at the level of both goal and activity. The men believe that sufficient effort on their part as free agents will so order the world, human and nonhuman, that good results human and nonhuman will thenceforward and thereby be determined. The women believe that a sufficient exploration of and recognition of and adaptation to the determinacies in human and nonhuman affairs will lead toward an increase in autonomy, in freedom, in objective, effective agency.

3. Immutability and Perfectibility.—The same kind of double contradiction between the sexes, and on the levels of both ideology and action,
obtains with respect to attitudes toward human perfectibility.

The women incline ideologically toward the view of human perfectibility, taking their point of departure in the known plasticities of human
nature, the established variations (throughout history and across contemporary cultures) in the culturally sanctioned ways of doing things. If
this variety is possible, it is argued, so presumably is any amount of variation, which includes ever better constellations. This bare possibility is
further supported, as a matter of morale, by a rather vague inheritance from
religious or evolutionary ideology or both, which is given the interpretation
that, since things *may* get better, the universal process ensures that they
will do so.

The men incline more to the recognition of invariances in human behavior, to a definition either that human nature is unchanging or, with more
sophistication, *plus ça change, plus c'est la même chose.* Elevated or ex-
alted views of human nature as it exists are dismissed as naïve; similar
views about potentialities, as "utopian," in a pejorative sense.

Both sexes reverse themselves in action. It is the women who, by and
large, in action take count of the intractabilities and unchangeableness in
human beings, as given, and who "realistically" adapt themselves to these
facts and operate quietly in their context. It is the men who demand a
process of continuous perfecting in their operations, and who rail loudly
against anyone sufficiently implastic to be incapable of constant improvement.

It is this differing attitude to perfectibility generally that in the first
place underlies and in the second is a consequence of differing involvement with the psychological, human relations, or social science expert.

The feeling among women is widespread that, since human nature and
social life both *are* perfectible and *ought* rapidly to be perfected, the
answer to any given human problem from how to be happy in marriage
to how to age gracefully either is or ought to be readily available and can
be learned from the right expert, and, having been learned, will be put into
practice either automatically or with a modicum of effort.[9] The men, who
have long employed and subordinated the expert-in-reference-to-things,
confront the expert-in-reference-to-people with, first, a deep and sometimes
inveterate scepticism, and even where this is weakened, with a demand for
his aid in the achievement of ends which they (the men) have already
defined. Where this can be done, they can employ such experts also, but in
a subordinate capacity as facilitators, i.e., they can use the "intelligence-
testers" in the Selective Service system in wartime. Where the orientation
of the expert raises questions about the ends, however—as, at the moment,
in most cases it must—the tendency is to return to scepticism if not to move
on to irritation or anger.[10]

4. Emotionalism and Rationalism.—Not unrelated to, but not wholly included logically or psychologically in, the voluntarism-determinism polarity is another which may be called "rationality–emotionality" or "thought–feeling."

The orientations for the two sexes are again dissimilar both as to fact and as to ideal: as to what is and what ought to be supreme, ultimate, decisive, or determinative. Again, the women, at the ideological level, give greatest weight to the feeling or emotional process, and indeed take the view that this both is and ought to be the final determinant of behavior. Rationality is to be at the service of emotion, and first place must be given to emotional considerations. It is an easy step from "the child cannot learn unless he is happy" (happiness is a necessary condition) to "the child will learn if he is happy" (happiness is a sufficient condition), and, while the two positions are rarely clearly separated, the women tend toward the second. Typically, however, in action and especially for themselves, they adopt practices that would be thought logical consequences of the ideological position of the men: "one cannot be happy unless one learns" (a necessary condition) or "by learning one will be made happy" (a sufficient condition).

The position of the men ideologically and their actions, are, as might now be expected, the point-for-point opposite. They cleave ideologically to the view that feeling is or ought to be subordinate to thought; they act on the assumption that feeling, or the distillate of experience which is intuition, is sufficient for their practices. There is very nearly the acting out of a conviction as to the "Divine Right of Men"; they act on the assumption that, without the study and thought so necessary to the women, they will know decisively at any given point what is right, or at least best or most suitable. It is to women that they attribute intuitive powers; but it is to themselves that they arrogate exclusive right of intuition-based action.

What has been said so far might be represented in a table, in which it may be observed that the ideological tendency of each sex is "counterbalanced" by its own habits of action and by the prevailing ideology of the opposite sex: there is thus an inner and an outer check.[11]

Differences in Ideology and Action According to Sex

Sex	Sphere of Ideology	Sphere of Action
Male	Collectivist	Individualist
	Voluntarist	Determinist
	Immutabilist	Perfectionist
	Rationalist	Emotionalist
Female	Individualist	Collectivist
	Determinist	Voluntarist
	Perfectionist	Immutabilist
	Emotionalist	Rationalist

Habits of Thought and Action

Not quite identical with the ideology-action distinction between the sexes, is a similar distinction between characteristic habits or modes of thought and action.

1. Span of Matter.—It is most notable that in the realm of thought itself it is the women who are the great system-builders and system-seekers; and the men who notably invent or accept innumerable little islands of un-connected—indeed often incompatible—belief. The urge to "philoso-phize," to integrate experience in an intellectually consistent, comprehen-sive fashion is quite markedly a female characteristic; the urge to leave ex-perience as an enjoyable muddle, or, at most, to organize small areas of it intellectually *ad hoc* by crude rule-of-thumb, is quite definitely male.

In contrast, it is the women who are in action the great improvisers, inventors, and demonstrators and devotees of the value of spontaneity. It is they, and those influenced by them, who in an endless flow of minute-to-minute adaptations and improvisations fit action to unforeseen possibility or opportunity—to the point where men feel that directed movement is lost in the confusions of "tacking." For the man, any sense of direction in action, lies in habit, system, routine, rule, and institution to the point where, for the woman, his constancy of direction under shifting circumstance is a permanent or recurrent threat to arrival at the goal originally intended.

2. Span of Time.—Similar in its effects,[12] and perhaps necessary to the maintenance of the foregoing difference, is a difference with respect to the time span habitually taken for granted in thought or action. The women predominantly think in the long range, almost *sub specie aeternitatis,* in terms of ultimate effects, just as they do in terms of logical conclusions. Their thinking attaches less to the immediacies of time and place, and tends to take into imaginative consideration not only the here and now, but the new generation, the "children yet unborn," altered circumstance, and per-haps even a new society as yet only vaguely envisioned. The men, on the contrary, much more earth-bound and datum-driven, take into considera-tion an evanescent present or, at most, a very short-run future, in which things will be much as they are now and have always been. It is perhaps not a contradiction—on the assumption of changelessness—that the men, in action, are the makers of long-term plans and the builders of persistent material and social edifices. They, predominantly, are the authors of en-during buildings, indestructible dams, business and social organizations that are intended to and do have an immortality transcending their own lives. The women, again, adapt old buildings to new uses—homes as adult-education centers, schools as community recreation centers—and create the multiplicity of cliques, alignments, groups, temporary committees which they intend to be as short-lived as the purposes for which they were brought into being.

3. Optimism and Pessimism.—Perhaps just because of these different concentrations on a few large or many small expanses of time and sub- ject- or thought-matter, there is a corresponding differential distribution of optimisms and pessimisms between the two sexes. First recognizable is a primary distinction similar to those already encountered: on the male side, an optimism in action and with reference to the consequences of action, accompanied by a pessimism as to the validity, utility, or indeed, possibility of thought when at all removed from the immediacies and urgencies of act; on the female side, a want of optimism (perhaps not a true pessimism) with reference to action and in action, but in thought and dream a radical, not to say utopian, optimism.[13] In another dimension —which, psychologically, is not wholly independent of the foregoing— the men seem incredibly optimistic with reference to things; the women with reference to human beings, values, and ideas.

We shall have to touch, below, on a similar dichotomy of optimism and pessimism in the relation of means and ends, to which we may now turn.

Means and Ends

The relation of ends and means is, of course, not given in nature, but only in the nature of man. There are no things that are "naturally" means and others that are "naturally" ends. Objects are given an ends- means relation by the place they occupy in the schemes of a purposing and conscious being. Needless to say, such relations, then, tell us about purposes—and not about the natural order independent of human pur- pose.

The differences between men and women as to ends and means seem again to run through nearly every important category or modality of experience, and only some of the most striking will be touched on here.[14]

1. Basic Location.—More fundamental perhaps than any following dis- tinction is a difference between men and women as difficult to define in a single term as it is psychologically impressive and significant. We have called it one of "basic location" because it has to do with a funda- mental feeling which each sex expresses as to where it is most comfort- able, most secure, most "at home": the women among ends and ultimate or long-term purposes (about the means to which they are relatively uncertain and unclear); the men among a proliferation and elaboration of means (as to the ends or purposes which these are to serve, they are less sure, more uneasy, and less interested). It is to this difference that each sex points when it reports the difficulty of getting the other into "serious" discussion: for the men, this represents an accusation that the women's discussion of ends is irresponsible, relatively divorced as it is from the close consideration of means; for the women, the men's interminable discussion of mere means has, in the absence of clarified purposes, a futility so potent as to disbar any possible claim to seriousness.[15]

2. *Point and Duration.*—The fundamental orientation of the two sexes toward two aspects of time seems to provide the ground for a whole series of related distinctions in valuation. Both sexes, needless to say, experience time in all its modalities or significances especially both as a series of discrete points (a sum of evanescent presents) and as a continuum, an unbroken (in one sense, timeless) flow or duration. For the men, quite dominantly, duration has to be accepted for the sake of point, the spaces between for the sake of the crises that punctuate and enliven them, the states of being for the sake of the events that may be counted upon to follow and render them meaningful. For the women, with equal clarity, events are engineered for the sake of the states that are to follow, the points accepted for the sake of the durations they seem to prelude or promise. It is as though in a system that flows while it pulses and pulses while it flows, the men felt the pulse of experience and valued it, while the women felt and valued the flow.

This differentiation tends to distinguish the preference for and the reaction to virtually all other experience. To use present happiness as a take-off point for future excitements; to see life as a sum of episodes or exploits, interleaved by preparations; to see sharp boundaries around experiences and over-potent definitions: these are all male (or masculine) characteristics. Perhaps no deeper distinction can be reached, although there is reason to think something deeper does underlie it: the preoccupation of the women with the ego (and other egos), of the men with the non-ego; of the women with the reality of the subjective world, of the men with the objective world. Each, of course, in ascribing inferior reality to that which to the other seems most real, evidences radical objectivism or radical subjectivism.[16]

3. *Things and Personalities.*—It is probably only on the basis of this underlying distinction that the dominant preoccupation of men with the use of persons as a means to the production of things can be fully appreciated and understood, in contrast with the women's unequivocal view that mere things are for the sake of their effect on the production and refinement of personality. This is not to say—here or anywhere else— that men never see things as means to the formation or alteration of personality. Of course, like others, they induce loyalty in their employees (by incentive pay and other schemes) and they buy their children toys to make them good or happy or well-adjusted children. But here as elsewhere the question is which is the psychologically ultimate

term. For the women, the ultimate term is here at the personality level; a personality characteristic is a sufficient good. For the men, it is merely or chiefly a necessary good: an ingredient necessary to the thing-producing process. A good child is good because, or if, he is effective; his happiness is good because happy people work better; his adjustment is a good because adjustment makes for a smooth-running team, i.e., a team that makes a good game by counted goals of concrete achievement.[17]

4. *Order and Freedom.*—It is almost inescapable in terms of the system of beliefs and preferences so far described that women should regard order less as a good in itself and more as a grudgingly recognized means to freedom; and that men, primarily oriented to order, admit freedom as a safety-valve without which order would be in danger of an eruptive breach. This view seems consistently applied with reference to their own lives, with regard to ideals of personality for children, and in their aspiration for the good society. The women discipline themselves that the children and, if strength remains, they themselves may have room for impulse and spontaneity; the men indulge them, and occasionally themselves, so that routine and order may be returned to with fresh spirit and be preserved with a more permanent and closer fit.

5. *Happiness and Achievement.*—Here for the first time, in the analysis of the written and spoken material, we seem to run into a psychological inconsistency.[18] Men seem to be telling one another and their children and such others as their propaganda may reach: "To be happy you must achieve." Women say: "To achieve, you must be happy." The first proclamation seems to look upon happiness as the end, achievement as the means; the second, to look the other way. Surely this is on both sides "out of character."

Indeed it is, for what has here been intercepted in the propaganda war of the sexes is a "message to the enemy" couched by each side in the vocabulary of the other in order to get inside his psychological defenses. What the men are saying really is: "Even if you believe (mistakenly) that happiness is the end of life, it makes no difference; you can only get there by putting our first value, achievement, first. Then you may get happiness and not otherwise; and, if you don't, you will have achieved and that is what matters." Similarly the women are saying "Even the (mistakenly) achievement-oriented must know that happiness is indispensable to their aim, so they had better seek it first in the first place."

Miscellaneous

One could perhaps continue indefinitely, or at least as long as the patience of readers would allow. Other contrasting words which the data show to be operationally significant for male and female come to mind: hard and soft; outward-oriented, inward-oriented; thought-reliant, feeling-reliant; fact-led toward a realism which discounts potentiality, wish-led toward a romanticism which discounts reality; rule-oriented, role-oriented; game-centered, player-centered; literal, symbolic—and so on. But since the object is to evoke a sufficient image of a primary orientation rather than to exhaust a definition, perhaps these examples will serve.

Summary

An attempt to summarize the difference in the belief systems of men and women in Crestwood Heights, without judging between or evaluating the issues, might justly conclude that the fundamental difference is in their basic orientation to two complementary aspects of living.

The men seem primarily concerned about the preservation of life against destruction, and they feel and believe accordingly. The women seem concerned about the creative and elaborative processes, and they believe and feel accordingly. The men attend to the *necessary* conditions for living; the women to the conditions that would make life *sufficing*. The men are oriented to the biological and social substratum, to minima; the women to the social and psychological superstratum, to maxima. The men are concerned with the prevention of positive "evils"; the women with the procurement of positive "goods." The men live psychologically in an emotional climate of scarcity requiring the close and calculated adaptation of means to ends; the women, correspondingly, live in a climate of abundance requiring the wise selection and utilization of the riches available. The men are for prevision—and provision accordingly; the women for vision—and enjoyment as of now. The men are sensitized to necessity: the women to choice. Compulsion, the *vis a tergo,* the drive from the past press with more weight on the men and order their behavior; yearning, "final cause," the pull of the future, lure or govern the women. Rousseau speaks more nearly for the women; Hobbes for the men.

The disappearance of the patriarchal family from practice as impossible and from ideology as immoral has, seemingly, left untouched in the men the more general orientations which it bespoke, and to which under the then-existing conditions of life it was probably the best answer.

The functional utility of this strong representation by male and female of the defense and the elaboration of life, respectively, is evident. In terms of material goods, it is not unlikely that we are now in North America at a transition point between the stages where a logic of scarcity was, and a logic of abundance is, an appropriate adaptation.[19] What is true of material goods is probably no less true of the new knowledge, of emerging art forms, of new modes of human relating, of developing possibilities in the formation of character and the structure of personality.

Perhaps this transition is—or seems to be—eternal, or at least coextensive in time with human life. In such situations, there appears invariably to be a party that would outrun the possibilities of change, go "too fast," and a party that would outwait these possibilities, go "too slow." These parties usually see one another as enemies, frequently as mortal ones. Where the parties are, as in the present instance, divided largely on sex lines, and where the life-conserving or life-defending and the life-enriching or life-developing impulses are pitted against one another in the area of greatest intimacy and co-operation, it might seem that the possibility of fruitful juncture had been sacrificed to the necessity of adequate representation.

This would indeed appear to be the case. To the degree that the picture represented is a true one, every child is assured of the experience of being pulled in two different directions with respect to all important matters. He must not only achieve an integration that will permit him to function adequately at each stage in the presence of two such opposed parent-figures, but he must further "choose" to make dominant the orientation appropriate to his sex unless he is to become or feel a social and occupational misfit. This he is quite generally able to do, but the task is rendered no easier by the playing down of social and psychological sex-differences that has accompanied the twentieth century's recognition and rewarding of anatomical and physiological ones.

37   *Kinship Terminology and the American Kinship System*

DAVID M. SCHNEIDER

and GEORGE C. HOMANS

The terms used in addressing or referring to relatives are one important tool by which anthropologists determine the structure of kinship systems. Professors Schneider and Homans, anthropologist and sociologist respectively, adapted this tool for large-scale administration in American society. In this paper they present the prevailing patterns as they have determined them. In addition, they discuss how kinship terminology conveys to the child broad principles of relationships and values which govern these relationships.

Introduction

The American kinship system is marked by bilateral descent, and the nuclear family and the kindred are the basic kin groups. Marriage is monogamous, residence neolocal, and inheritance by testamentary disposition. Succession is absent; a man gets no political or other office simply through kinship ties. The range of kinship is narrow, and kinship tends to be sharply divorced from other institutions such as the occupational system, the effect being to make kinship appear small beside such complex and ramifying institutions as economics and technology. The American kinship system appears to be "pushed to the wall" by other institutions, and much of its coloring derives from this.

For the light it may throw on the American kinship system, we shall describe here a study of American kinship terminology. We believe it may also illuminate certain problems of kinship terminology in general.

It appears at first glance, and many commentators have remarked, that the formal terms of American kinship are "Eskimo" in type. Fa is terminologically distinguished from FaBr, Mo from MoSi, while parents' siblings are grouped in categories distinguished from one another by sex but not collaterality. Cross and parallel cousins are grouped together and distinguished from siblings, while own children are differentiated from the children of siblings, who are differentiated from each other only on the basis of sex. Of this much, there seems little doubt.

Reprinted from *American Anthropologist,* LVII (December, 1955, 1194–1208, with the kind permission of the senior author.

These rather broad generalizations are clear enough, but at the time we began our study we were not sure what they implied or how far they held. Further investigation, we felt, might be useful. To this end we decided to collect some information on the terms Americans actually use for their kinsmen.

Obviously we could not sample, exhaustively and systematically, all age, sex, class, regional, and other groupings in America; indeed, we were not at all sure at the outset whether a genealogical, interview, or questionnaire method, or some combination of these, was the most fruitful approach. We therefore set up a pilot study, using a variety of techniques to assemble data on kinship usages, with students and faculty in the Department of Social Relations at Harvard as informants, but supplementing these with data from certain similar sources.

Our informants were 209 in number, of whom 154 were male and 55 female. We carried out intensive interviews from one to four hours in length, including, with 37 of the informants, 21 male and 16 female, the collection of full genealogies with the terms used for every kinsman. For the rest, we got completed forms for one version of a simplified questionnaire on terminology from 76 persons and, for another version, from 78.

Although the size of the sample is in one sense 209 persons, it is in another sense much larger. For example, data on terms used for uncles and aunts exist for 419 different persons: our 209 respondents had 419 different uncles and aunts.

Although we achieved a fair spread among age and sex groups and a thin coverage of most of the major regions of the United States, this was clearly no sample from which generalizations applicable to the whole American population might be derived with precisely stipulated probability values. It is our conviction that a fair picture of some of the major processes in American usage emerges, but this is a conviction, not a proved finding.

Certain Characteristics of the American Terminological System

Perhaps the fundamental characteristic of the American system of terms for kinsmen is the presence of a wide variety of alternate terms. Mother may be called "mother," "mom," "ma," "mummy," "mama," by her first name, nickname, diminutive, "old woman," and a variety of other less commonly used designations.

Father may be called "father," "pop," "pa," "dad," "daddy," by his first name, nickname, diminutive, "old man," "boss," and a variety of less commonly used designations. Uncles may be addressed or referred to as uncle-plus-first-name, first name alone, or uncle alone. Similarly for aunts.

The variety of alternate terms is increased by two other devices: the use of possessive pronouns—mother, for instance, may be "my mother" or just "mother"—and variations in specifying whom the relationship is *to*. We believe the latter mechanism has not been given enough attention in the literature on terminology. There are always at least three persons involved in the use of a term of reference: the speaker, the person spoken to, and the person referred to. In the United States, one may refer to a third person by his relationship to the speaker or to the person spoken to or even, as in teknonymy, to someone not necessarily present. Thus when speaking to mother's sister's son about mother's sister, the term of reference may be "your mother" or "Aunt Sally."

Closely related to the wide variety of alternate terms is the fact, which we documented far more fully than can be reported here, that forms of reference as well as address vary with situational context. In fact, it is not possible to give a single form of reference or a single form of address for a given class of kinsmen that is used in all contexts of address or reference. To put this in another way, the classic distinction between terms of address and terms of reference is not of much help in dealing with the American system. It tends to obscure certain important processes, partly, at least, because it presumes that there is a single term used in all referential contexts.

It is, of course, true that certain forms are never used in address and occur only in referential contexts. The term "second cousin" is one such term. But its use is confined to only one out of the total range of referential contexts. The term "second cousin" is confined to that situation in which the question is explicitly or implicitly, "Who is he to you?" or "How are you related?" But a variety of other referential contexts occurs in which the term "second cousin" is rarely, if ever, used. Ego, addressing his own mother or father, asks, "How is cousin John these days?" or "How is John these days?" He does not say, "And how is second cousin John these days?"

It is almost unnecessary to note the interdependence of alternate terms and the use of different forms in different contexts. If there were but one form available, this one form would have to be used in all contexts. If there are two forms, one for address and one for reference, then two general categories of context alone can be differentiated. In the contemporary American system, the wide variety of alternate forms allows them to differentiate a variety of different contexts.

Perhaps an example or two will make clear what we are describing. One informant would refer to his mother as "mother" when speaking with his father, as "ma" or "mom" when speaking to his brother, and as "my mother" when speaking with an uncle. Another informant, who usually calls his mother-in-law "mom" when speaking with his wife about her, conscientiously avoids calling her anything when his own mother and his mother-in-law are both present. Another informant calls his father's brother "Uncle Bill" when speaking with his father, "Bill" when speaking with the father's brother directly, and "my uncle" when telling stories about him to some friend who does not know him.

The distinction we found most useful in dealing with this efflorescence of terminology is one we believe to be universal for kinship terms. Each term has two aspects or functions: first, an *ordering* or *classifying* aspect and, second, a *role-* or *relationship*-designating aspect. By "ordering" aspect, we mean the class to which the various genealogically distinct categories of kinsmen are assigned. By "role-designating" aspect, we mean the pattern of behavior or relationship that the term symbolizes. A term like "father" thus does two things: it defines a class of kinsmen—in this case there is but a single genealogical category to the class—and it symbolizes the role which the person so classed is expected to play—in this case a relatively formal and authoritarian one.

The first question that arises in the light of this distinction is whether the various alternate terms are alternates in their role-designating or in their ordering aspects or in both. Put more simply, are the alternate terms mere synonyms for one another or do they have some perceptible and significant differences in meaning? If there are differences of meaning, do these differences center on the mode of classifying kinsmen or on the roles they play or on both these dimensions?

In the series "father," "papa," "pa," "pop," "dad," "daddy," we find that the ordering aspects of all these terms is identical; they refer to ego's presumed genitor. In the "mother," "ma," "mom," "mummy," "mama" series the same is true; each refers, in its classifying aspect, to the same class of kinsmen, in this case the single category of own mother.

If we go on to inspect the alternates that occur throughout the system, we discover that they never transgress the basic scheme of Eskimo-type classification. Fa is never classed with FaBr or MoBr; Mo is never classed with MoSi or FaSi; Br and Si are never classed with parallel or cross-cousins; So and Da are never classed with BrCh or SiCh. Some of the alternates do cross certain of the lines of classification. Thus the term *parents* classes Mo with Fa, *children* classes So with Da, and the newly invented and rapidly spreading *silbing* classes Br with Si, overriding in every case the criterion of sex but not disturbing the basic criteria for Eskimo systems. Certain other alternates, like first names, nicknames, and diminutives, leave the field of kinship entirely. We shall soon return to instances of these last two sorts.

On the other hand, what about the role-designating aspects of these terms? It is precisely here that the differences lie. The different alternates designate different roles or relationships or, more precisely in some cases, differently emphasized aspects of a given relationship.

Space limitations preclude a full inventory of the evidence we have collected on this point. Nor will it be possible to explore all the implications of the differences of role designation from term to term. We shall therefore confine ourselves to illustrations that we feel have particular interest.

Terms for father and mother have already been mentioned. One interesting feature is that only rarely did an informant confine himself to the use of a single term. More usually informants reported that they used a "principal" term and one or more "variant" terms. The principal term most frequently reported was "dad" by males, "daddy" by females. The most frequent variant term reported by males was "father"; by females, "dad." But, further investigation indicated that, if an informant used "father" as either a principal or variant term, he would never use "pop" or "pa" as an alternate. Conversely, those who used "pop" or "pa" as either a principal or variant term would never use "father" as an alternate. Both groups would use "dad"; the one used "father" and would not use "pop" or "pa," the other used "pop" or "pa" but would not use "father." Those who used "father" explained that they would not use "pop" or "pa" because it was too familiar, too egalitarian, and would verge on disrespect. They sometimes added that, "Father is no authority figure or stern old patriarch, but it just wouldn't seem right to call him 'Pop.' " On the other hand, those who used "pop" or "pa" invoked the same problem, but in reverse, explaining that they could not use "father" because their father was "not that sort of person; he is not a stern authority figure, he's much too friendly." The term "father" connotes formality and some qualified implications of authority and its attendant variety of respect; "pop" or "pa" connotes informality and familiarity, and, although authority and respect are by no means absent, they are not the primary implications. "Dad" seems to indicate an area where the formal and the friendly roles overlap.

The situation seemed to be different with mother terms. Here, no informant said that he would not use one of the alternates, and we got the impression that the roles designated by these terms were so close as to be seen by most informants as almost interchangeable. That is, while "pop" and "father" implied mutually incompatible roles—ego picks one or the other but cannot play both—no such sharp line divided the mother terms. Nonetheless, perceptible differences among mother terms are brought out when informants are divided by sex of speaker. Female speakers use "mother" predominantly; the term "ma" is reported by our female informants only rarely. Male speakers, on the other hand, use "mom" most frequently, and "mother" and "ma" occur much less frequently.

The formal term "father" is used far less frequently than the formal term "mother," and the evidence suggests that there is no simple symmetry between the terms "father" and "mother." "Father" has formality and respect implications which are lacking in the term "mother." For instance, some male informants reported that when they would argue with their fathers they would avoid any form of address, and one informant reported that if, during an argument with his father, he used the term, he would feel forced to abandon the argument: "You shouldn't argue with your father." By avoiding the use of the term, he was not forced to face the transgression of the norm.

On the other hand, male informants who reported that they would avoid any form of address while arguing with father stated that an argument with mother included such exclamations as, "Oh, mother" and, "But mom, how can you say such a thing," etc. That is, there was no such inhibition on the use of the mother term as there was on the use of the father term.

One implication of these data is that there is a kind of homogeneity among the alternate mother roles which is not entirely present with the father roles. There is instead a kind of split in the father roles, starting with the term "dad," which everyone either employed or said he would see no reason not to employ, and dividing either toward formality, respect, and authority or away from this toward familiarity, companionship, and a more egalitarian relationship. These two directions of variation are in some degree seen as "either-or" choices.

If in one respect our informants used father-terms very differently from mother-terms, in another respect they used them the same way. Among our other questions, we asked about changes over time in the use of kinship terms. We found that, as small children, both males and females reported using "daddy" and "mommy" or "mummy"—that is, fairly "informal" or diminutive terms. But the men reported changing, as they grew up, to "dad" for father and "mom" or "ma" for mother, and the women reported keeping "daddy" for father but shifting to "mother" for mother. That is, if we consider "dad" and "mother" more formal than "daddy" and "ma," our informants tended, with time, to become relatively more formal with the parent of the same sex as their own and remained relatively less formal with the parent of different sex. Have we to do here with the Oedipus complex, with the possibility that father is more apt to exert authority over son, mother over daughter, or that as the children grow up they become increasingly rivals with the parent of the same sex?

One rather interesting process emerged from a study of terms for aunts and uncles. Although the combination of aunt- or uncle-plus-first-name is the most frequently employed term, many informants reported the use of first name alone. In working over particular genealogies with informants, we encountered a sizeable group which did not apply any particular term consistently for all aunts or for all uncles. That is, one informant called his mother's elder brother "Uncle Jim" and his mother's younger brother "Bill." Another reported that he called his mother's sister "Aunt Jane" and his mother's sister's husband "John."

We spent some time trying to determine when the aunt or uncle term plus-first-name would be used as against the use of the first name alone, and a few interesting facts emerged.

First, there was a tendency for more first-name-alone designations to be applied to aunts and uncles on the mother's side than on the father's. About as many uncles as aunts were called by first names, and about as many affinal uncles and aunts as consanguineal ones. The only apparently significant difference was the side of the family they happened to be on. Does this represent a patrilateral tendency, in a society with a patripotestal bias, for ego's close and warm ties to be with his mother's kin?

Second, there was a slight tendency for male speakers to use the first name alone more often than female speakers. This may mean that women are more concerned with and perceptive of kinship obligations and relations than men, or that women still think of themselves as being of somewhat lower status than men and so are less willing to assert the equality implied by the use of the first name, or, finally, that women are less inclined to allow themselves the display of affect that is also, as we shall see, implied by the first name alone.

Third, some informants reported that they dropped aunt and uncle terms and used first names alone after they started going to college. Here, far more surely, the use of the first name implies a role of equality with uncle and aunt. The formal term is dropped when children view themselves, and are viewed, as being grown-up and so almost on the same plane as uncle and aunt.

Fourth, we ran across a number of situations of the following sort. An informant with three uncles would call one "John," one "Uncle Bill," and the other "Jim." When pressed to explain why he called the first uncle just plain "John," he would reply by saying that the person was a dirty so-and-so and that he would not dignify the man by calling him uncle. (This, by the way, was never said of mother or father.) The next question would be, "Well, how about your other uncle, Jim? Why don't you call him Uncle Jim?" And the explanation would be, "Jim is a wonderful guy! He and I have always been the closest friends. When I was a kid we would . . ." and out would come a picture of an idyllic relationship. The final question, of course, would be, "What about Uncle Bill?" And Uncle Bill would usually prove to be liked—a nice guy—"He's o.k.," or some such mildly positive or mildly negative sentiment.

The pattern seemed to be that wherever there was strong affect, either positive *or* negative, the "uncle" form would be dropped and the first name alone used. Alternatively, if we think of these terms as status designators, the first name may imply either the equality of the speaker with the person referred to *or* the inferiority of the latter. Where the affect was mild, one way or the other, and the relative statuses were simply those expected in the kinship norms, the uncle term was used.

It is, of course, a statement of some significance about the nature of the American kinship system that there can be three broad possibilities in the relationship between ego and uncles or aunts; the relationship may be intensely close, warm and intimate with egalitarian overtones; or it may be intensely hostile with or without the prominent display of this affect; or it can be mildly positive, mildly negative, or, to put it in another way, the affect can be subordinate to other, primarily kinship, considerations. Not all bilateral systems or even Eskimo-type systems permit ego to say quite bluntly: "I wouldn't dignify that S.O.B. by the use of a kinship term"; or even, conversely, "We are the closest of friends and always have been."

The use of first names as an alternate form of designation raises some more general problems. Let us look at the data. First, we found that first names occurred as alternate terms for all classes of kinsmen except grandparents. Our informants with but one exception never called their grandparents by first name. Second, they did call members of the parental generation by first name but not very often, whereas the first name was the dominant designation for kinsmen of ego's own or lower generations. That is, where some informants reported that they used father's first name as their primary designation, there were very few such informants. On the other hand, almost all informants reported that the principal term employed for them by their parents was first name, nickname, or diminutive. Third, as we have already seen, the use of first name as the principal term for uncle or aunt occurs where there is strong affect, either positive or negative.

If we review the actual cases in which strong affect occurs, it turns out that it is not the mere presence of the affect which is important but that the strong affect implies a relationship which is basically different from the general conception of what uncle (aunt)-nephew (niece) should be. Where strong positive affect was indicated, the relationship seemed far more a relationship of friendship than of kinship. Uncles were described as being "pals," "close friends all my life"; "I'd go talk over all my troubles with him, and we'd figure them out together." On the other hand, many informants reported real affection for an aunt or an uncle, but this was seen as a special attribute of the particular kinship relation, of the relationship which normally *should* obtain between uncle and nephew rather than of a fundamentally different sort, as in the case of friendship.

Where uncles or aunts were designated by their first names alone, the relationship seemed to be predominantly a person-to-person relationship, and whatever elements of kinship were implicit in it were kept at an implicit level. Its primary tone was of person to person; ego was either very close to or very hostile to him or her, as a person. Asked to describe why a particular uncle was not called "uncle," an informant would dwell on the particular person's personal qualities; he was mean, unpleasant, untrustworthy, etc. These are not the usual components of kinship relations. Similarly, on the other side, it was the personal qualities of, "We get along well" or, "We like the same things" that were cited in the cases where the affect was positive.

Our impression is that the use of first names designates relationships which have as their *dominant quality* considerations of a personal sort. When fathers address sons by their first names, this does not imply that the relationship is free from considerations of kinship, from the obligations that the son has to his father or the father to the son. What it does imply is that, from the point of view of the father, it is the personal qualities of his son which are of particular importance to him. How the son fulfills his kinship obligations are seen as particular qualities of the particular son. How the son behaves toward his mother are seen as qualities of the son as a person, and it is these that are the *emphasized* concerns of the father. Although there is clearly a kinship tie between them, with obligations and privileges based on their kinship, the aspect of the relationship that the parent stresses is the qualities of the child as a person, and his performance of his kinship role is seen not as the end, or even the primary concern, but only as one among a series of standards in terms of which the quality of the persons may be judged, guided, socialized.

If we make this interpretation of the use of personal names for members of the contemporary generation or below, are we justified in making the other obvious interpretation of the relatively greater use of formal kinship terms for members of older generations? Is it perhaps true that we Americans look on our contemporaries and descendants as individuals and our elders as representatives of the system? That we and our children are responsible to the self, our parents to society—that is, to us? At any rate, there is a thoroughgoing generational asymmetry in our kinship terminology.

It is worth noting the obvious point that in uncle and aunt designations the dominant tendency is neither toward the use of first name alone nor toward the use of the kinship term alone. Indeed, among our informants, first name alone was the more frequent designation than kinship term alone for uncles and aunts. Instead the dominant tendency is toward a combination of first name and kinship term. In a very important sense the American system classes all uncles together and then subdivides members of the class. That is, within the category of uncle, designations are practically descriptive since, even where two uncles have the same first name, they are almost always distinguished. The tendency, thus, is to particularize uncles and aunts and, in effect, to differentiate individuals within each class. This is clearly in line with the tendency to treat kinsmen as particular people with particular and unique qualities of a personal nature. Uncles, for instance, might be distinguished as elder, second, third, or younger and yield the same differentiation. But there the stress would be on the ranking among uncles and not, as in the American system, the stress on the person as such within the kinship setting.

In our study of the use of personal names for kin, especially for uncles and aunts, we have found reason to recur again to our fundamental point—that the nature of the relationship between the speaker and the person referred to is an important determinant of the term used. But in the uncle-aunt case, there are really only two available terms—"Jim" or "Uncle Jim"—yet the elements that enter the relationship are many: status similarities or differences, affect or lack of it, kinship or personal interest. The disproportion between the number of terms and the number of elements in the relationship means that, though the terms do reflect the relationship, they often do so crudely and sometimes ambiguously.

There can be no such complaint about the terms for husband and wife. Here the elaboration of alternate terms goes much further than it does anywhere else in the American system.

The terms fall into three rough categories: kinship terms, variants on given name (first name, diminutives, nicknames, etc.), and a group that might be given dignity by being labeled "terms of endearment." Kinship terms break down into two subcategories: first, terms used to indicate the order of kin, i.e., terms of reference mainly explaining who he or she is, such as "my wife," "my husband," "Mrs. X," "Mr. X"; second, parent terms, i.e., wife is called "mother," "mom," or "my old woman"; husband, "father," "dad," "papa," etc., or "my old man." "Terms of endearment" fall into a series of classes: saccharine terms (honey, sugar, sweet, cookie, etc.), affection terms (love, beloved, lover, etc.), animal and vegetable terms (kitten, bear-cat, pumpkin, etc.), and a large and varied collection of miscellaneous and idiosyncratic terms, some of them nonsense syllables (baby, pookums, etc.). We all are familiar with at least some of these terms. There is probably a greater variety of terms for wife than there is for husband.

Without going deeply into the wealth of detail here, we can make a few interesting inferences from the terminology. In the first place, the marital relationship seems either to center on a highly individual definition of a presumedly perpetual love affair, which is outside the realm of kinship altogether and has as its dominant element the particular harmony of the two unique persons involved, or it is a relationship defined by the presumption of children, so that the roles of husband and wife are predominantly the by-products of their roles as parents. Remember that we are not speaking here of the total relationship but of the elements in the total relationship which are stressed. That is, no matter how much saccharine terminology is employed, there is a relationship in which the law limits how far one or the other party may go in ignoring kinship rights and obligations. But it is not the rights and obligations that are stressed in terminology as predominant concerns; it is either the personal qualities of the pair or their common concerns as parents. In a very important sense, there is no clear-cut kinship relationship in marriage itself; there is either love or parenthood.

Yet another characteristic of the terminological system that reflects the stress on the individual as such is the importance placed on real genea-logical position, especially in the nuclear family. Only those who truly occupy the particular genealogical positions are seen as the proper persons to play the roles and receive the designations associated with those positions. Americans distinguish "father" from "stepfather," "mother" from "step-mother," real sibling from half-sibling and stepsibling, and so on. It is true that courtesy aunts and uncles occur, but there is never any doubt about their status as courtesy kin and not "real" kin. Further, the occupation of a structurally identical position and the playing of an identical role is not enough to warrant the use of the kinship term appropriate to that position and role. Thus, when a child is reared from infancy by its aunt or grand-parent, the aunt playing a maternal role toward the child, she is still not called "mother." Informants will state that, "She was just like a mother to me" and mean just that: she was *just like,* but she was still not the mother. The term "mother" is reserved for the person who occupies the correct genealogical category. This practice is very different from, for instance, the Zuni one, where a term is applied when it designates the role-relationship regardless of the appropriateness of the genealogical positions occupied by the persons concerned.

The manner of using personal pronouns may serve as our last bit of evi-dence that the great concern of the language of American kinship is indi-vidual persons. The possessive pronoun which is usually used by ego for any of his kinsmen is "my": "my father," "my uncle," "my mother," and so forth. The form "our father," "our mother," or "our brother" is only occasionally heard, though it is not uncommon in England. If the form "my" is inappropriate, as when one brother speaks to another brother about their father, then the kinship term is used without any qualifying possessive pronoun. Brothers seldom say to each other "our father"; they say "father" or "pop" or "dad."

Terminology, the Kinship System, and American Culture

We have suggested that the use of alternate terms for kinsmen in the American terminological system might vary with their classifying aspects or their role-designating aspects or both. What in fact happens is that variation is greatest along the dimension of role designation and least with respect to classification. Further, in the few places where there are alternate modes of classification, the basic scheme of Eskimo type is almost never transgressed.

One important implication of these data is that there is a single, basic pattern of kinship structure *within* which, but not across which, wide degrees of latitude for variation occur. That is, the American people do not show a wide variety of descent systems, a wide variety of kin-group types, or a wide variety of terminological types, but a single, basic form—bilateral descent, strongly emphasized nuclear family, and a distinct but secondarily important kindred. But within this framework there is considerable latitude for variation, and the variation is in terms of roles and relationships, not in terms of the basic kin-group affiliations or contrasting commitments to divergent kin groups or kinsmen.

To make this point in another way, it might be said that the American ideal of "unity in diversity" might better be phrased, in the kinship system at least, as "diversity centering on a basic unity."

A second implication of these data is further specification of what is already well known and widely commented on, and that is the central importance of the nuclear family in the kinship system. It is, after all, one of only two kin groups in the system, and the evidence suggests that the other, the loose, amorphous kindred, tends to vary in importance from time to time in the life-history of any given nuclear family, from region to region, from class to class, and from ethnic group to ethnic group. In some groups it looms large; in others it is held to a bare minimum. Upward mobile persons keep only shallow ties with members of their kindred, if they keep them at all; downward mobile persons may be neglected by their kindred; members of spatially static occupation groups can but need not, and so on.

The features reflecting the central importance of the nuclear family as against the kindred are many. First, there is elaborate role-differentiation within the nuclear families of orientation and procreation, and a much lower level of differentiation outside these groups. This situation is comparable to the high degree of internal differentiation found in lineage systems in the "own lineage" group as against the minimal differentiation within more distant groups such as, in matrilineal systems, father's matrilineage and mother's father's matrilineage. Second, there are those few alternate terms that present alternate modes of classification.

With only one exception, those alternate terms which vary in their classifying aspect occur either *within* the nuclear family or *outside* it, but the nuclear-family line is never crossed. Thus the term "parents" and its reciprocal "the children" or "the kids" makes a unit of Mo and Fa vis-à-vis the internally undifferentiated unit of So and Da. Here, in addition to the alternates for Fa and Mo, there is the additional alternate which groups them together into one unit. Similarly, and of more than passing interest, are the terms "old man" and "old woman" applied to Hu and Fa, Wi and Mo, respectively, and the term "father" or "dad" for both Hu and Fa, the term "mother" or "mom" for both Mo and Wi. It is our impression that the classes and the regions where "old man" and "old woman" refer to Hu-Fa and Wi-Mo, respectively, are not the same as the class or regions where "father" or "dad" and "mother" or "mom" group Hu-Fa and Wi-Mo, respectively. The fact that these occur in very different subgroups of the population suggests that a very general and basic process is at work and not merely class or regional styling. But the point of primary concern here is that this alternate mode of classification again is confined within the nuclear family and does not cut across that line.

It should be noted that, in the group we interviewed, neither of these two patterns for the grouping of Fa-Hu and Mo-Wi was at all common. Informants suggested that spouse is only called by a parental term in the presence of children, or at least after children come on the scene. We have too few cases of this sort to provide anything like a secure ground for generalization, but our impression is that in some cases the designation of the spouse by a parental term preceded the presence of children, and in some cases occurred among couples of sufficiently advanced age so that the prospect of children might be taken as unlikely and among couples whose children were full grown and far away.

It is interesting, too, that when one spouse uses a parental term for the other, the other does not reciprocate with a child term; that is, when husband is called "father," wife is not called "daughter"—this despite the frequent comment that one of the classic reefs on which marital relations may founder or, conversely, thrive is the psychological identification of the spouse with the parent of opposite sex. It is noteworthy that we did not discover a single terminological symbol of this psychological relationship, unless it be argued that, when husband calls wife "mother," she acts as mother to him, and he reciprocates by alternating his roles between father and son. We did not delve deeply enough to discover evidence either for or against this view.

Outside the nuclear family, the alternates are of a somewhat different sort. Where "parents," "the children," "old man," "old woman," "dad," and "mom" combine two otherwise differentiated genealogical categories, the alternate modes of classification outside the nuclear family tend toward what might be called "gross grouping," taking in a wide swath of genealogically distinct categories. The term "cousin" applied to cousins of each and every remove is one such term. Another is the appearance of such designations as "the Ohio Browns," "the bunch from Maine," "the Joneses," "the drunken Smiths." The one possible exception to the generalization that alternate modes of classification do not cut across the nuclear family is the designation "father's family" or "mother's side." Some informants were concerned to point out that, when they said "father's family" or "mother's family," they did not include father or mother but only their relatives. But other informants either implied or stipulated that father along with all his kinsmen were or were not held in high esteem, low esteem, or at any rate lumped together in some fashion by such terms.

We may now return to the problem of variation within the framework of bilateral kinship and emphasized nuclear family. The question is whether the variation is random or determinate.

The variation occurs along two distinct dimensions. One is variation from subgroup to subgroup within the American population, the sub-groups being regional, ethnic, class, age group, sex group, etc. Our sample was too small and unsystematically selected to show what we suspect to be the case—that this kind of variation is associated with what Florence Kluckhohn has called "variant value patterns."

The other kind of variation is in the forms any individual employs within a given relationship—what we call the use of alternate terms. As one informant said, "I usually call my father 'pop,' but if I want something from him I say, 'Dad, may I take the car tonight?' "

One of the determinants of the latter form of variation is the degree to which personal qualities or individualistic values are emphasized. We have already noted that the use of personal names reflects the value of personal qualities or the special value of the individual. We now want to say something about the over-all social arrangements within which this value may be more or less stressed.

Generally speaking, kinship terms are employed primarily when the person spoken to is senior in age or generation, but first names are employed between age and generation equals or when the speaker is senior in age or generation to the person addressed or referred to. Thus Fa calls So by the latter's first name, but the So usually uses some kinship term for Fa. Br calls Br or Si by first name, but BrCh usually calls FaBr by a designation involving a kinship term—"Uncle Bill," for instance.

As Linton noted, American culture is oriented about achieved rather than ascribed status, and parents are concerned that their children achieve some appropriate status. Ascribed status as a family member is insufficient to carry most people through life. If status is to be achieved, it has to be achieved, according to American values, on the merits of the person, his qualities and accomplishments as a person that meet value standards that Parsons has called "universalistic." Hence to go out and do the things that need to be done to achieve something, he must be relatively free of any encumbering bonds of kinship, and he must be motivated to do so. It is as part of this wider context, we suspect, that the older generation uses personal names rather than kinship terms toward the younger generation. Again, we repeat, this does not mean that the young person is freed from all kinship obligations. It only stresses personal qualities within the definition of his kinship role. It stresses the unique qualities of a person as he himself will have to stress his own initiative, his own inventiveness, if he is to achieve anything on his own.

On the other hand, there are two problems from the point of view of the younger generation. On the one hand, their view of the older generation is in part that the latter have achieved; they have arrived, so to speak. This is seen especially clearly in the usages of preschool children. In their view, almost all adults are mothers or fathers, depending on sex, if they are not otherwise designated as aunts, uncles, or grandparents. In a suburban housing project with the high birthrate characteristic of such units, where practically every family has at least one and usually more children, it was customary for all adults to be known teknonymously as "Johnny's daddy" or "Margaret's mother," etc. Here, one of the authors encountered a young man of about four engaged in a hopeless struggle with a knotted shoelace. The author did not know this child, and the child did not know the author. The child looked up and called out, "Somebody's daddy! Please fix my shoelace." Similarly, children of this age have difficulty comprehending the possibility that a woman might have any other status than mother. In this same housing project, it was repeatedly noted that small children would ask adult men to "Go ask your mother if you can come out and make a snowman with us." For the younger generation, there is an entirely imaginary quality of stability to the older generation: they are set, while the young are to make their way onward, upward, around, and past their elders. Hence their designation by kinship terms, that is, by terms that stress their status and their apparently eternal roles, is entirely appropriate.

On the other hand, the tasks of socialization and the responsibilities of parents all too often require that they act according to the long view of "what we want our child to be." They must exercise some discipline, however much or little they like, and this exercise must be stated in moral and rational terms and not as the product of transient states of mood or momentary emotions. In the nature of the case it is impossible to discipline an equal. The asymmetrical distribution of authority and the knowledge of right and wrong must be made clear as part of the institutionalized definitions of the respective roles. There is thus a problem, for the older generation, of maintaining the generational stratification or, as adults sometimes put it, of "keeping children in their place." When parent and child each uses first name, they tend to view one another as equals. Informants whose children used first names for them and informants who themselves used their parents' first names constantly indicated that the problem of maintaining the separation of status and blocking the tendency toward treating each other as equals was especially prominent. Parents always have the problem of dealing with children who, at certain ages, insist that, "If you can do it, why can't I?" But where first names are used reciprocally, we find that this problem is especially acute and especially difficult to handle. This is not to imply that *only because* first names are used is the relationship difficult; rather, the self-reciprocal use of first names reflects the definition of the relationship as one which tends toward equality.

The use of kinship terms from junior to senior is thus an affirmation of the authority and superordination of the elder and, equally, of the junior's view of the static position of the elder, which the junior is to equal or surpass. The use of first name from senior to junior thus affirms the elder's view of the junior as "up and coming" and emphasizes the qualities of junior as a unique person, an individual in his own right.

It is worth noting, in this connection, the very narrow range of kinship in America and the very narrow limits within which it is extended. In part, this is probably connected with the high value placed on the individual. But in part it is probably tied equally closely to the fact that the dominant social values center on achievement and not on ascription. The wider the range of extensions, the narrower the possibilities for achievement.

We have heard the view expressed that American kinship is "pushed to the wall" and "distorted by non-kinship considerations and values from outside the kinship system." By this is meant, of course, that kinship has a narrow range, not only in the sense that there are only a few kinsmen compared with an enormous number of non-kinsmen with whom ego interacts, but also in the sense that considerations of kinship are confined to only a small portion of the total activities which ego enters into. Occupational achievement is supposed to be outside the realm of kinship, and, where other societies view nepotism as an ideal, we treat it under certain circumstances as a crime.

We have no basic quarrel with this view, except that it is not the most useful formulation from which to work. The kinship system occupies a unique place in any culture, since it is almost always the context within which most socialization takes place. If the dominant values of a culture are to be transmitted and if the culture is to continue beyond the lifespan of any individual, then new recruits to the society must be taught that culture. The dominant values of the total culture must find expression in the kinship system, and they must be so expressed that they can be conveyed to children. This means, for one thing, that those values must be distilled and simplified. The first social system in which an individual acts is the reduced system of kinship. If he learns the lessons of kinship, he can go on. Kinship must, therefore, teach him more than the limited scope of pure kinship; *it must teach him the fundamentals of his whole culture.*

In a sense, the whole complex of kinship relations is informed by the system of which those relations are a part. The kinship system as a whole is therefore a socialization device, a "child-training practice," if you will, which looms considerably larger than any given child-training practice like weaning or toilet training or aggression control. Weaning and toilet training, to use two well-worn examples, are aspects of the kinship relation between mother and child, take their shape from this larger context, and therefore may be treated as expressions of it. Where it may be difficult to place an exact socialization value on weaning as such, it is much less difficult to discover the socialization values of a whole kinship system.

Far from being "pushed to the wall" and "distorted by values from outside kinship," the American kinship system embodies in clear and communicable form the essence of the dominant values of the whole culture even while it manages to discharge those functions universal to kinship systems, those social functions which are prerequisite to the maintenance of any social and cultural system.

38 *Family Structure and Sex-Role Learning by Children*

ORVILLE G. BRIM, JR.

Although there is apparently a universal principle of differentiation of roles by sex, there is also great variation in specific patterns that may be adopted. One of the functions the family performs is to inculcate patterns of sexual behavior appropriate to the individual, the family and the society. Dr. Brim, a sociologist, has studied the findings of Dr. Koch, a social psychologist, and has attempted to place her data within a framework of how families transmit, and how children acquire, patterns of sex-specific behavior.

The structure of a social group, delineated by variables such as size, age, sex, power, and prestige differences, is held to be a primary influence upon the patterns of interaction within the group, determining in major part the degree to which any two group members interact. It is held, second, that social roles are learned through interaction with others, such interaction providing one with the opportunity to practice his own role as well as to take the role of the other. On this basis, one may hypothesize that group structure, by influencing the degree of interaction between group members, would be related to the types of roles learned in the group: one would learn most completely those roles which he himself plays, as well as the roles of the others with whom he most frequently interacts. This argument is applied in this paper specifically to the relation between family structure, described in terms of age, sex, and ordinality of children, and the sex-role learning by the children.

The process of role learning through interaction, which has been described in detail by Mead,[1] Cottrell,[2] and others, can be sketched as follows. One learns the behavior appropriate to his position in a group through interaction with others who hold normative beliefs about what his role should be and who are able to reward and punish him for correct and incorrect actions. As part of the same learning process, one acquires expectations of how others in the group will behave. The latter knowledge is indispensable to the actor, in that he must be able to predict what others expect of him, and how they will react to him, in order to guide his own role performance successfully. Accurate or erroneous understanding and prediction are respectively rewarding and punishing to the actor, and

Reprinted from *Sociometry*, XXI (March, 1958), 1–16, with the kind permission of the author and publishers.

learning proceeds systematically through the elimination of incorrect responses and the strengthening of correct ones.

It has been the distinctive contribution of sociology to demonstrate that learning the role of others occurs through the actor's taking the role of the other, i.e., trying to act as the other would act. While this role-taking of the other can be overt, as with children who actively and dramatically play the role of the parent, it is commonly covert in adults, as with the husband who anticipates what his wife will say when he returns home late, or the employee who tries to foresee his employer's reaction when he asks for a raise.

It follows that, whether taking the role of others is overt or covert, certain responses belonging to the role of the other are in fact made, run through, completed, and rewarded if successful, i.e., accurate, and that this process adds to the repertoire of possible actions of a person those actions taken by others in their own roles. Such actions, as part of one's repertoire or pool of learned responses, are available for performance by an actor, not now simply in taking the role of the other, but as resources which he can use as part of his *own* role performances.

The critical fact is that the actor not only can, but *does,* make use of responses learned in role-taking in his own role performances. There are two senses in which this happens. The first, which does not concern us in this paper, involves the direct transfer of the role of the other to a new and parallel status of one's own, where there is a straightforward adoption of the other's role. Such transfer may be appropriate and rewarded, as where the oldest child performs the role of the parent to his sibs, or simply interesting and tolerated, as where the new assistant professor plays the department chairman to the graduate students.

The second sense, which is our major concern here, involves a more complex process of convergence between one's own role and that of the other which he takes, where there is a spill-over of elements belonging to another's role into one's own performance when it is not necessarily appropriate. Our basic hypothesis, set forth by Cottrell and others, is that interaction between two persons leads to assimilation of roles, to the incorporation of elements of the role of the other into the actor's role. Thus, one says, husbands and wives grow more alike through time, and long-time collaborators in research begin to think alike.

While not pretending to a full analysis of the process underlying assimilation, several causes can be described. First, the actor may note that the other is successful to a high degree in some of his behavior and consciously transfer to his own role such behavioral elements for trial. To the extent that they prove successful for him, in his performance, and are not eliminated through punishment from others for being inappropriate, he will adopt them. Second, faced with novel situations where his "own" behavior fails, the elements of others' roles are already learned and available for trial and hence would tend to be tried prior to the development of totally new responses; again, if successful, they tend to be assimilated to the role. Third, the actions learned by taking the roles of others are ordinarily performed implicitly and under limited conditions, e.g., in interaction with the other. However, the cues which guide and elicit one's own role performance may be difficult to differentiate from cues eliciting taking the role of the other. It would appear that for the young child this is especially difficult, and data indeed show that the child has difficulty discriminating between reality and fantasy, between what his role is or even what his self is, and what belongs in the category of the "other." In this way, behavior learned through role-taking and appropriate to the other is confused with and undifferentiated from behavior learned as part of one's own role. The latter becomes tinged or diluted with characteristics belonging to someone else's role.

Among the hypotheses which are derivative of the general hypothesis of assimilation through interaction, two are pertinent here. First, the process of discrimination between what belongs to oneself and what belongs to the other is aided by the guidance of other persons. Thus, the parent helps the son differentiate between what belongs to him and what belongs to his sister; the fledgling nurse is assisted in a proper demeanor and in separating her duties from those of the physician. Rewards and punishments administered by others govern the discrimination process. Where the process of assimilation comes primarily from inability to discriminate between roles, it follows that where greater attention is paid to helping the learner discriminate, the process of assimilation is to a greater degree arrested.

Second, given two other persons with whom one interacts and who differ in power over the actor, i.e., differ in the degree to which they control rewards and punishments for the actor, one would predict that the actor would adopt more of the characteristics of the powerful, as contrasted to the less powerful, other person. This follows from the fact that it is more important to the actor to predict the behavior of the powerful figure, that he is motivated more strongly to take his role, that the rewards and punishments are more impressive and the learning consequently better. Interaction between two figures of unequal power should give a parallel result, namely, there would be a greater assimilation of the role of the other into the actor's role for the less powerful figure, for the same reasons as above. Thus, the employee gravitates toward the boss more than the reverse, and the child becomes more like the parent than the other way round. However, this is not to imply that the more powerful figure need not take the role of the other, nor that he does not assimilate (to a lesser degree) elements from the other's role. The weaker figure always has some control over rewards and punishments, requiring therefore that his reaction be considered. The displeased employee can wound his boss through expressions of dislike, and the angry child can hurt his parents in a variety of ways, from refusing to eat to threatening to leave home.

Turning now to a consideration of sex-role learning specifically, pertinent reviews[3] of the data show that sex-role prescriptions and actual performance begin early. The accepted position is that children in a family learn their appropriate sex roles primarily from their parents. There is remarkably little data, other than clinical materials, on this topic, perhaps because of its obviousness. What systematic data there is, is not inconsistent with the role-learning propositions set forth above. Sears, Pintler, and Sears[4] have shown that in families where the father is absent the male child is slower to develop male sex-role traits than in families where the father is present, a finding predictable from the fact that there is no father whose role the child needs to take. Both Sears[5] and Payne and Mussen[6] have shown that father role-playing, identification with the father, and masculinity of attitudes are positively related to the father's being warm, affectionate, and rewarding. This strikes one as the same type of finding as the first, but at the other end of the interaction range; insofar as warm, affectionate, and rewarding fathers interact more with their sons, or are perceived as such because they interact more, it follows that the sons have more experience in taking their role.

In regard to the effects of sibling characteristics upon sex-role learning, there is again almost no information. Fauls and Smith[7] report that only children choose sex-appropriate activities more often than do children with older same-sex siblings, a finding which seems to fit none of our role-learning propositions. While one might hold that the only child has more interaction, because of sibling absence, with his same-sex parent, hence learns his sex role better, one might equally say, especially for the young boys, that it is the cross-sex parent with whom the child interacts and hence the only child should not learn his sex role well. In any case, the finding serves to stress the limitations of the data we are to report, namely, that they pertain to variations within two-child families, and that generalization to families of varying sizes is unwarranted. We return to this point later.

Even with respect to theory concerning the effects of siblings on sex-role learning, we have not noted any systematic predictions in the literature. It seems to us implicit in Parsons' recent analysis[8] of sex-role learning in the nuclear family that when the child begins his differentiation between the father and mother sex roles he would be helped in making the differentiation if he had a cross-sex sibling; this is not formally stated, however, and we may be guilty of misinterpretation.

It is against this background of comparative absence of research and theory on the effects of siblings on sex-role learning that our own report must be viewed. The very valuable data on personality traits of children presented in recent publications by Helen Koch[9] provide the opportunity to apply several of the general hypotheses set forth above to the substantive area of sibling effects on sex-role learning. The specific application of these hypotheses can be summarized as follows:

First, one would predict that cross-sex, as compared with same-sex, siblings would possess more traits appropriate to the cross-sex role. When taking the role of the other in interaction, cross-sex siblings must take the role of the opposite sex, and the assimilation of roles as delineated above should take place.

Second, one would predict that this effect would be more noticeable for the younger, as compared with the older, sibling in that the latter is more powerful and is more able to differentiate his own from his sibling's role.

Third, on the assumption that siblings close in age interact more than those not close in age, one would predict that this effect would be more noticeable for the siblings who are closest together in age. This is, in essence, an extension of the first hypothesis to deal with variations in interaction within the cross-sex sibling groups.

Procedures

Our description of procedures must of necessity be broken into two parts. The first consists of a brief description of the procedures in Helen Koch's original study; complete details are available in the publications cited previously. The second consists of our mode of further analysis of the reported data.

In her series of papers, Helen Koch has reported results from a major research project concerned with the relation between structural characteristics of the family, namely, sex of child, sex of sibling, ordinal position of child, and age difference between siblings, and the child's ratings on more than fifty personality traits. In her study, all subjects were obtained from the Chicago public schools and one large private school. The characteristics of the children used as subjects can be summarized as follows. All children were from unbroken, native-born, white, urban, two-child families. The children were five- and six-year-olds, free of any gross physical or mental defect. In most cases only one sibling in a family was a subject in the study.

The subjects numbered 384. "The experimental design included three sib-spacing levels, two ordinal positions, subjects of two sexes and siblings of two sexes. There were 48 children in each of the following categories— male with a male sib older, male with a male sib younger, male with a female sib older, male with a female sib younger, female with a male sib older, female with a male sib younger, female with a female sib older, and female with a female sib younger. Each of these groups of 48 children was composed of three subgroups of 16 children, representing the following three sibling-age-difference levels: siblings differed in age by under two years, by two to four years, and four to six years, respectively. Hence our basic subgroups of 16 numbered 24."[10] The groups were matched, approximately, on an individual subject basis with respect to age of child and father's occupational status.

Teachers' ratings were made for each child on 58 traits. The teachers, all of whom were women, were trained in a conference or two to make the ratings. No teacher rated a child with whom contact had been less than three months, and in most cases the contact ranged from six to nine months. The 58 traits included 24 of the Fels Child Behavior Scales, and 34 items from the California Behavior Inventory for Nursery School Children. All ratings were made on line scales, converted later to 9-point scales. Ratings on each trait were subsequently normalized, prior to analysis of the data.

The relation between personality-trait ratings and the structure of the family from which the children came was assessed by analysis of variance for each of the 58 traits. Helen Koch presents in her publications the findings from the variance analysis. It is these data on which we made our further study.

The procedures for the further analysis involved several steps. First, the writer, with the assistance of three professional persons as additional judges,[11] judged each of the 58 traits in terms of its pertinence to either a masculine or feminine role. Our conception of the characteristics of the two sex roles was based on recent empirical studies describing sex-role differences in small problem-solving groups[12] and in the nuclear family,[13] and on the major theoretical treatment of such differences by Talcott Parsons. In these studies, the now-familiar distinction between the instrumental or task role and the expressive or social-emotional role in a social group is shown to be related to sex-role differentiation, particularly in the family, with the male customarily taking the instrumental role and the female the expressive role. Hence in the judging process our decision as to whether a trait was masculine or feminine was essentially dependent on whether we believed the trait to belong to the instrumental or expressive role respectively.

Substantial descriptive data are available on sex-role differences in children for some of the traits which we judged. These findings, summarized by Terman and Tyler,[14] were consulted after the judging was completed and strongly corroborate our assignment of traits: e.g., male children are judged higher on traits we believed instrumental, such as dominance and aggression, and lower on traits we judged to pertain to the expressive role, such as affection and absence of negativism.

In judging the traits, it was recognized that many of them would be part of the role requirements for both roles. However, it was clear that there exists for each of the roles what is essentially a rank order of characteristics in terms of their importance for the role. Hence the basis for our judgments was whether the trait appeared to be higher in the rank order of requirements for the instrumental or the expressive role. Traits which seemed pertinent to neither, e.g., stammering, or for which

Table 1

Traits Assignable to Male (Instrumental) or Female (Expressive) Roles

Trait name	Pertains primarily to instrumental (I) or expressive (E) role	Trait is congruent (+) or incongruent (—) characteristic of role
1. Tenacity	I	+
2. Aggressiveness	I	+
3. Curiosity	I	+
4. Ambition	I	+
5. Planfulness	I	+
6. Dawdling and procrastinating	I	—
7. Responsibleness	I	+
8. Originality	I	+
9. Competitiveness	I	+
10. Wavering in decision	I	—
11. Self-confidence	I	+
12. Anger	E	—
13. Quarrelsomeness	E	—
14. Revengefulness	E	—
15. Teasing	E	—
16. Extrapunitiveness	E	—
17. Insistence on rights	E	—
18. Exhibitionism	E	—
19. Unco-operativeness with group	E	—
20. Affectionateness	E	+
21. Obedience	E	+
22. Upset by defeat	E	—
23. Responds to sympathy and approval from adults	E	+
24. Jealousy	E	—
25. Speedy recovery from emotional disturbance	E	+
26. Cheerfulness	E	+
27. Kindness	E	+
28. Friendliness to adults	E	+
29. Friendliness to children	E	+
30. Negativism	E	—
31. Tattling	E	—

no judgment of greater importance could be made, e.g., curiosity, were not ascribed to either role and were omitted from subsequent steps in the analysis. It was possible to assign 31 of the 58 traits to either the instrumental or expressive role. Twenty of the 31 traits pertain to the

Table 2

Instrumental and Expressive Traits for Five- and Six-year-old Girls

SUBJECTS	SIB AGE DIF-FERENCE	MALE (OR INSTRUMENTAL) TRAITS		FEMALE (OR EXPRESSIVE) TRAITS	
		High masculinity ratings	Low masculinity ratings	High femininity ratings	Low femininity ratings
Older girl with younger sister	0–2 years	2,5,7	4,6,9,10	13,14,15,16,17,18,19, 20,21,24,30	22,23,25,26, 27
	2–4 years	7	2,4,9,10, 11	13,14,15,16,17,18,19, 20,21,24,30	22,23,26,27, 28
	4–6 years	7	2,4,6,9, 10,11	13,14,15,16,17,18,19, 20,21,24,30	22,23,25,26, 27,28
Older girl with younger brother	0–2 years	1,2,3,4,5, 9,10	6	13,14,15,16,19,20,21, 25,26,27,30	22,24
	2–4 years	1,2,3,4,9, 10	6	13,14,15,16,19,20,25, 26,27,30,31	22,24
	4–6 years	1,2,3,4,7, 9,10	6	13,14,15,19,20,21,25, 26,27,28,30	22,24,31
Younger girl with older sister	0–2 years	2,5,6,7,8	3,4,9,10, 11	12,13,14,15,16,18,19, 20,21,22,23,30	17,25,26,27
	2–4 years	. .	3,4,5,8,9, 10,11	12,13,14,15,16,18,19, 20,21,22,23,30	17,25,26,27, 28
	4–6 years	6,7	2,3,4,9, 10,11	12,13,14,15,16,18,19, 20,21,22,23,30	17,25,26,27, 28
Younger girl with older brother	0–2 years	1,2,4,6,7 8,9,10,11	. .	12,13,14,15,16,18,19, 20,21,22,23,25,26,27, 28,30	
	2–4 years	1,4,6,7,10, 11	. .	12,13,14,15,16,18,19, 20,21,22,23,25,26,27, 28,30	
	4–6 years	2,4,5,10,11	. .	12,13,14,15,16,18,19, 20,21,22,23,25,26,27, 28,30	

Note: Trait numbers refer to listing in Table 1. Traits entered in high-masculinity rating column are male-congruent traits with high ratings, male-incongruent traits with low ratings. The reverse is true for low-masculinity rating column. Female trait entries are made in the same manner.

expressive role, the children evidently having been rated on a predominantly female cluster of traits.

Some of the traits were stated in a negative way which made them, while pertinent to the role, incongruent with the role conception. Thus, "unco-operativeness with group" seemed clearly to be relevant to the expressive role but as an incongruent trait. In like manner, both affectionateness and jealousy seemed most important as aspects of the expressive role, the former being congruent with the role conception, the latter incongruent. It therefore was necessary to make a second judgment regarding each trait, namely, whether it was a congruent or incongruent aspect of the role to which it pertained.

Table 1 lists the 31 traits, the role to which they seemed most pertinent, and the indication of whether the trait was a congruent or incongruent characteristic of the role.

With the judging of the traits completed, the next step was a careful reading of Helen Koch's findings. A tabulation was made of all differences on the 31 traits between the 16 basic subgroups reported by her as significant (close to or at the .05 level, based on the separate analyses of variance). Such differences involved single structural characteristics, e.g., first-born versus second-born; single interactions of characteristics, e.g., girls with brothers versus girls with sisters; and multiple interactions, e.g., first-born boys with sisters versus first-born boys with brothers. These significant differences in traits were then entered in some preliminary forms of Table 2 and 3. The procedure for entering differences was somewhat complicated and is described as follows:

First, with respect to a trait judged pertinent to the male or instrumental role, and considered a *congruent* aspect of that role: when any subgroup or groups were rated significantly higher than others on that trait, the number of the trait was entered in the high-masculinity column for such a group; the subgroup or groups they were higher than, i.e., the low groups, had the number of the trait entered in the low-masculinity column. Second, with respect to a male trait considered an *incongruent* aspect of the role: when any subgroup was rated higher than another on such a trait, the trait number was entered in the low-masculinity column for such a group; for the group it was higher than, i.e., the low group, the trait number was entered in the high-masculinity column. The procedure for the female or expressive traits was identical, except the female columns were used.

This procedure means that for any subgroup, entries in the high-masculinity column consist of congruent male traits on which the group is high, and incongruent male traits on which it is low; entries in the low-masculinity column consist of incongruent male traits on which the group is high, and congruent male traits on which it is low. Female column entries are read the same way. An example may be helpful at this point.

Consider in Table 3 the subgroup "Younger Boy with Older Brother" at the four- to six-year age difference. In the high-masculinity column, the entry of trait number 2 means that the group was rated significantly *high* on aggressiveness; the entry of trait number 10 means that the group was rated significantly *low* on wavering in decision. In the low-masculinity column, trait number 6 indicates a *high* rating on dawdling and procrastinating, while trait number 7 indicates a *low* rating on responsibleness.

Table 3

Instrumental and Expressive Traits for Five- and Six-year-old Boys

SUBJECTS	SIB AGE DIF-FERENCE	MALE (OR INSTRUMENTAL) TRAITS		FEMALE (OR EXPRESSIVE) TRAITS	
		High masculinity ratings	Low masculinity ratings	High femininity ratings	Low femininity ratings
Older boy with younger brother	0–2 years	9,10	1,2,7,11	..	12,13,14,15,16,19,22, 23,25,26,27,30
	2–4 years	4,9,10	1,2,5,7,11	..	12,13,14,15,16,19,20, 21,22,23,25,26,27,28, 30
	4–6 years	2,4,9,10	1,7,11	..	12,13,14,15,16,19,20, 22,23,25,26,27,30,31
Older boy with younger sister	0–2 years	11	2,4,7,9,10	25,26,27,31	12,13,14,15,16,17,18, 19,20,21,22,23,24,30
	2–4 years	2,3,5,11	4,7,9,10	25,26,27,28	12,13,14,15,16,17,18, 19,20,21,22,23,24,30
	4–6 years	3	2,4,7,9,10	25,26,27,28	12,13,14,15,16,17,18, 19,20,21,22,23,24,30
Younger boy with older brother	0–2 years	4,9,10	1,2,3,5,6,7,8	22,23,24	13,16,18,19,20,21,25, 26,27,28,30
	2–4 years	4,9,10	1,3,6,7	22,23,24	13,16,18,19,20,21,25, 26,27,28,30
	4–6 years	2,4,5,8,9,10	6,7	22,23,24,29	13,16,18,19,20,21,25, 26,27,28,30
Younger boy with older sister	0–2 years	..	2,4,5,6,7,8, 9,10	17,22,23,24, 25,26,27	13,19,30
	2–4 years	..	2,4,6,9,10	17,22,23,24, 25,26,27,28	13,16,19,20,21,30
	4–6 years	..	2,4,6,7,9,10 ..	17,22,23,24, 25,26,27,28	13,16,19,20,21,30

Note: See note to Table 2.

The preliminary forms of Tables 2 and 3 were complicated and two further steps toward simplification were taken before reaching the present form. The initial tables were marred by the occurrence of duplicate trait-number entries in the cells, arising primarily from the multiple reporting of the original data and the multiple differences emerging between the various subgroups. Hence, where duplicate trait-entries occurred, only one entry was kept. The result is to make each entry read that that subgroup is significantly higher (or lower) than some other group *or groups* on that particular trait. Second, the tables were complicated by the fact that for all subgroups there were at least some trait numbers which appeared in *both* the high and low subdivisions of either the male or female column. This indicated, of course, that a subgroup was higher (or lower) than some other group on that trait, but also lower (or higher) than still another group; i.e., on the ranking of mean ratings on the trait, the subgroup would have differed significantly from both the top and bottom ranks. To clarify the tables, and also substantially to increase the reliability of the subgroup differences reported here, all traits on which a subgroup had both high and low entries were dropped for that subgroup. In summary, the result of this step, combined with the one above, is to make *each entry in the final tables read that that subgroup is significantly higher (or lower) than one or more groups on that trait, and is significantly lower (or higher) than none.*

Results and Discussion

The data presented in Tables 2 and 3 can be brought to bear upon our hypotheses by considering the distribution by subgroups of the traits indicating high or low masculinity or femininity. Our concern is with the frequency of trait entries of the four types, rather than with the descriptive content of any particular trait. Essentially we give each separate trait an equal weight, then summarize in terms of masculinity (many high rating, few low rating entries) and of femininity, associated with each subgroup.

With respect to our first hypothesis, that through interaction and taking the role of the other the cross-sex sibs would have more traits of the opposite sex than would same-sex sibs, an examination of the distribution in Table 2 shows that this is clearly the case. Controlling for ordinality, the older girl with a younger brother has more high masculinity traits and fewer low masculinity traits, than does her counterpart, the older girl with a younger sister. This distribution of traits is even more pronounced for the girls in the second ordinal position, the younger girl with older brother being substantially higher on masculinity than her counterpart with an older sister. One will note that the acquisition of male traits does not seem to reduce the number of feminine traits of the girls with brothers. The more accurate interpretation is that acquisition of such traits adds to their behavioral repertoire, probably with a resultant dilution of their femininity in behavior, but not a displacement.

Examination of Table 3 with respect to this first hypothesis indicates that it holds for boys also. While not pronounced for the boys in the eldest child position, the boy with the sister is feminine to a greater degree than the boy with the brother. For the boys who are second-born, the difference is clear: the boy with the elder sister is substantially more feminine than his counterpart with an older brother. For the boy with the older sister, the acquisition of feminine traits would seem to have displaced, rather than simply diluted, his masculinity and he thus contrasts with the girls for whom this did not occur. We can offer no explanation for this, but it may provide a lead for further study in this area.

In connection with this result, the role of the parent requires attention. While all would agree that parents actively assist cross-sex sibs in separating their sex roles, the data show they are unsuccessful in completely arresting the process of assimilation. Perhaps in earlier times, when children's sex roles were stressed more strongly, and perhaps today for some parents making an extreme effort, the effects of interaction would be reduced. However, it certainly appears that the average parent today cannot completely avoid the effects of such sib interaction. Even were more attention given by parents to cross-sex as opposed to same-sex sibs in this matter, we believe that the tremendously greater cross-sex interaction of the former would leave its mark.

With respect to our second hypothesis, that, because of differences in control of rewards and punishments and in ability to discriminate between self and other roles, the effects of role-taking would be more pronounced for the younger child, an examination of Tables 2 and 3 again seems to support the hypothesis. While the younger, as contrasted with the older, girl with a brother manifests only a slightly greater degree of masculinity, this difference for boys is quite striking: the younger, as contrasted with the older, boy with a sister is substantially more feminine.

With respect to our third hypothesis, that on the assumption of interaction varying inversely with age-gap and greater interaction producing greater role-taking, the effects of role-taking would be largest for the sibs closest in age, the results in both tables are negligible. One might discern some such relationship for the boy with an older sister, and the girl with an older brother, but even here it is tenuous. Because the assumption that interaction varies with sib-age differences may in fact be untenable, we cannot in this instance say we have made a direct test of the hypothesis that more frequent interaction produces more role assimilation.

Since the first hypothesis, which in essence states the same point, was so strongly confirmed, our inclinations is to reject our assumption that interaction varies with age difference, at least to a degree sufficient to produce differences in role-taking.

There are two further aspects of Tables 2 and 3 which are quite noticeable and need comment. We refer first to the fact that girls with brothers appear to be masculine to a greater degree than do any of the males themselves. The simplest and most likely explanation, hence the one which we favor, is that this result occurs because of certain biases in the teachers' ratings. We submit that teachers implicitly rated boys and girls on different scales, i.e., girls were implicitly rated on a girls' scale, boys on a boys' scale. The girl with an extreme masculine trait—extreme, that is, for a girl—receives a very high rating; a boy with the same absolute degree of such a trait, or even more of it, would on the boys' scale not be extreme and his rating consequently would be reduced. In the subsequent analysis of variance, where the male and female ratings are treated as if on the same absolute scale, certain girls extremely high for girls would score significantly higher than even certain boys high on the trait. To some extent, we see the same effect in reverse for the younger boys with an older sister; while not being more feminine than girls, they almost tie certain girls, e.g., older girls with younger sisters. The probable use of different implicit rating scales, the implausibility of any group of girls being more masculine than all boys, and the important fact that when girls and boys are assuredly rated on the same absolute scale (e.g., 3, 17) boys regularly outscore girls on masculine traits, all tend to support this interpretation.

The second additional aspect of the tables which merits discussion is that all girls seem to be more feminine than the boys are masculine; indeed, the major characteristic of the boys is to be antifeminine, not masculine. In part, this is explained by the assumed bias in the ratings mentioned above; boys are outscored on their own traits by some girls. In part also, this is explained by the preponderance of feminine traits used in the ratings, so that boys could only express their masculinity, as it were, by being rated low on such traits. In part, and an intriguing part indeed, it may be explained by certain developmental processes commonly assumed in clinical theory and recently put in a role theory context by Parsons.[15] Parsons points out that both boy and girl first identify with the mother and tend to play an expressive role. In development, the boy must break away and establish a new identification with the father, which is difficult and involves much new learning, in the role-taking sense. At the same time, the boy must "push far and hard to renounce dependency." Girls, continuing identification with the mother and the expressive role, face neither of these problems. It may be, then, that the girls' femininity and the boys' antifemininity and yet lack of masculinity which shows itself in Tables 2 and 3 arises in part because the children have been caught by the raters at an age where the boy is trying to shift his identification from mother to father.

To conclude, our analysis of Helen Koch's data indicates that cross-sex siblings tend to assimilate traits of the opposite sex, and that this effect is most pronounced in the younger of the two siblings. There findings support the role-learning theory presented here, and also stand as a substantive contribution to the area of sex-role learning. We wish now to stress two points mentioned earlier.

First, these findings must be subject to strict limitations to two-child families. Not only does the Fauls and Smith study demonstrate this limitation with regard to only-child families, but observation suggests that in larger families other variables come into play; e.g., in the four-child family with a three and one sex split, parents may actively help the solitary child in differentiating sex roles; or in the four-child family with a two and two split, siblings may pair off by sex and the cross-sex role-taking effect is minimized.

Second, with respect to the substantive value of these results, we would point out that even though parents must remain as the major source of sex-role learning, almost every child has a mother and father to learn from. Hence the *variations* in type and amount of sex-role learning occur on top of this base, so to speak, and in this variability the effect of a same or a cross-sex sib may play as large or larger a role than variations in parental behavior, mixed versus single-sexed schooling, sex of neighborhood playmates, and the like. Speculations on the durable and considerable effects of sex of sib on sex-role learning thus seem warranted and lead one to consider problems such as the effect of sex of sibling on one's later role in the marital relation, on career choices, and on other correlates of the adult sex role.

Summary

This paper reports some relations between ordinal position, sex of sibling, and sex-role learning by children in two-child families. The findings are based on a further analysis of Helen Koch's data relating personality traits of children to their sex, sex of sibling, ordinal position, and age difference from sibling. In this analysis the personality traits were classified as pertaining either to the instrumental (masculine) role or the expressive (feminine) role. The distribution of such traits in children as a correlate of family structure was then assessed.

General propositions describing role learning in terms of interaction with others, including taking the role of the other, leads to hypotheses that cross-sex siblings will have more traits of the opposite sex than will same-sex siblings, and that this effect will be greater for the younger, as contrasted with the older, sibling. Both hypotheses are confirmed by the data presented.

PART IV

Family and Personality

---

39 *Parental Occupations and Children's Symptoms*

BRUNO BETTELHEIM
and EMMY SYLVESTER

The division of labor within the family usually involves one parent (typically the father in our society) having a major commitment to an occupation which is pursued outside the family. It is, thus, difficult for the father in his occupational role to serve as a readily accessible, easily comprehended model for children. Drs. Bettelheim and Sylvester have had wide experience in the treatment of severely disturbed children at the Orthogenic School at the University of Chicago. In this paper, they draw on that wide experience to show how, under certain conditions, the parental occupation becomes woven into the child's fantasy and behavior. The impact of this aspect of the family's adaptive patterns stands out very clearly in these disturbed cases. It is likely that what is highlighted in these cases is true in all families; various characteristics of parental occupations become assimilated into the personality structure of the developing child.

In our work with emotionally disturbed children, we have frequently noted the impact of cultural factors on personality development and particularly on the choice of symptomatic behavior. Of these factors, only one is singled out for discussion here, namely, parental occupation. In all instances mentioned below, parental occupation was the mold for certain aspects of the child's behavior, although the underlying disturbance was invariably a total one based on early and continuous difficulties in the central relationship of the child.

Children whose personality disturbances result from arrested or uneven growth generally manifest their disturbance by a fixation on primitive forms of mastery. For the infant, the perfection of instinctual functions is the central task of mastery in the service of survival. It is achieved within

---

Reprinted from *American Journal of Orthopsychiatry,* XX (October, 1950), 785–95, where it appeared under the title, "Notes on the Impact of Parental Occupations: Some Cultural Determinants of Symptom Choice in Emotionally Disturbed Children"; with the kind permission of the authors and the publishers.

the reality of the earliest phase of the mother-child relationship. Benign and predictable gratification during this period enables the child to give up his primitive narcissistic omnipotence for the realistic tools of mastery that are normally perfected during the latency period. It is then that the particular cultural setting assumes significance and reality for the child and is experienced in his relationship to the parent, who represents the external world. Only at late stages of maturation is cultural impact experienced directly, that is, without meditation through parental figures.

Like the normal infant, many emotionally disturbed children and adults are characterized by persistent magical concepts of the world around them. Lacking the tools of realistic mastery, they cling to an animistic view of external reality in attempts to complement their own unresolved needs. Since adequate evaluation in the approach to the outside world is normally acquired during a lengthy process of learning, deviations in the process may occur where the child's relationships to the mediators between himself and the external reality are unduly difficult. Thus, a child whose parents have failed to provide for his primitive needs will, at later stages of development, tend to experience all complexities of the outside world as replicas of the original frustrating parental behavior. This will especially be true whenever the connection between parental behavior and his own needs and actions lacks emotional logic for the child.

Such unresolved needs and their compensatory magic account for dysfunctions during the latency period, when cultural realities first become meaningful to the child. Our present-day culture presents all children with values and experiences that are often beyond their rational comprehension. Children whose personality structures predispose them to a magical rather than realistic approach tend to misinterpret wider sectors of the cultural reality in line with their own pressing needs.

Environmental factors are first realized through the medium of the child's experiences with significant adults. It is in his grasp of the culturally determined occupations and the culturally sanctioned preoccupations of the parents that the child of the latency period comes to test his fantastic beliefs about the world of adults.

The occupation of a parent, in particular, assumes personal meaning to the child only as it acquires direct bearing on the child's immediate welfare—whether as the source of livelihood, as the cause of the parent's absence from the home, or as a feature which makes the parent's image more awesome or more powerful. Occupation then expresses for the child such parental reactions as have already been tangibly experienced. Nevertheless, a child's unrealistic concept of parental occupation does not depend solely on his past relations to the parent; other factors, too, contribute to his inability to evaluate them correctly. The ways in which many parents today earn their livelihood are not readily observable to the child. Once the father enters his office, or the factory door closes behind him, his activities seem shrouded in mystery. It is only when the parent's occupation is open to the child's inspection, and within his comprehension, that observation may correct previous concepts or irrealistic elaborations. Yet in many cases, isolated activities, even when observed, do not necessarily clarify the parent's occupation for the child if these activities are meaningful only within a complex weave of interrelationships that are again beyond the child's comprehension and may therefore again seem "magic." If this is so, then the child may transfer the seemingly magical character of the parental occupation from the job to the parent.

With the growing division of labor, only few occupations remain meaningful per se. The complexity of modern employment also prevents the child from understanding the ways of adult work. This may force the child to interpret parental occupation in terms of emotional needs or magical thinking, rather than on the basis of a comprehensible transition between his own knowledge and the work of the parent. Again, in terms of the child's need to understand, isolated glimpses of the parent's occupation may themselves force him into fantastic elaborations, to fill the large gap between his capacity to understand and the incomplete information available to him. This means of establishing connections between the new and the already-known is by no means always a result of the parent's unwillingness to provide the necessary information; the inadequacy of the child's general knowledge and the immaturity of his judgment make it virtually impossible for the adult to give realistic information to the child. In a way, the child who knows nothing about his parent's occupation (other than the fact that the father spends a certain number of hours outside of the home) may be better off than the child who receives isolated, disconnected, and hence meaningless pieces of information which he tries unsuccessfully to synthesize.[1]

In each of our cases, too, the child's relation to his mother, and with it his normal development, was severely disturbed before he entered the Oedipal phase and developed greater interest in the father. Hence, these children were not turning to their fathers for emotional gratification and security solely because they were entering the latency period; they were also looking to the father for the gratification of emotional needs that should have been satisfied by the mother. Again, in turning to the father for assurance and emotional gratification, these children were not acting in simple trust, for bad relations to their mothers had already made them doubtful and anxious. They tended to evaluate the father, and his occupation along with him, in terms of their past experiences. Boys whose relationships to their mothers had been severely damaged turned to their fathers more in a spirit of despair than in terms of their natural development. Since earlier experiences with their mothers had already colored all their expectations with a fearful tint, it was difficult for them to envisage any adult's actions as non-threatening. In such instances, the father's incomprehensible occupation led the child to judge him by his occupation, as demonstrated in the following cases.

A small boy's experience with a cold and distant mother was aggravated by a visual defect which interfered quite seriously with his motor development. Since he was unable to judge either distance or objects, all efforts at crawling and walking were soon given up because they led to frustrating and painful experiences instead of any rewarding mastery of space. The mother's attempt at forceful drill of the child's motor performance met only with resistance. As a result, guilt and hurt pride increased her distance from the child, but she continued her fragmentized show of interest. In his helpless loneliness, the boy responded eagerly when his father began to show some interest in him. But in line with his previous experiences, the child reacted only to isolated segments of the father's advances and identified only with partial aspects of the father's personality.

No previous experience had supported any unified concept of his body in function, or his personality in communication with others. This was evidenced by his poor co-ordination long after correction of his vision, in his fear of injury, and above all in his infantile and nearly incomprehensible speech which had characteristics of autistic incantation rather than real communication.

When he entered the treatment institution, he was seven years old and his vision had been fully corrected for more than four years. Nevertheless he still moved as if spastic. When he walked down the stairs he had to hold to the rail for dear life and could move down to the next step only after both feet had reached it. Walking upstairs was possible only with one hand on the railing while another person held his other hand. It took him more than two years to gain normal and co-ordinated motility, and the development of speech as clear communication was parallel to that of motility.

For a long time, the boy was exclusively interested in the fanciful tales which the father would tell him by the hour. He began to imitate the father's tone of voice and repeated the stories to himself in soliloquy. These stories were more comprehensible to him than the father's attempts to entertain him with conventional toys. The boy's urgent request for his stories, as well as his inability and unwillingness to engage in other activities, increased the father's own pleasure in spinning out fantasies for his child. What had started as entertainment for the son soon became indulgence for the father, which unfortunately was detrimental to the son. The boy insisted on the word-by-word repetition of stories which began with the injury and abandonment of a little boy by an old witch and ended with the boy's miraculous salvation by a cunning hero who was powerful by virtue of the most modern of technical devices.

It is obvious that the boy began to perceive his father in terms of the megalomanic fantasies which had meant compensation and comfort to him during the time of his isolation and helplessness. With his father's participation, he was also able to deal with some of the hostility against his mother. Nevertheless, since he identified with his father only as a hero-rescuer, he derived no real strength from the relationship, and it did nothing to help him invalidate his previous grandiose fantasies.

As the boy grew older, the father's stockbroker office became a place of great fascination for him. His father explained the working of the stock market to him in terms of the skillful manipulation of figures, but he also impressed him with his concern about being able to provide the family with a constant flow of money. To the boy, this concern spelled a twofold insecurity: a repetition of the fears he experienced as an infant when he doubted the continued supply of vital needs, and a deflation of his father whom he had welcomed as a magic rescuer, although he had subsequently grown quite rivalrous toward him for achievement and power.

Since the parents, in the cultural tradition of their setting, stressed "realistic" attitudes toward the matter of money and equated wealth with security and status, the boy's new preoccupation had many determinants. His early experience of frustration and the persistence of magical thinking, now applied to exploration as well as to competition, led to intense and obsessional preoccupation with his father's incomprehensible profession— the more so as he began to doubt that anyone could maintain his life just by manipulating figures.

In line with his fantasies, he assumed that the father possessed secret, magical power which enabled him to produce money by the juggling of figures. The next logical step was to fear that this assumed secret power of his father's might be used against the boy. In order to test this and to see if figures actually possessed such magic powers—and if so, to acquire them himself—he obsessionally manipulated figures in nonsensical ways in an effort to find out the secret of the father's magic.[2] He spent hours and days in counting and writing down figures up to several thousand. The only subject he troubled to learn in class was arithmetic; when other subjects were being taught he withdrew into his counting obsessions. With progress in arithmetic, his manipulation of figures became more elaborate. For hours he made out and solved problems in addition or multiplication. The goal was always to reach higher and higher number combinations since he believed that these high figures gave him power, although actually they led him farther and farther from reality.

The boy's conception of his father's occupation was then seen to have resulted from his need for mastery through magic. In the therapeutic milieu of the psychiatric school, such magic proved a less acceptable way of identification and conformity than at home, and at the same time, new areas of assertion and achievement became available to the child.

In psychotherapy, means and ways to guarantee safety and subsistence were the central motif. These were in line with his strongest anxieties of the past—the result of inadequate gratification as an infant, and of the fear of injury through poor motor co-ordination. For some time, he was busily engaged in building complicated houses which, although high and imposing, were notable for their safeguards against falling or bumping oneself. While he juggled figures at school by the hour, he was more interested, with his therapist, in the problems of investment for lasting security. After he had experimented with physical safety in the building of apartment houses, schools, playgrounds, and swimming pools, he began to conduct burglar-proof bank buildings, then factories of which his father, and then he himself, was the owner and the sole recipient of goods.

In his rehabilitation, the achievement of mastery over his own body—in terms of adequate motility, the capacity for personal independence and co-ordinated social behavior—was equally as important as psychotherapy. His progress in these vital areas was much accelerated when, after having worked through his idea about his father's profession, he was free to devote his whole energy to the learning of previously disdained activities such as swimming, playing ball, and going on hikes. This task he could approach only after he had adequately solved and therefore relinquished his magic preoccupation with his father's profession.

The importance of cultural influence on symptom formation was particularly obvious among one group of severely damaged children, all of whom displayed high intelligence. A pseudo maturity made it possible for them to function in their family settings because their intellectuality enabled them to comply with the cultural demands of their parents. However, the instability of this pseudo integration became obvious when they were exposed to different sets of demands in the school, on the playground, or in living with their own age-mates.

These children, who were mainly, though insufficiently, supported by their intellectuality, seemed particularly influenced by the professional pursuits of their parents. Early interference with their ability in spontaneous mastery made it necessary for them to function by borrowed, rather than integrated, mechanisms. Their disturbances originated in their earliest relationships to their mothers. But the fathers, to whom they turned for compensation and comfort, seemed dangerous to them because so much of their lives was incomprehensible. Incomprehensible attitudes were adopted by these children in distorted form and accounted for the bizarre features in their personality structure.

One child in this group, an eight-year-old boy of superior intelligence, entered the residential institution because of his inability to function either scholastically or socially in the setup of the public schools. In the institution, the most bizarre feature of his disturbance was his preoccupation with guns, food, poison, and the celestial bodies. Relieved of the pressure of ordinary classroom learning or group participation, he would draw by the hour tiny models of guns, pistols or cannons; with the aid of a magnifying glass he would explain their mechanisms to a few adults whom he carefully selected, according to their willingness to feed him incessantly. With such persons he also engaged in scholarly conversation on the visibility of the stars and the feeding habits of prehistoric animals.

In psychotherapeutic sessions, some insight into the connection between his behavior and his father's profession was obtained. The father worked as a biochemist in the field of nutrition. He was greatly devoted to his profession, in which he had successfully sublimated many of his own emotional needs. The child, however, could not benefit from the successful mastery which these sublimations represented to the father. Sublimation had been the result of the father's personality growth, but the child was confronted with the finished results of intrapsychic processes. He had to use them for better or for worse and before he had grown to understand them.

The child's mother expressed her hostile competitiveness with all males in her need for prolificacy, but she was essentially cold to her first-born infant son. Within the first five years of his life, three siblings were born. The most primitive expression of the boy's hunger and destructiveness was first a refusal of food and, later, overeating. His alertness predisposed him to intense curiosity which was selectively indulged by the parents; they permitted him exploration in all but his most vital concern, the where and why about babies. The mother's rejection of the patient increased with the arrival of each new sibling and, with this growing distance, his need for acceptance by the father increased. New intellectual achievements made it possible for the boy to pay the price which the father unconsciously demanded for his devotion to the boy—that the child show interest in the father's emotional mainstay, his profession. Accordingly, the boy participated to his utmost in the father's professional interests and preoccupied himself in line with his needs, rather than in line with his childish and limited capacities for real understanding.

The father's work at the microscope became the expression of the boy's scoptophilic interests, of his wish to explore, and in his exploration to master the mother's fecundity; in this last, he eventually hoped to participate by making himself master of the gun which had significant symbolic meaning for him as a tool for procreation and destruction. The father's professional interest in food seemed to justify his own greed and cannibalistic tendencies, but even in taking over the father's interest he could only give form to his needs but never achieve mastery over them. His desperation was further expressed when he centered his interests on objects as distant from him in time and space as the stars and prehistoric animals. Since the tools which the child borrowed from the father brought no relief to his immediate situation, he experimented with them in a more removed way, applying them to stars and animals. Only by assuming grandiose proportions could these tools promise comfort in his immediate predicament.

In this way, the father's profession gave shape to the boy's delusional system, although they were not the cause of his disturbance. Borrowing techniques from the father increased the boy's distance from the pressing actuality of his life situation without offering relief through real mastery, and desperation found its expression in psychotic mechanisms, as he put incomprehensible parental practices in the service of his own needs for magic.

In the therapeutic milieu, the resolution of this delusional magic proceeded slowly. It happened in stages which paralleled his trust in the realistic potentialities for genuine mastery—because unconditional gratification was experienced in a thoroughly comprehensible way of life. Magic mastery, however, was not given up easily or without struggle, since the prestige offered by a rewarding life seemed infinitesimal when compared with the grandiose ideas implied in the delusional system.

Another case demonstrates how a child of superior intelligence used his misconception of parental profession to justify his persistent attempts at delusional mastery in real situations.

A ten-year-old boy was placed in the residential institution because of his general inability to stand tension of any kind. He was generally hyperactive and unable to accept any form of limitation. In the institution, his ability to spread excitement and confusion among his contemporaries persisted for a long time. He responded to all attempts at restriction by paranoid claims that the adult's behavior was logically incomprehensible, aimed at harming him as well as the children whom he involved in his near continuous upheavals. In psychotherapy, many aspects of his behavior began to make sense in terms of his unconscious identification with baffling aspects of his father's professional activities.

This responsive and intellectually precocious child was born to an elderly father and a young mother who was emotionally unsatisfied in her marriage. The mother's seductive attitude toward the boy aroused his anxiety and made him turn to the father for protection. Intellectual seduction by the father seemed less threatening to the boy at that time and he submitted to it. But immediate expression of competitive striving toward the father remained difficult because of the father's exclusive intellectual orientation, and because the boy considered him very vulnerable on account of his age and poor health. Identification with the father's intellectuality was therefore the less dangerous solution for the boy but confronted him with the need to adopt means of assertion which were beyond the scope of his emotional maturity. He could express them in token, however, since he was bright enough for that.

His bizarre reading habits were partly characteristic of his whole mode of functioning. He read voraciously with tremendous speed, minimal accuracy, and apparently no discrimination—but never failed to apply his spotty knowledge in an exhibitionistic way.

It appeared that at an early age he had begun to read the *Congressional*

Record compulsively, an achievement in which the father took great pride though he expressed it sarcastically. Understanding of this seemingly isolated feature in the child's makeup proved meaningful. His interest in the *Congressional Record* began with his knowledge that the father wrote political pamphlets under a pseudonym. At first this was a mystery to the boy and then turned into the apprehension that his father hid his name because he was in constant danger. If this were so, he felt he could forewarn him by finding out who the political powers were, since he identified them with reprisals against the father. The congressional records were clear and open to him, compared to the father's writings, which he understood as little as the intellectual exhibitions in which he had participated from his earliest years. This confusion and mystery he mirrored in his own behavior. He was participant, spy, judge, and prosecutor in relationship to his father, as well as in his attitudes toward staff and children at the school; there he was rebel, police officer, and reformer, in confused and confusing ways. Since the father's prestige had been unquestioned and real, the boy continued to function by attitudes borrowed from him which became a part of the dominant pattern of confusion.

Before this system was unraveled, the combination of discrepant attitudes in his behavior was as confusing to his environment as to himself. As those living with the child tried to decipher his reproachful accusations, they lent themselves to the gratification of his devious demands for a legitimate need of attention; in this way he remained tied to his mode of functioning as long as he could procure unlimited attention through his provocations.

He relinquished this pattern of behavior only when his relationship to the father became more realistic. Then he learned the real advantage of more self-contained, though less dramatic, behavior. For a long time, however, any disillusionment in his father or in father substitutes brought a recrudescence of his former need to prove his worth by provoking confusion, and by living according to patterns of provocative pamphlets about incomprehensible issues.

In other cases, the influence of the culture on the child's evaluation of parental occupations is most obvious where the occupation seems to give the father special prerogatives. In terms of the child's anxieties, such prerogatives may at any moment be turned against the child, and in this connection the child's guilt about the aggressions evoked by his bad relation to the parent should not be overlooked. Thus, emotionally disturbed children of physicians, particularly of surgeons, may develop the fear that their fathers are permitted—or at least able—to perform operations on them, operations which are often interpreted, in terms of the child's developmental stage, as implying castration.

To cite an example, the six-year-old daughter of a surgeon was receiving psychotherapy because of a tendency to withdraw from the members of her family. Whenever she was sick or required any of the common preventative treatment children receive, she reacted with continuous and violent displays of anxiety toward medical manipulation. She also proved herself to be well informed about her father's surgical practice and kept close check on all persons of her acquaintance whom the father had cared for. Her obsession was evidenced by her vocabulary, which was full of complicated medical terminology.

In the course of treatment, she became less hostile to the father, and then one of her favorite games was to play "Restaurant," in which the owner of a "Good Eating Place" took his whole family to his store for a special occasion. He was particularly skillful in giving his family the choice cuts of meat they wanted, because he had once been a doctor. Thus, in her play and her fantasy, she simply denied the father's mysterious and anxiety-evoking occupation and changed it into one that offered gratification of the most basic biological urge. By doing so, she also simplified the earning of a livelihood into one that provided for direct gratification in terms of her own understanding and needs.

The child's early fixation, in this case, lent support to her magical thinking and led to attempts at a magical mastery of the father's occupation by the mastery of medical terms she did not understand. With the change in her emotional relation to her father, he was changed from a threatening figure—engaged in a threatening occupation which had to be kept at bay through magic—into an indulging person providing oral gratification through his work.

The attitude of the culture toward the father's occupation was clearly reflected in this girl's anxiety about her contact with physicians. In our culture, the physician is invested with the privilege to hurt; he vaccinates the child, gives her penicillin shots, and so on. This privilege is interpreted by the child in terms of her own hostile tendencies, and she transforms all physicians (including her father) into anxiety-evoking persons. Similarly, the son of an obstetrician assumed that only obstetricians had the right to examine and understand sex organs. He did not dare to compete with the father and hence felt that sex exploration was prohibited for him. This led first to the impeding of all exploration and then to a severe learning inhibition.

But it is not only the occupation which carries special prerogatives, such as those of surgeons, which evokes such anxieties in the child. For example, the anxiety already created in one child by his disturbed relation to his father was further aggravated by the fact that his parent worked as a butcher in the stockyards. This increased his fears to the point where they became unbearable and he denied the existence of his father's occupation entirely. He viewed him, instead, only in terms of some of his leisure activities as a handy man doing chores around the neighbors' houses, activities in which the child actually participated, but always submissively and fearfully because of the father's known but denied occupation. While he thus degraded the father to a seemingly impotent role, he also tried to appease him by his docility. This boy, who in his own mind had changed the father's occupation as if in retaliation, had also to change himself to appear less manly: he tried to act and live like a girl. But in order to maintain this denial of the father's true occupation and his own masculinity, the boy had to pay the price of denying increasingly larger segments of reality and depriving himself of interpersonal relationships until he so lost contact that he had to be placed in a psychiatric institution.

In a less specific way, times of cultural changes also contribute to the difficulties of evaluating parental occupations and of identifying with parental values. More and more parents feel uneasy about the social significance of their occupations, or the two parents may feel differently about the matter. Their dissension is often conveyed to the child in such subtle ways that while doubt and insecurity are created, the elusiveness or absence of information about how and why this occupation is not fully accepted makes objective evaluation by the child impossible, and he falls back on fantastic elaborations that are in line with his emotional needs.

The mother of one delinquent boy was critical of her husband for her own neurotic reason. She felt superior to him because of his coarseness and also because of the crudeness of his occupation, which required manual skill. The boy, who had great manual dexterity himself, developed the notion that this precluded achieving higher status and gave up learning altogether. Identifying with his father—who under pressure of the mother moved in circles which felt superior to manual laborers—he not only gave up all efforts at intellectual achievement, but also began to fight society by delinquent action.

In general, however, children who are early and extensively damaged do not develop enough closeness to those around them to discern the fine points of parental attitudes or to be affected by nuances in parental behavior. Their evaluation of parental occupation is then chiefly affected by the ups and downs of their variable ambivalence toward the parents and is relatively untouched by the reality of the parent's occupational activities.

We do not intend to discuss further the defensive denial or misinterpretations of parental occupation and their consequences in symptomatic behavior. We wish only to point out that typical defensive mechanisms such as denial, isolation, projection, and so on are also applied to this element of the child's psychological reality, and *can* be applied because, in present-day society, so little reality testing is available to the child in the case of parental occupation that it contributes to further deviation, once personality disturbance has arisen.

40   *Family Living Space and Personality Development*

JAMES S. PLANT

Dr. Plant was a psychiatrist who was very sensitive to the social and cultural forces affecting the personality development of children. In his work as Director of the Child
Guidance Clinic in Essex County, New Jersey, he gained first-hand knowledge of these
effects. In this selection, he explores the impact of the family's use of living space on
their children and on their personality development. Dr. Plant sees the ramifications of
the patterns prevalent among families in overcrowded urban districts, and sees particularly the problems that can arise. Again, although the research evidence is not readily
available, a more general hypothesis seems warranted, namely, that the family's adaptation to the space in which it is free to move gets into the child's personality structure in
many ways.

The area under discussion[1] has a large number of industrial
plants interspersed in a general housing pattern of low rentals, large
families, and few rooms for each. In the working out of the problems of
life, what does this pattern mean to the individuals living within it?

Lack of Self-Sufficiency

Crowding seems very definitely to affect the self-sufficiency of children
—their ability to be alone. This is a matter entirely different from that of
the close-drawn walls about the ego which are built when others threaten.
Here we are dealing with a certain uncomfortable ill-at-ease-ness when
there are not many others about. The search is for games, for work, where
many others are close by. Also we have found difficulty in placing girls of
this area in house-servant positions, a difficulty made up of many elements
apparently, one of which at least is revealed by the girls' statement that
"the work is too lonely." Every social engineer has had the experience of
the loneliness of these children of crowded areas when placed in the country. It is as though they felt incomplete—without the necessary supports
to the personality. It seems that persistent and constant crowding from
early life destroys the sense of individuality—which without doubt is

Reprinted by permission of the publishers from James S. Plant, *Personality and the
Cultural Pattern* (Cambridge, Massachusetts: Harvard University Press, 1937), pp. 213–28.
Copyright, 1937, by The Commonwealth Fund.

fostered by opportunities for privacy. (McDougall in discussing this same phenomenon uses the term "incomplete personality."[2])

These children seek in all their activities situations in which there are others—the movies, the factory. Their panic over country placement is not due merely to the strangeness of the surroundings, as many do not show this when placed in equally new situations where there are plenty of people about—in other cities or in other parts of the same city. (Country children brought to the city similarly complain of "loneliness"—but this is a different matter. Here the child feels that he is no factor in all that goes on about him—that persons do not nod a "good morning"—that his place of importance in the community is lost.) Our work in suburban and rural districts has convinced us that periods of being alone, of playing alone, of having the privacy of one's own room, are important fostering agents in a feeling of individuality, of self-sufficiency.

The other side of the picture is that there is a certain sensing of the needs of others, a certain understanding of others that comes from always living with them, not provided otherwise. One often hears the complaint that the ward leader, the "typical politician," represents the crowded, less advantaged area, but one also hears the admission that he has a certain understanding of people that seems to come only from close contact with people in all their moods.

(The United States is rapidly being urbanized, and, if we see the effects of crowding correctly, its results should appear in our cultural pattern. Is our growing reputation as a nation of joiners in any sense dependent upon this same factor? Here seems again to be this feeling of incompleteness if there are not many around.)

Destruction of Illusions

Crowding serves to destroy the illusions which children build about other people. The word "illusion" is perhaps unwisely chosen. These images we build of others are of the material of our dreams and goals. They are of great dynamic power—leading us to the best we can attain. Indeed, the hero we thus invest is little more than the dramatizer, the personalization of what is perhaps otherwise too intangible a goal. We nevertheless use "illusion" here because its opposite has such a fixed and real meaning. When we speak of "disillusionment," we recognize the breaking of that which has been of tremendous worth.

There seems to be a certain optimum amount of contact for the construction of illusions. This differs for different individuals. At times, chance meeting serves for the building of a complete hero picture. This phenomenon is not common and depends entirely upon the extent to which some presenting symbol has been previously associated with an acceptable ideal image ("I *always* like people with that sort of hand"). Most of the children we see build much more definitely upon persons whom they know better—with whom they have carried through a number of conversations or projects. We have become quite certain that there is a point of contact beyond which these illusions stand the hazard of complete destruction. In this mechanism, the child puts into the individual what he would like to be there rather than accepting what actually is there. This means that with rare exceptions the process of disillusionment must come with better acquaintance and more frequent contact.

Crowding, as we have said, destroys these illusions. People are seen when not on dress parade, and they are seen often; they must be seen as they are rather than as they would wish to be or as one would wish to see them. For instance, the boys of this area do not want to follow in their fathers' footsteps. Of course, these families represent the least advantaged groups so that the children would naturally look to some other lines of work than those which seem so patently to have brought this lowly result. We have felt however that there is, too, the factor that the child knows his father too well. One idealizes out of dream material—the clatter and push of crowded living conditions too easily wake him up.

Does crowding prevent the formation of these illusions or break them down soon after they are formed? Our present feeling (without adequate data) is that the latter is the case. The discovery that these children continue the construction of these illusions (though now about new persons) would, in part, constitute such data. Would individuals show an insistent urge to form these idealized goals if they had never done so at least in embryo form? One may add, for what it is worth, the observation that the descriptions of persons which these children give carry that certain sort of crispness that comes from something broken ("Everybody is a gyp," "There isn't a one I'd really trust"). Admittedly, our data for this area only cover the delinquent group, which perhaps considerably skews the findings. The child describes his lack of goal images in the people about him with a certain attitude of rebuff. It is not alone that these children of crowded families are much more realistic about other people than are the children of well-to-do families. They are realistic on the negative or discouraging side—that they know that you cannot trust people, that people are fundamentally selfish and looking for the attainment only of their own ends. They are much more on the defensive as to other people.

If crowding actually prevented the formation of ideal images then we should find hero worship absent in these groups. But if, as we believe, crowding merely served to break the images which are formed, then in some form or other hero worship should be found quite as much as at other levels of social stratification. The latter is what we find in our group. The older children have their highly idealized heroes and follow their lead as best they can. But these heroes are now peculiarly depersonalized.

Thus, if one talks about some baseball hero he finds that nothing is known of the person. The hero is one of power and numbers. A home run is not a crisis met by a person but "his forty-first." Is this just the short-cut symbol for the more personal image? We think not; we have not been successful in getting back of batting averages and home-run accomplishments to the personality involved. This same "emptying" of the personality makes their description of the movies amusing. These children use the true names of the actors in describing their activities on the screen—again "protecting themselves" from the true personality of the movie hero or heroine. ("Clark Gable almost lost his life saving her.") Watching the face of the child through this gives ample evidence that the star is separated entirely from his or her own personality. If one now turns the child to the actual life of her favorite actress there is either a quick "Oh, I don't know anything about that" or a projection from a film that again leaves the star without much that she could really call her own.

Such observations led us to the following formulation: that the crowding of individuals does not prevent the development of image goals or hero worship; that the crowding of individuals repeatedly disillusions children, breaks the images that are formed; that what is left open to the child is an interesting form of depersonalized hero in which the name of an individual stands for such abstractions as numbers, high averages, power, or victory; that, in other words, the child learns that he cannot "afford" to worship a person *as such*.

This realism, this clearness of vision as to people, works peculiarly in another way, so that children seem to see more clearly what is "good" in people just as they see what is, for them, "bad." How else can one understand the ability of children to see the love that lies behind the harsh hand and voice? For often love is there—often it is precisely this force that impels the harshness. We have had some rather rude jolts from children in families where statistics as to tempests ran high—only to find ties of loyalty and love that seemed incomprehensible. "Sure the old man beat me up—lots of times—but it was because he loved me. He wouldn't a done it if he didn't care a lot." The child of the crowded home senses motives—sees what really lies behind conduct—and if this breaks his brittle idols it often too gives him strength and the sense of belongingness in the face of what seems to the objective outsider to be unreasonable and cruel treatment.

Sexual Maladjustment

Crowding also prevents the building of illusions about sex. (Again we impute a realism and dynamic power to "illusions" that is scarcely connoted in the word itself.) This demands that something be said of the meaning of sexual adjustments.

In any of the biological sciences it is difficult to set up a true dichotomy. If one sets up a dichotomy in the field of what sexual expression means to people, it is done only for the sake of clearer exposition; one accepts the premise that each of the two elements runs into the other, with indistinct borders between them. On this basis, sexual expression can be said to play two quite distinct roles which are in large measure separable though both have a part in most sexual acts.

Sexual phenomena, on the one hand, serve the individual in high degree as the source of direct pleasurable experiences. It is uncertain at how early an age this appears, though certainly, from birth, the genital region is provided with a greater concentration of sensory nerves than practically any other part of the body. The individual comes into the world already equipped to receive through this region satisfying responses which are not of a sexual nature as the adult knows it but rather of something merely more marked and striking than are other body reactions. However, the sexual connotations (in an adult sense) of these reactions rapidly grow, being aided by the biological process of the specialization of sensation and by the social process which hastens to give meaning to all life experiences. Thus, occasionally one finds children up to ten years old, let us say, who turn to stimulation of the genital region as a means of attaining a direct satisfying physical response (in distinction to those who use these activities for their social value—a group discussed in a moment). From ten years on, the opportunity for this direct satisfaction develops and is worked out largely in the problem of masturbation. We have seen both girls and boys who, we are convinced, have no phantasy life during masturbation beyond the contemplation of the pleasure of the act itself. Here one finds the establishment of various sorts of so-called perverted sexual acts because the individual is primarily interested in any procedure which will develop actual physical expression of the sexual hunger. Such an individual very soon loses all compunctions (as to following what society is pleased to call "normal" heterosexual procedures) and is quite ready to find expression in the homosexual or heterosexual, in the normal or perverted field, wherever gratification can be found.

Sexual phenomena on the other hand serve a high symbolic or language-value purpose for the individual. Just how early this begins is again unknown, although perhaps some of the rudimentary patterns are set down in late infancy when the child discovers that masturbation has a high social value in the temper tantrums his act causes in the nearby adults. Soon children learn that certain words serve the same purpose of attracting attention. By six, the boy learns that there are sexual acts which connote that one is grown up, and children of both sexes at this time, or before, use sexual information as valuable coin—buying respect and admiration from other children through particular bits of information. Most masturbation (at least this is true of our group) carries a high degree of heterosexual phantasy. By far the larger fraction of the "perversions" which we see at this period (sodomy and the like) are rich in heterosexual phantasy, are undertaken as a means of showing that one is "grown up" and spontaneously disappear just as soon as social sanctions allow of true ("normal") heterosexual experiences. The sexual phenomena through this whole adolescent period run rampant as the symbols of having grown up. One sees something of this as one listens to the tale of many a boy or girl who defies social condemnation in an effort to show through these fabrications that full growth has by now been attained. Similarly one talks with many of these children who actually dread definite heterosexual experience, but who try to drive themselves to it because it is their best established symbol of maturity. The boy who has attempted but failed to consummate the heterosexual act never comes to us with a story of physical thwarting or unpleasantness but with the shame that he is not yet grown up. So for the adolescent one could multiply by hundreds the examples of the use of the sexual life to attain in one's own eyes and the eyes of others, age, maturity, social prestige, victory in sibling rivalry, and the like.

Interwoven with the above and developing rapidly in adolescence is the use of the sexual life as a means of expressing relationships which are beyond the power of words. It is at this level that the sexual aspects of the marital relationships work themselves out. The intimacy ties involved in marriage are idiomatic for the individual; the partners labor to develop a feeling that here exists a relationship that could exist between no two others. The sexual act is of the highest importance here—entered upon only by "agreement" of both partners and turned to by them as a means of expressing some sort of idiomatic tie that seems to defy any other form of expression. So-called "perversions" (as Havelock Ellis long ago pointed out so well)[3] have frequently now a particular value as they represent to the partners symbols of "what other people wouldn't do."

Physical gratification of course plays a part in practically all the sexual phenomena. Equally, the symbolic values of the sexual life appear to some degree in most of its manifestations. The matter is one, then, of the relative degree to which each is present. We have dealt with boys and men who in fear and actual physical discomfort attempt to carry through various forms of sexual expression as symbolizing maturity. (This is apparently more common in girls and women—many of whom go through the entire sexual life with nothing beyond the experience of the sexual activities as the "proper thing to do" or what is "expected of one in marriage.") Of the existence of the various onanistic, homosexual, and heterosexual acts as no other than means of physical gratification, we are decidedly more certain.

What now are the "illusions" about sex? We think that they are the realistic, dynamic images that are set up in a vague way about this use of sex as a symbol of relationship. And what now does crowding do to these illusions, which ordinarily begin to appear at seven, eight, or nine years of age? If our observations are correct, then an individual can understand the use to which those who love each other put the sexual life only when he or she has had that experience. It is precisely the idiom of the relationship which defies teaching it to others. Yet our clinic records of crowded families quite abound in instances of children surreptitiously or more openly viewing those sexual activities to which they can give no other connotation than that of physical gratification. In other words, the "illusions" about sex are not formed because the child views the whole gamut of sex activities for those years during which he can give them practically no other connotation than that of direct physical gratification.

What meaning do such views give to "sexual perversion"? Evidently the important matter is whether or not the act leads towards a better heterosexual adjustment. Sexual acts carried out upon individuals of the same sex, or of a masturbatory nature, where the phantasy is entirely heterosexual and where the deterrance to heterosexual approach is social taboo, can hardly be called perversions—indeed, these individuals turn to "correct" heterosexual outlets as soon as the social sanctions allow. Similarly, the most eminently "proper" relations of the marital state may be carried through with so overwhelming a drive on the part of one of the partners for physical gratification and so complete a disregard for the language values of the sexual act in the expression of the affectional ties, as to constitute definitely a perversion. In other words, a perversion in sexual expression has nothing at all to do with the form of the act but only with its purpose (which, of course, has been already recognized by a number of writers).

Does crowding prevent the development of illusions about sex or does it break them down after they have been formed? We get the impression from our clinic children that these illusions are never formed. In talking with us they do not manifest the elements of disappointment—the sharpness as of something broken—that appears in the discussion of broken idols. It has been this, in part, that has built our theory that the symbolic language values of sexual phenomena appear later in childhood and are prevented from appearing where the child has first seen so much of what is to him meaningless ("meaningless" beyond their prevision of physical satisfaction) physical expression.

We are aware that a large and voluble group of psychoanalytic persuasion have felt that it has been precisely the illusions about sex that have led to most of our difficulties. They would have us realize that hiding from children the strength and undaunted drive of the sexual urge has been really what has led to neuroses and conflicts when the child actually meets the overpowering character of his or her own sexual hunger. This may be a correct view of the situation. If it is, then the various interesting (not to say exotic) mechanisms which this school has uncovered should be quite lacking in crowded families where children from tender years are accustomed to see a rather florid display of the sexual urge. Up to the present time, certain quite impelling urges have almost entirely prevented the psychoanalysts from investigations among the poor. Our experience is that among the poor these difficulties are at least as frequent as among their more advantaged cousins. We are still persuaded that any arrangement which brings to the child an important and insistent urge at a time when he is utterly unable to understand its perspective in the total life situation of the adults involved must color the child's whole future attitude.

We are also aware of the arresting nature of the facts supplied by the divorce courts. In the Los Angeles courts, for instance, it is reported that "the primary cause of discord was . . . mostly based on complaints of sexual maladjustments."[4] Data such as these have strengthened the present fervid group who seek to cure the ills of family life through sexual education. We would be willing to accept the validity of these findings. We have ourselves every indication that a difficulty in the affectional ties first shows itself in sexual expression. How can people talk if they have nothing to say? The most subtle rift in the affectional ties is quite obviously magnified and dramatized in the sexual act which is no less than a highly complicated mutual act of expression. The analogy from the field of speech seems fair. Because speech difficulties such as stammering are so very dramatic and noticeable, generations have been busily engaged in attempting to cure these through various exercises directed to the speech trouble itself. If those interested in speech trouble now see that their point of attack is the fundamental emotional adjustment of the individual, may we not hope that in time there will be similar recognition that the sexual act is a mode of expressing certain deeper relationships?

There is an interesting type of document developing with some rapidity at this time—the volumes devoted to the technique of the sexual act. These Emily Posts of the sexual field have convinced themselves that one can make people happily married by telling them what happily married people do. Nor would one too quickly turn from this approach—writers are aided by a larger vocabulary, artists by better colors, carpenters by a wider range of tools. But first there must be something to be expressed.

Similar considerations threaten any movement which is directed at merely a symptom of a relationship. The pleasure factors in the sexual relations—in distinction to the language factors—are indeed persistent. However, propaganda which stresses solely these pleasure factors and their enhancement through freedom from fear of consequences runs the danger of emphasizing what we would consider the least constructive and most rapidly disintegrating factor of the marital relationship. It would be difficult not to support the dissemination of sane and correct information concerning a matter which is very widely practiced at the present time—namely, birth control—so long as there continued through the whole procedure the proper primary emphasis of the part that the sexual life plays in the preservation and enrichment of the love relationship.

What does all this mean in the matter of sexual education for children and young adults? There is nothing to be gained in a program that keeps the nature of the physical acts of sex in the realm of mystery and taboo. It is equally fatuous to feel that we are covering the sexual education of youngsters by describing in detail the overt sexual phenomena. If children are to be given an insight into a vocabulary they must recognize that it is a vocabulary. The child eight or nine years old cannot understand why "people do such things." They have for him value only as objective phenomena. Admittedly, this is the only value which they have for many adults. This is not, however, the point here. Perhaps with children we can never go beyond the matter of teaching them that sex is "all right," that their questions about it are not taboo, that their interest is not evil. In other words, the important aspect of sexual education for young children is not the so-called "facts" which are taught them but the attitude with which these are taught. We have become rather certain that many parents have done more harm in blushing and blundering their way through a detailed and exact account of affairs than have others who have dispensed such old favorites as the magnanimity of the stork in a way that has made the child feel that it was all right to have asked the question.

But, frankly, we have felt that up to the present we could not answer the question of sexual education of the adolescent. The physical manifestations of the sexual life are not only highly individual but they attain, for any pair of persons who are what one calls "happily married," validity precisely on the basis of their individuality—or at least on the basis of their supposed individuality. Perhaps it is only this setting forth of principles that could ever be given to adolescents. The high degree of individuality in the sexual relationship of itself seems to defy further "teaching."

(Again we return to our parenthetical statements. If population-concentration grows and if it indeed skews the interest of the child toward the physical-gratification side of sexual phenomena, is there any general cultural trend which might be thought of as developing from this? In this light we have been interested in the development in our literature, as well as in psychiatric theory itself, of a marked increase in preoccupation with the sexual acts themselves rather than with them as an expression of the affectional ties.)

Mental Strain: Negativism and Irritability

A fourth effect of crowding we have called—for lack of a better term— "mental strain." It is that which arises from always having to "hold on to oneself." Walls are built about the ego to preserve its sanctity from prying eyes, and that these are walls of fear seems certain—nor can watchful guardianship over them be relaxed as long as many others are about. So one meets many adults—and some children—who "want to get away from everybody" they know, who feel the need of some surcease from this eternal vigilance. The results, when these periods of freedom are lacking, are either those of a somewhat forbidding negativism or of irritable outbursts of temper which belong definitely to the phenomena of fatigue. We see much of the latter either alone or associated with the former. The fatigue phenomenon seems to come from failure ever to be free from the task of guarding the status-preserving walls.

Or the matter may be expressed in another way—amounting, we guess, to the same thing. Earlier we pictured our children's inability to integrate the ego into a whole unit. Perhaps the walls of protection for the integrated ego are, in crowded families, never really completely formed. Perhaps this "mental strain," the fatigue phenomenon which we see, arises from the never-ending effort to integrate the ego under conditions which do not allow of this integration.

However this may be, one sees a constantly recurring picture of "touchy" reactions and irritability as the personality is pressed. Often one sees it covered, for protection, by an assumed nonchalance or braggadocio. When we realize that for many of these individuals from one year's end to the other, there is never a time that they are alone, we begin to get some picture of what this tension must be. Even the nights conspire to the same end; three to five children sleeping in the same bed means that even during the periods of relaxation and for the deeper levels of the unconscious there must always be this awareness of the imminence of others and the compromises and surrenders which this entails.

The reader recognizes that it is not alone the phenomenon of crowding that leads to this picture of mental strain. Nor, unfortunately, are touchy, irritable reactions confined to those of these less advantaged groups.

Lack of Objectivity

Finally, among these individuals of crowded areas and crowded families, there is what one describes as the phenomenon of being so much in the world that there is no chance to look at it. Objectivity has a basic importance to the developing personality. We believe that the degree of one's objectivity is largely if not entirely an inherent matter. However, even for individuals with a high degree of objectivity, this characteristic is in abeyance where the hurly-burly of life forever presses upon them. This is not a difficult matter to measure, our conclusions being based upon the relative ability of children from different areas to describe themselves and the situations in which they have been as onlookers rather than as participants.

41 *Effects upon Children of Their Mothers' Outside Employment*

ELEANOR E. MACCOBY

The employment of mothers outside the home is widely assumed to have harmful effects upon children. Dr. Maccoby, a social psychologist currently at Stanford University, examines a large body of evidence on the relationship of this aspect of the family's adaptive patterns. Although she does not doubt that the fact of the mother working outside the home has some impact upon the child's personality, Dr. Maccoby concludes that this characteristic of a family's adaptive patterns interacts with many other elements of family structure in the production of personality qualities.

Increasingly, women are taking jobs which take them away from their households for varying periods of the day. Many of them work only before marriage, or only during the first few years of marriage before children are born, withdrawing from the labor market during the period when their young children require closest care and returning to work when their children are grown. A sizeable group, however, continues to work during the child-rearing years, and it is with this group of mothers and their families that we shall be primarily concerned.

What are the effects upon children of the mother's absence during all or part of the day? Need we expect any repercussions in the children's emotional, intellectual, or moral development? Is there, for example, any relationship between maternal employment and the incidence of juvenile delinquency or school-adjustment problems? On the more positive side, does the mother's working stimulate the child, by example, to a greater interest in job achievement? This paper examines the available evidence bearing on these questions and, drawing upon theories of child development, poses what appear to be the important questions which are still unanswered.

For many centuries, there have been women who busied themselves with other activities than child care and who delegated the care of their children to others for all or part of the time. The situation prevalent in the United States, in which a mother cares for her young children in an isolated household with little sharing of her duties with relatives or servants, is by no means the prototype of family life from a historical or cross-cultural point of view. Most of the prominent men whose names figure in

Reprinted from *Work in the Lives of Married Women* (National Manpower Council; New York: Columbia University Press, 1958), pp. 150–172.

European history were raised primarily by "nannies" and governesses, not by their own mothers. In the poorer urban families, after the industrial revolution, many women worked long hours in factories; in agrarian communities, many worked in the fields, leaving their young children in the care of older siblings or grandparents. We do not know specifically how children were affected by these situations, except that many of them grew up without apparent detriment and, indeed, that some achieved notable success.

These considerations should remind us of an important point to be borne in mind throughout this discussion: a mother's working is only one of the very many factors bearing upon a child's development. It may even be a minor one, when viewed as part of a constellation which includes such other factors as the child's inherited intellectual and physical capacities, his parents' emotional stability, the number and characteristics of other children in the family, whether he is being raised in a city or on a farm, and whether he grows up in an extended or isolated nuclear family. When we undertake to discover the specific effects of the single factor of *maternal employment,* we must reconcile ourselves to the probability that the effects, if any, will be small. Furthermore, we must expect that the effects will not be the same on all, or even the majority of, children. The effects will depend upon the other features of the child's situation which will interact with the mother's presence or absence from the home to produce a discernible consequence.

First of all, let us examine what is known directly about the children of working mothers in terms of such gross indicators as delinquency, school-adjustment problems, and achievement motivation.

Juvenile Delinquency

Does the outside employment of mothers contribute to delinquency in their children? A positive relation has been widely assumed, and it is not uncommon to find a judge in a juvenile court delivering a strong reprimand to a working mother and urging her to stay at home. It is true that if one studies a population of juvenile delinquents, one is likely to find that a higher proportion of their mothers work than would be the case in the population at large. Obviously, however, most juvenile delinquents come from strata of the population where the mother's working is likely to be an economic necessity. Possibly, at this economic level, there is an equally large proportion of mothers working in the families where the children have *not* become delinquent, and if this is so, the relationship of the mother's employment to her child's antisocial behavior would be equivocal.

The study which provides the best control of such a factor as economic level is that conducted by the Gluecks[1] in the 1940's. In this study, a

group of 500 delinquent boys was compared with a group of non-delin-
quents who were like them in intelligence, ethnic background, age, and
residence in underprivileged areas. There was no difference between the
two groups of boys in the proportion of mothers who worked *regularly*
outside the home. But the delinquent group did contain a larger proportion
of boys (11.9 per cent more) whose mothers worked *sporadically*.
A hasty conclusion from these results might be that if a mother wishes to
work at all, she ought to work full time, since occasional employment seems
more closely associated with delinquency than either regular employment or
not working. But a more thoughtful reading of the results casts doubt upon
this conclusion. The association between irregular employment and delinquency suggests at the outset that it may not be the mother's absence from
home per se which creates adjustment problems for the children. Rather,
the cause may be found in the conditions of the mother's employment or the
family characteristics leading a mother to undertake outside employment.

What were these "occasionally employed" mothers like, who were
found with greater frequency in the family backgrounds of delinquent boys?
First of all, they tended to be women who had a history of delinquency
themselves; also they tended to be married to men who were emotionally
disturbed and who had poor work habits. Commonly, the husband and
wife formed an incompatible marriage pair whose members lacked self-
respect. It is a moot question, therefore, whether it is the mother's sporadic
employment as such which conduced to delinquency in the sons; equally
tenable is the interpretation that the emotionally disturbed and antisocial
characteristics of the parents produced both a sporadic work pattern on the
part of the mother and delinquent tendencies in the son.

One of the most interesting features of the Gluecks' findings concerns
the importance of the kind of supervision a mother arranges for her children in her absence if she does work. Table 1 presents a recomputation of

Table 1
**The Relation of Juvenile Delinquency to Maternal Employment
and the Quality of Child Supervision[a]**

	MOTHER'S EMPLOYMENT STATUS					
	Housewife		Regularly Employed		Occasionally Employed	
Supervision of child:	Good	Poor	Good	Poor	Good	Poor
Per cent delinquent	32	84	19	77	32	88
Number of cases	457	149	82	110	89	116

[a] To obtain these percentages, the two groups of children studied by the Gluecks (496 delinquent boys and a matched group of 497 non-delinquent boys) were combined into one population which was then subdivided on the basis of maternal employment and the quality of supervision provided for the child. This procedure sacrifices some of the benefits of the original matching, but it permits view-ing delinquency as a dependent variable.

the figures presented in Table 3 of the Gluecks' article, "Working Mothers and Delinquency."[2] It can be seen that, whether the mother is working or not, the quality of the supervision her child receives is paramount. If the mother remains at home but does not keep track of where her child is and what he is doing, he is far more likely to become a delinquent (within this highly selected sample), than if he is closely watched. Furthermore, if a mother who works does arrange adequate care for the child in her absence, he is no more likely to be delinquent (indeed, possibly less so!) than the adequately supervised child of a mother who does not work. But there is one more lesson to be learned from the data: among the working mothers, a majority did not in fact arrange adequate supervision for their children in their absence. This demonstrates the difficulty of obtaining good substitute care for the children of working mothers in these days of isolated nuclear families containing few grandmothers, maiden aunts, or older daughters who will assume a responsible role in child care.

An interesting comparison to the Gluecks' findings is provided by another study of delinquency recently done in California by Bandura and Walters,[3] as yet unpublished. This compared a group of *middle-class* delinquent boys (typified by nail-studded leather jackets, "D.A." haircuts, hot rod cars, and open defiance of authority) with a group similar in socio-economic status who were "good" boys and had not gotten into trouble with the authorities. Both groups studied were small, and the differences between them in the rate of maternal employment were not statistically significant. Nevertheless, it is interesting that there were more working mothers among the *non*-delinquent boys. Probably, when middle-class mothers work, they usually are in a position to arrange reliable care for their children. Thus, their children do not suffer from the neglect which often follows upon the employment of working-class mothers who cannot so easily afford sitters, housekeepers, or nursery-school care.

Problems of Adjustment

There have been a number of studies in which some association has been found between maternal employment and adjustment problems of children. Unfortunately, in the studies which this writer has been able to locate, such factors as economic status and emotional stability of the parents have not been held constant. Two of the available studies are worth examining, however, for they illustrate the kind of results reported and the problems in interpretation which arise. One is a study by Essig and Morgan,[4] in which a group of adolescent girls whose mothers worked full time was compared with a group whose mothers did not work. The daughters of working mothers, in response to questionnaires, more often indicated the following problems in adjustment:

They felt unwilling to discuss their activities and their problems with their parents.

They felt their parents didn't understand them when they *did* attempt to explain their conduct.

They felt that their families did not have a "good time" together and that family meals (especially breakfast) were gloomy affairs.

They felt rejected by their fathers; felt ashamed of how their fathers behaved in public; felt their fathers paid too little attention to family life; and "talked back" to their fathers quite often.

The two groups of girls were not matched according to economic level, and the following considerations immediately arise in interpreting the results. It is likely that the working mothers are concentrated in the low-income families; and it is known that child-rearing is somewhat less permissive, more punitive, less "democratic" in such families,[5] and, finally, that there is more tension between husbands and wives in working-class, as compared with middle-class, families. It is possible, therefore, that the attitudes of the daughters of working mothers may simply be a reflection of the interpersonal relationships prevailing in homes of this economic level whether or not the mother works.

A second interesting issue is raised in the relationship of these girls to their *fathers*. Curiously enough, there seemed to be more disturbance here in the families where the mother was working than in the relationship between mother and daughter. A possible explanation is that the mother's working in some way weakens or dilutes the father's role in the family, with the result that the daughter does not respect and esteem him as much as she would otherwise do. But an equally possible explanation is that a number of the mothers are working because, for some prior reason, their husbands are unstable. A man's instability might make it necessary for his wife to work—to supplement irregular earnings, for example—and at the same time produce negative feelings toward him on the part of both wife and daughter. If this were true, the daughter's low regard for her father in mother-working households would not be in any sense a *result* of the mother's employment. Until we can compare families which are initially similar in paternal stability and economic level, we will not know what is the effect of the mother's working per se on the adjustment of adolescent children.

A study by Rouman,[6] on school adjustment problems, provides some very interesting facts but presents similar issues in interpretation. Rouman studied a group of children referred to the guidance department of a large public school district for a variety of adjustment problems, including school failure, aggressiveness, excessive withdrawal, stealing, etc. Interestingly enough, most of the children of working mothers in this school district were never referred to the guidance office as "problem children." These children apparently adjusted adequately to the demands of school life, as also did most of the children of nonworking mothers. The children of working mothers who were referred as "problem children," however, were somewhat different from the children of nonworking mothers who were referred. The "problem children" of working mothers were (a) younger than other "problem children," and (b) less often referred for academic failure and more often for withdrawal tendencies.

We have some slight evidence, then, that in the small group of cases where the mother's working may contribute to school maladjustment, it is likely to do so at the time when the child first enters school, and that the child is more likely to suffer from a difficulty in relating adequately to other people (to both children and teachers) than he is to suffer from insufficient impulse control of the sort that would lead to aggression and stealing. But here again, we do not know whether it is the mother's working which is responsible for such problems as do appear, or whether both the problems and the mother's working are reflections of some other, deep-lying home factor.

Motivation for Achievement

We know very little about whether a mother's working stimulates her children to vocational achievement. Probably much depends upon the nature of the mother's work and the status it confers. Perhaps the example of serious interest in outside work on the mother's part makes both her sons and her daughters value such work more highly. We do know of a number of instances of notable scientific achievement on the part of men whose mothers had flourishing careers or other outside interests that must have kept them away from home for many daytime hours.[7]

We know that high-achievement motivation in children is often associated with the early application of parental pressure for independence.[8] If mothers who work (or who expect to work when the children reach school age) take special pains to train their children to do things by themselves, instead of relying upon others to help them, then we might expect that the children of working mothers would be especially self-reliant and oriented toward achievement. But there is always a possibility of a mother's working having the opposite effect, especially upon boys. If a woman's working makes her dominant—implies a devaluation of her husband and makes him appear ineffectual—then possibly her son will be in conflict about the acceptability of maleness and will find it difficult to succeed in the male world he must enter in adulthood. But quite evidently, there are many instances in which a husband approves and encourages his wife's working and does not feel that his masculinity is threatened by it. In such cases, the son's development should not be hampered. We do not have evidence as to the usual situation. We can only suspect that much depends upon what the mother's motivation is for working, and whether her husband views her work as helpful or threatening.

So far, we have focused our attention upon direct comparisons of children of working mothers with children of nonworking mothers, in so far as studies making such comparisons are available. We have raised far more questions than we have been able to answer with existing data.[9] Let us now turn to a consideration of the more basic processes which may mediate the impact of maternal employment.

From a psychological standpoint, the possible impact upon a child of the mother's being away from home for all or part of each day may be considered under three major headings:

1. Behavior Training.—At all stages of their development, children require detailed training in major and minor skills (how to dress, how to tell time, how to use a fork, how to keep house), but more importantly they require moral training. Under this heading would come training to tell the truth, to avoid hurting others, to respect the property of others, and to control sex impulses so that they will be expressed in socially approved channels. Does a mother's working affect the quality and effectiveness of training a child receives?

2. Dependency and Separation Anxiety.—Young children form strong emotional attachments to those who care for them. Separation from the person or persons upon whom the child is emotionally dependent has been found in some instances to be deeply disturbing to the child, with long-range effects alleged in the child's later interpersonal relationships and even in his cognitive capacities. Is the kind and duration of separation involved in a mother's working sufficient to produce separation trauma in a child?

3. Identification.—Much of what an individual becomes, according to psychoanalytic theory, is a function of the success with which he can, in early childhood, pattern himself upon his parents, particularly the parent of the same sex. Does a mother's working interfere with the orderly development of identification, and if so, what are the consequences of this?

Behavior Training

Child training is made up of thousands of episodes in which an adult caretaker distracts a child from undesired activity or interests him in desired activity; physically stops or prevents an act; guides a child's early performance of a skill; punishes or rewards an action which the child carries out spontaneously; or "reasons" with the child by labeling actions and events and their possible consequences clearly, so that the child will be able to recognize their recurrence and be able to act appropriately in the future. The common refrains of child training reflect these processes: "Don't touch, that's breakable." "Here, let me show you." "Wouldn't you like to . . .?" "Good boy!" "If you do that once more I'll spank." "This is a blueberry; it's not poisonous, you may eat it." "You musn't hit girls."

What determines whether all these myriad efforts at control and training are effective? First of all, the trainer must be present when significant events occur, to reward or punish or explain. Especially when the child is quite young, the more immediately the caretaker reacts to what the child has done, and the more explicitly the discipline or reward is associated with a specific action, the more likely it is that the training will be effective. The comment, "You've been very good today," spoken at bed time will undoubtedly please the child, but it does not help much to differentiate for him what the approved actions were. Second, the child's learning will be facilitated if the caretaker is consistent in what he demands of the child and how he reacts to the child's behavior. Third, the caretaker's effectiveness depends in part upon the nature of the disciplinary measures she employs. In general, physical punishment is less effective than other techniques,[10] although it often works better than no discipline at all,[11] and discipline is probably more effective when it is administered by a person who has a supportive relation to the child.

This last point, perhaps, needs amplification. The theory behind it is that punishment emanating from an individual whom the child does not love leads to fear and efforts upon the part of the child to escape or to conceal his misdeeds from the punisher. Punishment from a loved person, however, creates a different kind of problem for the child, for he wants the affection and approval of the disciplinarian, and he cannot get it by running away. He can only get it by conforming to the demands of the disciplinarian, or, if he does deviate from these demands, by confessing and being forgiven or by repairing the damage he has done. Ultimately, discipline administered by a loved agent is more conducive to the child's "internalizing" (accepting as his own) the values being taught him, so that he begins to enforce them upon himself without the continued need of outside discipline.

While it may seem bizarre to test this theory with animals, experiments growing out of the theory have indeed been conducted with dogs.[12] While the experimental work is in an early stage and it is by no means clear what the significant variables are, there is some evidence for the following conclusion: when one attempts to train a dog to "resist temptation" (e.g., to avoid a tabooed but delectable food when the trainer is out of the room), the training is more effective if the individual who administers it has a previously nurturant or "indulgent" relationship to the animal in puppyhood. Punishment by a stranger, or a person who has been primarily cold and restrictive toward the animal in puppyhood, does not seem to last very well in its effects when the trainer's back is turned.

The relevant point for our discussion here is that the effectiveness of discipline administered to the child of a working mother probably depends upon the total relationship the child has with his disciplinarian. If nurturant caretaking is divided between two people—the mother during evenings, weekends, and early morning, and a substitute during the day, for example—then discipline should be similarly divided. It would appear to be unwise for the mother to try to "make up" to the child for her absence by being exclusively nurturant while she is with him, to the point of not exercising control and discipline. Equally unwise would be a policy of delegating to her substitute only caretaking but not disciplinary functions.

What other implications are there for the training of children of working mothers that may be derived from the criteria for successful training listed above? The first question, one of primary importance, is whether there is an individual who assumes full responsibility for training and controlling the child in the mother's absence. In cases of delinquency, as has been seen, it is often found that the mother has not arranged for such care, so that after school hours the child roams the neighborhood unchecked (perhaps with a group of children in similar circumstances) until his mother comes home from work. It is obvious that under these conditions the risk is very great that the child will not learn the behavior society demands of him.

On the assumption that most working mothers try to arrange for at least minimum caretaking in their absence, it may be asked what kind of substitute caretaking is adequate from the standpoint of behavior training. The first point to make clear in answering this question is that the mothers themselves, if they remained at home, would differ enormously in the quantity and quality of control and training efforts they directed at the child. Some mothers are constantly warning, explaining, guiding, rewarding—to the point that the child may become "overcontrolled," passive, and lacking in initiative. Other mothers interact with the child very little. The busy farm mother, for example, who must feed livestock, process dairy products, tend a kitchen garden, cook for farm hands, and care for other children, may not have time to react to an individual child, except for routine caretaking or when an emergency arises. In the case of the overcontrolling mother, it is unlikely that any substitute person (unless it is a relative with very similar attitudes and habits) would exercise a similar degree of control. In the case of the mother who does not interact much with the individual child, it is quite likely that her substitute will expend at least as much effort (and possibly more) in child training.

In any case, the adequacy of the substitute caretaker depends in part, not on the amount of control she exercises nor on how she does it, but on how similar her reactions are to those of the mother when she is at home. For very young children a standard routine, even with respect to very minor matters, brings comfort and security. A child whose mother always puts on the left leg of his pajamas or play suits first, for example, will be confused by a sitter who tries to put on the right leg first, and may resist vigorously. More important, he will be confused if his mother allows him to suck his thumb and the sitter does not, or vice versa. If the mother and her substitute adhere closely to the same routine and react similarly to the child's actions, his learning task is simplified and his feelings of security enhanced. As the child grows older, of course, he can begin to discriminate what is expected and allowed by one person from what is expected and allowed by another, and can adjust his behavior accordingly. By the age of four or five and perhaps earlier, it is helpful to the child to begin to have some experience with adjusting himself to the idiosyncrasies of different caretakers, so that he will not become too rigid. Thus, he will be better prepared to adjust to the fact that, while the adults he deals with will agree fairly well on large values (e.g., he must not steal or lie), they will differ in their reactions to noise, to dirty hands, and the like, so that he must learn to behave according to the dictates of the setting in which he finds himself.

In answering the question, "What is adequate substitute caretaking from the standpoint of behavior training?" we must next ask how many children are being cared for by one person. Fairly often, the children of working mothers are left in day-care centers where the ratio of children to adults is high. In these situations, the adults are usually busy feeding the children, cleaning the rooms, setting out play materials, and supervising group activities. They tend to deal with an individual child only when there are signs of trouble, and not always then. Observations taken in two Israeli *kibbutzim*,[13] where the youngest children live in groups of six to a house (each house having its own "housemother"), reveal that the adult is so busy that very often a child's crying will go unheeded, or aggressive children will hit weaker children and snatch toys from them without adult interference. In such settings, the other children sometimes take over disciplinary functions and scold or hit one another in an attempt to stop the antisocial behavior of an individual child.[14] However, it is doubtful whether such reprisals are as effective as those administered by adults. The sanctions invoked by a child's peers are not always in the service of the values which adults would like to see inculcated, as we know in the case of delinquent gangs who punish deviations from the gang code but do not enforce the behavior demanded by the larger society.

Group caretaking does have some positive features. Often, the personnel in charge of children's groups are better trained, more patient, more objective in dealing with the children than the mothers would be. Playgroup teachers probably resort to physical punishment much less often than do mothers in their own homes. Furthermore, the child can be allowed greater freedom to run and climb and manipulate objects in the child-proofed, toy-filled atmosphere of the nursery than is possible in a home full of breakable and dangerous objects belonging to adults and older children. This greater freedom in group-care settings is reflected in the more rapid development of motor co-ordination in such children during the second year of life.[15] But the lower level of individual interaction with adults is reflected in slower language development and in slow toilet training with many relapses.

Studies on the effects of group care have been done primarily with children who lived almost exclusively in groups, and not with children who spent perhaps forty hours per week with a group of children and were regularly returned to a family setting, as is the case with the children of working mothers. Consequently, we must extrapolate from these findings with care. The most reasonable conclusions seem to be that, if the children of a working mother are cared for in groups while she works, there are certain features of behavior training that will not proceed as smoothly as they do with individual care; and, on the other hand, that in most group-care settings there will be some benefits flowing from the experience of "sharing" with other children and some stimulation from the variety of playmates, the freedom of movement, and the skill of the caretakers.

Dependency and Separation Anxiety

The work of such pioneering researchers as Spitz, Bowlby, Anna Freud, and Goldfarb[16] has made us aware of two kinds of dangers: (a) that of rearing a child in an institutional setting in which he does not have an opportunity to form a close attachment to a parent figure, and (b) that of separating a young child suddenly from the person or persons upon whom he has become emotionally dependent. While the conclusions of some of the individual studies in this field have been cogently criticized,[17] certain points are relevant for our interests:

1. Some young children, when separated from their parents for a period of a week or more (owing to the necessity for hospitalization, for example), go into a depressed, withdrawn, apathetic state (designated "anaclitic depression" by Spitz) from which it is difficult to rouse them. When they are reunited with their parents they do not recover at once from their grief, but may become excessively "clingy" and may show sleep disturbances that seem to reflect a fear that they will lose their parents again.

2. Children vary greatly in how vulnerable they are to separation trauma. Some seem to bear separation with little difficulty; others are deeply disturbed.

3. Very young infants show few such effects. Children between one and three years are most vulnerable. Later, children can begin to understand a little about the reasons for the separation and can be comforted by a promise that it will not last long.

4. While the most severe effects have been seen in separations lasting for a week or longer, many young children show disturbance of lesser degree with very brief separations—e.g., when their parents go out for the evening and leave them with a sitter. Commonly, however, such disturbance disappears shortly after the parents are out of sight.

Lasting damage to the child has been alleged from long-continued "maternal deprivation," such as that involved in institutional settings, especially if the child is institutionalized for the first three years of life.[18] It appears to the writer, however, that the problem involved in the mother's working is usually not one of "maternal deprivation" in the sense that is meant by writers on the subject. The child of a working mother has the attention and love of his mother during a predictable portion of his waking hours, and in her absence he has the attention (and perhaps also love) of her substitute. Unless he is cared for as a member of a very large group during the daytime hours and then neglected grossly by his mother when she is with him, we would not expect the kind of deterioration of function observed by Spitz and Goldfarb among institutional children.

Rather, the problem seems to lie in the area of separation anxiety. Is the child made anxious each day when his mother goes off to work? Does he feel rejected, abandoned? If so, are there lasting effects? Is the child handicapped, for example, in his ability to form close affectional ties later in life? So far we have very little systematic evidence on any of these questions. But let us see what we do know that is relevant.

A cross-cultural example may be enlightening as a starting point. In Okinawa, as in a number of other cultures, the mother of young children customarily goes to work in the fields during the day. In her absence, the infant or young child is cared for by a grandmother or an adolescent girl (not necessarily a sister, but usually a relative) until school is out. Then a girl between the ages of six and twelve takes the young child on her back in a sling and carries it with her during all her after-school activities until the mother returns home from the fields. Okinawan babies seldom cry when their parents go off to work in the morning, but they *are* upset by "back-weaning"—by being told that they are too old to be carried about constantly any more, so that they have to keep up with the play of the children's group by relying on their own small legs. Adult Okinawans are described as highly sociable, jolly, gregarious people. Possibly the fact that they dislike being alone is a reflection of dependency anxiety generated by the mothers' daily absence when they are young. However, it is more likely that it is a direct result of their becoming accustomed to constant close contact with some other person (not necessarily the mother) during all their waking hours.

From this example, we would judge that young children can easily adjust to caretaking divided between the mother and some regular substitute. Perhaps the example suggests further that the child's adjustment is made easier (a) if this division of responsibility is a common, indeed, taken-for-granted thing in the society; (b) if the mother's daily departure is begun in the child's infancy, so that there is no dramatic beginning of separation after the child has become accustomed to a single caretaker; and (c) if the substitute is a relative who presumably has very similar child-care techniques to those of the mother.

Probably, if the child is cared for by a number of familiar adults instead of being in the exclusive care of the mother, the affectional relationship between mother and child will be less intense—as indeed it is in very large families where the child interacts more with brothers and sisters than he does with his parents. We have no reason to believe that such attenuation of the mother-child relationship is necessarily harmful, although it probably produces a different kind of adult personality than an enduring, intense, and exclusive mother-child relationship does.

Earlier reference was made to the group-care situation prevailing in the *kibbutzim* of Israel, where the child sees his parents only for an hour or so each day. Does this great degree of dilution of the mother-child relationship seem to be associated with too *great* dependency or other symptoms of separation anxiety? Or is there too *little* dependency, presaging possible difficulties in the child's later establishment of mature emotional attachments? Observers have been astonished at how attached the *kibbutz* children are to their parents, in spite of seeing them so briefly. When playing with dolls, these children tend to act out dramas involving their parents, *not* scenes from daily life in the children's house involving the nurse and other children. While we have little evidence concerning the development of dependency and interpersonal ties specifically as children grow up in this environment, one clinical worker concerned himself with the development of "ego-strength," thought to be an important ingredient of normal personality functioning.[19] He found that while *kibbutz* children appeared to be somewhat behind a group of home-reared children at the age of one year, by the age of ten the *kibbutz* children were more mature in the features of personality development that were measured. Thus we see that whatever negative effects there were in early childhood in the group-care setting and the absence of constant close interaction with parents, these effects were not lasting.

Perhaps the study most directly relevant to the effects of the regular separations involved in a mother's working is that done by Heinicke[20] in England. Heinicke compared two groups of two-year-old children: a group in a residential nursery, who were repeatedly observed during their three-week stay, and a group in a day-care nursery, who were observed at the nursery during a three-week period in which they were brought in each morning by a parent and taken home again at the end of the day. The day-care children were all children of working mothers. This study gives us an opportunity to compare the effects of the regular, temporary separations experienced by children of working mothers with longer separations of the sort that have been the basis for much of the concern about the possible dangers of separation. Some of the most interesting findings of the Heinicke study are as follows:

1. On their first day in the nursery, both groups of children cried for their parents quite a bit (about 6 per cent of the time they were observed). As the three-week period progressed, however, "regain crying" practically disappeared among the day-nursery children. Instead, their efforts to regain their parents more often took the form of asking about them and seeking verbal reassurance that they were coming back. The residential group, however, continued to cry for their parents frequently during the three-week period.

2. The day-nursery group sought substitute attention in a more matter-of-fact way. They more often sought to be near the nurse or observer, while the residential children sought affection in a more intense way and accompanied their seeking by crying.

3. The residential children more often showed signs of severe hostility, and these increased as the three-week period wore on. The amount of hostility expressed by day-care children appeared normal.

4. The day-care children continued to be eager to see their parents at the end of the day. The residential children cried when their parents visited and sometimes failed to recognize them.

These and other findings from the Heinicke study suggest that, while there is an initial disturbance for the young child when the mother first leaves him with a substitute caretaker to go off to work, he quickly adjusts himself to the new routine and appears able to maintain a close affectional relationship with the mother during the parts of the day when they *are* together. Long separations, however, during which the child does not go home, are much more disturbing and the disturbance continues, having repercussions which last for at least some period beyond the time when the child is reunited with his family.

To balance our discussion of the possible dangers of separating the young child from his mother while she works, we should raise the issue of possible dangers of *not* separating the two often enough or early enough. It is possible for the dependency bond to become too strong, particularly if the mother has certain neurotic needs that she works out through a "smothering" attachment to the child.[21] Underlining the possible problems generated by a too-close mother-son relationship during the first two or three years of the child's life is a cross-cultural study done by Whiting, Kluckhohn, and Anthony.[22] A major finding was that if a society has early-childhood training practices that foster a very close dependency relationship between the mother and her young son (e.g., the son sleeps with the mother), then the society must later provide some drastic measures to break this bond and force the child to assume the male role. Cultural practices which Whiting and his colleagues believe have this function include: (a) sending the child to a relative's house in a different village when he is weaned, where he may remain for quite a long period (in some instances for the remainder of his childhood!); (b) subjecting the boy to initiation rites at puberty, including a separation from all women, that is strictly enforced and that may last for a long period, during which the boy resides in a special boys' house or "bachelors'" village. The relevant point of this study is that a too-strong dependency bond between mother and child developed during the early years may generate certain strains (by intensifying Oedipal rivalry, for example), with the result that much stress is involved for the family and, indeed, the whole society, in the process of the child's achieving the needed amount of independence. The mother's working may simplify the process of the gradual loosening of the dependency relationship with her children.

Identification

In discussing the relationship of maternal employment to a child's ability to "identify" with parental figures, we are probably on shakier ground than for any topic discussed so far. There is no general agreement on how the concept "identification" should be defined, and attempts to measure identification for research purposes are at a primitive stage. It is not possible here to do justice to the various points of view on the topic, and the following generalizations, which represent only one point of view, rest upon insecure evidence.

We can assume that one way in which children learn values (and specific items of behavior such as mannerisms and ways of speaking) is by patterning themselves on a model. While psychoanalytic theory has emphasized the importance of the parent of the same sex as a model for the child, there is reason to believe that the child can and does identify with more than one person, incorporating values and items of behavior from a number of sources. What determines the extent of a child's identification with a particular individual? It has been widely thought that affection is one of the prime determiners, but we have seen enough instances of an individual's adopting the characteristics of a strong figure in his life, even though that figure might be cold or hostile, that it has become a reasonable hypothesis that *power* is even more important than love in stimulating identification. That is, the child will generally identify himself with the person or persons having closest control over his destiny.

What are the implications of a mother's working for the likelihood of her children's identifying themselves with her? The answer should depend in part upon the mother's relationship with her substitute. If the mother delegates child care to a servant while she is at work, and the servant clearly respects the mother's authority, we would expect that the child would identify more with the mother than with the servant, as soon as he is able to perceive where the source of authority lies—and children perceive this surprisingly early. There is reason to believe that children cared for primarily by "nannies" and governesses, for example, still pattern themselves to a surprising degree upon the parents rather than upon their caretakers. If the mother is a working-class woman, on the other hand, and leaves her child at a day-care center in the charge of a teacher who thinks of herself as more about child rearing than the mother is, the chances are that the child would be more prone to pattern himself on this substitute caretaker. If care is divided between equal-status relatives, the child will probably incorporate material from each of them.

Does the child suffer from identifying partially with both the mother and a substitute caretaker? Anna Freud and Dorothy Burlingham report some instances in which they believe conflict is generated in this way in children of two and three. In one instance, a mother came periodically to visit her little girl who was in a residential nursery. The mother was fairly punitive and scolded the child harshly. After her visits, the child could be seen treating her doll in the same harsh manner, but as time passed, the child would revert to acting out in doll play the more patient care that was characteristic of the nursery "housemother." This example suggests that there will indeed be some conflict for the child in identifying with different people who embody very different values. This same kind of conflict arises, presumably, when the child's two parents differ widely in their ways of reacting to the child. But it is by no means clear that incorporating divergent values is always worse for the child than incorporating a single set of values. In the example above, we may well wonder whether the child was not better off in the conflict situation described than she would have been if she were exposed exclusively to the harsh, punitive treatment of the mother.

An important issue concerns the relationship between the children (particularly the son) and the father in a household where the mother works. For healthy development, the boy needs a strong masculine model. We have seen that there is some evidence of disturbance in the father-child relationship when the mother works.[23] We have also noted that the mother's working may not be the cause but the result of this disturbance. What effect would we expect the mother's working to have upon the children's ability to identify with their father? From one point of view, the dilution of the relationship between the mother and the children, by virtue of her absence from home during working hours, means that there is a greater opportunity for the father to play a strong role with the children. Unlike the situation which prevails in most families, where the mother is constantly present and mediates between the husband and children, the outside employment of the mother permits the father to interact directly with the children nearly as much as the mother.

On the other hand, there is the possibility that the very fact of the wife's working detracts from the husband's status—devalues him in the eyes of the children. It is true that in a household where the wife works and earns some of the money, it is less likely that the husband can play a strongly dominant, autocratic role. But it does not necessarily follow that the wife, therefore, becomes dominant or that the husband suffers loss of status. Equally possible is an arrangement of shared authority—a "democratic" relationship in which decisions are jointly made and mutual esteem exists—in which neither parent need be devalued in the eyes of the children when the mother goes to work. In other words, it is not whether the mother works that should determine her husband's stature as an identification model for the children; rather, the important factors should be the amount and kind of interaction between the father and the children, his own self-esteem, and the wife's underlying attitude toward him.

Concluding Comment

It is not possible to close this discussion with a box-score that will tell us whether maternal employment is, in sum, "good" or "bad" for children. It is clear that there is no single best way of organizing family life. Some mothers should work while others should not, and the outcome for the children depends upon many factors other than the employment itself. Some of these factors are: the age of the children, the nature of the mother's motivation to work, the mother's skill in child care and that of her substitute, the composition of the family (especially whether it contains a good substitute caretaker), the stability of the husband, and the pressure or absence of tension between the husband and wife. We cannot yet specify just how these factors influence the impact upon children of the mother's working. The necessary fact-finding has only just begun.

42   *Family Role Structure and Self-Blame*

ANDREW F. HENRY

One basic aspect of personality structure is how the individual handles aggressive or hostile feelings. As an earlier paper by Naegele pointed out, this can also be a problem for families. The late Dr. Henry's work was concerned with the relationship of discipline in the family and the direction an individual's aggression took. In this paper he presents evidence that children who direct their aggressive feelings inward, blaming themselves, have been reared in families in which the mother is perceived as the principal disciplinarian. Dr. Henry also refers to the fact that there is some evidence that the modes of handling aggression are related to different physiological modes of response to stress, in other words, that family structure gets built into the biological as well as the psychological system.

This paper reports findings supporting the hypothesis that male subjects who perceive their mother as playing the principal disciplinary role in the family will rank higher on attitudinal measures of self-blame than male subjects who perceive their father as playing the principal disciplinary role.

Dollard,[1] Menninger,[2] Rosenzweig,[3] and others have suggested that anger aroused by frustration may flow either outwardly against other persons or inwardly against the self. Anger aroused by experimental frustration is accompanied by one type of cardiovascular reaction when it is discharged outwardly against others and a different type of cardiovascular reaction when it is discharged inwardly in the form of anxiety or self-blame.[4] Subjects experiencing the type of cardiovascular reaction associated with the inward discharge of anger report their mother as the principal disciplinarian in the family.[5] This finding suggested the hypothesis that subjects who report on attitudinal measures that they would blame themselves will be more likely to perceive mother as principal disciplinarian than subjects who report on the same measures that they would not blame themselves. This hypothesis was tested in the course of a larger study

Reprinted from *Social Forces*, XXV (October, 1956), 34–38, with the kind permission of Mary L. Henry and the publisher.

with Louis Guttman to examine certain methodological hypotheses about higher components of attitudes generated by Guttman's scaling theory.[6]

A 34-page questionnaire was administered to a sample of enlisted personnel at a United States Air Force Base. Testing conditions were poor. Eight hundred subjects at a time gathered in a theater and were asked to fill in the questionnaire during a period of normally "free" time. The large size of the groups and the lack of motivation forced the removal of 17 per cent of the schedules which were incompletely filled out. Five per cent of the sample was female and these schedules were not analyzed. Another nine per cent failed to answer the question, "Who was the principal disciplinarian in your family?" Data here reported were gathered from 765 males who had completed at least a four-year high school education.

The questionnaire included two five-item Guttman scales—one designed to measure tendencies to blame the self and one designed to measure tendencies to blame the other person. Each of the scales poses a hypothetical conversation between the respondent and another person. The subject is asked to assume that the other person gets hurt by something which is said during the conversation. For example, the five items composing the "blame-self" scale are as follows:

> The questions which follow assume that the *other person* gets hurt by something which is said during a conversation with you.
> 1. Suppose the other person felt very deeply hurt. Would you have much feeling that you were to blame?
> 2. Suppose, in the heat of the discussion, you deliberately hurt the other person. Would you have much feeling that you were to blame?
> 3. Suppose the situation did not show the other person quite at his best. Would you have much feeling that you were to blame?
> 4. Suppose the situation made the other person look like quite a fool. Would you have much feeling that you were to blame?
> 5. Suppose, in the heat of the discussion, that the other person provoked you so that you said something which hurt his pride. Would you have much feeling that you were to blame?

The six response categories ranged from "yes, a great deal" to "no, none at all."

Scales.—Guttman's "image" technique[7] was used in constructing the self-blame scale. Since there is no simple summary statistic for assessing the reproductibility of an "image" scale, the conventional Guttman scale also was built using all five of the original items. It has a coefficient of reproductibility of 91.4 with 62 per cent of the cases falling into perfect scale types. Intensity computed by the "fold-over" technique[8] provided a rationale for dividing respondents into three groups. On the blame-self scale, 55 per cent of the respondents fall on the positive side of the zero point established by the plot of intensity of self-blame against content position on the self-blame scale. Thirteen per cent fall at the zero point and

32 per cent fall on the negative side of the zero point. In other words, about half of the subjects say they would blame themselves, a third say they would not blame themselves, and the rest beg the question. Forty-five per cent of those saying they would blame themselves report their mother as principal disciplinarian. Thirty-eight per cent of those falling at the zero point or on the negative side of the zero point report their mother as principal disciplinarian.[9] On the "blame-other" scale, 25 per cent fall on the positive side of the zero point saying they would blame the other person. A third say they would not blame the other person and 42 per cent beg the question.

Blame of Self and Blame of Another.—There is some positive correlation between our measure of self-blame and our measure of blame of the other person. Of those saying they would blame themselves, 27 per cent say they would not blame the other person. Of those saying they would not blame themselves, 44 per cent say they would not blame the other person. Those who are willing to blame the self are willing also to blame the other person. Those reluctant to blame the self also are reluctant to blame the other person. Given this correlation, it is possible that our relation between blame of self and perception of mother as disciplinarian only reflects a relation between perception of mother as disciplinarian and the tendency to assign blame irrespective of its target. However, among those who would blame the other person, the relation between blame of self and perception of mother as disciplinarian disappears. But the relation is significant beyond the .01 level among those who say they would not blame the other person. Among those saying they would not blame the other person, 53.6 per cent of those who would blame themselves perceive mother as disciplinarian compared with 35.2 per cent of those who would not blame themselves. Subjects saying they would blame themselves *and* would not blame the other person are most likely to perceive mother in the principal disciplinary role.

Relation between Behavioral and Normative Aspects of Self-Blame.— In addition to our content scales, a projective scale was built to measure the normative dimension of self-blame. The content scale asks the question "How much would you blame yourself?" The normative scale asks the question "How much should one blame himself?" One of the items in the normative scale is the following:

> Suppose two men, Mack and Larry, were talking excitedly about something important to both of them. In the heat of the discussion, Mack deliberately said something which hurt Larry very much. Some people would think it right and others would think it wrong if Mack felt he (Mack) was to blame for Larry getting hurt. In your opinion, how much should Mack feel that he himself was to blame?

Response categories ranged from "a great deal" to "not at all." Intensity also was computed for the normative scale providing a methodological rationale for dividing respondents into three groups. Those who say they would blame themselves tend to say that one should blame himself. And those who say they would not blame themselves tend to think one should not blame himself. But the correlation is far from perfect. One-fourth of those saying they would blame themselves also say that one should not blame one's self. And a third of those who say they would not blame themselves also say that one should blame one's self. Those viewing mother a disciplinarian were more likely to reveal a discrepancy in what they think one should do and what they say they actually would do than those viewing father as principal disciplinarian. Twenty-seven per cent of subjects perceiving mother as disciplinarian report this discrepancy between what they would do and what they should do. Only 22 per cent of those perceiving father as disciplinarian report this discrepancy.

Let us define as a "deviant" (1) a respondent who says one should blame one's self but who also says he would not blame himself; or (2) a respondent who says one should not blame one's self but also says he would blame himself. Deviants are respondents who say that their actual behavior fails to conform with the norms or values to which they subscribe. Conformists are those who say they would do what they think one ought to do; i.e., those whose reported behavior conforms with their verbalized norms. Those who perceive the mother as the principal disciplinarian tend to be deviants; those who see the father in the disciplinary role tend to be conformists.

The relation between self-blame and perception of disciplinarian holding constant the "should" or normative aspect of self-blame is significant. Among those saying they would blame themselves, 53.8 per cent of the "deviants" and 36.3 per cent of the "conformists" perceive mother as disciplinarian. Among those saying they would not blame themselves, only 29.6 per cent of the "deviants" and 28.1 per cent of the "conformists" perceive mother as disciplinarian. We noted above that subjects perceiving mother as disciplinarian were more likely to give a "deviant" response than subjects perceiving father as disciplinarian. The data show that perception of mother as disciplinarian is concentrated in only one of the two "deviant" groups—those saying they would blame themselves but should not. Among those saying they would not blame themselves, there is no difference in perception of disciplinarian between "deviants" and "conformists."

Self-Blame, Blame of Another, and Closure on Blame.—Also tested was the relation between self-blame and perception of mother as disciplinarian holding constant three variables—blame of another, the normative dimension of self-blame, and "closure" or the "third component" of blame.[10] Closure indexes whether the subject is clear in his own mind or unclear about whom he would blame. An example of one of the items in the closure on blame scale is the following:

Assume you and another person are talking excitedly about something important to both of you. Suppose, in the heat of the discussion, you deliberately hurt the other person. Now it is possible to have feelings that you were to blame, that the other person was to blame, that both of you were to blame, or that the situation was to blame. Is it clear to you against which of these you would have the strongest feelings of blame?

Response categories ranged from "yes, extremely clear" to "no, not at all clear."

It was found that those who would blame themselves are more likely to perceive mother as principal disciplinarian than those who would not blame themselves. And among those clear about whom they would blame and saying they both would and should blame themselves, the per cent perceiving mother as disciplinarian rises steadily from a low of 25.0 per cent for those willing to blame the other person to a high of 67.6 per cent for those unwilling to blame the other person.

Discussion

Subjects reporting that they would blame themselves and would not blame the other person are most likely to perceive mother as the principal disciplinarian. This finding is congruent with our research hypothesis derived from the fact that subjects experiencing the type of cardiovascular reaction associated with the outward discharge of anger report their father as the principal disciplinarian while those experiencing the type of cardiovascular reaction associated with the discharge of anger inwardly in the form of anxiety or self-blame report their mother as disciplinarian. Reluctance to blame the other person as well as willingness to blame the self both increase the likelihood that the mother will be viewed as principal disciplinarian.

Further, subjects reporting that they *would* blame themselves yet think one *should not* blame himself are most likely to perceive mother in the principal disciplinary role. The degree of correspondence between questionnaire reports of how a person would act and the way the person actually would act is unknown. Wide divergence often is assumed. This assumed divergence between questionnaire behavior and overt or actual behavior has led to the criticism that questionnaire research yields conventional or expected answers rather than true answers. Answers of the conformist—the subject who says he would do what he thinks one should do—are always suspect. His report of what he would do may merely reflect what he thinks one ought to do in the particular situation and have little or no relation to what he actually does. Unlike the conformist, the deviant cannot be accused of distorting reports of what he would do in favor of what he thinks one ought to do. In fact, we characterize him as a deviant because his report of what he would do does not correspond with what he thinks one ought to do. Therefore, on purely methodological grounds, we would have greater confidence in the report of the deviant than in the report of the conformist. If a subject tells us that he would blame himself even though he thinks one should not blame himself, we have more reason for believing him than if he tells us he would blame himself and thinks that one should blame himself.

There is a second possibility. Our findings indicate that the intropunitive subject is most likely to perceive mother as disciplinarian; further, that "deviant" subjects are more likely to perceive mother as disciplinarian. Is it not reasonable to suggest that a discrepancy between a statement of what one would and should do is in itself an instance if intropunitive behavior? But we are forced to reject this alternative. For if it were the true explanation, deviant subjects should be most likely to perceive mother as disciplinarian irrespective of their position on the content scale. This is not true. Deviance increases the likelihood of viewing mother as disciplinarian only among those who would blame themselves. It has no effect whatever among those who would not blame themselves.

Experimental data have shown a relation between perception of mother as disciplinarian and intropunitive behavior on the psycho-physiological level. Our data very tentatively suggest a relation between perception of mother as disciplinarian and intropunitive tendencies on the attitudinal level. The inference of causality from associated phenomena must always be avoided and the interpretation of this relationship—if buttressed by further supporting research—must await elaboration of the interaction between sociological or structural states on one hand and psycho-physiological states on the other. Yet one or two speculative remarks may be in order.

The emotion of anger has its roots in the physiological organism, and its discharge or inhibition is associated with the biochemistry of the autonomic nervous system. But the emotion of anger also is aroused by frustrations inherent in the interactive relationships between persons. And its control also is a function of the system of expectations operative in the subgroup and the sanctions imposed in their behalf. Perception of principal disciplinarian is related to birth order within the family.[11] The eldest child is exposed to a social environment radically different from that of the youngest child. Much further research is needed to see whether the locus of the person in the family structure is related to the control of the emotion of anger of the person and perhaps to the biochemical processes operating within his physiological structure. If these connections between sociological structures and physiological states become established, the balance of forces within the social system may prove to be one important determinant of the balance of forces within the physiological system.

43 The Family Constellation and Overt Incestuous Relations between Father and Daughter

IRVING KAUFMAN, ALICE L. PECK,

and CONSUELO K. TAGIURI

Incest is a pattern of sexual behavior which is strongly proscribed. When it occurs it is presumed that it both is preceded by and produces deviant personality development. Drs. Kaufman and Tagiuri and Miss Peck have studied and treated a number of cases of father-daughter incest in their work at the Judge Baker Guidance Center in Boston, Massachusetts. They find that incest, the "acting out of the Oedipal wish," cannot be explained in terms of the personalities of the mother and father alone. Rather, these families are characterized by a pattern in which both parents are involved and in which there is unconscious stimulus and permission of the incestuous behavior. Only when there is a certain constellation of role assignment, induction and reward, does incest occur. The fact, noted by the authors, that the daughters were guilty and anxious about the breakup of the home but not about the sexual behavior they had been involved in suggests how their personalities had been distorted by this family pattern.

We are presenting a preliminary report of our study of family relations and character formation in cases where girls have been involved in incestuous relationships with either father, stepfather, grandfather, foster father, or brother.[1] We plan a continued investigation and a more detailed report in the future.

Eleven girls, ranging in age from ten to seventeen, were referred to the Judge Baker Guidance Center for treatment. A protective agency referred seven patients and the court referred two. A family agency and a psychiatric clinic each referred one.

The age at which incest began ranged from six to fourteen years. The sexual relationship was a prolonged one, lasting a year or more in most cases, and in one instance as long as six years. Despite the long duration of the incestuous relationship, in only two cases did the mother report it to the authorities. The remainder of the cases came to the attention of the authorities through some external event such as a neighbor's reporting neglect of children.

The period of contact with these cases ranged from five interviews to two years of continuous treatment.

Reprinted from *American Journal of Orthopsychiatry*, XXIV (April, 1954), 266–77, with the kind permission of Dr. Kaufman and the publishers.

Only five of the eleven girls had sexual relations with their own fathers. There was a question as to two other girls.

We cannot detect from our material any apparent difference in the psychopathology of the participants regardless of whether the girls had relations with her father or with a father substitute.

Depression and guilt were universal as clinical findings in these girls. Other findings were as follows: learning difficulties in three girls, bossiness in two, sexual promiscuity in one, running away in one, and somatic complaints in four. Loss of appetite and abdominal distress were the most frequent somatic complaints. These abdominal symptoms appeared to be related to pregnancy fantasies in some of the girls.

Although learning difficulty was a presenting symptom in three cases, and one of these girls had had difficulties with school work prior to the detection of the incest, it became apparent during the course of treatment that following its detection all but one experienced specific or general learning disabilities. Learning became so painful in two cases that the girls left school.

Although only one girl was referred for promiscuity, it became apparent during treatment that at least two others were promiscuous. Stealing, present in three cases, never reached major proportions or caused legal action.

Because of length of contact or special disposition of the cases it was possible to test only seven of the eleven girls. They were given a battery of psychological tests including either the Stanford-Binet (Form L) or the Wechsler-Bellevue (Form I) intelligence tests, the Rorschach, the Thematic Apperception Test, and the Goodenough Draw-a-Man test. One girl was also given vocational guidance tests, and another girl had a group intelligence test at school.

It was the examiner's opinion that all the girls tended to perform below their ability. Performance scores were in general higher than verbal scores. The difference in one case between verbal and performance scores was 31 points; in another, 16.

The main trends which showed up in the Rorschach were depression, anxiety, confusion over sexual identification, fear of sexuality, oral deprivation, and oral sadism. The chief mechanisms of defense were denial, repression, and sometimes projection. These findings were substantiated by the TAT. The girls uniformly saw the mother figures in the latter test as cruel, unjust, and depriving. Father figures were sometimes described as nurturant, sometimes as weak and ineffectual, sometimes as frightening. The Draw-a-Man test further demonstrated the confused sexual identifications of these girls.

When we studied the parents, we found similar factors present in the background of both the mothers and the fathers.

Although most of our information came from the mothers,[2] we learned that all of the "fathers" came from backgrounds characterized by poverty, alcoholism, little education, inadequate housing, and little warmth or understanding from the paternal grandparents. Cases where we had more information about these men showed that they left home and school at an early age, as did the mothers of this study, to find work and to escape from their unpleasant environments.

The occupational history of these men indicated general irresponsibility. Some had been continually unemployed, but the largest number were employed either as merchant seamen or in some occupation closely allied with the sea, for example, as longshoremen.

All the fathers and stepfathers deserted their children at some time. This came about either as a result of divorce, living away from home, or just being away most of the time because of extreme alcoholism. At least eight of the men, and probably more, were alcoholic.

Just as the fathers and stepfathers deserted their families, so had the maternal grandfathers deserted their families, and so too did the mothers of the children included in this study in some way desert their husbands, leaving the daughters to assume the mother role. For example, one of the mothers in our study went upstairs to the maternal grandmother every night and left the children with the father and oldest daughter.

Generally, then, we see desertion and the reactions to this as being the prime common source of anxiety motivating all the individuals involved in the incest situation. When we studied the psychodynamics of the mothers, we were struck not only by the fact of desertion on the part of the maternal grandfathers, but by the striking similarity in the personality structure of the maternal grandmothers. They were stern, demanding, controlling, cold and extremely hostile women, who rejected their daughters and pampered their sons. They reacted to the desertion of their husbands by singling out one daughter whom they would describe as being like the maternal grandfather, and on whom they would displace their feelings of hostility and hurt at having been deserted by the maternal grandfather. These maternal grandmothers began the process of selecting one daughter to be the recipient of their resentments against the deserting maternal grandfather very early by continually pointing out how much of a tomboy the chosen daughter was, to the point where she would be denied pretty clothes and many of the normal feminine activities and interests.

The maternal grandmothers were generally employed as domestics, waitresses, etc., always in basically menial types of occupation. They were hard workers and masculine in character. As a rule they assumed most of the responsibility for the support of their families and gave their children good physical care but little real warmth and understanding.

The mothers of this study, like the fathers and stepfathers, left home and school at an early age to marry or seek employment. When first seen for interviews, they were described as hard, careless in dress and personal appearance, infantile, extremely dependent and intellectually dull. Most of them were poor housekeepers, panicky in the face of responsibility, and seemed on the surface to be satisfied to live in disorder and poverty. However, on closer study they emerged as brighter than average with a potential of achievement far beyond their actual performance. They married men who were also dependent and infantile. If they married a second time, the second partner was even more irresponsible and unsuccessful than the first. This was a repetition of the pattern set by the maternal grandmothers.

These mothers had described their unhappy marital experiences as "throwing myself away," a pattern wherein they acted out what they felt was expected of them by the maternal grandmothers, who had rejected, destroyed, and thrown them away.

The maternal grandmothers acted as though these mothers were no good. The mothers' reaction to this attitude was on the one hand to act and feel as though they were worthless, and on the other hand to hope to receive some denial of this poor opinion of themselves. This pathologic interaction was one of the reasons it was difficult to work with these mothers. They were tied to the maternal grandmothers—literally and psychologically unable to move away from them. Despite the misery and futility of their relationship, these mothers kept trying to return to the maternal grandmothers in constant hope they would receive the love and encouragement they never felt. These attempts to win the maternal grandmother's approval always failed. For example, whenever they achieved any success, they were immediately deflated by the maternal grandmothers who were unable to tolerate any signs of progress or independence in them.

These mothers went to any lengths to satisfy their need for affection, attention, and support, and to deny their feelings of worthlessness. Because of their personality orientation, they chose masochistic methods in their attempts to fulfill their needs. At least half of them attempted to satisfy these needs by promiscuity. Others neglected their health, hoping that someone would care enough to stop them. Some deliberately got into situations where they could have been injured physically.

The whole insidious process continued in the relationship between the mothers of this study and their daughters. The mothers singled out one daughter whom they treated in a special fashion. This daughter was given excellent physical care, was often overindulged materially, was encouraged to assume responsibility beyond her years, and gradually developed into a replica of the maternal grandmother. These mothers then displaced onto this chosen daughter all the hostility really felt for the maternal grandmother. They forced this daughter to become their confidante, helper with the other children, and adviser. They relinquished their responsibilities as parents so that they, in effect, became daughters again, and the daughter a mother. However, they became angry when the daughter became too directive, independent, and hostile. It seemed that the mothers acted out in this way because they had not resolved their anxiety over their Oedipal conflict. This resulted from the trauma of having been deserted by the maternal grandfathers. They dealt with this anxiety in other ways too, as we have mentioned, by choosing men who would desert them, and by deserting their husbands sexually. The mothers perpetuated their own experiences in these ways and finally created situations where they deserted the fathers, who then became involved in the incestuous relationship with the daughters. The mothers used the mechanism of denial to blind themselves to the incest, and when confronted with the evidence, they were more hostile toward the daughters than the husbands. This seemed to be because they projected onto the daughters the bad part of themselves which wanted to act out the Oedipal relationship.

We have found, too, that the mothers not only displaced the hostility felt toward maternal grandmothers onto the daughters, but also onto numerous older women with whom they invariably became involved. They tended to become very dependent upon these women to the point where they began to feel smothered and threatened. Then their hostility and consequent anxiety reached a panic state. On one level this seemed to represent a homosexual panic; fundamentally it appeared to be a manifestation of their extreme hostile dependence.

All the family members appeared to be searching for a mother figure. Their frustration tolerance to the anxiety of desertion was minimal and something in the unconscious of the family members, and their effect on each other caused them to handle their anxiety primarily by acting out.

Other cases known to us showed only one marriage partner with the personality structure we described as a prerequisite for the acting out of the incest, while the other partner showed some different personality structure. With this different family constellation, the father and daughter did not act out the incest but dealt with the Oedipal conflict in some other way. This problem and the problem of working with these mothers, we plan to discuss in a future paper.

One of the typical cases in our study was June Smith. She was 11 years, 2 months old at the time of her referral. The family group consisted of the mother, 38; the father, 42; a brother, 17; the patient; a brother, 8; a sister, 7; and baby sister, 4. There had been a stillborn child between the older brother and the patient.

They lived in a two-family house in a working-class neighborhood. The house was owned by the maternal grandmother who lived upstairs. They had moved there three years before referral to the clinic. Trouble between Mr. and Mrs. Smith began when they moved to this house. When they quarreled Mrs. Smith went upstairs to sleep with the maternal grandmother, leaving the children with Mr. Smith who often was drunk at these times. When Mrs. Smith deserted in this fashion, Mr. Smith began to have relations with June.

Two weeks before their incestuous relationship was discovered, Mr. Smith found June talking to some boys on a street corner. He became angry and dragged the patient home to her mother. The patient then became angry at her father and told her mother that her father had had sexual relations with her. Mrs. Smith used this evidence to obtain a divorce. Mr. Smith readily admitted the charge and was sent to prison for five years.

June was sent to camp the following summer and did well for the first three weeks. Then she had a severe attack of abdominal pain simulating appendicitis. This was diagnosed as hysteria.

When June returned home in the fall there were frequent quarrels with her mother which often culminated in physical battles; the two fought like children. June ran away several times but never went more than a few blocks from home. The tension and conflict became so difficult by November that June was moved to a protective group placement. Arrangements were made at this time for her to come to the Judge Baker Guidance Center for treatment.

Throughout the clinic contact (8 interviews), Mrs. Smith, a nice-looking woman, very plainly dressed, never showed evidence of any attempt to look attractive. Her appearance and attitude were martyrlike. She was stiff and expressionless at first. She was more than willing to leave everything concerning June in the hands of others. She said June needed more attention but that this should come from others. She had no idea of anything she could do about it.

June had always seemed older than her years to Mrs. Smith. She said that June seemed more like her mother than her daughter. Although she felt that June's ideas were those of an older girl, she couldn't describe what she meant. She added briefly that June menstruated at 11. Mrs. Smith commented that June could be very good when she wanted, taking over much of the care and responsibility of the home and children. Mrs. Smith said that she could only love little children and she hated to see them grow up.

Mrs. Smith's handling of June at home vacillated. At times she severely restricted the girl, locking her in her room and once even tying her hands and feet with a belt. At other times she gave her complete freedom, which she described as putting her on her own.

Mrs. Smith expressed the fear and the hope that June would run away. This preceded a runaway episode. Mrs. Smith had earlier expressed a similar wish about Mr. Smith. She wanted him out of the home since this would leave her free with the maternal grandmother and the younger children whom she could love; the older boy was going into the service very shortly.

Mrs. Smith never mentioned her own father. She described the maternal grandmother as a strict woman who lacked understanding. She said she was never allowed and never dared to "run around." The maternal grandmother nagged the mother and blamed her for June's behavior. Mrs.

Smith, however, was aware of her great dependence on the maternal grandmother.

Mrs. Smith did not give much information concerning her attitude toward Mr. Smith. She expressed fear of his hostility toward the older boy
and was concerned that he would kill his son. However, Mrs. Smith indicated that before moving to the maternal grandmother's home, she
was very dependent on Mr. Smith. This attitude changed on Mrs. Smith's
part when she turned her dependency back to the maternal grandmother.

The developmental history revealed nothing unusual. Mrs. Smith stated
that the pregnancy was normal and full term. There were no problems
associated with the birth or the puerperium. The child was bottle-fed, but
there was no feeding problem at any time. She walked and talked at the
average age.

The girl's psychological tests revealed an I.Q. of 100—not considered
optimum. The projective tests demonstrated a severe depression lying
close to the surface. The patient was busy constantly in an effort to blot
out traumatic memories. This spread into a general fear of retention of
any type of knowledge. There was tremendous expenditure of energy involved in warding off thoughts which threatened to destroy her ego
identity. There was guilt over the consequences of her incestuous relationship and feelings of worthlessness, of being irreparably damaged, and of
depression over the inevitable abandonment by her parents.

June had never been a school problem. Her grades were above average,
especially in arithmetic. The teachers described her as a very likable, con-
scientious child who might well have come from a superior home. She was
well liked by her classmates and often chosen by them as a leader.

June, a very tall, attractive 11-year-old, looked more like 13 or 14.
She was slender and secondary sex characteristics were precociously developed. She spoke freely and seemed to want to be friendly and make a
good impression.

June described her life as a happy one until her parents moved in with
the maternal grandmother. She said that the maternal grandmother tried
to come between her mother and father. Mrs. Smith never had her own
opinions; she always consulted the maternal grandmother. June often told
her mother that she wasn't grown-up. June had to take care of the little
ones and made her father's lunch. All the trouble was her mother's fault.
If her mother hadn't quarreled with her father and gone upstairs to sleep
with the maternal grandmother, there would not have been any trouble.
Her father drank sometimes, and it was when he was drinking that he
made sexual advances to June.

She said that she had wanted to do what was best for her father but
she was very sorry now that she had told anyone about it. She didn't know
that he would be put in prison for five years. Everyone told her nothing
would happen to him; even the judge had lied to her. She was always her

father's favorite and felt she could talk to him and never to her mother. She hated her eight-year-old sister, but loved the baby girl. She wanted to live with her father and the baby because this baby seemed like her own child.

She added that she wanted to be everything to her father because he had no one. Her mother was getting help and so was she, but nobody was doing anything to help her father. She felt terrible over putting him in prison. Everyone was against her because no one allowed her to see him. They didn't even give her the letters he wrote to her. Sometimes she became so angry that her stomach felt as if it were burning up. She was tired all the time and had no appetite.

During June's stay at the protective group placement, she showed wide extremes of mood and behavior. She was hyperactive at times, and she assumed much responsibility, especially in the care of younger children. The workers there commented that at such times it was difficult for them to remember that June was only 11, and that they often gave her responsibilities they would ordinarily give a 14- or 15-year-old. They were greatly puzzled and dismayed when she suddenly became a demanding, whining small child, sometimes seeming almost out of contact, curling up in a ball and crying, "I want my mummy," in a 3-year-old's tone of voice. Such periods of infantile regression alternated with or culminated in severe rage reactions during which June screamed and threw herself around, stiffened up rigidly, and hit out at anyone who came near her. As she gradually became worse, the director of the group placement asked for her removal and she was sent home to her mother until further plans could be made.

Her school work during the above period deteriorated rapidly, as well as her social adjustment with other children. She complained of their treatment of her, saying that they called her names and swore at her. She felt that wherever she was she spoiled things. She said that if she was not around, others had a good time. She said that when she was alone she thought that all the terrible things that happened were her fault.

June's behavior showed no essential change at home and she was placed in another group placement. Shortly afterward she ran away from there and was picked up by the police after having spent the night with several sailors who believed she was 18. She was sent to the training school for girls. When she was seen just before this episode, she continued to express the feeling that she was damaged, worthless, bad, and needed to be put in jail like her father. She begged to be allowed to see her father in prison and hated everyone for putting him there.

June represented a typical case which demonstrated many of the features characteristic of all these patients. When we reviewed all of the cases, certain facts stood out which we will present along with our conclusions and impressions.

The girls in this study were referred to the Judge Baker Guidance Center after the relationship with the father or stepfather had been detected and legal action had been taken. There was a disruption of the home and five of these girls were actually out of the home.

All of these girls were depressed and guilty. Their verbalized guilt, as far as our clinical material demonstrated, was in connection with the disruption of the home and not over the incest itself. The depression showed itself in many forms. Some of the girls verbalized their grief even to the extent of suicide threats; others demonstrated mood swings. Almost all had the somatic complaints characteristic of a depression. These included fatigue, loss of appetite, generalized aches and pains, inability to concentrate, and sleep disturbances. Their physical symptoms were often of such severity as to cause considerable concern for their health.

The patients demonstrated various methods of dealing with their anxiety, guilt, and depression:

Searching for punishment was one method. Some of the girls achieved this through somatic media such as submitting to painful medical procedures. Others verbalized this need; and others, by their provacative behavior, drew down upon themselves various forms of punishment. For example, June repeatedly said she wished she were imprisoned like her father and finally accomplished this through her delinquent behavior.

Another method of dealing with this anxiety was to seek forgiveness from the mother or mother figure. Some girls expressed this need by extensive gift-giving to the mother. Others searched for forgiveness by turning to religion.

Some of these girls became delinquent. This was another method of coping with their anxiety. The purpose of the sexual promiscuity seemed to be to relive the experiences with the father and hence, through the mechanism of the repetition compulsion, to work through their anxiety and at the same time achieve a restitution of the lost parent.

Although these girls during such a period of acting out seemed well integrated (almost expressing a hypomanic denial), they became depressed when they were confined and unable to act out. Their delinquency included several special problems. Since the sexuality of these girls led to the arrest and incarceration of the father and a disruption of the home, they had the experience of seeing their destructive omnipotent fantasies come true. This had a particularly damaging effect on their ego structure, which was intensified when further sexual activity led to the arrest of other men.

The resulting defect in the reality-testing function of the ego was overdetermined. Another factor was their disturbed object relationship. We see that these girls tended to act out rather than repress. This could be traced directly to their experiences with parents who did not help them to cope more adequately with their instinctual impulses.

Most of these girls at first appeared surprisingly mature and capable. Although many of them did well in school and were quite skilled and able in taking responsibility, it became clear during therapy that this was a façade.

Although these girls felt abandoned by both parents, they verbalized most of their hostility against the mother. They often idealized the father or father substitute and absolved him of guilt.

Incest usually began when the father and daughter felt the mother had abandoned them, either by giving birth to a new sibling, turning to the maternal grandmother, or developing some new interest outside the home. These girls in their loneliness and fear accepted the father's sexual advances as an expression of affection.

When the incest was associated with the birth of a new sibling, the girls often fantasied the child as theirs and father's. They then often expressed the wish to set up a new home with father and child and to push the mother out. They felt free to return the father's affection sexually because the mother had unconsciously given them permission. The mother did this, not only by being absent, but more actively by setting up a situation where this could occur. An example of this was one mother who felt very guilty over the incest, but when asked to discuss the circumstances said she could not tolerate her husband's snoring and went to sleep in another room. Then out of concern that he would be lonely she put the daughter in her place in bed with the husband. As a result of this parental acting out, these girls felt guilty not for the incest itself, which seemed to be condoned by both parents, but for the disruption of the home.

These girls had long felt abandoned by the mother as a protective adult. This was their basic anxiety. One way they dealt with this anxiety was to search for a mother figure who would care for and protect them. Their reality sense was sufficiently disturbed for them to continue to pursue this search in spite of repeated disappointments. However, reality testing was sufficiently adequate for the patients to realize their dissatisfaction and frustration in not achieving their wishes. Because of their painful experiences with their real mothers, they were never sure of gratification from any new mother figure. New relationships then held both the promise of fulfillment and the familiar fear of disappointment. Thus, as new relationships were formed in an effort to satisfy the need for a mother and to work through this anxiety, various complications ensued.

When many of these patients were placed in foster homes, the resultant dependent position caused them to regress and reveal their hostile demanding orality in the most primitive form. The regression which occurred in many of these girls approached psychotic states, such as prolonged confusional and stuporous periods or rage reactions.

These girls related to older women in a hostile dependent way and repeatedly made impossible demands, and if these could not be met, they became furious. Because of the sexualization of their object relationships to both men and women, the search for the mother often appeared in a homosexual form. Also, the trauma associated with the heterosexual experience with the father caused future heterosexual experiences to be a source of anxiety and so further motivated the turn to homosexuality.

These girls had difficulty working out their feelings toward both male and female figures since they had experienced hostility from mother and the pathologic relationship with father caused the breaking up of the home. This pathology in their identification figures and the conflicting ambiguous roles they assumed led to further complications in resolving their bisexual wishes. When some of these girls talked of their desire to be male, they expressed the wish and the fear both verbally and by various symptoms. For example, one adolescent who wet her bed tied this in with her fantasy that wetting represented male sexual activity.

The reactions to sexuality in these girls took various pregenital forms and ranged from promiscuity to asceticism and included homosexuality. Although the original sexual experience with the father was at a genital level, the meaning of the sexual act was pregenital and seemed to have the purpose of receiving some sort of parental interest.

The underlying craving for an adequate parent, then, dominated the lives of these girls.

Summary

Incest occurred in families of a similar psychopathology which was peculiarly conducive to the acting out of this Oedipal wish. The personality structure of the mother or of the father considered independently would not be sufficient to produce the acting out. The girls reacted to their mothers' unconscious desire to put them in the maternal role. They at the same time received gratification from the fathers as the parents who loved them in this pathologic way. However, they received no help in reality testing and superego development from either parent.

These girls showed a pseudo maturity, but this façade crumbled when they were placed in a dependent position and some experienced psychotic-like states.

When the incest was detected, these girls showed extreme guilt and anxiety over the disruption of the home, although they did not seem guilty over the incest which both parents condoned.

Some of these girls were extremely masochistic, searching for punishment in many ways. Some attempted to win their mothers' forgiveness. Others, by a repetition compulsion, attempted through promiscuity to bring back the lost father. They all tried, by these and other ways, to work through their depression, guilt and anxiety.

44 *Family Adjustment to the Brain-Damaged Child*

ALFRED M. FREEDMAN, WILLIAM HELME,

JOAN HAVEL, MARJORIE EUSTIS,

CONRAD RILEY, and WILLIAM S. LANGFORD

A child's biological and mental capacities (and limitations) are factors to which the family not only must adapt but keep as a framework, within which patterns of leadership and co-ordination are worked out. Dr. Freedman and his colleagues have made extensive studies of how the brain-damaged child fares in the family. In this paper they show how failure of the family to set expectations for the child appropriate to his limitations can transform a neurological disorder into a personality disturbance.

Familial dysautonomia, a chronic disease with a high mortality rate, which has both somatic and psychiatric features, was first described by Riley, Day, Greeley and Langford in 1949[1] and further elaborated subsequently.[2] It is a condition apparently of genetic origin occurring mostly in children of Jewish extraction.

The most striking manifestations are disturbances of autonomic functions. A consistent feature is the failure of production of tears in usual quantities when crying. Most patients show transient macular red blotches associated with excitement or eating. Perspiration is excessive, particularly under emotional stimulation. Blood pressure regulation is poor: all patients with the typical disease tested so far show postural hypotension, usually of slight degree but occasionally giving rise to syncope. Many patients show transient hypertension, often marked, under emotional stress. This is more characteristic of the older children. There is often pronounced swallowing difficulty which may give rise to feeding problems in infancy, prolonged drooling as the child grows, and may be associated with poor articulation and late speech development. Unexplained fever and undue febrile reaction to infection are common features.

There are other evidences of nervous system dysfunction which are difficult to explain. Deep tendon reflexes are usually diminished or absent. Motor co-ordination is slow to develop and poor. The patients show a

Reprinted from *American Journal of Orthopsychiatry*, XXVII (January, 1957), 96–104, where it appeared under the title, "Psychiatric Aspects of Familial Dysautonomia," with the kind permission of Dr. Freedman and the publishers.

definite and sometimes striking indifference to painful stimuli though there is no true anesthesia.

Disabling manifestations are frequent. Most common is a varying degree of emotional lability and instability which presents serious problems of management to the parents and teachers. In infancy many have alarming breath-holding spells. Urinary frequency is common.

Episodic vomiting is one of the most disturbing problems. The episodes may be frequent and severe enough to necessitate hospitalization. Repeated pulmonary infections in the early years, probably as a result of disturbance in swallowing reflexes with resultant aspiration, are common and have accounted for many deaths. The lack of tears and accompanying corneal anesthesia have apparently been the cause of repeated corneal ulceration leading to near-blindness in several patients.

Lastly, statural growth is often seriously impaired, with none of the patients having attained greater than mean height for the age, and many of them falling far below the mean.

So far, careful search of the brain in autopsied cases has shown no consistent lesion.

In order to gain more insight about these children over a broader field, studies have been carried out by a team, consisting of a pediatrician, neurologist, psychiatrists, psychologists, speech therapist, psychiatric social worker, and electroencephalographist as previously reported.[3] In this report, the emphasis will be on utilization of the resources of a team of psychiatrists, psychologists, and social worker. But it must be observed that this was preceded and accompanied by a most thorough somatic study by the pediatrician and neurologist.

The approach of the psychiatric team included the following aspects: (1) psychiatric interview of each child; (2) very detailed journal of the events of an entire week in the home life of each child, kept by the mother on a form provided; (3) interview with the parents (conducted by the psychiatrist and social worker) to extend and clarify the journal data; (4) systematic tabulation of all data in the hospital charts of the children by the psychiatrist and psychologists in collaboration; (5) psychological study of each child, particularly testing organizing functions with a wide variety of materials; (6) organization of a parent group, now in its third year, first as an aid to parents and, secondly, to delineate the many difficulties and problems parents experience.

Thus far, 14 children have been thoroughly studied by the entire clinical team, and the findings on this group will be presented.

The patients examined ranged in age from 3 years, 8 months, to 13 years, 4 months, at the time of the investigation. Six girls and eight boys were included.

In the psychiatric and social work-up, the emphasis was on the totality of the child's behavior; his physical and social relationship to the significant adults, including the physician; his verbalizations about himself, significant adults, peers, and siblings; his interests and aspirations; his inner life, particularly dreams and fantasies; and his neuropsychiatric status, with special attention to motility.

Motor retardation and slow speech development were frequently noted in the developmental histories of these children. From early infancy, relationships with parents were characterized by demands and dependency. These dependency struggles and demands were prominent through the years. Currently, the home situation is characterized by excessive and highly successful manipulation of the parents by the child.

These children seem to be very masterful in controlling people and particularly in playing parents off against each other. In many ways, they seem to operate almost exclusively on the manipulative level, scarcely ever dealing directly and spontaneously with anyone, including parents. Thus, in one child it may be overdependency, in another, overaffection. However, in every case the core of the relationship is concerned with methods of controlling the parents. There appears to be a continuous bargaining and haggling between parent and child, the parent very eager to avoid a physical crisis in the child's health and keeping clear of the child by avoiding intimacy. The child appears willing to accept this modified relationship in return for control. The *modus operandi* appears to be a highly structured relationship that is not close or intense.

In maternal relations, most of the children displayed marked dependency. Half of them displayed affection for their mothers; four were ambivalent and three were outwardly hostile. The majority of the patients were clinging and maintained close contact with the mother.

In their relations to father, most were dependent and half were predominantly affectionate. Interestingly enough, none of these children was described as being overtly hostile toward the father, although some degree of variable hostility toward the mother was frequent. Only two of them could be considered withdrawn from their fathers.

On the whole, the relationships of the dysautonomic subjects to siblings were more positive than toward the parents. Relationships with peers were poor for most of them. Only three could be said to maintain satisfactory relationships with other children. There was a tendency for many of the patients to be excessively submissive in order to maintain relationships, even going so far as to bribe other children to play with them.

Very few of the parents were fully accepting of their affected offspring. Most were ambivalent with superficial acceptance and deeper resentment and rejection. In some instances, one or both parents rejected the child completely. However, it is noteworthy that most of the subjects of the study who had an opportunity to deal with an adult other than the parents maintained excellent relationships with this adult, who might be an aunt, teacher, grandparent, neighbor, or domestic. This "other" adult was almost always a female. This again suggests a preference of the children for a relationship that is not too close or intense.

There seemed to be no consistent pattern in terms of the mother or father being the dominant parent. In more than half of the households the family revolved about the sick child.

The adaptation to the symptoms of dysautonomia was poor in eight of the fourteen patients; actually, only one could be said to have good adaptation to his symptoms.

In interviews, our children displayed little assertiveness, initiative or independence, instead seeking help and guidance from the physician. They were restless, hyperkinetic, impulsive, poorly controlled, inadequately co-ordinated, had a short attention span, and displayed desires for structure and rigidity in life.

A review of the daily journals indicates that these individuals are difficult to handle by ordinary standards and methods. This seemed particularly true in regard to periods of change in the daily cycle. Arising and going to bed, for example, were special periods of crisis for the dysautonomic child.

Motility abnormalities were observed in many of the patients. Eight out of ten over six years of age displayed tonic neck reflex whirling; this is pathological over the age of six.[4]

The psychological testing proved exceedingly valuable. A battery of tests was administered, primarily directly toward their "organizing behavior." The following areas were examined: "concept formation" by means of one verbal test and two non-verbal sorting tests, i.e., Similarities, Goldstein-Scheerer color-form tests, and Goldstein-Scheerer object sorting tests; "visual motor function" using figure drawing, Bender Gestalt, Marble Board, Block Design, Object Assembly, and Progressive Matrices; and planning skill by Porteus Mazes.

In the analysis of the psychometric studies, we were not only concerned with the specific content or scores of the tests, but also with the child's way of dealing with the materials. Thus, attention was given to whether he tended to handle materials in an expansive manner, or tended to restrict or control; whether he tended to differentiate the material, emphasizing different aspects or qualities, or whether he tended to integrate it, emphasizing the relation of parts to the whole.

Previous psychological tests and I.Q. determinations had led to the impression of mental retardation in some of the individuals in the study. However, because of motor problems displayed by many of them, specific areas were examined to determine whether any general retardation was present. These children do well in tests such as the "similarities"; performance on such tests avoids interchanges where problems of co-ordination and language skill are important, and probably quite closely reflects ability in abstract thinking. This leads us to feel that basically these patients are not retarded in general intellectual capacity and that with follow-up as they grow older, this finding will be confirmed.

By breaking down the findings according to age groups, it became apparent that there is a difference between the older and younger children. In the figure drawings, practically all the younger ones, from 3 years 8 months, to 6 years 10 months, displayed expansive qualities, while in the older group practically all demonstrated tendencies to rigid boundaries and overcontrol. In one older child, the boundaries were wavering and in another of the older group there were some expansive trends, but both of these individuals had severe visual disabilities as a result of corneal ulcer, and this may have interfered with control.

Qualitative ratings of the visual motor Gestalt tests reveal that tendencies to expansive reproductions and loss of control on the less structured figures appeared most marked in the younger children. Most of the reproduction in the older group was rigid and overcontrolled. On the more highly structured figures, most of the younger patients displayed expansive trends and only one of the older did so; this child was one with visual disabilities. Interestingly enough, the other children with eye disability showed strong controlling tendencies on the Gestalt test.

On the tasks requiring organization of a variety of different concrete materials, the younger children scored better than the older, due allowance being made for age. Thus, on the Progressive Matrices involving pattern recognition, the younger group earned weighted scores ranging from 7 to 13, while the older group ranged from 6 to 7. Throughout, 10 is the standard mean score with a normal range of 8–12. In the Block Design test, involving pattern reorganization, younger children earned scores of 10–12 while the older scored 7–9. In Object Assembly, involving construction of an unknown whole, the range in the younger group was from 6 to 10, while in the older it was from 3 to 7. On intellectual tasks requiring isolation of particular elements and one-to-one relations, the older equaled or excelled the younger group slightly. Thus, in the Porteus Mazes, the scores were in the same range, while in the similarities involving a one-to-one verbal relation, the median score for the younger was 9, and for the older it was 11.

In psychiatric interview, psychological testing, and neurological study, the subjects under study most closely resemble children suffering from diffuse, nonfocal organic disorders of the brain. We may state as a central hypothesis that dysautonomia is a diffuse organic disorder of the central nervous system with both primary and secondary effects on the functioning of the individual. These effects are measurable directly in terms of motor functioning, reflexes, electroencephalography, etc. They are measurable indirectly in terms of the social and intellectual functioning of the child.

It has been suggested by some that such children might in reality be suffering from childhood schizophrenia; as a matter of fact, one of the patients was so diagnosed at another clinic. Careful observation and study give little evidence to point in this direction. In the first place, there are no family histories of schizophrenia, nor is there the simultaneous precocity and retardation found in childhood schizophrenia. In no case has a child ever achieved a high level and slipped back. The ideational content of schizophrenia is absent here—the introjected bodies, bizarre concepts, experimentations with space and time, etc. It is true that the homeostatic problems in the physiological area[5] are reminiscent of schizophrenia and that there is a high incidence of immature reflexes such as whirling.

Emotional disturbance is evident in all cases studied. We have interpreted the dynamics of the emotional disturbance as a vicious circle. The point of departure in this circle would appear to be the congenital brain abnormality. As can be seen from the over-simplified schema, the brain disorder gives rise to problems in autonomic homeostasis and diffuse anxiety. Thus, the behavior of the patient is characterized by impulsivity and overreaction to emotional stimuli. The restlessness, anxiety, and frequent explosive outbursts of the child arouse anxiety and consequent resentment and guilt in the parents. The parents attempt to appease the child by excessive permissiveness and acceding to his wishes and whims. He continues to manipulate the parents but is distressed by being confronted by lack of stability in the external world; i.e., his parents' and his own helplessness in regard to his body and to the world as a whole. He frantically strives to attain equilibrium by further manipulation of the parents, thus increasing his own anxiety and insecurity. The cycle may be repeated indefinitely or come to a halt temporarily through physical crisis, such as vomiting. It was the over-all impression that such physical crises were often, but not always, precipitated by emotional crises. Sometimes organic illness such as respiratory disease seemed to be the "trigger."

Many parents, but not all, showed reactions that could not wholly be ascribed to the illness of their child. In studies of "brain-damaged" children, it has been a general impression that where parents are integrated, realistic and accepting, the behavioral disturbance is minimal. We cannot say at the present moment how much of the distress seen in the parents of dysautonomia victims preceded the birth of the patient, although this seems to have occurred fairly frequently. One can pose a very important question as to how sick these children would be if their parents were less anxious and more stable. Possibly in a study of cases that are less severe and younger, such a question can be answered, but in any event, much further work is necessary.

In this study, some notion of the dysautonomic child's self-concept has been achieved. He develops an image of himself in the world that is characterized by doubts about his own goodness, worth, and acceptance by others. This arises through perceiving three negative qualities about his difference from normal children: (1) that his disabilities are unique, (2) that his disabilities cause his parents trouble and disappointment, and (3) that he does not have adequate control of his own body. As a result, the dysautonomic patient develops a relationship to people and things about him which reflects his negative self-image and his need to establish a secure place and static order in his world. All the effects of dysautonomia are characterized by difficulties in complex organizations of behavior. As a result, the child experiences the most trouble in those stages of development where a reorganization of behavior is necessary and tends to cling to earlier organizations longer than does the child without diffuse organic disorders. The periods of change, whether in the daily cycle or the life cycle, are periods of special crises. These children cannot meet a fluctuation in the internal or external environment, handle it, and return to *status quo ante* in a normal fashion. This has been clearly demonstrated in the physiological area and appears to hold true psychologically as well. Thus, the children are most disturbed by any stimulus or stress out of keeping with the ordinary routine. They seem to strive defensively for a rigid pattern structure in daily living that will minimize the external and internal stress. As they grow older, they tend to achieve rigid structuring as a pattern. This suggests various therapeutic approaches.

One can try to minimize disturbing stimuli. Thus, one can strive for a stable, supporting home situation. This has been difficult, owing to the distress of the parents and the seriousness of the child's illness. The threat of death is always present in the household. We have attempted to reduce such disturbances in several ways. First, through the use of the parent groups, stability is encouraged through the sharing of experiences and consequent lessening of anxiety. Recently, we have been setting up rigid routines, in which every moment of the child's day is scheduled, to help in the development of useful and constructive patterns and minimize unpredictable change. Anxiety and guilt in the parents are controlled partially because this routine is established by an outside figure, the doctor. Further experience is necessary in the use of such schedules, but suggestively encouraging results have been attained in one girl thus far by this device, along with other therapies. The same routinization in school and elsewhere would be desirable. In a sense, we strive to achieve a compulsive character structure.

In difficult situations, the possibility of removing the child from the conflict of the home situation and placing him in a structured, patterned, impersonal, but warm hospital situation appears to be useful. One boy who was in repeated crisis, characterized by fainting spells, on two occasions completely lost this symptom by hospitalization alone.

The child himself can be made more resistant to stress and stimuli in two ways. (1) Drugs have been utilized to minimize the physical crisis. Chlorpromazine (Thorazine) has been found useful in the control of vomiting. (2) Individual psychotherapy might be expected to give the child more stability, and a better understanding of his disturbances. Experience, thus far, with such treatment is insufficient to draw specific conclusions.

This study has implications broader than understanding and management of dysautonomia. It affords a promising opportunity to understand how physiologic imbalance might upset the emotional balance; that is to say, the relationship of the vasovegetative system and the psyche. This would have wide applications in the field of psychiatry, particularly in childhood schizophrenia where homeostatic derangement is evidenced. The opposite is also true; we may gain some insight on how the emotions or affective stimuli might influence the physiology of the child.

It would be important to perform control studies to verify the conclusions drawn. It is our impression that the behavior of these children is different from that of other children who are chronically ill without involvement of the central nervous system. Also, these children differ from other "brain-damaged" children because of the periodic, severe, prostrating physical crises with the possibility of death. Thus, two groups of controls would be necessary; one, children with known brain damage, and the other, children with chronic illness in which death is a possibility. In this way, the origin of many of the symptoms of familial dysautonomia may be clarified.

45 *The Middle-Class Male Child and Neurosis*

ARNOLD W. GREEN

In a paper that is now a classic, Professor Green describes the extent and means of controlling children which prevails in middle-class families. He argues that when the mother has such an important role in the direction of male children, and when their direction is effected largely through the manipulation of love as a reward and punishment, the child is disposed to neurosis.

In another publication,[1] Erich Fromm's and Karen Horney's use of general-cultural data to explain neurosis was criticized. It was pointed out that while these two analysts have a concept of cultural neurosis (Horney) and pathological normalcy (Fromm) from which "the culture" is suffering, at the same time a clinical picture of neurosis is presented without reference to culture—the going awry of personal relationships, particularly of the child-in-family. While, in her earlier work in this country, Dr. Horney found love-frustration the key to the individual etiology of neurosis,[2] later, and indicating Dr. Fromm's influence, the key became the arbitrary imposition of authority within the family of orientation.[3]

Two things are being attempted in this paper: first, by a brief discussion of the socialization process taking place in a specific Polish-industrial community to demonstrate the inadequacy of a clinical etiology of neurosis in terms of either love-thwarting or the arbitrary exercise of authority; second, to explain in sociological terms the context in which "lack of genuine love" and "authority" operate to produce neurotic symptoms.

I

Sinclair Lewis failed to "see" Sauk Center until he had spent some time at Yale and in New York. Similarly, to evaluate what parts the "lack of genuine love" and "arbitrary authority" in themselves play in the etiology of neurosis, a comparison should be made of their effects in different contexts.[4]

The author spent his childhood and young adulthood in a Massachusetts industrial village of some three thousand population, most of which is

Reprinted from *American Sociological Review*, XI (February, 1946), 31–41, with the kind permission of the author and the publisher.

made up of immigrant Poles and their native-born children. It was previously pointed out how the middle-class norms governing courtship and marriage do not apply within this local Polish colony.[5] This is also true of parent-child relationships.

The local Polish parents emigrated before marriage from farm villages and small towns in Poland. While the old familistic tradition has been slowly deteriorating in rural Poland for several decades, enough of that tradition was brought with them so that their expectations of their American-born children's conduct reflected an alien peasant system of values.

An outstanding feature of peasant family life, in contradistinction to that of modern middle-class family organization, is the stress placed upon rules and work functions rather than personal sentiment, and parental authority is excessive by the standards of any comparable segment of the American population.[6] These rules of conduct and this parental authority are out of place in the American industrial slum. Second-generation Poles participate in a social world outside the home which their parents, because of language difficulties and previous conditioning, are incapable of sharing or even of understanding. As bewildered parents attempt to enforce old-world standards they are met with the anger and ridicule of their children. In answer to this, the parents have final recourse to a kind of authority which was unsanctioned in Poland: a vengeful, personal, irrational authority, which no longer finds support in the future hopes and ambitions of the children; this new authority is no longer controlled by both parents' families and a cohesive community. But this personal authority will not suffice to curb their wayward progeny, who have little respect for their parents as persons and who soon come to learn that their "American" playmates are not subjected to anything like it in their homes.

It is through this tragically antagonistic, mutually distrustful clash of wills that the relations of parents and children tend to be lacking in "love" (which is alien to the peasant mores anyway). At the same time, there is plenty of "irrational authority." In exasperation and fear of losing all control over their Americanized youngsters, parents apply the fist and whip rather indiscriminately. The sounds of blows, screams, howls, vexatious wails of torment and hatred are so commonplace along the rows of dilapidated mill-houses that the passerby pays them scant attention.

But those children do not become neurotic.[7] Why? Because parental authority, however harsh and brutal, is, in a sense, casual and external to the "core of the self." The Polish parents do not have the techniques and opportunity to *absorb the personality* of the child. In the first place, the child has many models of behavior to adopt both within the family (five to eight children are, in estimate, modal in the Polish section of the village) and outside. Siblings present a more or less united front in their rebellion against their parents. Parent-avoidance techniques are easily acquired because of the parents' halting use of English and the fact that both parents, typically, work in the local factory, leaving the younger children to the daytime supervision of older children, which frequently results in no supervision at all. The open woods and fields are close at hand and the children roam far. The homes are not particularly clean, nor do they contain bric-a-brac or furniture of any value, so that the local Polish child is spared the endless admonitions which bedevil the middle-class child not to touch this or that.

The children also develop a tolerant or openly malicious contempt for their parents as stupid, unknowing of American ways, concerning which the children regard themselves authorities. By and large, the parents are obstacles to be avoided or circumvented wherever possible. And while the resulting lack of identification with the parents virtually obviates demonstrations of affection, it also saves the children from feelings of guilt and repressed hostility.[8] The training of the child becomes, then, casual, haphazard, "free" in a sense, very similar to the training received in many primitive tribes, except for the negative other-regarding attitude of parent and child so typical in the village.

II

The claim has been made that "lack of love" and "irrational authority" do not, in and of themselves, cause the development of neurotic symptoms. These phenomena do operate, however, in individual etiologies of neurosis, but only within a certain context. The term "personality absorption" has already been used. Personality absorption is the physical and emotional blanketing of the child, bringing about a slavish dependence upon the parents. It is personality absorption, in conjunction with factors other than lack of love or irrational authority, that produces a certain type of neurosis.

To delineate the kind of socialization which maximizes personality absorption, it will be necessary to conceive of a parental type which simultaneously occupies several population segments: native-white, Protestant urban, college-educated, middle-class.[9] The training of children born to parents who can thus be characterized, is so experientially consistent it has a certain range of predictive value.

Now, how can we define the middle-class child's situation?[10] It has already been said that his personality is "absorbed,"[11] and to the extent that it has been absorbed, he is in danger of developing neurotic symptoms. But why is it absorbed?

Perhaps the best way to view his social conditioning is to consider his parents and their position in relation to him.[12] The father's work takes him far from the place of residence, where most of his associates are only slightly less strangers to him than they are to his family. He is a white-collar worker. As a salesman, office worker, minor bureaucrat, or professional man, his job-techniques revolve around manipulating the

personalities of others, instead of tools. Since he has internalized the supreme middle-class value, individual success, he tries to use his associates
as means to further his career; in fact, he has himself been conditioned to
view his associates, education, hobbies, intellectual interests, in terms of
their possible value to his career.[13] On the job he views himself not so
much as functionally associated with others in a common purpose as a
self-contained unit establishing "contacts" with others. His work relations
are not defined in fixed terms of status and role to the extent that they
were in the past, for he is on the move, or views himself in that way. He
has, then, a well-developed tendency to view his relations with others
in terms of what he, as a mobile, displaced person, can get out of them.

Yet the modern middle-class father cannot use his *child* either in the
new sense of manipulating others to his own advantage, nor, be it noted, in
the ways available in the past. In the old rural-familistic system, the child
served well three predominant interests of the father: he would soon
work on the farm, or, during the earlier days of the industrial revolution,
in the factory—become an economic asset to the father, in other words; he
would provide economic security in the father's old age;[14] and finally, he
would provide psychological security by preserving the family name, a
form of this-world immortality in a society which made the family the
primary repository of most social values.

In terms of dollars alone, the cost of raising a modern middle-class
child represents a serious threat to the personal ambition of the father.[15]
At the very time when, in terms of his primary success-goal, he should
have time and money available for further study if a professional man,
money for clothes, entertaining, household furniture, and an automobile,
for purposes of presenting a "front" in any event; at this time when his
career is in its initial and hence its crucial stage, the presence of the child
represents a diversion of energy and funds, so long, of course, as the career
remains his primary goal. A certain degree of ambivalence directed toward the child is inevitable. Not the depth, but the present height of
the middle-class birth-rate is the noteworthy phenomenon, indicating an
amazing vitality of the old rural-familistic values which find little support in modern social structure.

With the advancing individuation of modern society, not only has
individual success become a supreme value, but also individual, hedonistic
enjoyment. The child again presents an interference with most of the recreation available to the middle-class father, for whether commercialized
(movies, sports events, plays) or social (golf, bridge, tennis, dinner
parties), these are designed not for family-wide participation, but individual
or couple participation.

In conjunction with the above factors, the growing middle-class emphasis upon "scientific child care"[16] and the child's higher education
further increase the father's duties and obligations, while his rights steadily

diminish. What emerges from his total situation is an ambivalence toward his child which is more or less widespread, though very rarely admitted, even with confidantes.[17] Finally, children interfere with the companion and partner roles of husband and wife, which are more and more displacing the traditional patriarchal and housewife-and-mother roles.[18]

And how about the mother? She enters marriage and perhaps bears a child with no definite role and series of functions, as formerly. Her old role within the patriarchal family, with its many functions, its economic and emotional security, its round of community participations, is lost, but no well-defined role has taken its place. She feels inferior to men because comparatively she has been and is more restricted.[19] If she works after marriage she faces sex discrimination on the job and perhaps her husband's criticism if his traditional role of bread-winner is important to him.

Half-seriously she prepared for a career prior to marriage, half-seriously because a career is regarded by most middle-class girls as insurance against the grim possibility they will not be married; through a "good" marriage (the folk phrase "she married well" refers not to personality adjustment but to the bank balance and career prospects of the husband) the middle-class girl attains far more status than is possible through a career of her own. But the period of phantasy dalliance with a career, or an embarkation upon one, leaves her ill-fitted for the drudgery of housecleaning, diapers, and the preparation of meals. The freedom which the urban apartment and modern household devices have brought the middle-class housewife has been commonly misinterpreted as well as exaggerated. While the Victorian housewife had more work to do, that work was part of a well-integrated system of household and community activities. While the modern middle-class housewife has more leisure-time than either her mother or grandmother, she must still work at a number of household jobs for which she has not been trained, which are usually not an essential part of her value-system, and which are isolated from her social activities. One sociologist has expressed this dilemma facetiously: half her working day is spent doing something she does not like, the rest is spent thinking up ways of getting even with her husband. The resulting boredom frequently leads to a period of indecision early in the marriage over whether to have children or resume the career. This internal conflict has been well expressed by Thompson:

> In the present economic situation in the United States increase of population is not desired. The fact that small families are the rule is one of the factors driving women out of the home. Now that they are not in the home a kind of vicious circle is formed, for it is no longer convenient to be occupied in the home by one or two children. Much conflict centers here, for it is one of the problems of the culture which as yet has no generally satisfactory solution. Individual women have worked out ways

of having both children and a career, but most women still do one or the other; and in either case there are regrets and often neurotic discontent . . . the problem is not solved by going to the other extreme and trying to prove one's adequacy by having a child or two. The women of past generations had no choice but to bear children. Since their lives were organized around this concept of duty, they seldom became aware of dislike of the situation. . . . Nowadays, when women have a choice, the illusion is to the effect that unwanted children are less common, but women still from neurotic compulsion bear children they cannot love.[20]

And so it is inevitable that the child shall be viewed with some degree of ambivalence by both father and mother, for he represents a direct interference with most of the dominant values and compulsions of the modern middle class: career, social and economic success, hedonistic enjoyment. There is some doubt that under modern middle-class conditions, children automatically bring husband and wife closer together.[21]

To return to the consideration of the middle-class child. Personality absorption takes place against a background of parental ambivalence. The mother has little to do, in or out of the home; she is her single child's sole companion.[22] Modern "scientific child care" enforces a constant supervision and diffused worrying over the child's health, eating spinach, and ego-development; this is complicated by the fact that much energy is spent forcing early walking, toilet-training, talking, because in an intensively competitive milieu middle-class parents from the day of birth on are constantly comparing their own child's development with that of the neighbors' children. The child must also be constantly guarded from the danger of contacting various electrical gadgets and from kicking valuable furniture. The middle-class child's discovery that the living-room furniture is more important to his mother than his impulse to crawl over it, unquestionably finds a place in the background of the etiology of a certain type of neurosis, however absurd it may appear.

Under constant supervision, with limited play-area in a house touching other homes on all sides, or in an apartment, and lacking companions, the child's physiological expansiveness, fed by his boredom, persists in getting him into trouble: screaming, running around the apartment, upsetting daddy's shaving mug, rending teddy-bear in two, emptying his milk on the rug to observe what pattern will be formed. This "trouble" is all a matter of definition. Similar behavior, in modified form, would not be interpreted in primitive society as "trouble," and neither would it be by Polish parents in the community above described.

Already the parents have made "love" of supreme importance in their relation to the child, theirs for him and his for them, partly because of the love-complex of our time, which is particularly ramified within the middle class,[23] and partly as a compensation for the many sacrifices they have made for the child, long debated before and after its arrival. *The child's need for love is experienced precisely because he has been condi-*

tioned to need it. That the need is biological seems unlikely.[24] Now, the more ambivalent the parents are toward the child, the more seriously is the "trouble" he causes them interpreted. He should not act in such a way because of the sacrifices they have made in his behalf, and the least he can do is show his gratitude by "loving" them in turn, i.e., keeping out of "trouble." When the trouble inevitably occurs, the most effective punishment imaginable is the threat to withdraw their love from him. He "needs" that love because his personality has been absorbed by these two persons, because he has been conditioned to have a slavish-emotional dependence upon them. Not the need for parental love, but the constant threat of its withdrawal after the child has been conditioned to the need, lies at the root of the most characteristic modern neurosis. Mamma won't like you if you don't eat your spinach, or stop dribbling your milk, or get down from that davenport. To the extent that a child's personality has been absorbed, he will be thrown into a panic by this sort of treatment and develop guilt-feelings to help prevent himself from getting into further trouble. In such a child, a disapproving glance may produce more terror than a twenty-minute lashing in little Stanislaus Wojcik.

The threat of love-withdrawal is usually the mother's technique for controlling the child. At first the father may threaten to withdraw love, but as the child grows older the father finds a more subtle control—the expression of disapproval. The child is limited to his parents for modeling his behavior. While very young, he wants to set the table and sweep the floor "like mummy." In a few years standards of manly conduct are imposed and he wants to do things "like daddy." The father now controls him through the child's new self-conception, and it is not so much the use of "authority" as threatening the child's self-respect.[25] The child is not a person who amounts to very much, how does he ever expect to get along when he gets old enough to go to school, or join the Boy Scouts, or go to college, or get a job? Again, to the extent that the child's personality has been absorbed, he will be made to feel small, insignificant, unworthy. And, feeling absorbed, caught, and helpless, he must propitiate these combined god-monsters that he needs so desperately. Hence anxiety, guilt-feelings, the sense of inferiority; seek security at all costs, for he is living alone and afraid in a world he never made.[26]

As for authority, its exercise generates neurotic symptoms only under two conditions, both of which must be present; close identification of the child with at least one parent; the effective blocking-off of all avenues of authority-avoidance for twenty-four hours of the day. Neither of these conditions is met in the Polish homes described, and thus while the authority wielded by Polish parents is far more "irrational" (as defined by Fromm) than that likely to be encountered in many middle-class homes, neuroses are not developed. Indeed, it seems unlikely that Fromm's differentiation between rational and irrational authority has much psychological relevance. The child is hardly in a position to understand when authority is ". . . based on the competency of the person in authority to function properly with respect to the task of guidance he has to perform . . ."[27] and when it is ". . . based on the power which the authority has over those subjected to it and on the fear and awe with which the latter reciprocate."[28] Perhaps the Polish children do not experience irrational authority exactly as defined by Fromm, for while they fear parental authority, they also are hostile toward and contemptuous of their parents and thus are not in awe of them. Nevertheless, the important differentiation is not between rational and irrational authority but the extent to which any parental authority succeeds in absorbing the child's personality, which is itself dependent upon factors other than the imposition of arbitrary authority.

Yet when we have used the term "personality absorption" we have not by any means explained a neurosis etiology. The personality of the middle-class girl of the late nineteenth century was "absorbed" by her parents, she was subjected to the demands of "love" and unquestioning obedience, at least ideally; nevertheless, the rate of neurosis under those conditions was probably not too high, as nearly as can be judged at this later date. Why? Because she was not faced with inconsistent expectations of conduct on the part of others and herself. Because love and obedience were integrated within a role which changed relatively slightly from childhood into adolescence, courtship, and finally into marriage. In other words, her initial goals and self-conceptions were constantly re-enforced with each new life experience.

The modern middle-class child on the other hand, particularly the boy, who has found surcease from anxiety and guilt by blind obedience and "love" for his parents, is not allowed to stabilize his relationships with others on that basis. His play-group, which may be denied him until he has reached school age, makes him feel a certain shame and inadequacy in attempting to approach its members with familiar techniques.[29] He also early discovers that he is involved in competition with others, as an individual with his contemporaries, and as a representative of his family unit with other families.

If the abstraction "ours is a competitive society" is translated into terms of what happens to the child born to modern middle-class parents, it becomes quite relevant to the present discussion. Before the child has developed a real self-awareness he becomes part of a process of invidious comparison with other families: he uttered his first word two months earlier than the Jones' boy; he weighed so many pounds at the end of his first year. At Sunday School he received the Bible for perfect attendance; at public school his grades in arithmetic were higher than two-thirds of the other members of the class. He may take piano lessons in view of the day when Mrs. Smythe's pupils will be on public exhibition before the parents of the neighborhood. Everything he accomplishes or fails to accomplish becomes an inevitable part of the family's attempt to maintain or improve its standing in the community.

But effective competition demands a certain degree of independence, firmness of purpose, perhaps aggressiveness. Even for the "normal" middle-class child, the transition from submission to some degree of independent behavior is made difficult.[30] And for the child whose personality has been absorbed, an especially exacerbated conflict arises. He is expected to "do things," to accomplish, perhaps to lead in some endeavor, like other children, but his earliest social conditioning was dependence, submission, inferiority; his accomplishments, if any, are on a god-scale—in phantasy. He is desperately attempting to stabilize all later relationships on the basis of his earliest conditioning. Any pressure to compete only exaggerates his anxiety, guilt, and feelings of inadequacy. Life in the modern middle-class home insures that he shall feel that pressure.

There are, then, three elements in the etiology of what has been called the most characteristic neurosis of modern society; personality absorption; the reiterated threat to withdraw a love which has been made of paramount importance; a conflict between the resulting initial adjustment of submissive propitiation and the later assumption of goals of achievement and roles of independent action.

The child is not able to establish an integrated self-conception. Propitiation has meant obedience and "love" for the parents, leading to a compulsive repression of self-will. But he soon discovers that propitiation, in the sense of meeting new parental expectancies, means exhibiting independence, self-assertiveness, aggressiveness, *outside* the home. The father, as the child's mediator of the outside male world, rather than the mother, makes this demand uncompromisingly which may, incidentally, be one of the unsuspected sources of the so-called Oedipus complex. This seems more than likely since male neurotics often recall facing the father's ridicule of their fumbling efforts to meet the father's expectations of "manly" conduct.

With the new conflicting expectations, on the part of parents and contemporaries, the child's anxiety reaches new heights, a double set of guilt-feelings appear where previously there was only one: at first he felt guilty only if he failed to love and obey, and this guilt could be assuaged by the propitiation of submission; now, however, the god-monsters will be appeased only by a combination of submission in his role of child-in-family and assertiveness in his play-group, school-pupil, and other roles enacted outside of home. An integration of these conflicting roles is impossible. His conception of himself becomes one of abject failure. Any striving is painful for it violates the initial submissive adjustment. But he feels equally guilty for not making the effort to achieve. This is a key to much of his contradictory and self-blocking behavior: his desire to be the last man in the last regiment and his desire to conquer the world; his demand that everyone shall love him, and his settled conviction that no one could love a person as base as he; his inability to erect a hierarchy of values; his endless debate over the value of his own goals. He is damned if he does and damned if he doesn't. He is embraced by a psychological Iron Maiden: any lunge forward or backward only impales him more securely on the spikes.

46 *Pseudo-Mutuality in the Family Relations of Schizophrenics*

LYMAN C. WYNNE, IRVING M. RYCKOFF,

JULIANA DAY, and STANLEY I. HIRSCH

Many of the family processes significant for personality development are subtle, shift rapidly, and are thus difficult to observe. Dr. Wynne and his co-workers brought whole families into treatment and were able to study them very intensively. A quality they found characteristic of families in which one member was schizophrenic was pseudo-mutuality. This is a type of integration of the family in which an illusion of a well-integrated state is preserved even when that state is not supported by the emotional structures of the members. The preservation of such an illusion puts strains upon individual personalities. If the strains are severe and persistent enough this can, the authors hypothesize, contribute to the development of severe personality disturbance.

The purpose of this paper is to develop a psychodynamic interpretation of schizophrenia that takes into conceptual account the social organization of the family as a whole. We shall formulate a series of concepts and hypotheses applicable to various phases of schizophrenic processes—prepsychotic, acute, and chronic—in which we shall focus particularly upon the relevance of family relations to these processes.

In a sense, this has become a preliminary statement of a theory of schizophrenia, not by any means a theory attempting to account systematically for all schizophrenic phenomena, but, rather, a search for a coherent viewpoint about certain features of schizophrenia. We assume that other factors not included in this formulation may well combine on several levels of organization at various stages in the pathogenesis of schizophrenia, or the group of schizophrenias. In the present formulation we are content

Reprinted by special permission of the William Alanson White Psychiatric Foundation, Inc., from *Psychiatry*, XXI (May, 1958), 205–20, with the kind permission of Dr. Wynne and the publisher.

to hypothesize that those considerations which we do specify can make a significant contribution to the form taken by schizophrenic illness.

The work reported here is part of a long-range research program on the family setting of schizophrenic patients, begun in 1954 at the National Institute of Mental Health. In this program, a case is regarded as consisting of an entire family unit, including both parents and offspring. During the first phase of the program the schizophrenic patient received intensive psychotherapy in the hospital, parents were seen twice weekly on an out-patient basis by different psychiatrists or a psychiatric social worker, and data from other family members, as well as from the nursing staff and the ward administrator, were included in the reconstruction of family patterns.

We have used this kind of psychotherapeutic and observational study of the first group of families to generate the working hypotheses of this paper. Most of the clinical examples which we shall cite are drawn from work with four families, but some of the observations have been obtained from other families studied less thoroughly.

Our thinking thus far has mainly centered on schizophrenic illness in which the onset of psychosis occurred acutely in late adolescence or young adulthood, not in simple schizophrenia or "process" schizophrenia. The specification of the range of cases to which the present hypotheses apply is a problem of current and future research. Thus, our clinical examples are included for illustration and clarification, not for statistical verification.

The Concept of Pseudo-Mutuality

Let us first try to make explicit certain of our basic assumptions or postulates. We assume that movement into relation with other human beings is a fundamental principle or "need" of human existence. To restate this in psychoanalytic terminology, man is inherently object-related. For our present purposes, the striving for relatedness to other human beings may be regarded either as a primary,[1] or as an early and essential, although perhaps secondary, feature of the human situation.

Another key postulate for the formulation which follows is that every human being strives consciously and unconsciously, in a lifelong process, to develop a sense of personal identity. The sense of identity consists of those self-representations, explicit and implicit, which give continuity and coherence to experience despite a constant flux of inner and outer stimuli. Identity processes can be regarded as those ego functions through which the self is perceptually differentiated from objects. As Erikson points out, processes initially taking the form of what has been conceptualized as introjection and projection pave the way for multiple identifications, which are selectively repudiated, assimilated, and synthesized into the new configuration of identity.[2]

We consider that the universal necessity for dealing with *both* the problems of relation and identity[3] leads to three main "solutions." These three resultant forms of relatedness, or complementarity, are mutuality, non-mutuality, and pseudo-mutuality. Pseudo-mutuality is a miscarried "solution" of widespread occurrence. We shall hypothesize that this kind of relatedness, in an especially intense and enduring form, contributes significantly to the family experience of people who later, if other factors are also present, develop acute schizophrenic episodes.

Pseudo-mutuality refers to a quality of relatedness with several ingredients. Each person brings into the relation a primary investment in maintaining a *sense* of relation.[4] His need and wish for this particular relation is especially strong for one or more of a variety of possible reasons, such as, in adults, isolation from, or failure in, other relations because of personality or situational difficulties; or in children, painful earlier experiences of separation-anxiety. The past experience of each person and the current circumstances of the relation lead to an effort to maintain the idea or feeling, even though this may be illusory, that one's own behavior and expectations mesh with the behavior and expectations of the other persons in the relation.

Clearly, all interpersonal relations that persist are structured in terms of some kind of complementarity or fitting together. However, in describing pseudo-mutuality, we are emphasizing a predominant absorption in fitting together, at the expense of the differentiation of the identities of the persons in the relation. In contrast, each person brings to relations of genuine mutuality a sense of his own meaningful, positively-valued identity, and, out of experience or participation together, mutual recognition of identity develops, including a growing recognition of each other's potentialities and capacities.

With growth and situational changes, altered expectations inevitably come into any relation. Then, at least transient nonfulfillment of expectations—that is, non-complementarity—necessarily occurs. In pseudo-mutuality the subjective tension aroused by divergence or independence of expectations, including the open affirmation of a sense of personal identity, is experienced as not merely disrupting that particular transaction but as possibly demolishing the entire relation.

The alternative outcome is overlooked or cannot be awaited: that the recognition and exploration of difference may lead to an expanded or deepened, although altered, basis for the relation. Genuine mutuality, unlike pseudo-mutuality, not only tolerates divergence of self-interests but thrives upon the recognition of such natural and inevitable divergence. In terms of role theory, a relation of mutuality is experienced as having a larger context than a particular role so that particular items of role non-complementarity can occur as a stimulus rather than as a disruption to the relation as a whole.

In pseudo-mutuality, emotional investment is directed more toward maintaining the *sense* of reciprocal fulfillment of expectations than toward accurately perceiving changing expectations. Thus, the new expectations are left unexplored, and the old expectations and roles, even though outgrown and inappropriate in one sense, continue to serve as the structure for the relation.

The relation which persists can then neither be given up, except under very special or dire circumstances, nor be allowed to develop or expand. It is highly invested, often intensely charged emotionally, but at the same time constricts growth and impoverishes any sort of freshness of interpersonal experience. Ambivalence is inevitable in such relations that have the appearance of offering much on one level that is not confirmed on other levels. Without mutual perception and recognition of the identity of each person appropriate to the current life situation, the continuing relation increasingly becomes subjectively empty, barren, and stifling. Positive aspects of the relation cannot be explored and expanded; what outside observers might regard as coercive or manipulative negative aspects are interpreted *within* the relation as simply part of the effort to dovetail more fully with one another.

In short, the pseudo-mutual relation involves a characteristic dilemma: divergence is perceived as leading to disruption of the relation and therefore must be avoided; but if divergence is avoided, growth of the relation is impossible.

Clearly, many interpersonal relations are not characterized by either mutuality or pseudo-mutuality. The interchange of customer and sales clerk, for example, does not ordinarily involve, beyond the purchase of merchandise, a strong investment in excluding non-complementarity or in exploring what the relation has to offer either person. Such transactions, statistically frequent and generally quite highly institutionalized in form, do have an integration of reciprocal or complementary expectations, but this is *non-mutual* complementarity. Non-mutuality is usually role-limited; it is, applying Parsons' terms, functionally specific for a particular role rather than functionally diffuse for the relation.[5]

Non-mutual complementarity often evolves, especially if a relation persists in duration or heightens in significance to the participants, in the direction of either mutuality or pseudo-mutuality. For example, a customer and clerk who linger on, anxious about non-complementarity and hesitant to admit openly to each other that no sale is in prospect, become engaged in a mild form of pseudo-mutuality. Finally, some lame excuse about "coming back later" may be offered, but here the social context is strikingly different from the usual family setting. In family relations the persisting or recurrent necessity of dealing with the relations in some way or other may bring either richer possibilities of mutuality or more complex mechanisms for maintaining pseudo-mutuality.[6]

Let us now state more explicitly our first main hypothesis about the family relations of potential schizophrenics:

Hypothesis 1.—Within the families of persons who later develop acute schizophrenic episodes, those relations which are openly acknowledged as acceptable have a quality of intense and enduring pseudo-mutuality.

As we have already implied, pseudo-mutuality is not unique to the relations of schizophrenics but provides one kind of continuum between schizophrenic and other modes of relating. Hence, we do not mean to imply in this first hypothesis that pseudo-mutuality *in itself* is productive of schizophrenia, but we do hypothesize that it is a major feature of the kind of setting in which reactive schizophrenia develops when other factors are also present.

A further immediate qualification should be noted: In specifying that the pseudo-mutuality applies only to that part of the family social organization which is openly acknowledged, we are implying that this part of the family structure may be very sharply split off from other parts of the family organization which are not so acknowledged. The splitting off of these persons or roles that are not involved in the pseudo-mutuality may, as we shall indicate in discussing shared familial mechanisms, be highly functional for the family organization as a whole, even though these persons or roles may be consciously depreciated or ostracized.

We are, let us emphasize, still speaking of the family social organization before acute schizophrenic episodes have occurred. In these families, the predominant prepsychotic picture is a fixed organization of a limited number of engulfing roles. While the roles existing in the over-all family social organization tend to remain fixed, the particular persons who enact these roles may vary. Thus, there may be considerable competition and fluidity about who takes the role of the most dependent and helpless family member; the role structure may remain unchanged as child, mother, and father successively take this role.

> For example, in one family we have studied, the mother and one daughter maintained the pseudo-mutuality that the whole family *overtly* agreed was proper and desirable. The mother maintained a highly controlled, placid exterior, making a well-mannered social presentation to the outside world, and one of the daughters, from birth, was a model of "goodness" and of placid, quiet, completely conforming behavior that "never needed correction." In contrast, the father and the other daughter took roles which they themselves overtly deplored and which they felt did not represent the pseudo-mutual standards they too desired for the family.
>
> The father was expected by everyone in the family to take a domineering role punctuated with marked irritability and fiery temper outbursts, and one of the daughters was accepted as "wild," rebellious, and insolent since early childhood. During the course of psychotherapy with the mother, it became apparent that she was struggling to keep very similar "wild" impulses in herself in check; these impulses had been disturbingly displayed during her own adolescence. In late adolescence the "wild"

daughter became passive, quiet, and dutiful, and, in a sense, exchanged roles with her "good" sister who erupted with violently hostile rebellion in an acute schizophrenic episode. The family role structure as a whole thus remained essentially unchanged.

Such a family role structure may be already forming in the fantasy life of the parents before the birth of a child, who sometimes is expected to fill some kind of void in a parent's life. Lewis B. Hill has noted a number of instances in which the expected role of the child in the family was symbolically represented in the choice of name for the child. In later life the child never seemed to emerge from this early role assignment.[7]

While early expectations and role assignments occur in non-schizophrenic families, we feel that there is a difference in the rigidity of the family role structure. Normally, this structure both affects the personality development of the offspring and is reworked and modified, more or less continually, in accord with the changing needs and expectations of the family members toward each other. With pseudo-mutuality, however, expressions of the changing or emerging needs of family members are not reflected in changes in the role structure of the family. In schizophrenic family organization, the role structure may not be reshaped even in the face of such major characteristics as the sex, age, and degree of passivity or aggressiveness of the person. Depending upon the fit between native characteristics and the rigid family structure, the psychological experiences of the family members will vary.

From the observational standpoint, family pseudo-mutuality shows certain characteristics which can be readily noted: (1) A persistent sameness of the role structure of the family, despite physical and situational alterations in the life circumstances of the family members, and despite changes in what is going on and being experienced in family life. (2) An insistence on the desirability and appropriateness of this role structure. (3) Evidence of intense concern over possible divergence or independence from this role structure. (4) An absence of spontaneity, novelty, humor, and zest in participation together.

We are hypothesizing that non-complementarity is a more intense and enduring threat in the families of schizophrenics than it is in other families in which pseudo-mutuality may also appear. The threat to the established family role structure from independent or aggressive behavior is experienced as an impending disaster, often crystallized into specific anxieties. In one family with whom we have worked, open aggression between the family members was expected to produce a cerebral hemorrhage in the mother and a heart attack in the father. In instances where serious depression in a family member has previously occurred, a recurrence may be expected if one member makes moves toward psychological independence.

The ever-present menace of non-complementarity within these families leads to pseudo-mutuality as a way of life. Only a major crisis, such as an acute schizophrenic episode, is then experienced within the family as truly altering the meaning of family relations, and even then, as we shall note later, reinterpretation can quickly alter the meaning of the episode.

The concept of degrees of intensity and persistence of pseudo-mutuality suggests a dimension common to both schizophrenic and non-schizophrenic relations. The common element in this dimension is the presence of some degree of pseudo-mutuality. However, we feel that the differences in intensity and persistence are significant and considerable. Even more important are the differences in the kind and quality of shared mechanisms by which the pseudo-mutuality is maintained.[8]

Shared Mechanisms for Maintaining Pseudo-Mutuality

Hypothesis 2.—In the families of potential schizophrenics, the intensity and duration of pseudo-mutuality has led to the development of a particular variety of shared family mechanisms by which deviations from the family role structure are excluded from recognition or are delusionally reinterpreted. These shared mechanisms act at a primitive level in preventing the articulation and selection of any meanings that might enable the individual family member to differentiate his personal identity either within or outside of the family role structure. Those dawning perceptions and incipient communications which might lead to an articulation of divergent expectations, interests, or individuality are, instead, diffused, doubled, blurred, or distorted.

Here we wish to make clear that we are not simply referring to the concealment or masking of information or to direct efforts to coerce or elicit an attitude of a particular kind. These are characteristic "normal" and neurotic mechanisms for maintaining or restoring pseudo-mutuality, which, of course, are likely to occur in the families of schizophrenics in addition to the more specifically schizophrenic mechanisms. The willfulness and temper tantrums of the hysteric can be regarded as ways of forcibly inducing and defending an illusion of relation. Similarly, the substitutive, undoing, and isolating defenses of the obsessional dissociate and ward off the experience of non-complementarity. However, in characteristic schizophrenic relations, perceptual and communicative capacity is involved in an earlier and more primitive way. The problem is a more primary failure of the ego in articulating the meaning of experience and participation, not so much a defense by the ego against the conscious recognition of particular meanings.

In ordinary relations, contradictory or variant expectations are frequently communicated, often by differences between the content of verbalization and the setting or style of communication. Normally, however, shared cultural mechanisms and codes facilitate the selection of those aspects of the over-all communication to which attention will be paid. In contrast, in characteristically schizophrenic relations, when both of a pair of contradictory expectations are communicated, the shared mechanisms facilitate a *failure* in selection of meaning.[9] In the family relations of potential schizophrenics, it is not simply that divergence is kept out of awareness but rather that the discriminative perception of those events which might specifically constitute divergence is aborted and blurred. Jointly recognized divergence is, thus, never openly risked, but neither is the pervasive and diffuse danger of being divergent ever absent.

In the prepsychotic life of acute schizophrenics, we are hypothesizing that these shared family mechanisms serve to mitigate the full impact of chaotic, empty, and frightening experience by providing a role structure in which the person can pseudo-mutually exist without having developed a valued and meaningful sense of identity or its age-appropriate precursors. However, these shared mechanisms at the same time contribute to a failure by the potential schizophrenic in learning to discriminate or value who he is or where he is, except in terms of a blurred place in the family role structure. This difficulty of the potential schizophrenic in articulating a differentiation of himself from the family role structure means that the family role structure is experienced as all encompassing.

Normally, in this culture, the child's experiences are with persons who themselves participate in roles and relations outside as well as within the nuclear family. Certain of the needs and expectations of family members cannot normally be fulfilled within the nuclear family, necessitating a meaningful participation in the larger society, and parents normally anticipate and facilitate such expansion of the growing child's experiences beyond the nuclear family. The normal pattern or organization of family roles and relations therefore constitutes a differentiated subsystem of a society rather than a self-sufficient, complete social system.[10]

In contrast, when there is a continual effort in family relations to maintain pseudo-mutuality, the family members try to act as if the family could be a truly self-sufficient social system with a completely encircling boundary. Schizophrenic family members, in failing to articulate a differentiation of family member from family role structure, tend to shift and obscure the idea of the family boundaries. The unstable but continuous boundary, with no recognizable openings, surrounding the schizophrenic family system, stretches to include that which can be interpreted as complementary and contracts to extrude that which is interpreted as non-complementary. This continuous but elastic boundary we have called the rubber fence. This metaphor is a way of summarizing the effects of family pseudo-mutuality and the reinforcing shared family mechanisms in establishing a situation in which the person feels that he cannot trust his own perceptions and from which there seems no escape. We hasten to stress that we do not regard the potential schizophrenic as simply a passive victim of his family environment; in a subsequent section we shall bring up the active investment of the potential schizophrenic in helping to create and maintain this family structure.

While we shall not attempt to make a complete inventory of the mechanisms used in varying degrees to maintain this omnipresent pseudo-mutuality, some of them are illustrated by the following clinical examples. A very general kind of mechanism, subsuming some of the others to be described, is the creation of a pervasive familial subculture of myths, legends, and ideology which stress the catastrophic consequences of openly recognized divergence from the fixed family role structure. We have already mentioned that even minor divergence may be experienced as threatening to precipitate, for example, a heart attack. Family legends about fury and violence may be pervasive reminders of the supposed consequences of divergence.

Sometimes the subcultural ideology involves a desperate preoccupation with harmony in all relations within the family. As one mother again and again insisted, and the father echoed:

> We are all peaceful. I like peace even if I have to kill someone to get it. . . . A more normal, happy kid would be hard to find. I was pleased with my child! I was pleased with my husband! I was pleased with my life. I have *always* been pleased! We have had 25 years of the happiest married life and of being a father and mother.

Among the simplest of the family mechanisms we have studied is a bland, indiscriminate, but determined approval of the person's activities and interests, without differentiating whether they are actually incompatible with the family code of values. In some cases, the sweeping parental approval of any of the child's behavior is verbalized as respect for self-determination, "freedom," and family "democracy," and is typified by the oft-repeated response of one set of parents, "We only want you to do what you want to do." The open recognition of differences then becomes literally impossible, except by a truly violent, disruptive move, which the schizophrenic break seems to represent.

Often *all* of the behavior of the preschizophrenic child is perceived and approved by the parents as "good," in the sense of fulfilling the parental expectations. For example, one mother said about the prepsychotic relation with her daughter: "There were never any problems because she always knew what was right without being told." A father said about his daughter's childhood: "We didn't need to build a fence around our lot. It was as if there was an invisible line beyond which she knew she should not go."

Indiscriminate approval can be regarded as a mechanism by which a role important in the family can be maintained in the face of real and changing characteristics of the person assigned the role. Of course, when a child's "innate" characteristics initially happen to be attuned to a particular family role, it seems likely that the role will be more often taken by this child than by another sibling or a parent. Hence, when a child has been regarded as invariably "good" or docile, this parental report may represent a combination of actual "innate" docility, a stereotyped role assignment, and the child's learned skill in filling this stereotyped role assignment.

In one instance we had the opportunity, by comparing the parental report with the son's letters, to realize how undiscriminating was the evaluation of the son that continued right up to the time of his hospitalization for catatonic mutism. In order to document for us that "nothing had changed," the parents showed us the correspondence from him during the four months prior to hospitalization. These letters actually portrayed extremely vividly the marked changes in the son, which the parents were unable to recognize even when the letters were discussed with them directly.

At the beginning of his army experience, the son actively expressed in his letters many G.I. gripes and even made a "big fuss up the rank" to the lieutenant over being issued badly fitting shoes. Increasingly, however, he repetitively described a marked withdrawal to his bunk. The following are representative excerpts from his letters during the fourth month:

> Another weekend shot. Got off about seven yesterday threw my stuff from bag into footlocker made the bed and then called you. Afterwards came back and went to bed.
>
> Many of these guys hop out for town or movie first thing but would rather sleep.
>
> Haven't even dressed today [Sunday, 7 P.M.] Got up smoked one ate some apricots and got some out now. Went back till 2:00 then took shower and washed my boots and spent rest time rolling socks and arranging footlocker. Have still to read part of the papers and polish my boots. Spent some time rubbing crap off locker and shelves.
>
> Had today off as its Holiday [Monday, February 22] and have been loafing since Saturday. Had a parade, then got off at 9:30 A.M. Went to bed and slept right through till Sunday morning. Skipped Sat. lunch and dinner and Sun. breakfast and lunch. Did make supper though Sunday. Haven't written as just go to bed when get off.
>
> Been laying in bed all day and that's a good weekend. . . . Have yet to take a shower and shave but seems quite an effort could sack in for another day or three anyway. Not much to write as have been doing nothing but sleeping. Read the papers and ate a can of sardines and that's about it. After talked to you came back and also slept. Really can't think of anything to write just went and got some water but that doesn't seem to make much more to write. Was going to call tonight but decided to wait until later in the week. Lots of Love.

Yet the following is how the mother perceived her son's participation and experience before the parents were notified he had been hospitalized:

> Eddie always had a good time. He was always very active and was always a very happy and normal boy as far as we could see, and there was no suggestion of anything like this happening. That was why it was so

difficult for us to understand his illness. If he had been the kind of kid who wasn't friendly or active we might have been able to understand it. There wasn't a thing he missed out on.

Although indiscriminate approval can keep much behavior from being recognized as being disturbingly deviant, the intensity of anxiety about divergence may lead to contradictory scrutiny, judgment, and disapproval of the same behavior that has ostensibly been approved. Then, in order to maintain pseudo-mutuality, the contradiction itself, however blatant, may be reinterpreted or simply be blandly ignored.

> In one family, the parents of an adolescent only son, later to become schizophrenic, emphasized his right to decide privately, at 16, whether to get married or not. The parents, however, anxiously contacted his fiancée and filled her with questions and doubts until she became so perplexed and upset that she broke off the engagement. The parents remind the interviewer, as they state they did the boy, that they had left him entirely free to make his own decision. The boy seems to have made no complaint in the face of these two contradicting, mutually obscuring levels of communication, but, nine years later, he had never gone this far again in considering marriage.

A corollary to indiscriminate approval is secrecy, which results in the formula: *"That which cannot be approved will remain unknown."* Both mechanisms keep divergence from having a recognized and meaningful impact upon the family ideology and role structure. Each family member may be expected to conceal large areas of his experience and not open to communication with the others. Sometimes the expectations of secrecy are expressed in an exaggerated deference for what is labeled as privacy—that is, the invariable right of each family member to share only what he wishes.

Secrecy seems to be especially marked in schizophrenic family social organization for those roles which move in extrafamilial directions. Usually such roles and the personal attitudes and characteristics associated with them are kept dissociated from the rest of the family social organization. As an example, we have been impressed in these families with how unknown and foreign to the family are the personal characteristics which the father shows in his occupational role, even when he has been occupationally successful. Typically, the father collaborates with the other family members in acting as if the personal characteristics revealed by his occupational proficiencies do not exist.

Secrecy, however, like indiscriminate approval, may be simultaneously contradicted by its opposite. Driven by an anxious concern about the possible disruptive nature of concealed thoughts and interests, the family members may desperately attempt to anticipate, guess, or secretly investigate that which they simultaneously insist is inviolably private. The child is thus confronted—and the child comes to confront the parent—with simultaneous, contradictory expectations: to conceal large areas of his experience as private; to allow the intensive investigation of this same "private" experience. In addition, the contradiction itself, however obvious it may seem to be to an outside observer, is not recognized within the family.

> While emphasizing, vehemently, the right of their son to keep private his plans, wishes, and activities, the mother [of the same patient reported on above] engaged in an intensive encompassment of her son's experiences in the form of minute record-keeping, by means of which she was able to create a detailed, month-by-month report of her son's activities for his entire life. She spoke of her "files," in which she had all the original documents, and offered prepared duplicates of his school records, employment records, social security receipts, letters, and so on. It is perhaps not surprising, then, that this boy, two years prior to his overt psychotic breakdown, had transient paranoid ideas that he was being followed by detectives hired by his mother and that his best friend was spying on him at the mother's instigation.
>
> The father of another patient had major private objections to his daughter's interest in a foreign hospital attendant, but, unable to express his concern to her openly, he checked the mileage she used on the car and then calculated on a map whether she could have gone to his residence.

Such combinations of secrecy and investigation guard against any open recognition of differences or non-complementarity and also block any real clarification in the mind of either patient or parents as to when the family member is acceptably outside or independent of the family system.

As part of the exaggerated deference to "democracy" and "self-determination," there may be a tendency to formalize experiences that in less pathological families would be part of a free-flowing way of life. In one family, the parents instituted "Little-Boy Day" for their son during his younger years—a special day when he could choose the family's activity, such as going to the zoo or the movies. This was in response to his complaint that the grown-ups always did the deciding. However, this formalized mechanism for dealing with the complaint blocked any spontaneity in family participation, and pseudo-mutuality was heightened. In this family and in another, highly self-conscious "discussions," usually of such impersonal subjects as religion, sports, politics, and so on, were established as a carefully limited area for arguments. However heated they might become, such experiences were labeled in advance as not involving personal differences. Giving such a form to the experience helps eliminate possible areas of divergence and non-complementarity, while informality would leave room for the unexpected.

A common operation of these family systems is the use of intermediaries between the family members. Pseudo-mutuality may be more easily maintained and difference avoided if reciprocal expectations are communicated via the intermediaries. For example, whenever the parents of a hospitalized patient took their son out on pass, they wanted him to have a fresh shave beforehand. But, they said, he might refuse to go out if they took a stand on the shaving, and this would be too much of a risk. Hence, they asked the ward administrator to tell the attendant to tell their son to shave. When intermediaries participate in this way, the direct expectations within the family can be more easily blurred and the possible non-complementarity remain untested. In effect, intermediaries who fill such a role are incorporated into the family system temporarily; for a specific purpose the elastic boundaries have been stretched to include such persons, who are then not related to as separate identities.

> When the same patient was destroying a clock, radio, magazines, and food parcels that his parents brought to him, they felt that this behavior had nothing to do with them because they had left these objects with the nursing personnel to give to the patient. The nurses, feeling uncomfortable in this role and wishing to be free to deal with the patient in their own right, suggested that the parents deliver the parcels in person, even though they came at other than visiting hours. Immediately following this change in policy, the mother's anxiety increased, and, coincidence or not, her blood pressure suddenly rose so alarmingly that her family doctor forbade her from visiting.

Just as these nurse intermediaries who did not collaborate in helping to maintain the family pseudo-mutuality were extruded from the family system and were treated as outsiders thenceforth, so may members of the biological family be outside the rubber fence. In one family, the father was held responsible for a time for some of the patient's symptoms and felt ostracized in his own house. The threat of being cut off from family relations because of divergence was literally carried out.

Quite often, the family member labeled as schizophrenic is the one who is extruded from his family system. In some instances, prior to the onset of frank psychosis, the patient had been considered "peculiar" or the "black sheep" of the family, while in other cases, he was extruded from the overt family role structure only after hospitalization. In the conscious perceptions of the family members, all of the family non-complementarity is then localized in the one person who is overtly regarded as not fitting in. This person, unless he has achieved a sense of identity in his own right, shares with the rest of the family a negative valuation of himself and his role in the family, but everyone in the family will become very anxious if he disturbs the role structure by trying to abandon this role. From the observer's standpoint, the ostracized or scapegoated person thus takes an important covert family role in maintaining the pseudo-mutuality or surface complementarity of the rest of the family.

The problems within the family system can also be by-passed by focusing upon physical ailments or the schizophrenia itself as being responsible for upsetting "smooth" family relations. In effect, the schizophrenia is regarded as an intruder which is held accountable for interpersonal difficulties. It is then possible within the family to say that the patient "really means" to be agreeable, and his desperate efforts to be more direct, even though non-complementary, can be interpreted as not representing his intent.

> In one family, for example, the fact that the hospitalized son did not wear his glasses—he had smashed several pairs—was repeatedly interpreted by the parents as explanatory of the patient's negativism. He had begun voluntarily going to the recreation area until his parents heard about this change and took over his initiative by urging him to go. He stopped going immediately. His parents were puzzled, but concluded, even though he read newspapers in their presence, that he must be afraid of falling when walking without his glasses.
>
> At about the same time, the patient was returning his parents' letters to them unopened. His girl friend, who had become very much a part of the family system, also began writing to him, and he also forwarded these letters unopened to his mother. The mother was perplexed until she decided that he had not been able to read the address without his glasses. Thus, any interpersonal meaning of the son's action could remain unacknowledged.

Family pseudo-mutuality, as we have described it, does not require the physical presence of all members, since role expectations can be maintained at a distance. Thus geographical or situational changes, emphasized in the usual psychiatric social history, may not always be associated with significant changes in the underlying expectations or meanings of the person's family relations. Going away to college, for example, may be experienced as the continuation of an established role by a son who pleases his family by a particular kind of school achievement. In the case of one of our patients, the correspondence and telephone calls between her, when she was away at college, and her family provided very much the same degree and quality of communication for over a year as had occurred when she lived at home. Similarly, going into the army, moving to another city, even getting married and having children of one's own, may in some cases mean going through the motions of following social conventions as part of familial expectations, without a genuine sense of identity apart from the family system. In the hallucinations of one patient, she was still actively involved in establishing and warding off relations with her family members, all dead, in actuality, for many years.

Internalization of Family Role Structure

We take the view that, in the normal process of internalization, the over-all family role structure, together with the quality of relations and the shared subcultural mechanisms maintaining this system, is taken over into the child's personality structure. In psychoanalytic theory, the identifications with the parents and the internalization of parental codes are essential contributions to the quality of the child's ego and superego. This paper extends the more traditional view by emphasizing the significance of the internalization of the over-all family role structure.

We are using the term internalization to refer in a generalized way to the organized pattern of the *meanings* which external objects, events, and relations have acquired.[11] Thus, internalization includes the meanings a person finds attached to his position in the social structure of family and wider community. Also internalized are the ways of thinking and of deriving meaning, the points of anxiety, and the irrationality, confusion, and ambiguity that were expressed in the shared mechanisms of the family social organization.

Hypothesis 3.—The fragmentation of experience, the identity diffusion, the disturbed modes of perception and communication, and certain other characteristics of the acute reactive schizophrenic's personality structure are to a significant extent derived, by processes of internalization, from characteristics of the family social organization.

We have described how roles and role behavior in intense pseudo-mutual relations come to be largely dissociated from subjective experience. Such roles are not integrated into the functioning of an actively perceiving ego, but come to govern the person's behavior in an automatic, "reflex" fashion, having the quality of "going through the motions." These patterns of role behavior have been learned, are carried into new situations, and in a general sense are internalized into the personality, although they are not under the jurisdiction of an actively discriminating ego. In certain schizophrenics, the internalized family role structure and associated family subculture serve as a kind of primitive superego, which tends to determine behavior directly, without negotiation with an actively perceiving and discriminating ego.

The meaning of the self or of personal identity is buried in such a superego. It is only through experiencing the impact of non-complementarity and articulating its meaning that a perceiving ego begins to be differentiated with an identity of its own. However, the shared mechanisms operating in these families specifically interfere with the articulation of meanings that hint at non-complementarity. For a child who grows up and develops his perceptual capacities in a setting in which obvious contradictions are regarded as nonexistent, it seems reasonable to suppose that he may well come to regard his senses and emotional responses as a tenuous and unreliable guide to understanding the expectations he has of himself and others. Thus, modes of thinking, perceiving, and communicating built up in such a way render unavailable to the person the capacity to attach clear meanings to his own intrapsychic states, such as anger at the mother or disappointment. Instead, he may have a vague uneasiness, sometimes merging into panic. Under these conditions, the person becomes flooded with anxiety at precisely those moments when he is starting to articulate a meaningful indication of his individuality, in the same way that pseudo-mutual family relations became flooded with anxiety when non-complementarity threatened to emerge into shared recognition.

Individualized impulses, which are typically perceived as necessarily non-complementary in these family relations, are split off or dissociated from acknowledged family life by shared secrecy mechanisms. As we have noted, however, the same activity which, it is agreed, will be secret is simultaneously subject, by tacit agreement, to secret family investigation. We tentatively and metaphorically suggest that familial secrecy mechanisms have an internalized counterpart in the mechanisms of repression and dissociation and that the familial investigative mechanisms have a counterpart in anxious superego surveillance of that which has been dissociated. The result is a chronic, vague uneasiness about autistic experience that is constantly but obscurely re-exposed to awareness. The impulses and ideas of such autistic experience thus are neither clearly and fully dissociated nor sufficiently in the open to be directly confronted.[12] This situation, we feel, is the individual counterpart of the family patterns we have been describing.

Such processes, of course, can be expected to contribute to a marked constriction and impoverishment in ego functioning and development.[13] The potential schizophrenic, like other family members, tends to pick out in his perceptions that which can be seen as complementary and to exclude from his perceptions that which is seen as non-complementary. In the acute schizophrenic episode, the dissociation of non-complementarity breaks down and he becomes anxiously sensitive to the slightest hint of possible non-complementarity. This heightened sensitivity to a particular variety of expectations which are ferreted out in any and all situations cannot be regarded as genuine perceptiveness and imaginative capacity in any general sense. Imaginative capacity—the flexibility to discriminate, evaluate, and select meaning in a widely and freely ranging fashion—is closely related to what has been excessively condensed in the term "reality-testing."

Imaginative capacity of this sort is, clearly, not possible if there has been an internalization of a rubber fence beyond which one's experience may not wander without disaster. Instead, the characteristics of perception and thinking, whether stereotyped or amorphous, which occurred within the internalized rubber fence will be brought into all tasks and relations. The potential schizophrenic thus is particularly unprepared in ego skills and perceptions that would make possible the assumption of those roles, such as occupational and marital roles, which might be an expression of his personal identity, outside the family system of expectations, yet respected and valued by the family.

The formulation that we have been developing implies that, as internalization takes place, the child develops a reciprocal, active investment in maintaining the equilibrium of those family patterns which have contributed to the characteristics of his personality equilibrium. With various reinforcements or weakenings of his motivation arising from individual "constitutional" sources and from the effects of extra-familial experience, the potential schizophrenic typically develops considerable skill and an immense positive investment in fulfilling family complementarity and in saving the family as well as himself from the panic of dissolution. Indeed, the schizophrenic's ego identity often seems to consist of himself viewed as someone who takes care of the needs and expectations of his family or family-substitute. One preschizophrenic, even after a number of years of marriage, was frequently called at 11 or 12 o'clock at night by his parents to drive 15 miles to straighten out their quarrels. Later, he felt himself needed in a similar way by his wife, and, as he became overtly schizophrenic, he was filled with panic and suspicions that his usefulness to his wife had disappeared.

Acute Schizophrenic Episodes and Their Transition into Chronic States

The brittle and limited ego identity of the preschizophrenic, based upon an inner representation of the family system, is sorely strained in this culture as he approaches chronological adulthood. Through his own growth, the shift or loss of family figures and the exposure to new outside relations which are more seductive or coercive than earlier ones, there comes a time when he can no longer superimpose the family identity upon his ego identity. Erikson has described the resultant disorganization in terms of acute identity diffusion.[14] Acute schizophrenic panic and disorganization seem to represent an identity crisis in the face of overwhelming guilt and anxiety attendant upon moving out of a particular kind of family role structure. In the transition from the acute episode to a chronic state, pseudo-mutuality is re-established, usually at a greater psychological distance from family members, with an increase in guilt and anxiety over subsequent moves toward differentiation, and with heightened autism, loneliness, and emptiness of experience.

A more detailed example of such a sequence, in which an acute schizophrenic episode passed into a chronic catatonic state, may further show how some of these devices for maintaining family pseudo-mutuality operate.

The patient, a single man of 25, diagnosed as catatonic schizophrenic, was admitted to the hospital in a slowed-down state. He was largely mute with hospital personnel, but still somewhat responsive to visits from his parents and girl friend. During the first visit, the patient took his girl friend off to an empty recreation room and left his parents alone in his room. Later that day, the girl friend requested and was granted permission to visit the patient at a separate time from the parents. The parents, however, began intensive communication with the girl friend and induced her to visit the patient with them. During the next visit, the parents gave their encouragement to the patient and his girl friend's petting together in the patient's bedroom; the parents sat in the room with them, thumbing through magazines. When the necking became so heavy that the nursing staff intervened, the girl friend remarked to the nurse that she had wondered about it and had wanted to talk to the doctor about its advisability but had been told by the mother not to speak to the doctors about it.

The following is an excerpt from the transcript of a recorded interview with the mother about a parental visit a week later.

He had put the bolster up in front of him so he didn't see Jean at all, and all she saw of him was his feet, and I leaned over to him and said very quietly, "Eddie, have you thought of what you would like to have us get for you to give to Jean for Christmas?" Quietly, so she couldn't hear us. And he said, "I don't want to get her anything." And I said, "She'd feel very badly if you didn't." And he said loudly enough so you could hear him across the hall—I mean he wasn't hollering or anything, but he spoke right out and he said, "Unless I can buy my own Christmas presents and do my own Christmas shopping it's not Christmas as far as I'm concerned." He said, "This business of having everything done for you. You can't do anything for yourself." And then he was vulgar—it's the first time I've ever heard him talk like that—he said "You can't even—" he said, "as far as I'm concerned I can't even shit for myself." It was shocking for me—I mean I wasn't—I mean I was shocked at the fact that he felt the need to express himself that way, and I said, "Well, it's perfectly all right if you don't want me to. We won't do it. It's entirely up to you." . . . And a little while later I said to him, "Eddie," I said, "I believe the doctors out here—I just want to say that I can appreciate—we can all appreciate what you are going through and that it's a pretty tough time, and the doctors say that sometimes these things become pretty painful—not physically, but pretty painful to you mentally, and we do understand and appreciate that, and everybody around here does too." And he said, "Well, what do they want me to do?" And I said, "Well, I don't know what anybody wants you to do, Eddie, but everybody, regardless of what you think, they want you to do what you want to do. But I said that there are so many times that you don't express yourself, and if you don't tell us and if you don't tell the doctors here what you want, all we can do is kind of guess about what it is you want, unless you say definitely that you do or you don't. There isn't any way of anybody knowing what you want unless you let us know." And he said, "Well, what do they want me to do? What do I have to do to get well?" I said, "Well, the only thing that I could suggest that might help is to talk to them just like you are talking to me now. Tell them how you feel about things." And he said, "Why do I have to talk to them?" He said, "Are they God? Did they make me? Am I required to tell them my innermost feelings?" I started to say something and forgot what it was. Anyway, before I could say anything he said in a very controlled, and restrained, and courteous voice, as you would speak to an utter stranger on the streetcar, he said, "Would you please leave now." I said to him, "What did you say?" I couldn't believe my ears. He said, "I said, would you please leave now." And I said, "Eddie, you don't want me to go now. We've been looking forward to this visit all week, and I know that you have too." And he stood up and said, "Well, if you won't leave I will have to." He left the room and walked all the way down the corridor as far as he could possibly go . . . the very last door down there. So then we went outside.

This interchange signalled the onset of complete muteness and catatonia that continued for 13 months. It illustrates a serious disruption of the pseudo-mutuality which characterized the familial relations. The earlier background included an episode of violence on the part of the patient involving escaping from a hospital by scaling a ten-foot wall, threatening people in the vicinity with a knife, stealing a car, and finally being apprehended by the police in another city. The parents have never seen in this dramatic incident any expression of rage, but have attributed it solely to post electroshock confusion, specifically disclaiming this behavior as indicating a potential for rage within him. Thus the incident reported here occurs against a background of disruption and violence followed by withdrawal, passivity, and seeming submission to parental encompassment as an attempted restoration of earlier family relations.

In the incident cited, the parents clearly have taken over one of the few remaining areas of private experience and self-determination of the patient—his relation with his girl friend. This parental taking-over included being present during the sexual activity of the couple. The mother's whispered question, in front of the girl, about getting a present for him to give to her, was apparently the last straw, leading to an outburst of forcefully expressed resentment. The mother, although shocked, said this was "perfectly all right" and entirely up to him. Then, in a confusing denial of his explosive efforts to be direct in expressing his resentment, she suggests that his difficulty is in *not* expressing himself and, lastly, that the doctors would be the appropriate people to be the recipients of his feelings. This referral to the doctors is an attempt by the mother to heal the family breach by introducing outside persons into the picture. The patient is offended at this attempted deflection of his feeling to people who are unrelated to the immediate situation and asks, "Why do I have to talk to them?" It is additionally incredible and offensive since it violates the family code of keeping everything within the family. The patient seems to feel that his unprecedented effort to get his feelings across directly to his parents are hopeless, and he withdraws physically and psychologically.

However, his "polite" withdrawal is also his contribution to a restoration of pseudo-mutuality at a safer psychological distance. His own anxiety is thus reduced at the same time that he protects his parents from the intense anxiety which his continued open divergence would provoke in them. All three of the family members have demonstrated repeatedly in the past that they become anxious over any hint of disruption in their emotional attachment to each other; and both parents have frequently emphasized their vulnerability to cardiovascular disaster if they should become upset. In contrast to open divergence, the patient's subsequent muteness lends itself readily to a variety of interpretations, either disturbing or comforting, and hence this is a particularly appropriate vehicle for the expression of ambivalence.

During the following weeks and months the whole family set up a highly stable form of pseudo-mutuality. The incident described is re-interpreted by the parents: They developed the retrospective thesis that his withdrawal was out of anger at the nursing staff for intervening with the necking during the visit of the week before and that the whole incident had nothing whatsoever to do with them. They thus could quite comfort-ably resume visiting him as he lay silent, unresponsive, immobile, and certainly not openly aggressive toward them. Through his "collaboration" by appearing as a passively helpless object of parental concern, the parents were able to become "good parents" again. The new pseudo-mutuality with the son as a chronic schizophrenic was thus only quan-titatively different from that which prevailed in the prepsychotic state.

So far, we have been considering the incident as illustrative of the cycle of breakdown of pseudo-mutuality followed by attempted restitution to a new version of the old pattern of relatedness. But the psychotic episode as a whole, including this present incident, also represents a mis-carried attempt at attaining individuation. The initial breakdown in the pseudo-mutuality was motivated by the patient's drive toward individua-tion, and his behavior in this incident illustrates his wish for independence which he succeeds in attaining, in some ways, only by withdrawal. Thus, what may be considered a breakdown of relations within the family is simultaneously the attainment of some individuation, albeit of a seriously distorted kind.

However, in families in which strivings toward a separate personal identity are regarded as a non-integrated, crazy, or chaotic experience, *each* member of the family—not only the patient—experiences frustration of his needs for achieving a sense of identity. The overt psychosis, then, may have a covert function of giving expression to the family's collective, although dissociated, desires for individuality. One of the covert family roles the patient takes in becoming overtly schizophrenic, thus, may be to allow other family members to achieve vicariously some measure of individuation.

In contrasting pseudo-mutual complementarity with mutual and non-mutual forms of complementarity, we have attempted a new extension of role theory which takes into account the quality of subjective experience of the person taking a role. In mutuality, the complementarity has a larger context; individuation and non-complementarity of particular expectations give rise to perceptual exploration and participation together, which expands and deepens the basis for the relation. Imaginative flexibility and perceptual accuracy are essential in mutuality, especially in the perception of non-complementary expectations that may create for a time an element of alienation within the relation. In pseudo-mutuality, the full impact of alienation and loneliness is avoided, but a sense of relation unsupported by accurate perception of the realities of participation becomes a hollow and empty experience. In non-mutual complementarity, there is neither a strenuous effort to save the relation by warding off the perception of non-complementarity, nor is there any great interest in exploration of the meanings each person may have to offer the other.

In the families of certain schizophrenics, we hypothesize that pseudo-mutuality takes an especially intense and enduring form, in which the family members strive for a sense of relation by trying to fit into the family role structure. The social organization in these families is shaped by a pervasive familial subculture of myths, legends, and ideology which stress the dire consequences of openly recognized divergence from a relatively limited number of fixed, engulfing family roles.

The shared, familial efforts to exclude from open recognition any evidences of non-complementarity within the pseudo-mutual relation become group mechanisms that help perpetuate the pseudo-mutuality. In the families of schizophrenics, these mechanisms act at a primitive level in preventing the articulation and selection of any meanings that might enable the individual family member to differentiate himself either within or outside of the family role structure. Family boundaries thus obscured are continuous but unstable, stretching, like a rubber fence, to include that which can be interpreted as complementary and contracting to extrude that which is interpreted as non-complementary.

Role-taking in these families has not been modified by the events of actual participation or personal experience, and thus the roles cannot be integrated into the functions of a discriminating ego or become a valued part of a synthesizing ego identity. Rather, we hypothesize, the family role structure is taken into the personality functioning of these persons as an archaic superego which determines behavior directly, without negotiation with an actively perceiving ego.

In the acute schizophrenic episode can be found representations of the breakdown of pseudo-mutuality, its attempted restoration, the attainment of a distorted kind of individuation, and the vicarious expression of the need of the other family members for individuation. The chronic state that follows can be regarded as a return to pseudo-mutuality at a greater distance, with symptoms that represent a more stable compromise between an expression of individuation and a failure at individuation, between acceptance of a particular family role and nonacceptance, between achievement of relation and disruption of relation.

47 *Schism and Skew in the Families of Schizophrenics*

THEODORE LIDZ, ALICE R. CORNELISON, STEPHEN FLECK, and DOROTHY TERRY

Dr. Lidz and his associates have also studied schizophrenics and their families in great detail. Like Wynne and his co-workers, the Yale group found that the type of integration that the family has is a critical factor in the maintenance, and probably in the development, of schizophrenia. In contrast to Wynne's formulation, Lidz locates the critical factor as the integration into the family patterns of serious divisions and distortions of reality. Normally these would be disruptive for a family, but the fact that they have been successfully integrated into the family imposes severe strains on some particular member.

We are engaged in a long-term intensive study of the intrafamilial environment in which the schizophrenic patient grows up. Space does not permit an adequate exposition of the theoretic framework behind these investigations, and we shall seek to impart only an indication of our orientation. Previous studies have indicated that serious pathology of the family environment is the most consistent finding pertaining to the etiology of schizophrenia. We are considering schizophrenia as an extreme form of a social withdrawal, specifically characterized by efforts to modify reality into a tenable form by distorting the symbolization of reality, or through extreme limitation of the interpersonal environment. A theory of schizophrenia must explain both the patient's need to withdraw regressively and symbolically from the realm of shared living and meanings, and also his ability to do so. As the family is the primary teacher of social interaction and emotional reactivity, it appears essential to scrutinize it exhaustively. There is now considerable evidence that the schizophrenic's family can foster paralogic ideation, untenable emotional needs, and frequently offers contradictory models for identification which cannot be integrated. The importance of the very early mother-child relationship seems clear, but we are tentatively considering that deficiencies in this relationship may only establish a necessary *anlage* for the development of schizophrenia —or for certain other psychiatric and psychosomatic disorders. An *anlage* is not a cause. It remains possible that specific determinants may be found

Reprinted from *American Journal of Psychiatry*, CXIV (September, 1957), 241–48, where it appeared under the title, "The Intrafamilial Environment of Schizophrenic Patients: II. Marital Schism and Marital Skew," with the kind permission of Dr. Lidz and the publishers.

in the later difficulties in interpersonal relationships. We hypothesize that the ego weakness of the schizophrenic may be related to the introjection of parental weakness noted in the mother's dependency upon the child for fulfillment; to the introjection of parental rejection of the child in the process of early identification with a parent; and to the depreciated images for identification presented by the devaluation of one parent by the other.

The careful collection of data from 16 families has now continued for several years, through weekly interviews with family members; observation of their interaction with each other and the staff; visits to the home, by projective testing, and other techniques. The methodologic problems in collecting and assessing data are many, but technical difficulties cannot continue to bar exploration of an area which appears vital to the study of schizophrenics.

It is important to point out that the families studied are middle and upper class, able and willing to maintain a patient in a private psychiatric hospital for a long period. The only criteria for inclusion in the study are relative youth of the patient, hospitalization in the Yale Psychiatric Institute, and that the mother and at least one sibling are available as informants. By comparison with other groups, it has become quite certain that there is a bias toward the selection of better organized families of schizophrenics rather than toward the more disorganized.

The material which is being collected is complex, and its analysis is difficult and time-consuming. A year ago we reported briefly our initial survey of the fathers in 12 of these families,[1] calling attention to the serious psychopathology found in the fathers of schizophrenic patients which had previously been generally neglected because of the focusing of attention upon the early mother-child relationship and the pathology of the mothers. Today we report briefly on another fragment of the work in progress, namely, on the defects in the marital relations of parents of schizophrenic patients. The topic is selected because, like the psychopathology of the fathers and mothers, the marital difficulties stand out in bold relief; and also because these marital problems are basic to the study of the intrafamilial milieu. The potential relationship of these parental difficulties to the maldevelopment of the children will have to remain largely implicit in this paper.

From past experience, we know that we must emphasize as strongly as possible that we do not seek to establish a direct etiologic relationship between marital discord between parents and the appearance of schizophrenia in an offspring. It is obvious that bad marriages do not, in themselves, produce schizophrenic children. The presentation is simply one of a series of efforts to convey various facets of the family environment as they become apparent in our study. It is not a matter of conjecture but observation, amply documented, and it is unlikely that it does not have some relevance to the problem of schizophrenia.

The deficiencies in the relationships between parents of schizophrenic patients have been noted and studied by relatively few investigators. Lidz and Lidz,[2] in 1949, called attention to the frequency of broken homes, markedly unstable parents, and unusual patterns of child rearing, and found that at least 61 per cent of 33 patients had come from homes marked by strife. Tietze,[3] in 1949, reported that 13 of 25 mothers of schizophrenic patients reported that their marriages were very unhappy but that the statements by 9 that their marriages were "perfect" did not stand up under investigation, for the marriages were strained and far from happy. Helen Frazee,[4] in 1953, found that 14 of 23 parental couples were in severe conflict and none was "normal" or had "only moderate conflict," whereas 13 of the control parental couples were near normal or showed only moderate conflict. None of the parents of schizophrenic patients revealed any degree of marital stability, whereas well over one-half of the control group manifested only moderate conflict or had made a good marital adjustment. Gerard and Siegel[5] (1950) found open discord between 87 per cent of the parents of 71 male schizophrenics as against 13 per cent in the controls. Reichard and Tillman[6] cite the unhappy marriages of the parents of schizophrenics and analyze the sources of discord in terms of parental personalities. Of interest, too, is Murphy's report[7] (1952) of the family environment of 2 adopted children who became schizophrenic in which the marital relationship was filled with hostility and mutual recrimination between two seriously disturbed parents. Many individual case reports emphasize or mention the bad marital relationship between the parents.

In our efforts to study and describe marital relationships, it has become apparent—as it has to others—that one cannot adequately describe a family or even a marriage in terms of the personalities of each member alone. A family is a group and requires description in terms of group dynamics and the interaction among its members. We are indebted to Parsons and Bales and their co-workers;[8] to J. Spiegel and F. Kluckhohn;[9] Nathan Ackerman;[10] Reuben Hill and his co-workers;[11] Bradley Buell and the Community Research Associates,[12] and others for their efforts to analyze marital and family interrelationships. We are still searching for suitable frames of reference, but the deficiencies of descriptive method should not blur the basic consideration—that the parental relations are highly disturbed in all of the 14 cases whose study is nearly finished, as well as those which are still incomplete.

The requisites for successful marriage are unfortunately far from clear, but some essentials are emerging. A couple must find reciprocal interrelating roles with each other and in their respective roles with their children. Absence of such role reciprocity means making constant decisions, self-consciousness and tension. As Spiegel[13] has pointed out, role reciprocity requires common understanding and acceptance of each other's roles, goals and motivations, and a reasonable sharing of cultural value orientation. Mutual trust and effective communication between partners are important requisites given effect by support of the spouse's role and self-esteem during periods of loss of confidence. We have been particularly impressed by the need to maintain lines between generations: that is, not to confuse or blur distinctions between parents and children. Spouses cannot remain primarily in a dependent position to their parents to the exclusion of an interdependent marital relationship; nor can one behave primarily as the other's child; nor as a rival with one's own children for the spouse's attention, nor reject a parental role completely.[14] The need for both parents to form sources of primary love relationships for children and objects for stable identification will not be entered upon here, as we are concerned primarily with marital interaction.

It seems helpful to follow the lead of Parsons and Bales and consider the father's role in the family as primarily "adaptive-instrumental" and the mother's as "integrative-expressive." In broad terms, which may differ somewhat from Parsons', the father supports the family, establishes its position with respect to other families, determines prestige and the social patterns of interaction with other groups. The mother's basic functions pertain to intrafamilial interactions: tensions and their regulation; supplying the oral needs, both tangible and affectional. Each parent, in addition to filling his own role, must support the role of the other through his or her prestige, power, and emotional value to other family members.

The marriages of these parents of schizophrenics are beset by a wide variety of problems and ways of adjusting to them. However, the 14 marriages can be placed in two general groupings, which, of course, tend to overlap in places. Eight of the 14 couples have lived in a state of severe chronic disequilibrium and discord, which we are calling marital schism. This paper will focus primarily upon these eight couples. The other six couples have achieved some state of relative equilibrium, in which the continuation of the marriage was not constantly threatened; and the marital relationship could yield some gratification of needs to one or both partners. However, the achievement of parental satisfaction or the sacrifices of one parent to maintain marital harmony resulted in a distorted family environment for the children.

Marital Schism

In the eight families in which the state of disequilibrium designated as marital schism existed, both spouses were caught up in their own personality difficulties, which were aggravated to the point of desperation by the marital relationship. There was chronic failure to achieve complementarity of purpose or role reciprocity. Neither gained support of emotional needs from the other; one sought to coerce the other to conform to his or her expectations or standards but was met by open or covert defiance. These marriages are replete with recurrent threats of separation, which are not overcome by efforts at re-equilibration but through postponement of coming to grips with the conflict or through emotional withdrawal from one another—but without hope or prospect of improvement or ever finding any gratification in the marriage. Communication consists primarily of coercive efforts and defiance or of efforts to mask the defiance to avoid fighting. There is little or no sharing of problems or satisfactions. Each spouse pursues his needs or objectives, largely ignoring the needs of the other, infuriating the partner and increasing ill-will and suspiciousness. A particularly malignant feature in these marriages is the chronic "undercutting" of the worth of one partner to the children by the other. The tendency to compete for the children's loyalty and affection is prominent; at times to gain a substitute to replace the affection missing from the spouse, but at times perhaps simply to hurt and spite the marital partner. Absence of any positive satisfaction from the marital relationship (excluding the children) is striking, though strong dependency needs may be gratified in a masochistic fashion in a few instances. Mutual distrust of motivations is the rule and varies only in the degree with which realistic causes for mistrust extend into the paranoid.

In seven of these eight families, the husband retains little prestige in the home and with the children, either because of his own behavior or his wife's attitudes toward him. He becomes an outsider or a secondary figure who cannot assert his instrumental leadership, and when he strives to dominate in tyrannical fashion, he eventually forces the family to conspire to circumvent him. His instrumental role is basically limited to financial support, which he may have originally considered as a husband's basic function, or he is relegated to this position. The ineffectual role of the father applies equally to five of the six marriages in the other group in which marked schism is not present.

The wives will be considered only in respect to their wifely functions, excluding the complex maternal relationships which also cause marital discord because eccentric, cold, rigid, or over-indulgent attitudes toward the children antagonized the husband. All distrusted their husbands and had no confidence in them. They were openly defiant in major areas of interaction and rather habitually disregarded or circumvented their husbands' demands. They were emotionally cold and distant and, with one or two exceptions, sexually aloof. They competed for the attention and affection of the children and tried to instill their value systems, which differed from those of their husbands.

Communication in these marriages is greatly impeded by mutual withdrawal and by masking of motives from one another, but is further hindered because four wives show seriously scattered thinking and four husbands show paranoid thinking and rigidity. The imperviousness to the feelings of others, characteristic of many parents of schizophrenics, also creates communicative difficulties.

It seems of interest that in five of the eight marriages, the focus of the partners' loyalties remained in their parental homes, preventing the formation of a nuclear family in which the center of gravity rests in the home. The grandparents or the parental siblings often carried out much of the expressive and instrumental roles rather than the marital partners. The cardinal emotional attachment and dependency of one or both partners remained fixed to a parental figure and could not be transferred to the spouse.

The eight families can be grouped into three categories, according to the groupings of the Community Research Associates in their "Classification of Disorganized Families," which describes ten combinations of masculine and feminine personalities which are potentially hazardous to successful marital and family relationships.[15]

Four marriages seem best described as "Man Dominated Competitive Axes." The husband strives to assert his male dominance to a pathologic degree, rather clearly in reaction to his feminine dependent strivings. He needs an admiring wife who supports insatiable narcissistic needs and complies with his rigid expectations and is angered when she reacts with defiance and disregard. Indeed, her inadequacies as a wife or mother may well produce exasperated frustration. He distrusts her increasingly and undercuts her prestige with the children. The wives are disappointed and disillusioned in the father figure they married who cannot grasp their needs, and, if they are overwhelmed by force, they manage to gain their ends through circumvention. The husbands are rigid paranoids or obsessives, and the wives are poorly organized obsessives or schizophrenics. The marriages are marked by chronic severe mistrust without (except in the least serious instance) any semblance of affection. The family is split into two factions by the conflict and mutual undercutting. Although both members are fighting, it is the husband's moral brutality, his disregard and contempt for the wife whom he tries to force into compliance that dominates the picture.

> Mr. Reading, a forceful and successful but paranoidally suspicious man, sought to control his wife's behavior from the start of the marriage. He was infuriated and disillusioned when she joined a church group against his orders to remain aloof from any organizations. He was dependent upon his mother, who lived in the home for many years, following her advice in household matters in opposition to his wife's, whom he considered incompetent to furnish the house. Marked strife began with the birth of the elder of two daughters, for he was clearly jealous of the attention the wife paid the child. He disapproved of everything she did in raising the child, often with good reason, but he competed rather than supported. Mrs. Reading was obviously overprotective

of the children, whereas her husband wished to inure them to the hard knocks of life. Violent scenes, filled with Mr. Reading's dire threats and marred by occasional violence, were commonplace. The marriage further disintegrated into a hostile battleground after Mrs. Reading discovered that her husband was having an affair, which she reported to her mother-in-law to gain an ally her husband feared. Mr. Reading never forgave his wife for this betrayal and, apparently to spite her, sold their home in the best section of the city to move into a two-family house in an undesirable neighborhood. Thus, he struck a foul blow at Mrs. Reading's major preoccupations—her social aspirations and her insistence that her daughters associate with only "proper" companions. The family, previously split into two groups, now united against Mr. Reading and refused to eat meals with him. The difficulties engendered by the wife's indecisive obsessiveness and the husband's paranoid trends cannot be depicted here. Both partners used interviews primarily to incriminate the other and persuade the interviewer to judge in their favor against the spouse.

The second group of two families may be categorized as "Woman Dominated Competitive Axes," according to the "Classification of Disorganized Families." The outstanding common feature is the wife's exclusion of the passive and masochistic husband from leadership and decision-making. She derogates him in word and deed and is emotionally cold and distant to him. Her attention is focused on her narcissistic needs for completion and admiration. These wives are extremely castrating and their husbands are vulnerable. The husband withdraws from the relationship in an effort to preserve some integrity when defeated in the struggle and may find solace in alcohol. The husband's function in the family is restricted to providing a living or, if willing, to supporting the wife in her domination of the family. The wife does not fill an expressive, supportive role to her husband, and her expressive functions with the children are seriously distorted.

> Both Mr. and Mrs. Farell were closely tied to their parental families. Mrs. Farell, the youngest of three sisters, was very dependent upon her eldest sister, a masculine aggressive woman with open contempt for men, who tended to dominate the Farell household. Mrs. Farell refused to live at any distance from her family and spent two months each year with them away from her husband. She was an extremely cold, narcissistic woman and a "tease," who flirted constantly but denied her husband sexual relations. Mr. Farell was a passive man who sought to assert a pseudo-domination of his family when his men friends were about. He formed fawning attachments to men, which increased his wife's contempt for him. He was excluded increasingly from the family circle, his opinions disregarded, and felt like an outsider who was barely tolerated. He was closely attached to his mother, whom he helped to support. Mr. Farell finally took steps to separate unless his wife would detach herself from her sisters. She capitulated but became pregnant in the process of reconciliation. She was ashamed and concealed the pregnancy, and then took it out on her husband. Separated from her sisters, she began to drink heavily and carried on open flirtations, or perhaps affairs, neglecting her baby. The discord heightened. After Mrs. Farell was seriously disfigured in an

accident for which her husband was responsible, she became depressed and withdrew into seclusion until plastic surgery restored her appearance. Mr. Farell then tried to make amends through becoming a weak and spineless husband who mothered the youngest neglected child. However, he soon developed cancer and his wife displayed a physical abhorrence for him, fearing that she might catch the disease. She refused to nurse him during his terminal illness.

The remaining two marriages may be classified as "Dual Immature Dependency Axes." Mutual withdrawal of the spouses and dependency on members of the parental families was outstanding. It is difficult to say which spouse dominated the marriage, though both tried and at the same time resented not having a strong figure who would provide leadership. Resentment of the mates' attachments to their families was prominent. The inability to gain mutual gratification of needs and support to mounting disregard of the other and increasing emptiness of both lives. These marriages were replete with threats of separation by both members, but each tended to go his or her own way, undermining the other to the children by deeds and attitudes more than by words. Despite the long duration of both marriages, they remained tentative, as if both partners were awaiting and contemplating release.

The Nussbaums' dissension had started shortly after their marriage 25 years ago. Mr. Nussbaum had been largely supported by his elder brother, whom he regarded as a father. Mrs. Nussbaum's father had been fatally injured following business reverses, which her family blamed upon his affiliation with Mr. Nussbaum's brother. Mrs. Nussbaum appeared to side with her family in their accusation of her husband's brother. Mr. Nussbaum considered her attitude to show utter disloyalty as it furnished the finishing blow to his feelings of being excluded by her close-knit family. There was little or no discussion of the matter, but they drew apart. Mrs. Nussbaum was very sensitive lest her husband dominate her and stood her ground with the help of a violent temper. She refused to accompany him on social engagements essential to his career and antagonized his friends. Mr. Nussbaum felt unloved and unwanted and constantly deprecated. He stayed away from home much of the time and fostered the impression that he was having affairs, either to spite his wife or to mask his impotence, or both. Weeks would pass when the couple would not speak to one another. The wife found solace in her relationship to her son and the husband in his seductive attachment to his daughter, our patient.

Although the Newbergs had been in violent disagreement and there had been repeated threats of separation, some elements of good-will toward each other could be uncovered. Mr. Newberg is a very disturbed man, pushing numerous impractical schemes that are often grandiose; talking incessantly in a loud voice; seeking to dominate but with faulty judgment and, although a steady and hardworking provider, he had frightened his wife for years lest he leave his job and launch upon one of his impracticable schemes. He spent little time with his family, partly because of his attachment to his mother and partly because of his wife's attachment to her sisters, which forced the family to live in a home two hours from his job. Mr. Newberg resented his wife's attachment to her three sisters and mother and her domination by one sister who constantly disparaged him to his wife and children. Mrs. Newberg claimed that she remained dependent upon her sisters because her husband provided her neither emotional support nor help in raising the children. She considered him impossible to live with because of his demands, his thoughtlessness, and the constant confusion he produced in the home. She remained with him only because she felt the children needed a father but found she had to treat him as a child, humoring him to avoid strife. They blame each other's families for interfering and discourage and disparage each other's interests. The situation reached a crisis when Mr. Newberg wished to move to the West Coast because his mother and brother were moving there. He threatened to leave his wife if she would not move and she threatened to leave him if he tried to force the move. Both had intense needs which the other could not begin to satisfy. Although Mr. Newberg had strong paranoid trends and Mrs. Newberg had difficulties in being close, and the hostility was marked, this family offered the best chance of any for some reconciliatory movement, because both showed potential ability to recognize the other's need as well as their own difficulties.

The portrayals of these marriages are little more than symbolic fragments of the wealth of material collected. Still, they indicate the virtual absence of complementarity in each marriage. Husband and wife do not support each other's needs and the marital interaction increases the emotional problems of both, deprives the spouses of any sense of fulfillment in life, and deteriorates into a hostile encounter in which both are losers. Instead of any reciprocal give and take, there is demand and defiance leading to schism between partners that divides the entire family, leaving the children torn between conflicting attachments and loyalties.

Marital Skew

In six of the fourteen marriages, this type of schism did not exist, although the family life was distorted by a skew in the marital relationship. In all, the rather serious psychopathology of one marital partner dominated the home. In some, the dissatisfaction and unhappiness of one spouse is apparent to the other and to the children, but husband and wife manage to complement or support each other sufficiently to permit a degree of harmony. In the others, the distorted ideation of one partner was accepted or shared by the other, creating an atmosphere of *folie à deux,* or even of *folie à famille* when the entire family shared the aberrant conceptualizations.

In all of these families, one partner who was extremely dependent or masochistic had married a spouse who had appeared to be a strong and protecting parental figure. The dependent partner would go along with or even support the weaknesses or psychopathologic distortions of the parental partner because dependency or masochistic needs were met. In contrast to the marriages with overt schism, one partner could gratify rather than combat a spouse's narcissistic needs. It may be significant that no member of these six marriages had intense emotional bonds to the parental family, and it is possible that the absence of such alternative sources of gratification tended to hold these spouses together. A striking feature in all cases was the psychopathology of the partner who appeared to be dominant, creating an abnormal environment which, being accepted by the "healthier" spouse, may have seemed to be a normal environment to the children. Considerable "masking" of potential sources of conflict occurred, creating an unreal atmosphere in which what was said and admitted differed from what was actually felt and done. Two and perhaps three of the marriages may be classified as "Woman Oriented Self-depreciatory Axes," according to the "Classification of Disorganized Families," in which the wife's masochistic self-sacrifice to support a narcissistic and disappointing husband was striking. One, and perhaps two, of the marriages could be designated as "Man Oriented, Self-depreciatory Axes" in which a husband with a meek and self-effacing disposition supported a wife who was an ambulatory schizophrenic.

We shall cite examples in cursory fashion primarily to illustrate that even though these marriages provided some gratification to the marital partners, the family milieu was as distorted and disturbed as in the case of the schismatic marriages.

> The Schwartz family was completely dominated by a paranoid mother who supported the family. Her husband had left her on one occasion, unable to tolerate her demands, but had returned long before the patient, the youngest son, had been born. Soon thereafter the father suffered a nervous breakdown, after which he lived as a sort of handyman around the house and worked as a menial helper in the wife's business. The wife was extremely ambitious for her four sons, pushing them and dominating their lives, as well as making it clear that they must not become like their father. She was paranoidally fearful of outsiders, believing that their telephone was tapped and that the family was physically endangered because they were Jewish. A severe schism actually existed despite the peace between the marital couple. The mother was intensely protective of her oldest son, a gambler and embezzler, who consumed all of her attention as well as much of the family income. A chronic ambivalent conflict existed between them that tended to exclude the husband and the other sons. The husband did not intervene, but merely told his sons that the trouble in the family existed because they did not obey their mother as he did.

Here the father had abdicated and the mother was a paranoid instrumental leader, while the father supplied no masculine image with whom the younger sons could identify.

> Illustrative of the *folie à deux* and the *folie à famille* group, the Dollfuss family lived as European landed gentry in a New England suburb.

isolated from their neighbors. The family life was centered in the needs and opinions of Mr. Dollfuss, a successful but paranoidally grandiose inventor. The children were raised by a seductive nursemaid of whom the cold and distant mother was intensely jealous. However, Mrs. Dollfuss devoted her life to her husband, catering to his whims, and keeping the children out of his way. Mr. Dollfuss' major interest was an oriental religious sect. He believed that he and a friend were among the few select souls who would achieve a particular type of salvation. Both Mrs. Dollfuss and the nursemaid virtually deified him. They and the children shared his beliefs as well as his grandiose notions of himself, living in what we termed a *folie à famille*. Here, the children were largely excluded from the lives of the parents, the model of the father was an unrealistic one for the son, and the intellectual and emotional environment was estranged from that of the larger culture into which they had to emerge.

In all of these six families, the fathers were particularly ineffectual, assuming little responsibility for family leadership other than earning a livelihood. They were either weak, ineffectual men who went along with wives who were schizophrenic or at least questionably so, or they were disturbed men who could maintain an outward form of capability and strength because of the support of a masochistic wife. In all instances, the psychopathology that pervaded the home was masked or treated as normal.

The analysis of the pathologic environment in these last six cases and of the effects upon the children, cannot be gone into here, but I trust we have shown that we have not simply discarded less disturbed family environments in choosing to focus this paper upon the eight marriages in which overt schism between the partners existed. In considering the eight schismatic marriages we do not seek, as emphasized previously, to relate directly the appearance of schizophrenia in an offspring to the marital disorganization. There are many other factors in the family environment which we are studying that affect the children, but they all bear some relationship to the personalities of the parents and the atmosphere created by their interaction. We are only seeking to describe bit by bit what this family environment is like, until we can assemble the fragments into a meaningful description of the whole. We are still occupied with the grossest factors, for unless we start with what appears fairly obvious, these factors may be overlooked during our preoccupation with subtleties. In this presentation, we have paid minimal attention to the individual personalities of the parents in order to concentrate upon problems created by their interaction.

Discussion

We find a number of features in these marriages that are theoretically adverse to the "normal" developmental process of a child. In these families, each parent constantly denigrates and undercuts the other, making it clear to the children that each does not respect or value, but rather dislikes or hates, the other. Each parent more or less openly expresses fears that a child will resemble the other, and a child's resemblance to one parent is a source of concern or rejection by the other parent. One or both parents seek to win the child away from the other. The boundary between the generations is violated. A child may feel the burden of being expected or required to complete the life of one or both parents; and this creates a block to growth into an independent individual. A child may be used and needed as a replacement for the spouse. There is excellent opportunity for intensification of the Oedipal rivalry rather than for its resolution. The child can insert himself in the wedge between the parents, becoming inordinately adept at widening the breach and becoming caught in the incestuous concern that the parent can be seduced or might seduce, as well as in the guilt over hostile-destructive impulses toward the other parent. A parent of the same sex with whom the child should identify during latency and adolescence who is not an acceptable love object to the other parent but is hated and despised, cannot provide a model through which a child can achieve mature identity. Potential homosexual trends, which play a large role in schizophrenia, are opened. Many other serious impediments are placed in the way of the child's achievements of a stable identification with a parental figure, a requisite to the formation of a stable ego-identity by the end of adolescence. In addition, children of a rejected marriage are likely to feel rejected themselves. Caught in the anxiety that a needed parental love-object can be lost through separation of the parents, the children may devote much energy toward balancing the precarious marriage. The stronger the incestuous tendencies, the greater the need for protection by the presence of both parents. When one or both parents have paralogic and scattered ways of thinking and behaving, the difficulties are further heightened.

Summary

The careful scrutiny of the fourteen families containing schizophrenic offspring reveals that the marital relationships of all parents were seriously disturbed. Eight of the families were split into two factions by the overt schism between the parents. In these schismatic families, the parents repeatedly threatened to separate; one spouse sought to coerce the other to conform to rigid expectations and aroused defiance; difficulties of almost any type engendered recriminations between parents rather than mutual support. The parents derogated and undercut one another, and thus the child could not use one parent as a model for identification or as a love object without antagonizing the other parent. The other six couples lived together in reasonable harmony, but the family environments provided by their marriages were badly distorted or "skewed" because in each marriage the serious psychopathology of the dominant parent was accepted or shared by the other. Studies now in progress will seek to clarify further the difficulties in these marriages, the personalities involved, and the effects upon the children.

48 The "Cult of Personality" and Sexual Relations

ARNOLD W. GREEN

*The point of view has been held throughout this volume that system-to-system rela-
tionships are not one-way patterns of influence. Many of the papers in this part have
dealt more with the family's effects on the personality of a member than vice versa.
This paper by Professor Green is concerned with the reverse side of the coin. He
analyzes the difference between lower-class Polish-Americans and middle-class Americans,
as regards their orientation to love and sexual relations. The Polish-Americans do not
have the "cult of personality" which dictates that standards applied within the family
apply outside the family,* that individuals be accorded autonomy, and that coercion
not take place. The Polish-Americans do not have these norms and controls built into
their personalities; thus, they approach heterosexual relations with a very different
outlook. The resultant marriages are stable, even though they are not love matches, and
they are stable not in spite of but because of the personality characteristics. In other
words, given a certain type of personality, a particular type of marriage (and family)
results, a type that is integrated on bases other than the idealization of sex and spouse.*

Probably because of his middle-class background, the sociologist tends to assume that the norms governing middle-class courtship
and marriage appear constant throughout society.[1] Deviations from these
norms are almost invariably treated as abnormalities, and moral depre-
cation is freely exercised.

This paper describes the dominant patterns of sexual relations found
among second-generation Poles in a small industrial New England village,
patterns that could no more be labeled "abnormal" than Mohammedan
polygamy, because their orientation is outside the scope of our society's
middle-class norms and, since they could not conceivably be punished by
law, uncontrolled by them.[2]

The patterns described are abstracted from a localized population, from
a community in a severe state of disorganization. For purposes of valid
generalization, more data will have to be collected concerning the sexual
relations of the proletarian children of old-world parents. It is believed,
nevertheless, that the patterns here described constitute a more accurate

---

* Cf. E. C. Banfield, *The Moral Basis of a Backward Society* (Glencoe, Ill.: The Free
Press, 1958). This account describes an Italian peasant village where such norms are also
absent, where standards applied within the family do not carry outside the family. Editors.

Reprinted by special permission of the William Alanson White Psychiatric Foundation.
Inc., from *Psychiatry*, IV (1941), 343–48, with the kind permission of the author and the
publisher.

forecast of what will be discovered than do the discussions of sexual relations now available in the literature.

Modern courtship practices are no longer rooted in the rural-familistic system, since they too have been swept into the social whirlpool created by urbanism, mobility, and industrialism.[3]

In that system, ordering and forbidding techniques functioned smoothly to control courtship behavior, which was rigidly controlled in terms of status and role. A given couple had numerous reference points: home, family, church, which all worked together to demand virtue from the woman and restraint on the part of the man. Every step of involvement was carefully blue-printed in advance by the community, which channelized involvement toward inevitable marriage.

With the breakdown of the rural-familistic system, what Durkheim called the "cult of personality" has increasingly supplanted the old formal, rigid controls of courtship. From one who adheres to the cult, it exacts a respect for, and a deference to, the individual personalities of his associates. The cult has aptly been interpreted for courtship behavior:

> It is possible to be an ethical person amid a confusion of ethics. . . .
> *He must apply his code without personal discrimination.* If a boy, for example, he cannot sanction certain behavior in his girl friend and condemn it in his sister, merely because of his different relations to them. He cannot sanction in himself what he condemns in another. Finally, he must be honest. He must not exploit a fellow being by deceit or concealment of his true motives and character.[4]

The cult of personality is early imposed upon the life-organization of the middle-class child by his family. It conditions a fine, subtle awareness of the personalities of others which prompts a deference to their wishes, at least overtly, to gain personal ends, including the regard of others operating within the cult, since the sanction inhering is the fear of being considered a boor. For the middle classes, the cult serves as a reference point in personal relations, as a guide in an ever-widening undefined social area.

Of course, the cult functions on a much higher plane than serving merely as a technique for manipulating social situations. Upon thorough internalization, it can afford many psychic satisfactions.[5]

The cult is moralistic, but not in the familistic sense. Since the cult does not demand from its adherents respect for a rigid set of impersonal rules, but a respect for the autonomy of the other "individual," if that autonomy can be directed toward behavior which would be immoral within the familistic system, the cult is still operative. Seduction can take place within the cult when no misrepresentation is present, when both have an equally exact knowledge of all the factors in the situation.

Logically, a person might simulate operating within the cult while adopting the techniques of fraud and deception—logically, but rarely in fact. The middle-class boy is aware of the bitter condemnation awaiting him who practices deceit on a "nice" girl to obtain sexual favors. Only a few are capable of orienting their behavior toward the cult for the express purpose of transgressing it.

But even if fraud is practiced, it must be verbalized in terms of wishing the other well. There must be offered the other an emotional or intellectual rationalization, such as "love" or emancipated individualism, which will allow the other the believed retention of self-autonomy.

There is a control mechanism at work here. Wanton attacks on the other's ego are inadmissible. It is unlikely that the courtship situation will continue when it has degenerated to open and avowed conflict.[6]

The material following is a description of the sexual relations found among the second-generation Poles in a western Massachusetts village of some three thousand population. The Poles constitute the main ethnic-group in the village, but there are many French-Canadians and northern and southern Irish: of the old Yankee stock there is but a small residue left. The village is non-farm, and the factory, which was its reason for being, has been shut down completely for over five years. The youth of the village are faced by an economic stone wall.[7]

Courtship Patterns of a Localized Ethnic-Group: Thrill-seeking Behavior through Casual Dating[8]

There are three public dance-halls in the vicinity which are much frequented by the local youth. Not all the Polish girls accept dances from strangers and chance-acquaintances, but many do.

The local boys usually drive to the surrounding towns and villages for their pick-ups, so that the village's Main Street is the hunting ground for out-village boys. The following is a scene that is many times almost duplicated every night of good weather.

Three girls are parading Main Street in all their finery, keeping a sharp although carefully screened look-out for the cruising automobiles. A car slows to a stop. One of the three male occupants announces, "Isn't it a nice night." One of the girls draws up short with feigned surprise, snaps out a cool "Is it?"

The other girls simulate anxiety to continue their walk, but apparently resign themselves to the whim of their bolder companion, albeit with poor grace. Then the conversation becomes general, the boys adopting a blatant pose of sophistication, the girls a tone of mockery.

By silent, subtle communication the girls agree that the boys are sufficiently attractive, and, since none of them has previously had a distressing experience with one of the boys, they place their feet on the running-board of the car.[9] The conversation continues, loud and raucous; the boys disparage the size of the village, the girls counter with wise-cracks gleaned from the movies and radio. Finally, the girls enter the car.

One of the boys announces he is not feeling well, cannot drink any beer, so they go for a ride.[10] The car is soon parked in a secluded road for a period of necking.

After the initial group-date, the most impressed boy may attempt to date one of the girls individually, either at a dance, on the street, or, rarely, by calling at the girl's home. If she is willing to continue seeing him, on that night or shortly thereafter, he tries to seduce her. The girl either submits or struggles, on a physical basis.

This is the social jungle, where frustration of the male calls forth aggression in the form of violence, the justification for which is this: that the girl has made her person in some degree accessible, and since there is no known code to which she can refer him as reason for resisting his advances, then it must be in slighting terms of personal dismissal, a flagrant affront to the boy's ego. In such a situation, rape is not uncommon.

In this type of behavior, members of one sex group exhibit no interest in members of the other as persons. Rapport is crude and unorganized, based upon sexual excitation.[11] Each sex group manifests a profound distrust of the other. The boys consider themselves gulled and derided when refused intercourse. The girls travel together as a sort of mutual aid society. As between them and the boys there is little feeling of friendliness, but rather a situation approximating open warfare.[12]

Exploitative Relations

This type of courtship is the continued going together of a pair, both of whom usually live in the village. It is more general than casual dating, claiming many more of the Polish youth.[13] Its greater frequency is occasioned by the girls' preference and the shortage of funds among the boys. Continued going together constitutes an exploitative relation, for it redounds even more certainly than casual dating to the control of the boy.

Usually, the girl who goes steadily with a boy is more reserved, less promiscuous and foolhardy than those who date indiscriminately. For any of a complex of reasons[14] she does not flaunt her person on the open street or freely invite the attentions of strangers.

Status on the basis of occupation is denied the girl, for the local region offers nothing better than the sweat-shop or domestic service in a near-by city. Intense boredom and irritation are her lot in a home where privation rules and where Polish speaking parents do not understand her or her problems.

The girl is not inculcated with the cult of personality, which is largely dependent upon the family for imposition, but she has taken over all of the superficialities of American life. She reads American magazines, attends an American school, wears American clothes, speaks the latest American radio slang, and has become an American swing-addict.

She is conversant with a world that her parents do not know, but which they suspect, and against which they attempt to retaliate by using the coercive measures the girl knows are not sanctioned in the American culture. While for the most part conforming outwardly, the girl holds the dictates of her parents in either tolerant or bitter contempt.

Her milieu fails to offer her the steady, uncompromising set of habits of purposeful industry, unreflecting loyalty to family welfare, which rural-familism affords, nor, the cheap commercialized amusement available in cities, nor yet, a new purposeful life-organization to supplant that which cared for her parents.

One result of this *impasse* has been the burgeoning of in-groups among the girls whose main activity is the reading and discussion of romantic fiction and true-confessional magazines. So much time spent in vicarious experience of idealized love has made the romantic interest paramount in the girl's life.

In the eyes of her companions she gains status by attracting and holding the attention of some young man. Losing him means losing face, for there are no other interests to which to turn, no work that can be made important as a defense. And her bargaining position is such that she is allowed to have no one in reserve.

Most important of all, she cannot disparage the relationship to her sex in-group, or declare herself not really involved, for she has already, naïvely, made an open confession of deepest involvement. She does not have the bourgeois trait of close-mouthedness, of training in secrecy, which is invaluable to efficient competition and bargaining.

When her young man makes sexual demands of her, threatens to terminate the relationship if refused, she is literally caught in a trap. The ultimatum creates a problem for her; but very little moral indignation is aroused, for her training has not led her to expect kindliness and deference. Pride and the fear of becoming the butt of cruel jokes prompt her to yield.

To her, marriage is the only available career, and she is hoping the boy will ultimately marry her so that she may escape her conflict-ridden home. The loss of her "virtue" does not compare with the disaster that non-marriage would bring. And since she is not an economic asset to her parents, they also are anxious that she marry; they would make her life considerably more uncomfortable than it is if she sent the boy away. Because the lack of understanding in her home precludes a familial discussion of the problem, she follows the line of least resistance.

The question might be raised whether the nature of her romantic interest, fed by love-story book and magazine, does not lead her to expect noble sacrifice and idealism in her own romantic relationship and thus prompt her to refuse the boy's demands. Such is not the case. The boys whom she knows exhibit little differentiation of personality. They are unemployed or unskilled laborers, have a uniform small amount of formalized education, similar outlook on life, similar backgrounds, the same narrowly circumscribed set of interests, and they all conform to the dead level of mediocrity demanded by the village.

For this reason her state of in-loveness attaches easily, almost impersonally seeks out a love-object. Instead of idealizing the personality of the love-object, she continues to idealize the ideal. Since the transition to the idealization of the person is not made, since her love-phantasies are projected out of sight, that is, are not applicable to any of the boys she knows, the boy's ultimatum does not force her to hate him or to revise her set of values.

The boy, in contradistinction to the girl, is usually involved in both types of courtship at the same time. It is legitimate to speak of the attitude and value complex he brings to the courtship arena as a constant factor; it will not be necessary to introduce even a crude descriptive dichotomy such as was used in sorting the girls.

The boy has a reduced success drive.[15] He does not exercise the caution, foresight, and repression of impulse that the middle-class boy must use in courtship, as in all other relationships, to ensure that the channels of vertical mobility be kept open to him. In terms of social and economic betterment, the local Polish boy has little either to gain or lose by marrying: he gains a better opportunity of holding a job, since, locally, single men are the first to be laid off; and his chances of securing work on the WPA, or getting on relief, are bettered. He loses freedom of action in sexual adventure.

Thus a passive-resistant, uncalculating attitude is maintained toward marriage. Its coming soon or late means little to the boy's life organization: while contraceptives are always carried during casual dating, he often grows careless in steady dating. Most of the marriages in the Polish parish are precipitated by pre-marital pregnancy.

He maintains an aggressive-sexual attitude toward women, is not interested in them as persons. He does not have the romantic concept of love.[16] Three indices illustrate this:

The boy, of whatever age, scornfully rejects the love-theme in his reading matter. From the local library he secures adventure, detective, and mystery yarns. Not only "love stuff," but any book which deals with emotional problems irritates him.

At the local movie house, when the hero pauses in pursuit of the villain to proffer the heroine a tender sentiment, whistling and foot-stamping greet his fall from grace; and the lights go up, the old janitor scampers about aimlessly, pleading for quiet amidst the deafening uproar, when a movie approximating the problem-play is presented.

Over the beer-bottles, in tavern and club, the code of toughness is eulogized. Sexual exploits, actual and imaginary, are discussed in terms of successful hunting. Imputed failure to bring an affair to its natural conclusion is met with caustic ridicule. Because sexual success is a sure road to status, the sexual interest is almost as important to the boy as the romantic interest is to the girl.[17]

It is doubtful that the boy is capable of falling in love, if love be considered a striving toward a person, generating ideation and emotion to overcome cultural blocks.[18] His background does not foster idealization of the other's personality. Any block he encounters he personalizes. His milieu prompts and enables him to exploit the girl sexually. He is only too well aware of the strength of his bargaining position. He makes the most of it.

The Resultant Marriages

There are two polar points of view which may be adopted in making an evaluation of the marriages resulting from the courtship practices described: first, that of society, which is interested in seeing that a marriage remains legally unbroken, that divorce or desertion does not occur; second, that of the person, who is primarily concerned with satisfying his own physical, psychic, and social needs.

The Polish parish has had but one divorce and two cases of desertion in the past five years.[19] Ethnic-group solidarity is still strong enough in this rural community to enforce outer conformity.

Yet, one might wonder why the local marriage remains unbroken when it is entered by a reluctant boy, by a girl who has been coerced during courtship, by a couple who do not feel the ecstatic "oneness" which typically precipitates middle-class marriage. The answer is that while the cult of personality offers many psychic satisfactions, in this instance its *absence* fosters institutional stability!

Like members of the middle class, the local couple yearn for ego-gratification, but on a different level. Attacks and unreflective self-assertions of the other that would bring a "hurt response," and the necessity for a re-definition of the situation in a middle-class marriage do not mean significant changes for the local marriage. Precisely because the pair are not "one," as demanded by middle-class ideology, the marriage can bear up under insults, vulgarities, aggressions, that would utterly ruin a middle-class marriage.[20]

The local couple have not idealized a tremendous expectation for their marriage. The marriage relation is not intensive. There is not a ceaseless seeking-out of the other's motivation, no rigid set of expectations to which the other must conform, with the feeling of betrayal if the other does not conform. Conflict is concrete, specific, limited in time and area of interaction and, while violent, rarely summatory, typically subsiding, through sheer lack of further momentum, with no new definition of the situation.

The cult of personality, in courtship and marriage, demands its price: a psychic defenselessness against real or putative attacks on the ego by the beloved, a quivering sensitivity which, without moralizing, might be posited as a luxury the poor can ill afford.

The local couple, having largely renounced the success-drive, are spared the frustrations the middle-class husband experiences in striving to advance himself when he is blocked, and the pique the middle-class wife feels in being married to such a man. The shocks of a contracting economy to the aspirations of the middle class make the psychic necessity of the cult of personality in marriage even more acute, while at the same time the tensions engendered make the cult more unmanipulable and its constancy, in idealized form, more uncertain.

49 *The Communication of Neurotic Patterns over Two and Three Generations*

SEYMOUR FISHER and DAVID MENDELL

It is usual to view neurosis as the maladaptation of the individual to his life experiences. Dr. Fisher, a psychologist, and Dr. Mendell, a psychiatrist, bring a slightly different perspective to the problem. They view neurosis as a pattern of behavior which is characteristic of some families and is communicated by them over two and even three generations.

This paper is the first report on a study of similarities in the patterning of fantasy and behavior in two or more generations of various family groups. The investigators, a psychiatrist and a psychologist, have assumed that members of the same family are often pressed by similar conflicts; this study is an attempt to document the extent of this similarity from one generation to another. It has further been the intent to study the process whereby neurotic patterns are communicated from one generation to another. The psychiatrist's data are based on psychiatric interviews, and the psychologist's on the Rorschach and the Thematic Apperception Test. For purposes of this paper, most of the observations and analyses have been made by the psychologist on the basis of projective test data which are somewhat easier to integrate than the more complex interview data.

The incentive and opportunity for the over-all study have evolved out of the working philosophy of the psychiatrist who has for some time assumed in his own practice that the individual patient should be dealt with in terms of his membership in the family group and that all the members of the family, including the one who comes for therapy, should be treated. It

Reprinted by special permission of the William Alanson White Psychiatric Foundation, Inc., from *Psychiatry*, XIX (February, 1956), 41–46.

was this orientation which made it possible for the investigators to evaluate entire families intensively.

In this study, six families, with three generations of kin, and fourteen families, with two generations of kin, were examined by the psychiatrist through interviews, and by the psychologist with the Rorschach and the Thematic Apperception Test. Within five of the families, the children, the mother, the father, and either a paternal or maternal grandparent were studied. In one family, the mother, child, and maternal grandmother were evaluated. There were no grandparents available for study in the other fourteen families.

It is, of course, widely accepted that the wishes and fantasies of the parents significantly influence the child. Indeed, there are numerous lines of evidence that such fantasies and wishes are integrated by the child into his personality system and become a part of him. Several studies have focused on just how this communication occurs and have particularly pointed up the specificity of the need fantasies that are passed on from the parent to the child. Thus, Sperling[1] has shown in rich clinical detail how the child may sense certain repressed needs of the mother and act them out in a literally correlated fashion. Similarly, Frenkel-Brunswick[2] has abundantly illustrated how patterns of social and cognitive outlook may be transmitted almost unaltered from parents to child.

Henry,[3] taking the viewpoint of an anthropologist, has constructed, in our opinion, the most formal and systematic schema concerning the long-term transmission of patterns of behavior within the family group. He has sought to describe the process in terms of group interaction and "fields of forces." He hypothesizes that certain rigid and pathogenic modes of inter-action characterize given families. Furthermore, he feels that the modes of interaction within these families tend to be perpetuated from generation to generation, with the result that such families are characterized by a "core family neurosis," which in a sense is not the expression of any one member of the family, but rather of the family groups as a whole.

Since Rorschach and TAT data were available for either two or three generations of the families which were examined, there was afforded a rather unique opportunity to compare the fantasy trends characteristic of each generation in a manner more definite than would usually be possible from interview data alone. The Rorschach and TAT data make it possible to compare the responses of each generation to equivalent patterns of stimuli that were presented under uniform conditions. This permits a spe-cificity of comparison which would be more difficult to attain from inter-view data. There have been some scattered attempts[4] in the past to compare the projective test response of kin, but such attempts have been restricted to just a few cases and have not led to systematic formulations.

In the process of analyzing the projective responses of the various family members, each set of projective tests was first evaluated on a blind basis and a personality profile was written out for the person concerned. The over-all personality pattern of each family member was then compared with the over-all pattern of each of the other members of the same family; and generalizations were recorded concerning similarities and differences. In addition, a large chart was prepared for the family which made possible a detailed comparison of the exact responses given by each family member to the various Rorschach cards and TAT cards. Of course, there was also available a mass of clinical data concerning each family.

The first important finding that emerges from the data is that each family tends to be characterized by a special "flavor" or "atmosphere." The projective responses of the members of a family manifest certain themes in common, as if there were a key motif that concerned the members of this particular group. Illustratively, in one family all seven of the members, at three different generation levels, show an unusual preoccupation with themes of exhibitionism and self-display. In still another family, the inclusive theme is one of concern with death or a fear of destructive loss of self-control. In another family, the theme is a disturbed concern with body image, a feeling of unusual body distortion. The personality defenses of each of the various members of these families seem to be significantly focused on the problem of coping with the area of disturbance specific to the family. It is indeed striking to observe an area of conflict that is prominent in the test responses of one woman and then to observe the same area of conflict equally prominent in the test responses of her grandchild, who may have had a very limited relationship with her during his lifetime. One can best describe this family "atmosphere" phenomenon by taking a detailed illustrative look at the test responses of two typical families involved in the study.

Four members of one particular family were examined—mother, father, son, and maternal grandmother. The family first came under observation when the mother sought psychiatric help for feelings of anxiety, depression, and listless weariness. One of the prominent traits she had shown in her past life was a need to sacrifice herself for others. She found it difficult to say "no" to anyone and spent a good part of her time taking up the burdens of others. When her projective test responses were evaluated, it was found that her fantasies were full of a sense of unworthiness and dirtiness in reaction to strong unacceptable wishes to besmirch and hurt significant figures in her life. To an unusual degree, she was preoccupied with a feeling of being dirty, of needing to cleanse herself. Her Rorschach record contained many references to things being "messy looking" and "smeared." In her TAT stories, she kept noting that things looked "dirty"—for instance, "There is dirt on the floor." Her response to the TAT picture of a boy with a violin focused on the idea that the "violin was dropped in the mud." The other three family members also showed a preoccupying concern in the projective tests with the themes of dirt, cleanliness, and unclean repulsiveness. Thus, the son gave an unusual number of responses that made reference to concepts such as "people covered with soap suds" and "hyena." The husband made repeated references to the Rorschach cards as "stinkers," and he was concerned with concepts such as messy scraps of meat and "horse's anus." The maternal grandmother phrased many of her Rorschach images in forms such as "roach" and "pig." In one of her TAT stories she interpreted a small shadowy detail in the TAT picture as a pipe leaking dirty water.

In another family group, one of the children was seen psychiatrically because he had exposed himself to young girls on many occasions. His projective responses teemed with symbols of exhibitionistic self-display. These symbols are illustrated by such Rorschach responses as "peacock" and "medallion." His maternal grandmother's responses followed a similar trend. The following is an illustrative percept from her Rorschach: "Man coming out from between clouds or curtains. Stepping out nicely on a stage."

The father produced a Rorschach record in which the focus was almost completely on the exposed genitals of women. The mother's responses were not as explicitly concerned with exhibitionistic themes; but her most clear-cut reference to a human figure in the Rorschach was that of a "dandy."

The illustrations given above are qualitative and were arbitrarily selected from the data. It would, of course, be more striking if one could demonstrate in an objective quantitative manner that the similarity in projective responses of those in each family is greater than one would expect to find in a chance aggregation of people. Some preliminary attempts to quantify the data were made by asking raters to pick out and match the test protocols of members of the same family, when all obvious clues of family identification had been removed from the materials. However, with the masses of data involved, this was found to be a prodigious task that no rater could be sufficiently motivated to undertake.

The quantification of the data remains an unsolved methodological problem, and for the present an impressionistic overview has been substituted. On that basis, the data seems to support the hypothesis that each family is characterized by a basic problem area. That is, there seems to be a fairly specific core neurotic pattern which pervades the projective expressions of members of each given family group. It is, of course, true that one does not find that every single member of a family fits the pattern for his family. There are instances in which the pattern is found in the mother, the child, and the maternal grandmother, but does not characterize the father. Similarly, there are instances in which the pattern is found in the father, the child, and the paternal grandmother, but does not characterize the mother. Differences in pattern between husband and wife are more frequent than those between any of the other levels of relationship in the family; at the same time their patterns are more frequently alike than different. Indeed, of tne 18 husband-wife pairs studied, 13 showed a similar concern with a particular core personality problem. In the instance of such pattern correspondence between child and parent, it can easily be postulated that the child learns the pattern from the parents. However, such similarity between husband and wife must represent some kind of a mutual selection process. The husbands and wives involved in the present study apparently chose each other in an attempt to perpetuate an atmosphere familiar to them in terms of their past family experiences. One can only speculate about the purpose of such attempts to perpetuate association with other persons whose core problems are similar. Does each of the persons involved expect greater tolerance for his area of disturbance from someone sensitive in a similar area? Does the association represent an attempt to work out a problem area by joint or group effort, rather than by individual effort? One could conceptualize each family as a group attempting to work out a principal anxiety-laden problem common to its various members or to set boundaries to such a problem. In fact, it would seem to be possible for this family effort toward seeking a solution to embrace a number of generations and to extend over long periods of time.

Another point that stands out in the projective test data is the often extreme specificity of similarity between responses given by different family members. Thus, a woman gives an unusual response to a Rorschach card and her grandchild produces the same unusual response in reaction to the particular card. At times, every member of a particular family will give either the same or a similar unusual response to a particular stimulus. To illustrate this specificity some examples may be cited. The following are the various interpretations of Card III of the Rorschach which were given by four members of the same family: (1) "The earth all to pieces." (2) "Roosters that are dead." (3) "A house burned down." (4) "A pirate or a miscarriage." Each family member sees in Card III a representation of uncommon violence or destruction; and the imagery used tends to be atypical of that usually evoked by Card III.

In another family, Card I of the Rorschach was interpreted by the four family members as follows: (1) "Some structures leaning on one another." (2) "Elephants balancing themselves on a mutual object." (3) "Bird flown up and sitting on an arm." (4) "A bat that is prone." In all four of these responses there is the implication of leaning, resting, and being supported. Such similarity in imagery would seem not to be of chance occurrence.

The members of still another family each noted with some anxiety that the middle red area of Card III of the Rorschach did not fit into the picture and should not be there. Each emphasized this point and seemed to be concerned about the meaning of the middle red area.

Unusual similarities in response were noted in the TAT data also.

For example, five members of one family each told a comparable story about TAT Card II. The story revolved about a girl with high ambitions who was hindered in her aspirations by her mother, a weak person without ambition. This particular story theme is not one typically evoked by Card II; and it is noteworthy to find all five members of the same family projecting the theme into their stories. An example of an even more dramatic similarity in response to the TAT occurred in the test protocols of a woman and her mother. The woman perceived in picture 13G a pipe that was dripping dirty water. Her perception of a pipe in this picture is very uncommon. However, her mother in turn observed and became concerned with the very same pipe in picture 13G.

Examples of strikingly specific similarities in response are found, to a greater or lesser degree, in each and every one of the families that were studied. Such similarities lead one to speculate that the transmission of core personality patterns from parent to child in the family group may occur in a much more specific and exact manner than has been suspected. The transmission process seems to be one in which there can be pinpointed accentuation of given issues. The clinical interview data available concerning each family gives one the impression that this transmission process occurs primarily in terms of that which is denied, forbidden, and concealed. That is, the child comes to learn in great detail from parental prohibitions what the parents most fear in themselves and what they would secretly most like to do. For example, the parents with strong repressed exhibitionistic wishes reveal this to the child by anxiously denying self-display outlets to him. But further, the parents may reveal the intensity, gradations, and particular pattern of their exhibitionistic wishes in terms of the number and kinds of self-display behaviors they deny to the child.

A puzzling question is why a particular member of a family group breaks down as the result of his struggles with issues that actually trouble the other members of the family also. Since the other family members are wrestling with a similar problem area, why does one family member, and not another, finally get so disturbed that he requires psychiatric help?[5] This question cannot actually be answered in terms of the information available from the present study. There are, of course, two over-all hypotheses with which one might approach the question. One might assume that the particular member seeks help because of some individual, personal motivation which is not directly related to his membership in the family. Or one might assume that the family "chooses," in a sense, a special "representative" to seek outside help in an attempt to heal the issues which disturb the entire family.

In other words, one may consider that the primary motivation comes from the individual member or from the family itself. For the purposes of this paper, we shall emphasize the latter possibility. If one does take as a frame of reference for considering this question the concept of the family as a group of people working together on an important problem, it is feasible to raise some provocative questions. Thus, if the family group somehow chooses a special representative to obtain outside help, how might such a choosing process occur? There is evidence from previous observation of various types of groups that group members are able to apply pressures to individuals within the group and cause them to act out tensions which involve all of the others.[6] For example, in group therapy situations the members of the group may produce associations which indicate that they are angry at the therapist. However, instead of expressing this feeling toward the therapist, they may turn it against a group member and disturb him to the point where he in turn finds it necessary to express himself strongly and angrily to the therapist. Unconsciously, the group has incited one of its members to do something which they all have a wish to do, in order to relieve a disturbing tension.

One can theorize about the particular factors which might lie behind the family choice of one of its members rather than of any of the others to seek outside help. To begin with, would not these factors be quite complex and vary considerably with the situation? In one family, the members might choose as their outside representative the individual who was most in communication with their feelings and most sensitive to them. This person might, because of his more direct communication with the others, be in a position of most actively feeling the impact of their disturbed attitudes and consequently have greater motivation than the others to find a way of reducing the existing tension. In another family, the members might select as the outside representative the person most sensitive to withdrawal of their support and deviously threaten such withdrawal unless he attached himself to an outside source of help which would at least partially relieve their load. Perhaps in still another family the members might choose as their outside representative the person who was very dissatisfied and fed up with things as they were, and who had the greatest motivation to bring about constructive changes in himself. They might see in him a leader who could attempt for all of them that which they could not individually attempt themselves. Various other hypotheses about the family choice of someone to seek outside help could be suggested; but those enumerated are sufficient to illustrate a way of thinking about the problem which has grown out of the present study.[7]

50 The Transmission of Superego Defects in the Family

MARY E. GIFFIN, ADELAIDE M. JOHNSON, and EDWARD M. LITIN

Values, and the motivation to adhere to them, are not always transmitted from one generation to the next in an intact fashion. Drs. Giffin, Johnson, and Litin have had wide psychiatric experience with families in which a child has shown a problem in this area, in the form of delinquent or acting-out behavior. Their formulation* describes the problem as one of superego lacunae or defects being transmitted to the child. The defects are in specific areas; other parts of the superego may develop appropriately and remain intact. The authors look to the conflicts of the parents for the explanation of why certain parts of the superego develop defectively.

Delinquency is unquestionably on the increase in this country. The individuals involved in such behavior, if unassociated with any gang group, can be treated, but only with the enormous expenditure of energy by highly trained people. Successful therapy of children at home can be accomplished only by intensive collaborative treatment of parents and child. Successful treatment of the average *neurotic* adolescent is a simple task, by contrast.

For treatment to be rational, etiology must be explicit. Arrival at our understanding of clinical evidence for etiology has necessitated drastic changes in our previous understanding of traditional psychoanalytic theory. Psychoanalysts' first interest was in the neuroses, and with few exceptions research has been concerned largely with this aspect of psychopathology. In understanding the neuroses one conceives of a too-punitive superego. Until recently, pathology of the superego was viewed only in terms of its being too punishing to patients. For years any antisocial acting out was explained in terms of a patient's being excessively guilty about conflicts or being driven by constitutionally unmanageable instinctual drives. The reflected preventative attitude for all patients has been "Do not repress the child so drastically, or he will become neurotic or act out."

Therapists, as well as parents, have become greatly confused, thinking

* Dr. Johnson has discussed this subject at greater length in a recent publication, "Juvenile Delinquency," in Silvano Arieti (ed.), *American Handbook of Psychiatry* (New York: Basic Books, 1959). Editors.

From *American Journal of Orthopsychiatry*, XXIV (October, 1954), 668–84, where it appeared under the title, "Specific Factors Determining Antisocial Acting Out," with the kind permission of the authors and the publisher.

that prohibitions in all forms lead to too much guilt and thus, neurosis. Some therapists have unwittingly permitted and fostered acting out in, especially, the sexual sphere. Prohibitions in themselves do not lead to unhealthy guilt; rather, they are an important aspect of security. So far as the prevention of neurosis is concerned, the prohibition of antisocial activity merely requires the presence of a parent sufficiently well integrated to accept in legitimate ways the hostility expressed by the child over the limit-setting that society demands.

It has become increasingly clear that many parents, particularly those with poorly integrated impulses, have become uneasy about setting limits, even concerning matters which are specifically destructive to society, such as stealing, sexuality, or even murderous intent. Yet it is evident that certain specific things, such as stealing, fire-setting, murder, and sexual destructiveness, cannot be countenanced in our society—they must be prohibited completely and definitively. As most of us clearly recognize, there is, then, specific behavior, the expression of which should arouse guilt in everyone. The guilt alone is not unhealthy. Neurosis need be feared only if great rage has been repressed, along with the prohibition of such antisocial activity.

Our concern in this paper is with the development of that form of pathologic superego which permits antisocial behavior. Clinical evidence shows it to be lacunar, weak in some respects, punitive in some, and normal in still other areas.

Many people have strong latent antisocial impulses, yet never act out such fantasies. We are concerned with defining the specific stimulus to the acting-out behavior. We shall first consider the problems of the direct acting out of forbidden antisocial impulses; namely, stealing, truancy, fire-setting, and direct sexual acting out. Later in the paper, we shall consider the problems found in those *structurally* more complicated cases in which acting out is associated with perversions.

Since the early work of Szurek and one of us (Johnson),[1] collaborative studies on antisocial acting out have continued. From the initial studies emerged the thesis that antisocial acting out in a child is unconsciously initiated, fostered, and sanctioned by the parents, who vicariously achieve gratification of their own poorly integrated forbidden impulses through a child's acting out. One or both parents, in addition, unconsciously experience gratification for their own hostile and destructive wishes toward the child, who is repeatedly destroyed by his behavior. It is possible in every case adequately studied to trace the specific conscience defect in the child to a mirror image of similar type and emotional charge in the parent. The focus of these observations has been not on the activities of the kind seen among deprived and other sociologically determined gang groups, but rather among individual children of poor or of privileged class, frequently from families of "good" reputation and high social standing.

The superego defects in these children are frequently in only one or two areas and are rarely widespread. A child may steal, but never be truant. Another may set fires and do nothing else that is antisocial. In another, only the sexual sphere will be implicated through the acting out. To be sure, like other people, these patients have neuroses with conflict and guilt, but they have also the superego weakness in one or more areas, permitting discharge of tension.

There is frequently confusion regarding the use of the phrase "acting out." The expression "acting in the transference" was first used recurrently by Freud to refer to the phenomenon which was seen during psychoanalytic therapy in which the neurotic patient repeated in the transference, without insight, certain salient episodes of his earlier life.

Eduardo Weiss[2] aptly described it in the following way: "By acting-out is meant the behavior of a person who repeats without insight an unconscious psychic situation out of his past in terms of current reality. A man, for instance, repeats intense feelings of hostility towards his brothers and sisters by quarreling with his fellow workers."

Weiss continued, "Freud considered transference as a form of acting out. According to Freud one acts out instead of remembering. However, psychoanalytic experience teaches us that patients in analysis often act out emotional situations which they have already remembered." Weiss stated that "Freud's formulation can be modified by saying that one acts-out instead of remembering fully with the appropriate attending emotions." He continued, "While acting-out is a substitute for recall, it does not have the therapeutic effect of the latter. The patient who acts out has still to acknowledge that *his present behavior is a reproduction of past experiences*." Weiss concluded, "I agree fully with Anna Freud who says that the patient who acts-out *exclusively* cannot be analyzed."

In more recent years the phrase "acting out" has come to be used almost exclusively in referring to that behavior against authority which is specifically forbidden by our society. Actually, except for the moral issue, there is no sharp line of demarcation between the acting in the transference and the kind of phenomenon expressed by the unconscious acting-out problems with which we are here dealing. This is in keeping with the view commonly held today: That ego and superego are not separate entities, but merge imperceptibly on the spectrum of reality testing. At one end are observed highly moral aspects of the ego; here there can be no alternatives to conforming morally. Proceeding to the opposite end of the spectrum, increasingly complicated alternatives and choices become obviously permissible, since ethics is not involved; it is more in this latter area that acting out during analysis occurs.

The provocative contributions of Reich,[3] Alexander and Healy,[4] Healy and Bronner,[5] Schmideberg,[6] Gardner,[7] and many others have been extensively reviewed in our previous communications. It was Aichhorn[8] whose contributions first unquestionably moved delinquency out of the nihilistic depths of constitutional inheritance, into the realm of dynamic understanding. Every worker in the field of childhood and adolescent acting out has been stimulated by and greatly indebted to this man who genuinely understood delinquents.

We follow the emphasis of Szurek,[9] who as early as 1942 described the psychopathic personality as being only a delinquent grown older, as an individual defective in personality organization, specifically in the individual's conscience. Szurek distinguished those individuals from the sociologically stimulated gang lawbreakers, and presented one of the earliest contributions to the dynamic understanding of these problems. He wrote, "Clinical experience leaves the impression that the definition of psychopathic personality is no greater mystery than other syndromes in psychopathology. Almost literally, in no instance in which adequate psychiatric therapeutic study of both parent and child has been possible has it been difficult to obtain sufficient evidence to reconstruct the chief dynamics of the situation. Regularly, the more important parent, usually the mother, although the father is always in some way involved, has been seen unconsciously to encourage the amoral or antisocial behavior of the child."

It is impossible to understand the dynamic concepts behind the behavior of these individuals unless one has clearly in mind the development of the normal superego. One must understand the reaction of the well-integrated parent and the subtle conscious and unconscious ways in which this behavior directs the development of the child's superego. Identification with the parent consists of more than incorporation of the manifest behavior of the parent; it necessarily involves inclusion of the subtleties of the parent's conscious and unconscious image of the child. The healthy parent fantasies his child as capable of becoming law-abiding. The well-integrated, mature mother does not immediately check on a child following an order or request; she unconsciously assumes that the order will be carried out. The neurotic mother, who immediately checks or warns that if the job is not done dire consequences will follow, merely conveys to the child that an unstated alternative exists in the mother's mind. It is frequently with this alternative image in the mother's thoughts that the child more strongly identifies. This is true because the child senses the peculiar parental emotional need conveyed in the anxious, vacillating tone of the parent's expression.

The child internalizes, then, not only the positive, socially consistent attitudes of the parent, but also the frequently unexpressed, ambivalent antisocial feelings. We cannot agree with those who state that the child identifies only with idealized aspects of the parent. The child identifies with all facets of the parent—to be sure, repressing those parental characteristics which cause conscious confusion, anxiety, and shame.

The patients with whom we are specifically concerned in this paper are those manifesting what are frequently called "superego lacunae." The apparent "punched-out" aspect of this kind of superego is misleading except from the point of view of society. From the point of view of the patient, there is a positive, undeniable drive toward acting in the manner in which the parent unconsciously wishes, even though it be antisocial in direction. The conception of a deficit within the superego structure must be elaborated to include the overwhelming parentally determined dynamic push toward antisocial behavior which the child senses and with which he necessarily complies. Although we are not here concerned with sociologically delinquent gang members, there is frequently overlapping of the individuals who act out antisocially, these latter often moving into gangs.

If our thesis is correct that parents unconsciously initiate and foster antisocial behavior in order to experience gratification for themselves, accurate documentary evidence must be defined in answer to two basic questions:

1. How is sanctioning communicated to the child?

2. Why is one child implicated in a family in which all of the other children are quite conforming?

Not only is it possible by careful questioning and observation to define the process by which a specific child is chosen and the dynamic factors behind the choice of a particular form of socially disapproved behavior, but it is also possible to detect the highly personal technique by which the parent transmits the double talk, interest, permissive tone, or structured situation by which the activity is fostered.

During the process of definitive treatment, it is clearly seen why one child becomes emotionally chosen to be the outlet of expression for these forbidden impulses. An adopted child, whose behavior can be blamed on heredity, becomes a natural victim through whom to express antisocial trends, with simultaneous expression of hostile feelings in the parent toward this child. Sometimes the only son of a woman who is disturbed by unresolved hostile dependent problems with her own father, and permitted by her own mother to carry on petty stealing, may become the means of expressing both her unconscious anger and her poorly integrated stealing impulses through her fostering such socially destructive activities in her child.

Proper understanding of case material is impossible unless one is aware of the many innuendoes of communication which occur without conscious awareness between parents and child. Such communications are by all conceivable means of approach sometimes errors of omission, frequently ones of frank commission. Knowing *what* to listen for, and *how,* the diagnostician gradually defines these operations from direct quotations, double talk, facial expressions, and often through histrionic portrayal by some parents who dramatize the actual interchange between themselves and the child. In the more subtle cases, the casuistic, disingenuous rationalization of these parents can reduce the whole spirit of an ethical principle to a quibbling absurdity.

The specific manner in which, for instance, the truancy from home was handled on a particular day must be obtained; frequently, when this is done, one finds that the mother met the girl with the comment, "If you don't like us and our house, find another; we can get along without you." If this mother is merely asked for adjectival descriptions of the relationship between herself and Jennie she will, without realizing it, forget to indicate this kind of response.

The entranced parental facial expression apparent to the child describing a stealing episode, a sexual misdemeanor, or a hostile attitude toward a teacher conveys to the child that the parent is achieving some pleasurable gratification. No amount of subsequent punishment will act as a deterrent against the recurrences of the acting out. A child wishes to do the thing which he senses gives the parent pleasure, even though he may be punished. We frequently see parents who describe the child's delinquent behavior with obvious pleasure. Suspicious questioning often conveys the parents' unconscious wish that the child comply by doing the thing verbally warned against.

Frequently, parents verbalize evasion and deceptions such as, "Here is an extra quarter, but don't tell your father"; "You can get into the movie for half-price, since you certainly don't look twelve years old"; "Fires are dangerous, but if you must get it out of your system, then we'll set some in the yard."

A mother can make such a suggestion, yet she would never recommend that her child take a trial run in front of cars on the street. The mother of a 14-year-old girl was not genuinely interested in prohibiting her child's stealing; she said to her daughter, "Why did you take the money from your *aunt's* purse instead of from mine?"

Children hear their parents gloating about shortchanging the grocer; naturally they sense the parental pleasure. Some parents do not follow through when the facts of stealing are perfectly clear. For instance, they hesitate to go with the child to the dime store to make proper restitution for a stolen trinket. A mother who has poorly integrated prohibitions concerning her own hostile sexual impulses may fantasy that her eight-year-old daughter will "get into sexual difficulties" as adolescence approaches. With her provocative warnings accompanied by anxiety, she is a predictable stimulus to vacillating sexual behavior in such a child.

We frequently have patients whose parents tell the child to ask the physician for permission to do something they already well understand to be forbidden. Parents complain of *children's* breaking family rules when the parents themselves consciously or unconsciously break rule after rule and promise after promise without apology or comment.

The process of vicarious gratification now becomes clearer. The antisocial behavior of the implicated child becomes a means of parental expression by which poorly integrated antisocial impulses of the parent are expressed through the child. As Emch[10] lucidly stated it, the child is "acting-out the caricatured reproduction of past parental behavior." In addition to this use as a mode of expression for parental impulses, such a child is the recipient of a hostile destructive drive in the parent; in close relationship lie vicarious gratification through the child and the wish to destroy this same child. Such family behavior in the end is destructive to both the parent's ego organization and that of the child.

For purposes of research, particularly, but also for the proper controlled therapy of nonresidential acting-out patients, collaborative therapy is the only adequate technique. There continues to be misunderstanding about the actual procedure, and it must therefore be pointed out that the term "collaborative therapy," as we use it, refers to that particular form of dynamic psychotherapy in which the individual treatment hours of each patient are reviewed in great detail, hour by hour, among all the psychiatrists acting as therapists. It is not the task of a social work follow-up, nor is it concomitant therapy in which two individuals of the same family unit are undergoing therapy during the same period of time; it is a form of highly specialized therapy in which the individual treatment is intensive and the interchange between therapists is regular and frequent. The availability of each physician to the other must be immediate. Material pertinent to the current problem is discussed openly between therapists and with the patients, as it may be useful to them. Transference problems arising from such interchange of timely material are actively analyzed. The purpose and advantage lie in the convenient interchange of information between therapists, material which helps the understanding of each patient and hastens the treatment of all. By means of it, adequate and suitably timed limit-setting is possible, long before its need might be apparent in individual therapy.

Antisocial Acting Out: Illustrative Cases

Scientific proof of causation is not satisfied merely by demonstrating the invariable presence of the suspected cause (unwitting parental permissiveness) whenever the effect (antisocial behavior of children) is observed. In addition, it must also be shown that whenever the suspected cause is present, the effect is also seen. Our first case demonstrates the factors that must be satisfied for scientific proof of causation.

Stealing. Ten years ago one of us was asked to treat a young single woman of 22 years who was depressed. Her married sister, the only relative in that city, came to give some family history and assist with medical arrangements. At that interview, this sister, in commentng on the personalities of her *own* three children, said of her only son, 9-year-old Mark, "He runs circles around us all—he is so brilliant that schoolwork is no challenge to him. I often wish he had been born more dumb so he would be forced to work hard. I tell him that since his schoolwork requires no effort, he will never learn how hard it is to make an honest living. He has not stolen yet, that I know of, but I cannot see him working hard to make an honest living."

We were very interested at the time in recording these exact words because they indicated a hostile wish and image that the boy not be a straightforward citizen. In the course of 2½ years' treatment of Mark's 22-year-old maternal aunt, it was observed that her oldest brother, Bob, a brilliant fellow, was always permitted by his parents to cut corners to the point of frank cheating and stealing. Although his parents ostensibly favored him over the girls by this sanctioning, they were literally destroying him, and the law finally intervened. He was imprisoned for a few years, to the bitter humiliation of our patient and Mark's mother.

By the time Mark was 12 years old his parents came to see us because he had been caught with another boy stealing four jackknives from a sporting-goods store. Needless to say, when questioned closely the parents had absolute evidence of stealing from the mother's purse for at least a year; the only punishment for such transgressions had been a casual remark, which is now so familiar to us, "You are just Uncle Bob over again." In brief, when that mother became our patient, it was unmistakably clear that all Mark's life she had identified him with her hated brother and conveyed this image to the boy in countless ways.

The most alarming attitudes were those expressed quite unconsciously in the diagnostic interview with the parents as they related the episode of the stolen jackknives. When the parents were asked if they had any ideas as to why the child had stolen the knives, the mother immediately answered, *and* to the father's great discomfort, "Children don't realize it, but grownups know that stealing and cheating are on the short route to seriously injuring someone."

The husband burst out angrily, "Jean, your wild ideas run away with you. What do you mean? Mark has never hurt anyone. You've always had him so scared stiff of you that he won't even play a little baseball, let alone hurt anyone."

To this the wife responded angrily, "You don't listen to me—I've been telling you that for the past year when I slap him his eyes blaze with anger —there's terrible temper there, even if he does not *say* anything." Later in her treatment the mother's fantasies that this boy could steal and murder *"if driven to it"* had to be actively dealt with as a manifestation of her own fantasies. The normal parent neither anticipates impending disaster nor dismisses monetary or other transgressions as trivial.

When one discovers the presence of stealing in one family member, its occurrence in at least one other is predictable. Such a relationship is also true of fire-setting, truancy, and direct hostile or sexual acting out. A case of the last is appropriate.

Direct murderous acting out. Very attractive, prominent parents in a large city came with their 14-year-old adopted son for study. There were three older sisters, and one older bother, all unadopted. The parents' only concern was that sexually their son might not be developing normally—that his slight plumpness might be an endocrine problem. Fortunately, this boy was away in a private school from the age of 10 years, yet when he came home on vacations the mother bathed him, cleaned his penis thoroughly, and felt of his testes, ostensibly to ascertain if they were firm and large enough. She laughingly spoke of her amusement when her son called her by the name of a currently enticing actress as she herself strutted about in the nude. She complained bitterly of how defiant her boy was, yet when questioned by her husband, she could not describe any real naughtiness. The boy did surreptitiously take out anger in mild ways on colleagues—yet never had he dared an open battle. When this mother was alone with us, without the father's being present, she described fantasies which aptly reflect her image of her son's future. We could hardly believe the material spontaneously given by this well-dressed, intelligent, attractive woman.

"He is very affectionate—he hugs and kisses me. The school wanted his eyes checked for blinking. I wanted his male organs checked—they seem too small. His brother's seem bigger and firmer. He says I'm prettier than he—nicer in the breasts. We like our baths together. I'm afraid to turn him loose with boys for what he might do—a bad blow—afraid for him to have a gun. I worry he might rape or butcher someone—not just sexually. There are cases of boys who carved up people's organs, heads, and faces. I have the feeling that an attraction to a girl would develop in him a wish to mutilate her—stab her in the back, slice her throat, cut her from head to foot."

When the father was seen alone, he was, of course, not told of the mother's fantasies given to us, but in relating the family history he described his wife's background. Her father was brutal to her mother when he was drunk, a condition which was habitual. He was always kindly to our patient and she adored him. When she was 6 years old she saw her intoxicated father beat up the mother and throw her cruelly across the room. The 20-year-old son in the family picked up a bat and crushed his father's skull, killing him. This son, the maternal uncle of our 14-year-old patient, was imprisoned for a time. Our unfortunate parent, bewildered at what could happen and indeed did happen before her eyes as a child, had no capacity within herself to believe in her own son's control. It was not surprising that the mother, however, implicated the adopted son's heredity.

The boy himself, attractive and well built, showed the most rigid compulsive defensive attempt at inner control associated with considerable depression. His unconscious fantasy life was filled with murder, retribution, and "then everyone lived happily in the end."

In the foregoing case we see the poorly integrated seductive and hostile components of the mother's personality tragically coercing her son into mounting rage over the seduction, rage completely frightening in view of *her* concept of how anger is handled. These are truly terrifying cases, and often initially in treatment, for safety's sake, the child is treated best by removal to the medical floor of a hospital. The apparent mystery of adolescent homicides can be quickly dissipated if adequate background material is available.

Problems of Sexual Aberration

As with the direct activities of stealing and fire-setting, so with the perversions: One can invariably detect, with proper study, the interdigitation of parent-and-child conflicts. These are dynamically more complicated cases because of the additional regressive step which will be elaborated. Many individuals become aware, particularly during the course of psychotherapy, of strong latent homosexual, transvestite, or exhibitionistic trends, yet it never occurs to them to act out such fantasies, just as many neurotics show tendencies to set fires or steal, yet never act out such desires. We are here concerned with evaluating the specific stimuli to the overt behavior.

The etiology of perverse behavior follows a similar, but more complicated, pattern to that of direct acting out. With proper means of research it is possible to define (1) the specific details of a confused and unsatisfactory parental relationship; (2) evidences of pathologic seduction of a particular child, with condoning by the other parent; (3) a pattern of genital frustration following the initial pattern of seduction; (4) the impetus from the parent toward an abnormal pattern of sexual behavior.

As in antisocial acting out, the choice of the specific child in terms of the parents' background and neurosis is similarly definable. This is a very simplified statement of the factors entering into the acting out of aberrant sexuality. One must keep in mind that this is no simple one-to-one relationship, but rather, a relationship which depends upon all of these factors' interrelating with the total intrapyschic life of the patient.

It is necessary to understand that by the term "seduction," we are referring to a pathologic form of a parental sexual temptation which is completely inappropriate temporally for the child. Under the guise of tenderness, it confronts the child with an ambivalent, genital passion which he cannot understand or begin to integrate. Faced with what is overtly parental love, he becomes unconsciously aware of the hostile parental feelings; in incest or with genital frustration, the hostile guilty, shameful feelings of the parent are absorbed by the child, who experiences in himself confusion, guilt, fear of detection, and anxiety. Out of the parents' own guilt another form of personally acceptable sexual expression must be defined. Unconsciously, this has been previously emphasized by the parent during the polymorphous sexual period of the child.

How is the defining of a permitted regressed (perverse) outlet to the tension *generated* by seduction and frustration? Here we must observe the very early pregenital behavior of the child and mother, beginning with the ambivalence of the oral dependency on up to the genital struggles. In these cases of perversion, we always see overstressing of at least one aspect of polymorphous sexual behavior of the young child, such as to lead to unusual selective hypertrophy. Although at such an early age there is no orgasm, and therefore this cannot be called a "perversion," still the hypertrophy can be so *profound* and *organized* that we cannot accept this as just the unorganized sexuality of the polymorphous perverse child. We shall not include here a report on a child of this age; a case in which extreme transvestitism began in a child at 2½ years is now in press.[11]

We shall present only one case of adolescent perversion, that of exhibitionism.

A 17-year-old boy was apprehended by the police while exhibiting himself to three young women in a park. Investigation revealed that although the boy's transgressions never had been brought to the attention of the police before, certain neighbors had complained of his behavior to his parents for the three years preceding the incident in question. Medical help was not spontaneously sought by the moderately wealthy parents, both of whom were active in civic organizations.

Both parents were seen separately and together diagnostically. The father was humiliated and filled with rage and contempt toward the boy.

"I've been telling his mother for years that that kid would come to a bad end with her coddling and drooling over him like a spoiled pup. I despise her youngest brother, who was pampered and coddled by his mother—he isn't worth a darn. Of course, I admit his father never paid an hour's attention to him in his life, and then probably only to pull a few strings with politicians to bail him out of jams. I know my wife has been ashamed a hundred times of her brother, but she gets furious if I say one word of truth about the bum."

The mother was first interviewed by a man. The interviewer was immediately aware of her frank, rather intimate, seductive approach. No sign of anxiety was apparent in this woman.

When asked what she thought about the immediate problem, she said, "I don't understand Don—we have always been completely frank with each other about everything, but when I try to talk to him about this, he won't talk."

When the interviewer remained silent, she went on, "He is our only son and so many terrible mistakes were made with my youngest brother that I vowed to keep things friendly and frank with our boy. I've answered all his questions and he has told me everything until now. I admit he didn't tell me about these other things with women, and I didn't talk to him because I knew he would tell me in due time—my husband was so angry that I wouldn't let him talk to Don, but I can't trust my husband—he gets so angry and rigid with the child."

At this point the psychiatrist asked the mother if she could give some elaboration of how frank and confidential the boy had been with her. This opened a recital of wholly unconscious tragic seduction and unhealthy intimacy between this mother and Don. There were no restrictions on nudity, or the bathroom, and talk was endless about sexual matters. The mother went into great detail with the boy about her own sexual life, to the point of revealing frequency of intercourse, her husband's hostile demands, and her rearing concerning the duties of a wife.

The 15-year-old daughter, from 7 years on, would have none of this frankness; she demanded privacy in the bathroom and would not be lured into sexual discussions.

The father frequently rebuked the mother for carrying on her "long harangues" with the boy and shouted that he would be better off "learning stuff the hard way on the streets," as he did.

There is no need to include the boy's great detail in describing his mother's appearance, her breasts and other anatomic attributes; these attitudes of her son were given by the mother with a dreamy, pleasurable expression. She herself expanded at length about her son's fine physique, including what she called his "beautiful masculine endowment." The seduction between mother and son was obvious to any listener.

But how did this boy come to choose exhibitionism as a means of discharging his rage and sexual drive? The mother fostered and showed the keenest interest in exhibiting herself and in looking at the nude boy from his earliest years. Until Don was 13, he and the mother often showered together, especially when the father was away on trips. The mother commented, "Loneliness brings one closer to a child."

The boy hated his father; as this mutual dislike mounted, Don and the mother became even closer. Subsequent interviews with the mother revealed a most unhappy marriage, the husband being engrossed in business as well as openly flirtatious with other women; the mother was humiliated, but unable, because of her own background and conflicts, truly to enter a love relationship with her husband.

Don, a handsome, strongly built boy, was barely defending himself against murderous feelings toward both parents. His identifications with them were so confused as to suggest that no treatment was safe without his initial removal from home. Intensive therapy for Don, his mother, and father was necessary.

Summary

In this communication, we have discussed the etiology of individual antisocial acting out, and of sexual aberrations. Latent unconscious impulses to steal, set fires, and murder, as well as fantasies about such practices as homosexuality and transvestitism, are frequently seen in many patients. We have been concerned with defining the specific stimuli to their becoming overt.

Antisocial acting out is seen as a superego defect which stems from unconscious parental initiation and fostering because of poorly integrated forbidden impulses in the parents. These impulses and their permission to be acted upon are communicated usually unconsciously to the child. In his acting out, the child affords to the parents vicarious gratification for their own forbidden impulses and concomitantly satisfies parental destructive feelings toward the child. Such behavior is destructive toward both the child's and parent's ego organization, as well as toward society, unless adequate collaborative therapy is instituted.

Sexual aberrations are seen to develop as a result of ego adaptation to highly specific, often unconscious, family attitudes impinging on the child; these attitudes subtly coerce and distort the child's psychosexual development. The parent, because of his own problems, unconsciously seduces the child, then sets *genital* limits and unwittingly defines the direction for regressed perverse outlets.

The emphasis of this paper has been on factors in etiology. The basic tenets important in intensive collaborative therapy of parents and children stem from a more rational concept of etiology. Our thesis necessitates the early establishment of definite limits to behavior, the timing of which varies with the case. As has been seen, the concepts emerging in this paper place the emphasis in acting-out problems on a pathologic superego which is weak in certain specific areas; this is in contrast to the neurotic superego, which is too punitive.

It is the responsibility of psychiatrists to resolve the confusion in the treatment of individuals with weak superego structure. To be sure, we are cognizant of the confusion which accompanies transition from puritanic mores of a culture to greater individuation. But it is not alone this transition which has led to many improper treatment plans and far too permissive, ill-defined, so-called preventive psychiatric suggestions to parents. With clearer definition of etiologic factors in this group of patients, we are in a better position to be definitive about when we should be permissive of anger in order to offset neurosis, and when we must be prohibitive of amoral impulses in order to prevent acting out. No one should give tacit consent to behavior which acts against the individual's best interests in our society. Parents increasingly can be helped to absorb and to channel in constructive fashion the child's hostilities when society's prohibitions are imposed emphatically. When psychiatrists achieve greater clarity, parents, educators, and those executing the law will function with less confusion.

51 *The Superego*
and the Theory of Social Systems

TALCOTT PARSONS

Virtually all the papers included in Part IV, "Family and Personality," are reports of empirical work. Most of these are by clinicians and deal with examples from the pathological end of the scale. This final selection is a more general, abstract, and theoretical paper by Professor Parsons. In this paper, Parsons attempts to show the conceptual and theoretical convergences between the nature of social systems and the superego aspect of personality. In his formulations, Parsons focuses on the common culture as the "core of the stabilizing mechanisms of the system of social interaction" and as the orientations and "moral" content of what is internalized as part of the personality structure. Parsons phrases his discussion in terms of any social system, although, as he himself suggests, his formulations are directly applicable to that basic, prototypical group, the family.

In the broadest sense, perhaps, the contribution of psychoanalysis to the social sciences has consisted of an enormous deepening and enrichment of our understanding of human motivation. This enrichment has been such a pervasive influence that it would be almost impossible to trace its many ramifications. In the present paper, I have chosen to say something about one particular aspect of this influence, that exerted through the psychoanalytic concept of the superego, because of its peculiarly direct relevance to the central theoretical interests of my own social-science discipline, sociological theory. This concept, indeed, forms one of the most important points at which it is possible to establish direct relations between psychoanalysis and sociology, and it is in this connection that I wish to discuss it.

Psychoanalysis, in common with other traditions of psychological thought, has naturally concentrated on the study of the personality of the individual. Sociology, on the other hand, has equally naturally been primarily concerned with the patterning of the behavior of plurality of individuals as constituing what, increasingly, we tend to call a social system. Because of historical differences of perspective and points of departure, the conceptual schemes arrived at from these two starting points have in general not been fully congruent with each other; this fact has occasioned a good deal of misunderstanding. However, recent theoretical work[1] shows

---

that, in accord with convergent trends of thought, it is possible to bring the main theoretical trends of these disciplines together under a common frame of reference, that which some sociologists have called the "theory of action." It is in the perspective of this attempt at theoretical unification that I wish to approach the analysis of the concept of the superego.

One of the principal reasons for the selection of this concept lies in the fact that it has been, historically, at the center of an actual process of convergence. In part at least, it is precisely because of this fact that Freud's discovery of the internalization of moral values, as an essential part of the structure of the personality itself, constituted such a crucial landmark in the development of the sciences of human behavior. Though there are several other somewhat similar formulations to be found in the literature of roughly the same period, the formulation most dramatically convergent with Freud's theory of the superego was that of the social role of moral norms made by the French sociologist, Emile Durkheim—a theory which has constituted one of the cornerstones of the subsequent development of sociological theory.

Durkheim's insights into this subject slightly antedated those of Freud.[2] Durkheim started from the insight that the individual, as a member of society, is not wholly free to make his own moral decisions but is in some sense "constrained" to accept the orientations common to the society of which he is a member. He went through a series of attempts at interpretation of the nature of this constraint, coming in the end to concentrate on two primary features of the phenomenon: first, that moral rules "constrain" behavior most fundamentally by moral authority, rather than by any external coercion; secondly, that the effectiveness of moral authority could not be explained without assuming that, as we would now say, the value patterns were internalized as part of personality. Durkheim, as a result of certain terminological peculiarities which need not be gone into here, tended to identify "society" as such with the system of moral norms. In this very special sense of the term society, it is significant that he set forth the explicit formula that "society exists only in the minds of individuals."

In Durkheim's work, there are only suggestions relative to the psychological mechanisms of internalization and the place of internalized moral values in the structure of personality itself. But this does not detract from the massive phenomenon of the convergence of the fundamental insights of Freud and Durkheim, insights not only as to the fundamental importance of moral values in human behavior, but of the internalization of these values. This convergence, from two quite distinct and independent starting points, deserves to be ranked as one of the truly fundamental landmarks of the development of modern social science. It may be likened to the convergence between the results of the experimental study of plant breeding by Mendel and of the microscopic study of cell division—a convergence which resulted in the discovery of the chromosomes as bearers of the genes. Only when the two quite distinct bodies of scientific knowledge could be put together did the modern science of genetics emerge.

The convergence of Freud's and Durkheim's thinking may serve to set the problem of this paper: how can the fundamental phenomenon of the internalization of moral norms be analyzed in such a way as to maximize the generality of implications of the formulation, both for the theory of personality and for the theory of the social system? For if it is possible to state the essentials of the problem in a sufficiently generalized way, the analysis should prove to be equally relevant in both directions. It should thereby contribute to the integration of the psychoanalytic theory of personality and of the sociological theory of the social system, and thus to the further development of a conceptual scheme which is essentially common to both.

The essential starting point of an attempt to link these two bodies of theory is the analysis of certain fundamental features of the interaction of two or more persons, the process of interaction itself being conceived as a system. Once the essentials of such an interactive system have been made clear, the implications of the analysis can be followed out in both directions: the study of the structure and functioning of the personality as a system, in relation to the other personalities; and the study of the functioning of the social system as a system. It may be surmised that the difficulty of bringing the two strands of thought together in the past has stemmed from the fact that this analysis has not been carried through; and this has not been done because it has "fallen between two stools." On the one hand, Freud and his followers, by concentrating on the single personality, have failed to consider adequately the implications of the individual's interaction with other personalities *to form a system*. On the other hand, Durkheim and the other sociologists have failed, in their concentration on the social system as a system to consider systematically the implications of the fact that it is *the interaction of personalities* which constitutes the social system with which they have been dealing, and that, therefore, adequate analysis of motivational process in such a system must reckon with the problems of personality. This circumstance would seem to account for the fact that this subject has been so seriously neglected.

It may first be pointed out that two interacting persons must be conceived to be objects to each other in two primary respects, and in a third respect which is in a sense derived from the first two. These are (1) cognitive perception and conceptualization, the answer to the question of *what the object is,* and (2) cathexis—attachment or aversion—the answer to the question of *what the object means* in an emotional sense. The third mode by which a person orients himself to an object is by evaluation—the integration of cognitive and cathectic meanings of the object to form a system, including the stability of such a system over time. It may be maintained that no stable relation between two or more objects is possible without all three of these modes of orientation being present for *both* parties to the relationship.[3]

Consideration of the conditions on which such a stable, mutually oriented system of interaction depends leads to the conclusion that on the human level this mutuality of interaction must be mediated and stabilized by a common culture—that is, by a commonly shared system of symbols, the meanings of which are understood on both sides with an approximation to agreement. The existence of such symbol systems, especially though not exclusively as involved in language, is common to every known human society. However the going symbol systems of the society may have developed in the first place, they are involved in the socialization of every child. It may be presumed that the prominence of common symbol systems is both a consequence and a condition of the extreme plasticity and sensitivity of the human organism, which in turn are essential conditions of its capacity to learn and, concomitantly, to mislearn. These features of the human organism introduce an element of extreme potential instability into the process of human interaction, which requires stabilizing mechanisms if the interactive system, as a system, is to function.

The elements of the common culture have significance with reference to all three of the modes of orientation of action. Some of them are primarily of cognitive significance; others are primarily of cathectic significance, expressive of emotional meanings or affect; and still others are primarily of evaluative significance. Normative regulation for the establishing of standards is characteristic of all of culture; thus there is a right way of symbolizing any orientation of action in any given culture. This is indeed essential to communication itself: the conventions of the language must be observed if there is to be effective communication.

That a person's cathexis of a human object—that is, what the object means to the person emotionally—is contingent on the responsiveness of that object is a fact familiar to psychoanalytic theory. It may be regarded as almost a truism that it is difficult if not impossible in the long run to love without being loved in return. It is more difficult to see that there is an almost direct parallelism in this respect between cathexis and cognition. After all, a person's cathexis of an inanimate object, such as a food object, is not directly dependent on the responsiveness of the object; it is surely anthropomorphism to suggest that a steak likes to be eaten in the same sense in which a hungry man likes to eat the steak. Similarly, the cognition of the inanimate object by a person is not directly dependent on the object's reciprocal cognition of the person. But where the object is another person, the two, as ego and alter, constitute an interactive system. The question is what, in a cognitive sense, *is* alter from the point of view of ego, and vice versa. Clearly, the answer to this question must involve the place—or "status," as sociologists call it—of ego and alter in the structure of the interactive system. Thus, when I say a person is my mother, or my friend, or my student, I am characterizing that person as a participant in a system of social interaction in which I also am involved.

Therefore, not only the cathectic attitudes, but also the cognitive images, of persons relative to each other are functions of their interaction in the system of social relations; in a fundamental sense the same order of relationship applies in both cases.

Thus, a social system is a function of the common culture, which not only forms the basis of the intercommunication of its members, but which defines, and so in one sense determines, the relative statuses of its members. There is, within surprisingly broad limits, no intrinsic significance of persons to each other independent of their actual interaction. In so far as these relative statuses are defined and regulated in terms of a common culture, the following apparently paradoxical statement holds true: what persons *are* can only be understood in terms of a set of beliefs and sentiments which define what they *ought to be*. This proposition is true only in a very broad way but is none the less crucial to the understanding of social systems.

It is in this context that the central significance of moral standards in the common culture of systems of social interaction must be understood. Moral standards constitute, as the focus of the evaluative aspect of the common culture, the core of the stabilizing mechanisms of the system of social interaction. These mechanisms function, moreover, to stabilize not only attitudes—that is, the emotional meanings of persons to each other— but also categorizations—the cognitive definitions of what persons are in a socially significant sense.

If the approach taken above is correct, the place of the superego as part of the structure of the personality must be understood in terms of the relation between personality and the total common culture, by virtue of which a stable system of social interaction on the human levels becomes possible. Freud's insight was profoundly correct when he focused on the element of moral standards. This is, indeed, central and crucial, but it does seem that Freud's view was too narrow. The inescapable conclusion is that not only moral standards, but *all the components of the common culture* are internalized as part of the personality structure. Moral standards, indeed, cannot in this respect be dissociated from the content of the orientation patterns which they regulate; as I have pointed out, the content of both cathectic-attitudes and cognitive-status definitions have cultural, hence normative, significance. This content is cultural and learned. Neither what the human object *is*, in the most significant respects, nor what it *means* emotionally, can be understood as given independently of the nature of the interactive process itself; and the significance of moral norms themselves very largely relates to this fact.

It would seem that Freud's insight in this field was seriously impeded by the extent to which he thought in terms of a frame of reference relating a personality to its situation or environment without specific reference to the analysis of the social interaction of persons as a system. This perspective, which was overwhelmingly dominant in his day, accounts for two features of his theory. In the first place, the cognitive definition of the object world does not seem to have been problematical to Freud. He subsumed it all under "external reality," in relation to which "ego-functions" constitute a process of adaptation. He failed to take explicitly into account the fact that the frame of reference in terms of which objects are cognized, and therefore adapted to, is cultural and thus cannot be taken for granted as given, but must be internalized as a condition of the development of mature ego-functioning. In this respect, it seems to be correct to say that Freud introduced an unreal separation between the superego and the ego—the lines between them are in fact difficult to define in his theory. In the light of the foregoing considerations, the distinction which Freud makes between the superego and the ego—that the former is internalized by identification and that the latter seems to consist of responses to external reality rather than of internalized culture—is not tenable. These responses are, to be sure, learned responses; but internalization is a special kind of learning which Freud seemed to confine to the superego.

If this argument raises questions about cognitive function and therefore about the theory of the ego, there are implications, *ipso facto,* for the superego. The essential point seems to be that Freud's view seems to imply that the object, as cognitively significant, is given independently of the actor's internalized culture and that superego standards are then applied to it. This fails to take account of the extent to which the constitution of the object and its moral appraisal are part and parcel of the same fundamental cultural patterns; it gives the superego an appearance of arbitrariness and dissociation from the rest of the personality—particularly from the ego—which is not wholly in accord with the facts.

The second problem of Freud's theory concerns the relation of cathexis or affect to the superego. In a sense, this is the obverse of its relation to cognition. The question here is perhaps analogous to that of the transmission of light in physics: how can the object's cathectic significance be mediated in the absence of direct biological contact? Indeed, embarrassment over this problem may be one source of the stressing of sexuality in Freudian theory, since sexuality generally involves such direct contact.

To Freud, the object tends, even if human, to be an inert something on which a "charge" of cathectic significance has been placed. The process is regarded as expressive of the actor's instincts or libido, but the element of mutuality tends to be treated as accessory and almost arbitrary. This is associated with the fact that, while Freud, especially in his *Interpretation of Dreams,* made an enormous contribution to the theory of expressive or cathectic symbolism, there is a very striking limitation of the extension of this theory. The basis of this may be said to be that Freud tended to confine his consideration of symbolism in the emotional context to its directly expressive functions and failed to go on to develop the analysis of its communicative functions. The dream symbol remained for him the prototype of affective symbolism. It is perhaps largely because of this fact that Freud did not emphasize the common culture aspect of such symbolism but tended to attempt to trace its origins back to intrinsic meanings which were independent of the interactive process and its common culture. More generally, the tenor of the analysis of affect was to emphasize a fundamental isolation of the individual in his lonely struggle with his id.[4]

This whole way of looking at the problem of cathexis seems to have a set of consequences parallel to those outlined above concerning cognition; it tends to dissociate the superego from the sources of affect. This derives from the fact that Freud apparently did not appreciate the presence and significance of a common culture of expressive-affective symbolism and the consequent necessity for thinking of the emotional component of interaction as mediated by this aspect of the common culture. Thus, the aspect of the superego which is concerned with the regulation of emotional reactions must be considered as defining the regulative principles of this interaction system. It is an integral part of the symbolism of emotional expression, not something over, above, and apart from it.

The general purport of this criticism is that Freud, with his formulation of the concept of the superego, made only a beginning at an analysis of the role of the common culture in personality. The structure of his theoretical scheme prevented him from seeing the possibilities for extending the same fundamental analysis from the internalization of moral standards—which he applied to the superego—to the internalization of the cognitive frame of reference for interpersonal relations and for the common system of expressive symbolism; similarly, it prevented him from seeing the extent to which these three elements of the common culture are integrated with each other.

This very abstract analysis may become somewhat more understandable if examples are given of what is meant by the cognitive reference or categorization system and by the system of expressive symbolism, considering both as parts of the internalized common culture.

One of the most striking cases of the first is that of sex categorization— that is, the learning of sex role. Freud speaks of the original "bisexuality" of the child. The presumption is that he postulated a constitutionally-given duality of orientation. In terms of the present approach, there is at least an alternative hypothesis possible which should be explored.[5] This hypothesis is that some of the principal facts which Freud interpreted as manifestations of constitutional bisexuality can be explained by the fact that the categorization of human persons—including the actor's categorization of himself taken as a point of reference—into two sexes is not, except in its somatic points of reference, biologically given but, in psychological significance, must be learned by the child. It is fundamental that children of both sexes start life with essentially the same relation to the mother, a fact on which Freud himself rightly laid great stress. It may then be suggested that the process by which the boy learns to differentiate himself in terms of sex from the mother and in this sense "identify" with the father, while the girl learns to identify with the mother, is a learning process. One major part of the process of growing up is the internalization of one's own sex role as a critical part of the self-image. It may well be that this way of looking at the process will have the advantage of making the assumption of constitutional bisexuality at least partly superfluous as an explanation of the individual's sex identification. In any case, it has the great advantage of linking the determination of sex categorization directly with the role structure of the social system in a theoretical as well as an empirical sense. Every sociologist will appreciate this since he is familiar with the crucial significance of sex-role differentiation and constitution for social structure.

An example of the second role, that of common expressive symbolism, may be found in terms of the process by which a reciprocal love attitude between mother and child is built up. Freud quite rightly, it seems, points to the origin of the child's love attitude as found in his dependency on the mother for the most elementary sources of gratification, such as food, elementary comforts, and safety. Gradually, in the process of interaction, a system of expectations of the continuation and repetition of these gratifications comes to be built up in the child; and these expectations are bound together as a result of the fact that a variety of such gratifications comes from the single source, the mother.

In this process, one may assume that well before the development of language there begins to occur a process of generalization, so that certain acts of the mother are interpreted as signs that gratifying performances can be expected—for example, the child becomes able to interpret her approaching footsteps or the tone of her voice. It is suggested that one of the main reasons why the erotic component of the child's relation to the mother is so important lies in the fact that, since bodily contact is an essential aspect of child care, erotic gratifications readily take on a symbolic significance. The erotic element has the extremely important property that it is relatively diffuse, being awakened by any sort of affectionate bodily contact. This diffuseness makes it particularly suitable as a vehicle of symbolic meanings. By this process, then, gradually, there is a transition from the child's focus on erotic stimulation as such, to his focus on the mother's *attitude* which is expressed by the erotically pleasurable stimulation. Only when this transition has taken place can one correctly speak of the child's having become dependent on the *love* of the mother and not merely on the specific pleasures the mother dispenses to him. Only when this level is reached, can the love attitude serve as a motivation to the acceptance of disciplines, since it can then remain stable—even though many specific gratifications which have previously been involved in the relationship are eliminated from it.

The essential point for present purposes is that, in its affective aspect, the child's interaction with the mother is not only a process of mutual gratification of needs, but is on the child's part a process of learning of the symbolic significance of a complicated system of acts on the part of the mother— of what they signify about what she feels and of how they are interdependent with and thus in part consequences of his own acts. That is to say, there is developed a complex language of emotional communication between them. Only when the child has learned this language on a relatively complex level, can he be said to have learned to love his mother or to be dependent on her love for him. There is, thus, a transition from "pleasure dependence" to "love dependence." One primary aspect of learning to love and to be loved is the internalization of a common culture of expressive symbolism which makes it possible for the child to express *and communicate* his feelings and to understand the mother's feelings toward him.

It would seem that only when a sufficiently developed cognitive reference system and a system of expressive symbolism have been internalized is the foundation laid for the development of a superego; for only then can the child be said to be capable of understanding, in both the cognitive and the emotional senses, the meaning of the prescriptions and prohibitions which are laid upon him. The child must mature to the point where he can begin to play a responsible role in a system of social interaction, where he can understand that what people feel is a function of his and their conformity with mutually held standards of conduct. Only when he has become dependent on his mother's love can he develop meaningful anxiety, in that then he might jeopardize his security in that love by not living up to her expectations of being a good boy.

The above considerations have important implications for the nature of the process of identification in so far as that is the principal mechanism by which the superego is acquired. If this analysis is correct, the crucial problem concerns the process of internalization of the common culture, including all three of its major components—the cognitive reference system, the system of expressive symbolism, and the system of moral standards.

In the first place, it would seem to be clear that only cultural symbol systems can be internalized. An object can be cathected, cognized, and appraised, but it cannot as such be taken into the personality; the only sense in which the latter terminology is appropriate is in calling attention to the fact that the common culture is indeed part of the personality of the object, but it is only an aspect, not the whole of it. Two persons can be said to be identified with each other in so far as they share important components of common culture. But since roles in the social system are differentiated, it should be noted that it is always important to specify what elements of culture are common.

Secondly, it is important to point out that the learning of the common culture may lead to the assumption either of a role identical with that of the object of identification or of a role differentiated from that object's role. Thus in the case of the boy vis-à-vis his mother, the learning of his sex categorization enables him to understand and accept the fact that with respect to sex he is different from her. The standards of proper behavior for both sexes are shared by the members of both, but their application is differentiated. The usage of the term identification has often been ambiguous, since it has been used to imply a likeness both of standards and of application. From the present point of view it is quite correct to speak of a boy learning his sex role by identification with the mother—in that he learns the sex categorization partly from her—and by the fact that he and she belong to different sex categories, which has important implications for his behavior. This is different from identification with his father in the sense that he learns that, with respect to sex, he is classed with his father and not with his mother.

Thirdly, there seems to be excellent evidence that while identification cannot mean coming *to be the object*, it is, as internalization of common culture, dependent on *positive cathexis of the object*. The considerations reviewed above give some suggestions as to why this should be true. Internalization of a culture pattern is not merely knowing it as an object of the external world; it is incorporating it into actual structure of the personality as such. This means that the culture pattern must be integrated with the affective system of the personality.

Culture, however, is a system of generalized symbols and their meanings. In order for the integration with affect, which constitutes internalization, to take place, the individual's own affective organization must achieve levels of generalization of a high order. The principal mechanism by which this is accomplished appears to be through the building up of attachments to other persons—that is, by emotional communication with others so that the individual is sensitized to the attitudes of the others, not merely to their specific acts with their intrinsic gratification-deprivation significance. In other words, the process of forming attachments is in itself inherently a process of the generalization of affect. But this generalization in turn actually is in one major aspect the process of symbolization of emotional meanings—that is, it is a process of the acquisition of culture. The intrinsic difficulty of creation of cultural patterns is so great that the child can only acquire complex cultural generalization through interaction with others who already possess it. Cathexis of an object as a focal aspect of identification is then another name for the development of *motivation* for the internalization of cultural patterns, at least for one crucially important phase of this process.

The conditions of socialization of a person are such that the gratifications which derive from this cathexis of objects cannot be secured unless, along with generalization of emotional meanings and their communication, he also develops a cognitive categorization of objects, including himself, and a system of moral norms which regulate the relations between himself and the object (a superego). This way of looking at the process of identification serves perhaps to help clear up a confusing feature of Freud's method of treatment. Freud, it will be remembered, denies that the very young child is capable of object cathexis and speaks of identification, in contrast with object cathexis, as "the earliest form of emotional tie with an object." He then speaks of identification with the father in the Oedipus situation as a reversion to the more "primitive" form of relation to an object.

I would agree that the child's early attachment to the mother and his later cathexis of her are not the same thing. It seems probable that the earliest attachment is, as it were, precultural, while true object cathexis involves the internalization of a cultural symbol system. But it seems extremely doubtful whether the relation to the father in the Oedipus situation can be correctly described as a reversion to a presymbolic level. It is impossible to go into this problem fully here; but it may be suggested that the Oedipus situation might be better interpreted as the strain imposed on the child by forcing him to take a major further step in growing up, in the process of which the father becomes the focus of his ambivalent feelings precisely because the child dare not jeopardize his love relation to the mother. Although regressive patterns of reaction would be expected under such a strain, these are not the core of the process of identification; however important, they are secondary phenomena.

If the foregoing account of the internalized content of personality and of the processes of identification points in the right direction, it would seem to imply the necessity for certain modifications of Freud's structural theory of personality. The first point is that it is not only the superego which is internalized—that is, taken over by identification from cathected social objects—but that there are involved other important components which presumably must be included in the ego—namely, the system of cognitive categorizations of the object world and the system of expressive symbolism.

If this is correct, it would seem to necessitate, secondly, an important modification of Freud's conception of the ego. The element of organization, which is the essential property of the ego, would then not be derived from the "reality-principle"—that is, from adaptative responses to the external world alone. Instead it would be derived from two fundamental sources: the external world as an environment, and the common culture which is acquired from objects of identification. Both are, to be sure, acquired from outside, but the latter component of the ego is, in origin and character, more like the superego than it is like the lessons of experience.

Third, there are similar problems concerning the borderline between the ego and the id. A clue to what may be needed here is given in Freud's own frequent references to what have here been called "expressive symbols," as representatives to the ego of the impulses of the id. It seems to be a necessary implication of the above analysis that these symbolized and symbolically organized emotions are not only representatives *to* the ego; they should also be considered as integral *parts of* the ego. This may be felt to be a relatively radical conclusion—namely, that emotions, or affect on the normal human adult level, should be regarded as a *symbolically generalized* system, that it is never "id-impulse" as such. Affect is not a direct expression of drive-motivation but involves it only as it is organized and integrated with both the reality experience of the individual and the cultural patterns which he has learned through the processes of identification.

More generally, the view of personality developed in this paper seems to be broadly in line with the recent increasing emphasis in psychoanalytic theory itself on the psychology of the ego and the problems of its integration and functioning as a system. Freud's structural theory was certainly fundamentally on the right track in that it clearly formulated the three major points of reference of personality theory—the needs of the organism, the external situation, and the patterns of the culture. In view of the intellectual traditions within which Freud's own theoretical development took place, it was in the nature of the case that the cultural element, as he formulated it in the concept of the superego, should have been the last of the three to be developed and the most difficult to fit in.

In the light of the development of the more general theory of action, however, the cultural element must, as I have attempted to show, certainly occupy a very central place. For if the ego and the id in Freud's formulations are taken alone, there is no adequate bridge from the theory of personality to the theoretical analysis of culture and of the social system. The superego provides exactly such a bridge because it is not explicable on any other basis than that of acquisition from other human beings, through the process of social interaction.

Essentially what this paper has done has been to examine the concept of the superego in the light of the maturing bodies of theory in the fields of culture and of the social system; and it has attempted to follow through the implications of the appearance of the superego in Freud's thinking for the theory of personality itself. The result has been the suggestion of certain modifications in Freud's own theory of personality.

In this sense, the paper has contained a good deal of criticism of Freud, which may appear to be out of place in a paper dealing with the contributions of psychoanalysis to social science. It is, however, emphatically not the intent of the author to have this appear as primarily a critical paper. It has been necessary to emphasize the critical aspect at certain points, since the psychiatric or psychoanalytic reader is not likely to be adequately familiar with the developments in sociological theory which are so importantly related to the concept of the superego. The essential intent, however, is to contribute to the development of a common foundation for the theoretical analysis of human behavior which can serve to unify all of the sciences which take this as their subject matter. The massive and fundamental fact is that Freud formulated the concept of the superego and fitted it into his general analysis of human motivation. This and the parallel formulations in the field of sociology are the solid foundations on which we must build. I believe it can truthfully be said that we are now in a position to bring the theory of personality and the theory of the social system within essentially the same general conceptual scheme. Freud's contribution of the concept of the superego has been one of the important factors making this possible.

Notes

TOWARD A FRAMEWORK FOR THE FUNCTIONAL ANALYSIS OF FAMILY BEHAVIOR

1. This is, however, not the statistically normal unit. In 1953, only 28.6 per cent of household units consisted of a married couple and their own children under 18 years of age. See Paul C. Glick, *American Families* (New York: Wiley, 1957), p. 2.

2. Various references are available on the subject. See Robert K. Merton "Manifest and Latent Functions," in Merton, *Social Theory and Social Structure* (Glencoe, Ill.: The Free Press, 1949); Marion J. Levy, *The Structure of Society* (Princeton, N.J.: Princeton University Press, 1952); Walter Buckley, "Structural-functional Theory in Modern Sociology," in Howard Becker and Alvin Boskoff, *Modern Sociological Theory in Continuity and Change* (New York:Dryden Press, 1957).

3. Talcott Parsons, *The Social System* (Glencoe, Ill.: The Free Press, 1951) Cf. Ludwig Von Bertalanffy, "An Outline of General Systems Theory," *British Journal for the Philosophy of Science*, I (1950), 134–65.

4. John P. Spiegel, "A Model for Relationships among Systems," in Roy R. Grinker (ed.), *Toward a Unified Theory of Human Behavior* (New York: Basic Books, Inc., 1956). See also John P. Spiegel and Norman W. Bell, "The Family of the Psychiatric Patient," in Silvano Arieti (ed.), *American Handbook of Psychiatry* (New York: Basic Books, Inc., 1959).

5. Talcott Parsons and Neil Smelser, *Economy and Society* (Glencoe, Ill.: The Free Press, 1956).

6. For a good brief account, see David Greenwood, "The Study of Family Group Patterns" and "Institutional Development of the Family" in *Essays in Human Relations* (Washington, D.C.: Public Affairs Press, 1956).

7. Spiegel and Bell, *loc. cit.*

8. Nathan Ackerman and M. L. Behrens, "Child and Family Psychopathy: Problems of Correlation," in P. H. Hoch and J. Zubin (eds.), *Psychopathology of Childhood* (New York: Grune and Stratton, 1955), p. 182.

9. This analysis is based in part on the functional subsystems of society as treated by Talcott Parsons. See Talcott Parsons and Neil Smelser, *Economy and Society*.

10. For example, in a recent study by Kent Geiger, it was shown that the family was more united by the arrest of a member by the state than by the failure of the husband to earn an adequate income. Apparently the inability to earn an adequate wage is something regarded as the family's responsibility, in comparison with reference groups. See Kent Geiger, "Deprivation and Solidarity in the Soviet Urban Family," *American Sociological Review* XX (1955), 57–68. Cf. selection 14, this volume.

11. See, for example, E. E. Evans-Pritchard, *Marriage and Kinship among the Nuer* (London: Oxford University Press, 1951).

12. See Florence Kluckhohn, "Dominant and Variant Value-Orientations," in Clyde Kluckhohn, Henry A. Murray, and David M. Schneider (eds.), *Personality in Nature, Society and Culture* (New York: Knopf, 1953). Cf. selection 24, this volume.

13. In a recent study of London families, Michael Young has noted wide variations in the way goods are distributed within a family. Michael Young, "The Distribution of Income within the Family," *British Journal of Sociology*, III (1952), 305–21.

14. See George C. Homans, *The Human Group* (New York: Harcourt, Brace, and Co., 1950).

15. See Mirra Komarovsky, *The Unemployed Man and His Family* (New York: Dryden Press, 1940).

16. For some comments on studies on authority, see René König, "Family and Authority: The German Father in 1955," *Sociological Review*, V (1957), 107–25.

17. See, for example, Reuben Hill, *Families Under Stress* (New York: Harper and Brothers, 1949).

18. See, for example, Alex Inkeles, "Social Change and Social Character: The Role of Parental Mediation," *Journal of Social Issues* II, No. 2 (1955), 12–23.

19. Spiegel and Bell, *loc. cit.*

20. F. L. Strodtbeck, "Family Interaction, Values, and Achievement," in David McClelland *et al.*, *Talent and Society* (Princeton, N.J.: Van Nostrand, 1958), gives a good account of the relation of authority and leadership processes in the family to the son's achievement motivation.

1. THE UNIVERSALITY OF THE NUCLEAR FAMILY

1. The terms "polygamy" and "polygamous" are used in their recognized technical sense as referring to any form of plural marriage; "polygyny" will be employed for the marriage of one man to two or more women and "polyandry" for the marriage of one woman to two or more men.

2. Cf. M. K. Opler, "Woman's Social Status and the Forms of Marriage," *American Journal of Sociology*, XLIX (1943), 144; A.

R. Radcliffe-Brown, "The Study of Kinship Systems," *Journal of the Royal Anthropological Institute*, LXXI (1941), 2.

3. R. H. Lowie, *Primitive Society* (New York, 1920), pp. 66–67. Cf. also F. Boas *et al*, *General Anthropology* (Boston, 1938), p. 411; B. Malinowski, "Kinship," *Encyclopaedia Britannica* (14th ed.; London, 1929), XIII, 404.

4. R. Linton, *The Study of Man* (New York, 1936), pp. 153 (quoted), 154–55.

5. Cf. R. F. Kaindl, "Aus der Volksuberlieferung der Bojken," *Globus*, LXXIX (1901), 155.

6. A cross-cousin is the child of a father's sister or of a mother's brother. The children of a father's brother and of a mother's sister are technically known as "parallel cousins."

7. See, for example, E. Westermarck, *The History of Human Marriage* (5th ed.; New York, 1922), I, 72; A. M. Tozzer, *Social Origins and Social Continuities* (New York, 1925), p. 145.

8. J. Lippert, *Kulturgeschichte der Menschheit in ihrem organischen Aufbau* (Stuttgart, 1886–87), I, 70–74; II, 5.

9. See, for example, R. Briffault, *The Mothers* (New York, 1927), I, 608; W. G. Sumner and A. G. Keller, *The Science of Society* (New Haven, 1927), III, 1495–98, 1517; P. Vinogradoff, *Outlines of Historical Jurisprudence*, I (New York, 1920), 203.

10. See Sumner and Keller, *op. cit.*, III, 1505–18.

11. *Ibid.*, I, 111–40.

12. See G. P. Murdock, "Comparative Data on the Division of Labor by Sex," *Social Forces*, XV (1937), 551–53, for an analysis of the distribution of economic activities by sex in 224 societies.

13. Cf. M. Mead, *Sex and Temperament in Three Primitive Societies* (New York, 1935).

14. The term "sibling" is employed in its technical sense as designating either a brother or a sister irrespective of sex.

15. Cf. Linton, *op. cit.*, p. 155.

4. THE ATTEMPT TO ABOLISH THE FAMILY IN RUSSIA

1. See, for instance, Nathan Berman, "Juvenile Delinquency in the Soviet Union," *American Journal of Sociology*, March, 1937.

2. A. Kollontay, "The Family and the Communist State" (Russian; 1919), p. 8; N. Bukharin, *Proceedings of the XIII Congress of the Communist Party* (Russian; 1924), p. 545.

3. Cf. John Hazard in "Law and the Soviet Family," *Wisconsin Law Review*, 1939, p. 245.

4. First by the decree of December 17 and 18, 1917, later on consolidated and expanded by the Family Code of October 22, 1918.

5. New Economic Policy.

6. Decision of the Supreme Court of the RSFSR, reported in *Sudebnaya Praktika*, 1929, No. 20.

7. *Izvestia*, July 7, 1935.

8. *Pravda*, June 4 and 26, 1935; *Molodaya Gvardiya*, 1935, No. 1.

9. *Sotsialisticheskaya Zakonnost*, 1939, No. 2.

10. A group of workers pledged to work

substantially faster and better than required by regulations.

11. *Izvestia*, September 9, 1935; *Pravda*, September 11, 1935.

12. *Izvestia*, July 7, 1937; *Krasyaya Gazeta*, November 4, 1934.

13. *New York Times*, November 18, 1936.

14. *Izvestia*, February 12, 1937.

15. *New York Times*, July 11, 1944.

16. For instance, by Arkhangelski, member of the Academy of Sciences, *Izvestia*, June 5, 1935.

17. The second antidivorce law (1944) substantially increased the advantages granted to mothers of numerous children. Honorary titles were granted to mothers of seven or more children.

18. Young Communist League.

19. *Komsomolskaya Pravda*, June 7 and September 29, 1935; *Pravda*, August 4, 1935.

20. *Sovetskaya Yustitsia*, 1939, No. 4.

21. *Izvestia*, October 23, 1935.

5. IS THE FAMILY UNIVERSAL?—THE ISRAELI CASE

1. G. P. Murdock, *Social Structure* (New York: The Macmillan Co., 1949), p. 11.

2. *Ibid.*

3. *Ibid.*, p. 10.

4. The field work, on which statements concerning the *kibbutz* are based, was conducted in the year 1951–52.

5. *Ibid.*, p. 1.

6. *Ibid.*, p. 8.

7. *Ibid.*

8. Other terms, "young man" (*bachur*) and "young woman" (*bachura*), are also used in place of "husband" and "wife." If more than

one person in the *kibbutz* has the same proper name, and there is some question as to who is being referred to when the name is mentioned in conversation, the person is identified by adding, "the *bachur* of so-and-so," or "the *bachura* of so-and-so."

9. M. Zborowski and E. Herzog, *Life Is with People* (New York: International Universities Press, 1952), p. 308.

10. Murdock, *op. cit.*, p. 10.

11. R. Redfield, "The Folk Society," *American Journal of Sociology*, LII (1947), 297, 301.

12. For a report on the *kibbutz* and its family relations, see Melford E. Spiro, *Kibbutz: Venture in Utopia* (Cambridge, Mass.: Harvard University Press, 1956) and *Children of the Kibbutz* (Cambridge, Mass.: Harvard University Press, 1958).

6. IS THE FAMILY UNIVERSAL?—THE NAYAR CASE

1. The fieldwork on which this paper is based was carried out in three villages of Kerala between September, 1947, and July, 1949, with the aid of a William Wyse Studentship from Trinity College, Cambridge, England. Writing it has formed part of a project financed by the American Social Science Research Council.

2. *Notes and Queries on Anthropology* (6th ed.; London: Routledge and Kegan Paul, Ltd., 1951).

3. E. E. Evans-Pritchard, *Kinship and Marriage among the Nuer* (London: Oxford University Press, 1951), pp. 108–9.

4. In America, Miss Alisa S. Lourié, Douglass College, Rutgers University, has recently worked on this problem and I have been much stimulated by correspondence with her and by reading an unpublished paper of hers, *Concepts in Family Sociology*. In this paper Miss Lourié formulates a definition of marriage which is narrower than mine, but when her work is published readers will see that I was helped toward my definition by her analysis. I have also profited much from discussions with my husband, David F. Aberle.

5. E. R. Leach, "Polyandry, Inheritance and the Definition of Marriage," *Man,* No. 199 (1955), pp. 182–86.

6. *Ibid.,* p. 183.
   A. To establish the legal father of a woman's children.
   B. To establish the legal mother of a man's children.
   C. To give the husband a monopoly in the wife's sexuality.
   D. To give the wife a monopoly in the husband's sexuality.
   E. To give the husband partial or monopolistic rights to the wife's domestic and other labor services.
   F. To give the wife partial or monopolistic rights to the husband's labor services.
   G. To give the husband partial or total rights over property belonging or potentially accruing to the wife.
   H. To give the wife partial or total rights over property belonging or potentially accruing to the husband.
   I. To establish a joint fund of property —a partnership—for the benefit of the children of the marriage.
   J. To establish a socially significant "relationship of affinity" between the husband and his wife's brothers.

7. E. Kathleen Gough, "Changing Kinship Usages in the Setting of Political and Economic Change among the Nayars of Mala-

bar," *Journal of the Royal Anthropological Institute,* LXXXII (1952), Part 1. Also, "The Traditional Lineage and Kinship System of the Nayars," Unpublished manuscript in the Haddon Library, Cambridge, England, 1955.

8. Gough, "The Traditional Lineage and Kinship System. . . ."

9. *Ibid.*

10. Leach, *loc. cit.*

11. Gough, "Changing Kinship Usages. . . ," *J. R. Anthrop. Inst.*

12. E. Kathleen Gough, "Female Initiation Rites on the Malabar Coast," *Journal of the Royal Anthropological Institute,* LXXXV (1955), Parts I and II, pp. 45–80.

13. Alexander Hamilton, *A New Account of the East Indies,* 1727, in John Pinkerton, *A General Collection of Voyages and Travels* (London: Longman, 1811), p. 374.

14. Francis (Hamilton) Buchanan, *A Journey from Madras through Mysore, Canara and Malabar* (3 vols.; London: T. Cadell and W. Davies, 1807).

15. G. P. Murdock, *Social Structure* (New York: Macmillan, 1949), chap. i.

16. A. R. Radcliffe-Brown and D. Forde (eds.), *African Systems of Kinship and Marriage* (London: Oxford University Press, 1950). Radcliffe-Brown expressed this view most recently and fully in the Introduction to the aforenamed book, pp. 73 ff.

17. Leach, *loc. cit.*

18. Gough, "Changing Kinship Usages. . . ," *J. R. Anthrop. Inst.,* p. 73.

19. *Notes and Queries . . .* p. 24, line 5.

20. I agree with Dr. Leach that the Iravas of Central Kerala had true fraternal polyandry. My own enquiries produced evidence supporting Aiyappan's view that the brothers shared equally both sexual rights in the wife and also legal paternity of the children, in the same manner in which they were co-owners of the ancestral property. The eldest living brother at any given time was simply the legal representative of this corporation.

I do not know whether the Nayars believed it possible for two or more men to contribute to the formation of one embryo. I think it possible that they did, for I found this belief among villagers of the Tamil country. Among these castes it formed part of a belief that several acts of intercourse are necessary to "feed" the embryo and assist it to grow.

21. Evans-Pritchard, *op. cit.,* pp. 21, 26.

22. H. R. H. Prince Peter of Greece and Denmark, "For a New Definition of Marriage," *Man,* No. 46 (1956), p. 48.

23. H. R. H. Prince Peter of Greece and Denmark, "For a New Definition of Marriage," *Man,* No. 35 (1957), p. 32.

24. W. H. R. Rivers, *The Todas* (London, New York: Macmillan Co., Ltd., 1906), p. 526.

25. I agree with Dr. Fischer that Prince Peter's definition of marriage is a tautology and so of no assistance (*Man*, 1956, 92). All that Prince Peter's second note shows (*Man*, 1957, 35) is that several peoples of his acquaintance have different terms for different kinds of relationships between men and women. But unless we approach these with some guiding concepts of our own in mind, we cannot decide which of them to translate as "marriage" and which as "concubinage."

7. THE STABILITY OF THE AMERICAN FAMILY SYSTEM

1. Emphasized particularly by W. F. Ogburn. See, for instance, chap. xiii, "The Family and Its Functions," *Recent Social Trends in the U.S.*, Report of President's Research Committee on Social Trends, 1933.

2. "Two-thirds of those couples obtaining divorce are childless; one-fifth have only one child. In fact, there seems to be a definite relationship between childless marriages and divorce. That a relatively small number of children in the United States have divorced parents—may be owing, in part, to the fact that many couples do not stay married long enough to have a large family. Over 35 per cent of those divorced in 1940 had been married less than four years. The average length of marriages ending in divorce is less than six years." H. E. Barnes and O. M. Ruedi, *The American Way of Life* (New York: Prentice Hall, Inc., 1951), pp. 652–53.

3. A consistent rise started in 1940. Even the lowest war year, 1945, was only down to 20.4 per thousand population, and the rate has remained substantially above the level of the thirties since. Source: National Office of Vital Statistics, "Summary of Natality Statistics, United States, 1950," *Vital Statistics—Special Reports, National Summaries*, Vol. XXXVII (May 19, 1953).

The national office estimates that a slight drop from the 1947 boom (itself caused by demobilization) is accountable by the following: drop in first children because of lowered marriage rates, 1946–49; but rise in births of second, third, and fourth children during 1946–49.

4. It is not possible to find figures which exclude private multiple-family units, but general evidence is that the proportion of these has decreased, not increased. Source for building rates: Bureau of Labor Statistics, *New Construction, Expenditures 1915–51, Labor Requirements, 1939–51*, 1953.

5. T. N. Carver, *Essays in Social Justice* (Cambridge, Mass.: Harvard University Press, 1915).

8. THE IMPACT OF URBAN CIVILIZATION UPON NEGRO FAMILY LIFE

1. Frank A. Ross, "Urbanization of the Negro," *Publications of the American Sociological Society*, XXVI, 118.

2. *Ibid.*, p. 21. For literature on the movement of the Negro to northern cities one should consult Louise V. Kennedy, *The Negro Peasant Turns Cityward* (New York, 1930). This study lists books, articles, and editorials by 159 authors and organizations.

3. A detailed discussion of these four types may be found in E. Franklin Frazier, "Traditions and Patterns of Negro Family Life in the United States," in E. B. Reuter (ed.), *Race and Culture Contacts* (New York, 1934), pp. 191–207.

4. *The Transient Unemployed* (Research Monograph III [Washington, 1935]), p. 33.

5. From the records of the Unattached and Transient Division.

6. See E. Franklin Frazier, *The Negro Family in Chicago* (Chicago, 1932), chap. vi, for detailed information on the character of these zones as well as the method used in defining them.

7. See E. Franklin Frazier, "Negro Harlem: An Ecological Study," *American Journal of Sociology*, July, 1937.

8. See Frazier, *The Negro Family in Chicago*, pp. 150 ff.

9. See Frazier, "Negro Harlem: An Ecological Study," *loc. cit.*

10. See Frazier, *The Negro Family in Chicago*, chap. vii.

11. Warren S. Thompson and P. K. Whelpton, *Population Trends in the United States* (New York, 1933), p. 280.

12. Clyde V. Kiser, "Fertility of Harlem Negroes," *The Milbank Memorial Fund Quarterly*, XIII (July, 1935), 273–85.

13. See Frazier, *The Negro Family in Chicago*, pp. 136–44.

14. *Ibid.*, pp. 101–5.

10. MIDDLE-CLASS FATHERS' OCCUPATIONAL ROLE AND ATTITUDES TOWARD CHILDREN

1. In one sense these matters are universal. In all societies the child is eventually weaned and toilet-trained, and some regulation is imposed on sexual expression. Means and goals of training, of course, vary widely. But regardless of the degree to which these particular disciplines are regarded as crucial, it is probable that the techniques used and the

goals pursued with respect to any specific socialization problem are in part reflections of general parental value attitudes. Techniques and goals in socialization reflect a commitment to a style of life. This is a convenient assumption, however, and not a proven fact and should not prevent researchers from being alert to apparent or real contradictions and inconsistencies in parents' socialization practices.

2. This is not presented as a universally useful definition. One may equally well analyze socialization from the point of view of the person socialized, rather than from that of the socializer, or as a reciprocal process, involving mutual learning. In terms of our definition, socialization efforts are directed at individuals throughout life, whenever new roles are taken on or anticipated. It is assumed that the impact of early experiences with socializing agents and practices is of very great importance.

3. There may be major inconsistencies between the expectations for, say, a twelve-year-old boy in a particular society and expectations for that same boy's behavior as an adult; see R. F. Benedict, "Continuities and Discontinuities in Cultural Conditioning," *Psychiatry*, I (1938), 161–67. This involves complexities beyond the scope of this paper.

4. W. L. Warner, M. Meeker, and K. Eells, *Social Class in America* (Chicago: Science Research Associates, 1949).

5. Talcott Parsons, "The Kinship System of the Contemporary United States," *Essays in Sociological Theory, Pure and Applied* (Glencoe, Ill.: The Free Press, 1949), pp. 233–50.

6. Talcott Parsons, "The Professions and Social Structure," *ibid.*, pp. 185–99.

7. For present purposes the middle class is treated as if it were homogeneous. In fact, as Rosow has pointed out, there are undoubtedly subdivisions within any class as regards of life and life goals, some of which may cut across class lines; see I. Rosow, "Home Ownership Motives," *American Sociological Review*, XIII (1948), 751–55. Nevertheless, our particular group is fairly homogeneous with respect to the matters discussed here. Additional complexities are therefore overlooked, but their possible importance deserves mention.

8. That is not to say that all lower-class fathers will project lower-class futures for their sons. The orientation of an individual to the total social system in which he participates is more complex than that. Fathers of whatever class may hold upward social mobility as a value. If a lower-class father does so, he will project middle-class status for his son. When he does so, however, his picture of middle-class status and its demands and his consequent evaluation of his child's conduct should be effected by his lower-class status and experience. It should not be identical with that of the middle-class father. This is an empirical question well worth analysis, but one on which we have no information.

9. Sexual disciplines were discussed rarely with mothers, almost never with fathers. This limitation came about partly because of the newness of the Human Relations Service and its insecure position in the community. People had expressed fears that the Service aimed either at another Kinsey report or another Middletown, and at the time it seemed important to minimize such fears. In addition, however, the problem under analysis required other emphases.

10. Thus Sears indicates that first-born children are more dependent (R. R. Sears, "Ordinal Position in the Family as a Psychological Variable," *American Sociological Review*, XV [1950], 397–401). If this were so, then we would expect fathers to react more negatively to the dependency feelings of male first-born children than to those of female first-borns. Also, Duvall asserts that parents are more self-conscious about the raising of their first children (E. M. Duvall, "Conceptions of Parenthood," *American Journal of Sociology*, LII [1946], 193–203). But the literature on birth order and personality is so loaded with contradictions as to make these speculations hazardous; cf. G. Murphy, L. C. Murphy, and T. M. Newcomb, *Experimental Social Psychology* (revised ed.; New York: Harper, 1937), pp. 348–63, for a review of the literature through 1937.

11. A. Davis and R. J. Havighurst, "Social Class and Color Differences in Child-Rearing," in C. Kluckhohn and H. A. Murray (eds.), *Personality in Nature, Society, and Culture* (New York: Alfred A. Knopf, 1948), pp. 252–64.

11. THE EFFECTS OF THE WIFE'S EMPLOYMENT ON THE FAMILY POWER STRUCTURE

1. Alver H. Jacobson, "Conflict of Attitudes Toward the Roles of Husband and Wife in Marriage," *American Sociological Review*, XVII (April, 1952), 146–50.

2. Compare William F. Whyte's discussions of power as the "origination of action" in his *Street Corner Society, Human Relations in the Restaurant Industry*, and *Pattern for Peace*.

3. For a similar formulation, see Amos Hawley, *Human Ecology* (New York: Ronald Press, 1950), p. 221. See also Harold D. Lasswell, *Politics: Who Gets What, When, and How* (New York: McGraw-Hill, 1936).

4. Clifford Kirkpatrick, "Inconsistency in Marriage Roles and Marriage Conflict," in Judson T. Landis and Mary G. Landis, *Readings in Marriage and the Family* (New York: Prentice Hall, 1952), p. 387.

5. The demographic characteristics of the

controlled samples are as follows: Of the working wives, 16 per cent are school teachers and an addititional 80 per cent are engaged in other white-collar work, the remainder being self-employed or blue-collar workers (2 per cent each). Taking the working and non-working wives together, 42 per cent of their husbands are engaged in upper-middle class occupations, 27 per cent in lower-middle, 10 per cent in upper-lower class jobs, and the remaining 21 per cent are students. Five per cent of the wives have had some graduate study, 28 per cent are college graduates, 25 per cent partially finished college, 36 per cent are high school graduates, and 6 per cent did not finish high school. Sixty-two per cent of the wives are Protestant, 17 per cent Jewish, and 14 per cent Catholic, while 2 per cent have other faiths and 5 per cent none. The typical (median) wife is 26 years old (range 18 to 54), has been married four years, and has one child.

6. Alver H. Jacobson, "Conflict in Attitude Toward Marital Roles," *Research Studies of the State College of Washington*, XIX (1951), 105–6. These 18 items had proven scalable with college students in previous research by the junior author.

7. Several previous researchers have suggested or used the formula: "One initial suggestion which is adopted by the group equals one unit of power." This formula probably produces valid results if a sufficiently large and representative sample of decisions is used. See Robert L. Hamblin, "An Experimental Study of the Relationship of Communication, Power Relationships, Specialization, and Social Atmosphere to Group Size" (Unpublished Ph.D. dissertation, University of Michigan). Also William F. Whyte, *op. cit.*; and Ronald Lippitt *et al.*, "The Dynamics of Power: A Field Study of Social Influence in Groups of Children," in G. E. Swanson *et al.*, *Readings in Social Psychology* (New York: Henry Holt and Co., 1952), pp. 623–36.

8. Compare the senior author's ecological interpretation of the urban husband's greater share in the housework in spite of the farm wife's greater economic productivity, to be published in *Marriage and Family Living* as "The Division of Labor in City and Farm Families."

9. P. G. Herbst, "The Measurement of Family Relationships," *Human Relations*, V (1952), 3–35.

10. Alternative sources of family power will be analyzed at length in Robert O. Blood, Jr., and Donald M. Wolfe, *Husbands and Wives* (Glencoe, Ill.: The Free Press, 1960).

11. Charles H. Cooley, *Social Organization* (New York: Charles Scribner and Sons, 1922), pp. 273–82.

12. CAREERS AND CONSUMER BEHAVIOR

1. Boys bought slightly fewer, but more expensive, items than girls—a sign perhaps of the future "male" shopper, extravagant but narrow, as if overdetailed or sparing purchasing of household items were "women's work." Boys, of course, would be less likely than girls to identify with their mothers in the role of shopper.

2. This concept owes much to Robert K. Merton's formulations; cf. his article with Alice S. Kitt, "Contributions to the Theory of Reference-Group Behavior," in R. K. Merton and Paul F. Lazarsfeld (eds.), *Continuities in Social Research: Studies in the Scope and Method of "The American Soldier"* (Glencoe, Ill.: The Free Press, 1950), pp. 87–89. We may think of anticipatory socialization as a kind of psychological hope-and-fear chest the individual accumulates as he imaginatively transcends his membership group.

3. Some political consequences of this painfulness are suggested in D. Riesman and N. Glazer, "The Intellectuals and the Discontented Classes," *Partisan Review*, XXII (January–February, 1955), 47–72.

4. Manford H. Kuhn, "Factors in Personality: Socio-cultural Determinants as Seen through the Amish," in Francis L. K. Hsu (ed.), *Aspects of Culture and Personality* (New York: Abelard-Schumann, Inc., 1954). We need not stop to encompass the irony of the Amana Society, whose handsome freezers and refrigerators, products of co-operative asceticism, may often be the prime adornments of an urban housewife's menage.

5. Cf. the stages set forth in Jean Piaget *et al.*, *Moral Judgment of the Child*, trans. Marjorie Gabain (Glencoe, Ill.: The Free Press, 1948).

6. Cf. Eliot Freidson, "The Relation of the Social Situation of Contact to the Media of Mass Communication," *Public Opinion Quarterly*, XVII (1953), 230–38.

7. See further, D. Riesman, "Teachers Amid Changing Expectations," *Harvard Educational Review*, XXIV (Spring, 1954), 106–17.

8. Especially, T. Parsons, R. F. Bales, and E. A. Shils, *Working Papers in the Theory of Action* (Glencoe, Ill.: The Free Press, 1953), chap. iii; also Parsons, "The Integration of Economic and Sociological Theory," The Alfred Marshall Lectures, Cambridge, England, 1953 (unpublished).

9. George Katona, *Psychological Analysis of Economic Behavior* (New York: McGraw-Hill Book Co., Inc., 1951), p. 105.

10. "Income, Spending, and Saving Patterns of Consumer Units in Different Age Groups," in *Studies in Income and Wealth* (New York: National Bureau of Economic Research, 1952), XV, 77–102. As against this, we must set the rise in savings of the most recent years,

and also perhaps the education in saving given many by the G.I. Bill's nest egg provisions. Cf. also James Duesenberry's works, especially *Income, Saving and the Theory of Consumer Behavior* (Cambridge, Mass.: Harvard University Press, 1949).

11. Marvin B. Sussman, "The Help Pattern in the Middle-Class Family," *American Sociological Review,* XVIII (February, 1953), 22–28.

12. See table of magazine reading in W. L. Warner and P. S. Lunt, *The Social Life of a Modern Community* ("Yankee City Series," Vol. I; New Haven: Yale University Press, 1941).

13. S. Kuznets, *Shares of Upper Income Groups in Income and Saving* (New York: National Bureau of Economic Research, 1953); the Editors of Fortune, *The Changing American Market* (New York: Hanover House, 1955).

14. S. S. Sargent, "Class and Class Consciousness in a California Town," *Social Problems,* I (June, 1953), 22–27.

15. B. S. Rowntree, *Poverty: a Study of Town Life* (2nd ed.; New York: Longmans, Green and Company, Inc., 1922).

16. In their valuable paper, "Savings and the Income Distributions," Dorothy S. Brady and Rose D. Freidman emphasize, as Katona's work also does, the importance of the reference group for a relativistic income analysis: if real income rises for "everyone," everyone will think himself no better off and will not save new increments. *Studies in Income and Wealth* (National Bureau of Economic Research, 1947), X, 247–64.

17. Statement in a letter to the authors.

18. Owing to these attitudes, working-class girls often have an easier time attaining white-collar jobs and lower-middle class status than their male compeers do, and their ability to pass their aspirations on to their sons has been a continuing dynamic in the American drive for upward mobility. Mark Benney also reminds us of the "concealed" mobility the lower-class girl may have in affairs with men of higher social position—after which the girls are never quite lower class again. Moreover, he has noticed how continuously working girls give each other gifts—at showers and like occasions—and comments that gift buying, in all classes, tends to be the most socially sensitive form of consumption, analogous to

the money girls persuade their boy friends to spend on them.

19. *Ibid.*

20. See William H. Whyte, Jr., *Is Anybody Listening?* (New York: Simon and Schuster, Inc., 1952).

21. J. H. S. Bossard, *The Sociology of Child Development* (New York: Harper & Bros., 1954).

22. New York: Reinhold Publishing Corp., 1953. Cf. also R. J. Neutra, *Survival Through Design* (New York: Oxford University Press, 1954).

23. Citing W. H. Whyte, Jr., "The Transients," *Fortune,* May–August, 1953.

24. *Mademoiselle,* September, 1954, p. 101.

25. E. E. LeMasters, "Social Class Mobility and Family Integration," *Marriage and Family Living,* XVI (1954), 226–32.

26. These examples are taken from Irwin Deutscher's unpublished study of "Husband-Wife Relations in Middle Age," based on long interviews with parents whose children have left home.

27. "The Career of the Funeral Director" (Ph.D. dissertation, University of Chicago, 1954).

28. E. D. Baltzell, "Urbanization in Lower Bucks County," *Social Problems,* II (1954), 40.

29. C. C. McArthur, "Long-Term Validity of the Strong Interest Test in Two Subcultures," *Journal of Applied Psychology,* XXXVIII (1954), 346–53; also, McArthur and Lucia B. Stevens, "The Validation of Expressed Interests As Compared with Inventory Interests: A 14-Year Follow-up," *Journal of Applied Psychology,* XXXIX (1955), 184–89.

30. A. de Tocqueville, *Democracy in America,* ed. Phillips Bradley, (New York: Alfred A. Knopf, Inc., 1945), II, p. 132; see also pp. 105, 128–29, 134–35.

31. W. J. Cash, *The Mind of the South* (New York: Doubleday Anchor Books, 1954), p. 293.

32. Harper & Bros., 1952.

33. See "The Scientific Corps—A Sixth Estate?" *Confluence,* III (1954), 220–29. This paper as a whole draws heavily on the bibliography concerning leisure compiled by Professor Denney as well as on many specific suggestions by him.

34. *Ibid.*

35. *Ibid.*

13. FAMILY STRUCTURE AND ECONOMIC CHANGE IN NINETEENTH-CENTURY EUROPE

1. There is a useful comparative account of inheritance systems in Ernest Roguin, *Traité de droit civil comparé,* III–VII (Paris, 1904–12). J. W. Hedelmann, *Die Fortschritte des Zivilrechts im XIX Jahrhundert* (Berlin, 1910–35), II, also contains relevant material on the law of the subject. The fullest source on the history of inheritance practices in

Germany is the officially commissioned work, Max Sering (ed.), *Die Vererbung des ländlichen Grundbesitzes in Königreich Preussen* (Berlin, 1908). Of the volumes in this series, I have obtained most help from VII, *Erbrecht und Agrarverfassung in Schleswig-Holstein,* written by Sering himself; this also contains an account of inheritance in Norway. See also

I, *Oberlandsgerichtsbezirk Köln*, by W.
Wygodzinski. There is considerable historical
material in the more recent work of Max
Sering and C. von Dietze, *Die Vererbung
des ländlichen Grundbesitzes in der Nach-
kriegszeit* (Munich, 1930). For a discussion
of the effects of inheritance customs in a
restricted area in the present century see
Hans Bittorf, *Die Vererbungsgewohnheiten
des bäuerlichen Grundbesitzes in Landkreis
Hildburghausen* (Thesis, Jena, 1930), pp. 43–
72.
  2. See the discussion in Rougin, *op. cit.*,
IV, 389.
  3. Max Sering, *Deutsche Agrarpolitik*
(Leipsig, 1934), pp. 46–49.
  4. See, for example, the mixture of systems
in middle Germany, described by Sering and
von Dietze, *op. cit.*, I, 219ff. There is a good
account of variations of custom within a
single area in Fritz Elsas, "Zur Frage des
Anerbenrechts in Württemberg," *Schmollers
Jahrbuch* (1913), pp. 264–67.
  5. Sering and von Dietze, *op. cit.*, I, 228.
  6. There is an interesting discussion in J.
Bertillon, *La dépopulation en France* (Paris,
1911). Three reasons suggest that the low
French birth rate should not be ascribed to
the provisions of the Civil Code relating to
succession. (a) The desire to avoid partition
by limiting births could have operated with
great force only among the more substantial
peasantry. Were these numerous enough to
have had a significant effect on the birth rate
for the country as a whole? (b) Belgium and
Baden, both areas of division, showed substantial population increases. (c) The French
law of 1909, which allowed the creation of
inalienable rural property and so obviated
any necessity for a limitation of births to
achieve this end, was rarely used.
  7. Friedrich List, *Schriften, Reden, Briefe*,
ed. Erwin von Beckerath *et. al.* (Berlin, 1927–
35), IV: *Die Ackerverfassung, die Zwerg-
wirtschaft und die Auswanderung*.

  8. Valentin Steinert, *Zur Frage der Natural-
teilung* (Lucka, 1906), pp. 53–61; Ludwig
Fick, *Die Bäuerliche Erbfolge in rechts-
rheinischen Bayern* (Stuttgart, 1895), pp. 34,
276.
  9. For the view that *Anerbensitte* favored
migration, see Adolph Buchenberger, *Agrar-
wesen und Agrarpolitik*, I, 442–45; Fick, *op.
cit.*, and von der Goltz, *Die agrarischen
Aufgaben der Gegenwart* (Jena, 1894). The
contrary view was taken by Sering and
Wygodzinski in the works already cited, but
the method by which they arrived at their
conclusions was statistically faulty; see R.
Kuczynski, *Der Zug nach der Stadt* (Stuttgart, 1897), pp. 235–50.
  10. H. Boker and F. W. Von Bulow, *The
Rural Exodus in Czechoslovakia* (I. L. O.
Studies and Reports, Series K [Agriculture],
No. 13 [Geneva, 1935]).
  11. *Ibid.*
  12. G. C. Homans, *English Villagers of the
Thirteenth Century* (Cambridge, Mass.:
Harvard University Press, 1941) contains a
discussion of inheritance customs in medieval
England.
  13. In Austria, between 1868 and 1892,
958,876 cases of inheritance resulted in 543,-
747 new mortgages, incurred to compensate
heirs, which averaged 25 per cent of the value
of the land. E. H. Kaden, "The Peasant Inheritance Law in Germany," *Iowa Law Review*, XX (1934–35), 350–88.
  14. That question of the effect of inheritance customs on productivity is difficult to
resolve because the fertility of an area may
have helped to determine its inheritance
system. In Bavaria, according to the study of
Fick, the harvest yield was greatest in areas
where division was the ruling custom, but
this may well have been due to the fact that
it was the more fertile land that was the most
suitable for division. In any case, in Bavaria
the differences do not appear to have been
significant.

14. CHANGING POLITICAL ATTITUDES IN TOTALITARIAN SOCIETY: A CASE STUDY OF THE ROLE OF THE FAMILY

  1. Carl J. Friedrich (ed.), *Totalitarianism:
Proceedings of a Conference Held at the
American Academy of Arts and Sciences*
(Cambridge, Mass., 1954). See especially the
papers and discussion included in Part III,
"Totalitarianism and Ideology," pp. 87–137.
  2. Accounts in English of various aspects
of totalitarian youth movements may be
found in the following: Merle Fainsod, "The
Komsomols—A Study of Youth Under
Dictatorship," *American Political Science
Review*, XLV (March, 1951), 18–40; Herbert
S. Lewin, "Hitler Youth and the Boy Scouts
of America: A Comparison of Aims," *Human
Relations*, I (1947), 206–27; Robert A. Brady,
The Spirit and Structure of German Fascism,
(New York, 1937), especially chap. v

"Training the Youth to Become Soldiers of
Labor," pp. 161–98; Herman Finer, *Mus-
solini's Italy* (London, 1935), especially
chap. xv, "The Fascist Party: Youth Organization," pp. 426–54.
  3. Compare Kingsley Davis, "The Sociology
of Parent-Youth Conflict," *American Sociological Review*, V (August, 1940), 523–35.
Davis notes that rapid social change, when
taken in conjunction with the slower rates of
socialization of older persons, results in a
general tendency for attitudes of parents to
lag behind those of their children in modern
industrial society.
  4. All ages are as of 1950; father's occupation is the last one reported prior to World
War II.

5. It was frequently noted that this was done only after the children were old enough to be trusted, or that the children were carefully warned to keep silent about such matters when outside the family.

6. Isolated, that is, in the sense that members of the larger kin group are in the typical case not particularly close in either a residential or emotional sense to the members of the immediate individual family. In this respect, the Soviet family, at least in its urban Slavic variety, does not differ from the predominant family type in the United States. See Talcott Parsons, "The Kinship System of the Contemporary United States," *American Anthropologist*, XLV (January, 1943), 22–38.

7. The advantage to the individual parent of peace within the family is clearly expressed in the following exchange:
(How did you explain to your children those events in the U.S.S.R. whose negative side was clear to you?) On this question, the children had much instruction in school, and in order not to become upset, I kept silent. (56-year-old female, bookkeeper)

8. Compare with the role of children in the first-generation immigrant family in the United States. For example: "In the face of this whole development [i.e., the pressures and attractions of American life] the immigrants were helpless. They had neither the will nor the ability to turn their offspring into other directions. The nominal authority of the fathers was often half-heartedly used; they were cruelly torn by the conflicting wishes that their sons be like themselves and yet lead better lives than they. Sensing that the school and street would tear the next generation away, the parents knew not how to counteract those forces without injuring their own flesh and blood." From Oscar Handlin, *The Uprooted* (Boston, 1951), pp. 252–53. See also W. Lloyd Warner and Leo Srole, *The Social Systems of American Ethnic Groups* (New Haven, 1945), especially chap. vi, "The Family," pp. 103–55.

9. Changes in family relationships subsequent to regime-induced deprivations are discussed at length in Kent Geiger, "Deprivation and Solidarity in the Soviet Urban Family," *American Sociological Review*, XX (January, 1955), 57–68.

10. Consult Fainsod, *op. cit.*, especially p. 36, for information on the weaknesses of youth organization in rural areas. The differential exposure of various populations groups to the mass media is discussed in Peter H. Rossi and Raymond A. Bauer, "Some Patterns of Soviet Communications Behavior," *Public Opinion Quarterly*, XVI (Winter, 1952–53), 653–70. Rossi and Bauer characterize the Soviet collective farmer as a person who is "almost isolated from the communications network" (p. 658).

11. In 1937, Y. Yaroslavsky, head of the League of Militant Atheists, estimated that about two-thirds of the urban adult population over 16 called themselves atheists, whereas in the country from one-half to two-thirds were believers. Cited in N. S. Timasheff, *Religion in Soviet Russia, 1917–1942* (New York, 1942), p. 65. Harvard Project data on refugee attitudes toward religion also indicate that religious belief increases in strength as one descends in the social-class hierarchy.

12. Lorimer concludes that the net migration from rural areas to cities must have been at least 23 million persons in the inter-census period, 1926 to 1939. Frank Lorimer, *The Population of the Soviet Union: History and Prospects* (Geneva, 1946), pp. 145–50.

13. Alex Inkeles, "Social Stratification and Mobility in the Soviet Union: 1940–1950," *American Sociological Review*, XV (August, 1950), 465–79.

14. There is, however, some evidence to the contrary. It is likely that a considerable portion of the frustration engendered by difficult material living conditions is expressed and dissipated within the context of the family itself. See Geiger, *op. cit.*

15. Geiger, *op. cit.*, pp. 65–66.

16. Forms of property ownership, relations between church and state, etc.

15. THE FAMILY AND THE POLITICAL BEHAVIOR OF YOUTH

1. Angus Campbell, Gerald Gurin, and Warren E. Miller, "Political Issues and the Vote," *American Political Science Review*, XLVII (June, 1953), 389; Paul F. Lazarsfeld, Bernard Berelson, and Hazel Gaudet, *The People's Choice* (New York: Harcourt Brace, 1952), p. 44.

2. Lazarsfeld, *op. cit.*, pp. 140ff.

3. Hadley Cantril, *Public Opinion, 1935–46* (Princeton, N. J.: Princeton University Press, 1951), pp. 591, 602, 627, and 644; Campbell, *loc. cit.*

4. Richard Centers, *The Psychology of Social Class* (Princeton, N. J.: Princeton University Press, 1949), pp. 165ff.

5. Lazarsfeld, *op. cit.*, pp. 23ff.

6. Samuel Lubell, *The Future of American Politics* (New York: Harper and Brothers, 1952).

7. A sample of youth, as might be expected, is extremely mobile and difficult to locate for interviewing: 24 per cent of the young people called upon had moved and could not be traced to a new address; 10 per cent had been drafted; and a further sizeable group were not at home after repeated call-backs.

Comparisons with census figures show that the group who were reached for interview include too many who are married and too many at the upper end of the 21–24 age bracket.

8. To determine party preference, the following question was asked: "In general which party do you like best, Republican or Democratic?" For candidate choice, the question was: "How did you vote for President in the election that's just past?" For the relatively small group who did not vote, this question was worded: "If you had voted in the last election, how do you think you would have voted for president?"

9. For this study, SES level has been measured by rating the respondent's occupation on the Warner seven-point scale of occupational status. Students were not rated, since their occupational status is not yet established. For a description of the scale, see W. L. Warner, Marcia Meeker, and K.

Eells, *Social Class in America* (Chicago: Science Research Associates, 1949).

10. Centers, *op. cit.*

11. L. Festinger, "Informal Social Communication," *Psychological Review*, LVII (1950), 271–82.

12. For married women, social mobility was measured by comparing the occupation of the young woman's husband with that of her father.

13. T. Newcomb, *Personality and Social Change* (New York: Dryden Press, 1943).

14. E. Havemann and Patricia S. West, *They Went to College* (New York: Harcourt, Brace, 1952).

15. Of the 48 young people with college educations who have left college, 16 became more Republican than their parents, 12 more Democratic. Among the 32 people still in college, 4 became more Republican, 11 more Democratic.

16. POLITICAL ISSUES AND HUSBAND-WIFE INTERACTION

1. See Talcott Parsons and Edward A. Shils (eds.), *Toward a General Theory of Action* (Cambridge, Mass.: Harvard University Press, 1951), especially pp. 23–26, 54–55.

2. See David B. Truman, *The Governmental Process* (New York, 1951), pp. 189–91; Harold D. Lasswell and Abraham Kaplan, "On Power and Influence," in Lasswell, *Power and Personality* (New York, 1948), p. 223.

3. This is, of course, the usual reason given for consciously planned specialization in the organization of work.

4. A more frequently noted consequence for the individual personality is almost directly opposite of this—the increase in boredom and/or fatigue. See Herbert A. Simon, Donald W. Smithburg, and Victor A. Thompson, *Public Administration* (New York, 1950), pp. 141–42. Without wishing to deny the complexity of the relationships involved or the absence of systematically organized empirical information, we can consider the ego-destructive effects of specialization (e.g., boredom) as being activated ordinarily toward the extreme of specialization.

5. The fact that much of the literature concerning managerial problems and techniques is devoted to methods for overcoming the special problems of integration introduced by the division of labor should not conceal the fact that this division probably considerably reduces the internal friction that would otherwise exist.

6. See Louise M. Young, "The Political Role of Women in the United States," a paper presented to the Hague Congress of the International Political Science Association, September 8–12, 1952.

7. See Fred L. Strodbeck, "Husband-Wife Interaction over Revealed Differences,"

American Sociological Review, XVI (1951), 468–73.

8. *Ibid.*, p. 473.

9. The expression of opinion-giving acts is ordinarily quite properly perceived as "attempted" influence, requiring the "acceptance" of the person to whom it is directed before it is incorporated into that person's orientation to the situation. However, in an ongoing social group, such as a married couple, the expectation is that the relationship between "attempted" and "accepted" influence will be virtually one-to-one. To check this a priori assumption against the present data, an independent measure of influence was examined. Each of the twelve questions was evaluated according to the proportion of decisions (i.e., final position adopted in cases of disagreement) "won" by the husbands. A ranking of questions on this basis was correlated with a ranking according to the proportion of opinion-giving acts originated by the husbands. The rank difference correlation between these two rankings is significant at the .05 level of significance. As an experimental gauge of influence, the "opinion-giving acts" criterion is preferred to the "decisions won" criterion because of its greater sensitivity. In particular, it has the considerable advantage of providing an evaluation of relative power even in those frequent cases where no overt disagreement is recorded between the married pair.

10. See Robert F. Bales, *Interaction Process Analysis* (Cambridge, Mass., 1950).

11. Since the interactions in the present study are scored from a recording, it is not possible to score those acts that are entirely soundless (e.g., a sneer).

12. The convention utilized for testing this

joint prediction of concordance and direction
(i.e., Labor > Foreign > Local) is one based
upon Kendall and developed by Strodtbeck.
See Maurice G. Kendall, *Rank Correlation
Methods* (London, 1948), p. 146; Fred L.
Strodtbeck, "Representing the Outcome of
Successive Ranking of Three Alternatives," a
paper presented to the March, 1952, meeting
of the Connecticut Chapter of the American
Statistical Association.

13. Since these data are not taken from the
recording, information is available for all
nine couples (i.e., all eighteen individuals).

14. See E. G. Olds, "The 5 per cent Signifi-

cance Levels for Sums of Squares of Rank
Differences and a Correction," *Annals of
Mathematical Statistics*, XX (1949), 117–18.

15. One intuitively obvious fact should be
noted. The Labor-Foreign-Local categorization by no means exhausts the complexity of
the interpersonal relationship. Thus, in the
present study there is some persuasive evidence to indicate that a "foreign policy"
question on policy toward the United Nations
evokes a substantially different pattern of
husband-wife interaction from a "foreign
policy" question on policy toward Communist
China.

17. DIVORCE LAW AS SOCIAL CONTROL

1. Such factors as industrialization, urbanization, happiness of parents, personality
factors are illustrative of the types of factors
which are thought to influence family
breakup. Ernest W. Burgess and Harvey J.
Locke, *The Family: From Institution to
Companionship* (2nd ed.; New York: American Book Co., 1953), pp. 407–29.

2. William F. Ogburn, "The Changing
Functions of the Family," in Robert F. Winch
and Robert McGinnis (eds.), *Selected
Studies in Marriage and the Family* (New
York: Henry Holt and Co., 1953), pp. 74–
81.

3. Essentially two types of social-psycho-
logical theory have been used to support the
view that punishment affects non-violators.
One is typified by Alexander and Staub
(Franz Alexander and Hugo Staub, *The
Criminal, The Judge, and The Public*, trans.
Gregory Zilboorg [New York: Macmillan
Co., 1931]), and the other is typified by
Durkheim (Emile Durkheim, *The Division
of Labor*, trans. George Simpson [1st and 5th
eds.; Glencoe, Ill.: The Free Press, 1947],
Book I, "The Function of the Division of
Labor," chap. ii, "Mechanical Solidarity
through Likeness," pp. 70–110), and by
Mead (George H. Mead, "The Psychology of
Punitive Justice," *American Journal of
Sociology*, XXIII [1917–18], 577–602).

4. James P. Lichtenberger, *Divorce* (New
York and London: Whittlesey House, Mc-
Graw-Hill Book Co., 1931); Max Rheinstein, "Trends in Marriage and Divorce Law
of Western Countries," *Law and Contemporary Problems*, XVIII (Winter, 1953), 4.
Rheinstein, though agreeing that divorce
laws have historically embodied the concept
of punishment, would not agree that the
punishment was intended to prevent breakdown.

5. Irving Mandell and Richard McKay,
Law of Marriage and Divorce (2nd ed.; New
York: Oceana Publications, 1952), pp. 75–
76.

6. *Ibid.*, p. 76.

7. *Ibid.*, pp. 77–78.

8. The only ground for divorce in New
York is adultery, which may be prosecuted
as a crime by the district attorney in proceedings independent from those which are
constituted by the spouse who wishes to
obtain a divorce.

9. Harriet F. Pilpel and Theodore Zavin,
Your Marriage and the Law (3rd ed. rev.;
Chicago: J. B. Lippincott Co., 1939), p. 363.

10. Durkheim, *op. cit.*, pp. 70–110; Mead,
op. cit., pp. 577–602.

11. See Walter C. Reckless, *The Crime
Problem* (New York: Appleton-Century-
Crofts, 1950), pp. 165ff. Actually, the formulations of Mead and Durkheim as stated in
this paper take the variable of social organization into account in a very limited sense.
They do not really deal with the factor of
power. The effects of public punishment
might be directly contrary depending on
whether the deviant comes from a high-
powered or low-powered group. In this paper
there will be no extended discussion of the
role of social organization.

12. See Pilpel and Zavin, *op. cit.*, chap.
xix, "Divorce: The Law and Fact," pp.
297–306.

13. See Rheinstein, *loc. cit.*, p. 18.

14. Generally speaking, divorce laws are
addressed to reducing breakup by opportunity, for they define the conditions under
which a married man can take a new spouse.

15. For a discussion of the law as therapy,
see Paul W. Alexander, "A Therapeutic Approach," *The Law School, the University of
Chicago, Conference on Divorce*, Conference Series No. 9 (February 29, 1952).

16. Unpublished manuscript provided by
Max Rheinstein. Max Beckman, "Divorce in
Sweden" (University of Stockholm, 1952).

17. For attempts to express this view, see
Robert K. Merton, "Social Structure and
Anomie," in Ruth Anshen (ed.), *The Family,
Its Functions and Destiny* (New York: Har-
per and Bros., 1949), pp. 226–57. See Talcott
Parsons, *The Social System* (Glencoe, Ill.:
The Free Press, 1951), especially chap. vii,

"Deviant Behavior and the Mechanisms of Social Control," pp. 249–321. See Nelson N. Foote and Leonard S. Cottrell, Jr., *Identity and Interpersonal Competence: A New Direction in Family Research* (Chicago: University of Chicago Press, 1955).

18. Talcott Parsons, "Age and Sex in the Social Structure of the United States," in Winch and McGinnis, *op. cit.*, chap. xii, pp. 330–45.

19. Ogburn, *op. cit.*, pp. 74–81. However, Burgess and Locke have pointed out the limitations of such an analysis, *op. cit.* (rev. ed.), pp. 713ff, especially 718.

20. For an illustration of other techniques which are more effective than lectures, see Kurt Lewin, "Group Decision and Social Change," in Theodore M. Newcomb and Eugene L. Hartley (eds.), *Readings in Social Psychology* (New York: Henry Holt and Co., 1947), especially pp. 334–40.

21. Foote and Cottrell, *op. cit.*

22. See Ernest W. Burgess and Paul Wallin, *Engagement and Marriage* (Chicago: J. B. Lippincott Co., 1953), especially pp. 624ff.

23. The Family Study Center at the University of Chicago is preparing a manual of these procedures under a grant from the Russell Sage Foundation.

18. INTRODUCTION TO THE ANALYSIS OF KINSHIP SYSTEMS

1. *The Early History of Institutions*, 1874, p. 214.

2. For an exposition of the theory, see A. R. Radcliffe-Brown, "The Study of Kinship Systems," *Journal of the Royal Anthropological Institute*, LXXI (1941), 1–18.

3. Quoted by Vinogradoff, *Outlines of Historical Jurisprudence*, I, p. 252, from Liebermann, *Gesetze der Angelsachsen*, I, p. 442. The "wedding" was the agreement or contract entered into by the kinsfolk of bride and bridegroom, equivalent to the Roman *sponsalia*, not the ceremony of handing over the bride (the Roman *traditio puellae*).

4. Belgian and some French writers made a similar misuse of the term "dot," which is a woman's marriage portion of which the annual income is under her husband's control.

5. This is the view of modern English law. If an unmarried woman is seduced her father can recover damages for the loss of her "services"; as though the only value attached to a daughter is as a servant.

6. P. Amaury Talbot, *Southern Nigeria*, III (1926), 437–40.

7. See Marcel Mauss, *Essai sur le don*.

8. Roscoe, *The Baganda*, 1911, p. 129.

9. Werner, in *Journal of the African Society*, XIII (1914), 139.

10. J. F. Cunningham, *Uganda and Its Peoples*, 1905, pp. 54, 331.

11. A. R. Radcliffe-Brown, "On Joking Relationships," *Africa*, XIII (July, 1940), 195–210.

12. *Ibid.*; R. E. Moreau, "The Joking Relationship (*Utani*) in Tanganyika," *Tanganyika Notes and Records*, XII, 1941, pp. 1–10, and "Joking Relationships in Tanganyika," *Africa*, XIV (July, 1944, 386–400.

13. After a lecture given more than thirty years ago in which this theory was explained, a member of the audience asked: "Would it not be a good thing to introduce this custom (the avoidance of the wife's mother) amongst ourselves?" His question aroused a roar of laughter from the audience, which, I imagine, was what he aimed at.

14. Lindblom, *The Akamba*, which gives a good account of the relations between *athoni* (avoidance relatives).

19. CONJUGAL ROLES AND SOCIAL NETWORKS

1. In sociological and anthropological literature, the term "group" is commonly used in at least two senses. In the first sense, it is a very broad term used to describe any collectivity whose members are alike in some way; this definition would include categories, logical classes, and aggregates as well as more cohesive social units. The second usage is much more restricted. In this sense, the units must have some distinctive interdependent social relationships with one another; categories, logical classes, and aggregates are excluded. To avoid confusion, I use the term "organized group" when it becomes necessary to distinguish the second usage from the first.

2. The idea of network is often met in anthropological, sociological, and psychological literature, although it does not always bear this name, e.g., Rivers' concept of the "kindred," Fortes' "web of kinship," Armstrong's "grouping"; see W. H. R. Rivers, *Social Organization* (London: Kegan Paul, Trench, Trubner, 1924); M. Fortes, *The Web of Kinship Among the Tallensi* (London: Oxford University Press, 1949); W. E. Armstrong, *Rossel Island* (London: Cambridge University Press, 1928). See also R. K. Merton, "Patterns of Influence: A Study of Interpersonal Influence and of Communications Behavior in a Local Community," in P. F. Lazarsfeld and F. N. Stanton (ed.), *Communications Research, 1948–1949* (New York: Harper and Bros., 1949), pp. 180–219; J. L. Moreno, *Who Shall Survive?* (Washington: Nervous and Mental Disease Publishing Co., 1934); C. P. Loomis *et al.*,

Turrialba (Glencoe, Ill.: The Free Press, 1953). Most of these authors are more concerned with the fact that a person has relationships with a number of people than with the pattern of relationships among these other people themselves. Radcliffe-Brown used the term metaphorically, as in his definition of social structure as "a complex network of social relations." A. R. Radcliffe-Brown, "On Social Structure," *Journal of the Royal Anthropological Institute*, LXX (1940), 1–12.

In finding it convenient to use the term "network" to describe a set of social relationships for which there is no common boundary, I follow the recent usage of John Barnes: "Each person is, as it were, in touch with a number of people, some of whom are directly in touch with each other and some of whom are not. . . . I find it convenient to talk of a social field of this kind as a *network*. The image I have is of a net of points some of which are joined by lines. The points of the image are people, or sometimes groups, and the lines indicate which people interact with each other." J. A. Barnes, "Class and Committees on a Norwegian Island Parish," *Human Relations*, VII, No. 1, p. 43.

20. COMMUNITY STATUS AND FAMILY STRUCTURE IN BRITISH GUIANA

1. See Talcott Parsons, *The Social System* (Glencoe, Ill.: The Free Press, 1951), pp. 59–61.

2. This term is used in the sense defined by S. F. Nadel, *The Foundations of Social Anthropology* (London, 1951), pp. 45–47.

3. See W. M. Cousins, "Slave Family Life in the British Colonies 1800–34," *Sociological Review*, Vol. XXVII (1935).

4. See A. R. Radcliffe-Brown, "Introduction," in A. R. Radcliffe-Brown and D. Forde (eds.), *African Systems of Kinship and Marriage* (London, 1950), p. 77.

5. See F. Eggan, *Social Organization of the Western Pueblos* (Chicago: University of Chicago Press, 1950).

6. K. Gough, "Changing Kinship Usages in the Setting of Political and Economic Change among the Nayars of Malabar," *Journal of the Royal Anthropological Institute*, Vol. LXXXII (1952).

7. See L. Braithwaite, "Social Stratification in Trinidad: A Preliminary Analysis," *Social and Economic Studies*, Vol. II (Kingston, Jamaica).

8. E. R. Leach, *Political Systems of Highland Burma: A Study of Kachin Social Structure* (London, 1954).

21. THE FAMILY AND PEER GROUPS

1. Luckily enough, maids and governesses, who are part of the style of life of the upper-middle class, are apt to be more lenient than the parents; as long as the child leaves them in peace, they will care little with whom the child plays. Freedom, then, is seen as a sort of illicit commodity, secure through the complacence of inferiors and secure only as long as it does not disturb the adult's routine.

2. The courting relationship is the only basic exception to this statement. Here, the "sexual-prowess" imperative permits a man to attempt to meet a strange woman and to push the relationship as far as he possibly can, without ridicule.

3. Thursday is the equivalent of Saturday in American schools.

4. Achievement must still remain within the limits of the family norm qua peer group. Otherwise, there can be such a thing as too much success, which humiliates the other nuclear families. On the other hand, a Frenchman rarely feels successful unless the extended family ratifies the judgment of the outside world.

5. Jean Jacques Rousseau, in his *Emile* (1762) gave a sort of eighteenth-century version of progressive education.

6. The writing of essays in French literature and history are, of course, the part of the curriculum where this is easiest. Latin and Greek tend to check this tendency, for, as in mathematics, it is difficult to do anything but be right or wrong in a translation, although the teacher will require "elegance" in the presentation of correct results.

7. The child is made to return to school Thursday and even Sunday for study periods —the length of which are determined by the amount of punishment to be given.

8. The power applied is not physical force, but symbolic force, since all that is necessary is to muster enough *pions* (proctors) and enough teachers willing to note down the distribute the hours of *consigne* which are necessary to disorganize the peer group. Pity is the administration's worst enemy; it must keep up the myth of the student group as a tribe of savages who must be tamed by sheer terror. (*Maté* is the French word.)

9. This figure has been computed from a sample of 260 students interviewed in 1951–54.

10. Even relatively unpopular teachers may receive a gift which is more in the nature of a bribe than a token of affection.

11. They are addressed by the familiar *tu* in this case.

12. Cf. the description of the reception given to Charles Bovary when he enters the college in Flaubert's *Madame Bovary* (1857). According to all informants, the treatment

granted the *nouveaux* who did not know how to make peace with the peer group had not changed one hundred years later, including the fixation on the nouveau's hat.

13. In France, as anywhere else, there will exist peer groups where, for special reasons, the commitment of the individual members is very high. When this peer group does not have to enter into exchange with adult structures, in the form of playful commercial or recreational activities, or when there are no legitimate facilities available, aberrant behavior is likely to occur. Cf. André Colin, *Les Jeux Sauvages* (Paris: Julliard, 1947); André Gide, *Les Faux Monnayeurs* (Paris: Gallimard, 1925); and the various J3 scandals which have occurred in the upper and middle class. Cf. *Le Monde,* June, 1953, *passim,* and the recent movie *Les Tricheurs,* (1958).

14. Laurence Wylie in his book, *Village in the Vaucluse* (Cambridge: Harvard University Press, 1957) has a very good description of the process, pp. 83–84.

15. It is interesting in this light to compare the themes in popular fiction regarding the hero's relationship to the peer group. In America, a frequent theme is the undercover agent: membership in any peer group must always be subordinated to societal values. In the name of these values a peer group can be left behind, or even destroyed. The bad policeman becomes a good policeman again and arrests the members of the gang who had befriended him. In France, the theme is more frequently the competition between the peer group, particularly of male friendship dyads, and love for a woman. The hero has to choose between loyalty to his friend and love for the latter, though he tries to combine the two as long as possible.

16. Our respondents indicated overwhelmingly a choice of best friends made at age 13–14 which was still strong when the respondents were aged 18–24. A good description of these intense friendships can be found in Margaret Mead and Rhoda Metraux, *The Study of Culture at a Distance* (Chicago: University of Chicago Press, 1959) pp. 188–192.

17. There are indications that political consciousness has declined in the last ten years, in favor of the first manifestations of an American type "youth culture" much more oriented to dating, jazz, and sports. In the same way, the Boy Scout movement has suffered from the loss of interest in the late teen-agers who used to provide its cadre.

18. The period of military service, which every French youth must accomplish, is an important socializer in the patterns of adult peer grouping, and would deserve an essay in itself.

19. Without mentioning the aristocracy, formally dedicated until World War I to the exiled sovereign, a large section of the bourgeoisie has always been politically in opposition to every French regime since the Revolution with the exception of the early days of both the First and Second Empire, and the presidency of Mr. Thiers.

20. The four main police systems are: La Préfecture de Police de la Seine, La Police Judiciaire, La Défense du Territoire, Le Deuxième Bureau, (ubiquitous name which covers the espionage and counterespionage activities of the various branches of the armed services).

21. The illicit love affair can be seen as such a delinquent community in relation to the demands of family value and organization.

22. Arnold Rose, *Theory and Method in the Social Sciences* (Minneapolis: University of Minnesota Press, 1954) pp. 50–115. See also Orville R. Gallagher, "Voluntary associations in France," *Social Forces,* XXXVI (December, 1957), 153–60.

23. CULTURE CONFIGURATIONS IN THE AMERICAN FAMILY

1. I have adhered to Clyde Kluckhohn's definition of configuration in his chapter, "Patterning as Exemplified in Navaho Culture," in Leslie Spier, A. Irving Hallowell, and Stanley S. Newman (eds.), *Language, Culture, and Personality* (Menasha, Wis.: Sapir Memorial Publication Fund, 1941), pp. 109–30, and exemplified in part in Clyde Kluckhohn and Dorothea Leighton, *The Navaho* (Cambride, Mass.: Harvard University Press, 1946), pp. 216–38. My indebtedness is considerable to Ruth Benedict, "Configurations of Culture in North America," *American Anthropologist,* XXXIV (1932), 1–27, and *Patterns of Culture* (Boston: Houghton Mifflin Co., 1934). For the study of value systems, configuration has appeared to be a more useful concept than most, in that it refers to positive rules which organize behavior into patterns, while the mores are generally stated as unitary negative injunctions (see William Graham Sumner, *Folkways* [Boston: Ginn & Co., 1906], p. 30; and William Graham Sumner and Albert Galloway Keller, *The Science of Society,* Vol. I [New Haven: Yale University Press, 1927], 33–35). Bronislaw Malinowski has used the concept of "charter" in his definition of a social institution as a means of studying values (*A Scientific Theory of Culture and Other Essays* [Chapel Hill: University of North Carolina Press, 1944], pp. 52–53). Alfred McClung Lee has analyzed social values from an interesting and useful approach in "Levels of Culture as Levels of Social Generalization," *American Sociological Review,* X (1945), 485–95, and in "Social

Determinants of Public Opinions," *International Journal of Opinion and Attitude Research*, I (1947), 12–29.

2. Erich Fromm, *Man for Himself* (New York: Rinehart & Co., 1947), p. 241.

3. Sumner, *op. cit.*, pp. 5–6.

4. John Sirjamaki, "A Footnote to the Anthropological Approach to the Study of American Culture," *Social Forces*, XXV (1947), 253–63; Clyde Kluckhohn, "The American Culture: Definition and Prophecy. Part II. The Way of Life," *Kenyon Review*, III (1941), 160–79; Clyde Kluckhohn and Florence R. Kluckhohn, "American Culture: Generalized Orientations and Class Patterns," in Lyman Bryson, Louis Finkelstein, and R. M. MacIver (eds.), *Conflicts of Power in Modern Culture* (New York: Harper & Bros., 1947), pp. 106–28; Andrew G. Truxal and Francis E. Merrill, *The Family in American Culture* (New York: Prentice-Hall, 1947), pp. 29–199; Robert S. Lynd, *Knowledge for What?* (Princeton, N.J.: Princeton University Press, 1939), pp. 63–99; Robert S. Lynd and Helen Merrell Lynd, *Middletown: A Study in American Culture* (New York: Harcourt, Brace & Co., 1929), and *Middletown in Transition* (New York: Harcourt, Brace & Co., 1937); and Oscar Waldemar Junek, "What Is the Total Pattern of Our Western Civilization? Some Preliminary Observations," *American Anthropologist*, XLVIII (1946), 397–406.

5. *Sixteenth Census of the United States, 1940, Population*, IV, Part I, 16.

6. *Fifteenth Census of the United States, 1930, Population*, II, chapter on marital condition.

7. Willard Waller, "The Rating and Dating Complex," *American Sociological Review*, II (1937), 727–34.

8. Weston LaBarre, "Social Cynosure and Social Structure," *Journal of Personality*, XIV (1946), 171.

9. Ernest R. Groves, *Marriage* (New York: Henry Holt & Co., 1933), pp. 89–90.

10. Ralph Linton, *The Study of Man* (New York: D. Appleton-Century Co., 1936), p. 175.

11. LaBarre, *loc. cit.*, p. 179.

12. Sumner and Keller, *op. cit.*, p. 464.

13. Margaret Park Redfield, "The American Family: Consensus and Freedom," *American Journal of Sociology*, LII (1946), 177.

14. W. Lloyd Warner and Paul S. Lunt, *The Social Life of a Modern Community* (New Haven: Yale University Press, 1941), pp. 92–111; and Allison Davis, Burleigh B. Gardner, and Mary R. Gardner, *Deep South* (Chicago: University of Chicago Press, 1941), pp. 84–136.

15. Joseph K. Folsom, *The Family and Democratic Society* (New York: John Wiley & Sons, 1943), p. 184.

16. *Ibid.*, p. 105.

17. Abram Kardiner, *The Psychological Frontiers of Society* (New York: Columbia University Press, 1945), p. 361.

18. Edward A. Strecker, *Their Mothers' Sons* (Philadelphia: J. B. Lippincott Co., 1946), and Philip Wylie, *Generation of Vipers* (New York: Farrar & Rinehart, 1942).

19. Mass-Observation, London, "Portrait of an American?" *International Journal of Opinion and Attitude Research*, I (1947), 96.

20. In lecture at Yale University, May 2, 1947.

21. Alfred C. Kinsey, Wardell B. Pomeroy, and Clyde E. Martin, *Sexual Behavior in the Human Male* (Philadelphia: W. B. Saunders Co., 1948).

22. Lewis M. Terman, *Psychological Factors in Marital Happiness* (New York: McGraw-Hill Book Co., 1938), pp. 145–66.

23. Constantine Panunzio, *Major Social Institutions* (New York: Macmillan Co., 1939), p. 430.

24. Mirra Komarovsky, "Cultural Contradictions and Sex Roles," *American Journal of Sociology*, LII (1946), 184–89.

25. Ferdinand Lundberg and Marynia F. Farnham, *Modern Woman: The Lost Sex* (New York: Harper & Bros., 1947).

24. VARIATIONS IN THE BASIC VALUES OF FAMILY SYSTEMS

1. Clyde Kluckhohn *et al.*, "Values and Value-Orientations in the Theory of Action," in Talcott Parsons and Edward A. Shils (eds.), *Toward a General Theory of Action* (Cambridge, Mass.: Harvard University Press, 1952), Part IV, chap. ii, pp. 409–10.

2. For a fuller discussion of this classification scheme and the theory of variation in value orientations, see two articles by the author, "Dominant and Substitute Profiles of Cultural Orientations: Their Significance for the Analysis of Social Stratification," *Social Forces*, XXVIII, No. 4 (1950), 276–93, and "Dominant and Variant Value Orientations," in Clyde Kluckhohn, Henry A. Murray and David M. Schneider (eds.), *Personality in Nature, Society, and Culture* (2nd ed.; New York: Alfred A. Knopf, 1953), pp. 342–57.

A still more complete version of the theory, as well as the results of testing it in five cultures, will appear in *Variations in Value Orientations* (Evanston, Ill.: Row, Peterson & Co., to be published), a forthcoming monograph written by the author in collaboration with Fred L. Strodtbeck and others.

3. In the research done on five subcultures in the American Southwest—Zuni, Navaho, Spanish-Americans, Mormons, and Texans—a research instrument was developed for a direct testing. The instrument and the results

obtained with it will appear in *Variations in Value Orientations.*

4. Erik H. Erikson, *Childhood and Society* (New York: W. W. Norton & Co., 1950).

5. The best single source of information on the lineal *relational* structure of modern rural Ireland is Conrad M. Arensberg and Solon T. Kimball, *Family and Community in Ireland* (Cambridge, Mass.: Harvard University Press, 1940).

25. PRESSURES TO REMARRY:
INSTITUTIONALIZED PATTERNS AFFECTING THE DIVORCED

1. Of course, many contemporary analysts do maintain that our high divorce rate does create major disruptive forces in the society.

2. Kingsley Davis, "Statistical Perspective on Marriage and Divorce," *Annals,* CCLXXII (1950), 9–21, asserts that our divorce rate will not continue to rise, but will level off.

3. *Statistical Bulletin,* XXVI, No. 5 (1945), 1–3.

4. For a particularly good, succinct presentation of this position, see Kingsley Davis, *Human Society* (New York: Macmillan, 1949), chap. xv.

5. Corroborating data are in Hadley G. Cantril and Mildred Strunk, *Public Opinion 1935–1946* (Princeton, N.J.: Princeton University Press, 1951).

6. Howard Becker and Reuben Hill, *Family, Marriage and Parenthood* (Boston: Heath, 1942), chap. xxii.

7. Willard Waller, *The Old Love and the New* (New York: Liveright, 1930), chap. iv.

8. Correspondingly, parents with no strong convictions regarding religion may feel that it is their moral responsibility to send their children to church. If they do not feel this responsibility, their *neighbors* believe that they ought to do so.

9. We are inclined to believe, in addition, that there is a gradually increasing feeling on the part of friends of the divorcee that he or she "deserves a break." That is to say, he or she *deserves* a spouse and a good marriage.

26. ROLE DIFFERENTIATION IN THE NUCLEAR FAMILY:
A COMPARATIVE STUDY

1. Most notably the Nayar. See, for instance, E. K. Gough, "The Traditional Kinship Systems of the Nayars of Malabar," prepared for the Social Science Research Council Seminar on Kinship (unpublished). Also, Gough, "Changing Kinship Usages in the Setting of Political and Economic Change Among the Nayars of Malabar," *Journal of the Royal Anthropological Institute,* Vol. XCII (1952).

2. In Chap. v of *Family, Socialization and Interaction Process.*

3. The framework for this analysis is provided in T. Parsons, R. F. Bales, and E. A. Shils, *Working Papers in the Theory of Group Action* (Glencoe, Ill.: The Free Press, 1953); and Parsons, *The Social System* (Glencoe, Ill.: The Free Press, 1951).

4. Because resources do not necessarily cluster around the immediate residence of the family, and typically a mother stays near the home partly, we may suppose, to symbolize the latent system.

5. There are several implicit assumptions here; for instance, that if you are inhibiting emotions in order to perform instrumental tasks, you cannot at the same time release them in integrative-expressive behavior. So that it is no solution to the problem to try to do both at once.

27. TASK DIFFERENTIATION OF HUSBAND AND WIFE IN FAMILY ACTIVITIES

1. These studies, of which Mr. Herbst's is an integral part, have been reported in O. A. Oeser and S. B. Hammond (eds.), *Social Structure and Personality in a City* (London: Routledge and Kegan Paul, Ltd., 1954). See also O. A. Oeser and F. E. Emery, *Social Structure and Personality in a Rural Community* (London: Routledge and Kegan Paul, Ltd., 1954). Editors.

2. There are grounds for believing the results to be representative of all Australian city families. Since the original publication of this article, a number of replications of the study have been made in Australia. The first to be published is by Dr. R. Taft, "Some Sub-Cultural Variables in Family Structure in Australia," *Australian Journal of Psychology,* IX, No. 1 (1957), 69–90. The study was carried out in Perth, western Australia, employing a matched population sample of the same size as that used in the Melbourne study.

3. Without taking into consideration the 16 cases of husbands who participate in all regions, which would increase the prediction ratio unduly.

28. ILLNESS, THERAPY, AND THE MODERN URBAN AMERICAN FAMILY

1. The limitations on space have made it necessary to omit some of our more "psychologistic" points. We hope that such deletions in no way impair our foremost intent, which is to show how the simultaneous use of psychological and sociological theory can serve to illuminate a given problem area.

2. For a grounding of this classification of types of deviant orientation, see T. Parsons, *The Social System* (Glencoe, Ill.: The Free Press, 1951), chap. vii; and R. K. Merton, "Social Structure and Anomie," chap. iii of *Social Theory and Social Structure* (Glencoe, Ill.: The Free Press, 1949).

3. Cf. Parsons, "Sources and Patterns of Aggression in the Social Structure of the Western World," in *Essays in Sociological Theory* (Glencoe, Ill.: The Free Press, 1949), chap. xii.

4. As we will point out in a later section of this article, despite the paring-down process which our family system has undergone, its residual functions as primary socializer, social-control agent, and emotional bulwark, are so crucial that the over-all importance of kinship in our society has not diminished. Indeed, as Robin Williams phrases it in his study of *American Society* (New York: Alfred A. Knopf Inc., 1951), though "the scope of family activities has narrowed, the emotional significance of the surviving relations has, in one sense, increased" (p. 77).

A brief analysis of these features of the American family will be found in T. Parsons, R. F. Bales, and E. A. Shils, *Working Papers in the Theory of Group Action* (Glencoe, Ill.: The Free Press, 1953), chap. v, section 8.

5. We know how important (particularly at the Oedipal period) the significance of the parental marriage solidarity is to children, and how sensitive they are to a feeling of being excluded.

6. It must not be forgotten that the sick role has a *positive* function in American society. There is much reason to believe that illness is less harmful to the society than other forms of deviant behavior—for example, crime and some types of political involvement. For sickness not only exposes the actor to the counteractive therapy of the doctor and his adjuncts, but (with the important exception of "magic-mountain-like" communities of the chronically ill) illness usually prevents the individual from attaching himself to a solidary subculture of similarly oriented deviants. Thus, the inability of the family to tolerate the illness of its members runs counter to a social need to increase, rather than decrease, the relative amount of illness. This is not to say that illness is positively valued in our culture. It is merely to point out that there is pressure to divert unavoidable deviant motivation from other channels into this one—with a net functional gain for the

society. (The situation is analagous to the positive function of the national debt. From the point of view of private finance, debt is undesirable; but from the point of view of economy as a whole, it has certain positive functions.) On this aspect of illness, cf. Parsons, *The Social System*, chaps. vii and x.

7. The discomforts of the double-dependency characteristic of the patient role would undoubtedly be experienced more acutely by an activistically oriented personality type, for example, than by a more compliantly organized individual. We are assuming, however, that even in the case of motivated illness, wherein the acquiescence is "chosen" by the actor, this choice is always an ambivalent one; and thus, the difficulties experienced by the patient-initiate, though perhaps milder in degree, will be qualitatively the same.

8. In outlining the components of therapy, we are assuming that not only the psychiatrist's role, but the role of the physician in the more general sense, is psychotherapeutic. Indeed, it is clear that "the basic structuring of the physician's role in our society did not come about through the application of theories of the ideal situation for psychotherapy. It was a spontaneous, unplanned development of social structure which psychiatry was able to utilize and develop. . . ." Parsons, *The Social System*, p. 462.

9. In regard to the latter type of case, see Renée C. Fox, *Experiment Perilous* (Glencoe, Ill.: The Free Press, 1959), which describes a hospital ward comprised of patients ill with chronic, progressively debilitating diseases, demonstrating this phenomenon clearly.

10. To reiterate an earlier point: the fact that the patient is a partially socialized adult, whose tolerance of dependence has upper limits, is relevant here, too. What is more, the sick actor's difficulties in accepting the passive-dependent obligations of the patient role is one of the best pieces of evidence we know for correcting the common tendency to regard the child and the sick person as psychologically identical.

11. Cf. D. M. Levy, *Maternal Overprotection* (New York: Columbia University Press 1943).

12. The role of the physician, however, is more closely analogous to the father role than to that of the mother. In this special sense, mother, father, and therapist may be said to vary over a continuous range: with the mother giving the highest level of permissiveness and support; the physician, the greatest incentive to acceptance of discipline.

13. It is not easy, of course, for the hospital staff—with its bureaucratic structuring and its multiple technical responsibilities to large groups of patients—to provide such

personalized care. In this respect, it resembles the school more than the family.

14. Even so, the restoration of the actor to his kinship unit, to his job, and to his other non-sick orbits, is usually problem-laden. For one thing, we have already shown

that at this juncture we encounter the well-known phenomenon of secondary gain—a possible consequence if the transference relationship of patient and physician, and the supportive-exemptive features of illness are not adequately controlled.

29. THE RESOLUTION OF ROLE CONFLICT WITHIN THE FAMILY

1. See, for example, Nathan W. Ackerman, " 'Social Role' and Total Personality," *American Journal of Orthopsychiatry*, XXI (1951), 1–17; Nathan W. Ackerman and Raymond Sobel, "Family Diagnosis: An Approach to the Preschool Child," *American Journal of Orthopsychiatry*, XX (1950), 744–53; Talcott Parsons and Robert F. Bales, *Family, Socialization and Interaction Process* (Glencoe, Ill.: The Free Press, 1955); Otto Pollak, *Social Science and Psychotherapy for Children* (New York: Russell Sage Foundation, 1952); John P. Spiegel, "The Social Roles of Doctor and Patient in Psychoanalysis and Psychotherapy," *Psychiatry*, XVII (1954), 369–76.

2. See the following: Arthur F. Bentley, "Kennetic Inquiry," *Science*, CXII (1950), 775–83; John Dewey and Arthur F. Bentley, *Knowing and the Known* (Boston: Beacon Press, 1949); Florence R. Kluckhohn and John P. Spiegel, *Integration and Conflict in Family Behavior* (Report No. 27; Topeka, Kansas: Group for the Advancement of Psychiatry, 1954); John P. Spiegel, "A Model for Relationships Among Systems," in Roy R. Grinker (ed.), *Toward a Unified Theory of Human Behavior* (New York: Basic Books, 1956), pp. 16–26.

3. The expression *role conflict* has been used in two different ways. In the first and perhaps more common usage, it refers to a situation in which ego is involved in a difficult or impossible choice between two different roles toward two different alters. No matter what decision he makes, he is in trouble with one or the other of his role partners in the situation. In the second usage, ego and alter have conflicting or incompatible notions of how to play their reciprocal roles. The conflict is not over which of several possible roles to take, but rather how to enact the role each has decided to take. It is the second definition which is used in this paper. Settlement of the terminological problem should not prove too difficult, but will have to be postponed for the present.

4. Adelaide M. Johnson and S. A. Szurek, "The Genesis of Antisocial Acting Out in Children and Adults," *Psychoanalytic Quarterly*, XXI (1952), 323–43; Adelaide M. Johnson, "Factors in the Etiology of Fixations and Symptom Choice," *Psychoanalytic Quarterly*, XXII (1953), 475–96.

5. Talcott Parsons, Robert F. Bales, and Edward A. Shils, *Working Papers in the Theory of Action* (Glencoe, Ill.: The Free Press, 1953), chap. v.

6. In this context, *equilibrium* does not denote a rigid, static state, but rather a balancing of process in a moving or changing state. The phrase *moving equilibrium* might, perhaps, be a better name.

7. Such roles are described by Ralph Linton in *The Study of Man* (New York: Appleton-Century, 1936), chap. viii.

8. *Ibid.*

9. Florence R. Kluckhohn, "Dominant and Variant Value Orientations," in Clyde Kluckhohn, Henry A. Murray, and David M. Schneider (eds.), *Personality in Nature, Society, and Culture* (New York: Alfred A. Knopf, Inc., 1953), pp. 342–57. See also Florence R. Kluckhohn, *Variations in Value Orientations* (Evanston, Ill.: Row, Peterson, forthcoming).

10. Harry Stack Sullivan used the term *induction* for the process through which anxiety in the parent elicits anxiety in the child. However, Sullivan applied the word only to the transmission of anxiety, whereas in this paper it refers to a variety of interpersonal influences. A further distinction is that Sullivan regarded the process as somewhat mysterious—a unitary phenomenon, incapable of analytical penetration. For further details, see Harry Stack Sullivan, *The Interpersonal Theory of Psychiatry*, eds. Helen Swick Perry and Mary Ladd Gawel (New York: Norton, 1953), pp. 53–55.

11. Kenneth Burke, *A Rhetoric of Motives* (New York: Prentice-Hall, 1950).

12. Sullivan, *op. cit.*, chap. xiii.

13. Like *role conflict*, the expression *role reversal* has been used in two different ways. In one usage, it refers to a situation in which ego and alter permanently exchange roles. For example, a husband and wife settle on an arrangement in which the husband stays home and looks after the house and children, while the wife takes a job and earns the income for the family. In the second usage, the phrase refers to a process in which ego and alter temporarily exchange roles, in action or in imagination, for the sake of gaining insight into each other's feelings and behavior. This definition has been extensively used by J. L. Moreno and his associates, to whom I am much indebted. For examples, see J. L. Moreno, "The Discovery of the Spontaneous Man—With Special Emphasis on the Technique of Role Reversal," *Group Psychotherapy*, VIII (1955), 103–29.

14. George Herbert Mead, *Mind, Self, and Society* (Chicago: University of Chicago Press, 1936).

15. Georg Simmel, "Quantitative Aspects of Groups," in Kurt H. Wolff (ed.), *The Sociology of Georg Simmel* (Glencoe, Ill.: The Free Press, 1950), pp. 85–177.

16. T. M. Mills, "Power Relations in Three-Person Groups," in D. Cartwright and A. Zander (eds.), *Group Dynamics* (Evanston, Ill.: Row, Peterson, 1953), pp. 428–42; T. M. Mills, "The Coalition Pattern in Three-Person Groups," *American Sociological Review*, XIX (1954), 657–67.

30. THE EMOTIONALLY DISTURBED CHILD AS THE FAMILY SCAPEGOAT

1. Sir James Frazer, *The Golden Bough* (abridged ed.; New York: Macmillan, 1927).

2. *Ibid.*, p. 562.

3. *Ibid.*, p. 575.

4. In addition to Frazer, *op. cit.*, see also Emile Durkheim, "Deux lois de l'évolution pénale," *L'Année Sociologique*, IV (1899), 55–95; Henri Hubert and Marcel Mauss, "Essai sur la nature et la fonction du sacrifice," *L'Année Sociologique*, II (1897), 29–138; William Robertson Smith, *The Religion of the Semites* (London: A. and C. Black, Ltd., 1927); Roger Money-Kyrle, *The Meaning of Sacrifice* (London: Hogarth Press, 1930); George Herbert Mead, "The Psychology of Punitive Justice," *American Journal of Sociology*, XXIII (1918), 577–620; Ruth S. Eissler, "Scapegoats of Society," in Kurt R. Eissler (ed.), *Searchlights on Delinquency* (New York: International Universities Press, 1949), 288–305; and Clyde Kluckhohn, "Navaho Witchcraft," *Papers of the Peabody Museum of American Archaeology and Ethnology, Harvard University*, Vol. XXII (1944).

5. This is not to deny relevance of psychological aspects. The same facts can be related to a number of different theoretical systems, but here focus is on the group dynamics.

6. For other reports of this research, see John P. Spiegel, "The Resolution of Role Conflict Within the Family," *Psychiatry*, XX (1957), 1–16; Florence Rockwood Kluckhohn, "Family Diagnosis: Variations in the Basic Values of Family Systems," *Social Casework*, XXXIX (1958), 1–11; and John P. Spiegel, "Some Cultural Aspects of Transference and Countertransference," in Jules H. Massermann (ed.), *Individual and Family Dynamics* (New York: Grune and Stratton, Inc., 1959). A more inclusive statement of the conceptual framework will be published in the near future as, John P. Spiegel, "The Structure and Function of Social Roles in the Doctor-Patient Relationship." Lectures delivered at Tulane University, 1958.

7. It should be noted that only families which had never been separated or divorced were included in the present sample. Of course, there are also cases of emotionally disturbed children where only one parent is living with the children and cases in which one parent is living with other relatives. Hence, tensions between parents cannot be the universal cause of emotional disturbance. A more general hypothesis would be that the emotionally disturbed child is always the focus of primary-group tension.

8. This is spelled out in more detail in Ezra F. Vogel, "The Marital Relationship of Parents and the Emotionally Disturbed Child" (Unpublished Ph.D. thesis, Harvard University, 1958).

9. See Florence R. Kluckhohn, *loc. cit.;* and F. Kluckhohn, Fred L. Strodtbeck and others, *Variations in Value Orientations* (Evanston, Ill.: Row, Peterson & Co., forthcoming).

10. Well families, by contrast, had bridged the gap between the orientations of different ethnic or class groups. They had succeeded in neutralizing old orientations before taking on new ones. Usually such families were changing in a slower and more orderly fashion.

11. Discussed at length in Norman W. Bell, "The Impact of Psychotherapy Upon Family Relationships" (Unpublished Ph.D. thesis, Harvard University, 1959).

12. The one family which did occasionally express antagonism directly to outsiders was the most disturbed family in the sample. The expression of hostility to neighbors was filled with such conflicts and added complications that it inevitably proved inadequate and the family returned to the scapegoating of their child.

While many members of these families did express prejudice towards minority groups, this prejudice did little to drain the severe tensions within the family. Perhaps the minority group was not symbolically appropriate for the handling of any of the family conflicts, or perhaps they were not sufficiently available to serve as a continual focus of family tensions.

13. While in virtually all these families, there were considerable problems about achievement, another family seen by one of the authors as part of another investigation was very closely tied to the traditional ethnic patterns and had not yet seriously begun to incorporate American achievement values. In this family, there was one child, seriously substandard in intelligence, with very ugly physical features, who had epileptic seizures. There were also some children who were above average in intelligence. This family had no serious conflicts about achievement, and none of the children were scapegoated.

14. Alfred Adler, *Understanding Human Nature* (New York: Greenberg, 1927), and Alfred Adler, "The Cause and Prevention of

Neurosis," *Journal of Abnormal and Social Psychology*, XXIII (1928), 4–11.

15. In the well families, there were cases of comparable physical illness which did not result in the same type of anxieties in the family.

16. No adequate large-scale studies are available to provide an estimate of the proportion of emotional disturbances found in the eldest child. Many small-scale studies have been made, but they are inconsistent and contradictory. See John P. Spiegel and Norman W. Bell, "The Family of the Psychiatric Patient," in Silvano Arieti (ed.), *American Handbook of Psychiatry* (New York: Basic Books, Inc., 1959). In the present study, slightly more than half were eldest children, a finding similar to that in another small sample of emotionally disturbed children: Sydney Croog, "The Social Backgrounds of Emotionally Disturbed Children and their Siblings" (Unpublished Ph.D. thesis, Yale University, 1954). It has also been noted that eldest sons are more likely to be involved in problems of inheritance and rivalry, and are more likely to be adult-oriented. See such diverse studies as George Peter Murdock, *Social Structure* (New York: Macmillan, 1949); Sigmund Freud, *Moses and Monotheism* (New York: Alfred A. Knopf, 1939); and Charles McArthur, "Personalities of First and Second Children," *Psychiatry*, XIX (1956), 47–54.

17. The way the parent gives the child implicit approval to act out his own unconscious wishes has already been well described for the relationship between a single parent and a single child. Adelaide M. Johnson, "Sanctions for Superego Lacunae of Adolescents," in Kurt R. Eissler (ed.), *Searchlights on Delinquency* (New York: International Universities Press, 1949); Melitta Sperling, "The Neurotic Child and his Mother: A Psychoanalytic Study," *American Journal of Orthopsychiatry*, XXI (1951), 351–64. For a more detailed account of family role-induction methods, see Spiegel, "The Resolution of Role Conflict within the Family" (Reprinted in this volume).

18. Here again, the analogy to the individual personality system is instructive. Just as Freud's hysteric patients expressed a *belle indifference* to their symptoms and a surprising reluctance to change them, so did these parents have a *belle indifference* to the symptoms of their children. Just as the individual's symptom represents an expression of his own unconscious wish, so does the child's

symptom represent an expression of his parents' unconscious wishes.

19. While the control imposed by parents in well families sometimes appeared to be extremely aggressive and punitive, this aggression was not such a massive critical attack on the child and did not carry the threat of such severe sanctions as did the aggression by the disturbed parents. In the well families, the punishment of the child was not regarded by the child as so damaging, and there was ordinarily the possibility of escaping further punishment by behaving in a different, desired way. There were few possibilities for the child to escape this hostility in the disturbed family.

20. In one well family, when there was considerable marital tension it was handled in a very overt fashion, and marital problems were not dealt with through the child.

21. At adolescence, the time when more demands for independent existence are made, a large number of acute disturbances appear. Many who were adequately adjusted to the roles they were assigned within the family, were unable to meet the new adjustment outside the family. See, for example, Nicholas J. Demerath, "Adolescent Status and the Individual" (Unpublished Ph.D. thesis, Harvard University, 1942). A large number of acute psychoses also occur as soon as the army recruit leaves home and enters military service. Under ordinary circumstances, the socialization of the child prepares him for the social demands of external society. See, for example, Talcott Parsons, "The Incest Taboo in Relation to Social Structure and the Socialization of the Child," *British Journal of Sociology*, V (1954), 101–17; and David Aberle and Kaspar Naegele, "Middle-Class Fathers' Occupational Roles and Attitudes toward Children," *American Journal of Orthopsychiatry*, XXII (1952), 566–78 (reprinted in this volume).

22. The importance of difficulties with the associations outside the nuclear family in directing the family for psychiatric treatment has long been recognized by clinicians. See, for example, Anna Freud, "Indications for Child Analysis," in *The Psychoanalytic Study of the Child*, Vol. I (New York: International Universities Press, 1945).

23. See, for example, the analysis of the case of Long John's nightmares in William F. Whyte, *Street Corner Society* (Chicago: University of Chicago Press, 1943); and a report of Asch's experiments in Solomon E. Asch, *Social Psychology* (New York: Prentice-Hall, 1952).

31. LEGITIMACY AND THE INCEST TABOO

1. Bronislaw Malinowski, "Kinship," *Encyclopaedia Brittanica*, 14th ed., p. 406; "Parenthood—The Basis of Social Structure" in V. F. Calverton and S. D. Schmalhausen, *The New Generation* (New York: Macauley, 1930), pp. 134–46; *Sex and Repression in Savage Society* (London: Harcourt, Brace, 1927), pp. 212–14.

2. Malinowski, "Parenthood . . . ," *loc. cit.*, p. 137. Cf. Kingsley Davis, "The Forms of Illegitimacy," *Social Forces*, XVIII (October, 1939), 77–89; and "Illegitimacy and the Social Structure." *American Journal of Sociology*. XLV (September, 1939), 215–33.

3 Malinowski, "Parenthood . . . ," *loc. cit.*, p. 138.

4. *Ibid.*, p. 140.

5. For an analysis of the causes and kinds of illegitimacy, see Davis, "The Forms of Illegitimacy," *loc. cit.*

6. This is what happens in actual cases, where the daughters are often less than ten years of age. See Jacob A. Goldberg and Rosamond W. Goldberg, *Girls on City Streets* (New York: American Social Hygiene Asso-

ciation, 1935), pp. 185–217. Svend Riemer says nothing about the age of the daughters in Swedish court cases but analyzes the life histories and motives of the offending fathers; the father's use of his superior power and authority is quite apparent in the cases described. "A Research Note on Incest," *American Journal of Sociology*, XLV (January, 1940), 566–75.

7. A fuller analysis of incest taboos will be found in Brenda Seligman, "Incest and Descent: Their Influence on Social Organization," *Journal of the Royal Anthropological Institute*, LIX (January–June, 1929), 231–72; Reo Fortune, "Incest," *Encyclopedia of the Social Sciences;* and Malinowski, *Sex and Repression.* . . .

32. THE FAILURE OF SOLIDARITY

1. Talcott Parsons, "Actor, Situation, and Normative Pattern" (Unpublished manuscript, 1942), p. 114.

2. Ralph Linton, *The Study of Man* (New York: Appleton-Century, 1936), p. 152.

3. Cf. Margaret Mead, *Male and Female: A Study of the Sexes in a Changing World* (New York: Morrow, 1949), chap. xiii.

4. The literature on this phenomenon, in general, is, of course, very extensive. By reason of its summary of a considerable part of this literature having to do with ethnic differences as the source of strain upon family solidarity, one may be cited here to some good purpose, namely, William C. Smith, *Ameri-*

cans in the Making (New York: Appleton-Century, 1939).

5. Jean Piaget, *The Moral Judgment of the Child* (New York: Harcourt, Brace, 1932).

6. Cf. "Changing Societies as Family Contexts," in Howard Becker and Reuben Hill (eds.), *Marriage and the Family* (Boston: Heath, 1942), pp. 3–24.

7. Cf. Max Horkheimer (ed.), *Studien über Autorität und Familie* (Paris: Libraire Félix Alcan, 1939), pp. 63–68.

8. See, for example, Robert S. Lynd and Helen M. Lynd, *Middletown: A Study in American Culture* (New York: Harcourt, Brace, 1929).

33. SOME PROBLEMS IN THE STUDY OF HOSTILITY AND AGGRESSION IN MIDDLE-CLASS AMERICAN FAMILIES

1. The literature dealing with problems of "hostility" and "aggression" is extensive and cannot be surveyed here. Hostility and aggression are both assumed to involve (potential) injury, the former primarily in the medium of "hate" and the latter in the medium of "anger." The following are the most important references for purposes of the present project: Allison Davis, "American Status Systems and the Socialization of the Child," *American Sociological Review*, VI (1941), 345–56; Kingsley Davis, "Jealousy and Sexual Property," *Social Forces*, Vol. XVII, No. 1 (1938), and "The Sociology of Parent-Youth Conflict," *American Sociological Review*, I (1940), 523–35; J. Dollard, "Hostility and Fear in Social Life," *Social Forces*, Vol. XVII, No. 1 (1938); J. Henry, "Some Cultural Determinants of Hostility in Pilaga Indian Children," *American Journal of Orthopsychiatry*, X (1940), 230–35; A. Irving Hallowell, "Aggression in Saulteaux Society," in C. Kluckhohn and H. Murray (eds.), *Personality in Nature, Society and Culture* (New York: Alfred A. Knopf, Inc.,

1947); David M. Levy, "The Hostile Act," *Psychological Review*, XLVIII (1941), 356–61, and "Hostility Patterns," *American Journal of Orthopsychiatry*, XIII (1943), 441–61; Erich Lindemann, "Individual Hostility and Group Integration," *Human Organization*, VIII (1949), 5–9; R. Lippitt, "An Experimental Study of the Effect of Democratic and Authoritarian Group Atmospheres," in K. Lewin *et al.*, *Studies of Topological and Vector Psychology*, I ("University of Iowa Studies," *Studies in Child Welfare*, XVI, No. 3, 1939); R. K. Merton, "Social Structure and Anomie," in *Social Theory and Social Structure* (Glencoe, Ill.: The Free Press, 1949); Thomas M. Newcomb, "Autistic Hostility and Social Reality," *Human Relations*, I (1947), 69–85; Talcott Parsons, "Certain Primary Sources and Patterns of Aggression in the Western World," *Essays in Sociological Theory: Pure and Applied* (Glencoe, Ill.: The Free Press, 1949); "Round Table on the Treatment of Aggression," *American Journal of Orthopsychiatry*, XIII (1943), 384–440; R. Sears, "Research Frontiers in Human Relations," *Proceedings of the American Philosophical Society,* XC (1948), 325–410.

2. *Essays in Sociological Theory,* especially x, xi, and xii; "Theoretical Problems in the Study of Social Mobility" (Unpublished memorandum).

3. *Human Society* (New York: The Macmillan Co., 1949).

4. *The Family Revolution in Modern China* (Cambridge, Mass.: Harvard University Press, 1949).

5. For a systematic exposition of this point of view, see D. F. Aberle, A. K. Cohen, A. K. Davis, M. J. Levy, and F. X. Sutton, "The Functional Prerequisites of a Society," *Ethics,* LX (1950), 100–11; Talcott Parsons, unpublished manuscripts.

34. FAMILY RITUAL AND FAMILY INTEGRATION

1. Ernest W. Burgess and Leonard S. Cottrell, *Predicting Success and Failure in Marriage* (New York: Prentice-Hall, Inc., 1939).

2. Ernest W. Burgess and Harvey J. Locke, *The Family* (New York: The American Book Co., 1945), p. 579.

3. Elizabeth Kemper Adams, *The Aesthetic Experience* (Chicago: University of Chicago Press, 1907).

4. Frederick Henke, *A Study in the Psychology of Ritualism* (Chicago: University of Chicago Press, 1910), p. 84.

5. L. L. Bernard, *Social Control,* (New York: The Macmillan Co., 1939), p. 434.

35. NORMS AND IDEOLOGY: THE NORMAL FAMILY

1. See S. F. Nadel, *Foundations of Social Anthropology* (London: Cohen and West, 1951), p. 94; T. Parsons and R. F. Bales, *Family, Socialization and Interaction Process* (Glencoe, Ill.: The Free Press, 1955), p. 106; and A. R. Radcliffe-Brown, "On Social Structure," *Journal of the Royal Anthropological Institute,* LXX (1940), 1–12.

2. M. Gluckman, *The Judicial Process among the Barotse of Northern Rhodesia* (Manchester: Manchester University Press, 1955).

3. At first, I thought replies to direct questions were less "true" than spontaneous conversation. I now regard this as an error. Except for cases of conscious lying, I now think people express their views quite differently in different contexts without being aware of it. They may even hold different views in different contexts. This exemplifies Max Gluckman's point that flexibility and inconsistency in norms make them more rather than less useful socially; they can be adapted to suit immediate circumstances. M. Gluckman, *The Judicial Process Among the Barotse of Northern Rhodesia* (Manchester: Manchester University Press, 1955).

Informal discussions with other family sociologists suggest that they have fallen into the same error. In cases where questionnaires and unstructured interviews with the same informants have yielded very different results, research workers have tended to regard one technique as right and truth-revealing and the other as wrong and false. It would be more rewarding to regard both sets of results as "true" in the sense of revealing what people think in different research situations. The two sets of results could be compared closely to see if there were a consistent bias. Such a procedure would lead to greater understanding of the effects produced by different research techniques.

4. E. W. Burgess and H. J. Locke, *The Family: From Institution to Companionship* (2nd ed.; New York: American Book Co., 1953).

5. M. Sherif, *The Psychology of Social Norms* (New York: Harper and Bros., 1936); T. M. Newcomb, *Social Psychology* (London: Tavistock Publications, and New York: Dryden Press, 1950).

6. P. Heimann, "Certain Functions of Introjection and Projection in Early Infancy," in M. Klein, P. Heimann, S. Isaacs, and J. Riviere, *Developments in Psycho-Analysis* (London: Hogarth Press, 1952), pp. 122–68; M. Klein, *Contributions to Psycho-Analysis* (London: Hogarth Press, 1948).

7. G. H. Mead, *Mind, Self and Society* (Chicago: University of Chicago Press, 1934).

36. DIFFERENTIATION OF VALUES IN A MODERN COMMUNITY

1. The word "cleavage" may be ill-chosen, since it implies that there ought to be (as perhaps there ought not), or that there was expected to be (as indeed there was), a substantial degree of unity, at least among adults, and at least with reference to basic beliefs.

2. There is evidence that these sex differences are established or emerge early, for example at age ten or eleven, and perhaps earlier.

3. The differences in orientation between the sexes must derive from a multiplicity of sources—historical, social-structural, and perhaps biological.

4. The extension of knowledge as to the role that difference in sex, as biologically given and socially defined, plays in every sphere of activity has been paralleled by the seeming denial that the difference makes any difference. The freedom to discuss sex freely,

and the disappearance of the taboo against exchanging information on sexual activity (in its narrowest connotation), has been accompanied, for the women, by another taboo against discussing the proposition that men and women may have, on biogenic or sociogenic grounds or both, radically differing orientations towards critical issues and aspects of life.

5. A statistician might understand if it were said that women are "Q-oriented"; men, "R-oriented." Cf. W. Stephenson, *The Study of Behavior: Q-Technique and Its Methodology* (Chicago: University of Chicago Press, 1953), pp. 47–61.

6. It is perhaps more on this ground than on any other that the experts (and also some religious leaders) are felt by the men as "feminine"; the experts, like the women, stress the primacy of inner meanings over outer similarities.

7. These polarities, which emerged as data of observation out of intimate contact with men and women individually, in the operation of a women's seminar (five years) and a men's group (much more briefly), and out of direct questions about aspiration, find strong suggestive support in material taken in a wholly different frame of reference. Cf. S. Ferenczi, *Sex in Psychoanalysis*, trans. E. Jones (New York: Basic Books, 1950), and E. Fromm, *The Forgotten Language: An Introduction to the Understanding of Dreams, Fairy Tales and Myths* (New York: Rinehart & Co., 1951), pp. 195–263.

8. This statement applies with one noteworthy exception—as to the role of biological heredity. The women lay much greater stress on the effects of environment, and the men proportionately greater stress on the effects of heredity. In actual mating behavior, however, the women pay careful attention to biological characteristics dispassionately considered; the men respond more impulsively to the immediate environment.

9. Cf. R. de Roussey de Sales, "Love in America," *Atlantic Monthly*, May, 1938, pp. 645–51, where he observes this attitude in reference to love as "a national problem," but mistakenly, we think, attributes to the people generally what is characteristically dominantly middle-class and feminine. That he should do so, moving in intellectual circles of "experts," themselves representative of the "feminine" view, is understandable.

10. On the basis of this material on perfectability and on attitude to the expert, which indicates a tendency for males to maintain ego and institution intact while strains mount unnoted, and for females to sacrifice ego and institution to the attempt to maintain continuous adjustment, one might expect, in the field of mental-health phenomena: (1) continuous strain and gradualness of onset of trouble in the women; and (2) crisis (personal and institutional) and suddenness of onset in the men. Whether this expectation

could be confirmed or not, we do not *know*. We have a strong impression (where there *is* pathology) of long-sustained harried tension in women and of eruptive phenomena (for example, sudden neurotic break-through, ulcers, etc.) in men; but it is no more than an impression.

11. The ideology-action distinction presupposes a conscious argument, an ideology, logically and otherwise elaborated, pursued as a program of thought, and "recommended." What we subsequently call "thought-ways" are mere ways of thinking, which are mostly not conscious, do not constitute a "program," and would not be recommended by either party. How—if at all —they are related to ideology, it is difficult to say.

12. Similar in the sense that philosophic "system" implies a large span of matter, and "long-range," a large span of events.

13. "Utopian" not now in its pejorative sense, but in the sense of a capacity to imagine a different and better state in the future, and to believe in its possibility without either flying in the face of established knowledge or leaning exclusively upon it. Cf. D. Riesman, *Individualism Reconsidered* (Glencoe, Ill.: The Free Press, 1954), pp. 70–98.

14. It is taken for granted that the reader will understand throughout that it is a relation of value, not of cause and effect, that is spoken of. The question is which is "for the sake of" what. Religion may or may not contribute to "peace of mind," but those who value it for the sake of peace make it, for themselves, a means to peace as an end. Whether or not it is an efficient means is a quite separate question, and one for psychology to determine; though one would suppose that here as elsewhere the perception of the behavior would also affect the effect of what is perceived.

15. Again, the ethnic minority follows the pattern of the domestic one; among them was noted a pronounced tendency to clear ultimate purposes first, indeed to proceed from whole to part, from generalization to particular.

16. They do not use the terms, but psychologically the women are at home with "phenomenology"; the men with "behaviorism."

17. A partial qualification must be entered here, and would be relevant also at many other points. Several men—some top executives—were ready to admit individually and under cross-examination that for them also the personal satisfactions were primary goods, and the production-bonus, if it occurred, a mere rationalization of or defense for their "humane" impulses. But a Puritan culture did not permit them to avow, nor in most cases to recognize, such gentle, "non-male" desires.

18. Not to be confused with a logical in-

consistency. By a psychological inconsistency, is understood here what would be felt as emotionally (or aesthetically) inharmonious or clashing: something that prevents the formation of *Gestalt* in the personality. A logical inconsistency may do so—for logical people —but there is little, if any, necessary relation.

19. Cf. D. Riesman (in collaboration with R. Denney and N. Glazer), *The Lonely Crowd: A Study of the Changing American Character* (New Haven: Yale University Press, 1950), pp. 6–25.

38. FAMILY STRUCTURE AND SEX-ROLE LEARNING BY CHILDREN

1. A. Strauss, *The Social Psychology of George Herbert Mead* (Chicago: Phoenix Books, University of Chicago Press, 1956).

2. L. S. Cottrell, Jr., "The Analysis of Situational Fields in Social Psychology," *American Sociological Review,* VII (1942), 370–82.

3. O. G. Brim, Jr., "The Parent-Child Relation as a Social System: I. Parent and Child Roles," *Child Development,* XXVIII (1957), 344–64; M. Zelditch, Jr., "Role Differentiation in the Nuclear Family: A Comparative Study," in T. Parsons and R. F. Bales, *Family, Socialization and Interaction Process* (Glencoe, Ill.: The Free Press, 1955).

4. R. R. Sears, M. H. Pintler, and P. S. Sears, "Effect of Father Separation on Preschool Children's Doll Play Aggression," *Child Development,* XVII (1946), 219–43.

5. P. S. Sears, "Childrearing Factors Related to Playing of Sex-Typed Roles," *American Psychologist,* VIII (1953), 431 (abstract).

6. D. E. Payne and P. H. Mussen, "Parent-Child Relations and Father Identification Among Adolescent Boys," *Journal of Abnormal and Social Psychology,* LII (1956), 359–62.

7. L. B. Fauls, and W. D. Smith, "Sex-Role Learning of Five-Year-Olds," *Journal of Genetic Psychology,* LXXXIX (1956), 105–17.

8. T. Parsons, "Family Structure and the Socialization of the Child," in T. Parsons and R. F. Bales, *op. cit.*

9. "The Relation of 'Primary Mental Abilities' in Five- and Six-Year-Olds to Sex of Child and Characteristics of His Sibling," *Child Development,* XXV (1954), 210–23; "Some Personality Correlates of Sex, Sibling Position, and Sex of Sibling Among Five- and Six-Year-Old Children," *Genetic Psychology Monographs,* LII (1955), 3–50; "The Relation of Certain Family Constellation Characteristics and the Attitudes of Children toward Adults," *Child Development,* XVI (1955), 13–40; "Attitudes of Children toward Their Peers as Related to Certain Characteristics of Their Sibling," *Psychological Monographs,* Vol. LXX, No. 19 (1956); "Children's Work Attitudes and Sibling Characteristics," *Child Development,* XXVII (1956), 289–310; "Sibling Influence on Children's Speech," *Journal of Speech and Hearing Disorders,* XXI (1956), 322–28; "Sissiness and Tomboyishness in Relation to Sibling Characteristics," *Journal of Genetic Psychology,* LXXXVIII (1956), 231–44.

10. Koch, "Attitudes of Children toward Their Peers . . . ," *loc. cit.,* p. 289.

11. Dr. John Mann, Mr. David Glass, and Mr. David Lavin.

12. F. L. Strodtbeck and R. D. Mann, "Sex Role Differentiation in Jury Deliberations," *Sociometry,* IX (1956), 3–11.

13. Zelditch, *op. cit.*

14. L. M. Terman and L. E. Tyler, "Psychological Sex Differences," in L. Carmichael (ed.), *Manual of Child Psychology* (2nd ed.; New York: Wiley, 1954).

15. *Op. cit.,* pp. 95–101.

39. PARENTAL OCCUPATIONS AND CHILDREN'S SYMPTOMS

1. Of course, if the relationships between child and parent are positive, then parental occupation, whatever it may be, is viewed by the child within the dominant frame of reference of love, respect, and security. If the parent is loved, it is taken for granted that his occupation is important and desirable.

2. Although adults do not always understand the whole complex working of the stock exchange, this lack of understanding does not interfere with their emotional adjustment as long as they do not feel that their entire security depends upon its function.

40. FAMILY LIVING SPACE AND PERSONALITY DEVELOPMENT

1. A crowded area of Newark, New Jersey.

2. William McDougall, *Character and the Conduct of Life* (New York: Putnam's, 1927).

3. In various places; particularly see Havelock Ellis, *Studies in the Psychology of Sex* (Philadelphia: F. A. Davis, 1927), VI, 523, 531n, 544, and 554.

4. J. E. Wallace Wallin, *Personality Maladjustments and Mental Hygiene* (New York: McGraw-Hill, 1935).

41. EFFECTS UPON CHILDREN OF THEIR MOTHERS' OUTSIDE EMPLOYMENT

1. Sheldon Glueck and Eleanor Glueck, *Unraveling Juvenile Delinquency* (New York: Commonwealth Fund, 1950).

2. Sheldon Glueck and Eleanor Glueck, "Working Mothers and Delinquency," *Mental Hygiene*, XLI, No. 3 (1957), 327 ff.

3. Albert Bandura and R. H. Walters, "Adolescent Aggressive Behavior Disorders" (Unpublished manuscript, University of Toronto).

4. Mary Essig and D. H. Morgan, "Adjustment of Adolescent Daughters of Employed Women," *Journal of Educational Psychology*, Vol. XXXVII (1946).

5. Robert R. Sears, Eleanor E. Maccoby, and Harry Levin, *Patterns of Childrearing* (Evanston, Ill.: Row, Peterson & Co., 1957), chap. xii.

6. Jack Rouman, "School Children's Problems as Related to Parental Factors," *Journal of Education Research*, Vol. L (1956–57).

7. Anne Roe, *The Making of a Scientist* (New York: Dodd, Mead & Co., 1952).

8. See references to M. R. Winterbottom in David McClelland, John W. Atkinson, Russell A. Clark, and Edgar L. Lowell, *The Achievement Motive* (New York: Appleton-Century, 1953), esp. pp. 302, 303, 305.

9. New research is being initiated that should illuminate a number of the issues discussed above. Parallel studies are being undertaken in Australia and the United States of the effects of maternal employment upon family relations and child development, and the studies will embody closer control of demographic variables than has previously been attempted. In the United States, part of this work is being undertaken by the U.S. Public Health Service, Institute of Mental Health, under the direction of Dr. Marian Radke Yarrow; another segment will be done at Stanford by Drs. Lois Stolz and Alberta E. Siegel.

10. Sears *et al.*, *Patterns of Childrearing*, chap. xii.

11. William McCord and Joan McCord, *Origins of Crime* (New York: Columbia University Press, 1959).

12. Abraham Black, Richard L. Solomon, and J. W. M. Whiting, "Resistance to Temptation as a Function of Antecedent Dependency Relationships in Puppies" (Unpublished paper read at the Eastern Psychological Association meetings, 1954); D. G. Freedman, "The Effects of Indulgent and Disciplinary Rearing on Four Breeds of Dog," Abstract, *American Psychologist*, XII (1957), 398.

13. Helen Faigin, "Social Behavior of Young Children in the Kibbutz," *Journal of Abnormal and Social Psychology*, LVI (1958), 117–29.

14. *Ibid.*; Anna Freud and Dorothy Burlingham, *Infants without Families* (New York: International Universities Press, 1944).

15. *Ibid.*

16. R. A. Spitz, "Hospitalism: An Inquiry into the Genesis of Psychiatric Conditions in Early Childhood (I)," *The Psychoanalytic Study of the Child*, Vol. I; J. Bowlby, *Maternal Care and Mental Health* (Geneva: World Health Organization Monograph Series No. 2, 1952); Freud and Burlingham, *op. cit.*; Anna Freud and Sophie Dann, "An Experiment in Group Upbringing," *The Psychoanalytic Study of the Child*, Vol. II; W. Goldfarb, "Psychological Privation in Infancy and Subsequent Adjustment," *Journal of Orthopsychiatry*, Vol. XV (1945).

17. Samuel R. Pinneau, "The Infantile Disorders of Hospitalism and Anaclitic Depression," *Psychological Bulletin*, Vol. LII (1955).

18. W. Goldfarb, "Psychological Privation in Infancy and Subsequent Adjustment," *Journal of Orthopsychiatry*, Vol. XV (1945).

19. A. I. Rabin, "Infants and Children under Conditions of 'Intermittent Mothering' in the Kibbutz" (Unpublished paper delivered at the annual meeting of the American Orthopsychiatric Association, 1957).

20. Christoph M. Heinicke, "Some Effects of Separating Two-Year-Old Children from Their Parents: A Comparative Study," *Human Relations*, Vol. IX (1956).

21. David Levy, *Maternal Overprotection* (New York: Columbia University Press, 1943).

22. J. W. M. Whiting, Richard Kluckhohn, and Albert Anthony, "The Function of Male Initiation Ceremonies at Puberty," in Maccoby, Newcomb, and Hartley (eds.), *Readings in Social Psychology* (New York: Henry Holt and Co., 1958).

23. Mary Essig and D. H. Morgan, "Adjustment of Adolescent Daughters of Employed Women," *Journal of Educational Psychology*, Vol. XXXVII (1946); and Sheldon Glueck and Eleanor Glueck, "Working Mothers and Delinquency," *loc. cit.*

42. FAMILY ROLE STRUCTURE AND SELF-BLAME

1. John Dollard *et al.*, *Frustration and Aggression* (New Haven: Yale University Press, 1939).

2. Karl Menninger, *Man against Himself* (New York: Harcourt, Brace and Co., 1938).

3. S. Rosenzweig, "The Picture Association Method and Its Application in a Study of Reactions to Frustration," *Journal of Personality*, XIV (1945), 3–23.

4. Stanley H. King, "Emotional and Car-

diovascular Responses During Stress—An Experimental Study" (Unpublished Ph.D. dissertation, Harvard University, 1953).

5. Stanley H. King and Andrew F. Henry, "Aggression and Cardiovascular Reactions Related to Parental Control over Behavior," *Journal of Abnormal and Social Psychology*, L (March, 1955), 206–10.

6. Louis Guttman and Andrew F. Henry, "An Empirical Study of Some Higher Components of Attitudes" (in preparation).

7. Louis Guttman, "The Israel Alpha Technique for Scale Analysis," in M. W. Riley, J. W. Riley, Jr. and J. Toby (eds.), *Sociological Studies in Scale Analysis* (New Brunswick,

N.J.: Rutgers University Press, 1954), chap. xix.

8. S. A. Stouffer *et al.*, *Measurement and Prediction: The American Soldier* (Princeton, N.J.: Princeton University Press, 1950), IV, 249–53.

9. Significant beyond the .05 level.

10. Louis Guttman, "The Principal Components of Scale Analysis," in Stouffer, *op. cit.*, Vol. IV, chap. ix.

11. A. F. Henry, "Sibling Structure and Disciplinary Roles" (Paper prepared for the 1956 meetings of the American Sociological Society).

43. THE FAMILY CONSTELLATION AND OVERT INCESTUOUS RELATIONS BETWEEN FATHER AND DAUGHTER

1. Hereafter when we refer to the male figure involved we will call him "father."

2. We had no contact with the "fathers" for the following reasons: the older brothers and foster fathers were out of the state; the paternal grandfather was dead; five of the

remaining men had been imprisoned by the time the cases were referred; the rest were unavailable for a variety of reasons, such as residence in another state or disappearance from home with whereabouts unknown.

44. FAMILY ADJUSTMENT TO THE BRAIN-DAMAGED CHILD

1. C. M. Riley *et al.*, "Central Autonomic Dysfunction with Defective Lacrimation: I. Report of Five Cases," *Pediatrics*, III (1949), 468–78.

2. C. M. Riley, "Familial Autonomic Dysfunction," *Journal of the American Medical Association*, CIL (1952), 1532–35.

3. C. M. Riley, A. M. Freedman, and W. S. Langford, "Further Observations on Familial Dysautonomia," *Pediatrics*, XIV (1954), 475–80.

4. J. D. Teicher, "Preliminary Survey of Motility in Children," *Journal of Nervous and Mental Disorders*, XCIV (1941), 277–304.

5. L. Bender and A. M. Freedman, "A Study of the First Three Years in the Maturation of Schizophrenic Children," *Quarterly Journal of Child Behavior*, IV (1952), 245–71.

45. THE MIDDLE-CLASS MALE CHILD AND NEUROSIS

1. Arnold W. Green, "The Sociological Analysis of Horney and Fromm," to be published in the *American Journal of Sociology*.

2. Karen Horney, *Neurotic Personality of Our Time* (New York: W. W. Norton & Co., 1937), p. 80: The "basic evil is invariably a lack of genuine warmth and affection." Since "love" represents a not-too-radical departure from "libido" and "Oedipus," it is not surprising that the initial revolt against Freudian theory should find Freudian-trained analysts huddling close to the fence of familiar pastures. See, for example, Adolph Stern, "Psychoanalytic Therapy in the Borderline Neuroses," *The Psychoanalytic Quarterly*, XIV (1945), 190–98. Stern finds "affect-hunger," especially in the relationship of mother and child, the root of borderline neuroses. The revolt probably stems more from a distate of the moral nihilism implicit in Sigmund Freud's theoretical structure,

rather than primarily from a rejection of the theory itself.

3. Eric Fromm, *New Ways in Psychoanalysis* (New York: W. W. Norton & Co., 1939), pp. 75–76. Fromm's position remains more theoretically consistent. In *Escape from Freedom* (New York: Farrar & Rinehart, 1941), institutional authority as developed in a historical framework is designated as the cause of both neurosis and "normal escapes" in modern western culture; as for the *individual* etiology of neurosis and "pathological normalcy," Fromm points to the experience of irrational authority in the family or orientation: see "Individual and Social Origins of Neurosis," *American Sociological Review*, IX (1944), 380–84.

4. This seems to conform to Robert M. MacIver's dictum:". . . any effective causal inquiry should be addressed to a specific difference between comparable situations," p. 85

of *Social Causation* (New York: Ginn and Co., 1942). The question might be raised that "comparable situations" are not being dealt with here, but both Fromm and Horney use "the family" and "the modern family" as generic terms, without differentiation according to class, ethnic group, etc.

5. Arnold W. Green, "The 'Cult of Personality' and Sexual Relations," *Psychiatry*, IV (1941), 343–48. (Reprinted in this volume.)

6. In all the relations between parents and children, the familial organization leaves no place for merely personal affection. Certainly this affection exists, but it cannot express itself in socially sanctioned acts. The behavior of the parents toward the children and the contrary must be determined exclusively by their situations as family members, not by individual merits or preferences. W. I. Thomas and Florian Znaniecki, *The Polish Peasant in Europe and America* (New York: Alfred A. Knopf, 1927), I, 94. In other words, parental authority, while usually unleavened with "love," is based not so much on personal caprice (Fromm's "irrational authority") but mutual respect for common rules of behavior and labor functions within the household unit.

Respect, not love, is the tie that binds in the peasant family. And within a rigid set of rules, parental authority is almost absolute: ". . . a rebellious child finds nowhere any help, not even in the younger generation, for every member of the family will side with the child's parents if he considers them right, and everyone will feel the familial will behind him and will play the part of a representative of the group" (*Ibid.*, I, 91–92). If the male child's will is considered, it is not because of respect for his individual personality, but because of the increasing power and control the child will assume; he will finally assume the father's place as head of the household.

7. The author is no psychiatrist, and the reader may wonder at the foolhardiness of making such a statement. Yet in the overt behavior of an entire generation in the village, whom the author has intimately known as children, adolescents, and young adults, there was no expression of anxiety, guilt feeling, rigidity of response, repressed hostility, and so on, the various symptoms described by Horney as characteristic of the basic neurotic character structure. It is impossible to check directly on the reasons for rejection at the local induction center, yet a Polish informant has assured me there is no known case of army rejection because of psychoneurosis within the local Polish community.

Of course, the argument might be raised that only a psychiatrist could discover the unconscious personality conflicts which were present. There is no adequate answer to this charge, just as there is not adequate answer to the orthodox Freudian's charge that only a Freudian can criticize classical psychoanalysis because only a Freudian can understand it.

Admittedly, this is no water-tight rebuttal; about all that can be said here is that the total description of the socialization process taking place in the local Polish community at least leaves open the door to the possibility that many who experienced it did not become neurotic. And it is pertinent to remember that analysts have knowledge of only upper middle-class and upper-class behavior.

According to Horney, the neurotic develops one of three trends, or some combination of them: masochistic (making the self small and insignificant), narcissistic (appearing unduly significant to one's self and insatiably craving admiration from others), and perfectionistic (need for others' recognition of the self's infallibility, particularly moral infallibility). These trends are all accessible to direct observation within a field of personal interaction, without psychoanalytic techniques. The only personality trend in these Polish youngsters that resembles any of Horney's formulations is the narcissistic; it is not so much "neurotic," however, as sheer crass egocentrism. According to middle-class standards, the socialization process has simply been left uncompleted, with but an elementary self- and social-awareness resulting. And it is *because* these youngsters remain egocentric, with little identification of self with others, that they are spared such neurotic symptoms as anxiety and guilt feelings. This does not mean they are never unhappy and miserable; far from it, but these feeling-states have nothing in common with the neurotic trends and symptoms described by psychoanalysts, which are all dependent upon intensive identification.

8. Demonstrations of affection are not altogether lacking, but they have little in common with the definitions of parent-child love found in the middle-class women's magazines. A fairly common positive attitude is a fleeting, rather grimly humorous appreciation of the other's alleged shortcomings. On occasions where an expression of sentiment would seem to be appropriate, such as a funeral within the family, parents and children are clumsy, awkward, embarrassed with one another. Too many avenues of approach have been sealed off in the past. Relations with parents tend to improve as the children become economically independent; while extremely rare, it does happen occasionally that a father and his grown son may be observed drinking beer together at one of the tables in the Polish Club. It must be remembered that while the local Polish community is an industrial slum, it is also a rural community, and there is sufficient cohesiveness within it to enforce at least the outward appearance of intrafamily solidarity; this is not experienced to any great degree, however, until the children reach young adulthood, and only if they take up residence within the community.

No claim is being made that the early training of all Polish youth in this community is exactly alike, nor that the attitudes of parents and children toward one another are exactly duplicated from family to family. It is here that the "subjective element" in insight (where the observer himself constructs patterns of behavior, at least in part, or merely interprets field-conjectures?) and in the participant-observer technique becomes potentially dangerous: a single description of a behavior-type or development is applied to various individual personalities, families, situations. And so, in the local Polish community, there is the boy who cripples his father in a fist-fight, runs away from home never to return; another lad, married and raising a family of his own, wistfully wishes he "had gotten to know the old folks better." One girl leaves home at sixteen to become a prostitute; another delays marriage to care for an ailing mother. Thus, reality, compressed into a single formulation, becomes distorted.

This is not the place for justification of abstraction. I am convinced, however, that if another observer could spend many years in the village and find some means of participating in the life of a large number of families representing all groups, as did the author, he would agree that the training of any second-generation Polish child would deviate but slightly from the above general description, while the training of any lower-middle-class Protestant child would deviate from that description to a marked degree.

9. The problem here is defining "middle class" in such a way as to maximize psychological relevance. Robert S. Lynd has defined middle class as that class which is off the economic floor (objective) and conceives of itself as going places (subjective). For present purposes, this can be revised as follows: the middle class is that class whose members have welded their attitudes and value into a lifelong striving toward an improvement of personal socio-economic position within the class structure. By this definition, the lower class then becomes made up of those who acquiesce to inferior status and the upper class those with an assured superior status. The only "objective criterion" which can be admitted in conjunction with the foregoing definition of middle class is that a given person not be permanently blocked in his striving by reason of race, color, ethnic group, which are essentially caste elements.

10. Not only has "middle class" been loosely defined, but also the claim is not being made that all middle-class children are equally affected by the ideal-type conditioning described, which is a deliberate exaggeration of the factor-conjunction which maximizes personality absorption. In individual cases, there will be different combinations of the factors enumerated, as well as deviations from individual factors.

11. Fromm's formulation of the "pseudo self" must not be confused with "personality absorption." Fromm views the self as having a dynamism of its own, apart from its social context, the pseudo self arises when the self accepts the ideas, values, and goals of others as its own. The present author accepts no such demarcation of self and social: the self is derived within the given social context; personality absorption occurs when that context is narrowed for the child to include little more than one or two adults.

12. Peculiarly enough, parents are viewed either as constant factors or as the villains in the piece in most discussions of "individual factors" in neurosis. But it is rather important to find out what there is to being a modern middle-class parent that fertilizes the soil of the child's neurosis, however the individual seed may be planted. It will not suffice to dismiss the matter with "the parents' own neuroses," as does Horney.

13. See Arnold W. Green, "Duplicity," *Psychiatry*, VI (1943), 411–24.

14. The obligation, as an individual experience, is fast passing. See Robert M. Kinkel, "Attitudes of Children toward Supporting Aged Parents," *American Sociological Review*, IX (1944), 370–79. The government bureaus are planning old-age assistance benefits on the assumption that an increasing proportion of the aged will fail to secure support from their children. See W. S. Woytinsky, *Labor in the United States* (Washington: Social Science Research Council, 1938).

15. Basing their estimates on a family income of $2,500, Dublin and Lotka figure that the parents spend between $9,180 and $10,485 in rearing a child through the age of 18. Quoted in Kingsley Davis, "Reproductive Institutions and the Pressure for Population," *Sociological Review*, XXIX (1937), 1–18 (a British publication).

16. The child must not be spanked, parents should be "patient" with him, his ego-growth must not be curbed, etc. The assumption of much of the child care literature seems to be that the parents have a combined culinary, nursing, and psychiatric function, and nothing more. But note that in a mobile, industrial, specialized job-world, with its emphasis upon contractual relations, that cooks, nurses, and psychiatrists are paid for what they do.

17. It would be impossible to ascertain directly the extent of this ambivalence. Asking a man whether or not he approves of the Bretton Woods Proposal differs from asking him whether he loves his little daughter—to be indicated on a ten-point scale. It differs, first, because Bretton Woods is relatively extraneous to the core of the self and is publicly defined as something upon which one may express a wide divergence of opinion, and, second, because a man's attitude toward his daughter is made up of a series of personal experiences, some delightful, others not, all complicated by a cultural compulsive to re-

press consciousness of ambivalence toward one's own children.

18. See Willard Waller, *The Family* (New York: Cordon, 1938).

19. The extent of the actual emancipation of women has been commonly exaggerated. Within all classes in our culture, as in all other cultures, women are trained to regard themselves as inferior to men in some degree. It is usually desired that the first child shall be a boy, by the wife as well as husband.

20. Clara Thompson, "The Role of Women in This Culture," *Psychiatry*, IV (1941), 6.

21. See Ernest W. Burgess and Leonard S. Cottrell, Jr., *Predicting Success or Failure in Marriage* (New York: Prentice-Hall, 1939), especially p. 413. In their sample they found a slight negative correlation between number of children and self-rating of marital adjustment. Lewis M. Terman *et al.*, *Psychological Factors in Marital Happiness* (New York: McGraw-Hill, 1938) apparently remain unaware that their characterization of "happily married women," derived from statistical manipulations, is a classic statement of the middle-class Victorian housewife-and-mother role. If "happiness" for married women must be something founded in a fading tradition, the future looks black. Fortunately, Terman and his associates have probably not established isolable unit-factors; instead, they have sifted elements out of a total middle-class cultural setting which is rapidly changing—i.e., their "factors" may not be applicable in the immediate future.

22. The addition of one more child, which is the outside limit in most middle-class homes, probably does nothing to diminish the possibility of the first child's developing a neurosis *if* there is an appreciate gap in their ages, because of the likelihood of sibling rivalry. See David M. Levy, *Maternal Overprotection* (New York: Columbia University Press, 1943). Levy's valuable monograph has not been used in the present discussion because Levy conceives of the overprotective mother as a person who has voluntarily renounced the world and all its works to devote her entire life to the sacred cause of her own child; the "middle-class mother" is here conceived as a type which has not resolved a conflict between "duty" and individualism. The latter is much more common.

23. Children are being more and more regarded by young middle-class couples as a symbol of romantic consummation. "And soon we'll be three," the popular song goes; the child is, then, considered more in terms of being a product of wedded egos than of having an integral place of his own in a family unit. Also, as parents no longer secure economic good and security from children, the affectional element is stepped up to give the parents a reason for having children. In fact, William F. Ogburn has made affection his only hope for preserving our present family form.

24. Margarethe Ribble, in "Disorganizing Factors of Infant Personality," *American Journal of Psychiatry*, XCVIII (1941), 463, says: "There is a necessity for a long and uninterrupted period of consistent and skillful 'psychological mothering' by one individual. This must continue at least until speech is well-developed and the child has acquired a feeling of self-security and voluntary control of his body equilibrium. . . . It seems that the tone of the gastro-intestinal tract in this early period depends in some special way on reflex stimulation from the periphery. Thus the touch of the mother has a definite biological implication in the regulation of the breathing and nutritive functions of the child." Two things should be noted here: while a certain amount of handling during infancy by one person may be necessary, that person need not be the biological mother; and it would be difficult to measure the extent of the need.

There are several excellent empirical studies of the socialization process now available, and in all of them a great deal is made of the child's need for love and affection. But in every single instance studied, the child had either been early conditioned to regard love as the most important thing in the world, or had had the opportunity of observing other youngsters receiving something which he did not have. This is not to deny that some affirmation of personal ties to others in primary-group relationships, if not a biological need, is at least universal, but it is doubtful that it need be the type of parent-child love discussed in such studies. Primitive children, brought up in large dwelling-units among many kinsmen, in a sense spread thin their affection over a wide area, and this affection is relatively less in total intensity as well. Polish children, in the village above described, receive short shrift from their mothers when they begin to walk, and even during infancy there is little dandling and cooing; in fact, after weaning, the child is most frequently literally handed over to the eldest daughter, who gives the child the strictest minimum of attention. Among the siblings there is little demonstrativeness: there is, however, the fierce loyalty of an in-group on the defensive; this loyalty comprises the principal matrix for the imposition of the actual moral code by which they live. Describing "genuine love" in and of itself as a necessity for preventing neurosis is sociologically naive.

25. I am immeasurably indebted to Dr. Franklin J. Shaw for long stimulating conversations about his work at the University of New Hamphire Psychological Clinic. He states that male students seeking psychotherapy invariably recall ridicule and ego-attacks by the father during the period of first testing male roles.

As for the "authority" formulation, is it not possible that it may be subsumed under "love withdrawal"? From the child's point of view, even corporal punishment becomes unbearable primarily because it represents the father's withdrawal of love and support. During adolescence, authority as such does become a problem for the child, but the "normal" child suffers from it then as much, and oftentimes more, than does the neurotic.

26. All middle-class children certainly do not become neurotic. But to the extent that their experience approaches the polar type described, they will tend to. This picture is often exaggerated by the parents' own unacknowledged hostile impulses toward the child, stemming from the individualistic values and strivings described.

27. Erich Fromm, "Individual and Social Origins of Neurosis," *American Sociological Review*, IX (1944), 381.

28. *Ibid.*

29. The play-group immeasurable sociolog-

ical significance, for it is secondary in importance only to the family of orientation in the socialization process. Unfortunately, the only good empirical studies of the play-group available are of institutionalized children or slum children whose gang behavior is regarded as a social problem.

30. See Ruth Benedict, "Continuities and Discontinuities in Cultural Conditioning," *Psychiatry*, I (1938), 161–67. On p. 161 appears this statement: "From a comparative point of view our culture goes to great extremes in emphasizing contrasts between the child and the adult. The child is sexless, the adult estimates his virility by his sexual activities; the child must be protected from the ugly facts of life, the adult must meet them without psychic catastrophe; the child must obey, the adult must command this obedience."

46. PSEUDO-MUTUALITY IN THE FAMILY RELATIONS OF SCHIZOPHRENICS

1. For example, see W. R. D. Fairbairn, *Psychoanalytic Studies of the Personality* (London: Tavistock Publications, 1952); Michael Balint, *Primary Love and Psychoanalytic Technique* (London: Hogarth Press, 1952).

2. Erik Homburger Erikson, "The Problem of Ego Identity," *Journal of the American Psychoanalytic Association*, IV (1956), 56–121.

3. See Martin Buber, "Distance and Relation," *Psychiatry*, XX (1957), 97–104, for a philosophical study of the issues involved in this necessity.

4. In an earlier version of this paper, the phrase "sense of complementarity" was used throughout, instead of "pseudo-mutuality." Because we attach so much importance to the difference between a sense or illusion of complementarity and genuine mutuality, we felt a more distinct difference in terms was warranted, since the qualifying words, "sense of," were easily overlooked.

5. See, in this connection, Talcott Parsons and Edward A. Shils (eds.), *Toward a General Theory of Action* (Cambridge, Mass.: Harvard University Press, 1951).

6. John P. Spiegel has been a valuable and helpful stimulus to our thinking about role theory. See John P. Spiegel, "The Social Roles of Doctor and Patient in Psychoanalysis and Psychotherapy," *Psychiatry*, XVII (1954), 369–76; "The Resolution of Role Conflict Within the Family," *Psychiatry*, XX (1957), 1–16. However, in distinguishing three varieties of complementarity—mutuality, pseudo-mutuality, and non-mutuality—we extend attention to the quality of subjective experience and personality functioning that occurs during role performance. When Spiegel speaks of role reciprocity as conferring spontaneity upon behavior by sparing a person "the necessity

of coming to decisions about most of the acts he performs" (*Psychiatry*, 1957, p. 4), we feel that he is referring only to the reciprocity of basically non-mutual relations. In pseudo-mutuality, decisions are spared a person but at the price of *blocking* spontaneity. In genuine mutuality decision-making and spontaneity are interwoven; spontaneity in the service of imaginative capacity is from the beginning an integral part of the relationship system. We question whether the physiological model of homeostasis can be transposed to human relations and still leave room for the imaginative, selective, non-automatic details of fully mutual complementarity. It is only the simpler situation of non-mutuality and in the pathological situation of pseudo-mutuality that the automaticity of homeostatic equilibration seems an appropriate analogy.

7. Personal communication.

8. The dimension along which some degree of pseudo-mutuality may be found includes the psychoneuroses and character disorders but also certain phases of normal development. For example, romantic infatuations in normal adolescent development in American culture can be regarded as a relatively transitory pseudo-mutual attempt to deal with the identity diffusion that occurs with the prospect of assuming new, adult roles. "Normally," in time, there is perceptual correction and recognition of dissatisfaction with these illusory romantic relations.

9. Our views on the importance of this aspect of schizophrenic relations were developed independently but seem to concur with those of Bateson and his co-authors, who have recently referred to this as a "double-bind" situation (Gregory Bateson *et al.*, "Toward a Theory of Schizophrenia," *Behavioral Science*, I [1956], 251–64).

10. Talcott Parsons and R. F. Bales,

Family, Socialization and Interaction Process (Glencoe, Ill.: The Free Press, 1955).

11. Talcott Parsons, "The Theory of Symbolism in Relation to Action," chap. ii in *Working Papers in the Theory of Action* (Glencoe, Ill.: The Free Press, 1953).

12. Compare Harry Stack Sullivan, *Clinical Studies in Psychiatry*, ed. Helen Swick Perry, Mary Ladd Gawel, and Martha Gibbon (New York: Norton, 1956). "The schizophrenic chance, I believe, is quite generally due to an inability to maintain dissociation. . . . Thus the schizophrenic has an unsure mental state in which he is clearly aware of the activity of the dissociated system but unable to get the thing into clear personal focus" (p. 187).

13. Our emphasis on familial experience, for purposes of exposition, does not, of course, exclude effects on ego development from other sources, such as hereditary and constitutional factors. On the contrary, we consider the interaction of multiple factors as very likely of crucial significance. We have indicated that the kind of fit between native characteristics and family structure will affect the kind of psychological experience any given person may have. As a simple and obvious example, a girl who is assigned a "feminine" role in a family will have a kind of experience different from that of a boy who is cast in the same feminine role.

14. Erikson, *op. cit.*

47. SCHISM AND SKEW IN THE FAMILIES OF SCHIZOPHRENICS

1. T. Lidz, B. Parker, and A. R. Cornelison, *American Journal of Psychiatry*, Vol. CXIII (July, 1956).

2. R. W. Lidz and T. Lidz, *American Journal of Psychiatry*, CVI (1949), 332.

3. T. Tietze, *Psychiatry*, XII (1949), 55.

4. H. E. Frazee, *Smith College Studies in Social Work*, XXIII (1953), 125.

5. D. L. Gerard and J. Siegel, *Psychiatric Quarterly*, XXIV (1950), 47.

6. S. Reichard and C. Tillman, *Psychiatry*, XIII (1950), 247.

7. B. Murphy, *Psychiatric Quarterly*, XXVI (1952), 450.

8. T. Parsons and R. Bales, *Family, Socialization and Interaction Process* (Glencoe, Ill.: The Free Press, 1955).

9. J. P. Spiegel, *Psychiatry*, XX (1957), 1.

10. N. Ackerman, *Social Casework*, XXXV (April, 1954).

11. Reuben Hill *et al.*, *Eddyville's Families* (Chapel Hill, N.C.: University of North Carolina Press, 1953).

12. B. Buell *et al.*, *Classification of Disorganized Families for Use in Family Oriented Diagnosis and Treatment* (New York: Community Research Associates, 1953).

13. J. P. Spiegel, *loc. cit.*

14. Parsons and Bales, *op. cit.*

15. B. Buell *et al.*, *op. cit.*

48. THE "CULT OF PERSONALITY" AND SEXUAL RELATIONS

1. There are notable exceptions, especially where the sociologist has specifically investigated lower-class sexual behavior. Even here, however, little attempt has been made to point out the salient differences between "lower-class" and "middle-class" sexual relations. What are referred to above are the works purporting to treat of sexual relations "in general."

2. In a sense, prostitution is governed by middle-class norms since it constitutes a transgression of them which is punishable by law, and is thus to some extent controllable.

3. Kingley Davis, "Reproductive Institutions and the Pressure for Population," *Sociological Review*, XXIX (1937), 1–18 (a British publication). See pp. 6–9 for an analysis of how these three forces have undermined familism.

4. J. K. Folsom, "Finding a Mate in Modern Society," in J. K. Folsom (ed.), *Plan for Marriage* (New York: Harper, 1938), p. 108.

5. What do we mean when we speak of a "perfect understanding" as between lovers or a married couple? Even Georg Simmel fell into popular error when he spoke of "self-revelation" and giving of the self "entirely"

(Georg Simmel, "The Sociology of Secrecy and Secret Societies," *American Journal of Sociology*, XI [1906], 441–98; in particular, p. 460). The "perfect understanding" does not involve the selves initially offered in the relationship. Nor is the "entire self" ever revealed. Rather, the establishment of the "perfect understanding" is a construction job in which each partner builds a set of idealized behavior patterns upon the personality of the other, and there results a mutual willingness to accept this superimposition as the *self to be presented*. This is by no means an impulsive process, but a slow realization of how conforming to the inferred means of delighting the other may be an integral part of the personality.

6. The middle-class boy would not necessarily exhibit restraint when dealing with girls of the lower classes or girls of his own class who had a reputation for being promiscuous.

7. Arnold W. Green, "Village Conditioning to Economic Failure" (Master's thesis, Pennsylvania State College, 1939). The thesis concerns the Village under present consideration and maintains that a combination of factors—familial conflict between old-world parents

and but superficially Americanized offspring, ethnic-group conflict, the lack of class differentiation to prompt emulation on, the necessity of traveling to school by bus to a larger community that holds the Village in contempt, the lack of recreational facilities, the paucity of organizations offering training in social intercourse, a virtually complete ignorance of the intellectual world, and the economic expectation of nothing better than sweat-shop labor, WPA, or relief—these all work together to produce a community-wide attitude of helplessness and an accommodation of comforting mediocrity which preclude the efficient use of any of the channels of vertical mobility which might occasionally be available in individual instances.

8. For a discussion of the middle-class counterpart of this behavior, refer to Willard Waller, *The Family* (New York: Cordon, 1938), in particular, "Dating in a University," pp. 230–35.

9. A local boy explained the significance of this act: "When 'they' put their feet on the running-board of your car, you know you've got 'em."

10. For the girl, this type of behavior does not offer the opportunity for economic exploitation that dating affords the middle-class girl. Usually it takes the combined resources of two or three lads to gasoline a car for an evening's entertainment.

11. Neither the community nor the Polish ethnic group offer any patterns for social relationships between the young of opposite sexes except on the basis of dating or "going together."

12. The printable terms used to refer to members of the opposite sex by the boys include "bag," "squash," "pig." These terms constitute aggression releases. They are used with special relish by social rejects, who thus express contempt—a hate derivative— for recalled blocking of the sexual impulse.

13. While the girl is rarely involved in both types of courtship at the same time, since the boy she is going with steadily would not countenance her dating other boys, and the power relationship is such that she is forced to accede, the boy usually does date other girls as much and as often as his pocket book will allow.

14. "The position of a girl in an immigrant family differs from that of a boy in the fact that the claims which the family puts upon her are greater. She is supposed to be under stricter control even after school age. She is expected to help in housework if she does not work outside and to turn all of her earnings into the home. Moreover, the old rule prohibiting sexual relations before marriage is still enforced upon her. Thus a few remnants of the traditional life-organization are preserved for her benefit; her rearing is on the average not as amoral as that of the boy." William I. Thomas and Florian Znaniecki, *The Polish Peasant in Europe and America* (New York: Alfred A. Knopf, 1927), p. 1800.

Sexual amorality in the Village has not advanced to the extreme stage described by Thomas and Znaniecki as current among urban immigrants. Differences of rural living, the modicum of commercialized amusement available, the virtual impossibility of anonymity, and the absence of a local leisure class to envy—all aid in maintaining a semblance of the old-world community organization among the local Poles. While parental control is weak, it seldom breaks down completely.

The local Polish families carry on a degree of social intercourse that would be impossible under urban conditions. They have a certain respectability stake in the community which exerts a constant pressure on the girl to at least outward conformity.

15. "Success drive" denotes a wish purposefully directed toward a specific economic-occupational goal. The wish is there, but it is little more than a vague hankering which is becoming increasingly timid of expression as obvious blocking makes it futile.

16. Thomas and Znaniecki point out how foreign the concepts of "love" and "immorality" are to the experience of the Polish peasant: *op. cit.*, pp.1705, 1737, 1797.

17. Blocking of the success drive releases much energy into sexual channels.

18. For an extended definition of love, turn to Waller, *op. cit.*, pp. 198–99, 206, and 258. A statement concerning the end state of love is given by Harry Stack Sullivan, "Conceptions of Modern Psychiatry," *Psychiatry*, III (1940), 20.

19. The local Polish population does not experience the hammer impact of alien American legal institutions that disrupts familial life among urban immigrants. Thomas and Znaniecki, *op. cit.*, p. 1751.

20. While drunk one recently married boy made a series of joking invitations to his companions to have coitus with his wife. She suffered ridicule on this score, yet the marriage survived.

49. THE COMMUNICATION OF NEUROTIC PATTERNS OVER TWO AND THREE GENERATIONS

1. Melitta Sperling, "The Neurotic Child and His Mother: A Psychoanalytic Study," *American Journal of Orthopsychiatry*, XXI (1951), 351–64.

2. Else Frenkel-Brunswick, "Patterns of Social and Cognitive Outlook in Children and Parents," *American Journal of Orthopsychiatry*, XXI (1951), 543–58.

3. Jules Henry and Samuel Warson, "Family Structure and Psychic Development," *American Journal of Orthopsychiatry*, XXI (1951), 59–73.

4. See, for instance, Saul Rosenzweig and A. C. Isham, "Complementary Thematic Apperception Test Patterns in Close Kin," *American Journal of Orthopsychiatry*, XVII (1957), 129–42; Rose Palm and David Abrahamsen, "A Rorschach Study of the Wives of Sex Offenders," *Journal of Nervous and Mental Disease*, CXIX (1954), 167–72; Saul Rosenzweig and Loretta K. Cass, "The Extension of Psychodiagnosis to Parents in the Child Guidance Setting," *American Journal of Orthopsychiatry*, XXIV (1954), 715–22.

5. S. A. Szurek has asked the same question. See Szurek, "Concerning the Sexual Disorders of Parents and Their Children,"

Journal of Nervous and Mental Disease, CXX (1954), 369–78.

6. See Florence B. Powdermaker and Jerome D. Frank, *Group Psychotherapy: Studies in Methodology of Research and Therapy* (Cambridge, Mass.: Harvard University Press, 1953).

7. It should be noted that Nathan W. Ackerman, in a recent publication, takes a similar line of thought. He is so impressed with the importance of a theoretical position which emphasizes family group phenomena that he speaks of a "psychotherapy of the family." He feels that therapy of the individual can frequently be only partially successful because it neglects to consider or change the equilibrium of family forces in which the patient lives. See Ackerman, "Interpersonal Disturbances in the Family," *Psychiatry*, XVII (1954), 359–68.

50. THE TRANSMISSION OF SUPEREGO DEFECTS IN THE FAMILY

1. Adelaide M. Johnson and S. A. Szurek, "The Genesis of Antisocial Acting Out in Children and Adults," *Psychoanalytic Quarterly*, XXI (1952), 323–43.

2. Eduardo Weiss, "Emotional Memories and Acting Out," *Psychoanalytic Quarterly*, XI (1942), 477–92.

3. Wilhelm Reich, *Der triebhafte Charakter* (Vienna: Internationaler Psychoanalytische Verlag, 1925).

4. Franz Alexander and William Healy, *Roots of Crime* (New York: Alfred A. Knopf, 1935).

5. Willam Healy and Augusta F. Bronner, *New Light on Delinquency and Its Treatment* (New Haven: Yale University Press, 1936).

6. Melitta Schmideberg, "The Mode of Operation of Psychoanalytic Therapy," *Inter-*

national Journal of Psychoanalysis, XIX (1938), 314.

7. George E. Gardner, personal communication to the authors.

8. August Aichhorn, *Wayward Youth* (trans. from 2nd German ed.; New York: Viking Press, 1935).

9. S. A. Szurek, "Notes on the Genesis of Psychopathic Personality Trends," *Psychiatry*, V (1942), 1–6.

10. Minna Emch, "On the 'Need to Know' as Related to Identification and Acting Out," *International Journal of Psychoanalysis*, XXV (1944), 13–19.

11. E. M. Litin, Mary E. Giffen, and Adelaide M. Johnson, "Parental Influence in Unusual Sexual Behavior in Children," *Psychoanalytic Quarterly*, XXV (1956), 37–55.

51. THE SUPEREGO AND THE THEORY OF SOCIAL SYSTEMS

1. Cf. Talcott Parsons and Edward A. Shils (eds.), *Toward a General Theory of Action* (Cambridge, Mass.: Harvard University Press, 1951). Also Talcott Parsons, *The Social System* (Glencoe, Ill.: The Free Press, 1951).

2. Durkheim's insights were first clearly stated in a paper, "Détermination du fait moral," published in the *Revue de Métaphysique et de Morale* in 1906, and were much further developed in *Les formes élémentaires de la vie religieuse*, his last book (Paris, F. Alcan, 1912). The earlier paper was reprinted in Charles Bougle (ed.), *Sociologie et Philosophie* (Paris: F. Alcan, 1929). Its theme is further elaborated in the posthumously published lectures, delivered at the Sorbonne in 1906, which carry the title, *L'Education morale* (Paris: F. Alcan, 1925). Strongly influenced by Durkheim is the work of the Swiss psychologist, Jean Piaget,

who has developed his view on the psychological side. See especially his *The Moral Judgment of the Child* (Glencoe, Ill.: The Free Press, 1948). I presume that the psychiatric reader is familiar with the relevant works of Freud. However, two of the most important discussions of the superego are found in *The Ego and the Id* (London: Hogarth Press, 1949) and the *New Introductory Lectures on Psychoanalysis* (New York: Norton, 1933).

3. Further development of this analytical starting point and of the reasons for assuming it will be found in Parsons and Shils (eds.), *Toward a General Theory of Action* (reference footnote 1). See especially the "General Statement" and Part II, "Values, Motives, and Systems of Action." The reader may also wish to consult Parsons, *The Social System* (reference footnote 1).

4. This view has certainly been modified

in subsequent psychoanalytic thinking, but it is the major framework within which Freud introduced the concept of the superego.

5. This is in no way meant to suggest that there is *no* element of constitutional bisexuality, but only that *some* things Freud attributed to it may be explicable on other grounds.

Index

Aberle, David F., 420
Abortion, 43, 56, 61–62
Achievement, 462, 478–80, 526–27
Acting-out of anti-social behavior, 624–26, 627–35
Action, 454–58, 459–60, 483; orientation of, 639
Activities, 6 n., 340–46
Activity orientation, 306, 308–9, 311
Adjustment, 524–26
Adolescence, 147, 180, 193, 515, 668
Adopted children, 1, 383
Adultery, 57, 300, 400
Affection, 214, 220, 297
Africa, 223, 226, 227–36, 243–44, 246
Age grading, 405
Age-sex matrix, 335
Aggression, 275–76, 278, 420–28
Agnatic kinship, 221, 222
Agnosticism, 407
Agriculture, 171
Allocative discrepancy, 366–69
Ambivalence, 565–72, 576
Amish, 145–46
Anaclitic depression, 531
Anger, 538, 543
Anti-social behavior, 624–26, 627–35
Antitraditionalism, 135
Anxiety, 552–54; see also Guilt
Approval, 18
Assimilation of roles, 483–85, 493
Athletics, 412
Attitudes: change in, in continuance of system, 332; change in, in therapeutic process, 355–57; differentiation in, 333; of patient, and severity of illness, 350; of task leader, 331; of society toward divorcee, 322–23, 325
Aunts, 470–74
Authority: and development of neurosis, 569–70; during period of unemployment, 118; and family power structure, 138–39, 141–42; kinship terminology as affirmation of, 479; and leadership, 23–24, 336; in nuclear and extended family, 6–7; and respect, 675; in Russian families, 177; variations in, 49, 423
Automobiles as status symbols, 156
Autonomic pattern, 341, 343

Bales, Robert F., 363
Bandura, Albert, 524
Bed-wetting, 391–92
Behavior, patterns of: acting-out of anti-social, 624–26, 627–35; of child as scapegoat, 390 ff.; consumer, 144–62; controlled by ritual activities, 432; culture configurations as, 295 ff.; differentiation of, 333; of divorcee, 316–17, 325–26; in kinship systems, 220 ff.; in inhabitants of close neighborhoods, 287–94; institutionalization

Behavior, patterns of (*cont.*)
of, 15; long-term transmission, 617–21; normal, 435–51; political, 189 ff.; of sociometric star, 331; of task leader, 330–31; training and maternal employment, 527–31; during unemployment, 114 ff.; and value systems, 17
Behavioral field, 340
Behavioral mode, 436
Being orientation, 308, 311
Being-in-becoming orientation, 308, 311
Belief systems; *see* Values
Bernard, L. L., 432
Bigamy, 56, 57
Bilateral family, 48
Biological factors, 21, 41, 298, 366, 671
Birth control, 518
Birth rate, 4, 58, 94, 108, 166–67, 171, 656
Birth status rights, 90–91
Blame, 538–43
Bloomberg, Warner, Jr., 150–51
Bourgeoisie, 293–94
Boy Scout movement (France), 282
Breakup, de facto, 208 ff.
Briffault, R., 3
British Guiana, 258–65
Bryson, Lyman, 161
Burgess, E. W., 5, 448
Burke, Kenneth, 372
Burlingham, Dorothy, 536

Canalization, 411–12, 416
Careers, 152–57
Cash, W. J., 160
Cathexis, 638, 639–40, 641–42
Catholics, 209, 211
Chicago, 105 ff.
Child rearing, 135–36, 288–91
Children: achievement, motivation for, 526–27; adjustment problems, 524–26; behavior training, 527–31; birth and care of, 42–43, 343; in British Guiana, 261; choice of playmates (France), 266–67; conflict, and parents' ambivalence, 570–72; consumer education, 146–47; control of, and pragmatic self-interest, 406–8; competition, 271–73, 570–71; in crowded living conditions, 510–20; dependency, 531 ff.; of divorced mother, 320–21; dysautonomic, 555–62; economic co-operation in family, 42; in educational system (France), 271–73; effect on conjugal roles of parents, 250–51; -father relationship, 115, 118, 130–34, 136, 274, 350, 399, 500–9, 525, 536–37, 566–67; father's occupation, concept of, 500–9; goal discrepancy, 365–66; identification, 535–37; and illness, 351, 353; importance in kinship institutions, 317; and inheritance patterns, 163–64; internalization of family role structure, 586–89; involvement in parents' role con-